Western Civilization
A Brief History

Other Books by Marvin Perry

An Intellectual History of Modern Europe

Sources of the Western Tradition
Third Edition
Perry/Peden/Von Laue

- Two-Volume Paperback
  Volume I: From Ancient Times to the Enlightenment
  Volume II: From the Renaissance to the Present

Western Civilization: Ideas, Politics, and Society
Fifth Edition
Perry/Chase/Jacob/Jacob/Von Laue

- One-Volume Paperback
  Complete (Chapters 1–35)

- Two-Volume Paperback
  Volume I: To 1789 (Chapters 1–18)
  Volume II: From the 1600s (Chapters 16–35)

- One-Volume Paperback
  From the 1400s (Chapters 13–35)

Western Civilization
A Brief History

THIRD EDITION

MARVIN PERRY

Baruch College
City University of New York

George W. Bock, *Editorial Associate*

Houghton Mifflin Company   BOSTON   NEW YORK

Senior Sponsoring Editor: Patricia A. Coryell
Senior Associate Editor: Jeffrey Greene
Project Editor: Helen Bronk
Production/Design Coordinator: Jennifer Waddell
Senior Manufacturing Coordinator: Priscilla Bailey
Marketing Manager: Clint Crockett

Cover Design: Len Massiglia
Image: Jan Vermeer, Dutch: *A Geographer in His Study,* 1669, Stadelsches Kunstinstitut, Frankfurt/A.K.G. Berlin/ Super Stock

Printed in the U.S.A.
Library of Congress Catalog Card Number: 96-76868
ISBN: 0-395-81110-4
 23456789-CS-00 99 98 97

❖ Contents

CHAPTER 9

**Political and Economic Transformation: National States,
Overseas Expansion, Commercial Revolution**   243

❖ Maps

❖ Chronologies

❖ Preface

Western civilization is a grand but tragic drama. The West has forged the instruments of reason that make possible a rational comprehension of physical nature and human culture, conceived the idea of political liberty, and recognized the intrinsic worth of the individual. But the modern West, though it has unravelled nature's mysteries, has been less successful at finding rational solutions to social ills and conflicts between nations. Science, a great achievement of the Western intellect, while improving conditions of life, has also produced weapons of mass destruction. Though the West has pioneered in the protection of human rights, it has also produced totalitarian regimes that have trampled on individual freedom and human dignity. And although the West has demonstrated a commitment to human equality, it has also practiced brutal racism.

Western Civilization: A Brief History, Third Edition, is an abridged version of *Western Civilization: Ideas, Politics, and Society,* Fifth Edition. Like the longer text, this volume examines the Western tradition—those unique patterns of thought and systems of values that constitute the Western heritage. While focusing on key ideas and broad themes, the text also provides economic, political, and social history for students in Western civilization courses.

The text is written with the conviction that history is not a meaningless tale. Without a knowledge of history, men and women cannot fully know themselves, for all human beings have been shaped by institutions and values inherited from the past. Without an awareness of the historical evolution of reason and freedom, the dominant ideals of Western civilization, commitment to these ideals will diminish. Without a knowledge of history, the West cannot fully comprehend or adequately cope with the problems that burden its civilization and the world.

In attempting to make sense out of the past, the author has been careful to avoid superficial generalizations that oversimplify historical events and forces and arrange history into too neat a structure. But the text does strive to interpret and synthesize in order to provide students with a frame of reference with which to comprehend the principal events and eras in Western history.

Changes in the Third Edition

For the third edition, most chapters have been reworked to some extent. The numerous carefully selected modifications and additions significantly enhance the text. Some changes deepen the book's conceptual character; others provide useful and illustrative historical details. The concluding essays in several chapters have been enlarged and improved. Several chapters treating intellectual history have been expanded, and the art essays have been reorganized.

Specific changes include a revised concluding essay, "The Religious Orientation of the Ancient Near East," in Chapter 1, "The Ancient Near East." A concluding essay, "The Legacy of the Ancient Jews," has been added to Chapter 2, "The Hebrews." In Chapter 3, "The Greeks," we have illuminated more fully the genius of Homer, Thucydides, and Euripides. Chapter 4, "Rome," contains some new material on Cicero, slavery, and Roman imperialism. The discussions of Jesus and Paul have been enriched in Chapter 5, "Early Christianity." Some additional information on town life and Jewish-Christian relations has been incorporated into Chapter 6, "The Rise of Europe." The concluding essay has been reworked in Chapter 7, "The Flowering and Dissolution of Medieval Civilization." A separate section on slavery has been added to Chapter 9, "Political and Economic Transformation." Chapter 10, "Intellectual Transformation," has been completely rewritten.

In recent years, historians have rethought the question: Was the French Revolution a bourgeois revolution? In Chapter 11, "The Era of the French Revolution," we have expanded the discussion of this issue. The relationship between romanticism and nationalism has been more carefully delineated in Chapter 12, "Thought and Culture in the Early Nineteenth Century." A new section, "Feminism: Extending the Principle of Equality," has been added to Chapter 15, "Thought and Culture in the Mid-Nineteenth Century." The treatment of irrationalism has been enlarged in Chapter 17, "Modern Consciousness." In Chapter 18, "World War I," the concluding essay, "The War and European Consciousness," has been expanded and deepened. The discussion of the Holocaust has been expanded in Chapter 21, "World War II." The concluding chapter, "The West in a Global Age," has been significantly restructured and brought up to date.

Distinctive Features

This brief edition was prepared for Western Civilization courses that run for one term only, for instructors who like to supplement the main text with primary source readers, novels, or monographs, and for humanities courses in which additional works on literature and art will be assigned. In abbreviating the longer text by about a third, the number of chapters has been reduced from 35 to 22. The emphasis on the history of ideas and culture has been retained, but the amount of detail has of necessity been reduced.

The text contains several pedagogical features. Chapter introductions provide comprehensive overviews of key themes and give a sense of direction and coherence to the flow of history. Chronologies at the beginning of most chapters show the sequence of important events discussed in the chapter. Many chapters contain concluding essays that treat the larger meaning of the material. Facts have been carefully selected to illustrate key relationships and concepts and to avoid overwhelming students with unrelated and disconnected data. Each chapter concludes with an annotated bibliography and review questions. The questions refer students to principal points and aim at eliciting thoughtful answers.

This text is published in both single-volume and two-volume editions. Volume I treats the period from the first civilizations in the Near East through the age of Enlightenment in the eighteen century (Chapters 1–10). Volume II covers the period from the Renaissance and the Reformation to the contemporary age (Chapters 8–22), and incorporates the last three chapters in Volume I: "Transition to the Modern Age: Renaissance and Reformation," "Political and Economic Transformation: National States, Overseas Expansion, Commercial Revolution," and "Intellectual Transformation: The Scientific Revolution and the Age of Enlightenment." Volume II also contains a comprehensive introduction that surveys the ancient world and the Middle Ages; the introduction is designed particularly for students who have not taken the first half of the course.

Ancillaries

Learning and teaching ancillaries, including a *Study Guide, Instructor's Manual with Test Items, Computerized Test Items,* and *Map Transparencies,* also contribute to the text's usefulness. The *Study Guide* has been prepared by Professor Lyle E. Linville of Prince George's Community College. For each text chapter, the *Study Guide* contains an introduction, learning objectives, words to know, identifications, a map study exercise, chronological/relational exercises, multiple-choice and essay questions, and a "transition," which reflects back on the chapter and looks forward to the next chapter's topic. The map study has outline maps, and students are asked to locate geographical features on them. A duplicate set of maps appears at the back of the book and may be removed for use in class quizzes. In the chronological/relational exercises, students are asked to put a list of items in their chronological order; then in an exercise that develops critical thinking skills, students are asked to write a paragraph indicating the relationship of the items to one another, along with their historical significance.

The *Instructor's Manual with Test Items* was prepared for the brief edition by Professor Diane Moczar of Northern Virginia Community College. The *Manual* contains chapter outlines, learning objectives, lecture topics, a film/video bibliography, essay and discussion questions, identifications, and multiple-choice questions and answers. The test questions are also available on computer disk (for Macintosh, IBM and IBM-compatible computers). In addition, a set of map transparencies is available on adoption.

Acknowledgments

In preparing this abridgment, I have made extensive use of the chapters written by my colleagues for *Western Civilization: Ideas, Politics, and Society*. Chapter 8, "Transition to the Modern Age: Renaissance and Reformation," and Chapter 9, "Political and Economic Transformation: National States, Overseas Expansion, Commercial Revolution," are based largely on James R. Jacob's and Margaret C. Jacob's chapters in the longer volume. Several sections of Chapter 12, "The Industrial Revolution: The Transformation of Society," and of Chapter 16, "Europe in the Late Nineteenth Century: Modernization, Nationalism, Imperialism," are drawn from Myrna Chase's chapters. Chapter 19, "The Soviet Union: Modernization and Totalitarianism," and the concluding chapter, "The West in a Global Age," are, to a large extent, abridgments of Theodore H. Von Laue's chapters. To a lesser or greater extent, my colleagues' material has been abridged, restructured, and rewritten to meet the needs of this volume. Therefore, I alone am responsible for all interpretations and any errors. I which to thank my colleagues for their gracious permission to use their words and thoughts.

I am also grateful to the staff of Houghton Mifflin Company who lent their considerable talents to the project. In particular I would like to thank Jeff Greene, developmental editor, and Helen Bronk, project editor, for their careful attention to detail, and Irmina Plaszkiewicz-Pulc, whose copyediting skills are reflected in the manuscript. This edition rests substantially on the editorial talents of Freda Alexander, who worked closely with me on previous editions of the text. I am especially grateful to my friend George Bock who read the manuscript with an eye for organization, major concepts, and essential relationships. As ever, I am grateful to my wife Phyllis G. Perry for her encouragement.

M.P.

Geography of Europe

The map on the following pages shows the continent of Europe and the countries around the Mediterranean Sea. It gives the names of countries and their capitals and indicates the physical features of the land, such as major rivers and other bodies of water, mountains, and changes in elevation. A knowledge of the geography of this area will help give a sense of the connection between geography and history: of how the characteristics of the terrain and the availability of rivers and other bodies of water affected the movement of people and the relationship between people and the environment throughout history.

Europe is the smallest continent in the world with the exception of Australia. The other continents are Africa, Asia, North America, South America, and Antarctica. The continent of Europe, which can be viewed as the western extension of the Asian landmass, is distinctive in its configuration. Peninsulas make up a significant portion of its land area. This feature gives Europe an unusually long coastline, equal in distance to one and a half times around the equator (37,877 miles). Europe's western boundary is the Atlantic Ocean; the Ural Mountains, Ural River, and Caspian Sea—in Russia and Kazakhstan—form its eastern boundary. The European continent extends southward to the Caucasus Mountains, the Black Sea, and the Mediterranean Sea, and northward to the Arctic Ocean. Off the mainland but considered by geographers to be part of Europe are thousands of islands, most notably the British Isles to the northwest.

The small size of the European continent often surprises North Americans. France, for example, covers less geographic area than Texas, and England is similar in size to Alabama. The distance from London to Paris is about the same as from New York to Boston; the distance from Berlin to Moscow is comparable to that from Chicago to Denver. And the entire continent of Europe is about the size of Canada.

Major Peninsulas and Islands   There are five major European peninsulas: the Iberian (Portugal and Spain); the Apennine (Italy); the Balkan (Albania, Bulgaria, Greece, and parts of the former Yugoslavian republics and Turkey); the Scandinavian (Norway and Sweden); and Jutland (Denmark). Ireland and the United Kingdom of England, Wales, and Scotland make up the British Isles. Major islands of the Mediterranean Sea include the Balearic Islands, Corsica, Sardinia, Sicily, Crete, and Cyprus.

Seas, Lakes, and Rivers   Europe's irregular coastline divides large areas of the surrounding waters into bays, gulfs, and seas. Located in the Mediterranean Sea are, from west to east, the Tyrrhenian Sea (bordered by Italy, Sicily, Sardinia, and Corsica), the Adriatic Sea (between Italy and the former Yugoslavian republics), the Ionian Sea (between Italy and Greece), and the Aegean Sea (between Greece and Turkey).

The Baltic Sea, in the north, is bordered by Finland, Estonia, Latvia, Lithuania, Poland, Germany, and Sweden. Narrow channels connect it to the North Sea, which lies between Great Britain and the countries of the northwestern mainland. The English Channel separates England and France, and the Bay of Biscay is bounded by the west coast of France and the north coast of Spain. The Black Sea, on the southern border of Russia and the Ukraine, is linked by water passages to the Aegean Sea. The Caspian Sea, which lies partly in Russia and Kazakhstan, and partly in Asia, is the world's largest saltwater lake. At ninety-two feet below sea level, it is also the lowest point in Europe.

Elevation

Meters	Feet
4,000	13,120
2,000	6,560
500	1,640
200	656
Sea level	Sea level
Below sea level	Below sea level

⊛ National capital
• Other city

ATLANTIC

OCEAN

North Sea

NORWAY

Oslo ⊛

SWEDEN

S

B

SCOTLAND

NORTHERN IRELAND

UNITED

IRELAND
Dublin ⊛

KINGDOM

ENGLAND

WALES

Thames

London •

DENMARK

Copenhagen ⊛

Elbe

NETHERLANDS
Amsterdam ⊛

Berlin ⊛

Brussels ⊛

GERMANY

PO

Seine

BELGIUM

LUXEMBOURG
Luxembourg •

Prague ⊛

CZECHOSLOVAKIA

English Channel

Loire

Paris •

FRANCE

Vienna ⊛

Bern ⊛

SWITZERLAND

AUSTRIA

Bay of Biscay

A L P S

SLOVENIA

Ljubljana ⊛

Zagreb ⊛

Be

CROATIA

PYRENEES

Ebro

Po

APENNINES

Adriatic Sea

BOSNIA AN
HERZEGOV

Sarajevo ⊛

PORTUGAL

SPAIN

Madrid ⊛

Corsica

Rome ⊛

(Y

MONTENEGR
Titograd •

Lisbon ⊛

ITALY

Balearic Is.

Sardinia

Tyrrhenian Sea

GIBRALTAR
(Gr. Br.)

Rabat ⊛

Algiers ⊛

Ion

MOROCCO

Tunis ⊛

Sicily

MALTA

TUNISIA

Tripoli ⊛

ALGERIA

0	100	200	300	400	500 Km.
0	100	200	300	400	500 Mi.

LIBYA

Europe's many rivers have served as transportation routes for thousands of years. Several of the major rivers, including the longest, flow across the Russian plain. The Volga, Europe's longest river (2,194 miles), rises west of Moscow and empties into the Caspian Sea; canals and other river systems link it to the Arctic Ocean and the Baltic Sea. The Dnieper flows south through the agricultural heartland of the Ukraine into the Black Sea.

The second longest river, the Danube (1,777 miles), is the principal waterway in southeastern Europe. Originating in Germany, it flows through Austria, Slovakia, Hungary, the former Yugoslavian republics, Bulgaria, and Romania and into the Black Sea. The Rhine winds northward from the Alps, through western Germany and the Netherlands, to the North Sea, which is also the destination of the Elbe River in eastern Germany. In France, the Rhône flows south into the Mediterranean, and the Seine and Loire flow west to the English Channel and the Bay of Biscay. Other important waterways are the Po in northern Italy, the Vistula in Poland, and the Thames in England.

The proximity of most areas of the European landmass to the coastline or to major river systems is important to understanding the historical development of European civilization. Trading routes evolved and major cities grew along these waterways, and rivers have served as natural boundaries.

Land Regions   Despite its small size, Europe presents a wide range of landforms, from rugged mountains to sweeping plains. These landforms can be separated into four major regions: the Northwest Mountains, the Great European Plain, the Central Uplands, and the Alpine Mountain System. The mountains of the northwest cover most of that region, running through northwestern France, Ireland, Scotland, Norway, Sweden, northern Finland, and the northwestern corner of Russia.

The Great European Plain spreads across almost the entire European part of the former Soviet Union, extending from the Arctic Ocean to the Caucasus Mountains. It stretches westward across Poland, Germany, Belgium, the western portion of France, and southeastern England.

The Central Uplands are a belt of high plateaus, hills, and low mountains. This belt reaches from the central plateau of Portugal, across Spain and the central highlands of France, to the hills and mountains of southern Germany, the Czech Republic, and Slovakia.

The Alpine Mountain System comprises several mountain chains. Within it lie the Pyrenees, between Spain and France; the Alps in southeastern France, northern Italy, Switzerland, and western Austria; and the Apennine range in Italy. Also included are the mountain ranges of the Balkan Peninsula, the Carpathian Mountains in Slovakia, Poland, and Romania, and the Caucasus Mountains between the Black and Caspian Seas. Throughout history, these mountain ranges have been formidable barriers and boundaries, affecting the movement of people and the relationship of people to each other and to the land.

When studying the map of Europe, it is important to notice the proximity of western regions of Asia—especially those at the eastern end of the Mediterranean Sea—to parts of North Africa. The cultures of these areas have not only interacted with those of Europe, but they have also played a significant role in shaping the history of Western civilization.

Western Civilization
A Brief History

❖ PART ONE

The Ancient World: Foundation of the West

TO A.D. 500

The Acropolis of Athens. (*Robert Harding Picture Library*)

	POLITICS AND SOCIETY	THOUGHT AND CULTURE
3000 B.C.	Rise of civilization in Sumer (c. 3200) Union of Upper and Lower Egypt (c. 2900) Rise of Minoan civilization (c. 2600)	Cuneiform writing in Sumer; hieroglyphics in Egypt
2000 B.C.	Rise of Mycenaean civilization (c. 2000) Hammurabi of Babylon builds an empire (1792–1750)	*Epic of Gilgamesh* (c. 1900) Code of Hammurabi (c. 1790) Amenhotep IV and a movement toward monotheism in Egypt (1369–1353) Moses and the Exodus (1200s)
1000 B.C.	Creation of a unified Hebrew monarchy under David (1000–961) Dark Age in Greece (c. 1100–800) Hellenic Age (c. 800–323) Persian conquest of Near East (550–525) Formation of Roman Republic (509)	Homer's *Iliad* and *Odyssey* (700s) Age of classical prophecy: flowering of Hebrew ethical thought (750–430)
500 B.C.	Persian Wars (499–479) Peloponnesian War (431–404) Conquest of Greek city-states by Philip of Macedonia (338) Conquests of Alexander the Great (336–323) Hellenistic Age (323–30) Roman conquest of Carthage and Hellenistic kingdoms (264–146)	Law of the Twelve Tables (450) Rise of Greek philosophy: Ionians, Pythagoreans, Parmenides (500s and 400s) Greek dramatists: Aeschylus, Sophocles, Euripides, Aristophanes (400s) Greek philosophers: Socrates, Plato, Aristotle (400s and 300s) Hellenistic philosophies: Epicureanism and Stoicism
100 B.C.	Political violence and civil wars in Rome (88–31) Assassination of Julius Caesar (44) Octavian takes the title Augustus and becomes first Roman emperor (27) Pax Romana: height of Roman Empire (27 BC–180 AD)	Roman philosophers during the Republic: Lucretius, Cicero (1st cent.) Rise and spread of Christianity: Jesus (d. 29 AD); Paul's missionary activity (c. 34–64) Gospel of Mark (c. 66–70) Roman historians, poets, and philosophers during the Pax Romana: Livy, Tacitus, Virgil, Horace, Ovid, Juvenal, Seneca, Marcus Aurelius
200 A.D.	Military anarchy in Rome (235–285) Goths defeat Romans at Adrianople (378) End of Roman Empire in the West (476)	Church fathers; Jerome, Ambrose, Augustine (300s and 400s)

❖ CHAPTER I

The Ancient Near East: The First Civilizations

*C*ivilization was not inevitable; it was an act of human creativity. The first civilizations emerged some five thousand years ago in the river valleys of Mesopotamia and Egypt. There, human beings established cities and states, invented writing, developed organized religion, and constructed large-scale buildings and monuments—all characteristics of civilized life. Humanity's rise to civilization was long and arduous. Some 99 percent of human history took place before the creation of civilization, in the vast ages of prehistory. ❖

Prehistory

The period called the Paleolithic Age, or Old Stone Age, began with the earliest primitive toolmaking human beings who inhabited East Africa nearly three million years ago. It ended about ten thousand years ago in parts of the Near East when people discovered how to farm. Our Paleolithic ancestors lived as hunters and food gatherers. Because they had not learned how to farm, they never established permanent villages. When their food supplies ran short, they abandoned their caves or tentlike structures of branches and searched for new dwelling places.

Human social development was shaped by this three-million-year experience of hunting and food gathering. For survival, groups of families formed bands consisting of around thirty people; members learned how to plan, organize, cooperate, trust, and share. Hunters assisted each other in tracking and killing game, finding cooperative efforts more successful than individual forays. By sharing their kill and bringing some back to their camp for the rest of the group, they reinforced the social bond. So, too, did women, who gathered nuts, seeds, and fruit for the group. Bands that did not cooperate in the hunt, in food gathering, or in food distribution were unlikely to survive.

Although human progress was very slow during the long centuries of the Paleolithic Age, developments occurred that influenced the future enormously. Paleolithic people developed spoken language and learned how to make and use tools of bone, wood, and stone. With these simple tools, they dug up roots, peeled the bark off trees, trapped, killed, and skinned animals,

4

Chronology 1.1 ❖ The Near East

3200 B.C.*	Rise of civilization in Sumer
2900	Union of Upper and Lower Egypt
2686–2181	Old Kingdom: essential forms of Egyptian civilization take shape
2180	Downfall of Akkadian empire
1792–1750	Hammurabi of Babylon brings Akkad and Sumer under his control and fashions a code of laws
1570	Egyptians drive out Hyksos and embark on empire
1369–1353	Reign of Amenhotep IV: a movement toward monotheism
1200	Fall of Hittite empire
612	Fall of Assyrian empire
604–562	Reign of Nebuchadnezzar: height of Chaldean empire
550–525 B.C.	Persian conquests form a world empire

*Most dates are approximations.

made clothing, and fashioned fishnets. They also discovered how to control fire, which allowed them to cook their meat and provided warmth and protection.

Like toolmaking and the control of fire, language was a great human achievement. Language enabled individuals to acquire and share knowledge, experiences, and feelings with one another. Thus, language was the decisive factor in the development of culture and its transmission from one generation to the next.

Most likely, our Paleolithic ancestors developed mythic-religious beliefs to explain the mysteries of nature, birth, sickness, and death. They felt that living powers operated within and beyond the world they experienced, and they sought to establish friendly relations with these powers. To Paleolithic people, the elements—sun, rain, wind, thunder, and lightning—were alive. The natural elements were spirits; they could feel and act with a purpose. To appease them, Paleolithic people made offerings. Gradually, there emerged shamans, medicine men, and witch doctors, who, through rituals, trances, and chants, seemed able to communicate with these spirits. Paleolithic people also began the practice of burying their dead, sometimes with offerings, which suggests belief in life after death.

Between thirty thousand and twelve thousand years ago, Paleolithic people sought out the dark and silent interior of caves, which they probably viewed

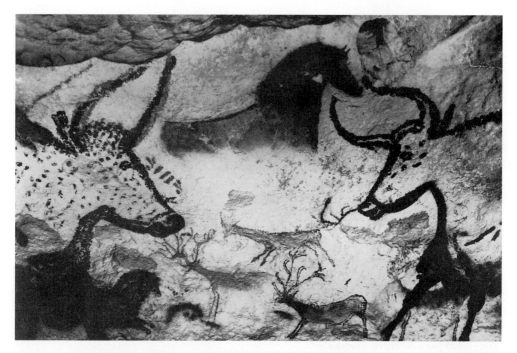

Paleolithic Cave Painting from Lascaux, France.   Produced as part of magical religious rites of hunting, these early paintings display considerable artistic skills. (*French Government Tourist Office*)

as sanctuaries, and, with only torches for light, they painted remarkably skillful and perceptive pictures of animals on the cave walls. When these prehistoric artists drew an animal with a spear in its side, they probably believed that this act would make them successful in hunting; when they drew a herd of animals, they probably hoped that this would cause game to be plentiful.

Some ten thousand years ago, the New Stone Age, or Neolithic Age, began in the Near East. During the Neolithic Age, human beings discovered farming, domesticated animals, established villages, polished stone tools, made pottery, and wove cloth. So important were these achievements that they are referred to as the Neolithic Revolution.

Agriculture and the domestication of animals revolutionized life. Whereas Paleolithic hunters and food gatherers had been forced to use whatever nature made available to them, Neolithic farmers altered their environment to satisfy human needs. Instead of spending their time searching for grains, roots, and berries, women and children grew crops near their homes; instead of tracking animals over great distances, men could slaughter domesticated goats or sheep nearby. Farming made possible a new kind of community. Since farmers had to live near their fields and could store food for the future, farming led to the rise of permanent settlements.

Villages changed the patterns of life. A food surplus freed some people to devote part of their time to sharpening their skills as basket weavers or tool-makers. The demand for raw materials and the creations of skilled artisans fostered trade, sometimes across long distances, and spurred the formation of trading settlements. An awareness of private property emerged. Hunters had accumulated few possessions, since belongings presented a burden when moving from place to place. Villagers, however, acquired property and were determined to protect it from one another and from outsiders who might raid the village. Hunting bands were egalitarian; generally, no one member had more possessions or more power than another. In farming villages, a ruling elite emerged that possessed wealth and wielded power.

Neolithic people made great strides in technology. By shaping and baking clay, they made pottery containers for cooking and for storing food and water. The invention of the potter's wheel enabled them to form bowls and plates more quickly and precisely. Stone tools were sharpened by grinding them on rock. The discoveries of the wheel and the sail improved transportation and promoted trade, and the development of the plow and the ox yoke made tilling the soil easier for farmers.

The Neolithic period also marked the beginning of the use of metals. The first to be used was copper, which was easily fashioned into tools and weapons. Copper implements lasted longer than those of stone and flint, and they could be recast and reshaped if broken. In time, artisans discovered how to make bronze by combining copper and tin in the proper ratio. Bronze was harder than copper, which made a sharper cutting edge possible.

During the Neolithic Age, the food supply became more reliable, village life expanded, and the population increased. Families that acquired wealth gained a higher social status and became village leaders. Religion grew more formal and structured; nature spirits evolved into deities, each with specific powers over nature or human life. Altars were erected in their honor, and ceremonies were conducted by priests, whose power and wealth increased as people gave offerings to the gods. Neolithic society was growing more organized and complex; it was on the threshold of civilization.

The Rise to Civilization

What we call *civilization* arose some five thousand years ago in the Near East (in Mesopotamia and Egypt) and then later in East Asia (in India and China). The first civilizations began in cities that were larger, more populated, and more complex in their political, economic, and social structure than Neolithic villages. Because the cities depended on the inhabitants of adjacent villages for their food, farming techniques must have been sufficiently developed to produce food surpluses. Increased production provided food for urban inhabitants, who engaged in nonagricultural occupations; they became merchants, craftsmen, bureaucrats, and priests.

The invention of writing enabled the first civilizations to preserve, organize, and expand knowledge and to pass it on to future generations. It also allowed government officials and priests to conduct their affairs more efficiently. Moreover, civilized societies possessed organized governments, which issued laws and defined the boundary lines of their states. On a scale much larger than Neolithic communities, the inhabitants erected buildings and monuments, engaged in trade and manufacturing, and used specialized labor for different projects. Religious life grew more organized and complex, and a powerful and wealthy priesthood emerged. These developments—cities, specialization of labor, writing, organized government, monumental architecture, and a complex religious structure—differentiate the first civilizations from prehistoric cultures.

Religion was the central force in these primary civilizations. It provided satisfying explanations for the workings of nature, helped ease the fear of death, and justified traditional rules of morality. Law was considered sacred, a commandment of the gods. Religion united people in the common enterprises needed for survival—for example, the construction and maintenance of irrigation works and the storage of food. Religion also promoted creative achievements in art, literature, and science. In addition, the power of rulers, who were regarded either as gods or as agents of the gods, derived from religion.

The emergence of civilization was a great creative act and not merely the inevitable development of agricultural societies. Many communities had learned how to farm, but only a handful made the leap into civilization. How was it possible for Sumerians and Egyptians, the creators of the earliest civilizations, to make this breakthrough? Most scholars stress the relationship between civilizations and river valleys. Rivers deposited fertile silt on adjoining fields, provided water for crops, and served as avenues for trade. But environmental factors alone do not adequately explain the emergence of civilization. What cannot be omitted is the human contribution: capacity for thought and cooperative activity. Before these rivers could be of any value in producing crops, swamps around them had to be drained, jungles had to be cleared, and dikes, reservoirs, and canals had to be built. To construct and maintain irrigation works required the cooperation of large numbers of people, a necessary condition for civilization.

In the process of constructing and maintaining irrigation networks, people learned to formulate and obey rules and developed administrative, engineering, and mathematical skills. The need to keep records stimulated the invention of writing. These creative responses to the challenges posed by nature spurred the early inhabitants of Sumer and Egypt to make the breakthrough to civilization, thereby altering the course of human destiny.

Mesopotamian Civilization

Mesopotamia is the Greek word for "land between the rivers." It was here, in the valleys of the Tigris and Euphrates Rivers, that the first civilization began.

The first people to develop an urban civilization in Mesopotamia (modern-day Iraq) were the Sumerians, who colonized the marshlands of the lower Euphrates, which, along with the Tigris, flows into the Persian Gulf.

Through constant toil and imagination, the Sumerians transformed the swamps into fields of barley and groves of date palms. Around 3000 B.C., their hut settlements gradually evolved into twelve independent city-states, each consisting of a city and its surrounding countryside. Among the impressive achievements of the Sumerians were a system of symbol writing on clay tablets (*cuneiform*) to represent ideas; elaborate brick houses, palaces, and temples; bronze tools and weapons; irrigation works; trade with other peoples; an early form of money; religious and political institutions; schools; religious and secular literature; varied art forms; codes of law; medicinal drugs; and a lunar calendar.

The history of Mesopotamia is marked by a succession of conquests. To the north of Sumer lay a Semitic* city, called Akkad. About 2350 B.C., the people of Akkad, led by Sargon the Great, the warrior-king, conquered the Sumerian cities. Sargon built the world's first empire, which extended from the Persian Gulf to the Mediterranean Sea. The Akkadians adopted Sumerian cultural forms and spread them beyond the boundaries of Mesopotamia with their conquests. Mesopotamian religion became a blend of Sumerian and Akkadian elements.

In succeeding centuries, the Sumerian cities were incorporated into various kingdoms and empires. The Sumerian language, replaced by a Semitic tongue, became an obscure language known only to priests, and the Sumerians gradually disappeared as a distinct people. But their cultural achievements endured. Akkadians, Babylonians, Elamites, and others adopted Sumerian religious, legal, literary, and art forms. The Sumerian legacy served as the basis for a Mesopotamian civilization, which maintained a distinct style for three thousand years.

Religion: The Basis of Mesopotamian Civilization

Religion lay at the center of Mesopotamian life. Every human activity—political, military, social, legal, literary, artistic—was generally subordinated to an overriding religious purpose. Religion was the Mesopotamians' frame of reference for understanding nature, society, and themselves; it dominated and inspired all other cultural expressions and human activities. Wars between cities, for instance, were interpreted as conflicts between the gods of those cities, and victory ultimately depended on divine favor, not on human effort. Myths—narratives about the activities of the gods—explained the origins of the human species. According to the earliest Sumerian myths, the first human beings issued forth from the earth like plant life, or were shaped from clay by

---

*Semites included Akkadians, Hebrews, Babylonians, Phoenicians, Canaanites, Assyrians, and Aramaeans. Hebrew and Arabic are Semitic languages.

divine craftsmen and granted a heart by the goddess Nammu, or were formed from the blood of two gods sacrificed for that purpose.

The Mesopotamians believed that people were given life so that they could execute on earth the will of the gods in heaven. No important decisions were made by kings or priests without first consulting the gods. To discover the wishes of the gods, priests sacrificed animals and then examined their entrails; or the priests might find their answers in the stars or in dreams.

The cities of Mesopotamia were sacred communities dedicated to serving divine masters, and people hoped that appeasing the gods would bring security and prosperity to their cities. Each city belonged to a particular god, who was the real owner of the land and the real ruler of the city; often a vast complex of temples was built for the god and the god's family.

Supervised by priests, the temple was the heart of the city's life. The temple probably owned most of the land in its city; temple priests collected rents, operated businesses, and received contributions for festivals. Most inhabitants of the city worked for the temple priests as tenant farmers, agricultural laborers, or servants. Anxious to curry favor with the gods who watched over the fields, peasants surrendered part of their crops to the temples. Priests coordinated the city's economic activity, supervising the distribution of land, overseeing the irrigation works, and storing food for emergencies. Temple scribes kept records of expenditures and receipts. By serving as stewards of the city's gods and managing their earthly estates, the priests sustained civilized life.

The Mesopotamians believed that the gods controlled the entire universe and everything in it. The moon, the sun, and the storm, the city, the irrigation works, and the fields—each was directed by a god. The Mesopotamians saw gods and demons everywhere in nature. There was a god in the fire and another in the river; evil demons stirred up sandstorms, caused disease, and endangered women in childbirth. To protect themselves from hostile powers, Mesopotamians wore charms and begged their gods for help. When misfortune befell them, they attributed it to the gods. Even success was not due to their own efforts, but to the intervention of a god who had taken a special interest in them. Compared with the gods, an individual was an insignificant and lowly creature.

Uncertainty and danger filled life in Mesopotamia. Sometimes, the unpredictable waters of the rivers broke through the dikes, flooding fields, ruining crops, and damaging cities. At other times, an insufficient overflow deprived the land of water, causing crops to fail. Mesopotamia had no natural barriers to invasion. Feeling themselves surrounded by incomprehensible and often hostile forces, Mesopotamians lived in an atmosphere of anxiety, which permeated their civilization.

Contributing to this sense of insecurity was the belief that the gods behaved capriciously, malevolently, and vindictively. What do the gods demand of me? Is it ever possible to please them? To these questions Mesopotamians had no reassuring answers, for the gods' behavior was a mystery to mere human beings.

A mood of uncertainty and anxiety, an awareness of the cosmos as unfath-

Wooden Soundbox of a Sumerian Harp, Ur, c. 2600 B.C.   The top panel features a heroic figure embracing two man-faced bulls made from shells inlaid in bitumen. Beneath are three panels with various animals carrying food or drink and musical instruments. The theme may depict a fable of some festive celebration or ritual myth. (*University Museum, University of Pennsylvania, Negative #S8–22097*)

omable and mysterious, a feeling of dread about the fragility of human existence and the impermanence of human achievement—these attitudes are as old as the first civilization. The *Epic of Gilgamesh*, the finest work of Mesopotamian literature, masterfully depicts this mood of pessimism and despair. The *Gilgamesh* deals with a profound theme: the human protest against death. Confronted with the reality of his own death, Gilgamesh yearns for eternal life. But he learns that when the gods created human beings, they made death part of their lot. "Where is the man who can clamber to heaven?

Only the gods live forever . . . but as for us men, our days are numbered, our occupations are a breath of wind."[1]

Government, Law, and Economy

Bestowed on a man by the gods, kingship was the central institution in Mesopotamian society. Unlike Egyptian pharaohs, Mesopotamian kings did not see themselves as gods, but rather as great men selected by the gods to represent them on earth. Gods governed through the kings, who reported to the gods about conditions in their land (which was the gods' property) and petitioned the gods for advice.

The king administered the laws, which came from the gods. The principal collection of laws in ancient Mesopotamia was the famous code of Hammurabi (c. 1792–c. 1750 B.C.), the Babylonian ruler. Unearthed by French archaeologists in 1901–1902, the code has provided invaluable insights into Mesopotamian society. In typical Mesopotamian fashion, Hammurabi claimed that his code rested on the authority of the gods; to violate it was to contravene the divine order.

The code reveals social status and mores in that area and time. Women were subservient to men, although efforts were made to protect women and children from abuse. By making death the penalty for adultery, the code probably sought to preserve family life. Punishments were generally severe—"an eye for an eye and a tooth for a tooth." The code prescribed death for housebreaking, kidnapping, aiding the escape of slaves, receiving stolen goods, and bearing false witness, but it also allowed consideration of extenuating circumstances. Class distinctions were expressed in the code. For example, a person received more severe punishment for harming a noble than for harming a commoner. Government officials who engaged in extortion or bribery were harshly punished. The code's many provisions relating to business transactions underscore the importance of trade to Mesopotamian life.

The economy of Mesopotamian cities depended heavily on foreign and domestic trade. To safeguard it, governments instituted regulations to prevent fraud, and business transactions had to be recorded in writing. Enterprising businessmen set up trading outposts in distant lands, making the Mesopotamians pioneers in international trade.

Mathematics, Astronomy, and Medicine

The Mesopotamians made some impressive advances in mathematics. They devised multiplication and division tables, including even cubes and cube roots. They determined the area of right-angle triangles and rectangles, divided a circle into 360 degrees, and had some understanding of the principles that centuries later would be developed into the Pythagorean theorem and quadratic equations. But the Babylonians, who made the chief contribution in mathematics, barely advanced to the level of devising theories; they did not formulate general principles or furnish proofs for their mathematical operations.

By carefully observing and accurately recording the positions of planets and constellations of stars, Babylonian sky watchers took the first steps in developing the science of astronomy, and they devised a calendar based on the cycles of the moon. As in mathematics, however, they did not form theories to coordinate and illuminate their data. They believed that the position of the stars and planets revealed the will of the gods. Astronomers did not examine the heavens to find what we call cause and effect connections between the phenomena. Rather, they aspired to discover what the gods wanted. With this knowledge, people could organize their political, social, and moral lives in accordance with divine commands, and they could escape the terrible consequences that they believed resulted from ignoring the gods' wishes.

Consistent with their religious world-view, the Mesopotamians believed that gods or demons caused disease. To cure a patient, priest-physicians resorted to magic; through prayers and sacrifices, they attempted to appease the gods and eject the demons from the sick body. Nevertheless, in identifying illnesses and prescribing appropriate remedies, Mesopotamians demonstrated some accurate knowledge of medicine and pharmacology.

Egyptian Civilization

During the early period of Mesopotamian civilization, the Egyptians developed their civilization in the fertile valley of the Nile. Without this mighty river, which flows more than four thousand miles from central Africa northward to the Mediterranean, virtually all Egypt would be a desert. When the Nile overflowed its banks, the floodwaters deposited a layer of fertile black earth, which, when cultivated, provided abundant food to support Egyptian civilization. The Egyptians learned how to control the river—a feat that required cooperative effort and ingenuity, as well as engineering and administrative skills. In addition to water and fertile land, the Nile provided an excellent transportation link between Upper (southern) and Lower (northern) Egypt. Natural barriers—mountains, deserts, cataracts (rapids) in the Nile, and the Mediterranean—protected Egypt from attack, allowing the inhabitants to enjoy long periods of peace and prosperity. Thus, unlike Mesopotamians, Egyptians derived a sense of security from their environment.

From the Old Kingdom to the Middle Kingdom

About 2900 B.C., a ruler of Upper Egypt, known as Narmer, or Menes, conquered the Nile Delta and Lower Egypt. By 2686 B.C., centralized rule had been firmly established, and great pyramids, which were tombs for the

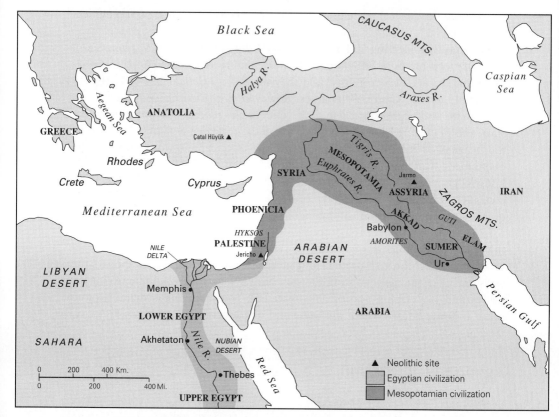

Map 1.1   Mesopotamian and Egyptian Civilizations

pharaohs, were being constructed. During this Pyramid Age, or Old Kingdom (2686–2181 B.C.), the essential forms of Egyptian civilization crystallized.

The Egyptians believed the pharaoh to be both a man and a god, the earthly embodiment of the deity Horus. He was an absolute ruler and kept the irrigation works in order, maintained justice in the land, and expressed the will of heaven. In time, the nobles who served as district governors gained in status and wealth and gradually came to undermine the divine king's authority. The nobles' growing power and the enormous expenditure of Egypt's human and material resources on building pyramids led to the decline of the Old Kingdom. From 2181 to 2040 B.C., a span of time called the First Intermediate Period, rival families competed for the throne, thus destroying the unity of the kingdom. The civil wars and the collapse of central authority required to maintain the irrigation system cast a pall over the land.

During what is called the Middle Kingdom (2040–1786 B.C.), strong kings reasserted pharaonic rule and reunited the state. The restoration of political stability reinvigorated cultural life, and economic activity revived. Pharaohs extended Egyptian control south over the land of Nubia (modern Sudan), which became a principal source of gold. A profitable trade was carried on with Palestine, Syria, and Crete.

Around 1800 B.C., central authority again weakened. In the era known as the Second Intermediate Period (1786–1570 B.C.), the nobles regained some of their power, the Nubians broke away from Egyptian control, and the Hyksos (a mixture of Semites and Indo-Europeans) invaded Egypt. The Hyksos dominated Egypt for about a hundred years, until the Egyptians drove them out in 1570 B.C. The period of empire building known as the New Kingdom (1570–1085 B.C.) then began.

The basic features of Egyptian civilization had been forged during the Old and Middle Kingdoms. Egyptians looked to the past, convinced that the ways of their ancestors were best. For almost three thousand years, Egyptian civilization sought to retain a harmony with the order of nature instituted at creation. Believing in a changeless universe, the Egyptians did not value change or development—what we call progress—but venerated the institutions, traditions, and authority that embodied permanence.

Religion: The Basis of Egyptian Civilization

Religion was omnipresent in Egyptian life and accounted for the outstanding achievements of Egyptian civilization. Religious beliefs were the basis of Egyptian art, medicine, astronomy, literature, and government. The great pyramids were tombs for the pharaohs, man-gods. Magical utterances pervaded medical practices, for disease was attributed to the gods. Astronomy evolved to determine the correct time for performing religious rites and sacrifices. The earliest examples of literature dealt wholly with religious themes. A sacrosanct monarch, the pharaoh served as an intermediary between the gods and human beings. The Egyptians developed an ethical code, which they believed the gods had approved.

Egyptian polytheism took many forms, including the worship of animals, for the people believed that gods manifested themselves in both human and animal shapes. The Egyptians also believed the great powers in nature—sky, sun, earth, the Nile—to be gods. Thus, the universe was teeming with divinities, and human lives were tied to the movements of the sun and the moon and to the rhythm of the seasons. In the heavens alive with gods, the Egyptians found answers to the great problems of human existence.

A crucial feature of Egyptian religion was the afterlife. Through pyramid-tombs, mummification to preserve the dead, and funerary art, the Egyptians showed their yearning for eternity and their desire to overcome death. Mortuary priests recited incantations to ensure the preservation of the dead body and the continuity of existence. Inscribed on the pyramids' interior walls were "pyramid texts," written in *hieroglyphics*—a form of picture writing, in which figures, such as crocodiles, sails, eyes, and so forth, represented words or sounds that would be combined to form words. The texts contained fragments from myths, historical annals, and magical lore and provided spells to assist the king in ascending to heaven. To the Egyptians, the other world offered the same pleasures as those enjoyed on earth: friends, servants, fishing, hunting, paddling a canoe, picnicking with family members, entertainment by musicians and dancers, and good food. But since earthly existence was not fundamentally unhappy, Egyptians did not long for death.

Divine Kingship

Divine kingship was the basic institution of Egyptian civilization. The Egyptians saw rule by a god-king as the only acceptable political arrangement: it was in harmony with the order of the universe, and it brought justice and security to the nation.

The pharaoh's power extended to all sectors of society. Peasants were drafted to serve in labor corps as miners or construction workers. Foreign trade was a state monopoly, conducted according to the kingdom's needs. As the supreme overlord, the pharaoh oversaw an army of government officials, who collected taxes, supervised construction projects, checked the irrigation works, surveyed the land, kept records, conducted foreign trade, and supervised government warehouses, where grain was stored as insurance against a bad harvest. All Egyptians were subservient to the pharaoh, whose word was regarded as a divine ordinance. Most pharaohs took their responsibilities seriously and tried to govern as benevolent protectors of the people.

The pharaoh was seen as ruling in accordance with Ma'at, which means justice, law, right, and truth. To oppose the pharaoh was to violate the order of Ma'at and to bring disorder to society. Because the Egyptians regarded Ma'at as the right order of nature, they believed that its preservation must be the object of human activity—the guiding norm of the state and the standard by which individuals conducted their lives. Those who did Ma'at and spoke Ma'at would be justly rewarded. Could anything be more reassuring than this belief that divine truth was represented in the person of the pharaoh?

Science and Mathematics

Like the Mesopotamians, the Egyptians made practical advances in the sciences. They demonstrated superb engineering skills in building pyramids and fashioned an effective system of mathematics, including geometry for measurements, which enabled them to solve relatively simple problems. The Egyptians' solar calendar, which allowed them to predict when the Nile would overflow, was more accurate than the Babylonians' lunar calendar.

In the area of medicine, Egyptian doctors were more capable than their Mesopotamian counterparts. They could identify illnessess and recognized that uncleanliness encouraged contagion. They also had some knowledge of anatomy and performed operations: circumcision and perhaps the draining of abscessed teeth. But their knowledge of medicine, like that of the Mesopotamians, was handicapped by their belief that spiritual forces caused illnesses.

**Pharaoh Mycerinus and His Queen,
c. 2525 B.C.** Swelling chests and
hips idealize the royal couple's humanity, but the cubic feeling of the
sculpture and rigid confidence of the
pose proclaim their unquestioned divinity. (*Harvard MFA Expedition.
Courtesy, Museum of Fine Arts,
Boston*)

The New Kingdom and the Decline of Egyptian Civilization

The New Kingdom began in 1570 B.C. with the war of liberation against the
Hyksos. This war gave rise to an intense militancy, which found expression in
empire building. Aggressive pharaohs conquered territory that extended as far
east as the Euphrates River. From its subject states, Egypt acquired tribute
and slaves. Conquests led to the expansion of the bureaucracy, the development of a professional army, and the increased power of priests, whose temples shared in the spoils. The formation of the empire ended Egyptian
isolation and accelerated commercial and cultural intercourse with other peoples. During this period, Egyptian art, for example, showed the influence of
foreign forms.

A growing cosmopolitanism was paralleled by a movement toward

The Eighteenth Dynasty King Akhenaton.   His religious revolution has intrigued historians. Here he is depicted with his wife Nefertiti and their daughter seated on her lap. The sun disc, representing the sole god Aton, looms above. (*Egyptian Museum Berlin/Bildarchiv Preussischer Kulturbesitz*)

monotheism during the reign of Pharaoh Amenhotep IV (c. 1369–1353 B.C.). Amenhotep sought to replace traditional polytheism with the worship of Aton, a single god of all people, who was represented as the sun disk. Amenhotep took the name Akhenaton ("It is well with Aton") and moved the capital from Thebes to a newly constructed holy city, called Akhataten (near modern Tell el Amarna). The city had palaces, administrative centers, and a temple complex honoring Aton. Akhenaton and his wife, Nefertiti, who played a prominent role in his court, dedicated themselves to Aton—the creator of the world, the sustainer of life, and the god of love, justice, and peace. Akhenaton also ordered his officials to chisel out the names of other gods from inscriptions on temples and monuments. With awe, Akhenaton glorified Aton:

> *How manifold are thy works!*
> *They are hidden from man's sight.*
> *O sole god, like whom there is no other.*
> *Thou hast made the earth according to thy desire.*[2]

Akhenaton's "monotheism" had little impact on the masses of Egyptians, who retained their ancient beliefs, and was resisted by priests, who resented his changes. After Akhenaton's death, a new pharaoh had the monuments to Aton destroyed, along with records and inscriptions bearing Akhenaton's name.

The most significant historical questions about Akhenaton are these two: Was his religion genuine monotheism, which pushed religious thought in a new direction? And if so, did it influence Moses, who led the Israelites out of Egypt about a century later? These questions have aroused controversy among historians. The principal limitation on the monotheistic character of Atonism is that there were really two gods in Akhenaton's religion: Aton and the pharaoh himself, who was still worshiped as a deity. Nor is there any evidence that Akhenaton influenced the monotheism of Moses. Moreover, the Hebrews never identified God with the sun or any other object in nature.

Late in the thirteenth century B.C., Libyans, probably seeking to settle in the more fertile land of Egypt, attacked from the west, and the Peoples of the Sea, as unsettled raiders from the Aegean Sea area and Asia Minor were called, launched a series of strikes at Egypt. A weakened Egypt abandoned its empire. In the succeeding centuries, Egypt came under the rule of Libyans, Nubians, Assyrians, Persians, and finally Greeks, to whom Egypt lost its independence in the fourth century B.C.

Egyptian civilization had flourished for nearly two thousand years before it experienced an almost one-thousand-year descent into stagnation, decline, and collapse. During its long history, the Egyptians tried to preserve the ancient forms of their civilization, revealed to them by their ancestors and representing for all time those unchanging values that they believed were the way of happiness.

Empire Builders

The rise of an Egyptian empire during the New Kingdom was part of a wider development in Near Eastern history after 1500 B.C.—the emergence of international empires. Empire building led to the intermingling of peoples and cultural traditions and to the extension of civilization well beyond the river valleys.

One reason for the growth of empires was the migration of peoples known as Indo-Europeans. Originally from a wide area ranging from southeastern Europe to the region beyond the Caspian Sea, Indo-Europeans embarked, around 2000 B.C., on a series of migrations, which eventually brought them into Italy, Greece, Asia Minor, Mesopotamia, Persia, and India. From a core Indo-European tongue emerged the Greek, Latin, Germanic, Slavic, Persian, and Sanskrit languages.

Hittites

Several peoples established strong states in the Near East around 1500 B.C.—the Hurrians in northern Mesopotamia, the Kassites in southern Mesopotamia, and the Hittites in Asia Minor. The Hittites wanted to control the trade routes that ran along the Euphrates River into Syria. In the 1300s, the Hittite empire reached its peak. Its leaders ruled Asia Minor and northern Syria, raided Babylon, and challenged Egypt for control of Syria and Palestine.

The Hittites borrowed several features of Mesopotamian civilization, including cuneiform, legal principles, and literary and art forms. Hittite religion blended the beliefs and practices of Indo-Europeans, native inhabitants of Asia Minor, and Mesopotamians. The Hittites were probably the first people to develop a substantial iron industry. Initially, they apparently used iron only for ceremonial and ritual objects, and not for tools and weapons. However, because iron ore was more readily available than copper or tin (needed for bronze), after 1200 B.C. iron weapons and tools spread throughout the Near East, although bronze implements were still used. Around 1200 B.C., the Hittite empire fell, most likely to Indo-European invaders from the north.

Small Nations

During the twelfth century B.C., there was a temporary lull in empire building, which permitted a number of small nations in Syria and Palestine to assert their sovereignty. Three of these peoples—the Phoenicians, the Aramaeans, and the Hebrews*—were originally Semitic desert nomads. The Phoenicians were descendants of the Canaanites, a Semitic people who had settled Palestine around 3000 B.C. The Canaanites who had migrated northwest into what is now Lebanon were called Phoenicians.

Settling in the coastal Mediterranean cities of Tyre, Byblos, Berytus (Beirut), and Sidon, the Phoenicians were naturally drawn to the sea. These daring explorers established towns along the coast of North Africa, on the islands of the western Mediterranean, and in Spain; they became the greatest sea traders of the ancient world. The Phoenicians (or their Canaanite forebears) devised the first alphabet, which was a monumental contribution to writing. Since all words could be represented by combinations of letters, it saved memorizing thousands of diagrams and aided the Phoenicians in transmitting the civilizations of the Near East to the western Mediterranean. Adopted by the Greeks, who added vowels, the phonetic alphabet became a crucial component of European languages.

The Aramaeans, who settled in Syria, Palestine, and northern Mesopotamia, performed a role similar to that of the Phoenicians. As great caravan traders, they carried both goods and cultural patterns to various parts of the Near East. The Hebrews and the Persians, for example, acquired the Phoenician alphabet from the Aramaeans.

Assyria

In the ninth century B.C., empire building resumed with the Assyrians, a Semitic people from the region around the upper Tigris River. Although they had made forays of expansion in 1200 and 1100 B.C., the Assyrians began their march to "world" empire three centuries later. In the eighth and seventh centuries, they became a ruthless fighting machine, which stormed through Mesopotamia—including Armenia and Babylonia—as well as Syria, Palestine, and Egypt.

The Assyrian king, who was the representative and high priest of the god Ashur, governed absolutely. Nobles appointed by the king kept order in the provinces and collected tribute. The Assyrians improved roads, established

---

*The Hebrews are discussed in Chapter 2.

messenger services, and engaged in large-scale irrigation projects to facilitate effective administration of their conquered lands and to promote prosperity. They exacted obedience by resorting to terror and by deporting troublemakers from their home territories.

Despite their harsh characteristics, the Assyrians preserved and spread the culture of the past. They copied and edited the literary works of Babylonia, adopted the old Sumerian gods, and used Mesopotamian art forms. The Assyrian king Ashurbanipal (669–626 B.C.) maintained a great library, housing thousands of clay tablets. After a period of wars and revolts by oppressed subjects weakened Assyria, a coalition of Medes from Iran and Chaldeans, or Neo-Babylonians, sacked the Assyrian capital of Nineveh in 612 B.C., destroying Assyrian power.

Persia: Unifier of the Near East

The destruction of the Assyrian empire made possible the rise of a Chaldean empire, which included Babylonia, Assyria, Syria, and Palestine. Under Nebuchadnezzar, who ruled from 604 to 562 B.C., the Chaldean, or Neo-Babylonian, empire reached its height. After Nebuchadnezzar's death, the empire was torn by civil war and threatened by a new power: the Persians, an Indo-European people who had settled in southern Iran. Under Cyrus the Great and his son and successor, Cambyses, the Persians conquered all lands between the Nile in Egypt and the Indus River in India. This conquest took twenty-five years, from 550 to 525 B.C.

The Near Eastern conception of absolute monarchy justified by religion reached its culminating expression in the person of the Persian king, who, with divine approval, ruled a vast empire, "the four quarters of the earth." Persian kings developed an effective system of administration—based in part on an Assyrian model—which gave stability and a degree of unity to their extensive territories. The Persian empire was divided into twenty provinces (*satrapies*), each one administered by a governor (*satrap*) responsible to the emperor. To guard against subversion, the king employed special agents— "the eyes and ears of the emperor"—who supervised the activities of the governors. Persian kings allowed the provincials a large measure of self-rule. They also respected local traditions, particularly in matters of religion, as long as subjects paid their taxes, served in the royal army, and refrained from rebellion.

The empire was bound together by a uniform language, Aramaic (the language of the Aramaeans of Syria), used by government officials and merchants. Aramaic was written in letters based on the Phoenician alphabet. By making Aramaic a universal language, the Persians facilitated written and oral communication within the empire. The empire was further unified by an elaborate network of roads, an efficient postal system, a common system of weights and measures, and an empirewide coinage based on an invention of the Lydians from western Asia Minor.

Besides providing impressive political and administrative unity, the Persians

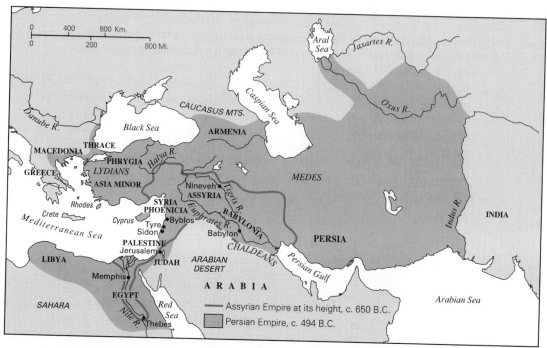

Map 1.2   The Assyrian and Persian Empires

fused and perpetuated the various cultural traditions of the Near East. Persian palaces, for example, boasted the terraces of Babylon, the colonnades of Egypt, the winged bulls that decorated Assyrian palace gates, and the craftsmanship of Median goldsmiths.

The political and cultural universalism of the Persian empire had its counterpart in the emergence of a higher religion, Zoroastrianism, which contained both monotheistic and dualistic elements and emphasized the individual's capacity to choose between good and evil. Named for its founder, the Persian prophet Zoroaster, who lived in the sixth century B.C., this religion taught belief in Ahura Mazda—the Wise Lord—god of light, justice, wisdom, goodness, and immortality. In addition to Ahura Mazda, however, there existed Ahriman, the spirit of darkness, who was evil and destructive; Ahriman was in conflict with the ultimately triumphant Ahura Mazda. People were free to choose whom they would follow. To serve Ahura Mazda, one had to speak the truth and be good to others; the reward for such behavior was life eternal in paradise, the realm of light and goodness. Followers of the evil spirit could be cast into a realm of darkness and torment. In contrast to the traditional religions of the Near East, Zoroastrianism rejected magic, polytheism, and blood sacrifices. Instead, it stressed ethics.

Persia unified the nations of the Near East into a world-state, headed by a divinely appointed king. It also synthesized the region's cultural traditions.

Soon it would confront the city-states of Greece, whose political system and cultural orientation differed from those of the Near East.

The Religious Orientation of the Ancient Near East

Religion dominated, suffused, and inspired all features of Near Eastern society: law, kingship, art, and science. It was the source of the vitality and creativity of Mesopotamian and Egyptian civilizations. Priest-kings or god-kings, their power sanctioned by divine forces, furnished the necessary authority to organize large numbers of people in cooperative ventures. Religion also encouraged and justified wars—including enslavements and massacres—which were seen as conflicts between the gods.

A Myth-Making World-View

A religious, or mythopoeic (myth-making), view of the world gives Near Eastern civilization its distinctive form and allows us to see it as an organic whole. Myth-making was humanity's first way of thinking; it was the earliest attempt to make nature and life comprehensible. Appealing primarily to the imagination and emotions, rather than to reason, mythical thinking, as expressed in language, art, poetry, and social organization, has been a fundamental formative element of human culture.

Originating in sacred rites, ritual dances, feasts, and ceremonies, myths depicted the deeds of gods, who, in some remote past, had brought forth the world and human beings. Holding that human destiny was determined by the gods, Near Eastern people interpreted their experiences through myths. Myths also enabled Mesopotamians and Egyptians to make sense out of nature, to explain the world of phenomena. Through myths, the Near Eastern mind sought to give coherence to the universe and make it intelligible. These myths gave Near Eastern people a framework with which to pattern their experiences into a meaningful order, justify their rules of conduct, and try to overcome the uncertainty of existence.

The civilizations of the ancient Near East were based on a way of thinking fundamentally different from the modern scientific outlook. The difference between scientific and mythical thinking is profound. The scientific mind views physical nature as an *it*—inanimate, impersonal, and governed by universal law. The myth-making mind of the Near East saw every object in nature as a *thou*—personified, alive, with an individual will. It saw gods or demons manipulating things. The sun and stars, the rivers and mountains, the wind and lightning were either gods or the dwelling places of gods. An Egyptian or a Mesopotamian experienced natural phenomena—a falling rock, a thunderclap, a rampaging river—as life facing life. If a river flooded the region, destroying crops, it was because it wanted to; the river or the gods desired to punish the people.

In other words, the ancients told myths instead of presenting an analysis or conclusions. We would explain, for instance, that certain atmospheric changes broke a drought and brought about rain. The Babylonians observed the same facts but experienced them as the intervention of the gigantic bird Imdugud which came to their rescue. It covered the sky with the black storm clouds of its wings and devoured the Bull of Heaven, whose hot breath had scorched the crops.[3]

The Egyptians believed that the sun rose in the morning, traveled across the sky, and set into the netherworld beyond the western horizon. Sometimes, it was maintained that the great Cow of Heaven every day gave birth to the sun, which was swallowed every evening by the sky goddess Nut. After warding off the forces of chaos and disruption, the sun reappeared the next morning. For the Egyptians, the rising and setting of the sun were not natural occurrences—a celestial body obeying an impersonal law—but a religious drama.

The scientific mind holds that natural objects obey universal rules; hence, the location of planets, the speed of objects, and the onset of a hurricane can be predicted. The myth-making mind of the ancient Near East was not troubled by contradictions. It did not seek logical consistency and had no awareness of repetitive laws inherent in nature. Rather, it attributed all occurrences to the actions of gods, whose behavior was often erratic and unpredictable. Witch doctors employed magic to protect people from evil supernatural forces that surrounded them. The scientific mind appeals to reason: it analyzes nature logically and systematically and searches for general principles that govern phenomena. The myth-making mind appeals to the imagination and feelings and proclaims a truth that is emotionally satisfying, not one that has been arrived at through intellectual analysis and synthesis. Mythical explanations of nature and human experience enrich perception and feeling. Thus, they made life seem less overwhelming and death less frightening.

Of course, Near Eastern people did engage in rational forms of thought and behavior. They certainly employed reason in building irrigation works, in preparing a calendar, and in performing mathematical operations. However, because rational, or logical, thought remained subordinate to a mythic-religious orientation, they did not arrive at a *consistently* and *self-consciously* rational method of inquiring into physical nature and human culture.

Thus, Near Eastern civilization reached the first level in the development of science: observing nature, recording data, and improving technology in mining, metallurgy, and architecture. But it did not advance to the level of self-conscious philosophical and scientific thought—that is, logically deduced abstractions, hypotheses, and generalizations. Mesopotamians and Egyptians did not fashion a body of philosophical and scientific ideas that were logically structured, discussed, and debated. They had no awareness of general laws that govern particular events. These later developments were the singular achievement of Greek philosophy. It gave a "rational interpretation to natural occurrences which had previously been explained by ancient mythologies. . . .

With the study of nature set free from the control of mythological fancy, the way was opened for the development of science as an intellectual system."[4]

Near Eastern Achievements

The Sumerians and the Egyptians demonstrated enormous creativity and intelligence. They built irrigation works and cities, organized governments, charted the course of heavenly bodies, performed mathematical operations, constructed large-scale monuments, engaged in international trade, established bureaucracies and schools, and considerably advanced the level of technology. Without the Sumerian invention of writing—one of the great creative acts in history—what we mean by *civilization* could not have emerged.

Many elements of ancient Near Eastern civilization were passed on to the West. The wheeled vehicle, the plow, and the phonetic alphabet—all important to the development of civilization—derive from the Near East. In the realm of medicine, the Egyptians knew the value of certain drugs, such as castor oil; they also knew how to use splints and bandages. The innovative divisions that gave 360 degrees to a circle and 60 minutes to an hour originated in Mesopotamia. Egyptian geometry and Babylonian astronomy were utilized by the Greeks and became a part of Western knowledge. The belief that a king's power issued from a heavenly source also derived from the Near East. In Christian art, too, one finds connections to Mesopotamian art forms—for example, the Assyrians depicted winged angel-like beings.

Both the Hebrews and the Greeks borrowed Mesopotamian literary themes. For instance, some biblical stories—the Flood, the quarrel between Cain and Abel, and the Tower of Babel—stem from Mesopotamian antecedents. A similar link exists between the Greek and the earlier Mesopotamian mythologies.

Thus, many achievements of the Egyptians and the Mesopotamians were inherited and assimilated by both the Greeks and the Hebrews. Even more important for an understanding of the essential meaning of Western civilization are the ways in which the Greeks and the Hebrews rejected or transformed elements of the older Near Eastern traditions to create new points of departure for the human mind.

Notes

1. *Epic of Gilgamesh*, with an introduction by N. K. Sandars (Baltimore: Penguin Books, 1960), pp. 69, 104.
2. Quoted in John A. Wilson, *The Culture of Ancient Egypt* (Chicago: University of Chicago Press, Phoenix Books, 1951), p. 227.
3. Henri Frankfort, et al., *Before Philosophy* (Baltimore: Penguin Books, 1949), p. 15.
4. Samuel Sambursky, *The Physical World of the Greeks* (New York: Collier Books, 1962), pp. 18–19.

Suggested Reading

Campbell, Bernard G., *Humankind Emerging* (1982). The world of pre-history.

David, Rosalie A., *The Ancient Egyptians* (1982). Focuses on religious beliefs and practices.

Frankfort, Henri, et al., *The Intellectual Adventure of Ancient Man* (1946); paperback edition is entitled *Before Philosophy*. Brilliant discussions of the role of myth in the ancient Near East by distinguished scholars.

Gowlett, John, *Ascent to Civilization* (1984). An up-to-date study, with excellent graphics.

Hallo, W. W., and W. K. Simpson, *The Ancient Near East* (1971). An authoritative survey of the political history of the Near East.

Moscati, Sabatino, *The Face of the Ancient Orient* (1962). An illuminating survey of the various peoples of the ancient Near East.

Oppenheim, A. L., *Ancient Mesopotamia* (1964). Stresses social and economic history.

Saggs, H. W. F., *Civilization Before Greece and Rome* (1989). Focuses on culture and society.

Wilson, John A., *The Culture of Ancient Egypt* (1951). An interpretation by a distinguished Egyptologist.

Review Questions

1. Why is the development of the Neolithic Age referred to as the Neolithic Revolution?
2. What is meant by civilization? Under what conditions did it emerge?
3. How did religion influence Mesopotamian civilization?
4. What did the Mesopotamians achieve in trade, mathematics, and science?
5. How did the Egyptians' religious beliefs affect their civilization?
6. What is the historical significance of Akhenaton?
7. How did the Persians give unity to the Near East?
8. What is myth? How does mythical thought differ from scientific thought?
9. What advances in science were made by Near Eastern civilization? How did a myth-making view of nature limit science?
10. What were the accomplishments of the civilizations of the Near East? What elements of Near Eastern civilizations were passed on to Western civilization?

❖ CHAPTER **2**

The Hebrews: A New View of God and the Individual

$\mathcal{A}$ncient Mesopotamia and Egypt, the birthplace of the first civilizations, are not the spiritual ancestors of the West; for the origins of the Western tradition we must turn to the Hebrews (Jews) and the Greeks. As Egyptologist John A. Wilson writes,

The Children of Israel built a nation and a religion on the rejection of things Egyptian. Not only did they see God as one, but they ascribed to him consistency of concern for man and consistency of justice to man. . . . Like the Greeks, the Hebrews took forms from their great neighbors; like the Greeks, they used those forms for very different purposes.[1]

In this chapter, we examine one source of the Western tradition, the Hebrews, whose conception of God broke with the outlook of the Near East and whose ethical teachings helped to fashion the Western idea of the dignity of the individual.   ❖

Early Hebrew History

The Hebrews originated in Mesopotamia and migrated to Canaan, a portion of which was later called Palestine. The Hebrew patriarchs—Abraham, Isaac, and Jacob, so prominently depicted in the Old Testament—were chieftains of seminomadic clans that roamed Palestine and occasionally journeyed to Mesopotamia and Egypt. The early Hebrews absorbed some features of Mesopotamian civilization. For example, there are parallels between biblical law and the Mesopotamian legal tradition. Several biblical stories—the Creation, the Flood, the Garden of Eden—derive from Mesopotamian sources.

Some Hebrews journeyed from Canaan to Egypt to be herdsmen and farmers, but they eventually became forced laborers for the Egyptians. Fearful of turning into permanent slaves of the pharaoh, the Hebrews yearned for an opportunity to escape. In the thirteenth century B.C., an extraordinary leader rose among them, called Moses, who was accepted by his people as a messenger of God. Leading the Hebrews in their exodus from Egypt, Moses transformed them during their wanderings in the wilderness of Sinai into a nation, united and uplifted by a belief in Yahweh, the one God.

The wandering Hebrews returned to Canaan to rejoin other Hebrew tribes that had not migrated to Egypt. The conquest and colonization of Canaan was a gradual process, which took many generations. Threatened by the Philistines (originally from the islands of the Aegean Sea and the coast of Asia Minor), the twelve Hebrew tribes united under the leadership of Saul, a charismatic hero, whom they acclaimed as their first king. Under Saul's successor, David, a gifted warrior and poet, the Hebrews (or Israelites) broke the back of Philistine power and subdued neighboring peoples.

David's son Solomon built a royal palace in Jerusalem and beside it a magnificent temple honoring God. Under Solomon, ancient Israel was at the height of its political power and prosperity, but opposition to Solomon's tax policies and his favored treatment of the region of Judah in the south led to the division of the kingdom after his death in 922 B.C. The tribes loyal to Solomon's son belonged to the Kingdom of Judah, whereas the other tribes organized the northern Kingdom of Israel.

In 722 B.C., Israel fell to the Assyrians, who deported many Hebrews to other parts of the Assyrian empire. These transplanted Hebrews merged with neighboring peoples and lost their identity as the people of the one God. In 586 B.C., the Chaldeans conquered Judah, destroyed Solomon's temple, devastated the land, and deported several thousand Hebrews to Babylon. This time was the darkest moment in the history of the Hebrews. Their state was gone, and neighboring peoples had overrun their land; their holy temple, built during the reign of King Solomon, was in ruins; thousands had died in battle or had been executed or had fled to Egypt and other lands; and thousands more were in exile in Babylon. This exile is known as the Babylonian Captivity.

Still, the Hebrews, now commonly called Jews, survived as a people—a fact that is a marvel of history. Although many of the exiles in Babylon assimilated Babylonian ways, some remained faithful to their God, Yahweh, and to the Law of Moses, and they longed to return to their homeland. Thus, their faith enabled them to endure conquest and exile. When the Persians conquered Babylon, King Cyrus, in 538 B.C., permitted the exiles to return to Judah, now a Persian province, and to rebuild the temple.

The Jews lost their independence to Rome in the first century B.C. and eventually became a dispersed people. But they never relinquished their commitment to God and his Law as recorded in the Hebrew Scriptures. Called *Tanak* by Jews (and Old Testament by Christians), these Scriptures consist of thirty-nine books* by several authors who lived in different centuries. Jews call the first five books—Genesis, Exodus, Leviticus, Numbers, and Deuteronomy— the Torah (which originally meant "teaching" or "instruction"). Often the Torah is referred to as the Pentateuch, a Greek word meaning "five books."

---

*In ancient times, the number of books was usually given as twenty-four. Certain books are now divided into two parts, and the twelve works by the minor prophets are now counted as individual books.

Chronology 2.1 ❖ The Hebrews

1250 B.C.*	Hebrew exodus from Egypt
1024–1000	Reign of Saul, Israel's first king
1000–961	Creation of a united monarchy under David
961–922	Reign of Solomon; construction of the first temple
750–430	Age of classical prophecy
722	Kingdom of Israel falls to Assyrians
586	Kingdom of Judah falls to Chaldeans; the temple is destroyed
586–539	Babylonian exile
538	Cyrus of Persia allows exiles to return to Judah
515 B.C.	Second temple is dedicated

*Most dates are approximations.

The Hebrew Scriptures represent Jewish written and oral tradition dating from about 1250 to 150 B.C. The record of more than a thousand years of ancient Jewish life, they include Jewish laws, wisdom, hopes, legends, and literary expressions. In describing an ancient people's efforts to comprehend the ways of God, the Scriptures emphasize and value the human experience; their heroes are not demigods but human beings. The Scriptures depict human strength as well as weakness. Some passages exhibit cruelty and unseemly revenge against the enemies of Israel, but others express the highest ethical values.

Compiled by religious devotees, not research historians, the Hebrew Scriptures understandably contain factual errors, imprecisions, and discrepancies. However, they also offer passages of reliable history, and historians find these Scriptures an indispensable source for studying the ancient Near East. Students of literature explore the Old Testament for its poetry, legends, and themes, all of which are an integral part of the Western literary tradition. But it is as a work of religious inspiration that the Hebrew Bible attains its profoundest importance. As set forth there, the Hebrew idea of God and his relationship to human beings is one of the foundations of the Western tradition.

God: One, Sovereign, Transcendent, Good

Monotheism, the belief in one God, became the central force in the life of the Hebrews, and marked a profound break with Near Eastern religious thought. Near Eastern gods were not truly free; their power was not without limits.

A Dead Sea Scroll, Judea, Second Century B.C.   The sacredness of the biblical texts and the authority of the recorded word of God remain a unifying factor in modern as well as ancient Jewish society. Many ancient Hebrew scrolls were found in caves near the west bank of the Dead Sea beginning in the late 1940s. The scroll depicted here contains the earliest existing copy of a complete Hebrew text of the book of the prophet Isaiah. It barely differs from more modern manuscripts. (© *John C. Trevor, 1970*)

Unlike Yahweh, Near Eastern gods were not eternal, but were born or created; they issued from some prior realm. They were also subject to biological conditions, requiring food, drink, sleep, and sexual gratification. Sometimes, they became ill or grew old or died. When they behaved wickedly, they had to answer to fate, which demanded punishment as retribution; even the gods were subject to fate's power.

The Hebrews regarded God as *fully sovereign.* He ruled all and was subject to nothing. Yahweh's existence and power did not derive from a preexisting realm, as was the case with the gods of other peoples. The Hebrews believed that no realm of being preceded God in time or surpassed him in power. They saw God as eternal, the source of all in the universe, and having a supreme will.

Whereas Near Eastern divinities dwelt within nature, the Hebrew God was *transcendent,* above nature and not a part of it. Yahweh was not identified with any natural force and did not dwell in a particular place in heaven or on earth. Since God was the creator and ruler of nature, there was no place for a sun god, a moon god, a god in the river, or a demon in the storm. Nature was God's creation but was not itself divine. Therefore, when the Hebrews confronted natural phenomena, they experienced God's magnificent handiwork, not objects with wills of their own. All natural phenomena—rivers, mountains, storms, stars—were divested of any supernatural quality. The stars and planets were creations of Yahweh, not divinities or the abodes of divinities. The Hebrews neither regarded them with awe nor worshiped them.

The removal of the gods from nature—the demythicizing of nature—is a necessary prerequisite for scientific thought. But concerned with religion and morality, the Hebrews did not create theoretical science. As testimony to God's greatness, nature inspired them to sing the praises of the Lord; it invoked worship of God, not scientific curiosity. When they gazed at the heavens, they did not seek to discover mathematical relationships but admired God's handiwork. They did not view nature as a system governed by self-operating physical principles or natural law. Rather, they saw the rising sun, spring rain, summer heat, and winter cold as God intervening in an orderly manner in his creation. The Hebrews, unlike the Greeks, were not philosophical or scientific thinkers. They were concerned with God's will, not the human intellect; with the feelings of the heart, not the power of the mind; with righteous behavior, not abstract thought.

Unlike the Greeks, the Hebrews did not speculate about the origins of all things and the operations of nature; they knew that God had created everything. For the Hebrews, God's existence was based on religious conviction, not on rational inquiry; on revelation, not reason. It was the Greeks, not the Hebrews, who originated rational thought. But Christianity, born of Judaism, retained the Hebrew view of a transcendent God and the orderliness of his creation: concepts that could accommodate Greek science.

The Hebrews also did not speculate about God's nature. They knew only that he was *good* and that he made ethical demands on his people. Unlike Near Eastern gods, Yahweh was not driven by lust or motivated by evil but was "merciful and gracious, long-suffering, and abundant in goodness and truth . . . forgiving inequity and transgression and sin" (Psalm 145:8).[2] In contrast to pagan gods, who were indifferent to human beings, Yahweh was attentive to human needs. By asserting that God was *one, sovereign, transcendent,* and *good,* the Hebrews effected a religious revolution that separated them entirely from the world-view held by the other peoples of the ancient Near East.

The Individual and Moral Autonomy

This new conception of God made possible a new awareness of the individual. In confronting God, the Hebrews developed an awareness of *self,* or *I:* the individual became conscious of his or her own person, moral autonomy, and personal worth. The Hebrews believed that God, who possessed total freedom, had bestowed on people moral freedom—the capacity to choose between good and evil.

Fundamental to Hebrew belief was the insistence that God did not create people to be his slaves. The Hebrews regarded God with awe and humility, with respect and fear, but they did not believe that God wanted people to grovel before him; rather, he wanted them to fulfill their moral potential by freely making the choice to follow or not to follow God's Law. Thus, in creating men and women in his own image, God made them autonomous and sovereign. In God's plan for the universe, human beings were the highest creation, subordinate only to God. Of all his creations, only they had been given the freedom to choose between righteousness and wickedness, between "life and good, and death and evil" (Deuteronomy 30:15). But having the power to choose freely, men and women must bear the responsibility for their choice.

God demanded that the Hebrews have no other gods and that they make no images "nor any manner of likeness, of any thing that is in heaven above, or that is in the earth beneath, . . . thou shalt not bow down unto them nor serve them" (Exodus 20:4–5). The Hebrews believed that the worship of idols deprived people of their freedom and dignity; people cannot be fully human if they surrender themselves to a lifeless idol. Hence, the Hebrews rejected images and all other forms of idolatry. A crucial element of Near Eastern religion was the use of images—art forms that depicted divinities—but the Hebrews believed that God, the Supreme Being, could not be represented by pictures or sculpture fashioned by human hands. The Hebrews rejected entirely the belief that an image possessed divine powers, which could be manipulated for human advantage. Ethical considerations, not myth or magic, were central to Hebrew religious life.

By making God the center of life, Hebrews could become free moral agents; no person, no human institution, and no human tradition could claim their souls. Because God alone was the supreme value in the universe, only he was worthy of worship. Thus, to give ultimate loyalty to a king or a general violated God's stern warning against the worship of false gods. The first concern of the Hebrews was righteousness, not power, fame, or riches, which were only idols and would impoverish a person spiritually and morally.

There was, however, a condition to freedom. For the Hebrews, people were not free to create their own moral precepts or their own standards of right and wrong. Freedom meant voluntary obedience to commands that originated with God. Evil and suffering were not caused by blind fate, malevolent demons, or arbitrary gods; they resulted from people's disregard of God's commandments. The dilemma is that in possessing freedom of choice, human beings are also free to disobey God, to commit a sin, which leads to suffering and death. Thus, in the Genesis story, Adam and Eve were punished for disobeying God in the Garden of Eden.

For the Hebrews, to know God was not to comprehend him intellectually, to define him, or to prove his existence; to know God was to be righteous and loving, merciful and just. When men and women loved God, the Hebrews believed, they were uplifted and improved. Gradually, they learned to overcome the worst elements of human nature and to treat people with respect and compassion. The Jews came to interpret the belief that man was created in God's image to mean that each human being has a divine spark in him or her, giving every person a unique dignity, which cannot be taken away.

Through their devotion to God, the Hebrews asserted the value and autonomy of human beings. Thus, the Hebrews conceived the idea of moral freedom: that each individual is responsible for his or her own actions. These concepts of human dignity and moral autonomy, which Christianity inherited, are at the core of the Western tradition.

The Covenant and the Law

Central to Hebrew religious thought and decisive in Hebrew history was the covenant, God's special agreement with the Hebrew people: if they obeyed his commands, they would "be unto Me a kingdom of priests, and a holy nation" (Exodus 19:6). By this act, the Israelites as a nation accepted God's lordship. Justice was the central theme of Old Testament ethics. The Israelites, liberated from slavery by a righteous and compassionate God, had a moral responsibility to overcome injustice, to care for the poor, the weak, and the oppressed.

The Hebrews came to see themselves as a unique nation, a "chosen people," for God had given them a special honor, a profound opportunity, and (as they could never forget) an awesome responsibility. The Hebrews did not claim that God had selected them because they were better than other peoples or because they had done anything special to deserve God's election. They believed that God had selected them to receive the Law so that their nation would set an example of righteous behavior and ultimately make God and the Law known to the other nations.

This responsibility to be the moral teachers of humanity weighed heavily on the Hebrews. They believed that God had revealed his Law—including the moral code known as the Ten Commandments—to the Hebrew people as a whole, and obedience to the Law became the overriding obligation of each Hebrew.

Israelite law incorporated many elements from Near Eastern legal codes and oral traditions. But by making people more important than property, by expressing mercy toward the oppressed, and by rejecting the idea that law should treat the poor and the rich differently, Israelite law demonstrated a greater ethical awareness and a more humane spirit than other legal codes of the Near East. Thus, there were laws to protect the poor, widows, orphans, resident aliens, hired laborers, and slaves:

> *Ye shall not steal; neither shall ye deal falsely, nor lie to one another. . . . Thou shalt not oppress thy neighbour nor rob him. . . . Ye shall do no unrighteousness in judgment; thou shalt not respect the person of the poor, nor favour the person of the mighty; but in righteousness shalt thou judge thy neighbor. . . . And if a stranger*

Wall Painting from the Synagogue in Dura-Europos.   Some time after 1050 B.C. the Israelites engaged the Philistines, formidable warriors who dominated Canaanite cities, in battle near Aphek. The Israelites brought the Ark of the Covenant into their camp, hoping that God's presence would produce victory. However, the Philistines decimated the Israelites and captured the ark. These events are described in 1 Samuel, Chapter 4. This painting from a third century synagogue in Roman Syria depicts the ark's capture. (*Yale University Art Gallery, Dura-Europos Collection*)

> *sojourn with thee in your land, ye shall not do him wrong. The stranger that sojourneth with you shall be unto you as the home born among you, and thou shalt love him as thyself. (Leviticus 19:11, 13, 15, 33, 34)*

Like other Near Eastern societies, the Jews placed women in a subordinate position. The husband was considered his wife's master, and she often addressed him as a servant or subject would speak to a superior. A husband could divorce his wife, but she could not divorce him. Only when there was no male heir could a wife inherit property from her husband or a daughter inherit from her father. Outside the home, women were not regarded as competent witnesses in court and played a lesser role than men in organized worship.

On the other hand, the Jews also showed respect for women. Wise women and prophetesses like Judith and Deborah were esteemed by the community and consulted by its leaders. Prophets compared God's love for the Hebrews with a husband's love for his wife. Jewish law regarded the woman as a person, not as property. Even female captives taken in war were not to be abused or humiliated. The law required a husband to respect and support his wife and never to strike her. One of the Ten Commandments called for honoring both father and mother.

The Hebrew Idea of History

Their idea of God made the Hebrews aware of the crucial importance of historical time. Holidays commemorating such specific historical events as the Exodus from Egypt, the receiving of the Ten Commandments on Mount Sinai, and the destruction of Solomon's temple kept the past alive and vital. Egyptians and Mesopotamians did not have a similar awareness of the uniqueness of a given event; to them, today's events were repetitions of events experienced by their ancestors. To the Jews, the Exodus and the covenant at Mount Sinai were singular, nonrepetitive occurrences, decisive in shaping their national history. This historical uniqueness and importance of events derived from the idea of a universal God profoundly involved in human affairs—a God who cares, teaches, and punishes.

The Jews valued the future as well as the past. Regarding human history as a process leading to a goal, they envisioned a great day when God would establish on earth a glorious age of peace, prosperity, happiness, and human brotherhood. This utopian notion has become deeply embedded in Western thought.

The Hebrews saw history as the work of God; it was a divine drama filled with sacred meaning and moral significance. Historical events revealed the clash of human will with God's commands. Through history's specific events, God's presence was disclosed and his purpose made known. When the Hebrews suffered conquest and exile, they interpreted these events as retribution for violating God's Law and as punishments for their stubbornness, sinfulness, and rebelliousness. For the Hebrews, history also revealed God's compassion and concern. Thus, the Lord liberated Moses and the Israelites at the Red Sea and appointed prophets to plead for the poor and the oppressed. Because historical events revealed God's attitude toward human beings, these events possessed spiritual meaning and therefore were worth recording, evaluating, and remembering.

The Prophets

Jewish history was marked by the emergence of spiritually inspired persons called *prophets,* who felt compelled to act as God's messengers. The flowering of the prophetic movement—the age of classical, or literary, prophecy—began in the eighth century B.C. Among the prophets were Amos, a shepherd from Judea in the south; his younger contemporary, Hosea, from Israel in the

Wall Painting from the Synagogue in Dura-Europos, Raman Syria, Early Third Century A.D.   This painting shows a Hebrew prophet reading from an open scroll. (*Yale University Art Gallery, Dura-Europos Collection*)

north; Isaiah of Jerusalem; and Jeremiah, who witnessed the siege of Jerusalem in the early sixth century B.C. The prophets cared nothing for money or possessions, feared no one, and preached without invitation. Often emerging in times of social distress and moral confusion, they pleaded for a return to the covenant and the Law. They exhorted the entire nation and taught that when people forgot God and made themselves the center of all things, they would bring disaster on themselves and their community. The prophets saw national misfortune as an opportunity for penitence and reform. They were remarkably courageous individuals, who did not quake before the powerful.

In attacking oppression, cruelty, greed, and exploitation, the classical prophets added a new dimension to Israel's religious development. These prophets were responding to problems emanating from Israel's changed social structure. A tribal society generally lacks class distinctions, but this situation had been altered by the rise of Hebrew kings, the expansion of commerce, and the growth of cities. By the eighth century, there was a significant disparity between the wealthy and the poor. Small farmers in debt to moneylenders faced the loss of their land or even bondage; the poor were often dispossessed by the greedy wealthy. To the prophets, these social evils were religious sins that would bring ruin to Israel. In the name of God, they denounced the hypocrisy and pomp of the heartless rich and demanded justice. God is compassionate, they insisted. He cares for all, especially the poor, the unfortunate, the suffering, and the defenseless. God's injunctions, declared Isaiah, were to

> *Put away the evil of your doings*
> *From before mine eyes,*
> *Cease to do evil;*
> *Learn to do well;*
> *Seek justice, relieve the oppressed,*
> *Judge the fatherless, plead for the widow.*
> (Isaiah 1:16–17)

Prophets stressed the direct spiritual-ethical encounter between the individual and God. The inner person concerned them more than the outer forms of religious activity. Holding that the essence of the covenant was universal righteousness, the prophets criticized priests whose commitment to rites and rituals was not supported by a deeper spiritual insight or a zeal for morality in daily life. To the prophets, an ethical sin was far worse than a ritual omission. Above all, said the prophets, God demands righteousness, living justly before God. To live unjustly, to mistreat one's neighbors, to act without compassion—these actions violated God's Law and endangered the entire social order.

The prophets thus helped shape a social conscience that has become part of the Western tradition. They held out the hope that life on earth could be improved, that poverty and injustice need not be accepted as part of an unalterable natural order, and that the individual was capable of elevating himself or herself morally and could respect the dignity of others.

Two tendencies were present in Hebrew thought: parochialism and universalism. Parochial-mindedness stressed the special nature, destiny, and needs of the chosen people, a nation set apart from others. This narrow outlook was offset by universalism: a concern for all humanity, which found expression in those prophets who envisioned the unity of all people under God. All people were equally precious to God.

The prophets were not pacifists, particularly if a war was being waged against the enemies of Yahweh. But some prophets denounced war as obscene and looked forward to its elimination. They maintained that when people glorify force they dehumanize their opponents, brutalize themselves, and dishonor God. When violence rules, there can be no love of God and no regard for the individual.

The prophets' universalism was accompanied by an equally profound awareness of the individual and his or her intrinsic worth. Before the prophets, virtually all religious tradition had been produced communally and anonymously. The prophets, however, spoke as fearless individuals, who, by affixing their signatures to their thoughts, fully bore the responsibility for their religious inspiration and conviction.

The prophets emphasized the individual's responsibility for his or her own actions. In coming to regard God's Law as a *command to conscience, an appeal to the inner person,* the prophets heightened the awareness of the human personality. They indicated that the individual could not know God only by following edicts and by performing rituals; the individual must experience God. Precisely this *I-Thou* relationship could make the individual fully conscious of self and could deepen and enrich his or her own personality. During the Exodus, the Hebrews were a tribal people who obeyed the Law largely out of awe and group compulsion. By the prophets' time, the Jews appeared to be autonomous individuals who heeded the Law because of a deliberate, conscious inner commitment.

The ideals proclaimed by the prophets helped sustain the Jews throughout their long and often painful historical odyssey, and they remain a vital force for Jews today. Incorporated into the teachings of Jesus, these ideals, as part of Christianity, are embedded in the Western tradition.

The Legacy of the Ancient Jews

For the Jews, monotheism had initiated a process of self-discovery and self-realization unmatched by other peoples of the Near East. The great value that westerners give to the individual derives in part from the ancient Hebrews, who held that man and woman were created in God's image and possessed free will and a conscience answerable to God.

Christianity, the essential religion of Western civilization, emerged from ancient Judaism, and the links between the two, including monotheism, moral autonomy, prophetic values, and the Hebrew Scriptures as the Word of God, are numerous and strong. The historical Jesus cannot be understood without examining his Jewish background, and his followers appealed to the Hebrew Scriptures in order to demonstrate the validity of their beliefs. For these reasons, we talk of a Judeo-Christian tradition as an essential component of Western civilization.

The Hebrew vision of a future messianic age, a golden age of peace and social justice, is at the root of the Western idea of progress—that people can build a more just society, that there is a reason to be hopeful about the future. This way of perceiving the world has greatly influenced modern reform movements.

Finally, the Hebrew Scriptures have been a source of inspiration for Western religious thinkers, novelists, poets, and artists to the present day. Historians and archaeologists find the Hebrew Scriptures a valuable source in their efforts to reconstruct Near Eastern history.

Notes

1. John A. Wilson, "Egypt—the Kingdom of the 'Two Lands,'" in *At the Dawn of Civilization*, ed. E. A. Speiser (New Brunswick, N.J.: Rutgers University Press, 1964), pp. 267–268. Vol. I in *The World History of the Jewish People*.

2. The scriptural quotations in this chapter come from *The Holy Scriptures* (Philadelphia: The Jewish Publication Society of America, 1917), and are used with the permission of The Jewish Publication Society of America.

Suggested Reading

Anderson, Bernhard, *Understanding the Old Testament*, 2nd ed. (1966). An excellent survey of the Old Testament in its historical setting.

Boadt, Lawrence, *Reading the Old Testament* (1984). A study of ancient Israel's religious experience by a sympathetic Catholic scholar.

Bright, John, *A History of Israel* (1972). A thoughtful, clearly written survey; the best of its kind.

Grant, Michael, *The History of Ancient Israel* (1984). A lucid account.

Heschel, Abraham, *The Prophets*, 2 vols. (1962). A penetrating analysis of the nature of prophetic inspiration.

Kaufmann, Yehezkel, *The Religion of Israel* (1960). An abridgment and translation of Kaufmann's classic multivolume work.

Kuntz, Kenneth J., *The People of Ancient Israel* (1974). A useful introduction to Old Testament literature, history, and thought.

Zeitlin, Irving M., *Ancient Judaism* (1984). A sociologist examines the history and thought of ancient Israel.

Review Questions

1. How did the Hebrew view of God mark a revolutionary break with Near Eastern religious thought?

2. How did Hebrew religious thought promote the idea of moral autonomy?

3. Provide examples showing that Hebrew law expressed a concern for human dignity.

4. Why did the Hebrews consider history to be important, and how did they demonstrate its importance?

5. What role did the prophets play in Hebrew history? What is the enduring significance of their achievements?

6. Why are the Hebrews regarded as one source of Western civilization?

❖ CHAPTER 3

The Greeks: From Myth to Reason

$\mathcal{T}$he Hebrew conception of ethical monotheism, with its stress on human dignity, is one source of the Western tradition. The other source derives from ancient Greece. Both Hebrews and Greeks absorbed the achievements of Near Eastern civilizations, but they also developed their own distinctive viewpoints and styles of thought, which set them apart from the Mesopotamians and Egyptians. The great achievements of the Hebrews lay in the sphere of religious-ethical thought; those of the Greeks lay in the development of rational thought.

The Greeks conceived of nature as following general rules, not acting according to the whims of gods or demons. They saw human beings as having a capacity for rational thought, a need for freedom, and a worth as individuals. Although the Greeks never dispensed with the gods, they increasingly stressed the importance of human reason and human decisions; they came to assert that reason is the avenue to knowledge and that people—not the gods—are responsible for their own behavior. In this shift of attention from the gods to human beings, the Greeks broke with the myth-making orientation of the Near East and created the rational humanist outlook that is a distinctive feature of Western civilization. ❖

Early Aegean Civilizations

Until the latter part of the nineteenth century, historians placed the beginning of Greek (or Hellenic) history in the eighth century B.C. Now it is known that two civilizations preceded Hellenic Greece: the Minoan and the Mycenaean. Although the ancient Greek poet Homer had spoken of an earlier Greek civilization in his works, historians believed that Homer's epics dealt with myths and legends, not with a historical past. In 1871, however, a successful German businessman, Heinrich Schliemann, began a search for earliest Greece. In excavating several sites mentioned by Homer, Schliemann discovered tombs, pottery, ornaments, and the remains of palaces of what hitherto had been a

Chronology 3.1 ❖ The Greeks

1700–1450 B.C.*	Height of Minoan civilization
1400–1230	Height of Mycenaean civilization
1100–800	Dark Age
c. 700	Homer
750–550	Age of Colonization
594	Solon is given power to institute reforms
507	Cleisthenes broadens democratic institutions
480	Xerxes of Persia invades Greece; Greek naval victory at Salamis
479	Spartans defeat Persians at Plataea, ending Persian Wars
431	Start of Peloponnesian War
404	Athens surrenders to Sparta, ending Peloponnesian War
387	Plato founds a school, the Academy
359	Philip II becomes king of Macedonia
338	Battle of Chaeronea: Greek city-states fall under dominion of Macedonia
335	Aristotle founds a school, the Lyceum
323 B.C.	Death of Alexander the Great

*Some dates are approximations.

lost Greek civilization. The ancient civilization was named after Mycenae, the most important city of the time.

In 1900, Arthur Evans, a British archaeologist, excavating on the island of Crete, southeast of the Greek mainland, unearthed a civilization even older than that of the Mycenaean Greeks. The Cretans, or Minoans, were not Greeks and did not speak a Greek language, but their influence on mainland Greece was considerable and enduring. Minoan civilization lasted about 1,350 years (2600–1250 B.C.) and reached its height during the period from 1700 to 1450 B.C.

The centers of Minoan civilization were magnificent palace complexes, whose construction attested the wealth and power of Minoan kings. The palaces housed royal families, priests, and government officials and contained workshops that produced decorated silver vessels, daggers, and pottery for local use and for export.

Judging by the archaeological evidence, the Minoans were peaceful. Generally, Minoan art did not depict military scenes, and Minoan palaces, unlike the Mycenaean ones, had no defensive walls or fortifications. Thus, the Minoans were vulnerable to the warlike Mycenaean Greeks, whose invasion contributed to the decline of Minoan civilization.

Who were these Mycenaeans? Around 2000 B.C., Greek-speaking tribes moved southward into the Greek peninsula, where, together with the pre-Greek population, they fashioned the Mycenaean civilization. In the Peloponnesus, in southern Greece, the Mycenaeans built palaces that were based in part on Cretan models. In these palaces, Mycenaean kings conducted affairs of state, and priests and priestesses performed religious ceremonies. Potters, smiths, tailors, and chariot builders practiced their crafts in the numerous workshops, much like their Minoan counterparts. Mycenaean arts and crafts owed a considerable debt to Crete. A script that permitted record keeping probably also came from Crete.

Mycenaean civilization, which consisted of several small states, each with its own ruling dynasty, reached its height in the period from 1400 to 1230 B.C. Following that, constant warfare among the Mycenaean kingdoms (and perhaps foreign invasions) led to the destruction of the palaces and the abrupt disintegration of Mycenaean civilization about 1100 B.C. But to the later Greek civilization, the Mycenaeans left a legacy of religious forms, pottery making, metallurgy, agriculture, language, a warrior culture and code of honor immortalized in the Homeric epics, and myths and legends that offered themes for Greek drama.

Evolution of the City-States

From 1100 to 800 B.C., the Greek world passed through the Dark Age, an era of transition between a dead Mycenaean civilization and a still unborn Hellenic civilization. The Dark Age saw the migration of Greek tribes from the barren mountainous regions of Greece to more fertile plains, and from the mainland to Aegean islands and the coast of Asia Minor. During this period the Greeks experienced insecurity, warfare, poverty, and isolation.

After 800 B.C., however, town life revived. Writing again became part of the Greek culture, this time with the more efficient Phoenician script. The population increased dramatically, there was a spectacular rise in the use of metals, and overseas trade expanded. Gradually, Greek cities founded settlements on the islands of the Aegean, along the coast of Asia Minor and the Black Sea, and to the west in Sicily and southern Italy. These colonies, established to relieve overpopulation and land hunger, were independent, self-governing city-states, not possessions of the homeland city-states. During these two hundred years of colonization (750–550 B.C.), trade and industry expanded and the pace of urbanization quickened.

Homer: Shaper of the Greek Spirit

The poet Homer lived during the eighth century B.C., just after the Dark Age. His great epics, the *Iliad* and the *Odyssey*, helped shape the Greek spirit and Greek religion. Homer was the earliest molder of the Greek outlook and character. For centuries, Greek youngsters grew up reciting the Homeric epics and admiring the Homeric heroes, who strove for honor and faced suffering and death with courage.

Homer was a poetic genius, who could reveal a human being's deepest thoughts, feelings, and conflicts in a few brilliant lines. His characters, complex in their motives and expressing powerful human emotions—wrath, vengeance, guilt, remorse, compassion, and love—would intrigue and inspire Western writers down into the twentieth century.

The *Iliad* deals in poetic form with a small segment of the last year of the Trojan War, which had taken place centuries before Homer's time, during the Mycenaean period. Homer's theme is the wrath of Achilles. In depriving "the swift and excellent" Achilles of his rightful war prize (the captive young woman Briseis), King Agamemnon has insulted Achilles' honor and violated the solemn rule that warrior heroes treat each other with respect. His pride wounded, Achilles refuses to rejoin Agamemnon in battle against Troy. Achilles plans to affirm his honor by demonstrating that the Greeks need his valor and military prowess. Not until many brave men have been slain, including his dearest friend Patroclus, does Achilles set aside his quarrel with Agamemnon and enter the battle.

Homer employs a *particular* event, the quarrel between an arrogant Agamemnon and a revengeful Achilles, to demonstrate a *universal* principle: that "wicked arrogance" and "ruinous wrath" will cause much suffering and death. Homer grasps that there is an internal logic to existence. For Homer, says British classicist H. D. F. Kitto, "actions must have their consequences; ill-judged actions must have uncomfortable results."[1] People, and even the gods, operate within a certain unalterable framework; their deeds are subject to the demands of fate, or necessity. With a poet's insight, Homer sensed what would become a fundamental attitude of the Greek mind: there is a universal order to things. Later Greeks would formulate it in scientific and philosophical terms.

In Homer, we also see the origin of the Greek ideal of *areté,* excellence. The Homeric warrior expresses a passionate desire to assert himself, to demonstrate his worth, to gain the glory that poets would immortalize in their songs. In the warrior-aristocrat world of Homer, *excellence* was principally interpreted as bravery and skill in battle. Homer's portrayal also bears the embryo of a larger conception of human excellence, one that combines thought with action. A man of true worth, says the wise Phoenix to the stubborn Achilles, is both "a speaker of words and a doer of deeds." In this passage, we find the earliest statement of the Greek educational ideal: the molding of a man who, says classicist Werner Jaeger, "united nobility of action with nobility of

Detail of an Amphora from Eleusis.   In the *Odyssey,* Homer describes the wiley
Hero Odyesseus assisted by two comrades blinding the drunken monster Polyphemus.
In this seventh-century vase painting, Odyesseus is painted in white. (*German Archeo-
logical Institute, Athens*)

mind," who realized "the whole of human potentialities."[2] Thus, in Homer
we find the beginnings of Greek humanism—a concern with man and his
achievements.

Essentially, Homer's works are an expression of the poetic imagination and
mythical thought. But his view of the eternal order of nature and his conception of the individual striving for excellence form the foundations of the
Greek outlook.

Although Homer did not intend his poetry to have any theological significance, his treatment of the gods had important religious implications for the
Greeks. In time, his epics formed the basis of the Olympian religion accepted
throughout Greece. The principal gods were said to reside on Mount Olym-
pus, and on its highest peak was the palace of Zeus, the chief deity. Religion
pervaded daily life, but in time, traditional religion was challenged and undermined by a growing secular and rational spirit.

The Break with Theocratic Politics

From 750 B.C. to the death of Alexander the Great in 323 B.C., Greek society comprised many independent city-states. The city-state based on tribal allegiances was generally the first political association during the early stages of civilization. Moreover, Greece's many mountains, bays, and islands—natural barriers to political unity—favored this type of political arrangement.

The scale of the city-state, or *polis,* was small; most city-states had fewer than 5,000 male citizens. Athens, which was a large city-state, had some 35,000 to 40,000 adult male citizens at its height in the fifth century B.C.; the rest of its population of 350,000 consisted of women, children, resident aliens, and slaves, none of whom could participate in lawmaking. The polis gave individuals a sense of belonging, for its citizens were intimately involved in the political and cultural life of the community.

In the fifth century B.C., at its maturity, the Greeks viewed their polis as the only avenue to the good life—"the only framework within which man could realize his spiritual, moral, and intellectual capacities," in Kitto's words.[3] The mature polis was a self-governing community that expressed the will of free citizens, not the desires of gods, hereditary kings, or priests. In the Near East, religion dominated political activity, and to abide by the mandates of the gods was the ruler's first responsibility. The Greek polis also had begun as a religious institution, in which the citizens sought to maintain an alliance with their deities. Gradually, however, the citizens de-emphasized the gods' role in political life and based government not on the magic powers of divine rulers, but on human intelligence as expressed through the community. The great innovation introduced by the Greeks into politics and social theory was the principle that law did not derive from gods or divine kings, but from the human community.

The emergence of rational attitudes did not, of course, spell the end of religion, particularly for the peasants, who retained their devotion to their ancient cults, gods, and shrines. Worshiping the god of the city remained a required act of patriotism, to which Greeks unfailingly adhered. Thus, the religious-mythical tradition never died in Greece but existed side by side with a growing rationalism, becoming weaker as time passed. When Athenian democracy reached its height in the middle of the fifth century B.C., religion was no longer the dominant factor in politics. Athenians had consciously come to rely on human reason, not divine guidance, in their political and intellectual life.

What made Greek political life different from that of earlier Near Eastern civilizations, as well as gave it enduring significance, was the Greeks' gradual realization that community problems are caused by human beings and require human solutions. The Greeks also valued free citizenship. An absolute king, a tyrant who ruled arbitrarily and by decree and who was above the law, was abhorrent to them.

The ideals of political freedom are best exemplified by Athens. But before turning to Athens, let us examine another Greek city, which followed a different political course.

Sparta: A Garrison State

Situated on the Peloponnesian peninsula, Sparta conquered its neighbors, including Messenia, in the eighth century B.C. Instead of selling the Messenians abroad, the traditional Greek way of treating a defeated foe, the Spartans kept them as state serfs, or *helots*. Helots were owned by the state rather than by individual Spartans. Enraged by their enforced servitude, the Messenians, also a Greek people, desperately tried to regain their freedom. After a bloody uprising was suppressed, the fear of a helot revolt became indelibly stamped on Spartan consciousness.

To maintain their dominion over the Messenians, who outnumbered them ten to one, the Spartans—with extraordinary single-mindedness, discipline, and loyalty—transformed their own society into an armed camp. Agricultural labor was performed by helots; trade and crafts were left to the *perioikoi*, conquered Greeks who were free but who had no political rights. The Spartans learned only one craft, soldiering, and were inculcated with only one conception of excellence: dying in battle for their city.

They were trained in the arts of war and indoctrinated to serve the state. Military training for Spartan boys began at age seven; they exercised, drilled, competed, and endured physical hardships. Other Greeks admired the Spartans for their courage, obedience to law, and achievement in molding themselves according to an ideal. Spartan soldiers were better trained and disciplined and were more physically fit than other Greeks. But the Spartans were also criticized for having a limited conception of areté.

Athens: The Rise of Democracy

The contrast between the city-states of Athens and Sparta is striking. Whereas Sparta was a land power and exclusively agricultural, Athens was located on the peninsula of Attica near the coast, possessed a great navy, and was the commercial leader among the Greeks. To the Spartans, freedom meant preserving the independence of their fatherland; this overriding consideration demanded order, discipline, and regimentation. The Athenians also were determined to protect their city from enemies, but unlike the Spartans, they valued political freedom and sought the full development and enrichment of the human personality. Thus, while authoritarian and militaristic Sparta turned culturally sterile, the relatively free and open society of Athens became the cultural leader of Hellenic civilization.

Greek city-states generally moved through four stages: rule by a king (monarchy), rule by landowning aristocrats (oligarchy), rule by one man who seized power (tyranny), and rule by the people (democracy). During the first stage, monarchy, the king, who derived his power from the gods, commanded the army and judged civil cases.

Oligarchy, the second stage, was instituted in Athens during the eighth century B.C. when aristocrats (*aristocracy* is a Greek word meaning "rule of the best") usurped power from hereditary kings. In the next century, aristocratic

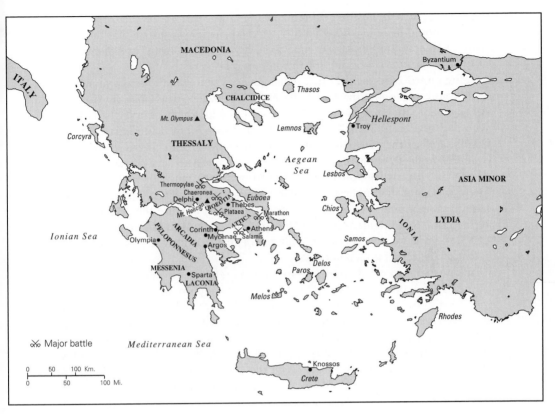

Map 3.1   The Aegean Basin

regimes experienced a social crisis. Peasants who borrowed from the aristocracy, pledging their lands as security, lost their property and even became enslaved for nonpayment of their debts. In Athens, the embittered and restless
peasants demanded and were granted one concession. In 621 B.C., the aristocrats appointed Draco to draw up a code of law. Although Draco's code let
the poor know what the law was and reduced the possibilities of aristocratic
judges behaving arbitrarily, penalties were extremely severe, and the code
provided no relief for the peasants' economic woes. As the poor began to organize and press for the cancellation of their debts and the redistribution of
land, Athens was moving toward civil war.

Solon, the Reformer   In 594 B.C., Solon (c. 640–559 B.C.), a traveler and
poet with a reputation for wisdom, was elected chief executive. He maintained that the wealthy landowners, through their greed, had disrupted community life and brought Athens to the brink of civil war. Solon initiated a
rational approach to the problems of society by de-emphasizing the gods'
role in human affairs and attributing the city's ills to the specific behavior of

individuals; he sought practical remedies for these ills; and he held that written law should be in harmony with *Diké*, the principle of justice that underlies the human community. At the same time, he wanted to instill in Athenians of all classes a sense of working for the common good of the city.

Solon aimed at restoring a sick Athenian society to health by restraining the nobles and improving the lot of the poor. To achieve this goal, he canceled debts, freed Athenians enslaved for debt, and brought back to Athens those who had been sold abroad, but he refused to confiscate and redistribute the nobles' land as the extremists demanded. He permitted all classes of free men, even the poorest, to sit in the Assembly, which elected magistrates and accepted or rejected legislation proposed by a new Council of Four Hundred. He also opened the highest offices in the state to wealthy commoners, who had previously been excluded from these positions because they lacked noble birth. Thus, Solon undermined the traditional rights of the hereditary aristocracy and initiated the process by which Athens was transformed from an aristocratic oligarchy into a democracy.

Solon also instituted ingenious economic reforms. Recognizing that the poor soil of Attica was not conducive to growing grain, he urged the cultivation of grapes for wine and the growing of olives, whose oil could be exported. To encourage industrial expansion, he ordered that all fathers teach their sons a trade and granted citizenship to foreign craftsmen willing to migrate to Athens. These measures and the fine quality of the native reddish-brown clay allowed Athens to become the leading producer and exporter of pottery. Solon's economic policies transformed Athens into a great commercial center. Solon's reforms, however, did not eliminate factional disputes among the aristocratic clans or relieve all the discontent of the poor.

Pisistratus, the Tyrant   In 546 B.C., Pisistratus (c. 605–527 B.C.), an aristocrat, took advantage of the general instability to become a one-man ruler, driving into exile those who had opposed him. Tyranny thus replaced oligarchy. Tyranny occurred frequently in the Greek city-states. Almost always aristocrats themselves, tyrants generally posed as champions of the poor in their struggle against the aristocracy. Pisistratus sought popular support by having conduits constructed to increase the Athenian water supply; like tyrants in other city-states, he gave to peasants land confiscated from exiled aristocrats and granted state loans to small farmers.

Pisistratus' great achievement was the promotion of cultural life. He initiated grand architectural projects, encouraged sculptors and painters, arranged for public recitals of the Homeric epics, and founded festivals, which included dramatic performances. In all these ways, he made culture, formerly the province of the aristocracy, available to commoners. Pisistratus thus launched a policy that eventually led Athens to emerge as the cultural capital of the Greeks.

Cleisthenes, the Democrat   Shortly after Pisistratus' death, a faction headed by Cleisthenes, an aristocrat sympathetic to democracy, assumed leadership.

By an ingenious method of redistricting the city, Cleisthenes ended the aristocratic clans' traditional jockeying for the chief state positions, which had caused so much divisiveness and bitterness in Athens. Cleisthenes replaced this practice, rooted in tradition and authority, with a new system, rationally planned to ensure that historic allegiance to tribe or clan would be superseded by loyalty to the city as a whole.

Cleisthenes hoped to make democracy the permanent form of government for Athens. To safeguard the city against tyranny, he introduced the practice of *ostracism*. Once a year, Athenians were given the opportunity to inscribe on a fragment of pottery (*ostracon*) the name of anyone who, they felt, endangered the state. An individual against whom enough votes were cast was ostracized, that is, forced to leave Athens for ten years.

Cleisthenes firmly secured democratic government in Athens. The Assembly, which Solon had opened to all male citizens, was in the process of becoming the supreme authority in the state. But the period of Athenian greatness lay in the future; the Athenians first had to fight a war of survival against the Persian Empire.

The Persian Wars

In 499 B.C., the Ionian Greeks of Asia Minor rebelled against their Persian overlord. Sympathetic to the Ionian cause, Athens sent twenty ships to aid the revolt. Bent on revenge, Darius I, king of Persia, sent a small detachment to Attica. In 490 B.C., on the plains of Marathon, the citizen army of Athens defeated the Persians—for the Athenians, one of the finest moments in their history. Ten years later, Xerxes, Darius' son, organized a huge invasion force—some 250,000 men and more than 500 ships—with the aim of reducing Greece to a Persian province. Setting aside their separatist instincts, most of the city-states united to defend their independence and their liberty.

The Persians crossed the waters of the Hellespont (Dardanelles) and made their way into northern Greece. Herodotus describes their encounter at the mountain pass of Thermopylae with three hundred Spartans, who, true to their training and ideal of areté, "resisted to the last with their swords if they had them, and if not, with their hands and teeth, until the Persians, coming on from the front over the ruins of the wall and closing in from behind, finally overwhelmed them."[4] Northern Greece fell to the Persians, who continued south, burning a deserted Athens.

When it appeared that the Greeks' spirit had been broken, the Athenian statesman and general Themistocles (c. 527–460 B.C.), demonstrating in military affairs the same rationality that Cleisthenes had shown in political life, lured the Persian fleet into the narrows of the Bay of Salamis. Unable to deploy their more numerous ships in this cramped space, the Persian armada was destroyed by Greek ships. In 479 B.C., a year after the Athenian naval victory at Salamis, the Spartans defeated the Persians in the land battle of Plataea. The inventive intelligence with which the Greeks had planned their military operations and a fierce desire to preserve their freedom had enabled them to defeat the greatest military power the Mediterranean world had yet seen.

The Persian Wars were decisive in the history of the West. The confidence and pride that came with victory propelled Athens into a golden age, but it also roused the Athenian urge for dominance in Greece. The Persian Wars had ushered in an era of Athenian imperialism, which had drastic consequences for the future. Immediately after the wars, more than 150 city-states organized a confederation, the Delian League (named after its treasury on the island of Delos), to protect themselves against a renewed confrontation with Persia. Because of its wealth, its powerful fleet, and the restless energy of its citizens, Athens assumed leadership of the Delian League. Athenians consciously and rapaciously manipulated the league for their own economic advantage, seeing no contradiction between imperialism and democracy. Athens forbade member states to withdraw, stationed garrisons on the territory of confederate states, and used the league's treasury to finance public works in Athens. Although member states did receive protection from both pirates and Persians, were not overtaxed, and enjoyed increased trade, they resented Athenian domination.

The Mature Athenian Democracy

Athenian imperialism was one consequence of the Persian Wars; another was the flowering of Athenian democracy and culture. The Athenian state was a direct democracy, in which the citizens themselves, not elected representatives, made the laws. In the Assembly, which was open to all adult male citizens and which met some forty times a year, Athenians debated and voted on key issues of state: they declared war, signed treaties, and spent public funds. The lowliest cobbler, as well as the wealthiest aristocrat, had the opportunity to express his opinion in the Assembly, to vote, and to hold office. By the middle of the fifth century, the will of the people, as expressed in the Assembly, was supreme.

The Council of Five Hundred (which had been established by Cleisthenes to replace Solon's Council of Four Hundred) managed the ports, military installations, and other state properties and prepared the agenda for the Assembly. Because its members were chosen annually by lot and could not serve more than twice in a lifetime, the Council could never supersede the Assembly. Some 350 magistrates, also chosen by lot, performed administrative tasks: collecting fines, policing the city, repairing streets, inspecting markets, and so forth. In view of the special competence that their posts required, the ten generals who led the army were not chosen by lot but were elected by the Assembly.

Athens has been aptly described as a government of amateurs; there were no professional civil servants, no professional soldiers and sailors, no state judges, and no elected lawmakers. Ordinary citizens performed the duties of government. Such a system rested on the assumption that the average citizen was capable of participating intelligently in the affairs of state and that he would, in a spirit of civic patriotism, carry out his responsibilities to his city. In Athens of the fifth century B.C., excellence was equated with good citizenship—a concern for the good of the community that outweighs personal aspirations.

Athenian democracy achieved its height in the middle of the fifth century B.C., under the leadership of Pericles (c. 495–429 B.C.), a gifted statesman, orator, and military commander. In the opening stage of the monumental clash with Sparta, the Peloponnesian War (431–404 B.C.), Pericles delivered an oration in honor of the Athenian war casualties. The oration, as reported by Thucydides, the great Athenian historian of the fifth century B.C., contains a glowing description of the Athenian democratic ideal:

> *We are called a democracy, for the administration is in the hands of the many and not of the few. But while the law secures equal justice to all alike in their private disputes, the claim of excellence is also recognized; and when a citizen is any way distinguished, he is [selected for] public service . . . as the reward of merit. Neither is poverty a bar, but a man may benefit his country whatever may be the obscurity of his condition. . . . There is no exclusiveness in our public life, and in our private intercourse we are not suspicious of one another, nor angry with our neighbor if he does what he likes; we do not put on sour looks at him which though harmless are unpleasant. . . . a spirit of reverence pervades our public acts; we are prevented from doing wrong by respect for authority and for the laws. . . .[5]*

Athenian democracy undoubtedly had its limitations and weaknesses. Modern critics point out that resident aliens were almost totally barred from citizenship and therefore from political participation. Slaves, who constituted about one-fourth of the Athenian population, enjoyed none of the freedoms that Athenians considered so precious. The Greeks regarded slavery as a necessary precondition for civilized life; for some to be free and prosperous, they believed, others had to be enslaved. Slaves were generally prisoners of war or captives of pirates. In Athens, some slaves were Greeks, but most were foreigners. Slaves usually did the same work as Athenian citizens: farming, commerce, manufacturing, and domestic chores. However, those slaves, including preadolescent children, who toiled in the mines suffered a grim fate.

Athenian women were another group denied legal and political rights. They were barred from holding public office and generally could not appear in court without a male representative. Since it was believed that a woman could not act independently, she was required to have a guardian—normally her father or husband—who controlled her property and supervised her behavior. A girl was usually married at fourteen to a man twice her age, and the marriage was arranged by a male relative. Although either spouse could obtain a divorce, the children remained with the father. In the belief that financial dealings were too difficult for women and that they needed to be protected from strangers, men did the marketing, not the women. Greek women received no formal education, although some young women learned to read and write at home.

The flaws in Athenian democracy should not cause us to undervalue its extraordinary achievement. The idea that the state represents a community of free, self-governing citizens remains a crucial principle of Western civilization. Athenian democracy embodied the principle of the legal state—a government based not on force, but on laws debated, devised, altered, and obeyed by free citizens.

This idea of the legal state could have arisen only in a society that was aware of and respected the rational mind. Just as the Greeks demythicized nature, so too they removed myth from the sphere of politics. Holding that government was something that people create to satisfy human needs, the Athenians regarded their leaders neither as gods nor as priests, but as men who had demonstrated a capacity for statesmanship.

Both democratic politics and systematic political thought originated in Greece. There, people first asked questions about the nature and purpose of the state, rationally analyzed political institutions, speculated about human nature and justice, and discussed the merits of various forms of government. It is to Greece that we ultimately trace the idea of democracy and all that accompanies it: citizenship, constitutions, equality before the law, government by law, reasoned debate, respect for the individual, and confidence in human intelligence.

The Decline of the City-States

Although the Greeks shared a common language and culture, they remained divided politically. A determination to preserve city-state sovereignty prevented the Greeks from forming a larger political grouping, which might have prevented the intercity warfare that ultimately cost the city-state its vitality and independence. But the creation of a Pan-Hellenic union would have required a radical transformation of the Greek character, which for hundreds of years had regarded the independent city-state as the only suitable political system.

The Peloponnesian War

Athenian control of the Delian League frightened the Spartans and their allies in the Peloponnesian League. Sparta and the Peloponnesian states decided on war because they saw a dynamic and imperialistic Athens as a threat to their independence. At stake for Athens was control over the Delian League, which gave Athens political power and contributed to its economic prosperity. Neither Athens nor Sparta anticipated the catastrophic consequences that the war would have for Greek civilization.

The war began in 431 B.C. and ended in 404 B.C. When a besieged Athens,

Attic Black-Figure Hydria, c. 510 B.C.   This hydria, or water jug, showing women drawing water from a fountainhouse dates from the sixth century B.C. These trips to the fountainhouse provided one of few opportunities for women to socialize outside of the home. (*William Francis Warden Fund. Courtesy, Museum of Fine Arts, Boston*)

with a decimated navy and a dwindling food supply, surrendered, Sparta dissolved the Delian League, left Athens with only a handful of ships, and forced the city to pull down its long walls—ramparts designed to protect it against siege weapons.

The Peloponnesian War shattered the spiritual foundations of Hellenic society. During its course, men became brutalized, selfish individualism triumphed over civic duty, moderation gave way to extremism, and in several cities, including Athens, politics degenerated into civil war between oligarchs and democrats. Oligarchs, generally from the wealthier segments of Athenian society, wanted to concentrate power in their own hands by depriving the lower classes of political rights. Democrats, generally from the poorer segment of society, sought to preserve the political rights of all adult male citizens. Strife between oligarchs and democrats was quite common in the Greek city-states even before the Peloponnesian War.

The Fourth Century

The Peloponnesian War was the great crisis of Hellenic history. The city-states never recovered from their self-inflicted spiritual wounds. The civic loyalty and confidence that had marked the fifth century waned, and the fourth century was dominated by a new mentality, which the leaders of the Age of

Pericles would have abhorred. A concern for private affairs superseded devotion to the general good of the polis. Increasingly, professionals, rather than ordinary citizens, administered the tasks of government, and mercenaries began to replace citizen soldiers.

In the fourth century, the quarrelsome city-states formed new systems of alliances and persisted in their ruinous conflicts. While the Greek cities battered one another in fratricidal warfare, a new power was rising in the north—Macedonia. To the Greeks, the Macedonians, a wild mountain people who spoke a Greek dialect and had acquired a sprinkling of Hellenic culture, differed little from other non-Greeks, whom they called barbarians. In 359 B.C., at the age of twenty-three, Philip II (382–336 B.C.) ascended the Macedonian throne. Converting Macedonia into a first-rate military power, he began a drive to become master of the Greeks.

Incorrectly assessing Philip's strength, the Greeks were slow to organize a coalition against Macedonia. In 338 B.C., at Chaeronea, Philip's forces decisively defeated the Greeks, and all of Greece was his. The city states still existed, but they had lost their independence. The world of the small, independent, and self-sufficient polis was drawing to a close, and Greek civilization was taking a different shape.

The Dilemma of Greek Politics

Philip's conquest of the city-states points to a fundamental weakness of Greek politics. Despite internal crisis and persistent warfare, the Greeks were unable to fashion any other political framework than the polis. The city-state was fast becoming an anachronism, but the Greeks were unable to see that, in a world moving toward larger states and empires, the small city-state could not compete. An unallied city-state, with its small citizen army, could not withstand the powerful military machine that Philip had created. A challenge confronted the city-states: the need to shape some form of political union, a Pan-Hellenic federation, that would end the suicidal internecine warfare, promote economic well-being, and protect the Greek world from hostile states. Because they could not respond creatively to this challenge, the city-states ultimately lost their independence to foreign conquerors.

The waning of civic responsibility among the citizens was another reason for the decline of the city-states. The vitality of the city-state depended on the willingness of its citizens to put aside private concerns for the good of the community. The Periclean ideal of citizenship dissipated as Athenians neglected the community to concentrate on private affairs or sought to derive personal profit from public office. The decline in civic responsibility could be seen in the hiring of mercenaries to replace citizen soldiers and in the indifference and hesitancy with which Athenians confronted Philip.

Greek political life demonstrated both the best and the worst features of freedom. On the one hand, as Pericles boasted, freedom encouraged active citizenship, reasoned debate, and government by law. On the other, as Thucydides lamented, freedom could degenerate into factionalism, demagoguery, unbridled self-interest, and civil war.

Greek politics also revealed both the capabilities and the limitations of reason. Originally, the polis was conceived as a divine institution, in which the citizen had a religious obligation to obey the law. As the rational and secular outlook became more pervasive, the gods lost their authority. When people no longer regarded law as an expression of sacred traditions ordained by the gods but saw it as a merely human contrivance, respect for the law diminished, weakening the foundations of the society. The results were party conflicts, politicians who scrambled for personal power, and moral uncertainty. Although the Greeks originated the lofty ideal that human beings could regulate their political life according to reason, their history, marred by intercity warfare and internal violence, demonstrates the extreme difficulties involved in creating and maintaining a rational society.

Philosophy in the Hellenic Age

The Greeks broke with the mythopoeic outlook of the Near East and conceived a new way of viewing nature and human society, which is the basis of the Western scientific and philosophical tradition. By the fifth century B.C., the Greeks had emancipated thought from myth and gradually applied reason to the physical world and to all human activities. This emphasis on reason marks a turning point for human civilization.

The development of rational thought in Greece was a process, a trend, not a finished achievement. The process began when some thinkers rejected mythical explanations for natural phenomena. The nonphilosophical majority of people never entirely eliminated the language, attitudes, and beliefs of myth from their life and thought. For them the world remained controlled by divine forces, which were appeased through cultic practices. Even in the mature philosophy of Plato and Aristotle, mythical modes of thought persisted. What is of immense historical importance is not the degree to which the Greeks successfully integrated the norm of reason, but the fact that they originated this norm, defined it, and applied it to their intellectual development and social and political life.

The first theoretical philosophers in human history emerged in the sixth century B.C., in the Greek cities of Ionia in Asia Minor. Curious about the essential composition of nature and dissatisfied with earlier creation legends, the Ionians sought physical, rather than mythic-religious, explanations for natural occurrences. In the process, they arrived at a new concept of nature and a new method of inquiry. They maintained that nature was not manipulated by arbitrary and willful gods and that it was not governed by blind chance. As the Ionians saw it, underlying the seeming chaos of nature were principles of order—general laws ascertainable by the human mind. This discovery marks the beginning of scientific thought. The early Greek thinkers are called cosmologists, because they were concerned with the nature of the universe, or Pre-Socratics, because they came before Socrates, a pivotal figure in the evolution of Greek thought.

The Cosmologists: A Rational Inquiry into Nature

Ionian philosophy began with Thales (c. 624–548 B.C.) of Miletus, a city in Ionia. A contemporary of Solon of Athens, he concerned himself with how nature came to be the way it was. Thales said that water was the basic element, the underlying substratum of nature, and that through some natural process—similar to the formation of ice or steam—water gave rise to everything else in the world.

Thales revolutionized thought because he omitted the gods from his account of the origins of nature and searched for a natural explanation of how all things came to be. Thales also broke with the commonly held belief that earthquakes were caused by Poseidon, god of the sea, and offered instead a naturalistic explanation for these disturbances: that the earth floated on water and when the water experienced turbulent waves the earth was rocked by earthquakes.

Anaximander (c. 611–547 B.C.), another sixth-century Ionian, rejected Thales' theory that water was the original substance. He rejected any specific substance and suggested that an indefinite substance, which he called the Boundless, was the source of all things. He believed that from this primary mass, which contained the powers of heat and cold, there gradually emerged a nucleus, the seed of the world. He said that the cold and wet condensed to form the earth and its cloud cover, while the hot and dry formed the rings of fire that we see as the moon, the sun, and the stars. The heat from the fire in the sky dried the earth and shrank the seas. From the warm slime on earth arose life, and from the first sea creatures there evolved land animals, including human beings. Anaximander's account of the origins of the universe and nature understandably contained fantastic elements. Nevertheless, by offering a natural explanation for the origin of nature and life and by holding that nature was lawful, it surpassed the creation myths.

Like his fellow Ionians, Anaximenes, who died about 525 B.C., made the transition from myth to reason. He also maintained that a primary substance, air, underlay reality and accounted for the orderliness of nature. Air that was rarefied became fire, whereas wind and clouds were formed from condensed air. If the process of condensation continued, it produced water, earth, and eventually stones. Anaximenes also rejected the old belief that a rainbow was the goddess Iris; instead, he said that the rainbow was caused by the sun's rays falling on dense air.

The Ionians have been called "matter philosophers" because they held that everything issued from a particular material substance. Other thinkers of the sixth century B.C. tried a different approach. Pythagoras (c. 580–507 B.C.) and his followers, who lived in the Greek cities in southern Italy, did not find the nature of things in a particular substance but in mathematical relationships.

The Pythagoreans discovered that the intervals in the musical scale can be expressed mathematically. Extending this principle of proportion found in sound to the universe at large, they concluded that the cosmos also contained an inherent mathematical order. Thus, the Pythagoreans shifted the emphasis from matter to form, from the world of sense perception to the logic of mathematics. The Pythagoreans were also religious mystics, who believed in the immortality and transmigration of souls. Consequently, they refused to eat animal flesh, fearing that it contained former human souls.

Parmenides (c. 515–450 B.C.), a native of the Greek city of Elea in southern Italy, challenged the fundamental view of the Ionians that all things emerged from one original substance. In developing his position, Parmenides applied to philosophical argument the logic used by the Pythagoreans in mathematical thinking. In putting forth the proposition that an argument must be consistent and contain no contradictions, Parmenides became the founder of formal logic. Despite appearances, asserted Parmenides, reality—the cosmos and all that is within it—is one, eternal, and unchanging. It is made known not through the senses, which are misleading, but through the mind; not through experience, but through reason. Truth is reached through abstract thought alone. Parmenides' concept of an unchanging reality apprehended by thought alone influenced Plato and is the foundation of metaphysics.

Democritus (c. 460–370 B.C.), from the Greek mainland, renewed the Ionians' concern with the world of matter and reaffirmed their confidence in knowledge derived from sense perception. But he also retained Parmenides' reverence for reason. His model of the universe consisted of two fundamental realities: empty space and an infinite number of atoms. Eternal, indivisible, and imperceptible, these atoms moved in the void. All things consisted of atoms, and combinations of atoms accounted for all change in nature. In a world of colliding atoms, everything behaved according to mechanical principles.

Concepts essential to scientific thought thus emerged in embryonic form with the early Greek philosophers: natural explanations for physical occurrences (Ionians), the mathematical order of nature (Pythagoras), logical proof (Parmenides), and the mechanical structure of the universe (Democritus). By giving to nature a rational, rather than a mythical, foundation and by holding that theories should be grounded in evidence and that one should be able to defend them, the early Greek philosophers pushed thought in a new direction. Their achievement made possible theoretical thought and the systematization of knowledge—as distinct from the mere observation and collection of data.

This systematization of knowledge extended into several areas. Greek mathematicians, for example, organized the Egyptians' practical experience with land measurements into the logical and coherent science of geometry. Both Babylonians and Egyptians had performed fairly complex mathematical operations, but unlike the Greeks, they made no attempt to prove underlying mathematical principles. In another area, Babylonian priests had observed the heavens for religious reasons, believing that the stars revealed the wishes of the gods. The Greeks used the data collected by the Babylonians, but not for a

The Parthenon, Athens, 447–432 B.C.   A masterpiece of the Doric style, the great temple dedicated to Athena Parthenos (the Maiden), the patron goddess of the city, was constructed through the efforts of Pericles. Its cult statue and sculptural reliefs under its roof line were designed by the outstanding sculptor of the age, Phidias. In post-Hellenistic times it served as a Christian church and subsequently an Islamic mosque until destroyed by an explosion in 1687. Between 1801–1812 the marble reliefs were removed by the English Lord Elgin and now reside in the British Museum, in London. (*Hirmer Fotoarchiv*)

religious purpose; they sought to discover the geometrical laws that underlie the motions of heavenly bodies.

A parallel development occurred in medicine. No Near Eastern medical text explicitly attacked magical beliefs and practices. In contrast, Greek doctors associated with the medical school of Hippocrates (c. 460–c. 377 B.C.) asserted that diseases have a natural, not a supernatural, cause.

The Sophists: A Rational Investigation of Human Culture

In their effort to understand the external world, the cosmologists had created the tools of reason. Greek thinkers then turned away from the world of nature and attempted a rational investigation of people and society. The Sophists exemplified this shift in focus. They were professional teachers who wandered from city to city teaching rhetoric, grammar, poetry, gymnastics, mathematics, and music. The Sophists insisted that it was futile to speculate about the first principles of the universe, for such knowledge was beyond the grasp of the human mind. Instead, they urged that individuals improve themselves and their cities by applying reason to the tasks of citizenship and statesmanship.

The Sophists answered a practical need in Athens, which had been transformed into a wealthy and dynamic imperial state after the Persian Wars. Because the Sophists claimed that they could teach *political* areté— the skill to formulate the right laws and policies for cities and the art of eloquence and persuasion—they were sought as tutors by politically ambitious young men, especially in Athens. The Western humanist tradition owes much to the Sophists, who examined political and ethical problems, cultivated the minds of their students, and invented formal secular education.

The Sophists were philosophical relativists; that is, they held that no truth is universally valid. Protagoras, a fifth-century Sophist, said that "man is the measure of all things." By this he meant that good and evil, truth and falsehood are matters of individual judgment; there are no universal standards that apply to all people at all times.

In applying reason critically to human affairs, the Sophists attacked the traditional religious and moral values of Athenian society. Some Sophists taught that speculation about the divine was useless; others went further and asserted that religion was just a human invention to ensure obedience to traditions and laws.

The Sophists also applied reason to law, with the same effect: the undermining of traditional authority. The laws of a given city, they asserted, did not derive from the gods; nor were they based on any objective, universal, and timeless standards of justice and good, for such standards did not exist. The more radical Sophists argued that law was merely something made by the most powerful citizens for their own benefit. This view had dangerous implications: since law rested on no higher principle than might, it need not be obeyed.

Some Sophists combined this assault on law with an attack on the ancient Athenian idea of *sophrosyne*—moderation and self-discipline—because it denied human instincts. Instead of moderation, they urged that people should maximize pleasure and trample underfoot those traditions that restricted them from fully expressing their desires.

In subjecting traditions to the critique of reason, the radical Sophists provoked an intellectual and spiritual crisis. Their doctrines encouraged disobedience to law, neglect of civic duty, and selfish individualism. These attitudes became widespread during and after the Peloponnesian War, dangerously weakening community bonds. Conservatives sought to restore the authority of law and a respect for moral values by renewing allegiance to those sacred traditions undermined by the Sophists.

Socrates: The Rational Individual

Socrates (c. 469–399 B.C.), one of the most extraordinary figures in the history of Western civilization, took a different approach. He attacked the Sophists' relativism, holding that people should regulate their behavior in accordance with universal values. While he recognized that the Sophists taught skills, he felt that they had no insights into questions that really mattered. What is the purpose of life? What are the values by which man should live? How does man perfect his character? Here the Sophists failed, said Socrates; they taught the ambitious to succeed in politics, but persuasive oratory and clever reasoning do not instruct a man in the art of living. According to Socrates, the Sophists had attacked the old system of beliefs, but had not provided the individual with a constructive replacement.

Socrates' central concern was the perfection of individual human character, the achievement of moral excellence. For Socrates, moral values did not derive from a transcendent God as they did for the Hebrews. Individuals attained them by regulating their lives according to objective standards arrived at through rational reflection, that is, by making reason the formative, guiding, and ruling agency of the soul. For Socrates, true education meant the shaping of character according to values discovered through the active and critical use of reason.

Socrates wanted to subject all human beliefs and behavior to the scrutiny of reason and in this way remove ethics from the realm of authority, tradition, dogma, superstition, and myth. He believed that reason was the only proper guide to the most crucial problem of human existence—the question of good and evil.

Dialectics   In urging Athenians to think rationally about the problems of human existence, Socrates offered no systematic ethical theory and no list of ethical precepts. What he did supply was a method of inquiry called *dialectics,* or logical discussion. As Socrates used it, a dialectical exchange between individuals, a *dialogue,* was the essential source of knowledge. It forced people out of their apathy and smugness and compelled them to examine their thoughts critically, to confront illogical, inconsistent, dogmatic, and imprecise assertions, and to express their ideas in clearly defined terms.

Dialectics demonstrated that the acquisition of knowledge was a creative act. The human mind could not be coerced into knowing; it was not a passive vessel into which a teacher poured knowledge. The dialogue compelled the individual to play an active role in acquiring the ideals and values by which to live. In a dialogue, individuals became thinking participants in a search for knowledge. Through relentless cross-examination, Socrates induced the persons with whom he spoke to explain and justify their opinions rationally, for only thus did knowledge become a part of one's being.

Dialogue implied that reason was meant to be used in relations between human beings and that they could learn from each other, help each other, teach each other, and improve each other. It implied further that the human mind could and should make rational choices. To deal rationally with oneself and others is the distinctive mark of being human.

The Execution of Socrates   Socrates devoted much of his life to his mission of persuading his fellow Athenians to think critically about how they lived their lives. Through probing questions, he tried to stir people out of their complacency and make them realize how directionless and purposeless their lives were.

For many years, Socrates challenged Athenians without suffering harm, for Athens was generally distinguished by its freedom of speech and thought. However, in the uncertain times during and immediately after the Peloponnesian War, Socrates made enemies. When he was seventy, he was accused of corrupting the youth of the city and of not believing in the city's gods but in other, new divinities. Underlying these accusations was the fear that Socrates was a troublemaker, a subversive who threatened the state by subjecting its ancient and sacred values to the critique of thought.

Socrates denied the charges and conducted himself with great dignity at his trial, refusing to grovel and beg forgiveness. Instead, he defined his creed:

> *If you think that a man of any worth at all ought to . . . think of anything but whether he is acting justly or unjustly, and as a good or a bad man would act, you are mistaken. . . . If you were therefore to say to me, "Socrates, we will not listen to [your accuser]. We will let you go, but on the condition that you give up this investigation of yours, and philosophy. If you are found following these pursuits again you shall die." I say, if you offered to let me go on these terms, I should reply: . . . As long as I have breath and strength I will not give up philosophy and exhorting you and declaring the truth to every one of you whom I meet, saying, as I am accustomed, "My good friend, you are a citizen of Athens . . . are you not ashamed of caring so much for making of money and for fame and prestige, when you neither think nor care about wisdom and truth and the improvement of your soul?"*[6]

Convicted by an Athenian court, Socrates was ordered to drink poison. Had he attempted to appease the jurors, he probably would have been given a light punishment, but he would not disobey the commands of his conscience and alter his principles even under threat of death.

Socrates did not write down his philosophy and beliefs. We are able to construct a coherent account of his life and ideals largely through the works of his most important disciple, Plato.

Plato: The Rational Society

Plato (c. 429–347 B.C.) used his master's teachings to create a comprehensive system of philosophy, which embraced both the world of nature and the social world. Virtually all the problems discussed by Western philosophers for the past two millennia were raised by Plato. We focus on two of his principal concerns, the theory of Ideas and that of the just state.

Theory of Ideas   Socrates had taught that universal standards of right and justice exist and are arrived at through thought. Building on the insights of his teacher, Plato postulated the existence of a higher world of reality, independent of the world of things that we experience every day. This higher reality, he said, is the realm of Ideas, or Forms—unchanging, eternal, absolute, and universal standards of beauty, goodness, justice, and truth.

Truth resides in this world of Forms and not in the world made known through the senses. For example, a person can never draw a perfect square, but the properties of a perfect square exist in the world of Forms. Similarly, the ordinary person derives an opinion of what beauty is only from observing beautiful things; the philosopher, aspiring to true knowledge, goes beyond what he sees and tries to grasp with his mind the Idea of beauty. The ordinary individual lacks a true conception of justice or goodness; such knowledge is available only to the philosopher, whose mind can leap from worldly particulars to an ideal world beyond space and time. Thus, true wisdom is obtained through knowledge of the Ideas and not through the imperfect reflections of the Ideas that the senses perceive.

A champion of reason, Plato aspired to study human life and arrange it according to universally valid standards. In contrast to sophistic relativism, he maintained that objective and eternal standards do exist.

The Just State   In adapting the rational legacy of Greek philosophy to politics, Plato constructed a comprehensive political theory. What the Greeks had achieved in practice—the movement away from mythic and theocratic politics—Plato accomplished on the level of thought: the fashioning of a rational model of the state.

Like Socrates, Plato attempted to resolve the problem caused by the radical Sophists: the undermining of traditional values. Socrates had tried to dispel this spiritual crisis through a moral transformation of the individual, based on reason, whereas Plato wanted the entire community to conform to rational principles. Plato said that if human beings are to live an ethical life they must do so as citizens of a just and rational state. In an unjust state, people cannot achieve Socratic wisdom, for their souls will mirror the state's wickedness.

Plato had experienced the ruinous Peloponnesian War and witnessed Socrates' trial and execution. Disillusioned by the corruption of Athenian morality and democratic politics, he concluded that under the Athenian constitution neither the morality of the individual Athenian nor the good of the state could be enhanced. He became convinced that Athens required moral and political reform founded on Socratic philosophy.

In his great dialogue, *The Republic,* Plato devised an ideal state based on standards that would rescue his native Athens from the evils that had befallen it. For Plato, the just state could not be founded on tradition (for inherited attitudes did not derive from rational standards) or on the doctrine of might being right (a principle taught by radical Sophists and practiced by Athenian statesmen). A just state, in his view, had to conform to universally valid principles and aim at the moral improvement of its citizens, not at increasing its power and material possessions. Such a state required leaders distinguished by their wisdom and virtue rather than by sophistic cleverness and eloquence.

Fundamental to Plato's political theory as formulated in *The Republic* was his criticism of Athenian democracy. An aristocrat by birth and temperament, Plato believed that it was foolish to expect the common man to think intelligently about foreign policy, economics, or other vital matters of state. Yet the common man was permitted to speak in the Assembly and to vote; he could also be selected, by lot, for executive office. A second weakness of democracy for Plato was that leaders were chosen and followed for nonessential reasons, such as persuasive speech, good looks, wealth, and family background.

A third danger of democracy was that it could degenerate into anarchy, said Plato. Intoxicated by liberty, the citizens of a democracy could lose all sense of balance, self-discipline, and respect for law: "The citizens become so sensitive that they resent the slightest application of control as intolerable tyranny, and in their resolve to have no master they end up by disregarding even the law, written or unwritten."[7]

As the democratic city falls into disorder, a fourth weakness of democracy will become evident. A demagogue will be able to gain power by promising to plunder the rich to benefit the poor. To retain his hold over the state, the tyrant "begins by stirring up one war after another, in order that the people may feel their need of a leader."[8] Because of these inherent weaknesses of democracy, Plato insisted that Athens would be governed properly only when the wisest people, the philosophers, attained power.

Plato rejected the fundamental principle of Athenian democracy: that the ordinary citizen is capable of participating sensibly in public affairs. People would not entrust the care of a sick person to just anyone, said Plato, nor would they allow a novice to guide a ship during a storm. Yet, in a democracy, amateurs were permitted to run the government and to supervise the education of the young; no wonder Athenian society was disintegrating. Plato believed that these duties should be performed only by the best people in the city, the philosophers, who would approach human problems with reason and wisdom derived from knowledge of the world of unchanging and perfect Ideas. He asserted that only these possessors of truth would be competent to rule.

Plato divided people into three groups: those who demonstrated philosophical ability should be rulers; those whose natural bent revealed exceptional courage should be soldiers; and those driven by desire, the great masses, should be producers (tradespeople, artisans, or farmers). In *The Republic,* the philosophers were selected by a rigorous system of education open to all children. Those not demonstrating sufficient intelligence or strength of character were to be weeded out to become workers or warriors, depending on their natural aptitudes. After many years of education and practical military and administrative experience, the philosophers were to be entrusted with political power. If they had been properly educated, the philosopher-rulers would not seek personal wealth or personal power; they would be concerned with pursuing justice and serving the community. The philosophers were to be absolute rulers. Although the people would have lost their right to participate in political decisions, they would have gained a well-governed state, whose leaders, distinguished by their wisdom, integrity, and sense of responsibility, sought only the common good. Only thus, said Plato, could the individual and the community achieve well-being.

Aristotle: Synthesis of Greek Thought

Aristotle (384–322 B.C.) stands at the apex of Greek thought because he achieved a creative synthesis of the knowledge and theories of earlier thinkers. The range of Aristotle's interests and intellect is extraordinary. He was the leading expert of his time in every field of knowledge, with the possible exception of mathematics.

Aristotle undertook the monumental task of organizing and systematizing the thought of the Pre-Socratics, Socrates, and Plato. He shared with the natural philosophers a desire to understand the physical universe; he shared with Socrates and Plato the belief that reason was a person's highest faculty and that the polis was the primary formative institution of Greek life.

Critique of Plato's Theory of Ideas   To the practical and empirically minded Aristotle, the Platonic notion of an independent and separate world of Forms beyond space and time seemed contrary to common sense. To comprehend reality, said Aristotle, one should not escape into another world. For him, Plato's two-world philosophy suffered from too much mystery, mysticism, and poetic fancy; moreover, Plato undervalued the world of facts and objects revealed through sight, hearing, and touch, a world that Aristotle valued. Like Plato, Aristotle desired to comprehend the essence of things and held that understanding universal principles is the ultimate aim of knowledge. But unlike Plato, he did not turn away from the world of things to obtain such knowledge. Possessing a scientist's curiosity to understand nature, Aristotle respected knowledge obtained through the senses.

For Aristotle, the Forms were not located in a higher world outside and beyond phenomena but existed in things themselves. He said that, through human experience with such things as men, horses, and white objects, the essence of man, horse, and whiteness can be discovered through reason; the Form of Man, the Form of Horse, and the Form of Whiteness can be determined. These universals, which apply to all men, all horses, and all white things, were for both Aristotle and Plato the true objects of knowledge. For Plato, these Forms existed independently of particular objects: the Forms for men or horses or whiteness or triangles or temples existed, whether or not representations of these Ideas in the form of material objects were made known to the senses. For Aristotle, however, universal Ideas could not be determined without examination of particular things. Whereas Plato's use of reason tended to stress otherworldliness, Aristotle brought philosophy back to earth.

By holding that certainty in knowledge comes from reason alone and not from the senses, Plato was predisposed toward mathematics and meta-physics—pure thought that transcends the world of change and material objects. By stressing the importance of knowledge acquired through the rational examination of sense experience, Aristotle favored the development of empirical sciences—physics, biology, zoology, botany, and other disciplines based on the observation and investigation of nature and the recording of data.

Ethical Thought   Like Socrates and Plato, Aristotle believed that a knowledge of ethics was possible and that it must be based on reason. For Aristotle, the good life was the examined life; it meant making intelligent decisions when confronted with specific problems. People could achieve happiness when they exercised the distinctively human trait of reasoning, when they applied their knowledge relevantly to life, and when their behavior was governed by intelligence and not by whim, tradition, or authority.

Aristotle recognized, however, that people are not entirely rational and that the passionate element in the human personality can never be eradicated or ignored. According to Aristotle, surrendering completely to desire meant descending to the level of beasts, but denying the passions and living as an ascetic was a foolish and unreasonable rejection of human nature. Aristotle maintained that by proper training people could learn to regulate their desires. They could achieve moral well-being, or virtue, when they avoided extremes of behavior and rationally chose the way of moderation. "Nothing in excess" is the key to Aristotle's ethics.

Political Thought   Aristotle's *Politics* complements his *Ethics*. To live the good life, he said, a person must do it as a member of a political community. Only the polis would provide people with an opportunity to lead a rational and moral existence, that is, to fulfill their human potential. With this assertion, Aristotle demonstrated a typically Greek attitude.

Like Plato, Aristotle presumed that political life could be rationally understood and intelligently directed. He emphasized the importance of the rule of law. He placed his trust in law rather than in individuals, for they are subject to passions. Aristotle recognized that at times laws should be altered but recommended great caution; otherwise, people would lose respect for law and legal procedure.

Tyranny and revolution, Aristotle said, can threaten the rule of law and the well-being of the citizen. To prevent revolution, the state must maintain "the spirit of obedience to law. . . . Men should not think it slavery to live according to the rule of the constitution, for it is their salvation."[9]

Aristotle held "that the best political community is formed by citizens of the middle class [that is, those with a moderate amount of property], and that those states are likely to be well-administered in which the middle class is large and stronger if possible than the other classes [the wealthy and the poor]." Both the rich, who excel in "beauty, strength, birth, [and] wealth," and the poor, who are "very weak or very much disgraced [find it] difficult to follow rational principle. Of these two the one sort grow into violence and great criminals, the other into rogues and petty rascals." The rich are unwilling "to submit to authority . . . for when they are boys, by reason of the luxury in which they are brought up, they never learn even at school, the habit of obedience." Consequently, the wealthy "can only rule despotically." On the other hand, the poor "are too degraded to command and must be ruled like slaves."[10] Middle-class citizens are less afflicted by envy than the poor and are more likely than the rich to view their fellow citizens as equals.

Art

The classical age of Greek art spans the years from the end of the Persian Wars (479 B.C.) to the death of Alexander the Great (323 B.C.). During this period, standards were established that would dominate Western art until the emergence of modern art in the late nineteenth century.

Greek art coincided with Greek achievement in all other areas. Like Greek philosophy and politics, it too applied reason to human experience and made the transition from a mythopoeic-religious world-view to a world perceived as orderly and rational. It gradually transformed the supernatural religious themes with which it was at first preoccupied into secular human themes. Classical art was representational—that is, it strove to imitate reality, to represent the objective world realistically, as it appeared to the human eye.

Artists carefully observed nature and human beings and sought to achieve an exact knowledge of human anatomy; they tried to portray accurately the body at rest and in motion. They knew when muscles should be taut or relaxed, one hip lower than the other, the torso and neck slightly twisted—in other words, they succeeded in transforming marble or bronze into a human likeness that seemed alive. Yet although it was realistic and naturalistic, Greek art was also idealistic, aspiring to a finer, more perfect representation of what was seen, depicting the essence and form of a thing more truly than it actually appeared. Thus, a Greek statue resembled no specific individual but revealed a flawless human form, without wrinkles, warts, scars, or other imperfections.

In achieving an accurate representation of objects and in holding that there were rules of beauty that the mind could discover, the Greek artist employed an approach consistent with the new scientific outlook. The Greek temple, for example, is an organized unity, obeying nature's laws of equilibrium and harmony; classical sculpture captures the basic laws that govern life in motion. Such art, based on reason, draws the mind's attention to the clear outlines of the outer world; at the same time it directs the mind's attention to the mind itself, making human beings the center of an intelligible world and the masters of their own persons.

Greek artists, just like Greek philosophers, proclaimed the importance and creative capacity of the individual. They exemplified the humanist spirit that characterized all aspects of Greek culture. Classical art placed people in their natural environment, made the human form the focal point of attention, and exalted the nobility, dignity, self-assurance, and beauty of the human being.

Poetry and Drama

Like philosophers and artists, Greek poets and dramatists gave expression to the rise of the individual and the emerging humanist values. One of the earliest and best of the Greek poets was Sappho; she lived around 600 B.C., on the island of Lesbos. Sappho established a school to teach music and singing to well-to-do girls and to prepare them for marriage. With great tenderness, Sappho wrote poems of friendship and love.

Pindar (c. 518–438 B.C.) was another Greek lyric poet. In his poem of praise for a victorious athlete, Pindar expressed the aristocratic view of excellence. Although life is essentially tragic—triumphs are short-lived, misfortunes are many, and ultimately death overtakes all—man must still demonstrate his worth by striving for excellence.

The high point of Greek poetry is drama, an art form that originated in Greece. In portraying the sufferings, weaknesses, and triumphs of individuals, Greek dramatists shifted attention from the gods to human beings. Greek drama evolved as a continuous striving toward humanization and individualization. Just as a Greek sculptor shaped a clear visual image of the human form, so a Greek dramatist brought the inner life of human beings, their fears and hopes, into sharp focus and tried to find the deeper meaning of human experience. Thus, both art and drama evidenced the growing self-awareness of the individual.

Drama originated in the religious festivals honoring Dionysus, the god of wine and agricultural fertility. A profound innovation in these sacred performances, which included choral songs and dances, occurred in the last part of the sixth century B.C. Thespis, the first actor known to history, stepped out of the chorus and engaged it in dialogue. By separating himself from the choral group, Thespis demonstrated a new awareness of the individual.

With only one actor and a chorus, however, the possibilities for dramatic action and human conflicts were limited. Then Aeschylus introduced a second actor in his dramas, and Sophocles a third. Dialogue between individuals thus became possible. The Greek actors wore masks, and by changing them, each actor could play several roles in the same performance. This flexibility allowed the dramatists to depict the clash and interplay of human wills and passions on a greater scale.

A development parallel to Socratic dialectics—dialogue between thinking individuals—occurred in Greek drama. By setting characters in conflict against each other, dramatists showed individuals as active subjects, responsible for their behavior and decisions.

Like the natural philosophers, Greek dramatists saw an inner logic to the

Floor Mosaic Depicting Dionysus, the Patron God of the Theater.   The panther's snarl, claws, and craning neck convey a fierceness that vividly contrasts with Dionysus' serene manner. (*Archeological Receipts Fund, Athens*)

universe, which they called Fate or Destiny. Both physical and social worlds obeyed laws. People paid a price for being stubborn, narrow-minded, arrogant, or immoderate; the order in the universe required it. In being free to make decisions, the dramatists said, individuals have the potential for greatness, but in choosing wrongly, unintelligently, they bring disaster to themselves and others.

Also like philosophy, Greek tragedy entailed rational reflection. Tragic heroes were not passive victims of fate. They were thinking human beings who felt a need to comprehend their position, explain the reasons for their actions, analyze their feelings, and respond to their fate with insight.

The essence of Greek tragedy lies in the tragic heroes' struggle against cosmic forces and insurmountable obstacles, which eventually crush them. But what impressed the Greek audience (and impresses us today) was not the vulnerability or weaknesses of human beings, but their courage and determination in the face of these forces.

The three great Athenian tragedians were Aeschylus (525–456 B.C.), Sophocles (c. 496–406 B.C.), and Euripides (c. 485–406 B.C.). Aeschylus believed that the world was governed by divine justice, which could not be violated with impunity; when individuals evinced *hubris* (overweening pride or arrogance), which led them to overstep the bounds of moderation, they had to be punished. Another principal theme was that through suffering people acquired knowledge: the terrible consequences of sins against the divine order should remind all to think and act with moderation and caution.

Sophocles maintained that individuals should shape their character in the way a sculptor shapes a form: according to laws of proportion. In his view, when the principles of harmony were violated by immoderate behavior, a person's character would be thrown off balance and misfortune would strike.

The rationalist spirit of Greek philosophy permeated the tragedies of Euripides. Like the Sophists, Euripides subjected the problems of human life to critical analysis and challenged human conventions. His plays carefully scrutinized the role of the gods, women's conflicts, the horrors of war, the power of passion, and the prevalence of human suffering and weakness. Euripides blended a poet's insight with the psychologist's probing to reveal the tangled world of human passions and souls in torment.

Greek dramatists also wrote comedies. Aristophanes (c. 448–c. 380 B.C.), the greatest of the Greek comic playwrights, lampooned Athenian statesmen and intellectuals and censured government policies. Behind Aristophanes' sharp wit lay a deadly seriousness; he sought an end to the ruinous Peloponnesian War and a reaffirmation of traditional values, which the Sophists had undermined.

History

The Mesopotamians and the Egyptians kept annals that purported to narrate the deeds of gods and their human agents, the priest-kings or god-kings. The Hebrews valued history, but believing that God acted in human affairs, they did not remove historical events from the realm of religious-mythical thought. The Greeks initiated a different approach to the study of history. For them, history was not a narrative about the deeds of gods, as it was for the Egyptians and Mesopotamians, or the record of God's wrath or benevolence, as it was for the Hebrews; instead, it dealt with the actions of human beings.

As the gods were eliminated from the nature philosophers' explanations for the origins of things in the natural world, mythical elements were also removed from the writing of history. Greek historians asked themselves questions about the deeds of people, based their answers on available evidence, and wrote in prose, the language of rational thought. They not only narrated events, but also examined causes.

Herodotus

Often called the "father of history," Herodotus (c. 484–c. 424 B.C.) wrote a history of the Persian Wars. The central theme of this book, entitled *The Histories,* is the contrast between Near Eastern despotism and Greek freedom and the subsequent clash of these two world-views in the wars. Though Herodotus found much to praise in the Persian Empire, he was struck by a lack of freedom and by what he considered barbarity. He emphasized that the mentality of the free citizen was foreign to the East, where men were trained to obey the ruler's commands absolutely. Not the rule of law but the whim of despots prevailed in the East.

Another theme evident in Herodotus' work was punishment for hubris. In seeking to become king of both Asia and Europe, Xerxes had acted arrogantly; although he behaved as if he were superhuman, "he too was human, and was sure to be disappointed of his great expectations."[11] Like the Greek tragedians, Herodotus drew universal moral principles from human behavior.

In several ways, Herodotus was a historian rather than a teller of tales. First, he asked questions about the past, instead of merely repeating ancient legends; he tried to discover what had happened and the motivations behind the actions. Second, he demonstrated at times a cautious and critical attitude toward his sources of information. Third, although the gods appeared in his narrative, they played a far less important role than they did in Greek popular mythology. Nevertheless, by retaining a belief in the significance of dreams, omens, and oracles and by allowing divine intervention, Herodotus fell short of being a thoroughgoing rationalist. His writings contain the embryo of rational history. Thucydides brought it to maturity.

Thucydides

Thucydides (c. 460–c. 400 B.C.) also concentrated on a great political crisis confronting the Hellenic world: the Peloponnesian War. Living in Periclean Athens, whose lifeblood was politics, Thucydides regarded the motives of statesmen and the acts of government as the essence of history. He did not just catalogue facts, but sought the general concepts and principles that the facts illustrated. In Thucydides' history, there was no place for myths, for legends, for the fabulous—all hindrances to historical truth. He recognized that a work of history was a creation of the rational mind and not an expression of the poetic imagination. The historian seeks to learn and to enlighten, not to entertain.

Rejecting the notion that the gods interfere in history, Thucydides looked for the social forces and human decisions behind events. Undoubtedly, he was influenced by Hippocratic doctors, who frowned on divine explanations for disease and distinguished between the symptoms of a disease and its causes. Whereas Herodotus occasionally lapsed into supernatural explanations, Thucydides wrote history from which the gods were absent, and he denied their intervention in human affairs.

From the Sophists, Thucydides learned that the motives and reactions of human beings follow patterns. Therefore, a proper analysis of the events of the Peloponnesian War, he believed, would reveal general principles that govern human behavior. He intended his history to be a source of enlightenment for future ages, indeed for all time, because he felt certain that the kinds of behavior that caused the conflict between Sparta and Athens would recur regularly through history.

In addition to being a historian, Thucydides was also a political philosopher, with a specific view of governments and statesmen. He warned against the dangers of extremism unleashed by the strains of war, and he believed that when reason was forsaken, the state's plight would worsen. He had contempt for statesmen who waged war lightly, acting from impulse, reckless daring, and an insatiable appetite for territory.

The Hellenistic Age: The Second Stage of Greek Civilization

Greek civilization, or Hellenism, passed through three distinct stages: the Hellenic Age, the Hellenistic Age, and the Greco-Roman Age. The Hellenic Age began around 800 B.C. with the early city-states, reached its height in the fifth century B.C., and endured until the death of Alexander the Great in 323 B.C. At that time, the ancient world entered the Hellenistic Age, which ended in 30 B.C., when Egypt, the last major Hellenistic state, fell to Rome. The Greco-Roman Age lasted five hundred years, encompassing the period of the Roman Empire up to the collapse of the Empire's western half in the last part of the fifth century A.D.

Although the Hellenistic Age absorbed the heritage of classical (Hellenic) Greece, its style of civilization changed. During the first phase of Hellenism, the polis had been the center of political life. The polis had given Greeks an identity, and only within the polis could a Greek live a good and civilized life. With the coming of the Hellenistic Age, this situation changed. Kingdoms and empires eclipsed the city-state in power and importance. Even though cities retained a large measure of autonomy in domestic affairs, they had lost their freedom of action in foreign affairs. No longer were they the self-sufficient and independent communities of the Hellenic period. Unable to stand up to kingdoms, the city-state had become an outmoded institution. The bonds between the individual and the city loosened. People had to deal with the feelings of isolation and insecurity produced by the decline of the polis.

As a result of Alexander the Great's conquests of the lands between Greece and India, tens of thousands of Greek soldiers, merchants, and administrators settled in eastern lands. This mixing of Greek and Near Eastern peoples and cultures defines the Hellenistic Age.

In the Hellenic Age, Greek philosophers had a limited conception of humanity, dividing the world into Greek and barbarian. In the Hellenistic Age, the intermingling of Greeks and peoples of the Near East caused a shift in focus from the city to the *oikoumene* (the inhabited world); parochialism gave way to cosmopolitanism and universalism as people began to think of themselves as members of a world community. Philosophers came to regard the civilized world as one city, the city of humanity.

Alexander the Great

After the assassination of Philip of Macedon in 336 B.C., his twenty-year-old son, Alexander, succeeded to the throne. Alexander inherited a proud and fiery temperament from his mother. From his tutor Aristotle, Alexander gained an appreciation for Greek culture, particularly the Homeric epics. Undoubtedly, the young Alexander was stirred by these stories of legendary heroes, especially of Achilles, and their striving for personal glory. Alexander acquired military skills and qualities of leadership from his father.

Alexander inherited from Philip an overriding policy of state: the invasion of Persia. With an army of thirty-five thousand men, Macedonians and Greeks combined, he crossed into Asia Minor in 334 B.C. and eventually advanced all the way to India. In these campaigns, Alexander proved himself to be a superb strategist and leader of men. Winning every battle, his army carved an empire that stretched from Greece to India.

The world after Alexander differed sharply from the one that existed before he took up the sword. Alexander's conquests brought West and East closer together, marking a new epoch. Alexander himself helped to implement this transformation. He took a Persian bride, arranged for eighty of his officers and ten thousand of his soldiers to marry Near Eastern women, and planned to incorporate thirty thousand Persian youths into his army. Alexander founded Greek-style cities in Asia, where Greek settlers mixed with the native population.

As Greeks acquired greater knowledge of the Near East, the parochialism of the polis gave way to a world outlook. As trade and travel between West and East expanded, as Greek merchants and soldiers settled in Asiatic lands, and as Greek culture spread to non-Greeks, the distinctions between barbarian and Greek lessened. Although Alexander never united all the peoples in a world-state, his career pushed the world in a new direction, toward a fusion of disparate peoples and the intermingling of cultural traditions.

The Competing Dynasties

In 323 B.C., Alexander, not yet thirty-three years old, died, after a sickness that followed a drinking party. After his premature death, his generals engaged in a long and bitter struggle to see who would succeed the conqueror.

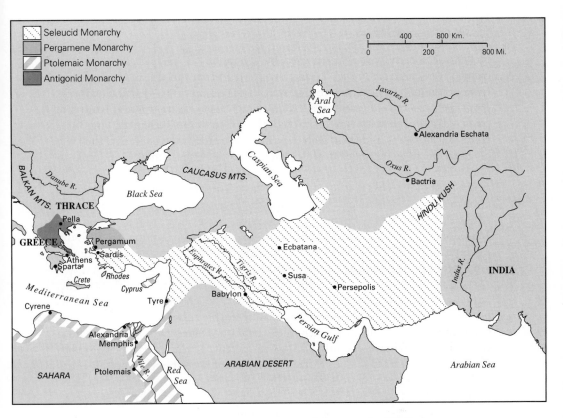

Map 3.2   The Division of Alexander's Empire and the Spread of Hellenism

Since none of the generals or their heirs had enough power to hold together Alexander's vast empire, the wars of succession ended in a stalemate. By 275 B.C., the empire was fractured into three dynasties: the Ptolemies in Egypt, the Seleucids in Asia, and the Antigonids in Macedonia. Macedonia, Alexander's native country, continued to dominate the Greek cities, which periodically tried to break its hold. Later, the kingdom of Pergamum in western Asia Minor emerged as the fourth Hellenistic monarchy.

In the third century B.C., Ptolemaic Egypt was the foremost power in the Hellenistic world. The Seleucid Empire, which stretched from the Mediterranean to the frontiers of India and encompassed many different peoples, attempted to extend its power in the west but was resisted by the Ptolemies. Finally, the Seleucid ruler Antiochus III (223–187 B.C.) defeated the Ptolemaic forces and established Seleucid control over Phoenicia and Palestine. Taking advantage of Egypt's defeat, Macedonia seized several of Egypt's territories.

Rome, a new power, became increasingly drawn into the affairs of the quarrelsome Hellenistic kingdoms. By the middle of the second century B.C., it had imposed its will upon them. From that time on, the political fortunes of the western and eastern Mediterranean were inextricably linked.

Cosmopolitanism

Hellenistic society was characterized by a mingling of peoples and an inter-change of cultures. Greek traditions spread to the Near East, while Mesopotamian, Egyptian, Hebrew, and Persian traditions—particularly reli-gious beliefs—moved westward. A growing cosmopolitanism replaced the parochialism of the city-state. Although the rulers of the Hellenistic kingdoms were Macedonians and their high officials and generals were Greeks, the style of government was modeled after that of the ancient oriental kingdoms. In the Hellenic Age, the law had expressed the will of the community, but in this new age of monarchy, the kings were the law. The Macedonian rulers encour-aged the oriental practice of worshiping the king as a god or as a representa-tive of the gods. In Egypt, for example, the priests conferred on the Macedonian king the same divine powers and titles traditionally held by Egyptian pharaohs; in accordance with ancient tradition, statues of the divine king were installed in Egyptian temples.

Following Alexander's lead, the Seleucids founded cities in the east pat-terned after the city-states of Greece. The cities, which were often founded to protect trade routes and as fortresses against hostile tribes, adopted the politi-cal institutions of Hellenic Greece, including a popular assembly and a coun-cil. Hellenistic kings generally did not intervene in the cities' local affairs. Thousands of Greeks settled in these cities, which were Greek in architecture and contained Greek schools, temples, theaters, where performances of classi-cal plays were staged, and gymnasia. Gymnasia were essentially places to ex-ercise, train in sports, and converse, but some had libraries and halls, where public lectures and competitions of orators and poets were held. Hellenistic kings brought books, paintings, and statues to their cities from Greece. Hel-lenistic cities, inhabited by tens of thousands of people from many lands and dominated by a Hellenized upper class, served as centers and agents of Hel-lenism, which non-Greeks adopted. The cities in Egypt and Syria saw the emergence of a native elite who spoke Greek, wore Greek-style clothing, and adopted Greek customs. *Koine,* a form of Greek, came to be spoken through-out much of the Mediterranean world.

The greatest city of the time and the one most representative of the Hel-lenistic Age was Alexandria in Egypt, founded by Alexander the Great. Strate-gically located at one of the mouths of the Nile, Alexandria became a center of commerce and culture. The most populous city of the Mediterranean world, Alexandria at the beginning of the Christian era contained perhaps a million people: Egyptians, Persians, Macedonians, Greeks, Jews, Syrians, and Arabs. The city was an unrivaled commercial center; goods from the Mediter-ranean world, east Africa, Arabia, and India circulated in its marketplaces. This cosmopolitan center also attracted poets, philosophers, physicians, as-tronomers, and mathematicians.

All phases of cultural life were permeated by cultural exchange. Sculpture showed the influence of many lands. Historians wrote world histories, not just local ones. Greek astronomers worked with data collected over the centuries by the Babylonians. The Hebrew Scriptures were translated into Greek for use by Greek-speaking Jews, and Jewish thinkers began to take note of Greek philosophy. Greeks increasingly demonstrated a fascination with oriental religious cults. Philosophers helped to break down the barriers between peoples by asserting that all inhabit a single fatherland.

The spread of Greek civilization from the Aegean to the Indus River gave the Hellenistic world a cultural common denominator, but Hellenization did not transform the East and make it one with the West. Hellenization was limited almost entirely to the cities, and in many urban centers it was often only a thin veneer. Many Egyptians in Alexandria learned Greek, and some assumed Greek names, but for most, Hellenization did not go much deeper. In the countryside, there was not even the veneer of Greek culture. Retaining traditional attitudes, the countryside in the East resisted Greek ways. In the villages, local and traditional law, local languages, and family customs remained unchanged; religion, the most important ingredient of the civilizations of the Near East, also kept its traditional character.

Hellenistic Thought and Culture

Hellenistic culture rested on a Hellenic foundation, but it also revealed new trends: a heightened universalism and a growing individualism.

History

The leading historian of the Hellenistic Age was Polybius (c. 200–118 B.C.), whose history of the rise of Rome is one of the great works of historical literature. Reflecting the universal tendencies of the Hellenistic Age, Polybius endeavored to explain how Rome had progressed from a city-state to a world conqueror. As a disciple of Thucydides, Polybius sought rational explanations for human events. Like Thucydides, he relied on eyewitness accounts (including his own personal experiences), checked sources, and strove for objectivity.

Art

Hellenistic art, like Hellenistic philosophy, expressed a heightened awareness of the individual. Whereas Hellenic sculpture aimed to depict ideal beauty— the perfect body and face—Hellenistic sculpture, moving from idealism to realism, captured individual character and expression, often of ordinary people. Scenes of daily life were realistically depicted.

Science

During the Hellenistic Age, Greek scientific achievement reached its height. When Alexander invaded Asia Minor, the former student of Aristotle brought

Clay Flask in the Shape of an African Boy, Late Third Century B.C. This common utensil in the shape of a squatting African boy symbolizes the multiethnic character of Hellenistic civilization in which numerous peoples were brought into contact with the Greeks and each other through Alexander's conquests. (*Martin von Wagner Museum of Art, University of Wuerzberg. Photo: K. Oehrlein*)

along surveyors, engineers, scientists, and historians, who continued with him into Asia. The vast amount of data in botany, zoology, geography, and astronomy collected by Alexander's staff stimulated an outburst of activity. Hellenistic science, says historian Benjamin Farrington, stood "on the threshold of the modern world. When modern science began in the sixteenth century, it took up where the Greeks left off."[12]

Because of its state-supported museum, Alexandria attracted leading scholars and superseded Athens in scientific investigation. The museum contained a library of more than half a million volumes, as well as botanical gardens and an observatory. It was really a research institute, in which some of the best minds of the day studied and worked.

Alexandrian doctors advanced medical skills. They improved surgical instruments and techniques and, by dissecting bodies, added to anatomical knowledge. Through their research, they discovered organs of the body not known until then, made the distinction between arteries and veins, divided nerves into those constituting the motor and the sensory systems, and identified the brain as the source of intelligence. Their investigations brought knowledge of anatomy and physiology to a level that was not significantly improved until the sixteenth century A.D.

Knowledge in the fields of astronomy and mathematics also increased. Eighteen centuries before Copernicus, Alexandrian astronomer Aristarchus (310–230 B.C.) said that the sun was the center of the universe, that the planets revolved around it, and that the stars were situated at great distances from the earth. But these revolutionary ideas were not accepted, and the belief in an earth-centered universe persisted. In geometry, Euclid, an Alexandrian mathematician who lived around 300 B.C., creatively synthesized earlier developments. Euclid's hundreds of geometrical proofs, derived from reasoning alone, are a profound witness to the power of the rational mind.

Eratosthenes (c. 275–194 B.C.), an Alexandrian geographer, sought a scientific understanding of the enlarged world. He divided the planet into climatic zones, declared that the oceans are joined, and, with extraordinary ingenuity and accuracy, measured the earth's circumference. Archimedes of Syracuse (287–212 B.C.), who studied at Alexandria, was a mathematician, a physicist, and an ingenious inventor. His mechanical inventions, including war engines, dazzled his contemporaries. However, in typically Greek fashion, Archimedes dismissed his practical inventions, preferring to be remembered as a theoretician.

Philosophy

Hellenistic thinkers preserved the rational tradition of Greek philosophy, but they also transformed it, for they had to adapt thought to the requirements of a cosmopolitan society. In the Hellenic Age, the starting point of philosophy was the citizen's relationship to the city; in the Hellenistic Age, the point of departure was the solitary individual's relationship to humanity, the individual's destiny in a complex world. Philosophy tried to deal with the feeling of alienation resulting from the weakening of the individual's attachment to the polis and sought a conception of community that corresponded to the social realities of a world grown larger. It aspired to make people ethically independent so that they could achieve happiness in a hostile and competitive world. In striving for tranquillity of mind and relief from conflict, Hellenistic thinkers reflected the general anxiety that pervaded their society.

Epicureanism   Two principal schools of philosophy arose in the Hellenistic world: Epicureanism and Stoicism. In the tradition of Plato and Aristotle, Epicurus (342–270 B.C.) founded a school in Athens at the end of the fourth century B.C. Epicurus broke with the attitude of the Hellenic Age in significant ways. Unlike classical Greek philosophers, Epicurus, reflecting the Greeks' changing relationship to the city, taught the value of passivity and withdrawal from civic life. To him, citizenship was not a prerequisite for individual happiness. Wise persons, said Epicurus, would refrain from engaging in public affairs, for politics could deprive them of their self-sufficiency, their freedom to choose and to act. Nor would wise individuals pursue wealth, power, or fame, as the pursuit would only provoke anxiety. For the same reason, wise persons would not surrender to hate or love, desires that distress the soul. They would also try to live justly because those who behave unjustly are burdened with troubles. Nor could people find happiness if they worried about dying or pleasing the gods.

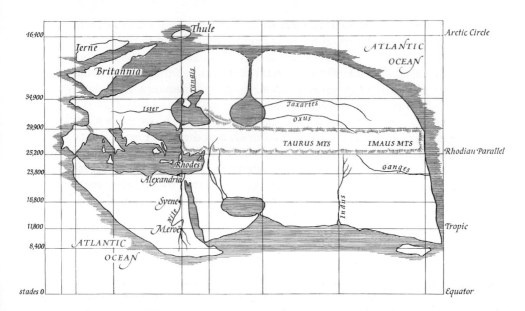

Reconstruction of the Map of the World by Eratosthenes (c. 275–194 B.C.).   Geographical knowledge expanded enormously among the Hellenistic Greeks. The first systematic scientific books on geography were credited to Eratosthenes, head of the Alexandrian Library, the greatest scientific and humanistic research center in the Hellenistic world. Eratosthenes estimated the circumference of the earth with remarkable accuracy for his time. His map illustrates the limits of the world known to the Greeks. (*From John Onians,* Art and Thought in the Hellenistic Age [*Thames and Hudson, 1979*]. *Reprinted by permission of Thames and Hudson Ltd.*)

To Epicurus, fear that the gods intervened in human life and could inflict suffering after death was the principal cause of anxiety. To remove this source of human anguish, he favored a theory of nature that had no place for the activity of gods. Therefore, he adopted the physics of Democritus, which taught that all things consist of atoms in motion. In a universe of colliding atoms, there could be no higher intelligence ordering things; there was no room for divine activity. Epicurus taught that the gods probably did exist but that they could not influence human affairs; consequently, individuals could order their own lives.

People could achieve happiness, said Epicurus, when their bodies were "free from pain" and their minds "released from worry and fear." Although Epicurus wanted to increase pleasure for the individual, he rejected unbridled hedonism. Because he believed that happiness must be pursued rationally, he urged avoidance of the merely sensuous pleasures that have unpleasant after-effects (such as overeating and excessive drinking). In general, Epicurus espoused the traditional Greek view of moderation and prudence. By opening his philosophy to men and women, slave and free, Greek and barbarian, and by separating ethics from politics, Epicurus fashioned a philosophy adapted to the post-Alexandrian world of kingdoms and universal culture.

Stoicism   Around the time when Epicurus founded his school, Zeno (335–263 B.C.) also opened a school in Athens. Zeno's teachings, called Stoicism (because his school was located in the *stoa,* or colonnade), became the most important philosophy in the Hellenistic world. By teaching that the world constituted a single society, Stoicism gave theoretical expression to the world-mindedness of the age. Through its concept of a world-state, the city of humanity, Stoicism offered an answer to the problem of community and alienation posed by the decline of the city-state. By stressing inner strength in dealing with life's misfortunes, it opened an avenue to individual happiness in a world fraught with uncertainty.

At the core of Stoicism was the belief that the universe contained a principle of order, variously called the Divine Fire, God—more the fundamental force of the universe than a living person—and Divine Reason (*Logos*). This ruling principle underlay reality and permeated all things; it accounted for the orderliness of nature. The Stoics reasoned that, being part of the universe, people too shared in the Logos that operated throughout the cosmos. The Logos was implanted in every human soul; it enabled people to act intelligently and to comprehend the principles of order that governed nature. Since reason was common to all, human beings were essentially brothers and fundamentally equal. Reason gave individuals dignity and enabled them to recognize and respect the dignity of others. To the Stoics, all people—Greek and barbarian, free and slave, rich and poor—were fellow human beings, and one law, the law of nature, applied to everyone. Thus, the Stoics, like the Hebrews, arrived at the idea of the oneness of humanity.

Like Socrates, the Stoics believed that a person's distinctive quality was the ability to reason and that happiness came from the disciplining of emotions by the rational part of the soul. Also like Socrates, the Stoics maintained that individuals should progress morally, should perfect their character. In the Stoic view, wise persons ordered their lives according to the natural law, the law of reason, that underlay the cosmos. This harmony with the Logos would give them the inner strength to resist the torments inflicted by others, by fate, and by their own passionate natures. Self-mastery and inner peace, or happiness, would follow. Such individuals would remain undisturbed by life's misfortunes, for their souls would be their own. Even slaves were not denied this inner freedom; although their bodies were subjected to the power of their masters, their minds still remained independent and free.

Stoicism had an enduring influence on the Western mind. To some Roman political theorists, the Empire fulfilled the Stoic ideal of a world community, in which people of different nationalities held citizenship and were governed by a worldwide law that accorded with the law of reason, or natural law, operating throughout the universe. Stoic beliefs—that by nature we are all members of one family, that each person is significant, that distinctions of rank and race are of no account, and that human law should not conflict with natural law—were incorporated into Roman jurisprudence, Christian thought, and modern liberalism. There is continuity between the Stoic idea of natural law—a moral order that underlies nature—and the principle of inalienable rights, stated in the American Declaration of Independence.

The Greek Achievement: Reason, Freedom, Humanism

Like other ancient peoples, the Greeks warred, massacred, and enslaved; they could be cruel, arrogant, contentious, and superstitious; and they often violated their own ideals. But their achievement was unquestionably of profound historical significance. Western thought begins with the Greeks, who first defined the individual by his capacity to reason. It was the great achievement of the Greek spirit to rise above magic, miracles, mystery, authority, and custom and to discover the means of giving rational order to nature and society. Every aspect of Greek civilization—science, philosophy, art, drama, literature, politics, historical writing—showed a growing reliance on human reason and a diminishing dependence on the gods and mythical thinking.

In Mesopotamia and Egypt, people had no clear conception of their individual worth and no understanding of political liberty. They were not citizens, but subjects marching to the command of a ruler whose power originated with the gods. Such royal power was not imposed on an unwilling population; it was religiously accepted and obeyed.

In contrast, the Greeks created political freedom. They saw the state as a community of free citizens who made laws in their own interest. The Greeks held that men are capable of governing themselves and they valued active citizenship. For the Greeks, the state was a civilizing agent, permitting people to live the good life. Greek political thinkers arrived at a conception of the rational, or legal, state: a state in which law was an expression of reason, not of whim or divine commands; of justice, not of might; of the general good of the community, not of self-interest.

The Greeks also gave to Western civilization a conception of inner, or ethical, freedom. People were free to choose between shame and honor, cowardice and duty, moderation and excess. The heroes of Greek tragedy suffered, not because they were puppets being manipulated by higher powers, but because they possessed the freedom of decision. The idea of ethical freedom reached its highest point with Socrates. To shape oneself according to ideals known to the mind—to develop into an autonomous and self-directed person—became for the Greeks the highest form of freedom.

During the Hellenistic Age, the Greeks, like the Hebrews earlier, arrived at the idea of universalism, the oneness of humanity. Stoic philosophers taught that all people, because of their ability to reason, are fundamentally alike and can be governed by the same laws. This idea is at the root of the modern principle of natural, or human, rights, which are the birthright of each individual.

Underlying everything accomplished by the Greeks was a humanist attitude toward life. The Greeks expressed a belief in the worth, significance, and dignity of the individual. They called for the maximum cultivation of human talent, the full development of human personality, and the deliberate pursuit of excellence. In valuing the human personality, the Greek humanists did not approve of living without restraints; they aimed at creating a higher type of man. Such a man would mold himself according to worthy standards and make his life as harmonious and flawless as a work of art. This aspiration required effort, discipline, and intelligence. Fundamental to the Greek humanist outlook was the belief that man could master himself. Although people could not alter the course of nature, for there was an order to the universe over which neither they nor the gods had control, the humanist believed that people could control their own lives.

By discovering theoretical reason, by defining political freedom, and by affirming the worth and potential of human personality, the Greeks broke with the past and founded the rational and humanist tradition of the West. "Had Greek civilization never existed," says the poet W. H. Auden, "we would never have become fully conscious, which is to say that we would never have become, for better or worse, fully human."[13]

Notes

1. H. D. F. Kitto, *The Greeks* (Baltimore: Penguin Books, 1957), p. 60.
2. Werner Jaeger, *Paideia: The Ideals of Greek Culture,* trans. Gilbert Highet (New York: Oxford University Press, 1945), 1:8.
3. Kitto, *The Greeks,* p. 78.
4. Herodotus, *The Histories,* trans. Aubrey de Sélincourt (Baltimore: Penguin Books, 1954), p. 493.
5. Thucydides, *The Peloponnesian War,* trans. B. Jowett (Oxford: Clarendon Press, 1881), bk. 2, chap. 37.
6. Plato, *Apology,* trans. F. J. Church, rev. R. D. Cummings (Indianapolis: Bobbs-Merrill, 1956), secs. 16–17.
7. Plato, *The Republic,* trans. F. M. Cornford (New York: Oxford University Press, 1945), p. 289.
8. Ibid., p. 293.
9. *Politics,* in *Basic Works of Aristotle,* ed. Richard McKeon (New York: Random House, 1941), pp. 1246, 1251.
10. Ibid., pp. 1220–21.
11. Herodotus, *The Histories,* p. 485.
12. Benjamin Farrington, *Greek Science* (Baltimore: Penguin Books, 1961), p. 301.
13. W. H. Auden, ed., *The Portable Greek Reader* (New York: Viking, 1952), p. 38.

Suggested Reading

Boardman, John, et al., *The Oxford History of the Classical World* (1986). Essays on all facets of Greek culture.

Copleston, Frederick, *A History of Philosophy,* vol. 1 (1962). An excellent analysis of Greek philosophy.

Cornford, F. M., *Before and After Socrates* (1968). The essential meaning of Greek philosophy clearly presented.

Ferguson, John, *The Heritage of Hellenism* (1973). A good introduction to Hellenistic culture.

Fine, John V. A., *The Ancient Greeks* (1983). An up-to-date, reliable analysis of Greek history.

Finley, M. I., ed., *The Legacy of Greece* (1981). Essays on all phases of Greek culture.

Frost, Frank J., *Greek Society* (1987). Social and economic life in ancient Greece.

Grant, Michael, *A Social History of Greece and Rome* (1992). Essays on the rich, the poor, women, slaves, and freedmen and freedwomen.

————, *From Alexander to Cleopatra* (1982). A fine survey of all phases of Hellenistic society and culture.

Hooper, Finley, *Greek Realities* (1978). A literate and sensitive presentation of Greek society and culture.

Jaeger, Werner, *Paideia: The Ideals of Greek Culture* (1939–1944). A three-volume work on Greek culture by a distinguished classicist. The treatment of Homer, the early Greek philosophers, and the Sophists in volume 1 is masterful.

Jones, W. T., *A History of Western Philosophy,* vol. 1 (1962). Clearly written; contains useful passages from original sources.

Kitto, H. D. F., *The Greeks* (1957). A stimulating survey of Greek life and thought.

Levi, Peter, *The Pelican History of Greek Literature* (1985). Sound insights into Greek writers.

Murray, Oswyn, *Early Greece* (1980). Good on relations with the Near East and lifestyles of the aristocracy.

Vernant, Jean-Pierre, *The Origins of Greek Thought* (1982). The movement from myth to reason.

Wallbank, F. W., *The Hellenistic World* (1982). A survey of the Hellenistic world; makes judicious use of quotations from original sources.

Webster, T. B. L., *Athenian Culture and Society* (1973). Discusses Athenian religion, crafts, art, drama, education, and so on.

Review Questions

1. Why is Homer called "the shaper of Greek civilization"?
2. How did the Greek polis break with the theocratic politics of the Near East?
3. Describe the basic features and the limitations of Athenian democracy.
4. What were the causes of the Peloponnesian War? What was the impact of this war on the Greek world?
5. Explain how Greek political life demonstrated both the best and the worst features of freedom and both the capabilities and the limitations of reason.
6. What was the achievement of the Ionian natural philosophers?
7. How did the Sophists advance the tradition of reason initiated by the natural philosophers? How did they contribute to a spiritual crisis in Athens?
8. What was Socrates' answer to the problems posed by the Sophists?
9. Describe the essential features of Plato's *Republic* and discuss the reasons that led him to write it.
10. How did Aristotle both criticize and accept Plato's theory of Ideas? What do Aristotle's political thought and ethical thought have in common?
11. Greek art was realistic, idealistic, and humanistic. Explain.
12. Why do the Greek plays have perennial appeal?
13. What were the basic differences between the Hellenic and Hellenistic ages?
14. How did Alexander the Great contribute to the shaping of the Hellenistic Age?

15. Hellenistic science stood on the threshold of the modern world. Explain.
16. What problems concerned Hellenistic philosophers?
17. What was the enduring significance of Stoicism?
18. The Greeks broke with the mythopoeic outlook of the ancient Near East and conceived a world-view that is the foundation of Western civilization. Discuss.

❖ CHAPTER 4

Rome: From City-State to World Empire

$\mathcal{R}$ome's great achievement was to transcend the narrow political orientation of the city-state and to create a world-state, which unified the different nations of the Mediterranean world. Regarding the polis as the only means to the good life, the Greeks had not desired a larger political unit and had almost totally excluded foreigners from citizenship. Although Hellenistic philosophers had conceived the possibility of a world community, Hellenistic politics could not shape one. But Rome overcame the limitations of the city-state mentality and developed an empirewide system of law and citizenship. The Hebrews were distinguished by their prophets, and the Greeks by their philosophers; Rome's genius found expression in law and government.

Historians divide Roman history into two broad periods. The period of the Republic began in 509 B.C. with the overthrow of the Etruscan monarchy; that of the Empire started in 27 B.C., when Octavian (Augustus) became in effect the first Roman emperor, ending almost five hundred years of republican self-government. By conquering the Mediterranean world and extending its law and, in some instances, citizenship to different nationalities, the Roman Republic transcended the parochialism typical of the city-state. The Republic initiated the trend toward political and legal universalism, which reached fruition in the second phase of Roman history, the Empire. ❖

Evolution of the Roman Constitution

By the eighth century B.C., peasant communities existed on some of Rome's seven hills near the Tiber River in central Italy. To the north stood Etruscan cities and to the south, Greek cities. The more advanced civilizations of both Etruscans and Greeks were gradually absorbed by the Romans. The origin of the Etruscans remains a mystery, although some scholars believe that they came from Asia Minor and settled in northern Italy. From them, Romans acquired architectural styles and skills in road construction, sanitation,

---

Chronology 4.1 ❖ Rome

509 B.C.	Expulsion of the Etruscan monarch
287	The end of the Struggle of the Orders
264–241	First Punic War; Rome acquires provinces
218–201	Second Punic War; Hannibal is defeated
133–122	Land reforms by the Gracchi brothers; they are murdered by the Senate
88–83	Conflict between Sulla and the forces of Marius; Sulla emerges as dictator
49–44	Caesar is dictator of Rome
27 B.C.	Octavian assumes the title *Augustus* and becomes, in effect, the first Roman emperor; start of the Pax Romana
A.D. 180	Marcus Aurelius dies; end of the Pax Romana
212	Roman citizenship is granted to virtually all free inhabitants of Roman provinces
235–285	Military anarchy; Germanic incursions
285–305	Diocletian tries to deal with the crisis by creating a regimented state
378	Battle of Adrianople: Visigoths defeat the Roman legions
406	Borders collapse, Germanic tribes move into the Empire
476	End of Roman Empire in the West

---

hydraulic engineering (including underground conduits), metallurgy, ceramics, and portrait sculpture. Etruscan words and names entered the Latin language, and Roman religion absorbed Etruscan gods.

The Etruscans had expanded their territory in Italy during the seventh and sixth centuries B.C., and they controlled the monarchy in Rome. Defeated by Celts, Greeks, and finally Romans, by the third century B.C. the Etruscans ceased to exercise any political power in Italy.

Rome became a republic at the end of the sixth century B.C.—the traditional date is 509 B.C.—when the landowning aristocrats, or patricians, overthrew the Etruscan king. As in the Greek cities, the transition from theocratic monarchy to republic offered possibilities for political and legal growth. In the opening phase of republican history, religion governed the people, dictated the law, and legitimized the rule of the patricians, who regarded themselves as the preservers of sacred traditions. Gradually, the Romans loosened

Etruscan Bronze Finial from a Candelabrum, 480–470 B.C.   The remarkable rise to power and wealth of the Etruscans was largely based upon their large-scale manufacture of bronze and iron wares. Merchants shipped weapons, armor, tools, and household utensils, as well as artistic works throughout Italy, Gaul, and central Europe. The Etruscans' capture of Rome c. 600 B.C. opened the way for the first real urbanization of the city. (*The Metropolitan Museum of Art, Rogers Fund, 1912* [*47.11.3*])

the ties between religion and politics and hammered out a constitutional system, which paralleled the Greek achievement of rationalizing and secularizing politics and law. In time, the Romans, like the Greeks, came to view law as an expression of the public will and not as the creation of god-kings, priest-kings, or a priestly caste.

The impetus for the growth of the Roman constitution came from a conflict—known as the Struggle of the Orders—between the patricians and the commoners, or plebeians. At the beginning of the fifth century B.C., the patrician-dominated government consisted of two elected executives, called consuls, the Centuriate Assembly, and the Senate. Patricians owned most of the land and controlled the army. The executive heads of government were the two annually elected consuls, who came from the nobility; they commanded the army, served as judges, and initiated legislation.

The Centuriate Assembly was a popular assembly, but because of voting procedures, it was controlled by the nobility. The Assembly elected consuls and other magistrates and made the laws, which also needed Senate approval. The Senate advised the Assembly but did not itself enact laws; it controlled public finances and foreign policy. Senators either were appointed for life terms by the consuls or were former magistrates. The Senate was the principal organ of patrician power.

The tension between patricians and commoners stemmed from plebeian grievances, which included enslavement for debt, discrimination in the courts, prevention of intermarriage with patricians, lack of political representation, and the absence of a written code of laws. Resenting their inferior status and eager for economic relief, the plebeians organized and waged a struggle for political, legal, and social equality.

The plebeians had one decisive weapon: their threat to secede from Rome, that is, not to pay taxes, work, or serve in the army. Realizing that Rome, which was constantly involved in warfare on the Italian peninsula, could not endure without plebeian help, the pragmatic patricians grudgingly made concessions. Thus, the plebeians slowly gained legal equality.

Early in the fifth century, the plebeians won the right to form their own assembly (the Plebeian Assembly, which was later enlarged and called the Tribal Assembly). This Assembly could elect tribunes, officials who were empowered to protect plebeian rights. As a result of plebeian pressure, around 450 B.C. the first Roman code of laws was written. Called the Twelve Tables, the code gave plebeians some degree of protection against unfair and oppressive patrician officials, who could interpret customary law in an arbitrary way. Other concessions gained later by the plebeians included the right to intermarry with patricians, access to the highest political, judicial, and religious offices in the state, and the elimination of slavery as payment for debt. In 287 B.C., a date generally recognized as the termination of the plebeian-patrician struggle, the Tribal Assembly acquired the power to make laws for all citizens without the Senate's approval.

Even though the plebeians had gained legal equality and the right to sit in the Senate and to hold high offices, Rome was still ruled by an upper class. The oligarchy that held power now consisted of patricians and influential plebeians who had joined forces with the old nobility. Marriages between patricians and politically powerful plebeians strengthened this alliance. As only wealthy plebeians became tribunes, they tended to side with the old nobility rather than to defend the interests of poor plebeians. By using bribes, the ruling oligarchy maintained control over the Assembly, and the Senate remained a bastion of aristocratic power. Deeming themselves Rome's finest citizens, the ruling oligarchy led Rome during its period of expansion and demonstrated a sense of responsibility and a talent for statesmanship.

During the two-hundred-year Struggle of the Orders, the Romans forged a constitutional system based on civic needs rather than on religious mystery. The essential duty of government ceased to be the regular performance of religious rituals and became the maintenance of order at home and the preservation of Roman might and dignity in international relations. Although the Romans retained the ceremonies and practices of their ancestral religion, public interest, not religious tradition or the prospect of divine punishment, determined the content of law. Public interest was also the standard by which all the important acts of the city were judged. In the opening stage of republican history, law was priestly and sacred, spoken only by priests and known only to men of religious families. Gradually, as law was written, debated, and altered, it became disentangled from religion. Another step in this process of secularization and rationalization occurred when the study and interpretation of law passed from the hands of priests to a class of professional jurists, who analyzed, classified, and systematized it and sought commonsense solutions to legal problems.

The Roman constitution was not a product of abstract thought, nor was it the gift of a great lawmaker, such as the Athenian Solon. Rather, like the unwritten English constitution, the Roman constitution evolved gradually and empirically in response to specific needs. The Romans, unlike the Greeks, were distinguished by practicality and common sense, not by a love of abstract thought. In their pragmatic and empirical fashion, they gradually developed the procedures of public politics and the legal state.

Roman Expansion to 146 B.C.

At the time of the Struggle of the Orders, Rome was also extending its power over the Italian peninsula. Without civic harmony and stability, it could not have achieved expansion. By 146 B.C., it had become the dominant power in the Mediterranean world.

Roman expansion occurred in three main stages: the uniting of the Italian peninsula, which gave Rome the manpower that transformed it from a city state into a great power; the collision with Carthage, from which Rome emerged as ruler of the western Mediterranean; and the subjugation of the Hellenistic states, which brought Romans in close contact with Greek civilization. As Rome expanded territorially, its leaders enlarged their vision. Instead of restricting citizenship to people having ethnic kinship, Rome assimilated other peoples into its political community. As law had grown to cope with the earlier grievances of the plebeians, so too it adjusted to the new situations resulting from the creation of a multinational empire. The city of Rome was evolving into the city of humanity—the cosmopolis envisioned by the Stoics.

The Uniting of Italy

During the first stage of expansion, Rome extended its hegemony over Italy, subduing in the process neighboring Latin kinsmen, semicivilized Italian tribes, the once dominant Etruscans, and Greek city-states in southern Italy.

Rome's conquest of Italy stemmed in part from superior military organization and discipline. Copying the Greeks, the Romans organized their soldiers into battle formations; in contrast, their opponents often fought as disorganized hordes, which were prone to panic and flight. Romans also willingly made sacrifices so that Rome might endure. In conquering Italy, they were united by a moral and religious devotion to their city strong enough to overcome social conflict, factional disputes, and personal ambition.

Despite its army's strength, Rome could not have mastered Italy without the cooperation of other Italian peoples. Instead of reducing adversaries to slavery and taking all their land—a not uncommon method of warfare in the ancient world—Rome endeavored, through generous treatment, to gain the loyalty of conquered people. Some defeated communities retained a measure of self-government but turned the conduct of foreign affairs over to Rome and contributed contingents to the army when Rome went to war. Other conquered people received partial or full citizenship. In extending its dominion over Italy, Rome displayed a remarkable talent for converting former enemies into allies and eventually into Roman citizens. No Greek city had ever envisaged integrating nonnatives into its political community.

The Conquest of the Mediterranean World

When Rome finished unifying Italy, there were five great powers in the Mediterranean area: the Seleucid monarchy in the Near East, the Ptolemaic monarchy in Egypt, the kingdom of Macedonia, Carthage in the western Mediterranean, and the Roman-dominated Italian Confederation. One hundred twenty years later—in 146 B.C.—Rome had subjected these states to its dominion.

Roman expansion beyond Italy did not proceed according to a set plan. Indeed, some Roman leaders considered involvement in foreign adventures a threat to both Rome's security and its traditional way of life. However, as its interests grew, Rome was drawn into conflicts and, without planning it, acquired an overseas empire.

Shortly after asserting supremacy in Italy, Rome engaged Carthage, the other great power in the western Mediterranean, in a prolonged conflict, the First Punic War (264–241 B.C.). Founded about 800 B.C. by Phoenicians, the North African city of Carthage had become a prosperous commercial center. The Carthaginians had acquired an empire comprising North Africa and coastal regions of southern Spain, Sardinia, Corsica, and western Sicily.

War between the two great powers began because Rome feared Carthage's designs on the northern Sicilian city of Messana. Rome was apprehensive about the southern Italian city-states that were its allies, fearing that Carthage would use Messana either to attack them or to interfere with their trade. Rome decided that the security of its allies required intervention in Sicily. Although Rome suffered severe losses—including the annihilation of an army that had invaded North Africa and the destruction of hundreds of ships in

Cast Made from Trajan's Column.   Emperor Trajan (98–117 A.D.) constructed a column to commemorate his campaigns. One of the reliefs depicts a Roman fleet landing at the port of Acona. During the First Punic War, Rome had become a naval power able to counter Carthage's fleet. (*Alinari/Art Resource, NY*)

battle and storms—the Romans never considered anything but a victor's peace. Drawing manpower from loyal allies throughout Italy, Rome finally prevailed over Carthage, which had to surrender Sicily to Rome. Three years later, Rome seized the islands of Corsica and Sardinia from a weakened Carthage. With the acquisition of these territories beyond Italy, which were made into provinces, Rome had the beginnings of an empire.

Carthaginian expansion in Spain precipitated the Second Punic War (218–201 B.C.). The Carthaginian army was commanded by Hannibal (247–183 B.C.), whose military genius astounded the ancients. Hannibal led a seasoned army, complete with war elephants for charging enemy lines, across mountain passes so steep and icy that men and animals sometimes lost their footing and fell to their deaths. Some twenty-six thousand men survived the crossing into Italy; fifteen thousand more were recruited from Gallic tribesmen of the Po Valley. At the battle of Cannae (216 B.C.), Hannibal's army completely destroyed a Roman army of sixty thousand soldiers—the largest single force Rome had ever put into the field.

These were the Republic's worst days. Nevertheless, says the Roman historian Livy, the Romans did not breathe a word of peace. Hannibal could not follow up his victory at Cannae with a finishing blow, for Rome wisely would not allow its army to be lured into another major engagement. Nor did Hannibal possess the manpower to capture the city itself. Rome invaded North Africa, threatening Carthage and forcing Hannibal to withdraw his troops from Italy in order to defend his homeland. Hannibal, who had won every battle in Italy, was defeated by Scipio Africanus at the battle of Zama in North Africa in 202 B.C., forcing Cathage to sue for peace. Carthage was compelled to surrender Spain and to give up its elephants and its navy.

The Second Punic War left Rome as the sole great power in the western Mediterranean; it also hastened Rome's entry into the politics of the Hellenistic world. In the year after Cannae, during Rome's darkest ordeal, Philip V of Macedonia entered into an alliance with Hannibal. Fearing that the Macedonian ruler might invade Italy, Rome initiated the First Macedonian War and won it in 205 B.C. To end Macedonian influence in Greece, which Rome increasingly viewed as a Roman protectorate, the Romans fought two other wars with Macedonia. Finally, in 148 B.C., Rome created the province of Macedonia.

Intervention in Greece led to Roman involvement in the Hellenistic kingdoms of the Near East and Asia Minor: Seleucia, Egypt, and Pergamum. The Hellenistic states became client kingdoms of Rome and consequently lost their freedom of action in foreign affairs.

In 146 B.C., the same year that Rome's hegemony over the Hellenistic world was assured, Rome concluded an unnecessary Third Punic War with Carthage. Rome had launched this war of annihilation against Carthage in 149 B.C. even though Carthage was by then a second-rate power and no longer a threat to Rome's security. The Romans were driven by old hatreds and the traumatic memory of Hannibal's near-conquest. Rome sold Carthaginian survivors into slavery, obliterated the city, and turned the territory into the Roman province of Africa. Rome's savage and irrational behavior toward a helpless Carthage was an early sign of the deterioration of senatorial leadership; there would be others.

Rome had not yet reached the limits of its expansion, but there was no doubt that by 146 B.C. the Mediterranean world had been subjected to its will. No power could stand up to Rome.

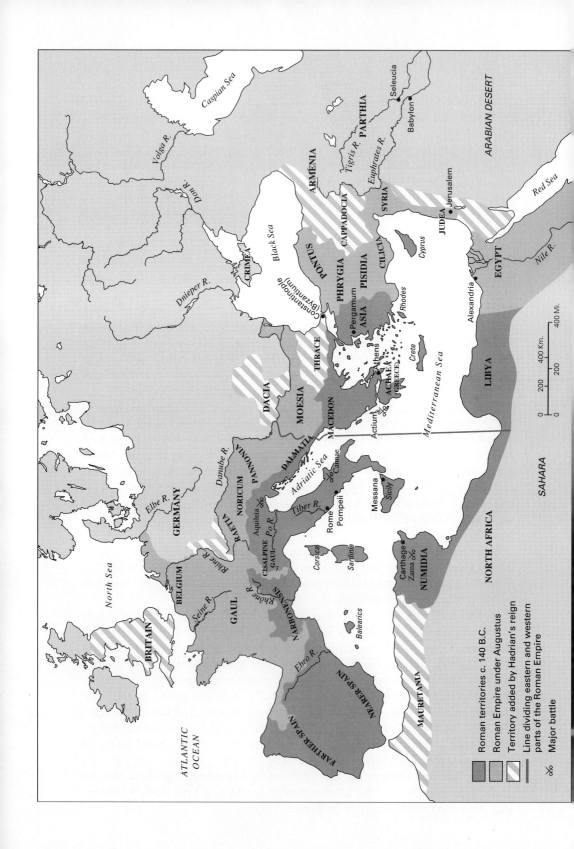

Roman territories c. 140 B.C.

Roman Empire under Augustus

Territory added by Hadrian's reign

Line dividing eastern and western parts of the Roman Empire

Major battle

ATLANTIC OCEAN

North Sea

BRITAIN

GERMANY

BELGIUM

GAUL

Seine R.

Rhine R.

Rhône R.

Elbe R.

NARBONENSIS

CISALPINE GAUL

RAETIA

NORICUM

PANNONIA

VINDONNA

DACIA

Danube R.

Ebro R.

FARTHER SPAIN

NEARER SPAIN

Balearics

Corsica

Sardinia

Sicily

Messana

Cannae

Rome

Pompeii

Tiber R.

Po R.

Aquileia

DALMATIA

MOESIA

MACEDON

THRACE

Adriatic Sea

Actium

ACHAEA (GREECE)

Athens

Crete

Rhodes

Mediterranean Sea

MAURETANIA

NORTH AFRICA

NUMIDIA

Carthage

Zama

Messana

SAHARA

LIBYA

Caspian Sea

Volga R.

Don R.

Dnieper R.

Black Sea

CRIMEA

Constantinople (Byzantium)

PONTUS

PHRYGIA

ASIA

Pergamum

PISIDIA

CILICIA

CAPPADOCIA

ARMENIA

Cyprus

SYRIA

JUDEA

Jerusalem

Alexandria

EGYPT

Nile R.

Tigris R.

Euphrates R.

PARTHIA

Seleucia

Babylon

ARABIAN DESERT

Red Sea

0   200   400 Km.

0   200   400 Mi.

The Consequences of Expansion

Expansion had important consequences for Rome and the Mediterranean world. Thousands of Greeks, many of them educated persons who had been enslaved as a result of Rome's eastern conquests, came to Rome. This influx accelerated the process of Hellenization begun earlier through Rome's contact with the Greek cities of southern Italy.

A crucial consequence of expansion was Roman contact with the legal experience of other peoples, including the Greeks. Demonstrating the Roman virtues of pragmatism and common sense, Roman jurists selectively incorporated into Roman law elements of the legal codes and traditions of these nations. Thus, Roman jurists gradually and empirically fashioned the *jus gentium,* the law of nations, or peoples, which eventually was applied throughout the Empire.

Roman conquerors transported to Italy hundreds of thousands of war captives, including Greeks, from all over the Empire. It is estimated that between 80 and 8 B.C. more than two million enslaved aliens were transported to Italy. By the middle of that century, slaves constituted about one-third of Italy's population, compared with about 10 percent before the Second Punic War. The more fortunate slaves worked as craftsmen and servants; the luckless and more numerous toiled on the growing number of plantations or died early laboring in mines. Roman masters often treated their slaves brutally. Although slave uprisings were not common, their ferocity terrified the Romans. In 135 B.C., slaves in Sicily revolted and captured some key towns, defeating Roman forces before being subdued. In 73 B.C., gladiators, led by Spartacus, broke out of their barracks and were joined by tens of thousands of runaways. Spartacus aimed to escape into Gaul and Thrace, the homelands of many slaves. His slave army defeated Roman armies and devastated southern Italy before the superior might of Rome prevailed. Some six thousand of the defeated slaves were crucified.

Roman governors, lesser officials, and businessmen found the provinces a source of quick wealth; they were generally unrestrained by the Senate, which was responsible for administering the overseas territories. Exploitation, corruption, looting, and extortion soon ran rampant. "No administration in history has ever devoted itself so whole-heartedly to fleecing its subjects for the private benefit of its ruling class as Rome of the last age of the Republic," concludes E. Badian.[1] The Roman nobility proved unfit to manage a world empire.

Despite numerous examples of misrule in the provinces, Roman administration had many positive features. Rome generally allowed its subjects a large measure of self-government and did not interfere with religion and local customs. Usually, the Roman taxes worked out to be no higher, and in some instances were lower, than those under previous regimes. Most important, Rome reduced the endemic warfare that had plagued these regions.

◀ **Map 4.1**   The Growth of Rome: From Republic to Empire

Culture in the Republic

One of the chief consequences of expansion was greater contact with Greek culture. During the third century B.C., Greek civilization started to exercise an increasing and fruitful influence on the Roman mind. Greek teachers, both slave and free, came to Rome and introduced Romans to Hellenic cultural achievements. As they conquered the eastern Mediterranean, Roman generals began to ship libraries and works of art from Greek cities to Rome. Roman sculpture and painting imitated Greek prototypes. In time, Romans acquired from Greece knowledge of scientific thought, philosophy, medicine, and geography. Roman writers and orators used Greek history, poetry, and oratory as models. Adopting the humanist outlook of the Greeks, the Romans came to value human intelligence and eloquent and graceful prose and poetry. Wealthy Romans retained Greek tutors, poets, and philosophers in their households and sent their sons to Athens to study. Thus, Rome creatively assimilated the Greek achievement and transmitted it to others, thereby extending the orbit of Hellenism.

Plautus (c. 254–184 B.C.), Rome's greatest playwright, adopted features of fourth- and third-century Greek comedy. His plays had Greek characters and took place in Greek settings; the actors wore the Greek style of dress. But the plays also contained familiar elements that appealed to Roman audiences: scenes of gluttony, drunkenness, womanizing, and the pains of love.

Another playwright, Terence (c. 185–159 B.C.), was originally from North Africa and had been brought to Rome as a slave. His owner, a Roman senator, provided the talented youth with an education and freed him. Terence's humor, restrained and refined, lacked the boisterousness of Plautus that appealed to the Roman audience, but his style was technically superior.

Catullus (c. 84–c. 54 B.C.), a native of northern Italy, is generally regarded as one of the world's great lyric poets. His father provided him with a gentleman's education. Tormented by an ill-fated love, Catullus wrote memorable poems dealing with passion and its anguish.

The leading Roman Epicurean philosopher, Lucretius (c. 96–c. 55 B.C.), was influenced by the conflict fostered by two generals, Marius and Sulla, which is discussed later in this chapter. Distraught by the seemingly endless strife, Lucretius yearned for philosophical tranquillity. In his work *On the Nature of Things,* Lucretius expressed his appreciation of Epicurus. Like his mentor, Lucretius denounced superstition and religion for fostering psychological distress and advanced a materialistic conception of nature, one that left no room for the activity of gods—mechanical laws, not the gods, governed all physical happenings. To dispel the fear of punishment after death, Lucretius marshaled arguments to prove that the soul perishes with the body. He proposed that the simple life, devoid of political involvement and excessive passion, was the highest good and the path that would lead from emotional turmoil to peace of mind.

Cicero (106–43 B.C.), a leading Roman statesman, was also a distinguished orator, an unsurpassed Latin stylist, and a student of Greek philosophy. His letters, more than eight hundred of which have survived, provide modern historians with valuable insights into the politics of the late Republic. His Senate speeches have served as models of refined rhetoric for all students of Latin. Dedicated to republicanism, Cicero sought to prevent one-man rule. He admired the Stoic goal of the self-sufficient sage who sought to accord his life with standards of virtue inherent in nature. He adopted the Stoic belief that natural law governs the universe and applies to all, that all belong to a common humanity, and that reason is the individual's noblest faculty. Stoicism was the most influential philosophy in Rome. Its stress on virtuous conduct and performance of duty coincided with Roman ideals, and its doctrine of natural law that applies to all nations harmonized with the requirements of a world empire.

The Collapse of the Republic

In 146 B.C., Roman might spanned the Mediterranean world. After that year, the principal concerns of the Republic were no longer foreign invasions but adjusting city-state institutions to the demands of empire and overcoming critical social and political problems at home. The Republic proved unequal to either challenge. Instead of developing a professional civil service to administer the conquered lands, Roman leaders attempted to govern an empire with city-state institutions, which had evolved for a different purpose. The established Roman administration proved unable to govern the Mediterranean world. In addition, the Republic showed little concern for the welfare of its subjects. Provincial rule worsened as governors, tax collectors, and soldiers shamelessly exploited the provincials.

During Rome's march to empire, all its classes had demonstrated a magnificent civic spirit in fighting foreign wars. With Carthage and Macedonia no longer threatening Rome, this cooperation deteriorated. Internal dissension tore Rome apart as the ferocious drive for domination formerly directed against foreign enemies turned inward, against fellow Romans. Civil war replaced foreign war.

Neither the Senate nor its opponents could rejuvenate the Republic. Eventually, it collapsed, a victim of class tensions, poor leadership, power-hungry demagogues, and civil war. Underlying all these conditions was the breakdown of social harmony and the deterioration of civic patriotism. The Republic had conquered an empire only to see the spiritual qualities of its citizens decay. In a high moral tone, the historian Sallust (c. 86–34 B.C.) condemned the breakdown of republican values:

> *Growing love of money, and the lust for power which followed it, engendered every kind of evil. Avarice destroyed honor, integrity, and every other virtue, and instead taught men to be proud and cruel, to neglect religion, and to hold nothing too sacred to sell. Ambition tempted many to be false. . . . At first these vices grew slowly and*

> *sometimes met with punishments; later on, when the disease had spread like a plague, Rome changed: her government, once so just and admirable, became harsh and unendurable.*[2]

The Gracchi Revolution

The downhill slide of the Republic began with an agricultural crisis. In the long war with Hannibal in Italy, farms were devastated, and with many Roman soldier-farmers serving long periods in the army, fields lay neglected. Returning veterans lacked the money to restore their land. They were forced to sell their farms to wealthy landowners at low prices.

Another factor that helped to squeeze out the small farm owners was the importation of hundreds of thousands of slaves to work on large plantations, called *latifundia*. Farmers who had formerly increased meager incomes by working for wages on neighboring large estates were no longer needed. Sinking ever deeper into poverty and debt, they gave up their lands and went to Rome to seek work. The dispossessed peasantry found little to do in Rome, where there was not enough industry to provide them with employment and where much of the work was done by slaves. The once sturdy and independent Roman farmer, who had done all that his country had asked of him, was becoming part of a vast urban underclass, poor, embittered, and alienated.

In 133 B.C., Tiberius Gracchus (163–133 B.C.), who came from one of Rome's most honored families, was elected tribune. Distressed by the injustice done to the peasantry and recognizing that the Roman army depended on the loyalty of small landowners, Tiberius made himself the spokesman for land reform. He proposed a simple and moderate solution for the problem of the landless peasants: he would revive an old law barring any Roman from using more than 312 acres of the state-owned land obtained in the process of uniting Italy. For many years, the upper class had ignored this law, occupying vast tracts of public land as squatters and treating this land as their own. By enforcing the law, Tiberius hoped to free land for distribution to landless citizens.

Rome's leading families viewed Tiberius as a revolutionary, who threatened their property and political authority. They also feared that he was seeking to stir up the poor in order to gain political power for himself. To preserve the status quo, with wealth and power concentrated in the hands of a few hundred families, senatorial extremists killed Tiberius and some three hundred of his followers, dumping their bodies into the Tiber.

The cause of land reform was next taken up by Gaius Gracchus (153–121 B.C.), a younger brother of Tiberius, who was elected tribune in 123 B.C. Gaius aided the poor by reintroducing his brother's plan for land distribution and by enabling them to buy grain from the state at less than half the market price. But like his brother, Gaius aroused the anger of the senatorial class. A brief civil war raged in Rome, during which Gaius Gracchus (who may have committed suicide) and three thousand of his followers perished. By killing the Gracchi, the Senate had substituted violence for reason and made murder a means of coping with troublesome opposition.

Soon the club and the dagger became common weapons in Roman politics, hurling Rome into an era of political violence, which ended with the destruction of the Republic. Although the Senate considered itself the guardian of republican liberty, in reality it was expressing the determination of a few hundred families to retain their control over the state. It is a classic example of a once creative minority clinging tenaciously to power long after it had ceased to govern effectively or to inspire allegiance. In the century after the Gracchi, Roman politics was bedeviled by intrigues, rivalries, personal ambition, and political violence. The Senate behaved like a decadent oligarchy, and the Tribal Assembly, which had become the voice of the urban mob, demonstrated a weakness for demagogues, an openness to bribery, and an abundance of deceit and incompetence. The Roman Republic had passed the peak of its greatness.

Rival Generals

Marius (157–86 B.C.), who became consul in 107 B.C., adopted a military policy that eventually contributed to the wrecking of the Republic. Short of troops for a campaign in Numidia in North Africa, Marius disposed of the traditional property requirement for entrance into the army and filled his legions with volunteers from the urban poor, a dangerous precedent. These new soldiers, disillusioned with Rome, served only because Marius held out the promise of pay, loot, and land grants after discharge. They gave their loyalty not to Rome but to Marius, and they remained loyal to their commander only as long as he fulfilled his promises.

Other ambitious commanders followed the example set by Marius. They saw that a general could use his army to advance his political career: that by retaining the confidence of his soldiers, he could cow the Senate and dictate Roman policy. No longer an instrument of government, the army became a private possession of generals. Seeing its authority undermined by generals appointed by the Assembly, the Senate was forced to seek army commanders who would champion the cause of senatorial rule. In time, Rome would be engulfed in civil wars, as rival generals used their troops to further their own ambitions or strengthen their political affiliations.

Meanwhile, the Senate continued to deal ineffectively with Rome's problems. When Rome's Italian allies pressed for citizenship, the Senate refused to make concessions. The Senate's shortsightedness plunged Italy into a terrible war, known as the Social War (91–88 B.C.). As war ravaged the peninsula, the Romans reversed their policy and conferred citizenship on the Italians. The unnecessary and ruinous rebellion petered out.

A conflict between Marius and Sulla (138–78 B.C.), who had distinguished himself in the Social War, over who would command an army in the east led to a prolonged civil war. Sulla won the first round, capturing the capital. But then Marius and his troops retook Rome and, in a frenzy, lashed out at Sulla's supporters. The killing lasted for five days and nights. Marius died shortly afterward. Sulla quickly subdued Marius's supporters on his return and instituted a terror that far surpassed Marius's violence.

Sulla believed that only rule by an aristocratic oligarchy could protect Rome from future military adventurers and assure domestic peace. Consequently, he restored the Senate's right to veto acts of the Assembly, limited the power of the tribunes and the Assembly, and reduced the military authority of provincial governors to prevent any march on Rome. To make the Senate less oligarchic, he increased its membership to six hundred. Having put through these reforms, Sulla retired.

Julius Caesar

The Senate, however, failed to wield its restored authority effectively. The Republic was still menaced by military commanders who used their troops for their own political advantage, and underlying problems remained unsolved. In 60 B.C., a triumvirate (a ruling group of three), consisting of Julius Caesar (c. 100–44 B.C.), a politician; Pompey, a general; and Crassus, a wealthy banker, conspired to take over Rome. The ablest of the three was Caesar.

Recognizing the importance of a military command as a prerequisite for political prominence, Caesar gained command of the legions in Gaul in 59 B.C. The following year he began the conquest of the part of Gaul outside of Roman control, bringing the future France into the orbit of Greco-Roman culture. The successful Gallic campaigns and invasion of Britain revealed Caesar's exceptional talent for generalship. Indeed, his victories alarmed the Senate, which feared that Caesar would use his devoted troops and soaring reputation to seize control of the state.

Meanwhile, the triumvirate had fallen apart. In 53 B.C., Crassus had perished with his army in a disastrous campaign against the Parthians in the east. Pompey, who was jealous of Caesar's success and eager to expand his own power, drew closer to the Senate. Supported by Pompey, the Senate ordered Caesar to relinquish his command. Caesar realized that without his troops he would be defenseless; he decided instead to march on Rome. After he crossed the Rubicon River into Italy in 49 B.C., civil war again ravaged the Republic. Pompey proved no match for so talented a general; the Senate acknowledged Caesar's victory and appointed him to be dictator, a legal office, for ten years.

Caesar realized that republican institutions no longer operated effectively and that only strong and enlightened leadership could permanently end the civil warfare destroying Rome. He fought exploitation in the provinces and generously extended citizenship to more provincials. To aid the poor in Rome, he began a public works program, which provided employment and beautified the city. He also relocated more than a hundred thousand veterans and members of Rome's lower class to the provinces, where he gave them land.

In February 44 B.C., Rome's ruling class, jealous of Caesar's success and power and afraid of his ambition, became thoroughly alarmed when his temporary dictatorship was converted into a lifelong office. The aristocracy saw this event as the end of senatorial government and their rule, which they equated with liberty, and as the beginnings of a Hellenistic type of monarchy. On March 15, a group of aristocrats, regarding themselves as defenders of republican traditions more than four and a half centuries old, assassinated Caesar.

The Republic's Last Years

The assassination of Julius Caesar did not restore republican liberty but plunged Rome into renewed civil war. Two of Caesar's trusted lieutenants, Mark Antony and Lepidus, joined with Octavian, Caesar's adopted son, and defeated the armies of Brutus and Cassius, conspirators in the plot against Caesar. After Lepidus was forced into political obscurity, Antony and Octavian fought each other, with control of Rome as the prize. In 31 B.C., at the naval battle of Actium, in western Greece, Octavian crushed the forces of Antony and his wife, Egypt's Queen Cleopatra. Octavian emerged as master of Rome and four years later became, in effect, the first Roman emperor.

The Roman Republic, which had amassed power to a degree hitherto unknown in the ancient world, was wrecked not by foreign invasion but by internal weaknesses: the degeneration of senatorial leadership, and the willingness of politicians to use violence; the formation of private armies, in which soldiers gave their loyalty to their commander rather than to Rome; the transformation of a self-reliant peasantry into an impoverished and demoralized city rabble; and the deterioration of the ancient virtues that had been the source of the state's vitality. Before 146 B.C., the threat posed by foreign enemies, particularly Carthage, forced Romans to work together for the benefit of the state. This social cohesion broke down when foreign danger had been reduced.

Augustus and the Foundations of the Roman Empire

After Octavian's forces defeated those of Antony and Cleopatra at the battle of Actium, no opponents could stand up to him. The century of civil war, political murder, corruption, and mismanagement had exhausted the Mediterranean world, which longed for order. Like Caesar before him, Octavian recognized that only a strong monarchy could rescue Rome from civil war and anarchy. But learning from Caesar's assassination, he also knew that republican ideals were far from dead. To exercise autocratic power openly, like a Hellenistic monarch, would have aroused the hostility of the Roman ruling class, whose assistance and good will Octavian desired.

Octavian demonstrated his political genius by reconciling his military monarchy with republican institutions: he held absolute power without abruptly breaking with a republican past. Magistrates were still elected and assemblies still met; the Senate administered certain provinces, retained its treasury, and was invited to advise Octavian. With some truth, Octavian could claim that he ruled in partnership with the Senate. By maintaining the facade of the Republic, Octavian camouflaged his absolute power and contained senatorial opposition, which had already been weakened by the deaths of leading nobles in battle or in the purges that Octavian had instituted against his enemies.

In 27 B.C., Octavian shrewdly offered to surrender his power, knowing that the Senate, purged of opposition, would demand that he continue to lead the state. By this act, Octavian could claim to be a legitimate constitutional ruler leading a government of law, not one of lawless despotism so hateful to the Roman mentality. In keeping with his policy of maintaining the appearance of traditional republican government, Octavian refused to be called king or even, like Caesar, dictator; instead, he cleverly disguised his autocratic rule by taking the inoffensive title *princeps* (first citizen); the rule of Augustus and his successors is referred to as the *principate*. The Senate also conferred on him the semireligious and revered name of *Augustus*.

The reign of Augustus signified the end of the Roman Republic and the beginning of the Roman Empire—the termination of aristocratic politics and the emergence of one-man rule. Despite his introduction of autocratic rule, however, Augustus was by no means a self-seeking tyrant, but a creative statesman. Heir to the Roman tradition of civic duty, he regarded his power as a public trust, delegated to him by the Roman people. He was faithful to the classical ideal that the state should promote the good life by protecting civilization from barbarism and ignorance, and he sought to rescue a dying Roman world.

Augustus instituted reforms and improvements throughout the Empire. He reformed the army to guard against the reemergence of ambitious generals like those whose rivalries and private armies had wrecked the Republic. He maintained the loyalty of his soldiers by assuring that veterans, on discharge, would receive substantial bonuses and land in Italy or in the provinces. For the city of Rome, Augustus had aqueducts and water mains built, which brought water to most Roman homes. He created a fire brigade, which reduced the danger of great conflagrations in crowded tenement districts, and he organized a police force to contain violence. He improved the distribution of free grain to the impoverished proletariat and financed the popular gladiatorial combats out of his own funds.

In Italy, Augustus had roads repaired, fostered public works, and arranged for Italians to play a more important role in the administration of the Empire. He earned the gratitude of the provincials by correcting tax abuses and fighting corruption and extortion, as well as by improving the quality of governors and enabling aggrieved provincials to bring charges against Roman officials. An imperial bureaucracy, which enabled talented and dedicated men to serve the state, gradually evolved.

The Pax Romana

The brilliant statesmanship of Augustus inaugurated Rome's greatest age. For the next two hundred years, the Mediterranean world enjoyed the blessings of the *Pax Romana,* the Roman peace. The ancient world had never experienced

Onyx Cameo of Roma and Augustus, First Century A.D.   The Emperor Augustus sits with the goddess Roma and is crowned with the laurel wreath of victory. At his foot is an eagle, emblem of the god Jupiter and totem of the Roman armies. To the left is a triumphal chariot with Nike, the goddess of Victory. The other figures are believed to be members of the imperial family. (*Kunsthistorisches Museum, Vienna*)

such a long period of peace, order, efficient administration, and prosperity. Although both proficient and inept rulers succeeded Augustus, the essential features of the Pax Romana persisted.

The Successors of Augustus

The first four emperors who succeeded Augustus were related either to him or to his third wife, Livia. They constituted the Julio-Claudian dynasty, which ruled from A.D. 14 to 68. Although their reigns were marked by conspiracies, summary executions, and assassinations, the great achievements of Augustus were preserved.

The Julio-Claudian dynasty came to an end when Emperor Nero committed suicide in A.D. 68. Nero had grown increasingly tyrannical and had lost the confidence of the people, the senatorial class, and the generals, who rose in revolt. In the year following his death, anarchy reigned as military leaders competed for the throne. After a bloody civil war, the execution of two emperors, and the suicide of another, Vespasian gained the principate. His reign (A.D. 69–79) marked the beginning of the Flavian dynasty. By having the great Colosseum of Rome constructed for gladiatorial contests, Vespasian earned the gratitude of the city's inhabitants. He also had nationalist uprisings put down in Gaul and Judea.

In Judea, Roman rule clashed with Jewish religious-national sentiments. Recognizing the tenaciousness with which Jews clung to their faith, the Roman leaders deliberately refrained from interfering with Hebraic religious beliefs and practices. Numerous privileges, such as exemption from emperor worship because it conflicted with the requirements of strict monotheism, were extended to Jews not only in Judea, but throughout the Empire. Sometimes, however, the Romans engaged in activities that outraged the Jews. For example, Emperor Caligula (A.D. 37–41) ordered that a golden statue of himself be placed in Jerusalem's temple, the central site and focus of Jewish religious life. To the Jews, this display of a pagan idol in their midst was an abomination. The order was rescinded when the Jews demonstrated their readiness to resist.

Relations between the Jews of Judea and the Roman authorities deteriorated progressively in succeeding decades. Militant Jews, who rejected Roman rule as a threat to the purity of Jewish life, urged their people to take up arms. Feeling a religious obligation to reestablish an independent kingdom in their ancient homeland and unable to reconcile themselves to Roman rule, the Jews launched a full-scale war of liberation in A.D. 66. In A.D. 70, after a five-month siege had inflicted terrible punishment on the Jews, Roman armies captured Jerusalem and destroyed the temple.

Vespasian was succeeded by his sons Titus (A.D. 79–81) and Domitian (A.D. 81–96). The reign of Titus was made memorable by the eruption of Mount Vesuvius, which devastated the towns of Pompeii and Herculaneum. After Titus's brief time as emperor, his younger brother Domitian became ruler. Upon crushing a revolt led by the Roman commander in Upper Germany, a frightened Domitian executed many leading Romans. These actions led to his assassination in A.D. 96, ending the Flavian dynasty.

The Senate selected one of its own, Nerva, to succeed the murdered Domitian. Nerva's reign (A.D. 96–98) was brief and uneventful. But he introduced a practice that would endure until A.D. 180: he adopted as his son and designated as his heir a man with proven ability, Trajan, the governor of Upper Germany. This adoptive system assured a succession of competent rulers.

During his rule (A.D. 98–117), Trajan eased the burden of taxation in the provinces, provided for the needs of poor children, and had public works built. With his enlarged army, he conquered Dacia (parts of Romania and Hungary), where he seized vast quantities of gold and silver. He made the territory into a Roman province, adding to the large frontier Rome had to protect.

Trajan's successor, Hadrian (A.D. 117–138), strengthened border defenses in Britain and fought the second Hebrew revolt in Judea (A.D. 132–135). After initial successes, including the liberation of Jerusalem, the Jews were again defeated by superior Roman might. The majority of Palestinian Jews were killed, sold as slaves, or forced to seek refuge in other lands. The Romans renamed the province Syria Palestina; they forbade Jews to enter Jerusalem, except once a year, and encouraged non-Jews to settle the land. Although the Jews continued to maintain a presence in Palestine, they had become a dispossessed and dispersed people.

After Hadrian came another ruler who had a long reign, Antoninus Pius (A.D. 138–161). He introduced humane and just reforms: limits on the right of masters to torture their slaves to obtain evidence and the establishment of the principle that an accused person be considered innocent until proven guilty. During his reign, the Empire remained peaceful and prosperous.

Marcus Aurelius (A.D. 161–180), the next emperor, was also a philosopher; his *Meditations* eloquently expressed Stoic thought. His reign was marked by renewed conflict in the east, with the kingdom of Parthia. The Roman legions were victorious in this campaign but brought back from the east an epidemic, which decimated the population of the Empire.

From the accession of Nerva in A.D. 96 to the death of Marcus Aurelius in A.D. 180, the Roman Empire was ruled by the "Five Good Emperors." During this period, the Empire was at the height of its power and prosperity, and nearly all its peoples benefited. The four emperors preceding Marcus Aurelius had no living sons, so they resorted to the adoptive system in selecting successors, which served Rome effectively. But Marcus Aurelius chose his own son, Commodus, to succeed him. With the accession of Commodus, a misfit and a megalomaniac, in A.D. 180, the Pax Romana came to an end.

The "Time of Happiness"

The Romans called the Pax Romana the "Time of Happiness." This period was the fulfillment of Rome's mission: the creation of a world-state that provided peace, security, ordered civilization, and the rule of law. Roman legions defended the Rhine-Danube river frontiers from incursions by German tribesmen, held the Parthians at bay in the east, and subdued the few uprisings that occurred. Nerva's adoptive system of selecting emperors provided Rome with internal stability and a succession of exceptionally able emperors. These Roman emperors did not use military force needlessly but fought for sensible political goals. Generals did not wage war recklessly; instead, they tried to limit casualties, avoid risks, and deter conflicts by a show of force.

Constructive Rule Roman rule was constructive. The Romans built roads, improved harbors, cleared forests, drained swamps, irrigated deserts, and cultivated undeveloped lands. The aqueducts they constructed brought fresh water for drinking and bathing to large numbers of people, and the effective sewage systems enhanced the quality of life. Goods were transported over roads made safe by Roman soldiers and across a Mediterranean Sea swept clear of pirates. A wide variety of goods circulated throughout the Empire. A stable currency, generally not subject to depreciation, contributed to the economic well-being of the Mediterranean world.

Scores of new cities sprang up, and old ones grew larger and wealthier. Although these municipalities had lost their power to wage war and had to bow to the will of the emperors, they retained considerable freedom of action in local matters. Imperial troops guarded against civil wars within the cities and prevented warfare between cities—two traditional weaknesses of city life in the ancient world. The municipalities served as centers of Greco-Roman civilization, which spread to the farthest reaches of the Mediterranean, continuing a process initiated during the Hellenistic Age. Citizenship, generously granted, was finally extended to virtually all free men by an edict of A.D. 212.

Improved Conditions for Slaves and Women   Conditions improved for those at the bottom of society, the slaves. At the time of Augustus, slaves may have accounted for a quarter of the population of Italy. But their numbers declined as Rome engaged in fewer wars of conquest. The freeing of slaves also became more common during the Empire. Freed slaves gained citizenship, with most of the rights and privileges of other citizens; their children suffered no legal disabilities whatsoever. During the Republic, slaves had been terribly abused; they were often mutilated, thrown to wild beasts, crucified, or burned alive. Several emperors issued decrees protecting slaves from cruel masters.

The status of women gradually improved during the Republic. In the early days of the Republic, a woman lived under the absolute authority first of her father, and then of her husband. By the time of the Empire, a woman could own property and, if divorced, keep her dowry. A father no longer forced his daughter to marry against her will. Women could make business arrangements and draw up wills without the consent of their husbands. Unlike their Greek counterparts, Roman women were not secluded in their homes but could come and go as they pleased. Upper-class women of Rome also had far greater opportunities for education than those of Greece. The history of the Empire, indeed Roman history in general, is filled with talented and influential women. Cornelia, the mother of Tiberius and Gaius Gracchus, influenced Roman politics through her sons. Livia, the dynamic wife of Augustus, was often consulted on important matters of state, and during the third century there were times when women controlled the throne.

World Community   From Britain to the Arabian Desert, from the Danube River to the sands of the Sahara, some 70 million people with differing native languages, customs, and histories were united by Roman rule into a world community. Unlike officials of the Republic, when corruption and exploitation in the provinces were notorious, officials of the Empire felt a high sense of responsibility to preserve the Roman peace, institute Roman justice, and spread Roman civilization.

In creating a stable and orderly political community with an expansive conception of citizenship, Rome resolved the problems posed by the limitations of the Greek city-state: civil war, intercity warfare, and a parochial attitude that divided people into Greek and non-Greek. Rome also brought to fruition an ideal of the Greek city-state: the protection and promotion of civilized life. By constructing a world community that broke down barriers between nations, by preserving and spreading Greco-Roman civilization, and by developing a rational system of law that applied to all humanity, Rome completed the trend toward universalism and cosmopolitanism that had emerged in the Hellenistic Age.

Roman Culture and Law During the Pax Romana

During the late Roman Republic, Rome had creatively assimilated the Greek achievement (see pages 93–95) and transmitted it to others, thereby extending the orbit of Hellenism. Rome had acquired Greek scientific thought, philoso-

Basalt Bust of Livia. Octavian's third wife Livia (58 B.C.–29 A.D.) was admired for her wisdom and dignity and the emperor valued her counsel. (*Alinari/Art Resource, NY*)

phy, medicine, and geography. Roman writers used Greek models; sharing in the humanist outlook of the Greeks, they valued human intelligence and achievement and expressed themselves in a graceful and eloquent style.

Literature and History Roman cultural life reached its high point during the reign of Augustus, when Rome experienced the golden age of Latin literature. At the request of Augustus, who wanted a literary epic to glorify the Empire and his role in founding it, Virgil (70–19 B.C.) wrote the *Aeneid,* a masterpiece of world literature. Virgil ascribed to Rome a divine mission to bring peace and civilized life to the world, and he praised Augustus as a divinely appointed ruler who had fulfilled Rome's mission. The Greeks might be better sculptors, orators, and thinkers, said Virgil, but only the Romans knew how to govern an empire.

> *For other peoples will, I do not doubt,*
> *still cast their bronze to breathe with softer features,*
> *or draw out of the marble living lines, plead causes better,*

trace the ways of heaven with wands and tell the rising
constellations; but yours will be the rulership of nations,
remember, Roman, these will be your arts:
to teach the ways of peace to those you conquer, to spare
defeated peoples, to tame the proud.[3]

In his *History of Rome,* Livy (59 B.C.–A.D. 17) also glorified Roman character, customs, and deeds. He praised Augustus for attempting to revive traditional Roman morality, to which Livy felt a strong attachment. Although Livy was a lesser historian than Thucydides or Polybius, his work was still a major achievement, particularly in its depiction of the Roman character, which helped make Rome great.

Roman writers who excelled in poetry include Horace (65–8 B.C.), the son of a freed slave. He broadened his education by studying literature and philosophy in Athens, and his writings reflect Greek ideals. Horace enjoyed the luxury of country estates, banquets, fine clothes, and courtesans, along with the simple pleasures of mountain streams and clear skies. His poetry touched on many themes—the joy of good wine, the value of moderation, and the beauty of friendship. Unlike Horace, Virgil, or Livy, Ovid (43 B.C.–A.D. 17) did not experience the civil wars during his adult years. Consequently, he was less inclined to praise the Augustan peace. His poetry showed a preference for romance and humor, and he is best remembered for his advice to lovers.

The writers who lived after the Augustan age were mostly of a lesser quality than their predecessors. The historian Tacitus (A.D. 55–c. 118) was an exception. Sympathetic to republican institutions, Tacitus denounced Roman emperors and the imperial system in his *Histories* and *Annals.* In *Germania,* he turned his sights on the habits of the Germanic peoples, describing the Germans as undisciplined but heroic, with a strong love of freedom. Another outstanding writer was the satirist Juvenal (A.D. c. 55–138). His works attacked evils of Roman society, such as the misconduct of emperors, the haughtiness of the wealthy, the barbaric tastes of commoners, the failures of parents, and the noise, congestion, and poverty of the capital.

Philosophy   Stoicism was the principal philosophy of the Pax Romana, and its leading exponents were Seneca (4 B.C.–A.D. 65), Epictetus (A.D. c. 60–c. 117), and Marcus Aurelius. Perpetuating the rational tradition of Greek philosophy, Rome's early Stoics saw the universe as governed by reason, and they esteemed the human intellect. Like Socrates, they sought the highest good in this world, not in an afterlife, and envisioned no power above human reason. Moral values were obtained from reason alone. The individual was self-sufficient and depended entirely on rational faculties for knowing and doing good. Stoics valued self-sufficient persons who attained virtue and wisdom by exercising rational control over their lives. The Stoic doctrine that all people, because of their capacity to reason, belong to a common humanity coincided with the requirements of the multinational Roman Empire.

The Stoic conception of God underwent a gradual transformation, reflecting the religious yearnings of the times. For the early Stoics, God was an intellectual necessity, an impersonal principle that gave order to the universe. For later Roman Stoics, God had become a moral necessity, comforting and reassuring people. While maintaining the traditional Stoic belief that the individual can attain virtue through unaided reason, Epictetus and Marcus Aurelius came close to seeking God's help to live properly. And Seneca showed an uncommon compassion for slaves and a revulsion for gladiatorial combat. The gap between Greek philosophy and Christianity was narrowing.

Science   The two most prominent scientists during the Greco-Roman Age were Ptolemy, a mathematician, geographer, and astronomer, who worked at Alexandria in the second century A.D., and Galen (A.D. c. 130–c. 201), who investigated medicine and anatomy. Ptolemy's thirteen-volume work, *Mathematical Composition*—more commonly known as the *Almagest*, a Greek-Arabic term meaning "the greatest"—summed up antiquity's knowledge of astronomy and became the authoritative text during the Middle Ages. In the Ptolemaic system, a motionless, round earth stood in the center of the universe; the moon, sun, and planets moved about the earth in circles or in combinations of circles. The Ptolemaic system was built on a faulty premise, as modern astronomy eventually showed. However, it did work—that is, it provided a model of the universe that adequately accounted for most observed phenomena. The Ptolemaic system was not challenged until the middle of the sixteenth century.

Just as Ptolemy's system dominated astronomy, so the theories of Galen dominated medicine down to modern times. By dissecting both dead and living animals, Galen attempted a rational investigation of the body's working parts. Although his work contains many errors, he made essential contributions to the knowledge of anatomy.

Art and Architecture   The Romans borrowed art forms from other peoples, particularly the Greeks, but they borrowed creatively, transforming and enhancing their inheritance. Roman portraiture continued trends initiated during the Hellenistic Age. Imitating Hellenistic models, Roman sculptors realistically carved every detail of a subject's face: unruly hair, prominent nose, lines and wrinkles, a jaw that showed weakness or strength. Sculpture also gave expression to the imperial ideal. Statues of emperors conveyed nobility and authority; reliefs commemorating victories glorified Roman might and grandeur.

The Romans most creatively transformed the Greek inheritance in architecture. The Greek temple was intended to be viewed from the outside; the focus was exclusively on the superbly balanced exterior. By using arches, vaults, and domes, the Romans built structures with large, magnificent interiors. The vast interior, massive walls, and overarching dome of the famous Pantheon, a temple built in the early second century A.D., during the reign of Hadrian, symbolize the power and majesty of the Roman world-state.

Engineering   The Romans excelled at engineering. In addition to amphitheaters and public baths, they built the finest roads in the ancient world. Roman engineers carefully selected routes with an eye for minimizing natural barriers and drainage problems. The great embanked roads constructed during the Empire were designed by military engineers. Stone bridges across rivers, as well as aqueducts, which carried water to Roman cities, still survive.

Law   Expressing the Roman yearning for order and justice, law was Rome's great legacy to Western civilization. Roman law passed through two essential stages: the formation of civil law (*jus civile*) and the formation of the law of nations (*jus gentium*). The basic features of the civil law evolved during the two-hundred-year Struggle of the Orders, at the same time as Rome was extending its dominion over Italy. The Twelve Tables, drawn up in the early days of the patrician-plebeian struggle, established written rules of criminal and civil law for the Roman state that applied to all citizens. Over the centuries, the civil law was expanded through statutes passed by the assemblies and through the legal decisions of jurisdictional magistrates, the rulings of emperors, and the commentaries of professional jurists, who, aided by familiarity with Greek logic, engaged in systematic legal analysis.

During the period of the Republic's expansion outside Italy, contact with the Greeks and other peoples led to the development of the second branch of Roman law, jus gentium, which combined Roman civil law with principles selectively drawn from the legal tradition of Greeks and other peoples. Roman jurists identified the jus gentium with the natural law (*jus naturale*) of the Stoics. The jurists said that a law should accord with rational principles inherent in nature: uniform and universally valid laws that can be discerned by rational people. Serving to bind different peoples together, the law of nations harmonized with the requirements of a world empire and with Stoic ideals. As Cicero pointed out,

> *True law is right reason in agreement with nature; it is of universal application, unchanging and everlasting. And there will not be different laws at Rome and at Athens or different laws now and in the future, but one eternal and unchangeable law will be valid for all nations and all times.*[4]

The law of nations came to be applied throughout the Empire, although it never entirely supplanted local law. In the eyes of the law, a citizen—and by A.D. 212, virtually all free people had been granted citizenship—was not a Syrian or a Briton or a Spaniard, but a Roman.

After the fall of the western Roman Empire, Roman law fell into disuse in western Europe. Gradually reintroduced in the twelfth century, it came to form the basis of the common law in all Western lands except Britain and its dependencies. Some provisions of Roman law are readily recognizable in modern legal systems, as the following excerpts illustrate:

> *Justice is a constant, unfailing disposition to give everyone his legal due.*
>
> *No one is compelled to defend a cause against his will.*

Aqueduct at Pont du Gard, Nîmes, France, 19 B.C.   The discovery and use of concrete allowed the Romans to carry out a vast program of public works—roads, bridges, aqueducts, harbor facilities, and fortifications. Without such aqueducts to bring clean water from distant sources, the Roman style of urban life would have been impossible. (*Foto Marberg/Art Resource*)

No one suffers a penalty for what he thinks.

In the case of major offenses it makes a difference whether something is committed purposefully or accidentally.

In inflicting penalties, the age . . . of the guilty party must be taken into account.[5]

Entertainment   Despite its many achievements, Roman civilization presents a paradox. On the one hand, Roman culture and law evidence high standards of civilization. On the other, the Romans institutionalized barbaric practices: battles to the death between armed gladiators and the tormenting and slaughtering of wild beasts. The major forms of entertainment in both the Republic and the Empire were chariot races, wild-animal shows, and gladiatorial combat. Chariot races were gala events, in which the most skillful riders and the finest and best-trained stallions raced in an atmosphere of rabid excitement.

The charioteers, many of them slaves hoping that victory would bring them freedom, became popular heroes.

The Romans craved brutal spectacles. One form of entertainment pitted wild beasts against each other or against men armed with spears. Another consisted of battles, sometimes to the death, between highly trained gladiators. The gladiators, mainly slaves and condemned criminals, learned their craft at schools run by professional trainers. Some gladiators entered the arena armed with a sword; others, with a trident and a net. The spectators were transformed into a frenzied mob that lusted for blood. If they were displeased with a losing gladiator's performance, they would call for his immediate execution. Over the centuries, these spectacles grew more bizarre and brutal. Hundreds of tigers were set against elephants and bulls; wild bulls tore apart men dressed in animal skins; women battled in the arena; dwarfs fought each other.

Signs of Trouble

The Pax Romana was one of the finest periods in ancient history. But even during the Time of Happiness, signs of trouble appeared; they grew to crisis proportions in the third century. The Empire's internal stability was always precarious. Unrest in Egypt, Gaul, and Judea demonstrated that not all people at all times welcomed the grand majesty of the Roman peace, that localist and separatist tendencies persisted in a universal empire. In the centuries that followed, as Rome staggered under the weight of economic, political, and military difficulties, these native loyalties reasserted themselves. Increasingly, the masses and even the Romanized elite of the cities withdrew their support from the Roman world-state.

Social and Economic Weaknesses

A healthy world-state required empirewide trade to serve as an economic base for political unity; expanding agricultural production to feed the cities; and growing internal mass markets to stimulate industrial production. But the economy of the Empire during the Pax Romana had serious defects. The means of communication and transportation were slow, which hindered long-distance commerce. Many nobles, considering it unworthy for a gentleman to engage in business, chose to squander their wealth rather than invest it in commercial or industrial enterprises. Lacking the stimulus of capital investment, the economy could not expand.

Ultimately, only a small portion of the population—the middle and upper classes of the cities, that is, landlords, merchants, and administrators—reaped the benefits of the Roman peace. They basked in luxury, leisure, and culture. These privileged classes bought off the urban poor with bread and circuses, but occasionally mass discontent expressed itself in mob violence. Outside the cities, the peasantry—still the great bulk of the population—was exploited to provide cheap food for the city dwellers. An enormous cultural gap existed between town and countryside. In reality, the cities were small islands of high culture surrounded by a sea of peasant barbarism.

Such a parasitical, exploitative, and elitist social system might function in periods of peace and tranquillity, but could it survive crises? Would the impoverished people of town and country—the overwhelming majority of the population—remain loyal to a state whose benefits barely extended to them and whose sophisticated culture, which they hardly comprehended, virtually excluded them?

Cultural Stagnation and Transformation

Perhaps the most dangerous sign for the future was the spiritual paralysis that crept over the ordered world of the Pax Romana. A weary and sterile Hellenism underlay the Roman peace. The ancient world was going through a transformation of values that foreshadowed the end of Greco-Roman civilization.

During the second century A.D., Greco-Roman civilization lost its creative energies, and the values of classical humanism were challenged by mythic-religious movements. No longer regarding reason as a satisfying guide to life, the educated elite subordinated the intellect to feelings and an unregulated imagination. No longer finding the affairs of this world to have purpose, people placed their hope in life after death. The Roman world was undergoing a religious revolution and was seeking a new vision of the divine.

The application of reason to nature and society was the great achievement of the Greek mind. Yet despite its many triumphs, Greek rationalism never entirely subdued the mythic-religious mentality, which draws its strength from human emotion. The masses of peasants and slaves remained attracted to religious forms. Ritual, mystery, magic, and ecstasy never lost their hold on the ancient world—nor, indeed, have they on our own scientific and technological society. During the Hellenistic Age, the tide of rationalism gradually receded, and the nonrational, an ever present undercurrent, showed renewed vigor. This resurgence of the mythical mentality could be seen in the popularity of the occult, magic, alchemy, and astrology. Burdened by danger, emotional stress, and fearing fate as fixed in the stars, people turned for deliverance to magicians, astrologers, and exorcists.

They also became devotees of the many Near Eastern religious cults that promised personal salvation. The proliferation of Eastern mystery religions was a clear expression of this transformation of classical values. During the Hellenistic era, slaves, merchants, and soldiers brought many religious cults westward from Persia, Babylon, Syria, Egypt, and Asia Minor. The various mystery cults possessed many common features. Converts underwent initiations and were bound by oath to secrecy. The initiates, in a state of rapture, attempted to unite with the deity after first purifying themselves through baptism (sometimes with the blood of a bull), fasting, having their heads shaved, or drinking from a sacred vessel. Communion was achieved by donning the

Stone Relief of Mithras Sacrificing a Bull.   The spread and popularity of Near Eastern mystery cults in the western Roman Empire was a sign of the cultural intermingling that prevailed in Roman imperial society. Among the most popular mystery cults, especially among soldiers, was that of Mithras, a Persian warrior deity also associated with the sun and justice. Mithras promised immortality to those who upheld high ethical standards of conduct and underwent cultic initiation rites. (*Cincinnati Art Museum, Gift of Mr. and Mrs. Fletcher E. Nyce, 1968*)

god's robe, eating a sacred meal, or visiting the god's sanctuary. Cultists were certain that their particular savior god would protect them from misfortune and ensure their soul's immortality. More and more people felt that the good life could not be achieved by individuals through their own efforts; they needed outside help.

Like the mystery religions, philosophy reached for something beyond this world in order to edify and comfort the individual. Philosophers eventually sought escape from this world through union with a divine presence greater than human power. In Neo-Platonism, which replaced Stoicism as the dominant school of philosophy in the Late Roman Empire, religious yearnings were transformed into a religious system that transcended reason. Plotinus (A.D. c. 205–c. 270), the most influential spokesman of Neo-Platonism, subordinated philosophy to mysticism. Plato's philosophy, we have seen, contained both a major and a minor key. The major key stressed a rational interpretation of the human community and called for reforming the polis on the basis of knowledge, whereas the minor key urged the soul to rise to a higher world of reality. Although Plotinus retained Platonic rationalism (he viewed the individual as a reasoning being and used rational argument to explain his religious orientation), he was intrigued by Plato's otherworldliness.

What Plotinus desired was union with the One, or the Good, sometimes called God—the source of all existence. Plotinus felt that the intellect could neither describe nor understand the One, which transcended all knowing, and that joining with the One required a mystical leap, a purification of the soul so that it could return to its true eternal home. For Plotinus, philosophy became a religious experience, a contemplation of the eternal. Compared with this union with the divine One, of what value was knowledge of the sensible world or a concern for human affairs? For Plotinus, this world was a sea of tears and troubles from which the individual yearned to escape. Reality was not in this world but beyond it, and the principal goal of life was not comprehension of the natural world nor the fulfillment of human potential nor the betterment of the human community, but knowledge of the One. Thus, his philosophy broke with the essential meaning of classical humanism.

By the time of the Late Roman Empire, mystery religions intoxicated the masses, and mystical philosophy beguiled the educated elite. Classical civilization was being transformed. Philosophy had become subordinate to religious belief; secular values seemed inferior to religious experience. The earthly city had raised its eyes toward heaven. The culture of the Roman world was moving in a direction in which the quest for the divine was to predominate over all human enterprises.

The Decline of Rome

In the third century A.D., the ordered civilization of the Pax Romana ended. Several elements caused this disruption. The Roman Empire was plunged into military anarchy, raided by Germanic tribes, and burdened by economic dislocations.

Third-Century Crisis

The degeneration of the army was a prime reason for the crisis. During the great peace, the army had remained an excellent fighting force, renowned for its discipline, organization, and loyalty. In the third century, however, there was a marked deterioration in the quality of Roman soldiers. Lacking loyalty to Rome and greedy for spoils, soldiers used their weapons to prey on civilians and to make and unmake emperors. Fearful of being killed by their unruly troops who wanted spoils or of being murdered by a suspicious emperor, generals were driven to seize the throne. Once in power, they had to buy the loyalty of their soldiers and guard against assassination by other generals. From A.D. 235 to 285, military mutiny and civil war raged, as legion fought legion. Many emperors were assassinated. The once stalwart army neglected its duty of defending the borders and disrupted the internal life of the Empire.

Taking advantage of the military anarchy, Germanic tribesmen crossed the Rhine-Danube frontier to loot and destroy. A reborn Persian Empire, led by the Sassanid dynasty, attacked and, for a while, conquered Roman lands in the east. Some sections of the Empire, notably in Gaul, attempted to break away; these moves reflected an assertion of local patriotism over Roman universalism. The "city of mankind" was crumbling.

These eruptions had severe economic repercussions. Cities were pillaged and destroyed, farmlands ruined, and trade disrupted. To obtain funds and supplies for the military, emperors confiscated goods, exacted forced labor, and debased the coinage, causing inflation. These measures brought ruin to the middle class. Invasions, civil war, rising prices, a debased coinage, declining agricultural production, disrupted transportation, and the excessive demands of the state caused economic havoc and famine in the cities. The urban centers of the ancient world, creators and disseminators of high civilization, were caught in a rhythm of breakdown.

Diocletian and Constantine: The Regimented State

The emperors Diocletian (A.D. 285–305) and Constantine (A.D. 306–337) tried to contain the awesome forces of disintegration. At a time when agricultural production was steadily declining, they had to feed the city poor and an expanded army of more than 500,000, strung out over the Empire. They also had to prevent renewed outbreaks of military anarchy, drive the Germans back across the Danube frontier, and secure the eastern region against renewed agression from Persia. Their solution was to tighten the reins of government and to squeeze more taxes and requisitions out of the citizens. In the process, they transformed Rome into a bureaucratic, regimented, and militarized state.

Cities lost their traditional right of local self-government, which consolidated a trend started earlier. To ensure continuous production of food and goods, as well as the collection of taxes, the state forced unskilled workers and artisans to hold their jobs for life and to pass them on to their children. For the same reasons, peasants were turned into virtual serfs, bound to the land that they cultivated. An army of government agents was formed to hunt down peasants who fled the land to escape crushing taxes and poverty.

Also frozen into their positions were city officials (*curiales*). They often found it necessary to furnish from their own pockets the difference between the state's tax demands and the amount that they could collect from an already overtaxed population. This system of a hereditary class of tax collectors and of crippling taxes to pay for a vastly expanded bureaucracy and military establishment enfeebled urban trade and industry. Such conditions killed the civic spirit of townspeople, who desperately sought escape. By overburdening urban dwellers with taxes and regulations, Diocletian and Constantine helped to shatter the vitality of city life on which Roman prosperity and civilization depended.

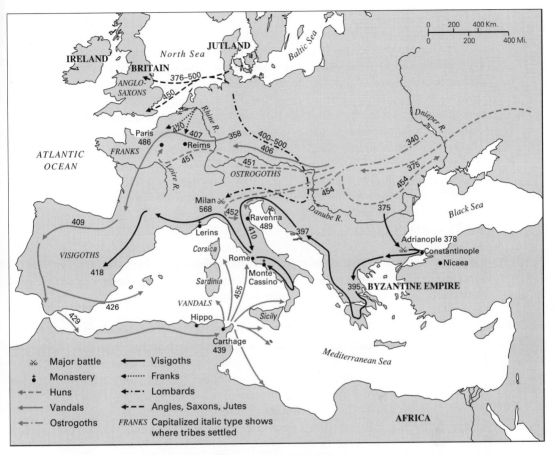

Map 4.2   Migrations and Incursions, c. A.D. 300–500

Rome was now governed by a highly centralized monarchy, regimenting the lives of its subjects. Whereas Augustus had upheld the classical ideal that the commonwealth was a means of fostering the good life for the individual, Diocletian adopted the despotic attitude that the individual lives for the state. To guard against military insurrection, he appointed a loyal general as emperor to govern the western provinces of the Empire while he ruled the eastern regions; although both emperors bore the title Augustus, Diocletian remained superior. Constantine furthered this trend of dividing the Empire into eastern and western halves by building an imperial capital, Constantinople, at the Bosporus, a strait where Asia meets Europe.

Tribal Migrations and Invasions

By imposing some order on what had been approaching chaos, Diocletian and Constantine prevented the Empire from collapsing. Rome had been given a reprieve. But in the last part of the fourth century, the problem of guarding the frontier grew more acute.

The Huns, a savage Mongol people from central Asia, swept across the plains of Russia and with their formidable cavalry put pressure on the Visigoths, a Germanic tribe that had migrated into southeastern Europe. Terrified of the Huns, the Goths sought refuge within the Roman Empire. Hoping to increase his manpower and unable to stop the panic-stricken Germans, Emperor Valens permitted them to cross the Danube frontier. But enraged by their mistreatment at the hands of Roman officials, the Visigoths took up arms. In 378, the Goths defeated the Romans in a historic battle at Adrianople. This battle signified that Rome could no longer defend its borders. The Visigoths were on Roman territory to stay. The Visigoths now plundered the Balkans at will. The Germanic tribes increased their pressure on the Empire's borders, which finally collapsed at the very end of 406, as Vandals, Alans, Suebi, and other tribes joined the Goths in devastating and overrunning the Empire's western provinces. In 410, the Visigoths looted Rome.

Economic conditions continued to deteriorate. Cities in Britain, Gaul, Germany, and Spain lay abandoned. Other metropolises saw their populations dwindle and production stagnate. The great network of Roman roads was not maintained, and trade in the west almost disappeared or passed into the hands of Greeks, Syrians, and Jews from the east.

In 451, Attila (c. 406–453), called "the Scourge of God," led his Huns into Gaul, where he was defeated by a coalition of Germans and the remnants of the Roman army. He died two years later, having come within a hairsbreadth of turning Europe into a province of a Mongolian empire. But Rome's misfortunes persisted. In 455, Rome was again looted, this time by the Vandals. Additional regions fell under the control of Germanic chieftains. Germanic soldiers in the pay of Rome gained control of the government and dictated the choice of emperor. In 476, German officers overthrew the Roman emperor Romulus and placed a fellow German, Odoacer, on the throne. This act is traditionally regarded as the end of the Roman Empire in the west.

Reasons for Rome's Decline

What were the underlying causes for the decline and fall of the Roman Empire in the west? Surely no other question has intrigued the historical imagination more than this one. Implicit in the answers suggested by historians and philosophers is a concern for their own civilization. Will it suffer the same fate as Rome?

To analyze so monumental a development as the fall of Rome, some preliminary observations are necessary. First, the fall of Rome was a process lasting hundreds of years; it was not a single event that occurred in A.D. 476. Second, only the western half of the Empire fell. The eastern half—wealthier, more populous, less afflicted with civil wars, and less exposed to barbarian invasions—survived as the Byzantine Empire until the middle of the fifteenth century. Third, no single explanation suffices to account for Rome's decline; multiple forces operated concurrently to bring about the fall.

The Role of the Germanic Tribes   The pressures exerted by the Germans along an immense frontier aggravated Rome's internal problems. The barbarian attacks left border regions impoverished and depopulated. The Empire imposed high taxes and labor services on its citizens in order to strengthen the armed forces, causing the overburdened middle and lower classes to hate the imperial government that took so much from them.

Spiritual Considerations   The classical mentality, once brimming with confidence about the potentialities of the individual and the power of the intellect, suffered a failure of nerve. The urban upper class, on whom the responsibility for preserving cosmopolitan Greco-Roman culture traditionally rested, became dissolute and apathetic, no longer taking an interest in public life. The aristocrats secluded themselves behind the walls of their fortified country estates; many did not lift a finger to help the Empire. The townspeople demonstrated their disenchantment by avoiding public service and by rarely organizing resistance forces against the barbarian invaders. Hounded by the state and persecuted by the army, many farmers viewed the Germans as liberators. The great bulk of the Roman citizenry, apathetic and indifferent, simply gave up, despite the fact that they overwhelmingly outnumbered the barbarian hordes.

Political and Military Considerations   The Roman government itself contributed to this spiritual malaise through its increasingly autocratic tendencies, which culminated in the regimented rule of Diocletian and Constantine. The insatiable demands and regulations of the state in the Late Roman Empire sapped the initiative and civic spirit of its citizens. The ruined middle and lower classes withdrew their loyalty. For many, the state had become the enemy, and its administration was hated and feared more than the Germans.

In the Late Roman Empire, the quality of Roman soldiers deteriorated, and the legions failed to defend the borders, even though they outnumbered the German invaders. During the third century, the army consisted predominantly of the provincial peasantry. These nonurban, non-Italian, semicivilized soldiers, often the dregs of society, were not committed to Greco-Roman civilization. They had little comprehension of Rome's mission, and at times used their power to attack the cities and towns. The emperors also recruited large numbers of barbarians into the army to fill depleted ranks. Ultimately, the army consisted mostly of barbarians, as both legionnaires and officers. Although these Germans made brave soldiers, they too had little loyalty to Greco-Roman civilization and to the Roman state. Moreover, barbarian units serving with the Roman army under their own commanders did not easily submit to traditional discipline or training. This deterioration of the Roman army occurred because many young citizens evaded conscription. No longer imbued with patriotism, they considered military service a servitude to be shunned.

Economic Considerations   Among the economic causes contributing to the decline of the Roman Empire in the west were the decrease in population, the failure to achieve a breakthrough in technology, the heavy burden of taxation, and the economic decentralization that abetted political decentralization.

Largely because of war and epidemics, the population of the Empire may have shrunk from seventy million during the Pax Romana to fifty million in the Late Roman Empire. This decrease adversely affected the Empire in at least three important ways. First, at the same time as the population was declining, the costs of running the Empire were spiraling, which created a terrible burden for taxpayers. Second, fewer workers were available for agriculture, the most important industry of the Empire. Third, population decline reduced the manpower available for the army, forcing emperors to permit the establishment of Germanic colonies within the Empire's borders to serve as feeders for the army. This situation led to the barbarization of the army.

The failure to expand industry and commerce was another economic reason for the Empire's decline. Instead of expanding industry and trade, towns maintained their wealth by exploiting the countryside. The Roman cities were centers of civilized life and opulence, but they lacked industries. They spent, but they did not produce. The towns were dominated by landlords whose estates lay beyond the city and whose income derived from grain, oil, and wine. Manufacturing was rudimentary, confined essentially to textiles, pottery, furniture, and glassware. The methods of production were simple, the market limited, the cost of transportation high, and agricultural productivity low— the labor of perhaps nineteen peasants was required to support one townsman. Such a fundamentally unhealthy economy could not weather the dislocations caused by uninterrupted warfare and the demands of a mushrooming bureaucracy and the military.

With the barbarians pressing on the borders, the increased military expenditures overstrained the Empire's resources. To pay for the food, uniforms, arms, and armor of the soldiers, taxes were raised, growing too heavy for peasants and townspeople. The state also requisitioned wood and grain and demanded that citizens maintain roads and bridges. The government often resorted to force to collect taxes and exact services. Crushed by these demands, many peasants simply abandoned their farms and sought the protection of large landowners or turned to banditry.

The growth of industries on latifundia, the large, fortified estates owned by wealthy aristocrats, also played a part in the economic decentralization. Producing exclusively for the local market, these estates contributed to the impoverishment of urban centers by reducing the number of customers available to buy goods made in the cities. As life grew more desperate, urban craftsmen and small farmers, made destitute by the state, sought the protection of these large landlords, whose estates grew in size and importance. The growth of latifundia was accompanied by the decline of cities and the transformation of independent peasants into virtual serfs.

These great estates were also new centers of political power, which the imperial government could not curb. A new society was taking shape in the Late Roman Empire. The center of gravity had shifted from the city to the landed estate, from the imperial bureaucrats to the local aristocrats. These developments epitomized the decay of ancient civilization and presaged the Middle Ages.

The Roman Legacy

Rome left the West a rich heritage, which has endured for centuries. The idea of a world empire united by a common law and effective government never died. In the centuries following the collapse of Rome, people continued to be attracted to the idea of a unified and peaceful world-state. By preserving and adding to the philosophy, literature, science, and art of ancient Greece, Rome strengthened the foundations of the Western cultural tradition. Latin, the language of Rome, lived on long after Rome perished. The Western church fathers wrote in Latin, and during the Middle Ages, Latin was the language of learning, literature, and law. From Latin came Italian, French, Spanish, Portuguese, and Romanian. Roman law, the quintessential expression of Roman genius, influenced church law and formed the basis of the legal codes of most European states. Finally, Christianity, the core religion of the West, was born within the Roman Empire and was greatly influenced by Roman culture and organization.

Notes

1. E. Badian, *Roman Imperialism in the Late Republic* (Ithaca, N.Y.: Cornell University Press, 1971), p. 87.
2. Sallust, *The Conspiracy of Catiline,* trans. S. A. Handford (Baltimore: Penguin Books, 1963), pp. 181–182.
3. *The Aeneid of Virgil,* trans. Allen Mandelbaum (Berkeley: University of California Press, 1971), pp. 160–161.
4. Cicero, *De Re Publica,* trans. C. W. Keyes (Cambridge, Mass.: Harvard University Press, Loeb Classical Library, 1928), p. 211.
5. Excerpted in Naphtali Lewis and Meyer Reinhold, eds., *Roman Civilization, Sourcebook II: The Empire* (New York: Harper & Row, 1966), pp. 535, 539, 540, 547, 548.

Suggested Reading

Balsdon, J. P. V. D., *Roman Women* (1962). Describes prominent women and treats various topics—marriage, divorce, concubinage—important to an understanding of the position of women.

Boardman, John, et al., eds., *The Oxford History of the Classical World* (1986). Essays on all facets of Roman culture.

Boren, H. C., *Roman Society* (1977). A social, economic, and cultural history of the Republic and the Empire; written with the student in mind.

Chambers, Mortimer, ed., *The Fall of Rome* (1963). A valuable collection of readings.

Christ, Karl, *The Romans* (1984). A good survey.

Crawford, M., *The Roman Republic* (1982). A reliable survey, with many quotations from original sources.

Dupont, Florence, *Daily Life in Ancient Rome* (1989). Social structure, religion, and notions of time and space.

Errington, R. M., *The Dawn of Empire: Rome's Rise to World Power* (1972). A study of Rome, the reluctant imperialist.

Ferrill, Arthur, *The Fall of the Roman Empire* (1986). A military explanation.

Grant, Michael, *History of Rome* (1978). A synthesis of Roman history by a leading classical scholar;

valuable in regard to both the Republic and the Empire.

Jenkyns, Richard, ed., *The Legacy of Rome* (1992). Essay on Rome's impact on western civilization.

Lewis, Naphtali, and Meyer Reinhold, eds., *Roman Civilization* (1966). A two-volume collection of source readings.

Ogilvie, R. M., *Roman Literature and Society* (1980). An introductory survey of Latin literature.

Veyne, Paul, ed., *A History of Private Life* (1987). All phases of Roman social life.

Wardman, Alan, *Rome's Debt to Greece* (1976). Roman attitudes toward the Greek world.

White, Lynn, ed., *The Transformation of the Roman World* (1973). A useful collection of essays on the transformation of the ancient world and the emergence of the Middle Ages.

Review Questions

1. What were the causes, results, and significance of the plebeian-patrician controversy?
2. What factors enabled Rome to conquer Italy? What were the consequences of Roman expansion?
3. How was Roman cultural life influenced by Greek civilization?
4. Analyze the reasons for the collapse of the Roman Republic.
5. The Roman world-state completed the trend toward cosmopolitanism and universalism that had emerged during the Hellenistic Age. Discuss this statement.
6. How did Roman law incorporate Stoic principles? What does modern law owe to Roman law?
7. Describe the crisis that afflicted Rome in the third century A.D.
8. How did Diocletian and Constantine try to deal with the Empire's crisis?
9. Discuss the spiritual, military, political, and economic reasons for the decline of the Roman Empire.

❖ CHAPTER 5

Early Christianity: A World Religion

*A*s confidence in human reason and hope for happiness in this world waned in the last centuries of the Roman Empire, a new outlook began to take hold. Evident in philosophy and in the popularity of Near Eastern religions, this viewpoint stressed escape from an oppressive world and communion with a higher reality. Christianity evolved and expanded within this setting of declining classicism and heightening otherworldliness. As one response to a declining Hellenism, Christianity offered a spiritually disillusioned Greco-Roman world a reason for living: the hope of personal immortality. The triumph of Christianity marked a break with classical antiquity and a new stage in the evolution of the West, for there was a fundamental difference between the classical and the Christian concepts of God, the individual, and the purpose of life. ❖

The Origins of Christianity

A Palestinian Jew named Jesus was executed by the Roman authorities during the reign of Tiberius (A.D. 14–37), who had succeeded Augustus. At the time, few people paid much attention to what proved to be one of the most pivotal events in world history. In the quest for the historical Jesus, scholars have stressed the importance of both his Jewishness and the religious ferment that prevailed in Palestine in the first century B.C. Jesus' ethical teachings are rooted in the moral outlook of Old Testament prophets. They must be viewed, says Andrew M. Greeley, a priest and student of religion, as

> *a logical extension of the Hebrew Scriptures . . . a product of the whole religious environment of which Jesus was a part. Jesus defined himself as a Jew, was highly conscious of the Jewishness of his message and would have found it impossible to conceive of himself as anything but Jewish. . . . The teachings of Jesus, then, must be placed squarely in the Jewish religious context of the time.*[1]

121

Judaism in the First Century B.C.

In the first century B.C., four principal social-religious parties, or sects, existed among the Palestinian Jews: Sadducees, Pharisees, Essenes, and Zealots. Composed of the upper stratum of Jewish society—influential landed gentry and hereditary priests, who controlled the temple in Jerusalem—the religiously conservative Sadducees insisted on a strict interpretation of Mosaic Law and the perpetuation of temple ceremonies. Challenging the Sadducees, the Pharisees adopted a more flexible attitude toward Mosaic Law; they allowed discussion and varying interpretations of the Law and granted authority to oral tradition, as well as to written Scriptures. The Pharisees had the support of most of the Jewish nation. The third religious party, the Essenes, established a semimonastic community near the Dead Sea. Another sect, the Zealots, demanded that the Jews neither pay taxes to Rome nor acknowledge the authority of the Roman emperor. Devoted patriots, the Zealots engaged in acts of resistance to Rome, which culminated in the great revolt of A.D. 66–70 (see page 102).

The concept of personal immortality is barely mentioned in the Hebrew Scriptures. Unlike the Sadducees, the Pharisees believed in life after death. A later addition to Hebrew religious thought, probably acquired from Persia, the idea had gained wide acceptance by the time of Jesus. The Essenes, too, believed in the physical resurrection of the body but gave this doctrine a more compelling meaning by tying it to the immediate coming of God's kingdom.

Besides the afterlife, another widely recognized idea in the first century B.C. was the belief in the Messiah, a redeemer chosen by God to liberate Israel from foreign rule. In the days of the Messiah, it was predicted, Israel would be free, the exiles would return, and the Jews would be blessed with peace, unity, and prosperity. Jesus (c. 4 B.C.–c. A.D. 29) performed his ministry within this context of Jewish religious-national expectations and longings. The hopes of Jesus' early followers stemmed from a lower-class dissatisfaction with the aristocratic Sadducees; the Pharisee emphasis on prophetic ideals and the afterlife; the Essene preoccupation with the end-of-days and the belief in the nearness of God and the need for repentance; and a conquered people's yearning for the Messiah, who would liberate their land from Roman rule and establish God's reign.

Jesus: Moral Transformation of the Individual

Jesus himself wrote nothing, and nothing was written about him during his lifetime. In the generations following his death, both Roman and Jewish historians paid him scant attention. Consequently, virtually everything we know about Jesus comes from the Bible's New Testament, which was written decades after Jesus' death by devotees seeking to convey a religious truth and to propagate a faith. Modern historians have rigorously and critically analyzed the New Testament; their analyses have provided some insights into Jesus and his beliefs, though much about him remains obscure.

Portrait of Christ.   Painted on a ceiling in the Catacomb of Domitilla around the second century A.D., this is among the oldest surviving portraits of Jesus. (*Alinari/Art Resource, NY*)

Around the age of thirty, no doubt influenced by John the Baptist, Jesus began to preach the coming of the reign of God and the need for people to repent—to undergo moral transformation so that they could enter God's kingdom. For Jesus, the coming of the kingdom was imminent; the process leading to its establishment on earth had already begun. A new order would soon emerge, in which God would govern his people righteously and mercifully. Hence, the present moment was critical—a time for spiritual preparedness and penitence—because an individual's thoughts, goals, and actions would determine whether he or she would gain entrance into the kingdom. People had to change their lives radically. They had to eliminate base, lustful, hostile, and selfish feelings; stop pursuing wealth and power; purify their hearts; and show their love for God and their fellow human beings.

Although Jesus did not intend to draw away his fellow Jews from their ancestral religion, he was distressed by the Judaism of his day. The rabbis taught the Golden Rule, as well as God's love and mercy for his children, but it seemed to Jesus that these ethical considerations were being undermined by an exaggerated rabbinical concern with ritual, restrictions, and the fine points of the Law. Jesus believed that the center of Judaism had shifted from prophetic values to obeying the rules and prohibitions regulating the smallest details of daily life. (To Jewish leaders, of course, these detailed regulations, governing eating, washing, Sabbath observance, family relations, and so forth, were God's commands, intended to sanctify all human activities.) To Jesus, such a rigid view of the Law distorted the meaning of prophetic teachings. Rules dealt only with an individual's visible behavior; they did not penetrate to the person's inner being and lead to a moral transformation. The

---

Chronology 5.1 ❖ Early Christianity

A.D. 29	Crucifixion of Jesus
c. 34–64	Missionary activity of Saint Paul
c. 66–70	Gospel of Mark is written
250–260	Decade of brutal persecution of Christians by the Romans
313	Constantine grants toleration to Christianity
325	Council of Nicaea rules that God and Christ are of the same substance, coequal and coeternal
391–392	Theodosius I prohibits public acts of pagan worship and the public profession of pagan religions; during his reign, Christianity becomes the state religion
430	Death of Saint Augustine
529	Saint Benedict founds monastery at Monte Cassino

---

inner person concerned Jesus, and it was an inner change that he sought. With the fervor of a prophet, he urged a moral transformation of human character through a direct encounter between the individual and God.

Jewish scribes and priests, guardians of the faith, regarded Jesus as a troublemaker who threatened ancient traditions and undermined respect for the Sabbath. Stated succinctly, Jewish leaders believed that Jesus was setting the authority of his person over Mosaic Law—an unpardonable blasphemy in their eyes. To the Romans who ruled Palestine, Jesus was a political agitator who could ignite Jewish messianic expectations into a revolt against Rome. After Jewish leaders turned Jesus over to the Roman authorities, the Roman procurator, Pontius Pilate, sentenced him to death by crucifixion, a customary punishment for someone guilty of high treason.

Believing that Jesus was an inspired prophet or even the long-awaited Messiah, some Jews had become his followers; the chief of these were the Twelve Disciples. But at the time of Jesus' death, Christianity was still just a small Hebrew sect, with dim prospects for survival. What established the Christian movement and gave it strength was the belief of Jesus' followers that he was raised from the dead on the third day after his burial. The doctrine of the Resurrection made possible the belief in Jesus as divine, a savior-god who had come to earth to show people the way to heaven.

In the years immediately following the Crucifixion, the religion of Jesus was confined almost exclusively to Jews, who could more appropriately be called Jewish-Christians. The word *Christian* derives from a name given Jesus:

Christ (the Lord's Anointed, the Messiah). Before Christianity could realize the universal implications of Jesus' teachings and become a world religion, distinct from a Jewish sect, it had to extricate itself from Jewish ritual, politics, and culture. This achievement was the work of a Hellenized Jew, named Saul—known to the world as Saint Paul.

Saint Paul: From a Jewish Sect to a World Religion

Saint Paul (A.D. c. 5–c. 67) came from the Greek city of Tarsus, in southeastern Asia Minor. He belonged to the Diaspora, or the "Dispersion"—the millions of Jews living outside Palestine. The non-Jews, or *Gentiles* (from Latin *gens*, or "nation"), who came into contact with Jews of the Diaspora were often favorably impressed by Hebrew monotheism, ethics, and family life. Some Gentiles embraced Hebrew monotheism but refused to adhere to provisions of the Law requiring circumcision and dietary regulations. Among these Gentiles and the non-Palestinian Jews who were greatly influenced by the Greco-Roman milieu, Jesus' Apostles would find receptive listeners.

At first, Saul persecuted the followers of Jesus, but then he underwent a spiritual transformation and became a convert to Jesus. Serving as a zealous missionary of Jewish Christianity in the Diaspora, Saint Paul preached to his fellow Jews in synagogues. Recognizing that the Christian message applied to non-Jews as well, Paul urged spreading it to the Gentiles. In the process of his missionary activity—and he traveled extensively through the Roman Empire—Paul formulated ideas that represented a fundamental break with Judaism and became the heart of this new religion. He taught that the crucified Messiah had suffered and died for our sins; that through Jesus God had revealed himself to all people, both Jews and Gentiles; and that this revelation supplanted God's earlier revelation to the Jewish people. Alone, one was helpless, possessed by sin, unable to overcome one's wicked nature. Jesus was the only hope, said Paul.

In attempting to reach the Gentiles, Saint Paul had to disentangle Christianity from a Jewish sociocultural context. Thus, he held that neither Gentile nor Jewish followers of Jesus were bound by the hundreds of rituals and rules that constitute Mosaic Law. As a consequence of Jesus' coming, Paul insisted, Mosaic regulations were obsolete and hindered missionary activity among the Gentiles. To Paul, the new Christian community was the true fulfillment of Judaism. The Jews regarded their faith as a national religion, bound inseparably with the history of their people. Paul held that Jesus fulfilled not only the messianic aspirations of the Jews, but also the spiritual needs and expectations of all peoples. For Paul, the new Christian community was not a nation, but an *oikoumene,* a world community. To this extent, Christianity shared in the universalism of the Hellenistic Age.

In preaching the doctrine of the risen Savior and insisting that Mosaic Law had been superseded, Paul (whatever his intentions) was breaking with his Jewish roots and transforming a Jewish sect into a new religion. Separating Christianity from Judaism enormously increased its appeal for the non-Jews

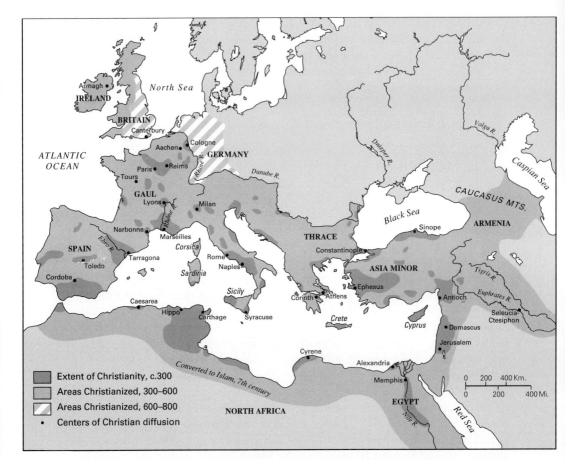

Map 5.1   The Spread of Christianity

who were attracted to Hebrew ethical monotheism but repelled by circumcision, dietary rules, and other strict requirements of Mosaic Law. Paul built on the personalism and universalism implicit in the teachings of Jesus (and the Hebrew prophets) to create a religion intended not for a people with its own particular history, culture, and land, but for all humanity.

The Spread and Triumph of Christianity

By establishing Christianity's independence from Judaism, Saint Paul made the new religion fit for export to the Greco-Roman world. But its growth was slow. Originating in the first century, Christianity took firm root in the second, grew extensively in the third, and became the official religion of the Roman Empire at the end of the fourth century.

The Appeal of Christianity

The triumph of Christianity was linked to a corresponding decline in the vitality of Hellenism and a shift in cultural emphasis: a movement from reason to emotion and revelation. Offering comforting solutions to the existential problems of life and death, religion demonstrated a greater capacity than reason to stir human hearts. Hellenism had invented the tools of rational thought, but the power of mythical thought was never entirely subdued. By the Late Roman Empire, science and philosophy could not compete with mysticism and myth. Mystery cults, which promised personal salvation, were spreading and gaining followers. Neo-Platonists yearned for a mystical union with the One. Astrology and magic, which offered supernatural explanations for the operations of nature, were also popular. This recoil from rational and worldly values helped prepare the way for Christianity. In a culturally stagnating and spiritually troubled Greco-Roman world, Christianity gave a new meaning to life and a new hope to disillusioned men and women.

The Christian message of a divine Savior and a concerned Father, as well as of brotherly love, inspired men and women who were dissatisfied with the world of the here-and-now—who felt no attachment to city or empire, derived no inspiration from philosophy, and suffered from a profound sense of loneliness. Christianity offered the individual what the city and the Roman world-state could not: an intensely personal relationship with God, an intimate connection with a higher world, and membership in a community of the faithful who cared for one another.

Stressing the intellect and self-reliance, Greco-Roman thought did not provide for the emotional needs of the ordinary person. Christianity addressed itself to this defect in the Greco-Roman outlook. The poor, the oppressed, and the slaves were attracted to the personality, life, death, and resurrection of Jesus, his love for all, and his concern for suffering humanity. They found spiritual sustenance in a religion that offered a hand of love and taught that a person need not be wellborn, rich, educated, or talented to be worthy. To people burdened with misfortune and terrified by death, Christianity held the promise of eternal life, a kingdom of heaven, where they would be comforted by God the Father. Thus, Christianity gave the common person what the aristocratic values of Greco-Roman civilization generally did not: hope, a sense of dignity, and inner strength.

Christianity succeeded not only through the appeal of its message, but also through the power of its institution, the Christian church, which grew into a strong organization uniting the faithful. For city dwellers, lonely, alienated, and disillusioned with public affairs—stranded mortals groping for a sense of community—the church that called its members brother and sister filled an elemental need of human beings to belong. The church welcomed women converts, who were often the first to join and brought their menfolk after them. Among the reasons that the church drew women was its command to husbands to treat their wives kindly, remain faithful, and provide for the children. The church won new converts and retained the loyalty of its members by furnishing social services for the poor and infirm, welcoming slaves, criminals, sinners, and other outcasts, and offering a hand of brotherhood and comfort during difficult times.

The ability of an evolving Christianity to assimilate elements from Greek philosophy and even from the mystery religions also contributed in no small measure to its growth. By utilizing Greek philosophy, Christianity was able to present itself in terms intelligible to those versed in Greek learning and thus attract educated people. Converts to Christianity trained in philosophy proved to be able defenders of their newly adopted faith. Because some Christian doctrines (the risen Savior-God, the Virgin and child, life after death, communion with the divine), practices (purification through baptism), and holy days (December 25 was the birth date of the god Mithras) either paralleled or were adopted from the mystery religions, it became relatively easy to win converts from these rivals.

Christianity and Rome

Generally tolerant of religions, the Roman government at first did not significantly interfere with the Christian movement. Indeed, Christianity benefited in many ways from its association with the Roman Empire. Christian missionaries traveled throughout the Empire, over roads and across seas made safe by Roman arms. The common Greek dialect, Koine, spoken in most parts of the Empire, facilitated the missionaries' task. Had the Mediterranean world been fractured into separate and competing states, the spread of Christianity might well have faced an insurmountable obstacle. The universalism of the Roman Empire, which made citizenship available to peoples of many nationalities, prepared the way for the universalism of Christianity, which welcomed membership from all nations.

As the number of Christians increased, Roman officials began to fear the Christians as subversives, preaching allegiance to God and not to Rome. To many Romans, Christians were enemies of the social order: strange people who would not accept the state gods, would not engage in Roman festivals, scorned gladiator contests, stayed away from public baths, glorified nonviolence, refused to honor deceased emperors as gods, and worshiped a crucified criminal as Lord. Romans ultimately found in Christians a universal scapegoat for the ills burdening the Empire, such as famines, plagues, and military reverses. In an effort to stamp out Christianity, emperors occasionally resorted to persecution. Christians were imprisoned, beaten, starved, burned alive, torn apart by wild beasts in the arena for the amusement of the Romans, and crucified. However, the persecutions did not last long enough to extirpate the new religion. Actually, they strengthened the determination of most of the faithful and won new converts, who were awed by the extraordinary courage of the martyrs willingly dying for their faith.

Unable to crush Christianity by persecution, Roman emperors decided to gain the support of the growing number of Christians within the Empire. In A.D. 313, Constantine, genuinely attracted to Christianity, issued the Edict of

Milan, granting toleration to Christians. By A.D. 392, Theodosius I had made Christianity the state religion of the Empire and declared the worship of pagan gods illegal.

Christianity and Greek Philosophy

Christianity synthesized both the Hebrew and the Greco-Roman traditions. Having emerged from Judaism, it assimilated Hebrew monotheism and prophetic morality and retained the Old Testament as the Word of God. As the new religion evolved, it also assimilated elements of Greek philosophy. The ability to combine a historic Judaic monotheism, which had many admirers in the Gentile world, with Greek rational philosophy was a crucial reason for Christianity's triumph in the Roman Empire. But there was a struggle between conservatives, who wanted no dealings with pagan philosophy, and those believers who recognized the value of Greek thought to Christianity.

To conservative church fathers—early Christian writers whose works are accepted as authoritative by the church—classical philosophy was all in error because it did not derive from divine revelation. As the final statement of God's truth, Christianity superseded both pagan philosophy and pagan religions. These conservatives feared that studying classical authors would contaminate Christian morality (did not Plato propose a community of wives, and did not the dramatists treat violent passions?) and promote heresy (was not classical literature replete with references to pagan gods?). For these church fathers, there could be no compromise between Greek philosophy and Christian revelation.

Some early church fathers, including several who had a Greek education, defended the value of studying classical literature. They maintained that Greek philosophy contained a dim glimmer of God's truth, a pre-Christian insight into divine wisdom. Christ had corrected and fulfilled an insight reached by the philosophical mind. Knowledge of Greek philosophy, they also contended, helped Christians explain their beliefs logically and argue intelligently with pagan critics of Christian teachings.

Utilizing the language and categories of Greek philosophy, Christian intellectuals transformed Christianity from a simple ethical creed into a theoretical system, a theology. This effort to express Christian beliefs in terms of Greek rationalism is referred to as the Hellenization of Christianity. Greek philosophy enabled Christians to explain rationally God's existence and revelation.

Christ was depicted as the divine Logos (reason) in human form. The Stoic teaching that all people are fundamentally equal because they share in universal reason could be formulated in Christian terms: that all are united in Christ. Christians could interpret the church to be the true fulfillment of the Stoic idea of a polity embracing the entire world. Stoic ethics, which stressed moderation, self-control, and brotherhood, was compatible with Christianity. Particularly in Platonism, which drew a distinction between a world perceived by the senses and a higher order, a transcendent world that should be the central concern of human existence—Christian thinkers found a congenial vehicle for expressing Christian beliefs. The perfect and universal Forms, or Ideas, which Plato maintained were the true goal of knowledge and the source of ethical standards, were held by Christians to exist in God's mind.

That Greek philosophy exerted an influence on church doctrine is of immense importance; it meant that rational thought, the priceless achievement of the Greek mind, was not lost. However, the Hellenization of Christianity did not mean the triumph of classicism over Christianity, but rather the reverse: Christianity triumphed over Hellenism. Greek philosophy had to sacrifice its essential autonomy to the requirements of Christian revelation; that is, reason had to fit into a Christian framework. Although Christianity made use of Greek philosophy, Christian truth ultimately rested on faith, not reason.

Development of Christian Organization, Doctrine, and Attitudes

Early in its history, the church developed along hierarchical lines. Those members of the Christian community who had the authority to preside over the celebration of the Mass—breaking bread and offering wine as Christ had done at the Last Supper—were called either priests or bishops. Gradually, the designation *bishop* was reserved for the one clergyman in the community with the authority to resolve disputes over doctrines and practices. Regarded as the successors to Christ's Twelve Disciples, bishops supervised religious activities within their regions. In creating a diocese that was supervised by a bishop and had its center in a leading city, the church adapted Roman administrative techniques.

The Primacy of the Bishop of Rome

The bishop of Rome, later to be called the pope, claimed primacy over the other bishops. In developing the case for their supremacy over the church organization, bishops of Rome increasingly referred to the famous New Testament passage in which Jesus says to his disciple Simon (also called Peter): "'And I tell you, you are Peter, and on this rock I will build my church'" (Matthew 16:18).[2] Because *Peter* in Greek means "rock" (petra), it was argued that Christ had chosen Peter to succeed him as ruler of the universal church. Since it was commonly accepted that Saint Peter had established a church in Rome and was martyred there, it was argued further that the Roman bishop inherited the power that Christ had passed on to Peter.

The Rise of Monasticism

Some devout Christians committed to living a perfect Christian life were distressed by the wickedness of the world about them, including the moral laxity of those clergy who chased after wealth and pomp. Seeking to escape from the agonies and corruptions of this world, some ardent Christians withdrew to deserts and mountains in search of spiritual renewal. In their zeal for holiness,

The Antioch Chalice: Roman Syria, Sixth Century. This richly ornamented silver chalice may have been used to hold the wine that Christians believed became the blood of Christ during the Eucharistic liturgy. (*The Metropolitan Museum of Art, The Cloisters Collection, 1950*)

they sometimes practiced extreme forms of asceticism: self-flogging, wearing spiked corsets, eating only herbs, or living for years on a column high above the ground. Gradually, colonies of these hermits sprang up, particularly in Egypt; in time, the leaders of these monastic communities drew up written rules that required monks to refrain from bodily abuses and to engage in manual labor.

The monastic ideal spread from east to west. The principal figure in the shaping of monasticism in the west was Saint Benedict (c. 480–c. 543), who founded a monastery at Monte Cassino, Italy, in 529. The Rule of Saint Benedict called for the monks to live in poverty and to study, labor, and obey the abbot, the head of the monastery. Monks were required to pray often, work hard, talk little, and surrender private property. In imposing discipline and regulations, Benedict eliminated the excessive and eccentric individualism of the early monks; he socialized and institutionalized the spiritual impulse that led monks to withdraw from the world. Benedict demonstrated the same genius for administration as the Romans had shown in organizing and governing their Empire. His rule became the standard for monasteries in western Europe.

The Scriptural Tradition and Doctrinal Disputes

Christ's sayings and actions were preserved by word of mouth. Sometime around A.D. 66–70, Saint Mark formulated the Christian message from this oral tradition and perhaps from some material that had been put in writing earlier. Later, Saint Matthew and Saint Luke, relying heavily on Mark's account, wrote somewhat longer Gospels. The Gospels of Mark, Matthew, and Luke are called *synoptic* because their approach to Jesus is very similar. The remaining Gospel, written by Saint John around A.D. 110, varies significantly from the synoptic Gospels. The synoptic Gospels, the Gospel of Saint John, Acts of the Apostles, the twenty-one Epistles, including those written by Saint Paul, and Revelation constitute the twenty-seven books of the Christian New Testament. Christians also accepted the Hebrews' Old Testament as God's Word.

The early Christians had a Bible and a clergy to teach it. But the Holy Writ could be interpreted differently by equally sincere believers, and controversies over doctrine threatened the unity of the early church. The most important controversy concerned how people viewed the relationship between God and Christ. Arius (A.D. 250–336), a Greek priest in Alexandria, led one faction. He denied the complete divinity of Christ, one of the basic tenets of the church. To Arius, Christ was more than man but less than God; there was no permanent union between God and Christ; the Father alone was eternal and truly God.

The Council of Nicaea (A.D. 325), the first assembly of bishops from all parts of the Roman world, was called to settle the controversy. The council condemned Arius and ruled that God and Christ were of the same substance, coequal and coeternal. The position adopted at Nicaea became the basis of the Nicene Creed, which remains the official doctrine of the church. Although Arianism, the name given the heresy of Arius, won converts for a time, it eventually lost supporters.

Christianity and Society

Although salvation was their ultimate aim, Christians still had to dwell within the world and deal with its imperfections. In the process, Christian thinkers challenged some of the mores of Greco-Roman society and formulated attitudes that would endure for centuries. Influenced by passages in the New Testament that condemned acts of revenge and the shedding of blood, some early Christians refused military service. Others, however, held that in a sinful world defense of the state was necessary, and, without concealment or apology, they served in the army. After Roman emperors professed Christianity, Christians began to serve the government more often. With the barbarians menacing the borders, these Christian officials could not advocate nonviolence. Christian theorists began to argue that under certain circumstances—to punish injustice or to restore peace—war was just. But even such wars must not entail unnecessary violence.

Sharing in the patriarchal tradition of Jewish society, Saint Paul subjected the wife to her husband's authority. "Wives, be subject to your husbands, as to the Lord. For the husband is the head of the wife as Christ is the head of the church" (Ephesians 5:22–23). But Paul also held that all are baptized in Christ: "There is neither Jew nor Greek, there is neither slave nor free, there is neither male nor female; for you are all one in Christ Jesus" (Galatians 3:28). Consequently, both sexes were subject to divine law; both men and women possessed moral autonomy. The early church held to strict standards on sexual matters. It condemned adultery and esteemed virginity pledged for spiritual reasons.

Christians waged no war against slavery, which was widely practiced and universally accepted in the ancient world. Saint Paul commanded slaves to obey their masters, and many Christians were themselves slave owners. However, Christians taught that slaves, too, were children of God, sought their conversion, and urged owners not to treat them harshly. In the modern world, the Christian teaching that all persons are spiritually equal before God would impel some Christians to fight for the abolition of slavery.

Christianity and the Jews

Numerous links connect early Christianity and Judaism. Jesus himself and his earliest followers, including the Twelve Apostles, were Jews who were faithful to Jewish law. Jesus' message was first spread in synagogues throughout the Roman Empire. Early Christianity's affirmation of the preciousness of the human being, created in God's image, its belief that God rules history, its awareness of human sinfulness, its call for repentance, and its appeal to God for forgiveness are rooted in Judaism. The Christian reference to God as a "merciful Father" derives from Jewish prayer. Also rooted in Judaism are the moral norms proclaimed by Jesus in the Sermon on the Mount and on other occasions. For example, "Thou shalt love thy neighbor as thyself" was the motto of the Jewish sage Hillel, a contemporary of Jesus who founded a school. Jesus' use of parables to convey his teachings, the concept of the Messiah, respect for the Sabbath, the practice of giving alms to the poor, and congregational worship likewise stem from Judaism. And, of course, Christians viewed the Hebrew Scriptures as God's Word.

Over the years, however, Christians forgot or devalued this relationship to Judaism, and some thinkers began to show hostility toward Judaism and Jews, which had tragic consequences in later centuries. Several factors fueled this anti-Judaism: resentment against Jews for their refusal to accept Jesus; the polemics of the Jewish establishment against the followers of Jesus; the role in Jesus' death ascribed to Jews by the New Testament; resentment against those Christians who Judaized, that is, continued to observe Jewish festivals and the Jewish Sabbath, to regard the synagogue as holy, and to practice circumcision; and anger that Judaism remained a vital religion, for this undermined the conviction that Christianity was the fulfillment of Judaism and the one true faith.

What made Christian anti-Judaism particularly ominous was the effort of some theologians to demonize the Jewish people. The myth emerged that Jews, murderers of the incarnate God who embodied all that was good, were a cursed nation, children of the Devil, whose suffering was intended by God. Thus, Origen (c. 185–c. 251) maintained that "the blood of Jesus falls not only on the Jews of the time but on all generations of Jews up to the end of the world." In the late fourth century, Saint John Chrysostom called the Jews "the most miserable of men, inveterate murderers, destroyers, men possessed by the Devil." The synagogue, he said, was "the domicile of the Devil, their rituals are criminal and impure, their religion is a disease." Since the Devil was very real to early and medieval Christians, the Jew became identified with evil. Christians developed a mindset, concludes the Reverend Robert A. Everett, that was "unable to see anything positive in Judaism. . . . Judaism and the Jewish people came to have no real value for Christians except as a negative contrast to Christianity."[3] Because of this "teaching of contempt" and the "diabolization of the Jew," the Christian ethic of love did not extend to Jews.

> . . . once it is established that God has cursed the Jews, how can one argue that Christians should love them? If Jews have been fated by God to have . . . a long history of suffering, who are Christians to alter their history by doing anything to relieve Jewish suffering? The theology of victimization thus precludes Christian love as a basis of relating to Jews.[4]

The diabolization of the Jew, which bore no relationship to the actual behavior of Jews or to their highly ethical religion, and the "theology of victimization," which held that the Jews were collectively and eternally cursed for denying Christ, became powerful myths. Over the centuries, these myths poisoned Christians' hearts and minds against Jews, spurring innumerable humiliations, persecutions, and massacres. Alongside this hatred of Jews and antipathy to their suffering, there also evolved the belief that Jews, faithless and perfidious though they were, should be permitted to survive, for one day they would see the light and convert to the true faith.

Saint Augustine: The Christian World-View

During the early history of Christianity, many learned men, "fathers of the church," explained and defended church teachings. Most of the leading early fathers wrote in Greek, but in the middle of the fourth century, three great Latin writers—Saint Jerome, Saint Ambrose, and Saint Augustine—profoundly influenced the course of Christianity in the West.

Saint Jerome (A.D. c. 340–420) wrote about the lives of the saints and promoted the spread of monasticism. But his greatest achievement was the translation of the Old and New Testaments from Hebrew and Greek into Latin. Jerome's text, the common, or Vulgate, version of the Bible, became the official edition of the Bible for the western church.

Saint Ambrose (A.D. 340–397), bishop of Milan, Italy, instructed the clergy to deal humanely with the poor, the old, the sick, and the orphaned. He urged clerics not to pursue wealth, but to practice humility and avoid favoring the

Apostle Peter. This silver plaque was found near Antioch, Syria and dates from the sixth century. (*Courtesy, Metropolitan Museum of Art, Fletcher Fund, 1950*)

rich over the poor. Ambrose sought to defend the autonomy of the church against the power of the state. His dictum that "the Emperor is within the church, not above it" became a cardinal principle of the medieval church.

The most important Christian theoretician in the Late Roman Empire was Saint Augustine (A.D. 354–430), bishop of Hippo, in North Africa, and author of *The City of God*. Augustine became the principal architect of the Christian outlook that succeeded a dying classicism.

In 410, when Augustine was in his fifties, Visigoths sacked Rome: a disaster for which the classical consciousness was unprepared. Throughout the Empire, people panicked. Non-Christians blamed the tragedy on Christianity. Even Christians expressed anxiety. Why were the righteous also suffering? Where was the kingdom of God on earth that had been prophesied? In *The City of God*, Augustine maintained that the worldly city could never be the central concern of Christians. The misfortunes of Rome, therefore, should not distress Christians unduly because the true Christian was a citizen of a heavenly city that could not be pillaged by ungodly barbarians but would endure forever. Compared with God's heavenly city, Rome and its decline were unimportant. What really mattered in history, said Augustine, was not the coming to be or the passing away of cities and empires, but the individual's entrance into heaven or hell.

Nevertheless, Augustine did not hold that by his death Christ had opened the door to heaven for all. The majority of humanity remained condemned to eternal punishment, said Augustine; only a handful had the gift of faith and the promise of heaven. People could not by their own efforts overcome a sinful nature; a moral and spiritual regeneration stemmed not from human will power, but from God's grace. The small number endowed with God's grace constituted the City of God. These people lived on earth as visitors only, for they awaited deliverance to the Kingdom of Christ. Most inhabitants of the earthly city were destined for eternal punishment in hell. A perpetual conflict existed between the two cities and between their inhabitants: one city stood for sin and corruption; the other, for God's truth and perfection.

For Augustine, the highest good was not of this world. Rather, it consisted of eternal life with God. His distinction between this higher world of perfection and a lower world of corruption remained influential throughout the Middle Ages.

Augustine repudiated the distinguishing feature of classical humanism: the autonomy of reason. For him, ultimate wisdom could not be achieved through rational thought alone; reason had to be guided by faith. Without faith, there could be no true knowledge, no understanding. Philosophy had no validity if it did not first accept as absolutely true the existence of God and the authority of his revelation. Thus, Augustine upheld the primacy of faith. But he did not necessarily regard reason as an enemy of faith, and he did not call for an end to rational speculation. What he denied of the classical view was that reason alone could attain wisdom. The wisdom that Augustine sought was Christian wisdom, God's revelation to humanity. The starting point for this wisdom, he said, was belief in God and the Scriptures. To Augustine, secular knowledge for its own sake was of little value; the true significance of knowledge lay in its role as a tool for comprehending God's will. Augustine adapted the classical intellectual tradition to the requirements of Christian revelation.

With Augustine, the human-centered outlook of classical humanism, which for centuries had been undergoing transformation, gave way to a God-centered world-view. The fulfillment of God's will, not the full development of human capacities, became the chief concern of life.

Christianity and Classical Humanism: Alternative World-Views

Christianity and classical humanism are the two principal components of the Western tradition. The value that modern Western civilization places on the individual derives ultimately from classical humanism and the Judeo-Christian tradition. Classical humanists believed that worth came from the

The Ascension of Jesus into Heaven: A Miniature Painting, c. A.D. 586. In a gospel book written by the monk Rabbula at Saint John's Abbey, Zagba, Mesopotamia, the upper zone of the painting reflects a vision of the prophet Ezekiel (1:3–28). The lower zone shows Jesus' apostles and his mother Mary with two angels as witnesses to Jesus' Ascension into heaven. (Acts 1: 7–14). (*Courtesy of Biblioteca Medicea Laurenziana, Florence. Photo by Donato Pineides.*)

capacity of individuals to reason and to shape their character and their life according to rational standards. Christianity, too, stresses the importance of the individual. In the Christian view, God cares for each person; he wants people to behave righteously and to enter heaven; Christ died for all because he loves humanity. Christianity espouses active love and genuine concern for fellow human beings.

But Christianity and classical humanism also represent two inherently different world-views. The triumph of the Christian outlook signified a break with the essential meaning of classical humanism; it pointed to the end of the world of antiquity and the beginning of an age of faith, the Middle Ages. With the victory of Christianity, the ultimate goal of life shifted. Life's purpose was no longer to achieve excellence in this world through the full and creative development of human talent, but to attain salvation in a heavenly city. A person's worldly accomplishments amounted to very little if he or she did not accept God and his revelation.

In the classical view, history had no ultimate end, no ultimate significance; periods of happiness and misery repeated themselves endlessly. In the Christian view, history is filled with spiritual meaning. It is the profound drama of individuals struggling to overcome their original sin in order to gain eternal happiness in heaven. History began with Adam and Eve's defiance of God and would end when Christ returns to earth, evil is eradicated, and God's will prevails.

Classicism held that there was no authority above reason: individuals had within themselves the ability to understand the world and life. For early Christianity, however, knowledge, without God as the starting point, was formless, purposeless, and prone to error. In classicism, ethical standards were laws of nature, which reason could discover. Through reason, individuals could arrive at the values by which they should regulate their lives. Reason would enable them to govern desires and will; it would show them where their behavior was wrong and how to correct it. Early Christianity, on the other hand, taught that ethical standards emanated from the personal will of God. Without obedience to God's commands, people would remain wicked forever; the human will, essentially sinful, could not be transformed by the promptings of reason. Only when individuals turned to God for forgiveness and guidance would they find the inner strength to overcome their sinful nature. People could not perfect themselves through scientific knowledge; spiritual insight and belief in God must serve as the first principle of their lives.

Thus, for classicism, the ultimate good came through independent thought and action; for Christianity, through knowing, obeying, and loving God. In early Christianity, the good life was identified not with worldly achievement, but with eternal life. Each person must make entrance into God's kingdom the central aim of life. For the next thousand years, this distinction between heaven and earth, this otherworldly, theocentric outlook, would define the Western mentality.

Notes

1. Andrew M. Greeley, "Hippie Hero? Superpatriot? Superstar? A Christmas Biography," *New York Times Magazine,* December 23, 1973, p. 28.
2. The biblical quotations are from the Holy Bible, Revised Standard Version (New York: Thomas Nelson & Sons, 1952). The Revised Standard Version is the text used for biblical quotations throughout, except where noted otherwise.
3. Randolph Braham, ed., *The Origins of the Holocaust: Christian Anti-Semitism* (Boulder, Colorado: Social Science Monographs and Institute for Holocaust Studies of the City University of New York, 1986), p. 36.
4. Ibid., p. 37.

Suggested Reading

Armstrong, Karen, *A History of God* (1994). Good material on early Christianity.
Benko, Stephen, *Pagan Rome and the Early Christians* (1984). How Romans and Greeks viewed early Christianity.
Chadwick, Henry, *The Early Church* (1967). A survey of early Christianity in its social and ideological context.
Davies, J. G., *The Early Christian Church* (1967). A splendid introduction to the first five centuries of Christianity.

Meeks, Wayne A., *The Moral World of the First Christians* (1986). Continuity and discontinuity between the moral outlook of early Christianity and that pervading Jewish and Greco-Roman thought.

Pelikan, Jaroslav, *The Christian Tradition* (1971), vol. 1, *The Emergence of the Catholic Tradition*. The first of a five-volume series on the history of Christian doctrine.

Perkins, Pheme, *Reading the New Testament* (1978). Introduces the beginning student to the New Testament.

Wilkin, Robert L., *The Christians as the Romans Saw Them* (1984). Pagan reaction to the rise of Christianity.

Review Questions

1. Why does the life of Jesus present a problem to the historian?
2. What were Jesus' basic teachings?
3. What is the relationship of early Christianity to Judaism?
4. How did Saint Paul transform a Jewish sect into a world religion?
5. What factors contributed to the triumph of Christianity in the Roman Empire?
6. Why did some early Christian thinkers object to the study of classical literature? What arguments were advanced by the defenders of classical learning? What was the outcome of this debate? Why was it significant?
7. What factors contributed to the rise of anti-Judaism among early Christians? Define and explain the historical significance of the "diabolization of the Jew," the "teaching of contempt," and the "theology of victimization."
8. How did Saint Augustine view the fall of Rome, the worldly city, humanity, and Greek philosophy?
9. Compare and contrast the world-views of early Christianity and classical humanism.

PART TWO

The Middle Ages: The Christian Centuries

500–1400

Stained Glass in La Sainte Chapelle Cathedral, Paris. (*Nicholas DeVore III/Bruce Coleman, Inc.*)

POLITICS AND SOCIETY	THOUGHT AND CULTURE
500 Germanic kingdoms established on former Roman lands (5th and 6th cent.) Saint Benedict founds monastery at Monte Cassino (529) Pope Gregory I sends missionaries to convert the Anglo-Saxons (596)	Boethius, *The Consolation of Philosophy* (523) Law Code of Justinian (529) Byzantine church Hagia Sophia (532–537) Cassiodorus establishes a monastic library at Vivarium (540)
600 Spread of Islam (622–732)	The Koran
700 Charles Martel defeats the Muslims at Tours (732)	Bede, *Ecclesiastical History of the English People* (c. 700) Muslim Golden Age (700s and 800s)
800 Charlemagne crowned emperor of Romans Muslim, Magyar, and Viking invasions of Latin Christendom (9th and early 10th cent.) Growth of feudalism (800–1100)	Carolingian Renaissance (768–814) Alfred the Great promotes learning in England (871–899)
900 German king Otto I becomes first Holy Roman Emperor (962)	
1000 Split between the Byzantine and Roman churches (1054) Norman conquest of England (1066) Start of First Crusade (1096)	Romanesque style in architecture (1000s and 1100s)
1100 Philip Augustus expands central authority in France (1180–1223) Development of common law and jury system in England (1100s) Pontificate of Innocent III: height of papal power (1198–1216)	Flowering of medieval culture (12th and 13th cent.): universities, Gothic architecture, scholastic philosophy, revival of Roman law
1200 Magna Carta (1215) Destruction of Baghdad by Mongols (1258)	Aquinas, *Summa Theologica* (1267–1273)
1300 Hundred Years' War (1337–1453) Black Death (1347–1351) Great Schism of papacy (1378–1417)	Dante, *Divine Comedy* (c. 1307–1321) Chaucer, *Canterbury Tales* (c. 1388–1400)

❖ CHAPTER 6

The Rise of Europe:
Fusion of Classical, Christian,
and Germanic Traditions

$\mathcal{T}$he triumph of Christianity and the establishment of Germanic kingdoms on once Roman lands constituted a new phase in Western history: the end of the ancient world and the beginning of the Middle
Ages, a period that spanned a thousand years. In the ancient world,
the locus of Greco-Roman civilization was the Mediterranean Sea.
The heartland of medieval civilization gradually shifted to the north,
to regions of Europe that Greco-Roman civilization had barely penetrated. During the Middle Ages, a common European civilization
evolved, integrating Christian, Greco-Roman, and Germanic traditions: Christianity was at the center of medieval civilization; Rome
was the spiritual capital, and Latin the language of intellectual life;
and Germanic customs pervaded social and legal relationships. In the
Early Middle Ages (500–1050), the new civilization was struggling to
take form; in the High Middle Ages (1050–1300), medieval civilization reached its peak.   ❖

The Medieval East

Three new civilizations based on religion emerged from the ruins of the
Roman Empire: Latin Christendom (western and central Europe) and two
Eastern civilizations, Byzantium and Islam.

Byzantium

Although the Roman Empire in the west fell to the German tribes, the eastern
provinces survived. They did so because they were richer, more urbanized,
and more populous and because the main Germanic and Hunnish invasions
were directed at the western regions. In the eastern parts, Byzantine civilization took shape. Its religion was Christianity; its language and culture, Greek;
and its machinery of administration, Roman. The capital, Constantinople,
was a fortress city, perfectly situated to resist attacks from land and sea.

Chronology 6.1 ❖ The Early and High Middle Ages

496	Clovis adopts Roman Christianity
596	Pope Gregory I sends missionaries to convert the Anglo-Saxons
732	Charles Martel defeats the Muslims at Tours
768	Charlemagne becomes king of the Franks
800	Charlemagne is crowned emperor of the Romans by Pope Leo III
c. 840s	Height of Viking attacks
962	Otto I crowned emperor of the Romans, beginning the Holy Roman Empire
987	Hugh Capet becomes king of France
1054	Split between Byzantine and Roman churches
1066	Norman conquest of England
1075	Start of the Investiture Controversy
1096	First Crusade begins
1198–1216	Pontificate of Innocent III: height of the church's power

During the Early Middle Ages, Byzantine civilization was economically and culturally far more advanced than the Latin West. At a time when few westerners (Latin Christians) could read or write, Byzantine scholars studied the literature, philosophy, science, and law of ancient Greece and Rome. Whereas trade and urban life had greatly declined in the West, Constantinople was a magnificent Byzantine city of schools, libraries, open squares, and bustling markets.

Over the centuries, many differences developed between the Byzantine church and the Roman church. The pope resisted domination by the Byzantine emperor, and the Byzantines would not accept the pope as head of all Christians. The two churches quarreled over ceremonies, holy days, the display of images, and the rights of the clergy. The final break came in 1054; the Christian church split into the Roman Catholic in the West and the Eastern (Greek) Orthodox in the East, a division that still persists.

Political and cultural differences widened the rift between Latin Christendom and Byzantium. In the Byzantine Empire, Greek was the language of religion and intellectual life; in the West, Latin predominated. Latin Christians refused to recognize that the Byzantine emperors were, as they claimed, successors to the Roman emperors. Byzantine emperors were absolute rulers who held that God had chosen them to rule and to institute divine will on earth. As successors to the Roman emperors, they claimed to rule all the lands that had once been part of the Roman Empire.

At its height, under Emperor Justinian, who reigned from 527 to 565, the Byzantine Empire included Greece, Asia Minor, Italy, southern Spain, and parts of the Near East, North Africa, and the Balkans. Over the centuries, the Byzantines faced attacks from the Germanic Lombards and Visigoths, Persians, Muslim Arabs, Seljuk Turks, and Latin Christians. The death blow to the empire was dealt by the Ottoman Turks. Originally from central Asia, they had accepted Islam and had begun to build an empire. They drove the Byzantines from Asia Minor and conquered much of the Balkans. By the beginning of the fifteenth century, the Byzantine Empire consisted of only two small territories in Greece and the city of Constantinople. In 1453, the Ottoman Turks broke through Constantinople's great walls and looted the city. After more than ten centuries, the Byzantine Empire had come to an end.

During its thousand years, Byzantium made a significant impact on world history. First, it prevented the Muslim Arabs from advancing into eastern Europe. Had the Arabs broken through Byzantine defenses, much of Europe might have been converted to the new faith of Islam. Another far-reaching development was the codification of the laws of ancient Rome under Justinian. This monumental achievement, the *Corpus Juris Civilis,* preserved Roman law's principles of reason and justice. Today's legal codes in much of Europe and Latin America trace their roots to the Roman law recorded by Justinian's lawyers. The Byzantines also preserved the philosophy, science, mathematics, and literature of ancient Greece.

Contacts with Byzantine civilization stimulated learning in both the Islamic world to the east and Latin Christendom to the west. Byzantium also carried its advanced civilization and Orthodox Christianity to some Slavic peoples of eastern and southeastern Europe, including the Russians. It gave those Slavs legal principles, art forms, and an alphabet (the Cyrillic, based on the Greek), which enabled them to put their own languages into writing.

Islam

The second civilization to arise after Rome's fall was based on the vital new religion of Islam, which emerged in the seventh century among the Arabs of Arabia. Its founder was Muhammad (c. 570–632), a prosperous merchant in the trading city of Mecca. When Muhammad was about forty, he believed that he was visited by the angel Gabriel, who ordered him to "recite in the name of the Lord!" Transformed by this vision, Muhammad was convinced that he had been chosen to serve as a prophet. Although most desert Arabs worshiped tribal gods, in the towns and trading centers many Arabs were familiar with Judaism and Christianity, and some had accepted the idea of one

Mosque of Mohammed Ali, Cairo, Twelfth Century A.D. This mosque was a gathering place for prayer, preaching, and study of the Koran. Mosques were usually rectangular buildings with arcaded porticos surrounding an open court. The focal point was an apse facing Mecca from which the local *Imam* led the congregation in prayer. Nearby was a pulpit for preaching and a copy of the Koran on a lectern. In the outer court were pools or fountains for ritual purification. In the Cairo mosque the fountains were covered by a domed building. Attached to the mosque was a *minaret* or tower from which the faithful were summoned for prayers five times a day. (*Courtesy of Trans World Airlines*)

God. Rejecting the many deities of the tribal religions, Muhammad offered the Arabs a new monotheistic faith, Islam, which means "surrender to Allah (God)."

Islamic standards of morality and rules governing daily life are set by the Koran, which Muslims believe contains the words of Allah as revealed to Muhammad. Muslims see their religion as the completion and perfection of Judaism and Christianity. They regard the ancient Hebrew prophets as messengers of God and value their message of compassion and the oneness of humanity. They also acknowledge Jesus as a great prophet but do not consider him divine. Muslims view Muhammad as the last and greatest of the prophets and see him as entirely human; they worship only Allah, the creator and ruler of heaven and earth, a single, all-powerful God, who is merciful, compassionate, and just. According to the Koran, on the Day of Judgment unbelievers and the wicked will be dragged into a fearful place of "scorching winds and seething water" and "sinners . . . shall eat . . . [bitter] fruit . . . [and] drink boiling water."[1] Faithful Muslims who have lived virtuously are promised paradise, a garden of bodily pleasures and spiritual delights.

In a little more than two decades, Muhammad united the often feuding Arabian tribes into a powerful force dedicated to Allah and the spreading of the Islamic faith. After Muhammad's death in 632, his friend and father-in-law, Abu Bakr, became his successor, or caliph. Regarded as the defender of the faith, whose power derived from Allah, the caliph governed in accordance with Muslim law as defined in the Koran. The Islamic state was a theocracy, in which government and religion were inseparable; there could be no distinction between secular and spiritual authority. Muslims viewed God as the source of all law and political authority and the caliph as his earthly deputy. Divine law regulated all aspects of human relations. The ruler who did not enforce Koranic law failed in his duties. Thus, Islam was more than a religion; it was also a system of government, society, law, and thought that bound its adherents into an all-encompassing community. The idea of a society governed by the Koran remained deeply embedded in the Muslim mind over the centuries and is still a powerful force today.

Islam gave the many Arab tribes the unity, discipline, and organization to succeed in their wars of conquest. Under the first four caliphs, who ruled from 632 to 661, the Arabs, with breathtaking speed, overran the Persian Empire, seized some of Byzantium's provinces, and invaded Europe. Muslim warriors believed that they were engaged in a holy war (*jihad*) to spread Islam to nonbelievers and that those who died in the jihad were assured a place in paradise. A desire to escape from the barren Arabian desert and to exploit the rich Byzantine and Persian lands was another compelling reason for expansion. In the east, Islam's territory eventually extended into India and to the borders of China; in the west, it encompassed North Africa and most of Spain. But the Muslims' northward push lost momentum and was halted in 717 by the Byzantines at Constantinople and in 732 by the Franks at the battle of Tours in central France.

In the eighth and ninth centuries, under the Abbasid caliphs, Muslim civilization entered its golden age. Islamic civilization creatively integrated Arabic, Byzantine, Persian, and Indian cultural traditions. During the Early Middle Ages, when learning was at a low point in western Europe, the Muslims had forged a high civilization. Muslim science, philosophy, and mathematics rested largely on the achievements of the ancient Greeks. The Muslims acquired Greek learning from the older Persian and Byzantine civilizations, which had kept alive the Greek inheritance. By translating Greek works into Arabic and commenting on them, Muslim scholars performed the great historical task of preserving the philosophical and scientific heritage of ancient Greece. Greek learning, supplemented by original contributions of Muslim scholars and scientists, was eventually passed on to Christian Europe.

The Arab empire, stretching from Spain to India, was unified by a common language (Arabic), a common faith, and a common culture. By the eleventh century, however, the Arabs began losing their dominance in the Islamic world. The Seljuk Turks, who had taken Asia Minor from the Byzantines, also conquered the Arabic lands of Syria, Palestine, and much of Persia. Although the Abbasid caliphs remained the religious and cultural leaders of Islam, political power was exercised by Seljuk sultans. In the eleventh and twelfth centuries, the Muslims lost Sicily and most of Spain to Christian knights, and European Crusaders carved out kingdoms in the Near East.

In the thirteenth century, Mongols led by Genghis Khan devastated Muslim lands; in the late fourteenth century, this time led by Tamerlane, they again plundered and massacred their way through Arab territory. After Tamerlane's death in 1404, his empire disintegrated, and its collapse left the way open for the Ottoman Turks.

The Ottoman Empire reached its height in the sixteenth century with the conquest of Egypt, North Africa, Syria, and the Arabian coast. The Ottomans developed an effective system of administration, but they could not restore the cultural brilliance, the thriving trade, or the prosperity that the Muslim world had known under the Abbasid caliphs of Baghdad.

Latin Christendom in the Early Middle Ages

The centuries of cultural greatness of both Islamic and Byzantine civilizations enriched the Western world. However, neither Islam nor Byzantium made the breakthroughs in science, technology, philosophy, economics, and political thought that gave rise to the modern world. That process was the singular achievement of Europe. During the Early Middle Ages (500–1050), Latin Christendom was culturally far behind the two Eastern civilizations, but by the twelfth century it had caught up. In succeeding centuries, it produced the movements that ushered in the modern age: the Renaissance, the Reformation, the Scientific Revolution, the Age of Enlightenment, the French Revolution, and the Industrial Revolution.

Political, Economic, and Intellectual Transformation

From the sixth to the eighth century, Europeans struggled to overcome the disorders created by the breakup of the Roman Empire and the deterioration of Greco-Roman civilization. In the process, a new civilization, with its own distinctive style, took root. It grew out of the intermingling of Greco-Roman civilization, the Christian outlook, and Germanic traditions. But centuries would pass before it would come to fruition.

In the fifth century, German invaders founded kingdoms in North Africa, Italy, Spain, Gaul, and Britain—lands formerly belonging to Rome. Even before the invasions, the Germans had acquired some knowledge of Roman culture and were attracted to it. Therefore, the new Germanic rulers did not seek to destroy Roman civilization but to share in its advantages. For example, Theodoric the Great (476–526), the Ostrogoth ruler of Italy, retained the Roman Senate, government officials, civil service, and schools, and rich aristocratic Roman families continued to hold high government offices. The Burgundians in Gaul and the Visigoths in Spain maintained Roman law for their conquered subjects. All the Germanic kingdoms tried to keep Roman systems of taxation; furthermore, Latin remained the official language of administration.

But the Germanic kingdoms, often torn by warfare, internal rebellion, and assassination, provided a poor political base on which to revive a decadent and dying classical civilization. Most of the kingdoms survived for only a short time and had no enduring impact. An exception to this trend occurred in Gaul and south-central Germany, where the most successful of the Germanic kingdoms was established by the Franks—the founders of the new Europe.

The Roman world was probably too far gone to be rescued, but even if it had not been, the Germans were culturally unprepared to play the role of rescuer. By the end of the seventh century, the old Roman lands in the west showed a marked decline in central government, town life, commerce, and learning. While vigorous and brave, the German invaders were essentially a rural and warrior people, tribal in organization and outlook. Their native culture, without cities or written literature, was primitive compared with the literary, philosophical, scientific, and artistic achievements of the Greco-Roman world. The Germans were not equipped to reform the decaying Roman system of administration and taxation or cope with the economic problems that had burdened the Empire. Nor could they maintain roads and irrigation systems, preserve skills in the arts of stoneworking and glassmaking, or breathe new life into the dying humanist culture.

The distinguishing feature of classical civilization, its vital urban institutions, had deteriorated in the Late Roman Empire. Under the kingdoms created by Germanic chieftains, the shift from an urban to a rural economy accelerated. Although towns did not vanish altogether, they continued to lose control over the surrounding countryside and to decline in wealth and importance. They were the headquarters of bishops, rather than centers of commerce and intellectual life. Italy remained an exception to this general trend. There, Roman urban institutions persisted, even during the crudest period of the Early Middle Ages. Italian cities kept some metal currency in circulation and traded with each other and with Byzantium.

In retreat since the Late Roman Empire, Greco-Roman humanism continued its decline in the centuries immediately following Rome's demise. The old Roman upper classes abandoned their heritage and absorbed the ways of their Germanic conquerors; the Roman schools closed, and Roman law faded into disuse. Aside from clerics, few people could read and write Latin, and even learned clerics were rare. Knowledge of the Greek language in western Europe was almost totally lost, and the Latin rhetorical style deteriorated. Many literary works of classical antiquity were either lost or neglected. European culture was much poorer than the high civilizations of Byzantium, Islam, and ancient Rome.

During this period of cultural poverty, the few persons who were learned generally did not engage in original thought but salvaged and transmitted remnants of classical civilization. In a rudimentary way, they were struggling to create a Christian culture that combined the intellectual tradition of Greece and Rome with the religious teachings of the Christian church.

An important figure in the intellectual life of this transitional period was Boethius (480–c. 525), a descendant of a noble Italian family. Aspiring to rescue the intellectual heritage of antiquity, Boethius translated into Latin some of Aristotle's treatises on logic and wrote commentaries on Aristotle, Cicero, and Porphyry (a Neo-Platonist philosopher). Until the twelfth century, virtually all that Latin Christendom knew of Aristotle came from Boethius's translations and commentaries. Similarly, his work in mathematics, which contains fragments from Euclid, was the main source for the study of that discipline in the Early Middle Ages. In his theological writings, Boethius tried to demonstrate that reason did not conflict with orthodoxy—an early attempt to attain a rational comprehension of belief, or, as he expressed it, to join faith to reason. Boethius's effort to examine Christian doctrines rationally, a salient feature of medieval philosophy, grew to maturity in the twelfth and thirteenth centuries.

Cassiodorus (c. 490–575), another Italian, collected Greek and Latin manuscripts and started the monastic practice of copying classical texts. Without this tradition, many key Christian and pagan works would undoubtedly have perished. In Spain, another "preserver" of ancient works, Isidore of Seville (c. 576–636), compiled an encyclopedia, *Etymologiae,* covering a diversity of topics, from arithmetic and furniture to God. Isidore derived his information from many secular and religious sources. Quite understandably, his work contained many errors, particularly in its references to nature. For centuries, though, the *Etymologiae* served as a standard reference work and was found in every monastic library of note.

The translations and compilations made by Boethius, Cassiodorus, and Isidore, the books collected and copied by monks and nuns, and the schools established in monasteries (particularly those in Ireland, England, and Italy) kept intellectual life from dying out completely in the Early Middle Ages.

The Church: Shaper of Medieval Civilization

Christianity was the integrating principle and the church was the dominant institution of the Middle Ages. During the Late Roman Empire, as the Roman state and its institutions decayed, the church gained power and importance. Its organization grew stronger, and its membership increased. Unlike the Roman state, the church was a healthy and vital organism. The elite of the Roman Empire had severed its commitment to the values of classical civilization, whereas the church leaders were intensely devoted to their faith.

When the Empire collapsed, the church retained the Roman administrative system and preserved elements of Greco-Roman civilization. A unifying and civilizing agent, the church provided people with an intelligible and purposeful conception of life and death. In a dying world, the church was the only institution capable of reconstructing civilized life. Thus, the Christian outlook, rather than the traditions of the German tribes, formed the foundation of medieval civilization. During the course of the Middle Ages, people came to see themselves as participants in a great drama of salvation. There was only one truth: God's revelation to humanity. There was only one avenue to heaven, and it passed through the church. Membership in a universal church replaced

Painting of St. Matthew from the Gospel Book of Charlemagne, c. 800–810.   Handwritten and very costly, sacred books were often lavishly illustrated with minature paintings. In this painting St. Matthew, wearing a Roman toga, is depicted with his pen poised writing his gospel. On the basis of its clear Hellenistic style, scholars believe the artist was trained in an Italian or Byzantine school. (*Kunsthistorisches Museum, Vienna*)

citizenship in a universal empire. Across Europe, from Italy to Ireland, a new society centered on Christianity was taking shape.

Monks helped build the foundation of medieval civilization. During the seventh century, intellectual life on the Continent continued its steady decline. In the monasteries of Ireland and England, however, a tradition of learning persisted. Early in the fifth century, Saint Patrick began the conversion of the Irish to Christianity. In Ireland, Latin became firmly entrenched as the language of both the church and scholars at a time when it was in danger of disappearing in many parts of the Continent. Irish monks preserved and cultivated Latin and even preserved some knowledge of Greek; they revived the use of Latin during their missionary activities on the Continent. In England, the Anglo-Saxons, both men and women, who converted to Christianity mainly in the seventh century, also established monasteries that kept learning alive. In the sixth and seventh centuries, Irish and Anglo-Saxon monks became the chief agents for converting people in northern Europe. Thus, monks and nuns made possible a unitary European civilization, based on a Christian foundation. By copying and preserving ancient texts, they also kept alive elements of ancient civilization.

During the Early Middle Ages, when cities were in decay, monasteries were the principal cultural centers; they would remain so until the rebirth of towns in the High Middle Ages. Monasteries also offered succor to the sick and the destitute and served as places of refuge for travelers. To the medieval mind, the monk's and nun's selfless devotion to God, adoption of apostolic poverty, and dedication to prayer and contemplation represented the highest expression of the Christian way of life; it was the finest and most certain path to salvation.

The Early Middle Ages were a formative period for the papacy, as well as for society in general. A decisive figure in the strengthening of the papacy was Gregory I, known as the Great (590–604). One of the ablest of medieval popes, Gregory used Roman methods of administration to organize effectively papal property in Italy, Sicily, Sardinia, Gaul, and other regions. He strengthened his authority over bishops and monks, dispatched missionaries to England to win over the Anglo-Saxons, and set his sights on an alliance with the Franks. Finally materializing 150 years later, this alliance helped shape medieval history.

The Kingdom of the Franks

From their homeland in the Rhine River valley, the Frankish tribes had expanded into Roman territory during the fourth and fifth centuries. The ruler Clovis united the various Frankish tribes and conquered most of Gaul. In 496, he converted to Roman Christianity. Clovis's conversion to Catholicism was an event of great significance. A number of other German kings had adopted the Arian form of Christianity, which the church had declared heretical. By embracing Roman Christianity, the Franks became a potential ally of the papacy.

Clovis's successors could not maintain control over their lands, and power passed to the mayor of the palace, the king's chief officer. Serving as mayor of the palace from 717 to 741, Charles Martel subjected all Frankish lands to his rule. In addition, at the battle of Tours in 732, he defeated the Muslims. Although the Muslims continued to occupy the Iberian Peninsula, they would advance no farther north into Europe.

Charles Martel was succeeded by his son Pepin the Short, who in 751 deposed the king. With the approval of the papacy and his nobles, Pepin was crowned king by Boniface, a prominent bishop. Two years later, Pope Stephen II anointed Pepin again as king of the Franks and appealed to him to protect the papacy from the Lombards, the last German tribe to invade formerly Roman territory. Pepin crossed into Italy, defeated the Lombards, and turned over captured lands to the papacy. This famous Donation of Pepin made the pope ruler of the territory between Rome and Ravenna, which became known as the Papal States.

The Era of Charlemagne

The alliance between the Franks and the papacy was continued by Pepin's successor, Charlemagne (Charles the Great), who ruled from 768 to 814. Charlemagne continued the Carolingian policy of expanding the Frankish kingdom. He destroyed the Lombard kingdom and declared himself king of

Map 6.1   The Carolingian World

the Lombards. He added Bavaria to his kingdom, and after long, terrible wars, he forced the Saxons to submit to his rule and convert to Christianity. He also conquered a region in northern Spain, the Spanish March, which served as a buffer between the Christian Franks and the Muslims in Spain.

Immense difficulties arose in governing the expanded territories. Size seemed an insuperable obstacle to effective government, particularly since Charlemagne's administrative structure, lacking in trained personnel, was primitive by Islamic, Byzantine, or Roman standards. The empire was divided into about 250 counties, administered by counts—nobles who were personally loyal to the ruler and who implemented the king's decisions.

On Christmas Day in Rome in the year 800, Pope Leo III crowned Charlemagne emperor of the Romans. The title signified that the tradition of a world empire still survived, despite the demise of the western Roman Empire three hundred years earlier. But because the pope crowned Charlemagne, the emperor now had a spiritual responsibility to spread and defend the faith. Thus, Roman universalism was fused with Christian universalism.

The Frankish empire, of course, was only a dim shadow of the Roman Empire. The Franks had no Roman law or Roman legions; there were no cities that were centers of economic and cultural activity; and officials were not trained civil servants with a world outlook, but uneducated war chieftains with a tribal viewpoint. Yet Charlemagne's empire did embody the concept of a universal Christian empire—an ideal that would endure throughout the Middle Ages.

The crowning of a German ruler as emperor of the Romans by the head of the church represented the merging of German, Christian, and Roman traditions, which is the essential characteristic of medieval civilization. This blending of traditions was also evident on a cultural plane, for Charlemagne, a German warrior-king, showed respect for classical learning and Christianity, both non-Germanic traditions.

Charlemagne believed that it was his religious duty to raise the educational level of the clergy so that they understood and could properly teach the faith. He also fostered education to train administrators who would be capable of overseeing his kingdoms and royal estates; such men had to be literate. To achieve his purpose, Charlemagne gathered some of the finest scholars in Europe. Alcuin of York, England (735–804), was given charge of the palace school, attended by Charlemagne and his family, high lords, and youths training to serve the emperor. Throughout Gaul, Alcuin expanded schools and libraries, promoted the copying of ancient manuscripts, and imposed basic literary standards on the clergy.

The focus of the Carolingian Renaissance—the cultural revival produced by Charlemagne's teachers and scholars—was predominantly Christian: an effort to train clergymen and improve their understanding of the Bible and the writings of the church fathers. This process raised the level of literacy and improved the Latin style. Most important, monastic copyists continued to preserve ancient texts, which otherwise might never have survived. The oldest surviving manuscripts of many ancient works are Carolingian copies.

Compared with the Greco-Roman past, with the cultural explosion of the twelfth and thirteenth centuries, or with the great Italian Renaissance of the fifteenth century, the Carolingian Renaissance seems slight indeed. But we must bear in mind the cultural poverty that prevailed before the era of Charlemagne. The Carolingian Renaissance reversed the process of cultural decay that characterized much of the Early Middle Ages. Learning would never again fall to the low level it had reached in the centuries following the decline of Rome.

During the era of Charlemagne, a distinct European civilization emerged. It blended the Roman heritage of a world empire, the intellectual achievement of the Greco-Roman mind, Christian otherworldliness, and the customs of the Germanic peoples. This nascent western European civilization differed from Byzantine and Islamic civilizations, and Europeans were growing conscious of the difference. But the new medieval civilization was still centuries away from its high point, which would be reached in the twelfth and thirteenth centuries.

Charlemagne's empire also engendered the ideal of a unified Latin Christendom: a single Christian community under one government. The ideal of a Christian world-state, Christendom, inspired many people, both clergy and laity. The influence of this ideal would reach its peak between the eleventh and the thirteenth centuries.

The Breakup of Charlemagne's Empire

After Charlemagne's death in 814, his son, Louis the Pious, inherited the throne. Louis aimed to preserve the empire, but the task was virtually impossible. The empire's strength rested more on the personal qualities of Charlemagne than on any firm economic or political foundation. Moreover, the empire was simply too large and consisted of too many diverse peoples to be governed effectively. Besides Frankish nobles, who sought to increase their own power at the emperor's expense, Louis had to deal with his own rebellious sons. After Louis died in 840, the empire was divided among the three surviving sons.

The Treaty of Verdun in 843 gave Louis the German the eastern part of the empire, which marked the beginning of Germany; to Charles the Bald went the western part, which was the start of France; and Lothair received the Middle Kingdom, which extended from Rome to the North Sea. This Middle Kingdom would be an area of conflict between France and Germany right into the twentieth century. As central authority waned, large landowners increasingly exercised authority in their own regions. Simultaneous invasions from all directions furthered this movement toward localism and decentralization.

In the ninth and tenth centuries, Latin Christendom was attacked on all sides. From bases in North Africa, Spain, and southern Gaul, Muslims ravaged coastal regions of southern Europe. The Magyars, originally from western Asia, had established themselves on the plains of the Danube; their horsemen launched lightning raids into northern Italy, western Germany, and parts of France. Defeated in Germany in 933 and again in 955, the Magyars withdrew to what is now Hungary; they ceased their raids and adopted Christianity.

Still another group of invaders, the Northmen, or Vikings, sailed south from Scandinavia on their long, wooden ships to raid the coasts and river valleys of western Europe. Villages were devastated, ports were destroyed, and the population was decimated. Trade came to a standstill, coins no longer circulated, and farms turned into wastelands. Already gravely weakened, the European economy collapsed. The political authority of kings disappeared, and cultural life and learning withered.

These terrible attacks heightened political insecurity and accelerated anew the process of decentralization that had begun with the decline of Rome. During these chaotic times, counts came to regard as their own the land that they administered and defended for their king. Similarly, the inhabitants of a district looked on the count or local lord as their ruler, for his men and fortresses protected them. In their regions, nobles exercised public power formerly held by kings. Europe had entered an age of feudalism, in which the essential unit of government was not a kingdom, but a county or castellany, and political power was the private possession of local lords.

Feudal Society

Arising during a period of collapsing central authority, invasion, scanty public revenues, and declining commerce and town life, feudalism attempted to provide some order and security. Feudalism was not a planned system derived logically from general principles, but rather an improvised response to the challenge posed by ineffectual central authority. Feudal practices were not uniform; they differed from locality to locality, and in some regions barely took root. Although it was only a stopgap means of governing, feudalism did bring some order, justice, and law during an era of breakdown, localism, and transition. It remained the predominant political arrangement until kings reasserted their authority in the High and Late Middle Ages.

Vassalage

Feudal relationships enabled lords to increase their military strength. The need for military support was the principal reason for the practice of vassalage, in which a knight, in a solemn ceremony, pledged loyalty to a lord. This feature of feudalism derived from an ancient German ceremony, during which warriors swore personal allegiance to the head of the war-band. Among other things, the vassal gave military service to his lord and received in return a *fief,* which was usually land. This fief was inhabited by peasants, and the crops that they raised provided the vassal with his means of support.

Besides rendering military assistance and supplying knights, the vassal owed several other obligations to his lord in return for the fief and the lord's protection. These duties included sitting in the lord's court and judging cases, such as the breach of feudal agreements between the lord and his other vassals; providing lodgings when the lord traveled through the vassal's territory; giving a gift when the lord's son was knighted or when his eldest daughter married; and raising a ransom should the lord be captured by an enemy.

Generally, both lord and vassal felt honor-bound to abide by the oath of loyalty. It became an accepted custom for a vassal to renounce his loyalty to his lord if the latter failed to protect him from enemies, mistreated him, or increased the vassal's obligations as fixed by the feudal contract. On the other hand, if a vassal did not live up to his obligations, the lord would summon him to his court, where he would be tried for treachery. If found guilty, the vassal could lose his fief and perhaps his life. At times, disputes between vassals and lords erupted into warfare. Because a vassal often held land from more than one lord and sometimes was himself a lord to vassals, situations frequently became awkward, complex, and confusing. On occasion, a vassal had to decide to which lord he owed *liege homage* (prime loyalty).

As feudalism evolved, the king came to be regarded as the chief lord, who had granted fiefs to the great lords, who in turn had divided them into smaller units and regranted them to vassals. Thus, all members of the ruling class, from the lowliest knights to the king, occupied a place in the feudal hierarchy. In theory, the king was the highest political authority and the source of land tenure, but in actual fact he was often less powerful than other nobles of the realm. Feudalism would decline when kings converted their theoretical powers into actual powers. The decline of feudalism was a gradual process; conflict between the crown and the aristocracy would persist, with varying degrees of intensity, for several centuries, but the future belonged to the centralized state being shaped by kings, and not to feudal fragmentation.

Feudal Warriors

Feudal lords viewed manual labor and commerce as degrading for men of their rank. They considered only one vocation worthy: that of warrior. Through combat, the lord demonstrated his valor, earned his reputation, measured his individual worth, derived excitement, added to his wealth, and defended his rights. Warfare gave meaning to his life. During the twelfth century, to relieve the boredom of peacetime, nobles staged gala tournaments, in which knights, fighting singly or in teams, engaged each other in battle to prove their skill and courage and to win honor. The feudal glorification of combat became deeply ingrained in Western society and endured into the twentieth century. Over the centuries, a code of behavior, called *chivalry,* evolved for the feudal nobility. A true knight was expected to fight bravely, demonstrate loyalty to his lord, and treat other knights with respect and courtesy.

In time, the church interjected a religious element into the warrior culture of the feudal knight. It sought to use the fighting spirit of the feudal class for Christian ends: knights could assist the clergy in enforcing God's will. Thus, a Christian component was added to the Germanic tradition of loyalty and courage. As a Christian gentleman, a knight was expected to honor the laws of the church and to wield his sword in the service of God.

Regarding the private warfare of lords as lawless violence that menaced social life, the church, in the eleventh century, imposed strictures called the

Portrait of a Convent. During the Middle Ages, it was believed that monks and nuns best exemplified the Christian way of life. In this scene from a convent, the abbess is holding a pastoral staff. *(British Library)*

Peace of God and the Truce of God. These restrictions limited feudal warfare to certain days of the week and certain times of the year. Although only relatively effective, the Peace of God did offer Christian society some respite from plundering and incessant warfare.

Noblewomen

Feudal society was very much a man's world. In theory, women were deemed to be physically, morally, and intellectually inferior to men; in practice, they were subjected to male authority. Fathers arranged the marriages of their daughters. Girls from aristocratic families were generally married at age sixteen or younger to men often twice their age; frequently, aristocratic girls who did not marry had to enter a convent. The wife of the lord was at the mercy of her husband; if she annoyed him, she might expect a beating. But as the lady of the castle, she performed important duties. She assigned tasks to the servants; made medicines; preserved food; taught young girls how to sew, spin, and weave; and despite her subordinate position, took charge of the castle when her husband was away. Although the church taught that both men and women were precious to God and that marriage was a sacred rite, some clergymen viewed women as agents of the Devil—evil temptresses who, like the biblical Eve, lured men into sin.

Agrarian Society

Feudalism was built on an economic foundation known as *manorialism*. Although pockets of free peasantry remained, a village community (manor) consisting of serfs bound to the land became the essential agricultural arrangement for much of the Middle Ages. The manorial village was the means of organizing an agricultural society with limited markets and money. Neither the lords who warred nor the clergymen who prayed performed economically productive work. Their ways of life were made possible by the toil of serfs.

The origins of manorialism can be traced in part to the Late Roman Empire, when peasants depended on the owners of large estates for protection and security. This practice developed further during the Early Middle Ages, especially during the invasions of Northmen, Magyars, and Muslims in the ninth and tenth centuries. Peasants continued to sacrifice their freedom in exchange for protection; in some cases, they were too weak to resist the encroachments of local magnates. Like feudalism, manorialism was not a neat system; it consisted of improvised relationships and practices that varied from region to region.

A lord controlled at least one manorial village; great lords might possess hundreds. A small manor had a dozen families; a large one had as many as fifty or sixty. The manorial village was never completely self-sufficient because salt, millstones, and metalware were generally obtained from outside sources. It did, however, constitute a balanced economic setting. Peasants grew grain and raised cattle, sheep, goats, and hogs; blacksmiths, carpenters, and stonemasons did the building and repairing; the village priest cared for the souls of the inhabitants; and the lord defended the manor and administered the customary law. The serf and his family lived in a dismal, one-room cottage, which they shared with chickens and pigs. In the center burned a small fire, the smoke escaping through a hole in the roof. In cold weather when the fire was strong, the room was filled with smoke. When it rained, water came through the thatched roof and turned the earth floor into mud. The odor from animal excrement was ever present.

When a manor was attacked by another lord, the peasants found protection inside the walls of their lord's house. By the twelfth century, in many places this building had become a well-fortified stone castle. Peasants generally lived, worked, and died on the lord's estate and were buried in the village churchyard. Few had any contact with the world beyond the village of their birth.

In return for protection and the right to cultivate fields and to pass these holdings on to their children, the serfs owed obligations to their lord, and their personal freedom was restricted in a variety of ways. Bound to the land, they could not leave the manor without the lord's consent. Before a serf could marry, he had to obtain the lord's permission and pay a fee. The lord could select a wife for his serf and force him to marry her. Sometimes, a serf, objecting to the lord's choice, preferred to pay a fine. These rules also applied to the serf's children, who inherited their parents' obligations. In addition to working their allotted land, the serfs had to tend the fields reserved for the lord. Other services exacted by the lord included digging ditches, gathering firewood, building fences, repairing roads and bridges, and sewing clothes. Probably somewhat more than half of a serf's workweek was devoted to fulfilling these labor obligations. Serfs also paid a variety of dues to the lord, including payments for using the lord's mill, bake-oven, and winepress.

Serfs did derive some benefits from manorial relationships. They received protection during a chaotic era, and they possessed customary rights, which the lord often respected, to cottages and farmlands. If a lord demanded more services or dues than was customary, or if he interfered with their right to cottages or strips of farmland, the peasants might demonstrate their discontent by refusing to labor for the lord. Until the fourteenth century, however, open rebellion was rare because lords possessed considerable military and legal power. The manorial system promoted attitudes of dependency and servility among the serfs; their hopes for a better life were directed toward heaven.

Economic Expansion During the High Middle Ages

Manorialism and feudalism presupposed a hierarchical, organic, and stable social order: clergy who prayed, lords who fought, and peasants who toiled. People believed that society functioned smoothly when all individuals accepted their status and performed their proper role. Consequently, a person's rights, duties, and relationship to law depended on his or her ranking in the social order. To change position was to upset the organic unity of society. And no one, serfs included, should be deprived of the traditional rights associated with his or her rank. This arrangement was justified by the clergy, who maintained that "God himself has willed that among men, some must be lords and some serfs."[2]

During the High Middle Ages (1050–1300), however, the revival of urban economy and the reemergence of central authority undermined feudal and manorial relationships. By the end of the eleventh century, Europe showed many signs of recovery. The invasions of Magyars and Vikings had ended, and powerful lords and kings imposed greater order in their territories. A period of economic vitality, the High Middle Ages witnessed an agricultural revolution, a commercial revolution, the rebirth of towns, and the rise of an enterprising and dynamic middle class.

An Agricultural Revolution

Important advances were made in agriculture during the Middle Ages. Many of these innovations occurred in the Early Middle Ages but were only gradually adopted and not used everywhere. In time, however, they markedly increased production. By the end of the thirteenth century, medieval agriculture had reached a technical level far superior to that of the ancient world.

One innovation was a heavy plow, which cut deeply into the soil. This new plow enabled farmers to work more quickly and effectively. As a result, they could cultivate more land, including the heavy, moist soils of northern Europe, which had offered too much resistance to the light plow. Another important advance in agricultural technology was the invention of the collar harness. The old yoke harness worked well with oxen, but it tended to choke horses—and horses, because they move faster and have greater stamina than oxen, are more valuable for agricultural work. The widening use of the water mill by the tenth century and the introduction of windmills in the twelfth century saved labor in grinding grain; these inventions replaced ancient hand-worked mills.

The gradual emergence of the three-field system of managing agricultural land, particularly in northern Europe, increased production. In the old, widely used two-field system, half the land was planted in autumn with winter wheat, while the other half was left fallow to restore its fertility. In the new three-field system, one third of the land was planted in autumn with winter wheat, a second third was planted the following spring with oats and vegetables, and the last third remained fallow. The advantages of the three-field system were that two-thirds of the land was farmed and only one-third left unused and that the diversification of crops made more vegetable protein available.

Higher agricultural production reduced the number of deaths from starvation and dietary disease and thus contributed to a population increase. Soon the farmlands of a manorial village could not support its growing population. Consequently, peasants had to look beyond their immediate surroundings and colonize trackless wastelands. Lords vigorously promoted this conversion of uncultivated soil into agricultural land because it increased their incomes. Monastic communities also actively engaged in this enterprise. Almost everywhere, peasants were draining swamps, clearing forests, and establishing new villages. Their endeavors during the eleventh and twelfth centuries brought vast areas of Europe under cultivation for the first time. New agricultural land was also acquired through expansion, the most notable example being the organized settlement of lands to the east by German colonists.

The colonizing and cultivation of virgin lands contributed to the decline of serfdom. Lords owned vast tracts of forests and swamps that would substantially increase their incomes if cleared, drained, and farmed. But serfs were often unwilling to move from their customary homes and fields to do the hard labor needed to cultivate these new lands. To lure serfs away from their villages, lords promised them freedom from most or all personal services. In many cases, the settlers fulfilled their obligations to the lord by paying rent rather than by performing services or providing foodstuffs, thus making the transition from serfs to freemen. In time, they came to regard the land as their own.

The improvement in agricultural technology and the colonization of new lands altered the conditions of life in Europe. Surplus food and the increase in population freed people to work at nonfarming occupations, making possible the expansion of trade and the revival of town life.

The Revival of Trade

Expanding agricultural production, the end of Viking attacks, greater political stability, and an increasing population brought about a revival of commerce. During the Early Middle Ages, Italians and Jews kept alive a small amount of long-distance trade between Catholic Europe and the Byzantine and Islamic worlds. In the eleventh century, sea forces of Italian trading cities cleared the Mediterranean of Muslim fleets that preyed on Italian shipping. As in Roman times, goods could circulate once again from one end of the sea to the other. In the twelfth and thirteenth centuries, local, regional, and long-distance trade gained such momentum that some historians describe the period as a commercial revolution that surpassed the commercial activity of the Roman Empire during the Pax Romana.

Crucial to the growth of trade were international fairs, where merchants and craftspeople set up stalls and booths to display their wares. Because of ever present robbers, lords provided protection for merchants carrying their wares to and from fairs. Each fair lasted about three to six weeks; then the merchants would move on to another site. The Champagne region in northeastern France was the great center for fairs.

The principal arteries of trade flowed between the eastern Mediterranean and the Italian cities; between Scandinavia and the Atlantic coast; between northern France, Flanders, and England; and from the Baltic Sea in the north to the Black Sea and Constantinople via Russian rivers.

Increased economic activity led to advances in business techniques. Since individual businessmen often lacked sufficient capital for large-scale enterprises, groups of merchants formed partnerships. By enabling merchants to pool their capital, reduce their risks, and expand their knowledge of profit-making opportunities, these arrangements furthered commerce. Underwriters insured cargoes; the development of banking and credit instruments made it unnecessary for merchants to carry large amounts of cash. The international fairs not only were centers of international trade, but also served as capital markets for international credit transactions. The arrangements made by fair-going merchants to settle their debts were the origin of the bill of exchange, which allowed one currency to be converted into another. The invention of double-entry bookkeeping gave merchants an overview of their financial situation: the value of their goods and their ready cash. Without such knowledge, no large-scale commercial activity could be conducted on a continuous basis.

Another improvement in business techniques was the formation of commercial law, which defined the rules of conduct for debts and contracts.

The Rise of Towns

In the eleventh century, towns emerged anew throughout Europe, and in the twelfth, they became active centers of commercial and intellectual life. Towns were a new and revolutionary force—socially, economically, and culturally. A new class of merchants and craftspeople came into being. This new class—the middle class—was made up of those who, unlike the lords and serfs, were not affiliated with the land. The townsman was a new man with a different value system from that of the lord, the serf, and the clergyman.

One reason for town growth was the increased food supply stemming from advances in agricultural technology. Surplus farm production meant that the countryside could support an urban population of artisans and professionals. Another reason for the rise of urban centers was the expansion of trade. Towns emerged in locations that were natural for trade: seacoasts, riverbanks, crossroads, and market sites; they also sprang up outside fortified castles and monasteries and on surviving Roman sites. The colonies of merchants who gathered at these places were joined by peasants skilled in crafts or willing to work as laborers. Most towns had a small population. The largest ones—Florence, Ghent, and Paris—had between fifty thousand and a hundred thousand inhabitants. Covering only small areas, these walled towns were crowded with people.

Merchants and artisans organized guilds to protect their members from outside competition. The merchant guild in a town prevented outsiders from doing much business. A craftsman new to a town had to be admitted to the guild of his trade before he could open a shop. Competition between members of the same guild was discouraged. To prevent one guild member from making significantly more money than another, a guild required its members to work the same number of hours, pay employees the same wages, produce goods of equal quality, and charge customers a just price. These rules were strictly enforced.

Women took an active part in the economic life of towns, working with men, usually their husbands, in the various crafts—as cobblers, tailors, hatters, bakers, goldsmiths, and so forth. Women brewed beer, made and sold charcoal, sold vegetables, fish, and poultry, and ran inns. In many towns, the wives and widows of master craftsmen were admitted to guilds. These guildswomen had many of the privileges of a master, including the right to train apprentices.

Because many towns were situated on land belonging to lords or on the sites of old Roman towns ruled by bishops, these communities at first came under feudal authority. In some instances, lords encouraged the founding of towns, for urban industry and commerce brought wealth to the region. However, tensions soon developed between merchants, who sought freedom from feudal restrictions, since they interfered with their pursuit of financial gain, and lords and bishops, who wanted to preserve their authority over the towns. Townspeople, or burghers, refused to be treated as serfs bound to a lord and liable for personal services and customary dues. The burghers wanted to travel, trade, marry, and dispose of their property as they pleased; they wanted to make their own laws and levy their own taxes. Sometimes by fighting, but more often by payments of money, the townspeople obtained charters from the lords giving them the right to set up their own councils. These assemblies passed laws, collected taxes, and formed courts that enforced the laws. Towns became more or less self-governing city-states, the first since Greco-Roman days.

In a number of ways, towns loosened the hold of lords on serfs. Seeking freedom and fortune, serfs fled to the new towns, where, according to custom, lords could no longer reclaim them after a year and a day. Enterprising serfs earned money by selling food to the townspeople. When they acquired a sufficient sum, they bought their freedom from lords, who needed cash to pay for goods bought from merchants. Lords increasingly began to accept fixed cash payments from serfs in place of labor services or foodstuffs. As serfs met their obligations to lords with money, they gradually became rent-paying tenants and, in time, were no longer bound to the lord's land. The manorial system of personal relations and mutual obligations was disintegrating.

The activities of townspeople made them a new breed; they engaged in business and had money and freedom. Their world was the market rather than the church, the castle, or the manor. Townspeople were freeing themselves from the prejudices both of feudal aristocrats, who considered trade and manual work degrading, and of the clergy, who cursed the pursuit of riches as an obstacle to salvation. The townspeople were critical, dynamic, and progressive—a force for change. Medieval towns nurtured the origins of the *bourgeoisie* (literally, "citizens of the burg," the walled town), the urban middle class, which would play a crucial role in modern European history.

The Rise of States

The revival of trade and the growth of towns were signs of the vitality of Latin Christendom. Another sign of strength was the greater order and security provided by the emergence of states. Aided by educated and trained officials who enforced royal law, tried people in royal courts, and collected royal taxes, kings expanded their territory and slowly fashioned strong central governments. These developments laid the foundations of European states. Not all areas followed the same pattern. Whereas England and France achieved a large measure of unity during the Middle Ages, Germany and Italy remained divided into numerous independent territories.

England

In 1066, the Normans—those Northmen who had first raided and then settled in France—conquered Anglo-Saxon England. Determined to establish effective control over his new kingdom, William the Conqueror (1027–1087), duke of Normandy, kept a sixth of conquered England for himself. In accordance with feudal practice, he distributed the rest among his Norman nobles, who swore an oath of loyalty to William and provided him with military assistance. But William made certain that no feudal baron had enough land or soldiers to threaten his power. Because he had conquered England in one stroke, his successors did not have to travel the long, painful road to national unity that French monarchs had to take.

To strengthen royal control, William retained some Anglo-Saxon administrative practices. The land remained divided into *shires* (counties) administered by *sheriffs* (royal agents). This structure gave the king control over local government. To determine how much money he could demand, William ordered a vast census to be taken of people and property in every village. These data were compiled in the *Domesday Book,* which listed the number of tenants, cattle, sheep, and pigs and the quantities of farm equipment throughout the realm. Thus, William knew his kingdom's assets better than any other monarch of his day.

A crucial development in shaping national unity was the emergence of common law. During the reigns of Henry I (1100–1135) and Henry II (1154–1189), royal judges traveled to different parts of the kingdom. Throughout England, important cases began to be tried in the king's court rather than in local courts, thereby increasing royal power. The decisions of royal judges were recorded and used as guides for future cases. In this way, a law common to the whole land gradually came to prevail over the customary law of a specific locality. Because common law applied to all England, it served as a force for unity. It also provided a fairer system of justice. Common law remains the foundation of the English legal system and the legal systems of lands settled by English people, including the United States.

Henry II made trial by jury a regular procedure for many cases heard in the king's court, thus laying the foundations of the modern judicial system. Twelve men familiar with the facts of the case appeared before the king's justices and under oath were asked if the plaintiff's statement was true. The justices based their decisions on the answers. Henry II also ordered representatives of a given locality to report under oath to visiting royal judges any local persons who were suspected of murder or robbery. This indictment jury was the ancestor of the modern grand jury system.

King John (1199–1216) inadvertently precipitated a situation that led to another step in the political development of England. Fighting a costly and losing war with the king of France, John coerced his vassals into giving him more and more revenue; he had also punished some vassals without a proper trial. In 1215, the angry barons rebelled and compelled John to fix his seal to a document called the *Magna Carta,* or Great Charter. The Magna Carta is

The Battle of Hastings A.D. **1066: Scene from the Bayeux Tapestry, France, Eleventh Century.**   This battle sealed the conquest of England by William, Duke of Normandy. The French-speaking Normans now governed the native Anglo-Saxons; eventually both Normans and Anglo-Saxons fused into a single people, the English. The Bayeux Tapestry depicted seventy scenes of the conquest and is significant as both a work of art and a historical source. (*Tapisserie de la Reine Mathilde, Ville de Bayeux, France*)

celebrated as the root of the unique English respect for basic rights and liberties. Although essentially a feudal document directed against a king who had violated the rights of feudal barons, the Magna Carta stated certain principles that could be interpreted more widely.

Over the centuries, these principles were expanded to protect the liberties of the English against governmental oppression. The Magna Carta stated that no unusual feudal dues "shall be imposed in our kingdom except by the common consent of our kingdom." In time, this right came to mean that the king could not levy taxes without the consent of Parliament, the governmental body that represents the English people. The Magna Carta also provided that "no freeman shall be taken or imprisoned . . . save by the lawful judgment of his peers or by the law of the land." The barons who drew up the document had intended it to mean that they must be tried by fellow barons. As time passed, these words were regarded as a guarantee of trial by jury for all men, a prohibition against arbitrary arrest, and a command to dispense justice fully, freely, and equally. Implied in the Magna Carta is the idea that the king cannot rule as he pleases but must govern according to the law—that not even the king can violate the law of the nation. Centuries afterward, when Englishmen sought to limit the king's power, they would interpret the Magna Carta in this way.

Anglo-Saxon England had retained the Germanic tradition that the king should consider the advice of the leading men in the land. Later, William the Conqueror continued this practice by seeking the opinions of leading nobles and bishops. In the thirteenth century, it became accepted custom that the king should not decide major issues without consulting these advisers, who assembled in the Great Council. Lesser nobility and townspeople also began to be summoned to meet with the king. These two groups were eventually called the House of Lords (bishops and nobles) and the House of Commons (knights and burghers). Thus, the English Parliament evolved; by the mid-fourteenth century, it had become a permanent institution of government. Frequently in need of money but unable to levy new taxes without the approval of Parliament, the king had to turn to that body for help. Over the centuries, Parliament would use this control over money matters to increase its power. The tradition grew that the power to govern rested not with the king alone, but with the king and Parliament together.

During the Middle Ages, England became a centralized and unified state. The king, however, did not have unlimited power; he was not above the law. The rights of the people were protected by certain principles implicit in the common law, the Magna Carta, and the emergence of Parliament.

France

In the 150 years after Charlemagne's death, the western part of his empire, which was destined to become France, faced terrible ordeals. Charlemagne's heirs fought each other for the crown; the Vikings raided everywhere their ships would carry them; Muslims from Spain plundered the southern coast; and strong lords usurped power for themselves. With the Carolingian family unable to maintain the throne, the great lords bestowed the title of king on one of their own. In 987, they chose Hugh Capet (987–996), the count of Paris. Because many great lords held territories far larger than those of Hugh, the French king did not seem a threat to noble power. But Hugh strengthened the French monarchy by having the lords also elect his son as his coruler. This practice continued until it became understood that the crown would remain with the Capetian family.

With the accession of Louis VI (1108–1137), a two-hundred-year period of steadily increasing royal power began. Louis started this trend by successfully subduing the barons in his own duchy. A decisive figure in the expansion of royal power was Philip Augustus (1180–1223). Philip struck successfully at King John of England (of Magna Carta fame), who held more territory as feudal lord in France than Philip did. When William, duke of Normandy, in western France, conquered England in 1066, he became ruler of England and Normandy; William's great-grandson Henry II acquired much of southern France through his marriage to Eleanor of Aquitaine (c. 1122–1204) in 1152. Thus, as a result of the Norman Conquest and intermarriage, the destinies of France and England were closely intertwined until the end of the Middle Ages. By stripping King John of most of his French territory (Normandy, Anjou, and much of Aquitaine), Philip trebled the size of his kingdom and became stronger than any French lord.

In the thirteenth century, the power of the French monarch continued to grow. Departing from feudal precedent, Louis IX (1226–1270) issued ordinances for the entire realm without seeking the consent of his vassals. Kings added to their lands through warfare and marriage. They also devised new ways of raising money, including taxing the clergy. A particularly effective way of increasing the monarch's power was by extending royal justice; many cases previously tried in lords' courts were transferred to the king's court.

At the beginning of the fourteenth century, Philip IV (the Fair) engaged in a struggle with the papacy. Seeking to demonstrate that he had the support of his subjects, Philip convened a national assembly—the Estates General—representing the clergy, the nobility, and the townspeople. This assembly would be called again to vote funds for the crown. But unlike the English Parliament, the Estates General never became an important body in French political life, and it never succeeded in controlling the monarch. Whereas the basis for limited monarchy had been established in England, no comparable checks on the king's power developed in France. By the end of the Middle Ages, French kings had succeeded in creating a unified state. But regional and local loyalties remained strong and persisted for centuries.

Germany

After the destruction of Charlemagne's empire, its German territories were broken into large duchies. Following an ancient German practice, the ruling dukes elected one of their own as king. The German king, however, had little authority outside his own duchy. Some German kings tried not to antagonize the dukes, but Otto the Great (936–973) was determined to control them. He entered into an alliance with German bishops and archbishops, who could provide him with fighting men and trained administrators—a policy continued by his successors. In 962, emulating the coronation of Charlemagne, the pope crowned Otto "Emperor of the Romans." (Later the title would be changed to Holy Roman Emperor.)

Otto and his successors wanted to dominate Italy and the pope—an ambition that embroiled the Holy Roman emperor in a life-and-death struggle with the papacy. The papacy allied itself with the German dukes and the Italian cities, enemies of the emperor. The intervention in papal and Italian politics was the principal reason that German territories did not achieve unity in the Middle Ages.

The Growth of Papal Power

In the High Middle Ages, a growing spiritual vitality accompanied economic recovery and the increased political stability. It was marked by several developments. Within the church, reform movements were attacking clerical abuses, and the papacy was gaining power. A holy war against the Muslims

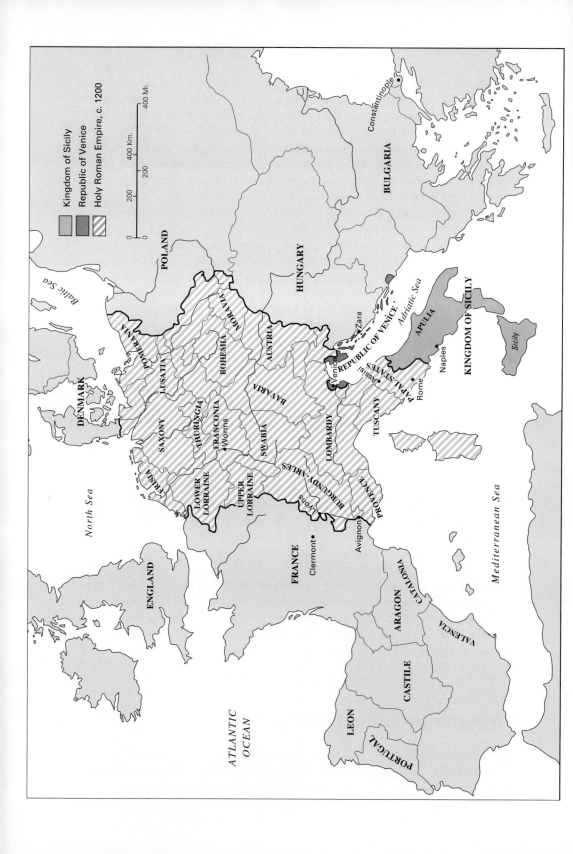

Kingdom of Sicily
Republic of Venice
Holy Roman Empire, c. 1200

400 Mi.
200
0

400 Km.
200
0

Baltic Sea

DENMARK

POMERANIA

North Sea

ENGLAND

FRISIA

SAXONY

LUSATIA

POLAND

THURINGIA

LOWER LORRAINE

FRANCONIA
• Worms

BOHEMIA

MORAVIA

HUNGARY

UPPER LORRAINE

BAVARIA

AUSTRIA

BULGARIA

Constantinople •

ATLANTIC OCEAN

FRANCE

Clermont •

BURGUNDY-ARLES

SWABIA

LOMBARDY

Lyons •

Avignon •

PROVENCE

TUSCANY

REPUBLIC OF VENICE

Venice •

PAPAL STATES

Assisi •

Rome •

Adriatic Sea

Zara •

APULIA

Naples •

KINGDOM OF SICILY

Sicily

Mediterranean Sea

PORTUGAL

LEON

CASTILE

ARAGON

CATALONIA

VALENCIA

was drawing the Christian community closer together. Furthermore, the church tried with great determination to make society follow divine standards: that is, it tried to shape all institutions and cultural expressions according to a comprehensive Christian outlook.

As the sole interpreters of God's revelation and the sole ministers of his sacraments—sacred rites—the clergy imposed and supervised the moral standards of Christendom. Divine grace was channeled through the sacraments, which could be administered only by the clergy, the indispensable intermediary between the individual and God. On those who resisted its authority, the church could impose the penalty of excommunication (expulsion from the church and denial of the sacraments, without which there could be no salvation).

Gregorian Reform

By the tenth century, the church was western Europe's leading landholder, owning perhaps a third of the land in Italy and vast properties in other lands. However, the papacy was in no position to exercise commanding leadership over Latin Christendom. The office of pope had fallen under the domination of aristocratic families; they conspired and on occasion murdered in order to place one of their own on the wealthy and powerful throne of Saint Peter. As the papacy became a prize for Rome's leading families, it was not at all unusual for popes themselves to be involved in conspiracies and assassinations. Also weakening the authority of the papacy were local lords, who dominated churches and monasteries by appointing bishops and abbots and by collecting the income from church taxes. These bishops and abbots, appointed by lords for political reasons, lacked the spiritual devotion to maintain high standards of discipline among the priests and monks.

What raised the power of the papacy to unprecedented heights was the emergence of a reform movement, particularly in French and German monasteries. High-minded monks called for a reawakening of spiritual fervor and the elimination of moral laxity among the clergy. They particularly denounced the concern for worldly goods, the taking of mistresses, and the diminishing commitment to the Benedictine rule. Of the many monasteries that took part in this reform movement, the Benedictine monks of Cluny, in Burgundy, France, were the most influential.

In the middle of the eleventh century, popes came under the influence of the monastic reformers. In 1059, a special synod, convened by the reform-minded Pope Nicholas II, moved to end the interference of Roman nobles and German Holy Roman emperors in choosing the pope. Henceforth, a select group of clergymen in Rome, called *cardinals*, would be responsible for picking a new pontiff.

◄   **Map 6.2**   The Holy Roman Empire, c. 1200

The reform movement found its most zealous exponent in the person of Hildebrand, who became Pope Gregory VII in 1073. For Gregory, human society was part of a divinely ordered universe, governed by God's universal law. As the supreme spiritual leader of Christendom, the pope was charged with the mission of establishing a Christian society on earth. As successor to Saint Peter, the pope had the final word on matters of faith and doctrine. All bishops came under his authority; so did kings, whose powers should be used for Christian ends. The pope was responsible for instructing rulers in the proper use of their God-given powers, and kings had the solemn duty to obey these instructions. If the king failed in his Christian duty, the pope could deny him his right to rule. Responsible for implementing God's law, the pope could never take a subordinate position to kings.

Like no other pope before him, Gregory VII made a determined effort to assert the preeminence of the papacy over both the church hierarchy and secular rulers. This determination led to a bitter struggle between the papacy and the German monarch and future Holy Roman emperor Henry IV. The dispute was a dramatic confrontation between two competing versions of the relationship between secular and spiritual authority.

Through his reforms, Gregory VII intended to improve the moral quality of the clergy and to liberate the church from all control by secular authorities. He forbade priests who had wives or concubines to celebrate Mass, deposed clergy who had bought their offices, excommunicated bishops and abbots who received their estates from a lay lord, and expelled from the church lay lords who invested bishops with their office. The appointment of bishops, Pope Gregory insisted, should be controlled by the church.

This last point touched off the conflict, called the Investiture Controversy, between Henry and Pope Gregory. Bishops served a dual function. On the one hand, they belonged to the spiritual community of the church; on the other, as members of the nobility and holders of estates, they were also integrated into the feudal order. Traditionally, emperors had both granted bishops their feudal authority and invested them with their spiritual authority. In maintaining that no lay rulers could confer ecclesiastical offices on their appointees, Pope Gregory threatened Henry's authority.

Seeking allies in the conflict with feudal nobility in earlier times, German kings had made vassals of the upper clergy. In return for a fief, bishops had agreed to provide troops for a monarch in his struggle against the lords. But if kings had no control over the appointment of bishops—in accordance with Pope Gregory's view—they would lose the allegiance, military support, and financial assistance of their most important allies. To German monarchs, bishops were officers of the state who served the throne. Moreover, by agreeing to Gregory's demands, German kings would lose their freedom of action and be dominated by the Roman pontiff. Henry IV regarded Gregory VII as a fanatic who trampled on custom, meddled in German state affairs, and challenged legitimate rulers established by God, thereby threatening to subordinate kingship to the papacy.

With the approval of the German bishops, Henry called for Pope Gregory to descend from the throne of Saint Peter. Gregory in turn excommunicated

Henry and deposed him as king. German lands were soon embroiled in a civil war, as German lords used the quarrel to strike at Henry's power. Finally, Henry's troops crossed the Alps, successfully attacked Rome, and installed a new pope, who crowned Henry emperor of the Romans. Gregory died in exile in 1085.

In 1122, the papacy and Emperor Henry V reached a compromise. Bishops were to be elected exclusively by the church and to be invested with the staff and the ring—symbols of spiritual power—by the archbishop, not the king. This change signified that the bishop owed his role as spiritual leader to the church only. But the king would grant the bishop the scepter, to indicate that the bishop was also the recipient of a fief and the king's vassal, owing feudal obligations to the crown. This compromise, called the Concordat of Worms, recognized the dual function of the bishop as a spiritual leader in the church and a feudal landowner. Similar settlements had been reached with the kings of France and England several years earlier.

The conflict between the papacy and the German rulers continued after the Concordat of Worms—a contest for supremacy between the heir of Saint Peter and the heir of Charlemagne. German monarchs wanted to control the papacy and the prosperous northern Italian cities. When Frederick I (1152–1190), known as Frederick Barbarossa (Red Beard), tried to assert authority over these cities, they resisted. In 1176, the armies of an alliance of Italian cities, supported by the pope, trounced Frederick's forces at the battle of Legnano. The Italian infantry showed that it could defeat knights on horseback, and Frederick was compelled to recognize the independence of the Italian cities. His numerous expeditions to Italy weakened his authority. German princes strengthened themselves at the expense of the monarchy, thereby continuing to preclude German unity.

The Crusades

Like the movement for spiritual renewal associated with the Cluniac reformers, the Crusades—wars to regain the Holy Land from the Muslims—were an outpouring of Christian zeal and an attempt by the papacy to assert its preeminence. Along with the renewal of commerce and the growth of towns, the Crusades signaled the increased vitality and self-confidence of western Europe. The victims of earlier Muslim attacks, Latin Christians now took the offensive.

The Crusades were also part of a general movement of expansion, which took place in Europe during the High Middle Ages. By the middle of the eleventh century, Genoese and Pisans had driven the Muslims from Sardinia. By 1091, Normans from France had taken Sicily from the Muslims and southern Italy from Byzantium. With the support of the papacy, Christian knights engaged in the long struggle to drive the Muslims from Spain; by 1248, after more than two centuries of conflict, only the small southern kingdom of Granada remained in Muslim hands. Germans conquered and colonized lands south of the Baltic coast inhabited by non-Christian Slavs, Balts, and Prussians. German settlers brought with them Christianity and German

Depiction of the Siege of Tyre in 1124.   The fall of the city gave Christians control of the Syrian coast. (*Biliothèque Nationale*)

language and culture. They cleared vast tracts of virgin land for farming and established towns, bishoprics, and monasteries in a region where urban life had been virtually unknown.

Seeking to regain lands taken from Byzantium by the Seljuk Turks, the Byzantine emperor Alexius appealed to the West for mercenaries. Pope Urban II, at the Council of Clermont (in France) in 1095, exaggerated the danger confronting Eastern Christianity. He called for a holy crusade against the heathen Turks, whom he accused of defiling and destroying Christian churches. A Christian army, mobilized by the papacy to defend the faith and to regain the Holy Land from nonbelievers, accorded with the papal concept of a just war; it would channel the endemic violence of Europe's warrior class in a Christian direction.

What motivated the knights and others who responded to Urban's appeal? No doubt, the Crusaders regarded themselves as armed pilgrims dedicated to rescuing holy places from the hated Muslims. Moreover, Urban declared that participation in a crusade was itself an act of penance, an acceptable way of demonstrating sorrow for sin. To the warrior nobility, a crusade was a great adventure, promising land, glory, and plunder, but it was also an opportunity to remit sins by engaging in a holy war. The enthusiasm with which knights became Christian warriors revealed to what extent Christian principles had permeated the warrior mentality of the nobles.

Stirred by popular preachers, the common people also became gripped by the crusading spirit. The most remarkable of the evangelists was Peter the Hermit. Swayed by this old man's eloquence, thousands of poor people abandoned their villages and joined Peter's march to Jerusalem. After reaching Constantinople, Peter's recruits crossed into Turkish territory, where they were massacred.

An army of Christian knights also departed for Constantinople. In June 1099, three years after leaving Europe, this army stood outside the walls of Jerusalem. Using siege weapons, it broke into the city and slaughtered the Muslim and Jewish inhabitants. Besides capturing Jerusalem, the Crusaders carved out four principalities in the Near East. Never resigned to the establishment of Christian states in their midst, Muslim leaders called for a jihad, or holy war. In 1144, one of the Crusader states, the County of Edessa, fell to the resurgent forces of Islam. Alarmed by the loss of Edessa, Pope Eugenius II called for the Second Crusade, which was a complete failure.

After 1174, Saladin, a brilliant commander, became the most powerful leader in the Muslim Near East. In 1187, he invaded Palestine, annihilating a Christian army near Nazareth and recapturing Jerusalem. This led to the Third Crusade, in which some of Europe's most prominent rulers took part—Richard I, the Lion-Hearted, of England, Philip Augustus of France, and Frederick Barbarossa of Germany. The Crusaders captured Acre and Jaffa, but Jerusalem remained in Muslim hands.

Pope Innocent III, who called the Fourth Crusade (1202–1204), was enraged by the actions of the Crusaders. They had first attacked the Christian port of Zara, controlled by the king of Hungary, and then looted and defiled churches and massacred Byzantines in Constantinople. This shameful behavior, along with the belief that the papacy was exploiting the crusading ideal to extend its own power, weakened both the crusading zeal of Christendom and the moral authority of the papacy. Other Crusades followed, but the position of the Christian states in the Near East continued to deteriorate. In 1291, almost two centuries after Pope Urban's appeal, the last Christian strongholds in the Near East fell.

The Crusades increased the wealth of the Italian cities that furnished transportation for the Crusaders and benefited from the increased trade with the East. They may have contributed to the decline of feudalism and the strengthening of monarchy because many lords were killed in battle or squandered their wealth financing expeditions to the Holy Land. Over the centuries, some have praised the Crusades for inspiring idealism and heroism. Others, however, have castigated the movement for corrupting the Christian spirit and unleashing religious intolerance and fanaticism—including the massacre of Jews in the Rhineland and of Muslims and Jews in Jerusalem—which would lead to strife in future centuries.

Dissenters and Reformers

Freedom of religion is a modern concept; it was totally alien to the medieval outlook. Regarding itself as the possessor and guardian of divine truth, the church felt a profound obligation to purge Christendom of heresy—beliefs that challenged Christian orthodoxy. To the church, heretics had committed treason against God and were carriers of a deadly infection. Heresy was the work of Satan; lured by false ideas, people might abandon the true faith and deny themselves salvation. In the eyes of the church, heretics not only obstructed individual salvation, but also undermined the foundations of society.

To compel obedience, the church used its power of excommunication. An excommunicated person could not receive the sacraments or attend church services—fearful punishments in an age of faith. In dealing with a recalcitrant ruler, the church could declare an interdict on his territory, which in effect denied the ruler's subjects the sacraments (although exceptions could be made). The church hoped that the pressure exerted by an aroused populace would compel the offending ruler to mend his ways.

The church also conducted heresy trials. Before the thirteenth century, local bishops were responsible for finding heretics and putting them on trial. In 1233, the papacy established the Inquisition, a court specially designed to fight heresy. The accused were presumed guilty until proven innocent; they were not told the names of their accusers, nor could they have legal defense. To wrest a confession from the accused, torture (which had been sanctioned by Roman law) was permitted. Those who persisted in their beliefs might be turned over to the civil authorities to be burned at the stake.

The Waldensians   Dissent in the Middle Ages was often reformist in character. Inspired by the Gospels, reformers criticized the church for its wealth and involvement in worldly affairs. They called for a return to the simpler, purer life of Jesus and the Apostles.

In their zeal to emulate the moral purity and material poverty of the first followers of Jesus, these reform-minded dissenters attacked ecclesiastical authority. The Waldensians, followers of Peter Waldo, a rich merchant of Lyons, were a case in point. In the 1170s, Peter distributed his property to the poor and attracted both male and female supporters. Like their leader, they committed themselves to poverty and to preaching the Gospel in the vernacular, or native tongue, rather than in the church's Latin, which many Christians did not understand.

The Waldensians considered themselves true Christians, faithful to the spirit of the apostolic church. Repelled by Waldensian attacks against the immorality of the clergy and by the fact that these laypeople were preaching the Gospel without the permission of ecclesiastical authorities, the church condemned the movement as heretical. Despite persecution, however, the Waldensians continued to survive as a group in northern Italy.

The Cathari   Catharism was the most radical heresy to confront the medieval church. This belief represented a curious mixture of Eastern religious movements that had competed with Christianity in the days of the Roman Empire. Cathari tenets differed considerably from those of the church. The Cathari believed in an eternal conflict between the forces of the god of good and those of the god of evil. Because the evil god, whom they identified with the God of the Old Testament, had created the world, this earthly home was evil. The soul, spiritual in nature, was good, but it was trapped in wicked flesh.

The Cathari taught that, since the flesh is evil, Christ would not have taken a human form; hence, he could not have suffered on the cross or have been resurrected. Nor could God have issued forth from the evil flesh of the Virgin. According to Catharism, Jesus was not God but an angel. In order to enslave people, the evil god created the church, which demonstrated its wickedness by pursuing power and wealth. Repudiating the church, the Cathari organized their own ecclesiastical hierarchy.

The center for the Catharist heresy was southern France, where a strong tradition of protest existed against the moral laxity and materialism of the clergy. When the Cathari did not submit to peaceful persuasion, Innocent III called on kings and lords to exterminate Catharism with the sword. Lasting from 1208 to 1229, the war against the Cathari was marked by brutality and fanaticism. Under Innocent's successor, Dominican and Franciscan inquisitors completed the task of exterminating them.

The Franciscans and the Dominicans   Driven by a zeal for reform, devout laypeople condemned the clergy for moral abuses. Sometimes, their piety and resentment exploded into heresy; at other times, it was channeled into movements that served the church. Such was the case with the two great orders of friars, the Franciscans and the Dominicans.

Like Peter Waldo, Saint Francis of Assisi (c. 1181–1226) came from a wealthy merchant family. After undergoing an intense religious experience, Francis abandoned his possessions and devoted his life to imitating Christ. Dressed as a beggar, he wandered into villages and towns, preaching, healing, and befriending the poor, the helpless, the sick, and even lepers, whom everyone feared to approach. The saintly Francis soon attracted disciples, called Little Brothers, who followed in their leader's footsteps.

As the Franciscans grew in popularity, the papacy exercised greater control over their activities. In time, the order was transformed from a spontaneous movement of inspired laymen into an organized agent of papal policy. The Franciscans served the church as teachers and missionaries in eastern Europe, North Africa, the Near East, and China. The papacy set aside Francis's prohibition against the Brothers owning churches, houses, and lands corporately. His desire to keep the movement a lay order was abandoned when the papacy granted the Brothers the right to hear confession. Francis's opposition to formal learning as irrelevant to preaching Gospel love was rejected when the movement began to urge university education for its members. Those who protested against these changes as a repudiation of Francis's spirit were persecuted, and a few were even burned at the stake as heretics.

The Dominican order was founded by Saint Dominic (c. 1170–1221), a Spanish nobleman, who had preached against the Cathari in southern France. Believing that those who were well versed in Christian teaching could best combat heresy, Dominic, unlike Francis, insisted that his followers engage in study. Eventually, Dominicans became some of the leading theologians in the universities. Like the Franciscans, they went out into the world to preach the Gospel and to proselytize. Dominican friars became the chief operators of the Inquisition. For their zeal in fighting heresy, they were known as the hounds of the Lord.

Innocent III: The Apex of Papal Power

During the pontificate of Innocent III (1198–1216), papal theocracy reached its zenith. More than any earlier pope, Innocent made the papacy the center of European political life; in the tradition of Gregory VII, he forcefully asserted the theory of papal monarchy. As head of the church, Vicar of Christ, and successor of Saint Peter, Innocent claimed the authority to intervene in the internal affairs of secular rulers when they threatened the good order of Christendom. According to Innocent, the pope, "lower than God but higher than man . . . judges all and is judged by no one."[3]

Innocent applied these principles of papal supremacy in his dealings with the princes of Europe. When King Philip Augustus of France repudiated Ingeborg of Denmark the day after their wedding and later divorced her to marry someone else, Innocent placed an interdict on France to compel Philip to take Ingeborg back. For two decades, Innocent III championed Ingeborg's cause, until she finally became the French queen. When King John of England rejected the papal candidate for archbishop of Canterbury, Stephen Langton, Innocent first laid an interdict on the country. Then he excommunicated John, who expressed his defiance by confiscating church property and by forcing many bishops into exile. However, when Innocent urged Philip Augustus of France to invade England, John backed down.

Innocent called the Fourth Crusade against the Muslims and a crusade against the heretical Cathari. The culminating expression of Innocent's supremacy was the Fourth Lateran Council, convened in 1215. Comprising some twelve hundred clergy and representatives of secular rulers, the council issued several far-reaching decrees. It maintained that the Eastern Orthodox church was subordinate to the Roman Catholic church. It prohibited the state from taxing the clergy and declared laws detrimental to the church null and void. It also made bishops responsible for ferreting out heretics in their dioceses and ordered secular authorities to punish convicted heretics. Furthermore, the council insisted on high standards of behavior for the clergy and required each Catholic to confess his or her sins to a priest at least once a year.

Christians and Jews

In their relations with heretics, pagans, and Muslims, medieval Christians demonstrated a narrow and hostile attitude, which ran counter to the Gospel message that all human beings were children of God and that Christ had suffered for all humanity. Muslims were seen, in the words of Pope Urban II, as a "vile breed," "infidels," and "enemies of God."

Medieval Christians also showed hatred for Jews—a visibly alien group in a society dominated by the Christian world-view. In 1096, bands of Crusaders massacred Jews in French and German towns. In 1290, Jews were expelled from England, and in 1306 from France. Between 1290 and 1293, expulsions, massacres, and forced conversions led to the virtual disappearance of a centuries-old Jewish community life in southern Italy. In Germany, savage riots periodically led to the torture and murder of Jews.

Several factors contributed to anti-Jewish feelings during the Middle Ages. To medieval Christians, the refusal of the Jews to embrace Christianity was an act of wickedness, particularly since the church taught that the coming of Christ had been prophesied by the Old Testament. Related to this prejudice was the portrayal of the Crucifixion in the Gospels. In the minds of medieval Christians, the crime of deicide—the killing of God—eternally tainted the Jews as a people. The flames of hatred were fanned by the absurd allegation that Jews, made bloodthirsty by the spilling of Christ's blood, tortured and murdered Christians, particularly children, to obtain blood for ritual purposes. This blood libel was widely believed and incited numerous riots, which led to the murder, torture, and expulsion of countless Jews, despite the fact that popes condemned the charge as groundless.

The role of Jews as moneylenders also provoked animosity toward them. Increasingly excluded from international trade and most professions, barred from the guilds, and in some areas from landholding as well, Jews found that virtually the only means of livelihood open to them was moneylending. This activity, which was in theory forbidden to Christians, aroused the hatred of individual peasants, clergy, lords, and kings who did the borrowing.

The policy of the church toward the Jews was that they should not be harmed, but that they should live in humiliation, a fitting punishment for their act of deicide and continued refusal to embrace Christianity. Thus, the Fourth Lateran Council barred Jews from public office, required them to wear a distinguishing badge on their clothing, and ordered them to remain off the streets during Christian festivals. Christian art, literature, and religious instruction depicted the Jews in a derogatory manner, often identifying them with the Devil, who was very real and very terrifying to medieval Christians. Such people deserved no mercy, reasoned medieval Christians. Indeed, nothing was too bad for them. Deeply etched into the minds and hearts of Christians, the distorted image of the Jew as a contemptible creature persisted in the European mentality into the twentieth century.

Despite their precarious position, medieval Jews maintained their faith, expanded their tradition of biblical and legal scholarship, and developed a flourishing Hebrew literature. The work of Jewish translators, doctors, and philosophers contributed substantially to the flowering of medieval culture in the High Middle Ages.

The foremost Jewish scholar of the Middle Ages was Moses ben Maimon (1135–1204), also called by the Greek name Maimonides. He was born in Córdoba, Spain, then under Muslim rule. After his family emigrated from Spain, Maimonides went to Egypt, where he became physician to the sultan. During his lifetime, Maimonides achieved fame as a philosopher, theologian, mathematician, and physician. He was recognized as the leading Jewish sage of his day, and his writings were respected by Christian and Muslim thinkers as well. Like Christian and Muslim philosophers, Maimonides sought to harmonize faith with reason, to reconcile the Hebrew Scriptures and the Talmud (Jewish biblical commentary) with Greek philosophy. In his writings on ethical themes, Maimonides demonstrated piety, wisdom, and humanity.

Notes

1. The Koran, trans. N. J. Dawood (Baltimore: Penguin Books, 1961), pp. 108–109.
2. Quoted in V. H. H. Green, *Medieval Civilization in Western Europe* (New York: St. Martin's Press, 1971), p. 35.
3. Excerpted in Brian Tierney, ed., *The Crisis of Church and State, 1050–1300* (Englewood Cliffs, N.J.: Prentice-Hall, 1964), p. 132.

Suggested Reading

Bark, W. C., *Origins of the Medieval World* (1960). The Early Middle Ages as a fresh beginning.

Dawson, Christopher, *The Making of Europe* (1957). Stresses the role of Christianity in shaping European civilization.

Gies, Frances, and Joseph Gies, *Women in the Middle Ages* (1978). The narrative weaves in valuable quotations from medieval sources.

———, *Life in a Medieval Castle* (1974). The castle as the center of medieval life; passages from journals, songs, and account books permit medieval people to speak for themselves.

Herrin, Judith, *The Formation of Christendom* (1987). The transition from antiquity to the Middle Ages.

Holmes, George, ed., *The Oxford History of Medieval Europe* (1988). Essays by several scholars; good opening essay on transformation of the Roman world.

Laistner, M. L. W., *Thought and Letters in Western Europe* A.D. 500 to 900 (1957). A comprehensive survey of European thought in the Early Middle Ages.

Lewis, A. R., *Emerging Medieval Europe* (1967). Good discussions of economic and social changes.

Lewis, Bernard, *The Arabs in History* (1966). A valuable survey.

Lopez, R. S., *The Commercial Revolution of the Middle Ages, 950–1350* (1976). How an undeveloped society succeeded in developing itself.

Lucas, Angela M., *Women in the Middle Ages* (1983). Women and religion, marriage, and letters.

Mayer, H. E., *The Crusades* (1972). A short, scholarly treatment.

Pounds, N. J. G., *An Economic History of Medieval Europe* (1974). A lucid survey.

Rorig, Fritz, *The Medieval Town* (1971). A study of medieval urban life.

Trachtenberg, Joshua, *The Devil and the Jews* (1961). The medieval conception of the Jew and its relationship to modern anti-Semitism.

White, Lynn, Jr., *Medieval Technology and Social Change* (1964). A study of medieval advances in technology.

Zacour, Norman, *An Introduction to Medieval Institutions* (1969). Comprehensive essays on all phases of medieval society.

Review Questions

1. What was the long-term influence of Byzantium on world history?
2. Characterize and discuss the significance of the Muslim intellectual achievement.
3. The civilization of Latin Christendom was a blending of Christian, Greco-Roman, and Germanic traditions. Explain this statement.
4. What was the significance of monks and nuns to medieval civilization?
5. What crucial developments occurred during the reign of Charlemagne? Why were they important?
6. What conditions led to the rise of feudalism? How did feudal law differ from Roman law?
7. What advances in agriculture occurred during the Middle Ages, and what effect did they have?
8. What factors contributed to the rise of towns? What was the significance of the medieval town?
9. Identify the following and explain their importance: William the Conqueror, common law, Magna Carta, and Parliament.
10. Why did Germany fail to achieve unity during the Middle Ages?
11. What prompted Urban II to call a crusade against the Turks? What caused lords and commoners to go on a crusade? What was the final importance and outcome of the Crusades?
12. Why did the church regard Waldensians and Cathari as heretics?
13. What factors contributed to the rise of anti-Semitism during the Middle Ages? How does anti-Semitism demonstrate the power of mythical thinking?
14. The High Middle Ages showed many signs of recovery and vitality. Discuss this statement.

❖ CHAPTER 7

The Flowering and Dissolution of Medieval Civilization

*E*urope in the High Middle Ages showed considerable vitality. The population increased, long-distance trade revived, new towns emerged, states started to take shape, and papal power grew. The culminating expression of this recovery and resurgence was the cultural flowering in philosophy, the visual arts, and literature. Creative intellects achieved on a cultural level what the papacy accomplished on an institutional level: the integration of life around a Christian viewpoint. The High Middle Ages saw the restoration of some of the learning of the ancient world, the rise of universities, the emergence of an original form of architecture (the Gothic), and the erection of an imposing system of thought, called *scholasticism*. Medieval theologian-philosophers fashioned Christian teachings into an all-embracing philosophy, which represented the spiritual essence, the distinctive style of medieval civilization. They perfected what Christian thinkers in the Roman Empire had initiated and what the learned men of the Early Middle Ages had been groping for: a synthesis of Greek philosophy and Christian revelation.   ❖

Revival of Learning

In the late eleventh century, Latin Christendom began to experience a cultural revival; all areas of life showed vitality and creativeness. In the twelfth and thirteenth centuries, a rich civilization with a distinctive style united the educated elite in the lands from Britain to Sicily. Gothic cathedrals, an enduring testament to the creativity of the religious impulse, were erected throughout Europe. Universities sprang up in many cities. Roman authors were again read and their style imitated. The quality of written Latin—the language of the church, learning, and education—improved, and secular and religious poetry, both in Latin and in the vernacular, abounded. Roman law emerged anew in Italy, spread to northern Europe, and regained its importance (lost since Roman times) as worthy of study and scholarship. Some key works of ancient Greece were translated into Latin and studied in universities. Employ-

---

Chronology 7.1 ❖ The High and Late Middle Ages

c. 1100	Revival of the study of Roman law at Bologna
1163	Start of the construction of the Cathedral of Notre Dame
1267–1273	Saint Thomas Aquinas writes *Summa Theologica*
1309–1377	Babylonian Captivity; the popes, all French, reside at Avignon and are influenced by the French monarchy
c. 1321	Dante completes *Divine Comedy*
1337–1453	Hundred Years' War between England and France
1347–1351	Black Death reaches Italian ports and ravages Europe
1377	Pope Gregory XI returns the papacy to Rome
1378–1417	Great Schism; Christendom has two and then three popes
1415	The battle of Agincourt: Henry V of England defeats the French; Jan Hus, a Bohemian religious reformer, is burned at the stake
1453	The English are driven from France, except Calais; the end of the Hundred Years' War
1460	Pope Pius II condemns the Conciliar Movement as heretical

---

ing the rational tradition of Greece, men of genius harmonized Christian doctrines and Greek philosophy.

Several conditions contributed to this cultural explosion, known as the Twelfth-Century Awakening. As attacks of Vikings, Muslims, and Magyars ended and kings and great lords imposed more order and stability, people found greater opportunities for travel and communication. The revival of trade and the growth of towns created a need for literacy and provided the wealth required to support learning. Increasing contact with Islamic and Byzantine cultures in Spain, Sicily, and Italy led to the translation into Latin of ancient Greek works preserved by these Eastern civilizations. By preserving Greek philosophy and science—and by commentating creatively on these classical works—Islamic civilization acted as a bridge between antiquity and the cultural revival of the High Middle Ages. What also prompted the Twelfth-Century Awakening was the legacy of the Carolingian Renaissance, whose cultural lights had dimmed but never wholly vanished in the period of disorder after the dissolution of Charlemagne's empire.

In the Early Middle Ages, the principal educational centers were the monastic schools. During the twelfth century, cathedral schools in towns gained importance. Their teachers, paid a stipend by a local church, taught grammar, rhetoric, and logic. However, the chief expression of expanding intellectual life was the university, a distinct creation of the Middle Ages. The first universities were not planned but grew spontaneously. They developed as students, eager for knowledge, gathered around prominent teachers. The renewed importance of Roman law for business and politics, for example, drew students to Bologna to study with acknowledged masters.

University students attended lectures, prepared for examinations, and earned degrees. They studied grammar, rhetoric, logic, arithmetic, geometry, astronomy, medicine, music, and, when ready, church law and theology, which was considered the queen of the sciences. The curriculum relied heavily on Latin translations of ancient texts, chiefly the works of Aristotle. Students in mathematics and astronomy read Latin translations of Euclid and Ptolemy, while those in medicine studied the works of two great medical men of the ancient world, Hippocrates and Galen.

Universities performed a crucial function in the Middle Ages. Students learned the habit of reasoned argument. Universities trained professional secretaries and lawyers, who administered the affairs of church, state, and the growing cities. These institutions of learning also produced theologians and philosophers, who shaped the climate of public opinion. Since the curriculum and the texts studied were essentially the same in all lands, the learning disseminated by universities tightened the cultural bonds that united Christian Europe. Medieval universities established in the West a tradition of learning that has never died. There is direct continuity between the universities of our own day and medieval centers of learning.

The Medieval World-View

A distinctive world-view, based essentially on Christianity, evolved during the Middle Ages. This outlook differed from both the Greco-Roman and the modern scientific and secular views of the world. In the Christian view, not the individual but the Creator determined what constituted the good life. Thus, reason that was not illuminated by revelation was either wrong or inadequate, for God had revealed the proper rules for the regulation of individual and social life. Ultimately, the good life was not of this world but came from a union with God in a higher world. This Christian belief, as formulated by the church, made life and death purposeful and intelligible; it dominated the thought of the Middle Ages.

The Universe: Higher and Lower Worlds

Medieval thinkers sharply differentiated between spirit and matter, between a realm of grace and an earthly realm, between a higher world of perfection and a lower world of imperfection. Moral values derived from the higher world,

Law Class at the University of Bologna. The core of the medieval curriculum included the *trivium* and the *quadrivium*. Students mastered grammar, rhetoric, and dialectic—the "three ways" (trivium)—and then proceeded to mathematics, geometry, astronomy, and music (quadrivium). The technique of teaching was the *disputatio*, or oral disputation between master and student. (*The Bodleian Library, Oxford, MS. Canon. Misc. 416, fol. 1r*)

which was also the final destination for the faithful. Two sets of laws operated in the medieval universe, one for the heavens and one for the earth. The cosmos was a giant ladder, with God at the summit; earth, composed of base matter, stood at the bottom, just above hell.

From Aristotle and Ptolemy, medieval thinkers inherited the theory of an earth-centered universe—the *geocentric theory*—which they imbued with Christian meaning. The geocentric theory held that revolving around the motionless earth at uniform speeds were seven transparent spheres, in which were embedded each of the seven "planets"—the moon, Mercury, Venus, the sun, Mars, Jupiter, and Saturn. A sphere of fixed stars enclosed this planetary system. Above the firmament of the stars were the three heavenly spheres. The outermost, the Empyrean Heaven, was the abode of God and the Elect. Through the sphere below—the Prime Mover—God transmitted motion to the planetary spheres. Beneath this was the lowest sphere, the invisible Crystalline Heaven.

An earth-centered universe accorded with the Christian idea that God had created the universe for men and women and that salvation was the primary aim of life. Because God had created people in his image, they deserved this central position in the universe. Although they might be living at the bottom rung of the cosmic ladder, only they, of all living things, had the capacity to ascend to heaven, the realm of perfection.

Also acceptable to the Christian mentality was the sharp distinction drawn by Aristotle between the world above the moon and the one below it. Aristotle held that terrestrial bodies were made of four elements: earth, water, air, and fire. Celestial bodies, which occupied the region above the moon, were composed of a fifth element, ether—too clear, too pure, and too perfect to be found on earth. The planets and stars existed in a world apart; they were made of the divine ether and followed celestial laws, which did not apply to earthly objects. Whereas earthly bodies underwent change—ice converting to water, a burning log converting to ashes—heavenly objects were incorruptible and immune to all change. Unlike earthly objects, they were indestructible.

Heavenly bodies also followed different laws of motion than earthly objects. Aristotle said that it was natural for celestial bodies to move eternally in uniform circles, such motion being considered a sign of perfection. According to Aristotle, it was also natural for heavy bodies (stone) to fall downward and for light objects (fire, smoke) to move upward toward the celestial world; the falling stone and the rising smoke were finding their natural place in the universe.

The Individual: Sinful but Redeemable

At the center of medieval belief was the idea of a perfect God and a wretched and sinful human being. God had given Adam and Eve freedom to choose; rebellious and presumptuous, they had used their freedom to disobey God. In doing so, they made evil an intrinsic part of the human personality. But God, who had not stopped loving human beings, showed them the way out of sin. God became man and died so that human beings might be saved. Men and women were weak, egocentric, and sinful. With God's grace they could overcome their sinful nature and gain salvation; without grace, they were utterly helpless.

The medieval individual's understanding of self depended on a comprehension of the universe as a hierarchy culminating in God. On earth, the basest objects were lifeless stones, devoid of souls. Higher than stones were plants, endowed with a primitive type of soul, which allowed reproduction and growth. Still higher were animals, which had the capacity for motion and sensation. The highest of the animals were human beings; unlike other animals, they could grasp some part of universal truth. Far superior to them were the angels, who apprehended God's truth without difficulty. At the summit of this graduated universe (the Great Chain of Being) was God, who was pure Being, without limitation, and the source of all existence. God's revelation reached down to humanity through the hierarchical order. From God, revelation passed to the angels, who were also arranged hierarchically. From the angels, the truth reached men and women; it was grasped first by prophets and apostles and then by the multitudes. Thus, all things in the universe, from God to angels to men and women to the lowest earthly objects, occupied a place peculiar to their nature and were linked by God in a great, unbroken chain.

Medieval individuals derived a sense of security from this hierarchical universe, in which the human position was clearly defined. True, they were sinners who dwelt on a corruptible earth at the bottom of the cosmic hierarchy. But they could ascend to the higher world of perfection above the moon. As children of God, they enjoyed the unique distinction that each human soul was precious and commanded respect.

Medieval thinkers also arranged knowledge in a hierarchical order: knowledge of spiritual things surpassed all worldly knowledge, all human sciences. To know what God wanted of the individual was the summit of self-knowledge and permitted entry into heaven. Thus, God was both the source and the end of knowledge. The human capacity to think and to act freely reflected the image of God within each individual; it ennobled men and women and offered them the promise of associating with God in heaven. Human nobility might derive from intelligence and free will, but if individuals used these attributes to disobey God, they brought misery on themselves.

Philosophy, Science, and Law

Medieval philosophy, or scholasticism, applied reason to revelation. It explained and clarified Christian teachings by means of concepts and principles of logic derived from Greek philosophy. Scholastics tried to show that the teachings of faith, although not derived from reason, were not contrary to reason. They tried to prove through reason what they already held to be true through faith. For example, the existence of God and the immortality of the soul, which every Christian accepted as articles of faith, could also, they thought, be demonstrated by reason. In struggling to harmonize faith with reason, medieval thinkers constructed an extraordinary synthesis of Christian revelation and Greek rationalism.

The scholastic masters used reason not to challenge but to serve faith: to elucidate, clarify, and buttress it. They did not break with the central concern of Christianity, that of earning God's grace and achieving salvation. Although this goal could be realized solely by faith, scholastic thinkers insisted that a science of nature did not obstruct the pursuit of grace and that philosophy could assist the devout in contemplating God. They did not reject Christian beliefs that were beyond the grasp of human reason and therefore could not be deduced by rational argument. Instead, they held that such truths rested entirely on revelation and were to be accepted on faith. To medieval thinkers, reason did not have an independent existence but ultimately had to acknowledge a suprarational, superhuman standard of truth. They wanted rational thought to be directed by faith for Christian ends and guided by scriptural and ecclesiastical authority. Ultimately, faith had the final word.

Not all Christian thinkers welcomed the use of reason. Regarding Greek philosophy as an enemy of faith (would not reason lead people to question belief in miracles?), a fabricator of heresies (would not reason encourage disbelief in essential church teachings?), and an obstacle to achieving communion of the soul with God (would not a deviation from church teachings, under the influence of pagan philosophy, deprive people of salvation?), conservative theologians opposed the application of reason to Christian revelation. In a sense, the conservatives were right. By giving renewed vitality to Greek thought, medieval philosophy nurtured a powerful force that would eventually shatter the medieval concepts of nature and society and weaken Christianity. Modern Western thought was created by thinkers who refused to subordinate reason to Christian authority. Reason proved a double-edged sword: it both ennobled and undermined the medieval world-view.

Saint Anselm and Abelard

An early scholastic, Saint Anselm (1033–1109) was abbot of the Benedictine monastery of Le Bec in Normandy. He used rational argument to serve the interests of faith. Like Augustine before him and other thinkers who followed him, Anselm said that faith was a precondition for understanding. Without belief there could be no proper knowledge. He developed philosophical proof for the existence of God. Anselm argued as follows: We can conceive of no being greater than God. But if God were to exist only in thought and not in actuality, his greatness would be limited; he would be less than perfect. Hence, he exists.

Anselm's motive and method reveal something about the essence of medieval philosophy. He does not begin as a modern might: "If it can be proven that God exists, I will adopt the creed of Christianity; if not, I will either deny God's existence (atheism) or reserve judgment (agnosticism)." Rather, Anselm accepts God's existence as an established fact because he believes what Holy Scripture says and what the church teaches. He then proceeds to employ logical argument to demonstrate that God can be known not only through faith, but also through reason. He would never use reason to subvert what he knows to be true by faith. In general, this attitude would characterize later medieval thinkers, who also applied reason to faith.

As a young teacher of theology at the Cathedral School of Notre Dame, Peter Abelard (1079–1142) acquired a reputation for brilliance and combativeness. His tragic affair with Héloise, whom he tutored and seduced, has become one of the great romances in Western literature. Abelard's most determined opponent, Bernard of Clairvaux, accused him of using the method of dialectical argument to attack faith. To Bernard, a monk and mystic, subjecting revealed truth to critical analysis was fraught with danger. Hearkening to Bernard's powerful voice, the church condemned Abelard and confined him to a monastery for the rest of his days.

Abelard believed that it was important to apply reason to faith and that careful and constant questioning led to wisdom. In *Sic et Non* (Yes and No), he took 150 theological issues and, by presenting passages from the Bible and the church fathers, showed that there were conflicting opinions. He suggested that the divergent opinions of authorities could be reconciled through proper use of dialectics. But like Anselm before him, Abelard did not intend to refute traditional church doctrines. Reason would buttress, not weaken, the authority of faith. He wrote after his condemnation in 1141: "I will never be a philosopher, if this is to speak against St. Paul; I would not be an Aristotle if this were to separate me from Christ. . . . I have set my building on the cornerstone on which Christ has built his Church. . . . I rest upon the rock that cannot be moved."[1]

Saint Thomas Aquinas: The Synthesis of Faith and Reason

The introduction into Latin Christendom of the major works of Aristotle created a dilemma for religious authorities. Aristotle's comprehensive philosophy of nature and man, a product of human reason alone, conflicted in many instances with essential Christian doctrine. Whereas Christianity taught that God created the universe at a specific point in time, Aristotle held that the universe was eternal. Nor did Aristotle believe in the personal immortality of the soul, another cardinal principle of Christianity.

Some church officials feared that the dissemination of Aristotle's ideas and the use of Aristotelian logic would endanger faith. At various times in the first half of the thirteenth century, they forbade teaching the scientific works of Aristotle at the University of Paris. But because the ban did not apply throughout Christendom and was not consistently enforced in Paris, Aristotle's philosophy continued to be studied. Rejecting the position of conservatives, who insisted that philosophy would contaminate faith, Saint Thomas Aquinas (c. 1225–1274) upheld the value of human reason and natural knowledge. He set about reconciling Aristotelianism with Christianity. Aquinas taught at Paris and in Italy. His greatest work, *Summa Theologica*, is a systematic exposition of Christian thought.

Can the teachings of faith conflict with the evidence of reason? For Aquinas, the answer was emphatically no. Since both faith and reason came from God, they were not in competition with each other but, properly understood, supported each other and formed an organic unity. Consequently, reason should not be feared, for it was another avenue to God. Because there was an inherent agreement between true faith and correct reason—they both ultimately stemmed from God—contradictions between them were only a misleading appearance. Although philosophy had not yet been able to resolve the dilemma, for God no such contradictions existed. In heaven, human beings would attain complete knowledge, as well as complete happiness. While on earth, however, they must allow faith to guide reason; they must not permit reason to oppose or undermine faith.

Thus, in exalting God, Aquinas also paid homage to human intelligence, proclaimed the value of rational activity, and asserted the importance of physical reality discovered through human senses. Therefore, he prized the natural philosophy of Aristotle. Correctly used, Aristotelian thought would aid faith. Aquinas's great effort was to synthesize Aristotelianism with the divine revelation of Christianity. That the two could be harmonized he had no doubt. He made use of Aristotelian categories in his five proofs of God's existence. In his first proof, for example, Aquinas argued that a thing cannot move itself. Whatever is moved must be moved by something else, and that by something else again. "Therefore, it is necessary to arrive at a first mover, moved by no other; and this everyone understands to be God."[2]

Aquinas upheld the value of reason. To love the intellect was to honor God and not to diminish the truth of faith. He had confidence in the power of the rational mind to comprehend most of the truths of revelation, and he insisted that in nontheological questions about specific things in nature—those questions not affecting salvation—people should trust only reason and experience. Thus, Aquinas gave new importance to the empirical world and to scientific speculation and human knowledge.

The traditional medieval view, based largely on Saint Augustine, drew a sharp distinction between the higher world of grace and the lower world of nature, between the world of spirit and the world of sense experience. Knowledge derived from the natural world was often seen as an obstacle to true knowledge. Aquinas altered this tradition by affirming the importance of knowledge of the social order and the physical world. He gave human reason and worldly knowledge a new dignity. Thus, the City of Man was not merely a sinful place from which people tried to escape in order to enter God's city; it was worthy of investigation and understanding. But Aquinas remained a medieval thinker, for he always maintained that secular knowledge should be supervised and corrected by revealed truth, and he never questioned the truth of the medieval Christian view of the world and the individual.

Science

During the Early Middle Ages, few scientific works from the ancient world were available to western Europeans. Scientific thought was at its lowest ebb since its origination more than a thousand years earlier in Greece. In contrast, both Islamic and Byzantine civilizations preserved and, in some instances, added to the legacy of Greek science. In the High Middle Ages, however, many ancient texts were translated from Greek and Arabic into Latin and entered Latin Christendom for the first time. Spain, where Christian and Muslim civilizations met, was one of the two principal centers of translation. The other was Sicily, which had been controlled by Byzantium up to the last part of the ninth century and then by Islam until Christian Normans completed the conquest of the island by 1091.

In the thirteenth and fourteenth centuries, a genuine scientific movement did occur. Impressed with the naturalistic and empirical approach of Aristotle, some medieval schoolmen spent time examining physical nature. Among them was the Dominican Albert the Great (Albertus Magnus, c. 1206–1280). Born in Germany, he studied at Padua, and taught at the University of Paris, where Thomas Aquinas was his student. To Albert, philosophy meant more than employing Greek reason to contemplate divine wisdom; it also meant making sense of nature. Albert devoted himself to editing and commenting on the vast body of Aristotle's works.

While retaining the Christian emphasis on God, revelation, the supernatural, and the afterlife, Albert (unlike many earlier Christian thinkers) considered nature a valid field for investigation. In his writings on geology, chemistry, botany, and zoology, Albert, like Aristotle, displayed a respect for the concrete details of nature, utilizing them as empirical evidence. Albert approved of inquiry into the material world, stressed the value of knowledge derived from experience with nature, sought rational explanations for natural occurrences, and held that theological debates should not stop scientific investigations.

Other scholars in the scientific movement included Robert Grosseteste (c. 1175–1253), the chancellor of Oxford University. He declared that the roundness of the earth could be demonstrated by reason. In addition, he insisted that mathematics was necessary in order to understand the physical world, and he carried out experiments on the refraction of light. Another Englishman, the monk and philosopher Roger Bacon (c. 1214–1294), foreshadowed the modern attitude of using science to gain mastery over nature. Bacon valued the study of mathematics and read Arabic works on the reflection and refraction of light. Among his achievements were experiments in optics and the observation that light travels much faster than sound. His description of the anatomy of the vertebrate eye and optic nerves was the finest of that era, and he recommended dissecting the eyes of pigs and cows to obtain greater knowledge of the subject.

Medieval scholars did not make the breakthrough to modern science. They retained the belief that the earth was at the center of the universe and that different sets of laws operated on earth and in the heavens. They did not invent analytic geometry or calculus or arrive at the concept of inertia—all crucial for modern science. Moreover, medieval science was never wholly removed from a theological setting. Modern science self-consciously seeks the advancement of specifically scientific knowledge, but in the Middle Ages, many questions involving nature were raised merely to clarify a religious problem.

Medieval scholars and philosophers did, however, advance knowledge about optics, the tides, and mechanics. They saw the importance of mathematics for interpreting nature, and they performed experiments. By translating and commenting on ancient Greek and Arabic works, medieval scholars provided future ages with ideas to reflect on and to surpass, a necessary precondition for the emergence of modern science. Medieval thinkers also developed an anti-Aristotelian physics, which, some historians of science believe, influenced Galileo, the creator of modern mechanics, more than two centuries later.

Recovery of Roman Law

During the Early Middle Ages, western European law essentially consisted of Germanic customs, some of which had been put into writing. Some elements of Roman law endured as custom and practice, but the formal study of Roman law had disappeared. The late eleventh and twelfth centuries saw the revival of Roman law, particularly in Bologna, Italy. Irnerius lectured on the *Corpus Juris Civilis*, codified by Byzantine jurists in the sixth century, and he made Bologna the leading center for the study of Roman law. Irnerius and his students employed the methods of organization and logical analysis that scholastic theologians used in studying philosophical texts.

Unlike traditional Germanic law, which was essentially tribal and parochial, Roman law assumed the existence of universal principles, which could be grasped by the human intellect and expressed in the law of the state. Roman jurists had systematically and rationally structured the legal experience of the Roman people. The example of Roman law stimulated medieval jurists to organize their own legal tradition. Intellectuals increasingly came to insist on both a rational analysis of evidence and judicial decisions based on rational procedures. Law codes compiled in parts of France and Germany and in the kingdom of Castile were influenced by the recovery of Roman law.

Literature

Medieval literature was written both in Latin and in the vernacular. Much of medieval Latin literature consisted of religious hymns and dramas depicting the life of Christ and saints. In their native tongues, medieval writers created different forms of poetry: *chansons de geste*, the *roman*, and *troubadour* songs, which emerged during the High Middle Ages.

The French *chansons de geste*—epic poems of heroic deeds that had first been told orally—were written in the vernacular of northern France. These poems dealt with Charlemagne's battles against the Muslims, with rebellious nobles, and with feudal warfare. The finest of these epic poems, *The Song of*

Roland, expressed the vassal's loyalty to his lord and the Christian's devotion to his faith. Roland, Charlemagne's nephew, was killed in a battle with the Muslims. The *Nibelungenlied,* the best expression of the heroic epic in Germany, is often called "the *Iliad* of the Germans." Like its French counterpart, it dealt with heroic feats.

The roman—a blending of old legends, chivalric ideals, and Christian concepts—combined love with adventure, war, and the miraculous. Among the romans were the tales of King Arthur and his Round Table. Circulating by word of mouth for centuries, these tales spread from the British Isles to France and Germany. In the twelfth century, they were put into French verse.

Another form of medieval poetry, which flourished particularly in Provence, in southern France, dealt with the romantic glorification of women. Sung by troubadours, many of them nobles, the courtly love poetry expressed a changing attitude toward women. Although medieval men generally regarded women as inferior and subordinate, courtly love poetry ascribed to noble ladies superior qualities of virtue. To the nobleman, the lady became a goddess worthy of all devotion, loyalty, and worship. He would honor her and serve her as he did his lord; for her love he would undergo any sacrifice.

Noblewomen actively influenced the rituals and literature of courtly love. They often invited poets to their courts and wrote poetry themselves. They demanded that knights treat them with gentleness and consideration and that knights dress neatly, bathe often, play instruments, and compose (or at least recite) poetry. To prove worthy of his lady's love, a knight had to demonstrate patience, charm, bravery, and loyalty. By devoting himself to a lady, it was believed, a knight would ennoble his character.

Courtly love did not involve a husband-wife relationship but a noble's admiration of and yearning for another woman of his class. Among nobles, marriages were arranged for political and economic reasons. The rituals of courtly love, it has been suggested, provided an outlet for erotic feelings condemned by the church. They also expanded the skills and refined the tastes of the noble. The rough warrior acquired wit, manners, charm, and skill with words. He was becoming a courtier and a gentleman.

The greatest literary figure of the Middle Ages was Dante Alighieri (1265–1321) of Florence. Dante appreciated the Roman classics and wrote not just in Latin, the traditional language of intellectual life, but in Italian, his native tongue. In this respect, he anticipated the Renaissance (see Chapter 8). In the tradition of the troubadours, Dante wrote poems to his beloved Beatrice.

In *The Divine Comedy,* Dante synthesized the various elements of the medieval outlook and summed up, with immense feeling, the medieval understanding of the purpose of life. Written while Dante was in exile, *The Divine Comedy* describes the poet's journey through hell, purgatory, and paradise. Dante arranges hell into nine concentric circles; in each region, sinners are punished in proportion to their earthly sins. The poet experiences all of hell's torments—burning sand, violent storms, darkness, and fearful monsters that

Virgil and Dante Watch Lucifer: A Miniature Painting in an Early Manuscript of *The Divine Comedy.*   Dante reserved the lowest depth of Hell for those guilty of treason. Lucifer, the angel who betrayed God, is depicted as a monster with three mouths. With these he perpetually chews the bodies of the arch-traitors Judas Iscariot, Brutus, and Cassius. *The Divine Comedy* exemplifies the medieval mind's overriding concern with God and the afterlife. (*Trivulzian Library, Milan*)

whip, claw, bite, and tear sinners apart. The ninth circle, the lowest, is reserved for Lucifer and traitors. Lucifer has three faces, each a different color, and two batlike wings. In each mouth he gnaws on the greatest traitors in history: Judas Iscariot, who betrayed Jesus, and Brutus and Cassius, who assassinated Caesar. Those condemned to hell are told: "All hope abandon, ye who enter in." In purgatory, Dante meets sinners who, although they undergo punishment, will eventually enter paradise. In paradise, an abode of light, music, and gentleness, the poet, guided by Beatrice, meets the great saints and the Virgin Mary. For an instant, he glimpses the Vision of God. In this mystical experience, the aim of life is realized.

Art as History:
The Ancient World
Through the Middle Ages

Historians rely on many different sources to arrive at a knowledge of the past. These sources include not only the written documents and literature of a people, but also their artistic creations—their architecture, sculpture, and painting. As you look at these works of art, what insights do they suggest about the historical times in which they were produced?

The Parthenon, Athens, 447–432 B.C. This Greek classical temple crowns the Acropolis above Athens. Dedicated to Athena, patron goddess of the city and of wisdom and the arts, the marble Parthenon once contained a huge ivory and gold statue of her. The temple ruins reveal the perfect proportions and placement of the Parthenon, but they do not show that its facade was painted, as were the life-size sculptures that filled the triangular spaces above the rows of columns. What do the structure and style of the Parthenon suggest about Greek civilization? *(Scala/Art Resource, NY)*

Metope from the Parthenon: Centaur and Lapith Fighting. Between the columns and the pediments of the Parthenon are relief sculptures called *metopes*. These squares contain simple compositions in high relief, that is, the figures stand out from the background, which was painted a strong color. The centaur (half man, half beast) and the Lapith (a Thessalonian Greek whose tribe defeated the centaurs) represent a mythological struggle. Why was this subject included in the temple decoration? *(Werner Forman/Art Resource, NY)*

Black-figured Amphora: Achilles and Ajax Playing a Board Game, 540–530 B.C. Greeks not only built beautiful temples and skillfully sculpted ideal figures possessing grace; they also imparted beauty to everyday utensils, such as this amphora, a "vase" used to hold wine or oil. Here, figures from Homer's *Iliad* are shown enjoying a respite from the siege of Troy. What does this vessel and its ornamentation reveal about the Hellenic Greeks? *(Scala/Art Resource, NY)*

Detail of Pompeian Wall Fresco: Lady Playing the Cithara. Upon the removal of lava
and ash from Pompeii, a first-century Roman city appeared, providing historians with
data on the daily life of almost twenty centuries ago. What does this fresco scene disclose about the state of Roman culture and the lives of Roman matrons?
(Copyright © 1996 by The Metropolitan Museum of Art, Rogers Fund, 1903)

Apse Mosaic: Justinian and Attendants, Church of San Vitale, Ravenna. Emperor Justinian, who ruled Byzantium from 527 to 565, appears in this mosaic as a symbol of Christ rather than as an ordinary ruler on earth. The golden halo and the presence of exactly twelve attendants, reminiscent of the Twelve Apostles, confirm this impression. The way in which an artist depicts the human figure reveals a lot about past cultures. What can we learn about Byzantium by comparing the portrayal of Justinian with that of the Roman matron playing the cithara on the previous page? *(Scala/Art Resource, NY)*

Stained Glass from Chartres Cathedral: Charlemagne Giving Orders for Building the Church of Saint James. Dating from the early thirteenth century, Chartres is one of the outstanding Gothic cathedrals. Its stained-glass windows shed light in jeweled colors on the interior of the sanctuary, uplifting the spirit and raising the eyes of the worshiper. These windows also instruct, however; they tell stories about heroes, such as Emperor Charlemagne, and about saints and the Trinity. What might a medieval churchgoer have learned from this window? *(Copyright Sonia Halliday and Laura Lushington)*

April from *Les très riches heures* of Jean, Duke of Berry. This page from a beautifully illustrated volume of prayers, which was made during 1413–1416, is one of the paintings of months appearing in this nobleman's book. What does this scene reveal about the lifestyle of nobles, both men and women?
(Giraudon/Art Resource, NY)

Domenico Veneziano (c. 1410–1461): *Madonna and Child with Saints,* c. 1445.
This Florentine master painted the altar panel (6' 7½" x 6' 11⅞") in a new style,
called *sacra conversazione* (sacred conversation). The enthroned Madonna and child
are framed by architectural elements and flanked by the formal, solemn figures of
saints, who seem to converse with her or between themselves, or even with the
onlooker. Saint John, to the left of the child and the Madonna, gazes out of the painting as he points to them, in effect directing the onlooker's eyes. In his color scheme,
Domenico uses sunlight and spots of bright primary colors, along with pastels, to present a glowing scene. What elements in the painting indicate that it is an Early
Renaissance work? *(Alinari/Art Resource, NY)*

Hubert or Jan van Eyck: *The Last Judgment,* c. 1420–1425. The major concern of medieval people was the salvation of their souls. At the Last Judgment, the good would be drawn to heaven while the damned would be sealed in hell. In *The Last Judgment,* the Flemish artist van Eyck depicts this final division in graphic detail. How does the relationship between man and the divine portrayed by van Eyck differ from the classical humanism of ancient Greek art? *(Copyright © 1996 by The Metropolitan Museum of Art, Fletcher Fund, 1933)*

The Romanesque Nave of the Cathedral of St. Sernin, Toulouse. The nave is covered by a stone barrel vault, replacing earlier wooden roofs which were susceptible to fire. The columns, thick walls, and small windows were required structurally to bear the great weight of the roof vaulting. Little light penetrated the interior. (*Caisse Nationale des Monuments Historiques, Paris*)

Written in the vernacular, *The Canterbury Tales* of Geoffrey Chaucer (c. 1340–1400) is a masterpiece of English literature. Chaucer chose as his theme twenty-nine pilgrims en route from London to the religious shrine at Canterbury. In describing the pilgrims, Chaucer displayed humor, charm, an understanding of human nature, and a superb grasp of the attitudes of the English. Few writers have pictured their times better.

Architecture

Two styles of architecture evolved during the Middle Ages: Romanesque and Gothic. The Romanesque style dominated the eleventh century and the greater part of the twelfth. In imitation of ancient Roman structures, Romanesque buildings had massive walls to support stone barrel and groin vaults with rounded arches. The thick walls were needed to hold up the great

The Gothic Nave and Choir of Notre Dame Cathedral, Paris, Twelfth Century.   The Gothic nave is wider than a Romanesque nave because pointed arches can bridge a wider space and carry a roof with less heavy vaulting. The walls are raised higher, are thinner and punctured with larger open spaces for windows than was possible in Romanesque buildings. The weight of the roof and walls is born by "flying buttresses," stone arched supports external to the walls. (*Jean Roubier*)

weight of the roofs. The walls left few spaces for windows, so little light entered the interior. However, the development of the pointed arch permitted supports that lessened the bearing pressure of the roof on the walls. This new style, called Gothic, allowed buildings to have lofty, vaulted ceilings and huge windows. The Romanesque building produced an impression of massive solidity; Gothic buildings created an illusion of soaring energy.

The Gothic cathedral gave visual expression to the medieval conception of a hierarchical universe. As historian Joan Gadol puts it, "Inside and out, the Gothic cathedral is one great movement upward through a mounting series of grades, one ascent through horizontal levels marked by arches, galleries, niches, and towers . . . the material ascends to the spiritual, the natural is assumed into the supernatural—all in a graduated rise."[3] This illusion is created by the tall and narrow proportions of the interior spaces, the springing pointed arches, and the marching patterns of closely spaced columns and colonettes.

The magnificently designed stained-glass windows and complex sculptural decoration of Gothic cathedrals depicted scenes from the Bible and the lives of saints—as well as scenes from daily life—for the worshipers, many of whom were illiterate. The reduction of wall space, which allowed these massive glass illustrations, was made possible by the flying buttresses on the buildings' exteriors. These great arcs of masonry carry the weight and thrust of the stone vaults out to the exterior walls.

The Gothic style was to remain vigorous until the fifteenth century, spreading from France to England, Germany, Spain, and beyond. Revived from time to time thereafter, it has proved to be one of the most enduring styles in Western art and architecture.

The Fourteenth Century: An Age of Adversity

By the fourteenth century, Latin Christendom had experienced more than 250 years of growth. On the economic level, agricultural production had expanded, commerce and town life had revived, and the population had increased. On the political level, kings had become more powerful, bringing greater order and security to large areas. On the religious level, the papacy had demonstrated its strength as the spiritual leader of Christendom, and the clergy had been reformed. On the cultural level, a unified world-view, blending faith and reason, had been forged.

During the Late Middle Ages (roughly the fourteenth century), however, Latin Christendom was afflicted with severe problems. The earlier increases in agricultural production did not continue. Limited use of fertilizers and limited knowledge of conservation exhausted the topsoil. From 1301 to 1314, there was a general shortage of food, and from 1315 to 1317, famine struck Europe. Throughout the century, starvation and malnutrition were widespread.

Adding to the economic crisis was the Black Death, or bubonic plague. This disease was carried by fleas on black rats and probably first struck Mongolia in 1331–32. From there, it crossed into Russia. Carried back from Black Sea ports, the plague reached Sicily in 1347. Spreading swiftly throughout much of Europe, it attacked an already declining and undernourished population. The first onslaught lasted until 1351, and other serious outbreaks occurred in later decades. The crowded cities and towns had the highest mortalities. Perhaps twenty million people—about one-quarter to one-third of the European population—perished in the worst natural disaster in recorded history.

Panic-stricken people drifted into debauchery, lawlessness, and frenzied forms of religious life. Organized bands of flagellants marched from region to region, beating themselves and each other with sticks and whips in a desperate effort to appease God, who, they believed, had cursed them with the plague. Art concentrated on morbid scenes of decaying flesh, open graves laden with worm-eaten corpses, dances of death, and the torments of hell. Sometimes, this hysteria was directed against Jews, who were accused of causing the plague by poisoning wells. Terrible massacres of Jews, often by mass burnings, occurred despite the pleas of the papacy.

The millions of deaths caused production of food and goods to plummet and some prices to soar. Economic and social tensions, some of them antedating the Black Death, escalated into rebellions. Each rebellion had its own specific causes, but a general pattern characterized the uprisings in the countryside. When kings and lords, breaking with customary social relationships, imposed new and onerous regulations, the peasants rose in defense of their traditional rights.

In 1323, the lords' attempt to reimpose old manorial obligations infuriated the free peasants of Flanders, whose condition had improved in earlier decades. The Peasants' Revolt lasted five bloody years. In 1358, French peasants took up arms in protest against the plundering of the countryside by soldiers. Perhaps twenty thousand peasants died in the uprising known as the *Jacquerie*. In 1381, English peasants revolted, angered over legislation that tied them to the land and imposed new taxes. Like the revolts in Flanders and France, the uprising in England failed. To the landed aristocracy, the peasants were sinners attacking a social system ordained by God. Possessing superior might, the nobility suppressed the peasants, sometimes with savage cruelty.

Social unrest also afflicted towns. The wage earners of Florence (1378), the weavers of Ghent (1382), and the poor of Paris (1382) rose up against the ruling oligarchies. These revolts were generally initiated not by the poorest and most downtrodden, but by those who had made some gains and were eager for more. The rebellions of the urban poor were crushed just like the peasant uprisings.

Compounding the adversity were the conflicts known as the Hundred Years' War (1337–1453). Because English kings had ruled parts of France, conflicts between the two monarchies were common. In the opening phase of the war, the English inflicted terrible defeats on French knights at the battles of Crécy (1346) and Poitiers (1356). Using longbows, which allowed them to shoot arrows rapidly, English archers cut down wave after wave of charging French cavalry. The war continued on and off throughout the fourteenth century. During periods of truce, gangs of unemployed soldiers roamed the French countryside killing and stealing, actions that precipitated the Jacquerie.

After the battle of Agincourt (1415), won by the English under Henry V, the English controlled most of northern France. It appeared that England would shortly conquer France and join the two lands under one crown. At this crucial moment in French history, a young and illiterate peasant girl, Joan of Arc (1412–1431), helped rescue France. Believing that God commanded her to drive the English out of France, Joan rallied the demoralized French troops, leading them in battle. In 1429, she liberated the besieged city of Orléans. Imprisoned by the English, Joan was condemned as a heretic and a

The Battle of Crécy, A.D. 1346.   English claims to the French throne led to the so-called Hundred Years' War between the French and the English monarchies. In the end, the English effort was unsuccessful. Although France was devastated by invading armies and internal revolts, the English kings lost almost all their French possessions. But the English victory at Crécy was catastrophic for the French mounted knights who fell in droves under the withering fire of English longbowmen. *(Photo Hachette)*

witch in 1431 by a handpicked church court. She was burned at the stake. Inspired by Joan's death, the French drove the English from all French territory except the port of Calais.

During the Hundred Years' War, French kings introduced new taxes, which added substantially to their incomes. These monies furnished them with the means to organize a professional army of well-paid and loyal troops. By evoking a sense of pride and oneness in the French people, the war also contributed to a growing, but still incomplete, national unity. The English too emerged from the war with a greater sense of solidarity. However, the war had horrendous consequences for the French peasants. Thousands of farmers were killed and valuable farmland was destroyed by English armies and marauding bands of mercenaries. In a portentous development, the later stages of the Hundred Years' War saw the use of gunpowder and heavy artillery.

The Decline of the Papacy

The principal sign of the decline of medieval civilization in the Late Middle Ages was the waning authority and prestige of the papacy. In the High Middle Ages, the papacy had been the dominant institution in Christendom, but in the Late Middle Ages its power disintegrated. The medieval ideal of a unified Christian commonwealth guided by the papacy was shattered. Papal authority declined in the face of the growing power of kings, who championed the parochial interests of states. As the pope became more embroiled in European politics, papal prestige and the pope's capacity to command diminished. Many pious Christians felt that the pope behaved more like a secular ruler than like an Apostle of Christ. Political theorists and church reformers further undermined papal authority.

Conflict with France

Philip IV of France (1285–1314) taxed the church in his land to raise revenue for war. In doing so, he disregarded the church prohibition against taxing its property without papal permission. In 1296, in the bull *Clericis Laicos,* Pope Boniface VIII (1294–1303) decreed that kings and lords who imposed taxes on the clergy and the clergy who paid them would be excommunicated. Far from bowing to the pope's threat, Philip acted forcefully to assert his authority over the church in his kingdom. Boniface backed down from his position, declaring that the French king could tax the clergy in times of national emergency. Thus, the matter was resolved to the advantage of the state.

A second dispute had more disastrous consequences for Boniface. Philip tried and imprisoned a French bishop despite Boniface's warning that this was an illegal act and a violation of church law and tradition, which held that the church, not the state, must judge the clergy. Philip summoned the first meeting of the Estates General to gain the backing of the nation. Shortly afterward, Boniface threatened to excommunicate Philip. The outraged monarch raided the papal summer palace at Anagni in September 1303 and captured the pope. Although Boniface was released, this shocking event proved too much for him, and a month later he died.

Boniface's two successors, Benedict XI (1303–1304) and Clement V (1305–1314), tried to conciliate Philip. In particular, Clement decided to remain at Avignon, a town on the southeastern French frontier, where he had set up a temporary residence.

From 1309 to 1377, a period known as the Babylonian Captivity, the popes were all French and resided in Avignon, not Rome. During this time, the papacy, removed from Rome and deprived of revenues from the Papal States in Italy, was often forced to pursue policies favorable to France. The growing antipapalism among the laity further damaged the papal image. Laypeople were repelled by the luxurious style of living at Avignon and by the appointment of high churchmen to lands where they did not know the language and showed little concern for the local population. Criticism of the papacy increased. The conflict between Boniface and Philip provoked a battle of words between proponents of papal supremacy and defenders of royal rights.

The most important critique of clerical intrusion into worldly affairs was *The Defender of the Peace* (1324) by Marsiglio of Padua (c. 1290–c. 1343). Marsiglio held that the state ran according to its principles, which had nothing to do with religious commands originating in a higher realm. Religion dealt with a supranatural world and with principles of faith that could not be proved by reason, wrote Marsiglio. Politics, on the other hand, dealt with the natural world and the affairs of the human community. Political thinkers should not try to make the earthly realm conform to articles of faith. For Marsiglio, the state was self-sufficient; it needed no instruction from a higher authority. Thus, Marsiglio denied the essential premises of medieval papal political theory: that the pope, as God's vicar, was empowered to guide kings; that the state, as part of a divinely ordered world, must conform to and fulfill supranatural ends; and that the clergy were above the laws of the state. Marsiglio viewed the church as a spiritual institution with no temporal power.

The Great Schism and the Conciliar Movement

Pope Gregory XI returned the papacy to Rome in 1377, ending the Babylonian Captivity. But the papacy was to endure an even greater humiliation: the Great Schism. Elected pope in 1378, Urban VI abused and imprisoned a number of cardinals. Fleeing from Rome, the cardinals declared that the election of Urban had been invalid and elected Clement VII as the new pope. Refusing to step down, Urban excommunicated Clement, who responded in kind. To the utter confusion and anguish of Christians throughout Europe, there were now two popes: Urban ruling from Rome and Clement from Avignon.

Prominent churchmen urged the convening of a general council—the Council of Pisa—to end the disgraceful schism, which obstructed the papacy from performing its sacred duties. Held in 1409 and attended by hundreds of churchmen, the Council of Pisa deposed both Urban and Clement and elected a new pope. Neither deposed pope recognized the council's decision, so Christendom then had three popes. A new council was called at Constance in 1414.

In the struggle that ensued, each of the three popes either abdicated or was deposed in favor of an appointment by the council. In 1417, the Great Schism ended.

During the first half of the fifteenth century, church councils met at Pisa (1409), Constance (1414–1418), and Basel (1431–1449) in order to end the schism, combat heresy, and reform the church. The Conciliar Movement attempted to transform the papal monarchy into a constitutional system, in which the pope's power would be regulated by a general council. Supporters of the movement held that the papacy could not reform the church as effectively as a general council representing the clergy. But the Conciliar Movement ended in failure. As the Holy Roman emperor and then the French monarch withdrew support from the councils, the papacy regained its authority over the higher clergy. In 1460, Pope Pius II condemned the Conciliar Movement as heretical.

Deeply embroiled in European power politics, the papacy often neglected its spiritual and moral responsibilities. Many devout Christians longed for a religious renewal, a return to simple piety. The papacy barely heard this cry for reform. Its failure to provide creative leadership for reform made possible the Protestant Reformation of the sixteenth century. By splitting Christendom into Catholic and Protestant, the Reformation destroyed forever the vision of a Christian world commonwealth guided by Christ's vicar, the pope.

Fourteenth-Century Heresies

Another threat to papal power and the medieval ideal of a universal Christian community guided by the church came from the radical reformers who questioned the function and authority of the entire church hierarchy. These heretics in the Late Middle Ages were forerunners of the Protestant Reformation.

The two principal dissenters were the Englishman John Wycliffe (c. 1320–1384) and the Bohemian (Czech) Jan Hus (c. 1369–1415). By stressing a personal relationship between the individual and God and by claiming the Bible itself, rather than church teachings, to be the ultimate Christian authority, Wycliffe challenged the fundamental position of the medieval church: that the avenue to salvation passed through the church alone. He denounced the wealth of the higher clergy and sought a return to the spiritual purity and material poverty of the early church.

To Wycliffe, the wealthy, elaborately organized hierarchy of the church was unnecessary and wrong. The splendidly dressed and propertied bishops had no resemblance to the simple people who first followed Christ. Indeed, these worldly bishops, headed by a princely and tyrannical pope, were really anti-Christians, the "fiends of Hell." Wycliffe wanted the state to confiscate church property and the clergy to embrace poverty. By denying that priests changed the bread and wine of communion into the substance of the body and blood of Christ, Wycliffe rejected the sacramental power of the clergy.

The church, in response, deprived the Lollards—an order of poor priests that spread Wycliffe's teachings—of their priestly functions. In the early fifteenth century, some of Wycliffe's followers were burned at the stake.

Wycliffe's ideas were enthusiastically received by Czech reformers in Bohemia led by Jan Hus. Like Wycliffe, Hus advocated vernacular translations of the Bible, which would be accessible to common people, and upbraided the upper clergy for their luxury and immorality.

Although both movements were declared heretical and Hus was burned at the stake, the church could not crush the dissenters' followers or eradicate their teachings. To some extent, the doctrines of the Reformation would parallel the teachings of Wycliffe and Hus.

Breakup of the Thomistic Synthesis

In the Late Middle Ages, the papacy lost power as kings, political theorists, and religious dissenters challenged papal claims to supreme leadership. The great theological synthesis constructed by the scholastic theologians of the twelfth and thirteenth centuries was breaking down. The process of fragmentation seen in the history of the church took place in philosophy as well.

Saint Thomas Aquinas's system had culminated the scholastic attempt to show the basic agreement of philosophy and religion. In the fourteenth century, a number of thinkers cast doubt on the possibility of synthesizing Aristotelianism and Christianity, that is, reason and faith. Denying that reason could demonstrate the truth of Christian doctrines with certainty, philosophers tried to separate reason from faith. Whereas Aquinas had said that reason proved or clarified much of revelation, fourteenth-century thinkers asserted that the basic propositions of Christianity were not open to rational proof. Whereas Aquinas had held that faith supplemented and perfected reason, some philosophers were now proclaiming that reason often contradicted faith.

To be sure, this new outlook did not urge abandoning faith in favor of reason. Faith had to prevail in any conflict with reason because faith rested on God, the highest authority in the universe. But the relationship between reason and revelation was altered. Articles of faith, it was now held, had nothing to do with reason; they were to be believed, not proved. Reason was not an aid to theology but a separate sphere of activity. This new attitude snapped the link between reason and faith that Aquinas had so skillfully forged. The scholastic synthesis was disintegrating.

The chief proponent of this new outlook was William of Ockham (c. 1285–1349). In contrast to Aquinas, Ockham insisted that natural reason could not prove God's existence, the soul's immortality, or any other essential Christian doctrine. Reason could only say that God probably exists and that he probably endowed human beings with an immortal soul. But it could not prove these propositions with certainty. The tenets of faith were beyond the reach of reason, said Ockham; there was no rational foundation to Christianity. For Ockham, reason and faith did not necessarily complement each other as they did for Aquinas; it was neither possible nor helpful to join reason to faith. He did not, however, seek to undermine faith—only to disengage it from reason.

In the process of proclaiming the authority of faith, Ockham also furthered the use of reason to comprehend nature. Ockham's approach, separating natural knowledge from religious dogma, made it easier to explore the natural world empirically, without fitting it into a religious framework. Ockham, thus, is a forerunner of the modern mentality, which is characterized by the separation of reason from religion and by an interest in the empirical investigation of nature.

The Middle Ages and the Modern World: Continuity and Discontinuity

Medieval civilization began to decline in the fourteenth century, but no dark age comparable to the three centuries following Rome's fall descended on Europe; its economic and political institutions and technological skills had grown too strong. Instead, the waning of the Middle Ages opened up possibilities for another stage in Western civilization: the modern age.

The modern world is linked to the Middle Ages in innumerable ways. European cities, the middle class, the state system, English common law, universities—all had their origins in the Middle Ages. During medieval times, important advances were made in business practices, including partnerships, systematic bookkeeping, and the bill of exchange. By translating and commenting on the writings of Greek and Arabic thinkers, medieval scholars preserved a priceless intellectual heritage, without which the modern mind could never have evolved. In addition, numerous strands connect the thought of the scholastics and that of early modern philosophers.

Feudal traditions lasted long after the Middle Ages. Up to the French Revolution, for instance, French aristocrats enjoyed special privileges and exercised power over local government. In England, the aristocracy controlled local government until the Industrial Revolution transformed English society in the nineteenth century. Retaining the medieval ideal of the noble warrior, aristocrats continued to dominate the officer corps of European armies through the nineteenth century and even into the twentieth. Aristocratic notions of duty, honor, loyalty, and courtly love have endured into the twentieth century.

During the Middle Ages, Europeans began to take the lead over the Muslims, the Byzantines, the Chinese, and all the other peoples in the use of technology. Medieval technology and inventiveness stemmed in part from Christianity, which taught that God had created the world specifically for

Wisdom Urges Medieval Scholars Forward.   During the Middle Ages, Europeans made considerable advances in technology. The astrolabe, quadrant, sundials, and mechanical clocks shown here illustrate medieval technical skills. (*Bibliothèque Royale Albert I, Brussels*)

human beings to subdue and exploit. Consequently, medieval people tried to employ animal power and laborsaving machinery to relieve human drudgery. Moreover, Christianity taught that God was above nature, not within it, so the Christian had no spiritual obstacle to exploiting nature—unlike, for instance, the Hindu. In contrast to classical humanism, the Christian outlook did not consider manual work degrading; even monks combined it with study.

The Christian stress on the sacred worth of the individual and on the higher law of God has never ceased to influence Western civilization. Even though in modern times the various Christian churches have not often taken the lead in political and social reform, the ideals identified with the Judeo-Christian tradition have become part of the Western heritage. As such, they have inspired social reformers who may no longer identify with their ancestral religion.

Believing that God's law was superior to state or national decrees, medieval philosophers provided a theoretical basis for opposing tyrannical kings who violated Christian principles. The idea that both the ruler and the ruled are bound by a higher law would, in a secularized form, become a principal element of modern liberal thought.

Feudalism also contributed to the history of liberty. According to feudal theory, the king, as a member of the feudal community, was duty-bound to honor agreements made with his vassals. Lords possessed personal rights, which the king was obliged to respect. Resentful of a king who ran roughshod over customary feudal rights, lords also negotiated contracts with the crown, such as the famous Magna Carta, to define and guard their customary liberties. To protect themselves from the arbitrary behavior of a king, feudal lords initiated what came to be called *government by consent* and the *rule of law*.

During the Middle Ages, then, there gradually emerged the idea that law was not imposed on inferiors by an absolute monarch but required the collaboration of the king and his subjects; that the king, too, was bound by the law; and that lords had the right to resist a monarch who violated agreements. A related phenomenon was the rise of representative institutions, with which the king was expected to consult on the realm's affairs. The most notable such institution was the British Parliament; although subordinate to the king, it became a permanent part of the state. Later, in the seventeenth century, Parliament would successfully challenge royal authority. Thus, continuity exists between the feudal tradition of a king bound by law and the modern practice of limiting the authority of the head of state.

Although the elements of continuity are clear, the characteristic outlook of the Middle Ages is as different from that of the modern age as it was from the outlook of the ancient world. Religion was the integrating feature of the Middle Ages, whereas science and secularism—a preoccupation with worldly life—determine the modern outlook. The period from the Italian Renaissance of the fifteenth century through the eighteenth-century Age of Enlightenment constituted a gradual breaking away from the medieval world-view: a rejection of the medieval conception of nature, the individual, and the purpose of life. The transition from medieval to modern was neither sudden nor complete, for there are no sharp demarcation lines separating historical periods. While many distinctively medieval ways endured in the sixteenth, seventeenth, and even eighteenth centuries, these centuries saw as well the rise of new intellectual, political, and economic forms, which marked the emergence of modernity.

Medieval thought began with the existence of God and the truth of his revelation as interpreted by the church, which set the standards and defined the purposes for human endeavor. The medieval mind rejected the fundamental principle of Greek philosophy: the autonomy of reason. Without the guidance of revealed truth, reason was seen as feeble.

Scholastics engaged in genuine philosophical speculation, but they did not allow philosophy to challenge the basic premises of their faith. Unlike either ancient or modern thinkers, medieval schoolmen ultimately believed that reason alone could not provide a unified view of nature or society. A rational soul had to be guided by a divine light. For all medieval philosophers, the natural order depended on a supernatural order for its origin and purpose. To understand the natural world properly, it was necessary to know its relationship to the higher world. The discoveries of reason had to accord with Scripture as interpreted by the church.

In the modern view, both nature and the human intellect are self-sufficient. Nature is a mathematical system that operates without miracles or any other form of divine intervention. To comprehend nature and society, the mind needs no divine assistance; it accepts no authority above reason. The modern mentality finds it unacceptable to reject the conclusions of science on the basis of clerical authority and revelation or to ground politics, law, or economics on religious dogma. It refuses to settle public issues by appeals to religious belief.

The medieval philosopher understood both nature and society to be a hierarchical order. God was the source of moral values, and the church was responsible for teaching and upholding these ethical norms. Kings acquired their right to rule from God. The entire social structure constituted a hierarchy: the clergy guided society according to Christian standards; lords defended Christian society from its enemies; and serfs, lowest in the social order, toiled for the good of all. In the hierarchy of knowledge, a lower form of knowledge derived from the senses, and the highest type of knowledge, theology, dealt with God's revelation. To the medieval mind, this hierarchical ordering of nature, society, and knowledge had divine sanction.

Rejecting the medieval division of the universe into higher and lower realms and superior and inferior substances, the modern view postulated the uniformity of nature and of nature's laws: the cosmos knows no privilege of rank; heavenly bodies follow the same laws of nature as earthly objects. Space is geometric and homogeneous, not hierarchical, heterogeneous, and qualitative. The universe was no longer conceived as finite and closed but as infinite, and the operations of nature were explained mathematically. The modern thinker studies mathematical law and chemical composition, not grades of perfection. Spiritual meaning is not sought in an examination of the material world. Roger Bacon, for example, described seven coverings of the eye and then concluded that God had fashioned the eye in this manner in order to express the seven gifts of the Spirit. This way of thinking is alien to the modern outlook. So, too, is the medieval belief that natural disasters, such as plagues and famines, are God's punishments for people's sins.

The outlook of the modern West also broke with the rigid division of medieval society into three orders: clergy, nobles, and commoners. The intellectual justification for this arrangement, as expressed by the English prelate John of Salisbury (c. 1115–1180), has been rejected by modern westerners: "For inferiors owe it to their superiors to provide them with service, just as the superiors in their turn owe it to their inferiors to provide them with all things needful for their protection and succor."[4] Opposing the feudal principle that an individual's obligations and rights are a function of his or her rank in society, the modern view stressed equality of opportunity and equal treatment under the law. It rejected the idea that society should be guided by clergy, who were deemed to possess a special wisdom; by nobles, who were entitled to special privileges; and by monarchs, who were thought to receive their power from God.

The modern West also rejected the personal and customary character of feudal law. As the modern state developed, law assumed an impersonal and objective character. For example, if the lord demanded more than the customary forty days of military service, the vassal might refuse to comply because he would see the lord's request as an unpardonable violation of custom and agreement, as well as an infringement on his liberties. In the modern state, with a constitution and a representative assembly, if a new law increasing the length of military service is passed, it merely replaces the old law. People do not refuse to obey it because the government has broken faith or violated custom.

In the modern world, the individual's relationship to the universe has been radically transformed. Medieval people lived in a geocentric universe, which was finite in space and time. The universe was small, enclosed by a sphere of stars, beyond which were the heavens. The universe, it was believed, was some four thousand years old, and, in the not-too-distant future, Christ would return and human history would end. People in the Middle Ages knew why they were on earth and what was expected of them; they never doubted that heaven would be their reward for living a Christian life. Preparation for heaven was the ultimate aim of life. J. H. Randall, Jr., a historian of ideas, eloquently sums up the medieval view of a purposeful universe, in which the human being's position was clearly defined:

> *The world was governed throughout by the omnipotent will and omniscient mind of God, whose sole interests were centered in man, his trial, his fall, his suffering and his glory. Worm of the dust as he was, man was yet the central object in the whole universe. . . . And when his destiny was completed, the heavens would be rolled up as a scroll and he would dwell with the Lord forever. Only those who rejected God's freely offered grace and with hardened hearts refused repentance would be cut off from this eternal life.*[5]

This comforting medieval vision is alien to the modern outlook. Today, in a universe some twelve billion years old, in which the earth is a tiny speck floating in an endless cosmic ocean, where life evolved over tens of millions of years, many westerners no longer believe that human beings are special children of God; that heaven is their ultimate goal; that under their feet is hell, where grotesque demons torment sinners; and that God is an active agent in human history. To many intellectuals, the universe seems unresponsive to the religious supplications of people, and life's purpose is sought within the limits of earthly existence. Science and secularism have driven Christianity and faith from their central position to the periphery of human concerns.

The modern outlook developed gradually in the period from the Renaissance to the eighteenth-century Age of Enlightenment. Mathematics rendered the universe comprehensible. Economic and political thought broke free of the religious frame of reference. Science became the great hope of the future. The thinkers of the Enlightenment wanted to liberate humanity from superstition, ignorance, and traditions that could not pass the test of reason. They saw themselves as emancipating culture from theological dogma and clerical authority. Rejecting the Christian idea of a person's inherent sinfulness, they held that the individual was basically good and that evil resulted from faulty institutions, poor education, and bad leadership. Thus, the concept of a rational and free society, in which individuals could realize their potential, slowly emerged.

Notes

1. Quoted in David Knowles, *The Evolution of Medieval Thought* (New York: Vintage Books, 1964), p. 123.
2. Thomas Aquinas, *Summa Theologica,* Pt. 1, question 2, art. 3. Excerpted in Anton C. Pegis, ed., *Introduction to Saint Thomas Aquinas* (New York: Modern Library, 1948), p. 25.
3. Joan Gadol, *Leon Battista Alberti,* *Universal Man of the Early Renaissance* (Chicago: University of Chicago Press, 1969), pp. 149–150.
4. John of Salisbury, *Policraticus,* trans. John Dickinson (New York: Russell & Russell, 1963), pp. 243–244.
5. J. H. Randall, Jr., *The Making of the Modern Mind* (Boston: Houghton Mifflin, 1940), p. 34.

Suggested Reading

Brooke, Christopher, *The Twelfth-Century Renaissance* (1969). Surveys schools, learning, theology, literature, and leading figures.

Copleston, F. C., *A History of Medieval Philosophy* (1974). A lucid, comprehensive survey of medieval philosophy.

Gilson, Etienne, *Reason and Revelation in the Middle Ages* (1966). A superb brief exposition of the medieval philosophical tradition.

Gimpel, Jean, *The Cathedral Builders* (1984). The financial, political, and spiritual forces behind the building of cathedrals.

Haskins, C. H., *The Renaissance of the Twelfth Century* (1957). Reprint of a still useful work.

Hay, Denys, *Europe in the Fourteenth and Fifteenth Centuries* (1966). A good survey of the Late Middle Ages.

Lerner, Robert E., *The Age of Adversity* (1968). A short, readable survey of the fourteenth century.

Ozment, Steven E., *The Age of Reform, 1250–1550* (1980). An intellectual and religious history of late medieval and Reformation Europe.

Pieper, Josef, *Scholasticism* (1964). Written with intelligence and grace.

Piltz, Anders, *The World of Medieval Learning* (1981). A clearly written, informative survey of medieval education and learning.

Wagner, David L., ed., *The Seven Liberal Arts in the Middle Ages* (1983). Essays on the place of the liberal arts in medieval culture.

Wieruszowski, Helene, *The Medieval University* (1966). A good survey, followed by documents.

Review Questions

1. What factors contributed to the revival of learning in the late eleventh and twelfth centuries?

2. Describe the essential features of the medieval view of the universe. How does it differ from the modern view?

3. The medieval individual's understanding of self was related to a comprehension of the universe as a hierarchy culminating in God. Explain this statement.

4. What were scholastic philosophers trying to accomplish?

5. What was the significance of Aquinas's thought?

6. Describe what each of the following tells about the attitudes and interests of medieval people: troubadour poetry, *The Canterbury Tales, The Divine Comedy,* and Gothic cathedrals.

7. What economic problems made the fourteenth century an age of adversity?

8. How was the church's authority weakened in the Late Middle Ages?

9. What is the legacy of the Middle Ages to the modern world?

10. How does the characteristic outlook of the Middle Ages differ from that of the modern age?

❖ PART THREE

The Rise of Modernity: From the Renaissance to the Enlightenment

1350–1789

Departure from Lisbon for Brazil, the East Indies, and America, by Theodore de Bry, 1562. (*Giraudon/Art Resource, NY*)

	POLITICS AND SOCIETY	THOUGHT AND CULTURE
1300	Hundreds Years' War (1337–1453)	Italian Renaissance begins (c. 1350)
1400	War of Roses in England (1455–1485) Rule of Ferdinand and Isabella in Spain (1469–1516) Charles VIII of France (1483–1498) Henry VII, beginning of Tudor dynasty in England (1485–1509) Columbus reaches America (1492)	Early Renaissance artists: Brunelleschi, Masaccio, van Eyck Printing with movable type (c. 1450) Humanists: Valla, Pico della Mirandola Late Renaissance artists: Botticelli, Leonardo da Vinci, Michelangelo, Raphael, Bellini, Giorgione, Titian Renaissance spreads to northern Europe (late fifteenth and early sixteenth cent.)
1500	Henry VIII of England (1509–1547) Francis I of France (1515–1547) Charles V, Holy Roman Emperor (1519–1556) Henry VIII of England breaks with Rome (1529–1536) Council of Trent (1545–1563) Peace of Augsburg in Germany (1555) Philip II of Spain (1556–1598) Elizabeth I of England (1558–1603) Religious wars in France (1562–1598) Revolt of the Netherlands from Spain (1566–1609) Defeat of Spanish Armada (1588)	Humanists: Castiglione, Erasmus, Montaigne, Rabelais, More, Cervantes, Shakespeare Machiavelli, *The Prince* (1513) Luther writes his Ninety-Five Theses (1517) Copernicus, *On the Revolution of the Heavenly Spheres* (1543)
1600	Thirty Years' War (1618–1648) English Revolution (1640–1660, 1688–1689) Louis XIV of France (1643–1715) Peter the Great of Russia (1682–1725)	Scientists: Kepler, Galileo, Newton Philosophers: Bacon, Descartes, Hobbes, Locke
1700	War of Spanish Succession (1702–1714) War of Austrian Succession (1740–1748) Frederick the Great of Prussia (1740–1786) Maria Theresa of Austria (1740–1780) Seven Years' War (1756–1763) American Declaration of Independence (1776) American Revolution (1776–1783) Beginning of French Revolution (1789)	Enlightenment thinkers: Voltaire, Montesquieu, Rousseau, Diderot, Hume, Adam Smith, Thomas Jefferson, Kant

❖ CHAPTER 8

Transition to the Modern Age: Renaissance and Reformation

*F*rom the Italian Renaissance of the fifteenth century through the Age of Enlightenment of the eighteenth century, the outlook and institutions of the Middle Ages disintegrated and distinctly modern forms emerged. The radical change in European civilization affected every level of society. On the economic level, commerce and industry expanded greatly, and capitalism largely replaced medieval forms of economic organization. On the political level, central government grew stronger at the expense of feudalism. On the religious level, the rise of Protestantism fragmented the unity of Christendom. On the social level, middle-class townspeople, increasing in number and wealth, began to play a more important role in economic and cultural life. On the cultural level, the clergy lost its monopoly over learning, and the otherworldly orientation of the Middle Ages gave way to a secular outlook in literature and the arts. Theology, the queen of knowledge in the Middle Ages, surrendered its crown to science, and reason, which had been subordinate to revelation, asserted its independence.

Many of these tendencies manifested themselves dramatically during the Renaissance (1350–1600). The word *renaissance* means "rebirth," and it is used to refer to the attempt by artists and thinkers to recover and apply the ancient learning and standards of Greece and Rome. During the Renaissance, individuals showed an increasing concern for worldly life and self-consciously aspired to shape their destinies, an attitude that is the key to modernity.

To be sure, the Renaissance was not a complete and sudden break with the Middle Ages. Many medieval ways and attitudes persisted. Nevertheless, the view that the Renaissance represents the birth of modernity has much to recommend it. Renaissance writers and artists themselves were aware of their age's novelty. They looked back on the medieval centuries as a "Dark Age" that followed the grandeur of ancient Greece and Rome, and they believed that they were experiencing a rebirth of cultural greatness. Renaissance artists and writers were fascinated by the cultural forms of Greece and Rome; they sought to imitate classical style and to capture the secular spirit of antiquity. In the process, they broke with medieval artistic and literary forms. They valued the full development of human talent and expressed a new excitement about the possibilities of life in this world. This outlook represents a break with the Middle Ages and the emergence of modernity.

The Renaissance, then, was an age of transition. It saw the rejection of certain elements of the medieval outlook, the revival of classical cultural forms, and the emergence of distinctly modern attitudes. This rebirth began in Italy during the fourteenth century and gradually spread north and west to Germany, France, England, and Spain during the late fifteenth and sixteenth centuries.

The Renaissance was one avenue to modernity; another was the Reformation. By dividing Europe into Catholic and Protestant, the Reformation ended medieval religious unity. It also accentuated the importance of the individual person, a distinctive feature of the modern outlook. It stressed individual conscience rather than clerical authority, insisted on a personal relationship between each man or woman and God, and called attention to the individual's inner religious capacities.   ❖

Italy: Birthplace of the Renaissance

The city-states of northern Italy that spawned the Renaissance were developed urban centers, where people had the wealth, freedom, and inclination to cultivate the arts and to enjoy the fruits of worldly life. In Italy, moreover, reminders of ancient Rome's grandeur were visible everywhere: Roman roads, monuments, and manuscripts intensified the Italians' links to their Roman past. Northern Italian city-states had developed as flourishing commercial and banking centers and had monopolized trade in the Mediterranean during the twelfth and thirteenth centuries. The predominance of business and commerce within these city-states meant that the feudal nobility, who held the land beyond the city walls, played a much less important part in government than they did elsewhere in Europe. By the end of the twelfth century, the city-states had adopted a fairly uniform pattern of republican self-government, built around the office of a chief magistrate.

This republicanism proved precarious, however. During the fourteenth and early fifteenth centuries, republican institutions in one city after another toppled, giving way to rule by despots. The city-states had come to rely on mercenary troops, whose leaders, the notorious *condottieri*—unschooled in and owing no loyalty to the republican tradition—simply seized power during emergencies.

Florence, the leading city of the Renaissance, held out against the trend toward despotism for a long time. But by the mid-fifteenth century, even Florentine republicanism was giving way before the intrigues of a rich banking family, the Medici. They had installed themselves in power in the 1430s with

Chronology 8.1 ❖ The Renaissance and the Reformation

1304–1374	Petrarch, "father of humanism"
c. 1445	Johann Gutenberg invents movable metal type
1513	Machiavelli writes *The Prince*
1517	Martin Luther writes his Ninety-five Theses and the Reformation begins
1520	Pope Leo X excommunicates Luther
1524–1526	German peasants revolt
1529	English Parliament accepts Henry VIII's Reformation
1534	Henry VIII is declared head of the Church of England; King Francis I of France declares Protestants to be heretics; Ignatius Loyola founds the Society of Jesus; Anabaptists, radical reformers, capture Münster in Westphalia
1535	Sir Thomas More, English humanist and author of *Utopia*, is executed for treason
1536–1564	Calvin leads the Reformation in Geneva
1545–1563	Council of Trent
1555	Peace of Augsburg

the return of Cosimo de' Medici from exile. Cosimo's grandson, Lorenzo the Magnificent, completed the destruction of the republican constitution in 1480, when he managed to set up a government staffed by his supporters.

New ways of life developed within the Italian city-states. Prosperous business people played a leading role in the political and cultural life of the city. With the expansion of commerce and industry, the feudal values of birth, military prowess, and a fixed hierarchy of lords and vassals decayed in favor of ambition and individual achievement, whether at court, in the counting house, or inside the artist's studio.

Art served as a focus of civic pride and patriotism. Members of the urban upper class became patrons of the arts, providing funds to support promising artists and writers. Just as they contended on the battlefield, rulers competed for art and artists to bolster their prestige. The popes, too, heaped wealth on artists to enhance their own flagging prestige. They became the most lavish patrons of all, as the works of Michelangelo and Raphael testify.

Some women of wealthy and noble Italian families were educated in classical languages and literature and served as patrons of the arts. Thus, Isabella

Ludovico Gonzaga, His Family and Court: A Fresco Painted by Andrea Mantegna, A.D. 1465–1474.   The Gonzaga family came to power as princes of Mantua, selling their services as condottieri to the Venetians, Milanese, or others as their interests dictated. Ludovico (1414–1478) presided over the city at a time of great prosperity. He commissioned the famous painter Andrea Mantegna to decorate his palace and the architect Leon Battista Alberti to build several churches. His patronage of humanistic scholars, poets, and philosophers added to the prestige of the city and its princely ruler. (*Scala/Art Resource, NY*)

d'Este, wife of the ruler of a small state in northern Italy, knew Latin and Greek, collected books, and displayed works of artists, which she had commissioned.

The result of this new patronage by popes and patricians was an explosion of artistic creativity. The amount, and especially the nature, of this patronage also helped shape both art and the artist. Portraiture became a separate genre for the first time since antiquity and was developed much further than ever before. Patrician rivalry and insecurity of status, fed by the Renaissance ethic of individual achievement and reward, produced a scramble for honor and reputation. This pursuit fostered the desire to be memorialized in a painting, if not in a sculpture. A painter like Titian was in great demand.

The great artists emerged as famous men by virtue of their exercise of brush and chisel. In the Middle Ages, artists had been regarded as craftsmen who did lowly (manual) labor and who, as a result, were to be accorded little, if any, status. Indeed, for the most part they remained anonymous. But the unparalleled Renaissance demand for art brought artists public recognition.

The Renaissance Outlook

Increasingly, a secular outlook came to dominate Renaissance society. Intrigued by the active life of the city and eager to enjoy the worldly pleasures that their money could obtain, wealthy merchants and bankers moved away from the medieval preoccupation with salvation. To be sure, they were neither nonbelievers nor atheists, but more and more, religion had to compete with worldly concerns. Consequently, members of the urban upper class paid religion less heed or at least did not allow it to interfere with their quest for the full life. The challenge and pleasure of living well in this world seemed more exciting than the promise of heaven. This outlook found concrete expression in Renaissance art and literature.

Individualism was another hallmark of the Renaissance. The urban elite sought to assert their own personalities, demonstrate their unique talents, and gain recognition for their accomplishments. Traditional feudal values of birth and place in a fixed hierarchy were superseded by the desire for individual achievement. Individual worth was interpreted far more broadly than it had been by feudal lords, who had equated worth with military prowess. Renaissance Italy produced a distinctive human type, the "universal man": a many-sided person, who not only showed mastery of the ancient classics, an appreciation of and even talent for the visual arts, and a concern for the day-to-day affairs of his city, but also aspired to mold his life into a work of art. Disdaining Christian humility, Renaissance individuals took pride in their talents and worldly accomplishments—"I can work miracles," said the great Leonardo da Vinci. Renaissance artists portrayed the individual character of human beings, captured the rich diversity of human personality, produced the first portraits since Roman times, and affixed their signatures to their works. Renaissance writers probed their own feelings and manifested a self-awareness that characterizes the modern outlook.

In later centuries, as the secular outlook gathered strength, it would focus even more intently on the individual. It led to the conviction that the individual should be freed from domination by otherworldly concerns, theological dogma, and ecclesiastical authority and should concentrate on the full development of human talents and on improving the quality of earthly existence.

During the Renaissance, the secular spirit and the concern with the individual found expression in the intellectual movement called humanism and in a political theory that separated politics from Christian principles.

Humanism

Humanism, the most characteristic intellectual movement of the Renaissance, was an educational and cultural program based on the study of ancient Greek and Roman literature. The humanist attitude toward antiquity differed from that of medieval scholars, who had taken pains to fit classical learning into a Christian world-view. Renaissance humanists did not subordinate the classics to the requirements of Christian doctrines. Rather, they valued ancient literature for its own sake—for its clear and graceful style and for its insights into human nature. From the ancient classics, humanists expected to learn much that could not be provided by medieval writings: for instance, how to live well in this world and how to perform one's civic duties. For the humanists, the classics were a guide to the good life, the active life. To achieve self-cultivation, to write well, to speak well, and to live well, it was necessary to know the classics. In contrast to scholastic philosophers, who used Greek philosophy to prove the truth of Christian doctrines, Italian humanists used classical learning to nourish their new interest in a worldly life. Whereas medieval scholars were familiar with only some ancient Latin writers, Renaissance humanists restored to circulation every Roman work that could be found. Similarly, knowledge of Greek was very rare in Latin Christendom during the Middle Ages, but Renaissance humanists increasingly cultivated the study of Greek in order to read Homer, Demosthenes, Plato, and other ancients in the original.

Although predominantly a secular movement, Italian humanism was not un-Christian. True, humanists often treated moral problems in a purely secular manner. Yet in dealing with religious and theological issues, they did not challenge Christian belief or question the validity of the Bible. They did, however, attack scholastic philosophy for its hairsplitting arguments and preoccupation with trivial matters. They stressed instead a purer form of Christianity, based on the direct study of the Bible and the writings of the church fathers.

One of the early humanists, sometimes called the father of humanism, was Petrarch (1304–1374). Petrarch and his followers carried the recovery of the classics further through their systematic attempt to discover the classical roots of medieval Italian rhetoric. Petrarch's own efforts to learn Greek were largely unsuccessful, but he advanced humanist learning by encouraging his students to master the ancient tongue. Petrarch was particularly drawn to Cicero, the ancient Roman orator. Following Cicero's example, he maintained that education should consist not only of learning and knowing things, but also of learning how to communicate one's knowledge and how to use it for the public good. Therefore, the emphasis in education should be on rhetoric and moral philosophy—wisdom combined with eloquence. This was the key to virtue in the ruler, the citizen, and the republic. Petrarch helped to make Ciceronian values dominant among the humanists. His followers set up schools to inculcate the new Ciceronian educational ideal.

Implicit in the humanist educational ideal was a radical transformation of the Christian idea of human beings. According to the medieval (Augustinian) view, men and women, because of their sinful nature, were incapable of attaining excellence through their own efforts. They were completely subject to divine will. In contrast, the humanists, recalling the classical Greek concept of human beings, made the achievement of excellence through individual striving the end not only of education, but of life itself. Moreover, because individuals were capable of this goal, it was their duty to pursue it as the end of life. The pursuit was not effortless; indeed, it took extraordinary energy and skill.

People, then, were deemed capable of excellence in every sphere and duty-bound to make the effort. This emphasis on human creative powers was one of the most characteristic and influential doctrines of the Renaissance. A classic expression of it is found in the *Oration on the Dignity of Man* (1486) by Giovanni Pico della Mirandola (1463–1494). Man, said Pico, has the freedom to shape his own life. Pico has God say to man: "We have made you a creature" such that "you may, as the free and proud shaper of your own being, fashion yourself in the form you may prefer."[1]

An attack on the medieval scholastics was also implicit in the humanist educational ideal. Humanists accused scholastics of corrupting the Latin style of ancient Rome and of dealing with useless questions. This humanist emphasis on the uses of knowledge offered a stimulus to science and art.

So hostile were the humanists to all things scholastic and medieval that they reversed the prevailing view of history. According to the Christian view, history was a simple unfolding of God's will and providence. The humanists, however, stressed the importance of human actions and human will in history—the importance of people as active participants in the shaping of events. They characterized the epoch preceding their own as a period of decline from classical heights—a dark age—and saw their own time as a period of rebirth, representing the recovery of classical wisdom and ideals. Thus, the humanists invented the notion of the Middle Ages as the period separating the ancient world from their own. To the humanists, then, we owe the current periodization of history into ancient, medieval, and modern. The humanist view also contained an element of today's idea of progress: they dared to think that they, "the moderns," might even surpass the ancient glories of Greece and Rome.

The humanist emphasis on historical scholarship yielded a method of critical inquiry that could help to undermine traditional loyalties and institutions. The work of Lorenzo Valla (c. 1407–1457) provides the clearest example of this trend. Educated as a classicist, Valla trained the guns of critical scholarship on the papacy in his most famous work, *Declamation Concerning the False Decretals of Constantine.* The papal claim to temporal authority rested on a document that purported to verify the so-called Donation of Constantine, through which the Emperor Constantine, when he moved the capital of the Roman Empire to Constantinople in the fourth century, had given the pope dominion over the entire western Empire. But Valla proved that the document was based on an eighth-century forgery because the language at certain points was unknown in Constantine's time and did not come into use until much later.

Also embedded in the humanist reevaluation of individual potential was a new appreciation of the moral significance of work. For the humanist, the honor, fame, and even glory bestowed by one's city or patron for meritorious deeds was the ultimate reward for effort. The humanist pursuit of praise and reputation became something of a Renaissance cult.

A Revolution in Political Thought

By turning away from the religious orientation of the Middle Ages and discussing the human condition in secular terms, Renaissance humanists opened up new possibilities for thinking about political and moral problems. Niccolò Machiavelli (1469–1527), a keen observer of Italian politics, saw the Italian city-states, ruled by men whose authority rested solely on their cunning and effective use of force, as a new phenomenon. He recognized that traditional political theory, concerned with ideal Christian ends, could not adequately explain it. Italian princes made no effort to justify their policies on religious grounds; war was endemic, and powerful cities took over weaker ones; diplomacy was riddled with intrigue, betrayal, and bribery. In such a tooth-and-claw world—where political survival depended on alertness, cleverness, and strength—medieval theorists, who expected the earthly realm to accord with standards revealed by God, seemed utterly irrelevant. Machiavelli simply wanted rulers to understand how to prepare and expand the state's power. In his book *The Prince,* he expounded a new political theory—one that had no place for Christian morality but coincided with the emerging modern secular state. He himself was aware that his study of statecraft in the cold light of reason, free of religious and moral illusions, represented a new departure.

For Machiavelli, survival was the state's overriding aim; it transcended any concern with moral or religious values and the interests of individual subjects. Removing questions of good and evil from the political realm, Machiavelli maintained that the prince may use any means to save the state when its survival is at stake. Successful princes, he contended, have always been indifferent to moral and religious considerations—a lesson of history that rulers ignore at their peril. Thus, if the situation warrants it, the prince can violate agreements with other rulers, go back on his word with his subjects, and resort to cruelty and terror.

Machiavelli broke with the distinguishing feature of medieval thought: the division of the universe into the higher world of the heavens and a lower earthly realm. To this extent, he did for politics what Galileo accomplished a century later for physics. Medieval thinkers believed that rulers derived their power from God and had a religious obligation to govern in accordance with God's commands. Rejecting completely this otherworldly, theocentric orientation, Machiavelli ascribed no divine origin or purpose to the state. He saw it as a natural entity; politics had nothing to do with God's intent or with moral precepts originating in a higher world. Machiavelli's significance as a political thinker rests on the fact that he removed political thought from a religious frame of reference and viewed the state and political behavior in the detached and dispassionate manner of a scientist. In secularizing and rationalizing political philosophy, he initiated a trend of thought that we recognize as distinctly modern.

Renaissance Art

The essential meaning of the Renaissance is conveyed through its art, particularly architecture, sculpture, and painting. Renaissance examples of all three art forms reflect a style that stressed proportion, balance, and harmony. These artistic values were achieved through a new, revolutionary conceptualization of space and spatial relations. To a considerable extent, Renaissance art also reflects the values of Renaissance humanism: a return to classical models in architecture, to the rendering of the nude figure, and to a heroic vision of human beings.

Medieval art served a religious function and sought to represent spiritual aspiration; the world was a veil merely hinting at the other perfect and eternal world. Renaissance art did not stop expressing spiritual aspiration, but its setting and character differ altogether. No longer a shroud, this world becomes the place where people live, act, and worship. The reference is less to the other world and more to this world, and people are treated as creatures who find their spiritual destiny as they fulfill their human one. At its most distinctive, Renaissance art represents a conscious revolt against the art of the Middle Ages. This revolt produced revolutionary discoveries, which served as the foundation of Western art up to this century.

In art, as in philosophy, the Florentines played a leading role in this esthetic transformation. They, more than anyone else, were responsible for the way artists saw and drew for centuries and for the way most Western people still see or want to see. The first major contributor to Renaissance painting was the Florentine painter Giotto (c. 1276–1337). Borrowing from Byzantine painting, he created figures delineated by alterations in light and shade. He also developed several techniques of perspective, representing three-dimensional figures and objects on two-dimensional surfaces so that they appear to stand in space. Giotto's figures look remarkably alive. They are drawn and arranged in space to tell a story, and their expressions and the illusion of movement they convey heighten the dramatic effect. Giotto's best works were *frescoes,* wall paintings painted while the plaster was still wet, or *fresh.* Lionized in his own day, Giotto had no immediate successors, and his ideas were not taken up and developed further for almost a century.

By the early fifteenth century, the revival of classical learning had begun in earnest. In Florence, it had its artistic counterpart among a circle of architects, painters, and sculptors who sought to revive classical art. The leader of this group was an architect, Filippo Brunelleschi (1377–1446). He designed churches reflecting classical models. To him we also owe a scientific discovery of the first importance in the history of art: the rules of perspective. Giotto had revived the ancient technique of foreshortening; Brunelleschi completed the discovery by rendering perspective in mathematical terms. Brunelleschi's devotion to ancient models and his new tool of mathematical perspective set the stage for the further development of Renaissance painting. Brunelleschi's young Florentine friend Masaccio (1401–1428) took up the challenge. Faithful to the new rules of perspective, Masaccio was also concerned with painting statuesque figures and endowing his paintings with a grandeur and

The Birth of Venus by Sandro Botticelli (1444–1510). A member of the Florentine circle of Neo-Platonists, Botticelli celebrated classical myths, such as the rising of Venus, goddess of love, who was born in the sea. The use of classical deities and myths in Western art and literature took on new force during the Renaissance. (*Alinari/Art Resource, NY*)

simplicity whose inspiration was classical. Perspective came with all the force of religious revelation.

In his work *On Painting,* Leon Battista Alberti (1404–1472), a humanist, scholar, and art theoretician, brought the Renaissance trend toward perspectival art to a summation by advancing the first mathematical theory of artistic perspective. By defining visual space and the relationship between the object and the observer in mathematical terms, Renaissance art and artistic theory paved the way for the development of the modern scientific approach to nature, which later found expression in the astronomy of Copernicus and the physics of Galileo.

Renaissance artists were dedicated to representing things as they are, or at least as they are seen to be. Part of the inspiration for this was also classical. The ancient ideal of beauty was the beautiful nude. Renaissance admiration for ancient art meant that artists for the first time since the fall of Rome studied anatomy; they learned to draw the human form by having models pose for them, a practice fundamental to artistic training to this day. Another member of Brunelleschi's circle, the Florentine sculptor Donatello (1386–1466), also showed renewed interest in the human form.

The great Renaissance artists included Leonardo da Vinci (1452–1519), Michelangelo Buonarroti (1475–1564), and Raphael Santi (1483–1520). All of them were closely associated with Florence. Leonardo was a scientist and engineer, as well as a great artist. He was an expert at fortifications and gunnery, an inventor, an anatomist, and a naturalist. Bringing careful observation of nature to his paintings, he combined it with powerful psychological insight to produce works of unsurpassed genius, though few in number. Among his most important paintings are *The Last Supper* and *La Gioconda,* or the Mona Lisa. The Mona Lisa is an example of an artistic invention of Leonardo's—what the Italians call *sfumato.* Leonardo left the outlines of the face a little vague and shadowy; this freed it of any wooden quality, which more exact drawing would impart, and thus made it more lifelike and mysterious.

Michelangelo's creation of artistic harmony derived from a mastery of anatomy and drawing. His model in painting came from sculpture: his paintings are sculpted drawings. He was, of course, a sculptor of the highest genius, whose approach to his art was poetic and visionary. Instead of trying to impose form on marble, he thought of sculpting as releasing the form from the rock. Among his greatest sculptures are *David, Moses,* and *The Dying Slave.* Michelangelo was also an architect; patronized by the pope, he designed the dome of the new Saint Peter's Basilica in Rome. But perhaps his most stupendous work was the ceiling of the Sistine Chapel in the Vatican, commissioned by Pope Julius II. In four years, working with little assistance, Michelangelo covered the empty space with the most monumental sculpted pictures ever painted, pictures that summarize the Old Testament story. *The Creation of Adam* is the most famous of these superlative frescoes.

Raphael, the last of these three artistic giants, is especially famous for the sweetness of his Madonnas. But he was capable of painting other subjects and conveying other moods, as his portrait of his patron, *Pope Leo X with Two Cardinals*, reveals.

The Spread of the Renaissance

Aided by the invention of printing, the Renaissance spread to Germany, France, England, and Spain in the late fifteenth and sixteenth centuries. In its migration northward, Renaissance culture adapted itself to conditions different from those in Italy—particularly the strength of lay piety. For example, the Brethren of the Common Life was a lay movement emphasizing education and practical piety. Intensely Christian and at the same time anticlerical, the people in such lay movements found in Renaissance culture tools for sharpening their wits against the clergy—not to undermine the faith, but rather to restore it to its apostolic purity.

Thus, northern humanists, just like those in Italy, were profoundly devoted to ancient learning. But nothing in northern humanism compares with the non-Christian trend of the Italian Renaissance. The northerners were chiefly interested in the question of what constituted original Christianity. They sought a model in the light of which they might reform the corrupted church of their own time.

Giovanni Arnolfini and His Bride by Jan van Eyck (c. 1390–1441). The painting uses the new technique of perspective and draws a careful, and idealized, portrait of a prosperous married couple in their bedroom. As such, it depicts a world that values privacy, sober prosperity, and intimacy of a certain kind: he stares out at us, while she looks deferentially at him. (*Reproduced by courtesy of the Trustees, The National Gallery, London*)

Humanism outside Italy was less concerned with the revival of classical values than with the reform of Christianity and society through a program of Christian humanism. The Christian humanists cultivated the new arts of rhetoric and history, as well as the classical languages—Latin, Greek, and Hebrew. But the ultimate purpose of these pursuits was more religious than it had been in Italy, where secular interests predominated. Northern humanists used humanist scholarship and language to satirize and vilify medieval scholastic Christianity and to build a purer, more scriptural Christianity. The discovery of accurate biblical texts, it was hoped, would lead to a great religious awakening. Protestant reformers, including Martin Luther, relied on humanist scholarship.

Erasmian Humanism

To Erasmus (c. 1466–1536) belongs the credit for making Renaissance humanism an international movement. He was educated in the Netherlands by the Brethren of the Common Life, which was one of the most advanced religious movements of the age, combining mystical piety with rigorous humanist pedagogy. Erasmus traveled throughout Europe as a humanist educator and biblical scholar. Like other Christian humanists, he trusted the power of words and used his pen to attack scholastic theology and clerical abuses and promote his philosophy of Christ. His weapon was satire, and his *Praise of Folly* and *Colloquies* won him a reputation for acid wit vented at the expense of conventional religion.

True religion, Erasmus argued, does not depend on dogma, ritual, or clerical power. Rather, it is revealed clearly and simply in the Bible and therefore is directly accessible to all people, from the wise and great to the poor and humble. Erasmian humanism stressed toleration, kindness, and respect for human rationality.

This clear but quiet voice was drowned out by the storms of the Reformation, and the Erasmian emphasis on the individual's natural capacities succumbed to a renewed emphasis on human sinfulness and dogmatic theology. Erasmus was caught in the middle and condemned on all sides; for him, the Reformation was both a personal and a historical tragedy. He had worked for peace and unity only to experience a spectacle of war and fragmentation. Erasmian humanism, however, survived these horrors as an ideal, and during the next two centuries, whenever thinkers sought toleration and rational religion, they looked back to Erasmus for inspiration.

French and English Humanism

François Rabelais (c. 1494–c. 1553), a former monk, exemplified the humanist spirit in France. In response to religious dogmatism, he asserted the essential goodness of the individual and the right to enjoy the world rather than be bound by the fear of a punishing God. His folk-epic, *Gargantua and Pantagruel,* celebrates earthly life and earthly enjoyments, expresses an appreciation for secular learning and a confidence in human nature, and attacks monastic orders and clerical education for stifling the human spirit.

According to Rabelais, once freed from dogmatic theology with its irrelevant concerns and narrow-minded clergy, who deprived them of life's joys, people could, by virtue of their native goodness, build a paradise on earth and disregard the one dreamed up by theologians. In *Gargantua and Pantagruel,* Rabelais imagined a monastery where men and women spend their lives "not in laws, statutes, or rules, but according to their own free will and pleasure." They slept and ate when they desired and learned to "read, write, sing, play upon several musical instruments, and speak five or six . . . languages and compose in them all very quaintly." They observed only one rule: "do what thou wilt."[2]

The most influential humanist of the early English Renaissance was Sir Thomas More (1478–1535), who studied at Oxford. His impact came from both his writing and his career. Trained as a lawyer, he was a successful civil servant and member of Parliament. His most famous book is *Utopia,* the first major utopian treatise to be written in the West since Plato's *Republic* and one of the most original works of the entire Renaissance. Many humanists had attacked private wealth as the principal source of pride, greed, and human cruelty. However, only More carried this insight to its logical conclusion: in *Utopia,* he called for the elimination of private property. He had too keen a sense of human weakness to think that people could become perfect, but he used *Utopia* to call attention to contemporary abuses and to suggest radical reforms.

More succeeded Cardinal Wolsey as lord chancellor under Henry VIII. But when the king broke with the Roman Catholic church, More resigned, unable to reconcile his conscience with the king's rejection of papal supremacy. Three years later, in July 1535, More was executed for treason because he refused to swear an oath acknowledging the king's ecclesiastical supremacy.

William Shakespeare (1564–1616), widely considered the greatest playwright the world has ever produced, gave expression to conventional Renaissance values: honor, heroism, and the struggle against fate and fortune. But there is nothing conventional about Shakespeare's treatment of characters possessing these virtues. His greatest plays, the tragedies (*King Lear, Julius Caesar,* and others), explore a common theme: men, even heroic men, despite virtue, are able to overcome their human weaknesses only with the greatest difficulty, if at all. What fascinated Shakespeare was the contradiction between the Renaissance image of nobility, which is often the self-image of Shakespeare's heroes, and humans' capacity for evil and self-destruction. The plays are thus intensely human, but so much so that humanism fades into the background; art transcends doctrine to represent life itself.

The Renaissance and the Modern Age

The Renaissance, then, marks the birth of modernity: in art; in the idea of the individual's role in history and nature; and in society, politics, war, and diplomacy. Central to this birth was a bold new view of human nature, which departed from the medieval view: that individuals in all endeavors are not constrained by a destiny imposed by God from the outside but are free to make their own destiny, guided only by the example of the past, the force of present circumstances, and the drives of their own inner nature. Set free from theology, individuals were seen as the products, and in turn the shapers, of history; their future would be the work of their own free will.

Within the Italian city-states where the Renaissance was born, rich merchants were at least as important as the church hierarchy and the old nobility. Commercial wealth and a new politics produced a new culture, which relied heavily on ancient Greece and Rome. This return to antiquity also entailed a rejection of the Middle Ages as dark, barbarous, and rude. The humanists clearly preferred the secular learning of ancient Greece and Rome to the clerical learning of the more recent past. The reason for this was obvious: the ancients had the same worldly concerns as the humanists; the scholastics did not.

The revival of antiquity by the humanists did not mean, however, that they identified completely with it. The revival itself was done too self-consciously for that. In the very act of looking back, the humanists differentiated themselves from the past and recognized that they were different. They were in this sense the first modern historians, because they could study and appreciate the past for its own sake and, to some degree, on its own terms.

In the works of Renaissance artists and thinkers, the world was, to a large extent, depicted and explained without reference to a higher supernatural realm of meaning and authority. This is clearly seen in Machiavelli's analysis of politics. Renaissance humanism exuded a deep confidence in the capacities of able people, instructed in the wisdom of the ancients, to understand and change the world.

This new confidence was closely related to another distinctive feature of the Renaissance: the cult of the individual. Both prince and painter were motivated in part by the desire to display their talents and to satisfy their ambitions. This individual striving was rewarded and encouraged by the larger society of rich patrons and calculating princes who valued ability. Gone was the medieval Christian emphasis on the virtue of self-denial and the sin of pride. Instead, the Renaissance placed the highest value on self-expression and self-fulfillment—on the realization of individual potential, especially of the gifted few. The Renaissance fostered an atmosphere in which talent, even genius, was allowed to flourish.

To be sure, the Renaissance image of the individual and the world, bold and novel, was the exclusive prerogative of a small, well-educated urban elite and did not reach down to include the masses. Nevertheless, the Renaissance set an example of what people might achieve in art and architecture, taste and refinement, education and urban culture. In many fields, the Renaissance set the cultural standards of the modern age.

Background to the Reformation: The Medieval Church in Crisis

The Renaissance had revitalized European intellectual life and in the process discarded the medieval preoccupation with theology. Similarly, the Reformation marked the beginning of a new religious outlook. The Protestant Reformation, however, did not originate in the elite circles of humanistic scholars. Rather, it was sparked by Martin Luther (1483–1546), an obscure German monk and brilliant theologian. Luther started a rebellion against the church's authority that, in less than one decade, shattered the religious unity of Christendom. Begun in 1517, the Reformation dominated European history throughout much of the sixteenth century.

The Roman Catholic church, centered in Rome, was the one European institution that transcended geographic, ethnic, linguistic, and national boundaries. For centuries, it had extended its influence into every aspect of

European society and culture. As a result, however, its massive wealth and power appeared to take precedence over its commitment to the search for holiness in this world and salvation in the next. Encumbered by wealth, addicted to international power, and protective of their own interests, the clergy, from the pope down, became the focus of a storm of criticism, starting in the Late Middle Ages.

In the fourteenth century, as kings increased their power and as urban centers with their sophisticated laity grew in size and number, people began to question the authority of the international church and its clergy. Political theorists rejected the pope's claim to supremacy over kings. The central idea of medieval Christendom—a Christian commonwealth led by the papacy—increasingly fell into disrepute. Theorists were arguing that the church was only a spiritual body and therefore its power did not extend to the political realm. They said that the pope had no authority over kings, that the state needed no guidance from the papacy, and that the clergy were not above secular law. During the late fourteenth century, Latin Christendom witnessed the first systematic attacks ever launched against the church. Church corruption—such as the selling of indulgences (see page 229), nepotism (the practice of appointing one's relatives to offices), the pursuit of personal wealth by bishops, and the sexual indulgence of the clergy—was nothing new. What was new and startling was the willingness of both educated and uneducated Christians to attack these practices publicly.

Thus, the Englishman John Wycliffe and the Bohemian Jan Hus (see pages 200–201), both learned theologians, denounced the wealth of the clergy as a violation of Christ's precepts and attacked the church's authority at its root by arguing that the church did not control an individual's destiny. They maintained that salvation depends not on participating in the church's rituals or receiving its sacraments, but on accepting God's gift of faith.

Wycliffe's and Hus's efforts to initiate reform coincided with a powerful resurgence of religious feeling in the form of mysticism. Late medieval mystics sought an immediate and personal communication with God; such experiences inspired them to advocate concrete reforms that aimed at renewing the church's spirituality. The church hierarchy inevitably regarded mysticism with some suspicion, for if individuals could experience God directly, they would seemingly have little need for the church and its rituals. In the fourteenth century, these mystical movements seldom became heretical. But in the sixteenth and seventeenth centuries, radical reformers often found in Christian mysticism a powerful alternative to institutional control and even to the need for a priesthood.

With the advent of Lutheranism, personal faith, rather than adherence to the practices of the church, became central to the religious life of European Protestants. Renaissance humanists had sought to reinstitute the wisdom of ancient times; Protestant reformers wanted to restore the spirit of early Christianity, in which faith seemed purer, believers more sincere, and clergy uncorrupted by luxury and power. By the 1540s, the Roman Catholic church had initiated its own internal reformation, but it came too late to stop the movement toward Protestantism in northern and western Europe.

Martin Luther and the Wittenberg Reformers by Lucas Cranach the Younger, Sixteenth Century. The central figure is Frederick, elector of Saxony, the patron and protector of Luther, who stands at the prince's right arm. Ulrich Zwingli, reformer of Zurich, is at his left. (*Toledo Art Museum, Gift of Edward Drummond Libbey*)

The Lutheran Revolt

Martin Luther, who had experienced the personal agony of doubting the church's power to give salvation, had the will and talent to convey that agony to all Christians and to win the support of powerful princes. In his youth, Luther at first fulfilled his father's wish and studied law, but at the age of twenty-one, he suddenly abandoned his legal studies to enter the Augustinian monastery at Erfurt. Luther began his search for spiritual and personal identity, and therefore for salvation, within the strict confinement and discipline of the monastery. He pursued his theological studies there and prepared for ordination.

The Break with Catholicism

As he studied and prayed, Luther grew increasingly terrified by the possibility of his damnation. As a monk, he sought union with God, and he understood the church's teaching that salvation depended on faith, works (meaning acts of charity, prayer, fasting, and so on), and grace—God's influence and favor, which sanctifies and regenerates human life. He participated in the sacraments of the church, which, according to its teaching, were intended to give grace. Indeed, after his ordination, Luther administered the sacraments. Yet he still felt the weight of his sins, and nothing the church could offer seemed to relieve that burden. Seeking solace and salvation, Luther increasingly turned to reading the Bible. Two passages seemed to speak directly to him: "For therein is the righteousness of God revealed from faith to faith: as it is written, 'He who through faith is righteous shall live'" (Romans 1:17); and "They are justified by his grace as a gift, through the redemption which is in Christ Jesus" (Romans 3:24). In these two passages, Luther found, for the first time in his adult life, some hope for his own salvation. Faith, freely given by God through Christ, enables the recipient to receive salvation.

The concept of salvation by faith alone provided an answer to Luther's spiritual quest. Practicing such good works as prayer, fasting, pilgrimages, and participation in the Mass and the other sacraments had never brought Luther peace of mind. He concluded that no amount of good works, however necessary for maintaining the Christian community, would bring salvation. Through reading the Bible and through faith alone, the Christian could find the meaning of earthly existence. For Luther, the true Christian was a courageous figure who faced the terrifying quest for salvation armed only with the hope that God had granted the gift of faith. The new Christian served others not to trade good works for salvation, but solely to fulfill the demands of Christian love.

The starting point for the Reformation was Luther's attack in 1517 on the church's practice of selling indulgences. The church taught that some individuals go directly to heaven or hell, while others go to heaven only after spending time in purgatory—a period of expiation necessary for those who have sinned excessively in this life but who have had the good fortune to repent before death. To die in a state of mortal sin meant to writhe in hell eternally. Naturally, people worried about how long they might have to suffer in purgatory. Indulgences were intended to remit portions of that time and were granted to individuals by the church for their prayers, attendance at Mass, and almost any acts of charity—including monetary offerings to the church. This last good work was the most controversial since it could easily appear that people were buying their way into heaven.

In the autumn of 1517, a Dominican friar, named John Tetzel, was selling indulgences in the area near Wittenberg. Luther launched his attack on Tetzel and the selling of indulgences by tacking on the door of the Wittenberg castle church his Ninety-five Theses. Luther's theses (propositions) challenged the entire notion of selling indulgences not only as a corrupt practice, but also as a theologically unsound assumption—namely, that salvation can be earned by good works.

At the heart of Luther's argument in the Ninety-five Theses and in his later writings were the beliefs that the individual achieves salvation through inner religious feeling, a sense of contrition for sins, and a trust in God's mercy, and that church attendance, fasting, pilgrimages, charity, and other good works did not earn salvation. The church, in contrast, held that *both* faith and good works were necessary for salvation. Luther further insisted that every individual could discover the meaning of the Bible unaided by the clergy; the church, however, maintained that only the clergy could read and interpret the Bible properly. Luther argued that in matters of faith there was no difference between the clergy and the laity, for each person could receive faith directly and freely from God. But the church held that the clergy were intermediaries between individuals and God and that, in effect, Christians reached eternal salvation through the clergy. For Luther, no priest, no ceremony, and no sacrament could bridge the gulf between the Creator and his creatures. Hope lay only in a personal relationship between the individual and God, as expressed through faith in God's mercy and grace. By declaring that clergy and church rituals do not hold the key to salvation, Luther rejected the church's claim that it alone offered men and women the way to eternal life.

Recognizing that he might be in danger if he continued to preach without a protector, Luther appealed for support to the prince of his district, Frederick, the elector of Saxony. The elector was a powerful man in international politics—one of seven lay and ecclesiastical princes who chose the Holy Roman emperor. Frederick's support convinced church officials, including the pope, that this monk would have to be dealt with cautiously. When in 1520 the pope finally acted against Luther, it was too late; Luther had been given the needed time to promote his views. He proclaimed that the pope was the Antichrist and that the church was the "most lawless den of robbers, the most shameless of all brothels, the very kingdom of sin, death and Hell."[3] When the papal bull excommunicating him was delivered, Luther burned it.

No longer members of the church, Luther and his followers established congregations for the purpose of Christian worship. Christians outside the church needed protection, and in 1520 Luther published the *Address to the Christian Nobility of the German Nation.* In it he appealed to the emperor and the German princes to reform the church and to cast off their allegiance to the pope, who, he argued, had used taxes and political power to exploit them for centuries. His appeal produced some success; the Reformation flourished on the resentment against foreign papal intervention that had long festered in Germany. In this and other treatises, Luther made it clear that he wanted to present no threat to legitimate political authority, that is, to the power of the German princes.

In 1521, Charles V, the Holy Roman emperor, who was a devout Catholic, summoned Luther to Worms, giving him a pass of safe conduct. There, Luther was to answer to the charge of heresy, both an ecclesiastical and a civil offense. When asked to recant, Luther replied: "Unless I am convinced of error by the testimony of Scripture or by clear reason . . . I cannot and will not recant anything, for it is neither safe nor honest to act against one's conscience. God help me. Amen." Shortly after this confrontation with the emperor, Luther went into hiding to escape arrest. During that one-year period, he translated the New Testament into German. His followers, or Lutherans, were eventually called *Protestants*—those who protested against the established church—and the term became generic for all followers of the Reformation.

The Appeal and Spread of Lutheranism

Rapidly disseminated by the new printing press, the tenets of Protestantism offered the hope of revitalization and renewal to its adherents. Lutheranism appealed to the devout, who resented the worldliness and lack of piety of many clergy. But the movement found its greatest following among German townspeople, who objected to money flowing from their country to Rome in the form of church taxes and payment for church offices. In addition, the Reformation provided the nobility with the unprecedented opportunity to confiscate church lands, eliminate church taxes, and gain the support of their subjects by serving as leaders of a popular and dynamic religious movement. The Reformation also gave the nobles a way of resisting the Catholic Holy Roman emperor, Charles V, who wanted to extend his authority over the German princes. Resenting the Italian domination of the church, many other Germans who supported Martin Luther believed that they were freeing German Christians from foreign control.

Lutheranism drew support from the peasants as well, for they saw Luther as their champion against their oppressors—both lay and ecclesiastical lords and the townspeople. Indeed, in his writings and sermons, Luther often attacked the greed of the princes and bemoaned the plight of the poor. Undoubtedly, Luther's successful confrontation with the authorities served to inspire the peasants. In 1524, these long-suffering people openly rebelled against their lords. The Peasants' Revolt spread to over one-third of Germany; some 300,000 people took up arms against their masters.

Luther, however, had no wish to associate his movement with a peasant uprising and risk alienating the nobility who supported him. As a political conservative, he hesitated to challenge secular authority; to him, the good Christian was an obedient subject. Therefore, he virulently attacked the rebellious peasants, urging the nobility to become "both judge and executioner" and to "knock down, strangle, and stab" the insurgents. By 1525, the peasants had been put down by the sword. The failure of the Peasants' Revolt meant that the German peasantry remained among the most backward and oppressed until well into the nineteenth century.

Initially, the Holy Roman emperor, who was at war with France over parts of Italy and whose eastern territories were threatened by the Ottoman Turks, hesitated to intervene militarily in the strife between Lutheran and Catholic princes—a delay that proved crucial. Despite years of warfare, Charles V was unable to subdue the Lutheran princes. The religious conflict was settled by the Peace of Augsburg (1555), which decreed that each territorial prince should determine the religion of his subjects. Broadly speaking, northern Germany became largely Protestant, while Bavaria and other southern territories remained in the Roman Catholic church. The Holy Roman emperor, who had been successfully challenged by the Lutheran princes, saw his power diminished. The decentralization of the empire and its division into Catholic and Protestant regions would block German unity until the last part of the nineteenth century.

The Spread of the Reformation

Nothing better illustrates people's dissatisfaction with the church in the early sixteenth century than the rapid spread of Protestantism. There was a pattern to this phenomenon. Protestantism grew strong in northern Europe—northern Germany, Scandinavia, the Netherlands, and England. It failed in the Latin countries, although not without a struggle in France. In general, Protestantism was an urban phenomenon, and it prospered where local magistrates supported it and where the distance from Rome was greatest.

Calvinism

The success of the Reformation outside Germany and Scandinavia derived largely from the work of John Calvin (1509–1564), a French scholar and theologian. Sometime in 1533 or 1534, Calvin met French followers of Luther and became convinced of the truth of the new theology. He began to spread its beliefs immediately after his conversion, and within a year he and his friends were in trouble with the civil and ecclesiastical authorities.

Calvin soon abandoned his humanistic and literary studies to become a preacher of the Reformation. Even early in his religious experience, he emphasized the power of God over sinful and corrupt humanity. Calvin's God thundered and demanded obedience, and the terrible distance between God and the individual was mediated only by Christ. Calvin embraced a stern theology, holding that God's laws must be rigorously obeyed, that social and moral righteousness must be earnestly pursued, that political life must be carefully regulated, and that human emotions must be strictly controlled.

Even more than Luther, Calvin explained salvation in terms of uncertain predestination: that God, who grants grace for his own inscrutable reasons, knows in advance who will be saved and who will be condemned to hell. Calvin argued that although people are predestined to salvation or damnation they can never know their fate with certainty in advance. This terrible decree could and did lead some people to despair. To others—in a paradox difficult for the modern mind to grasp—Calvinism gave a sense of self-assurance and righteousness, which made the saint, that is, the truly predestined man or woman, into a new kind of European. Most of Calvin's followers seemed to believe that in having understood the fact of predestination they had received a bold insight into their unique relationship with God.

Calvinists were individuals who assumed that only unfailing dedication to God's law could be seen as a sign of salvation; thus, Calvinism made for stern men and women, active in their congregations and willing to suppress vice in themselves and others. Calvinism could also produce revolutionaries willing to defy any temporal authorities perceived to be in violation of God's laws. For Calvinists, obedience to Christian law became the dominating principle of life. Forced to flee France, Calvin finally sought safety in Geneva, a small, prosperous Swiss city near the French border. There, he eventually established

John Calvin in His Study. According to Calvin, the Bible, the Word of God, was central to the life of all Protestants. For that reason painting a person's piety often meant painting them as readers. The Reformation also encouraged literacy, at least literacy in simple religious texts. (*Snark/Art Resource, NY*)

a Protestant church that closely regulated the citizens' personal and social lives. Elders of the Calvinist church governed the city and imposed strict discipline in dress, sexual mores, church attendance, and business affairs; they severely punished irreligious and sinful behavior. Prosperous merchants, as well as small shopkeepers, saw in Calvinism doctrines that justified the self-discipline they already exercised in their own lives and wished to impose on the unruly masses. They particularly approved of Calvin's economic views, for he saw nothing sinful in commercial activities, unlike many Catholic clergy.

Geneva became the center of international Protestantism. Calvin trained a new generation of Protestant reformers of many nationalities, who carried his message back to their homelands. Calvin's *Institutes of the Christian Religion* (1536), in its many editions, became (after the Bible) the leading textbook of the new theology. In the second half of the sixteenth century, Calvin's theology of predestination spread into France, England, the Netherlands, and parts of the Holy Roman Empire.

Calvin always opposed any recourse to violence and supported the authority of magistrates. Yet when monarchy became their persecutor, his followers felt compelled to resist. Calvinist theologians became the first political theoreticians of modern times to publish cogent arguments for opposition to monarchy, and eventually for political revolution. In France and later in the Netherlands, Calvinism became a revolutionary ideology, complete with an underground organization, composed of dedicated followers who challenged monarchical authority. In the seventeenth century, the English version of Calvinism—Puritanism—performed the same function. Thus, in certain circumstances, Calvinism possessed the moral force to undermine the claims of the monarchical state on the individual.

France

Although Protestantism was illegal in France after 1534, the Protestant minority, the Huguenots, grew, becoming a well-organized underground movement. Huguenot churches, often under the protection of powerful nobles, assumed an increasingly political character in response to monarchy-sponsored persecution. French Protestants became sufficiently organized and militant to challenge their persecutors, King Henry II and the Guise, one of the foremost Catholic families in Europe, and in 1562 civil war erupted between Catholics and Protestants. What followed was one of the most brutal religious wars in the history of Europe. In 1572, on Saint Bartholomew's Day, the gruesome slaughter of thousands of Protestant men, women, and children stained the streets with blood. So intense was the religious hatred at the time that the massacre inspired the pope to have a Mass said in thanksgiving for a Catholic "victory."

After nearly thirty years of brutal fighting throughout France, victory went to the Catholic side—but barely. Henry of Navarre, a Protestant leader, became King Henry IV, though only after he agreed to reconvert to Catholicism. Henry established a tentative peace by granting Protestants limited toleration. In 1598, he issued the Edict of Nantes, the first document in any national state that attempted to institutionalize a degree of religious toleration. In the seventeenth century, the successors of Henry IV (who was assassinated in 1610) gradually weakened and then in 1685 revoked the edict. The theoretical foundations of toleration, as well as its practice, remained tenuous in early modern Europe.

England

The king himself rather than religious reformers initiated the Reformation in England. Henry VIII (1509–1547) removed the English church from the jurisdiction of the papacy because the pope refused to grant him an annulment of his marriage to his first wife. The English Reformation thus began as a political act on the part of a self-confident Renaissance monarch. But the Reformation's origins stretched back into the Middle Ages, for England had a long tradition of heresy, as well as anticlericalism, rooted in Wycliffe's actions in the fourteenth century.

When Henry VIII decided that he wanted a divorce from the Spanish princess Catherine of Aragon, in 1527–28, the pope ignored his request. As the pope stalled, Henry grew more desperate: he needed a male heir and presumed that the failure to produce one lay with his wife. At the same time, he desired the shrewd and tempting Anne Boleyn. Henry VIII arranged to grant himself a divorce by severing England from the church. In 1534, with Parliament's approval, he had himself declared supreme head of the Church of England. In 1536, he dissolved the monasteries and seized their property, which was distributed or sold to his loyal supporters. In most cases, it went to the lesser nobility and landed gentry. By involving Parliament and the gentry, Henry VIII turned the Reformation into a national movement. Political considerations, not profound theological differences, were at the root of the English Reformation.

Henry VIII was succeeded by his son, Edward VI (1547–1553), a Protestant, who in turn was succeeded by Mary (1553–1558), the daughter of Henry VIII and Catherine of Aragon. A devout Catholic, Mary severely persecuted Protestants. With the succession of Elizabeth I, Henry's second daughter (by Anne Boleyn), in 1558, England again became a Protestant country. Elizabeth's reign, which lasted until 1603, was characterized by a heightened sense of national identity and the persecution of Catholics, who were deemed a threat to national security. Fear of invasion by Spain, which was bent on returning England to the papacy, contributed to English anti-Catholicism.

The English, or Anglican, church as it developed in the sixteenth century differed to only a limited degree in its customs and ceremonies from the Roman Catholicism it replaced. The exact nature of England's Protestantism became a subject of growing dispute. Was the Anglican church to be truly Protestant? Were its services and churches to be simple, lacking in "popish" rites and rituals and centered on Scripture and sermon? Obviously, the powerful Anglican bishops would accept no form of Protestantism that might limit their privileges, ceremonial functions, and power. These issues contributed to the English Revolution of the seventeenth century (see Chapter 9).

The Radical Reformation

The leading Protestant reformers generally supported established political authorities, whether they were territorial princes or urban magistrates. For the reformers, human freedom was a spiritual, not a social, concept. Yet the Reformation did help trigger revolts among the artisan and peasant classes of central and then western Europe. By the 1520s, several radical reformers arose, often from the lower classes of European society. They attempted to channel popular religion and folk beliefs into a new version of reformed Christianity, which spoke directly to the temporal and spiritual needs of the oppressed.

Radical reformers proclaimed that God's will was known by his saints—those predestined for salvation. They said that the poor would inherit the

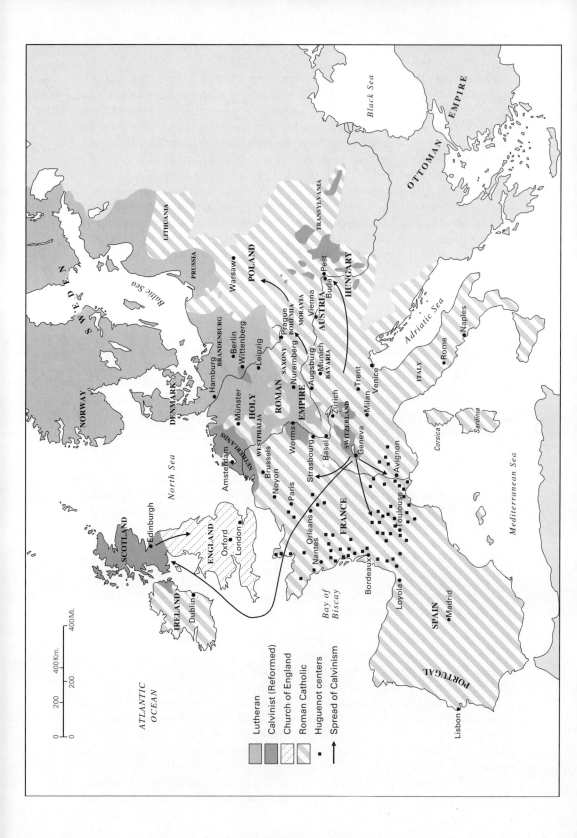

NORWAY

SWEDEN

DENMARK

Baltic Sea

LITHUANIA

PRUSSIA

POLAND

• Warsaw

Hamburg •
• Berlin
• Wittenberg
BRANDENBURG
• Leipzig

SAXONY
• Nuremberg
• Prague
BOHEMIA
MORAVIA
• Vienna
AUSTRIA
• Buda • Pest
HUNGARY

TRANSYLVANIA

Black Sea

OTTOMAN EMPIRE

Münster •
HOLY ROMAN EMPIRE
WESTPHALIA
Augsburg •
• Munich
BAVARIA
• Trent
• Milan
• Venice

NETHERLANDS
Amsterdam •
Brussels •
Worms •
Strasbourg •
Basel •
• Zürich
SWITZERLAND
• Geneva

Adriatic Sea

ITALY

• Rome

• Naples

North Sea

SCOTLAND
• Edinburgh

ENGLAND
Oxford •
• London

IRELAND
• Dublin

• Novon
• Paris

FRANCE

• Orléans
• Nantes

• Avignon
• Toulouse

• Bordeaux

Bay of Biscay

• Loyola

SPAIN
• Madrid

Corsica

Sardinia

Mediterranean Sea

PORTUGAL

• Lisbon

ATLANTIC OCEAN

400 Mi.
400 Km.
200
200
0
0

Lutheran
Calvinist (Reformed)
Church of England
Roman Catholic
Huguenot centers
Spread of Calvinism

earth, which at present was ruled by the Antichrist; the saint's task was to purge this earth of evil and thus make it ready for Christ's Second Coming. For the radicals, the Scriptures, which spoke of God's love for the wretched and lowly, became an inspiration for social revolution. Luther, Calvin, and other reformers vigorously condemned the social doctrines preached by the radical reformers.

The largest group in the Radical Reformation before 1550 has the general name of *Anabaptists*. Having received the inner light—the message of salvation—Anabaptists felt born anew and yearned to be rebaptized. Anabaptists were new Christians, new persons led by the light of conscience to seek reform and renewal of all institutions in preparation for Christ's Second Coming.

In 1534, Anabaptists captured the city of Münster in Westphalia, near the western border of Germany. They seized the property of nonbelievers, burned all books except the Bible, and in a mood of jubilation and sexual excess, openly practiced polygamy. All the while, the Anabaptists proclaimed that the Day of Judgment was close at hand. Provoked by their actions, Lutheran Prince Philip of Hesse and his army crushed the Anabaptists.

In early modern Europe, *Münster* became a byword for dangerous revolution. Determined to prevent these wild enthusiasts from gaining strength in their own territories, princes attacked them with ferocity. In Münster today, the cages still hang from the church steeple where the Anabaptist leaders were tortured and left to die as a warning to all would-be imitators.

By the late sixteenth century, many radical movements had either gone underground or grown quiet. But a century later, during the English Revolution (1640–1660), the beliefs and political goals of the Radical Reformation surfaced again, threatening to push the revolution in a direction that its gentry leaders desperately feared. Although the radicals failed in England, too, they left a tradition of democratic and antihierarchical thought. The radical assertion that saints, who have received the inner light, are the equal of anyone, regardless of social status, helped shape modern democratic thought.

The Catholic Response

The Protestant threat impelled the Roman Catholic church to institute reforms. At first, the energy for reform came from ordinary clergy, as well as laypeople such as Ignatius Loyola (1491–1556). Trained as a soldier, this pious Spanish reformer sought to create a new religious order, fusing the intellectual excellence of humanism with a reformed Catholicism that would appeal to powerful economic and political groups. Founded in 1534, the Society of Jesus, more commonly known as the Jesuits, became the backbone of

◀ **Map 8.1**   The Protestant and the Catholic Reformations

the Catholic Reformation in southern and western Europe. The Jesuits combined traditional monastic discipline with a dedication to teaching and an emphasis on the power of preaching. They sought to use both to win converts back to the church.

The Jesuits brought hope: a religious revival based on ceremony, tradition, and the power of the priest to offer forgiveness. In addition, they opened some of the finest schools in Europe. Just as the Lutherans in Germany sought to bring literacy to the masses so that they might read the Bible, the Jesuits sought to bring intellectual enhancement to the laity, especially to the rich and powerful. The Jesuits pursued positions as confessors to princes and urged them to intensify their efforts to strengthen the church in their territories.

By the 1540s, the Counter Reformation was well under way. The leaders of this Catholic movement attacked many of the same abuses that had impelled Luther to speak out, but they avoided a break with the doctrinal and spiritual authority of the clergy. The Counter Reformation also took aggressive and hostile measures against Protestantism. The church tried to counter the popular appeal of Protestantism by emphasizing spiritual renewal through faith, prayer, and religious ceremony. It also resorted to sterner means. The Inquisition—the church court dealing with heretics—expanded its activities, and wherever Catholic jurisdiction prevailed, unrepentant Protestant heretics were subject to death or imprisonment. Catholics did not hold a monopoly on persecution: wherever Protestantism obtained official status—in England, Scotland, and Geneva, for instance—Catholics or religious radicals also sometimes faced persecution.

One of the Catholic church's main tools was censorship. By the 1520s, the impulse to censor and burn dangerous books intensified dramatically as the church tried to prevent the spread of Protestant ideas. In the rush to eliminate heretical literature, the church condemned the works of reforming Catholic humanists, as well as those of Protestants. The Index of Prohibited Books became an institutional part of the church's life. Over the centuries, the works of many leading thinkers were placed on the Index, which was not abolished until 1966.

The Counter Reformation policies of education, vigorous preaching, church building, persecution, and censorship did succeed in bringing thousands of people, Germans and Bohemians in particular, back into the church. Furthermore, the church implemented some concrete changes in policy and doctrine. In 1545, the Council of Trent met to reform the church and strengthen it for confronting the Protestant challenge. Over the many years that it was convened (until 1563), the council modified and unified church doctrine; abolished many corrupt practices, such as the selling of indulgences; and vested final authority in the papacy, thereby ending the long and bitter struggle within the church over papal authority. The Council of Trent purged the church and gave it doctrinal clarity on such matters as the roles of faith and good works in attaining salvation. It passed a decree that the church shall be the final arbiter of the Bible. All compromise with Protestantism was re-

The Council of Trent.   When they met, the representatives to Trent were an angry lot, distressed by the long delay in calling them. The Pope resisted Councils because they threatened his authority, but at Trent a great deal was accomplished that put the Church back on the offensive against the Protestants. (*John Freeman*)

jected (not that Protestants were eager for it). The Reformation had split western Christendom irrevocably.

The Reformation and the Modern Age

At first glance, the Reformation would seem to have renewed the medieval stress on otherworldliness and reversed the direction toward secularism taken by the Renaissance. Attracted to the ancient Stoic doctrine of the autonomous will, Renaissance humanists had broken with Augustine's stern view of original sin—a corrupt human nature and the person's inability to achieve salvation through his or her own efforts. Both Luther and Calvin, however, saw human beings as essentially depraved and corrupt and rejected completely the notion that individuals can do something for their own salvation; such an assertion of human will, they held, revealed a dangerous self-confidence in human beings.

Yet in several important ways, the Reformation contributed to the shaping of modernity. By dividing Christendom into Catholic and Protestant, the Reformation destroyed the religious unity of Europe, the distinguishing feature of the Middle Ages, and weakened the church, the chief institution of medieval society. By strengthening monarchs at the expense of church bodies, the Reformation furthered the growth of the modern secular and centralized state. Protestant rulers repudiated all papal claims to temporal authority and extended their power over the newly established Protestant churches in their lands. In Catholic lands, the weakened church was reluctant to challenge monarchs whose support it now needed more than ever. This subordination of clerical authority to the throne permitted kings to build strong centralized states, a characteristic of political life of the modern West.

While absolute monarchy was the immediate beneficiary of the Reformation, indirectly Protestantism contributed to the growth of political liberty—another feature of the modern West. To be sure, neither Luther nor Calvin championed political freedom. For Luther, a good Christian was an obedient subject. Thus, he declared that subjects should obey their rulers' commands: "It is no wise proper for anyone who would be a Christian to set himself up against his government, whether it act justly or unjustly."[4] And again, "Those who sit in the office of magistrate sit in the place of God, and their judgment is as if God judged from heaven. . . . if the emperor calls me, God calls me."[5] Calvinists created a theocracy in Geneva, which closely regulated the citizens' private lives, and Calvin strongly condemned resistance to political authority as wicked. He held that rulers were selected by God and punishment of bad rulers belonged only to God and not to the ruler's subjects.

Nevertheless, the Reformation also provided a basis for challenging monarchs. Some Protestant theorists, mainly Calvinists, supported resistance to political authorities whose edicts, they believed, contravened God's law as expressed in the Bible. This religious justification for revolution against tyrannical rule helped fuel the resistance of English Calvinists, or Puritans, to the English monarchy in the seventeenth century.

The Reformation advanced the idea of equality. Equality is rooted in the Judeo-Christian belief that all people are the creatures of a single God. In two important ways, however, medieval society contravened the principle of equality. First, feudalism stressed hereditary distinctions between nobles and commoners. Medieval society was hierarchical, arranged in an ascending order of legal ranks, or estates: commoners, nobles, and clergy. Second, the medieval church taught that only the clergy could administer the sacraments, which provided people with the means of attaining salvation; for this reason, they were superior to the laity. Luther, in contrast, held that there was no spiritual distinction between the laity and the clergy. There was a spiritual equality of all believers: all were equally Christian; all were equally priests.

The Reformation also contributed to the creation of an individualistic ethic, which characterizes the modern world. Since Protestants, unlike Catholics, had no official interpreter of Scripture, the individual bore the awesome responsibility of interpreting the Bible according to the dictates of his or her conscience. Protestants confronted the prospect of salvation or damnation entirely on their own. No church provided them with security or certainty, and no priesthood interceded between them and God. Piety was not determined by the church, but by the autonomous individual, whose conscience, illuminated by God, was the source of judgment and authority.

For the Protestant, faith was personal and inward. This new arrangement called for a personal relationship between each individual and God and called attention to the individual's inner religious capacities. Certain that God had chosen them for salvation, many Protestants developed the inner self-assurance and assertiveness that marks the modern individual. Thus, the Protestant emphasis on private judgment in religious matters and on an inner personal conviction accentuated the importance of the individual and helped to mold a new and distinctly modern European.

The Reformation's stress on individual conscience may have contributed to the development of the capitalist spirit, which underlies modern economic life. So argued German sociologist Max Weber in *The Protestant Ethic and the Spirit of Capitalism* (1904). Weber acknowledged that capitalism existed in Europe before the Reformation; merchant bankers in medieval Italian and German towns, for example, engaged in capitalistic activities. But, he contended, Protestantism (particularly Calvinism) made capitalism more dynamic. Protestant businesspeople believed that they had a religious obligation to make money, and their faith gave them the self-discipline to do so. Convinced that prosperity was God's blessing and poverty his curse, Calvinists had a spiritual inducement to labor industriously and to avoid laziness.

According to Calvin's doctrine of predestination, God had already determined in advance who would be saved; salvation could not be attained through any worldly actions. Although there was no definite way of discovering who had received God's grace, Calvin's followers came to believe that certain activities were signs that God was working through them, that they had indeed been elected. Thus, Calvinists viewed hard work, diligence, dutifulness, efficiency, frugality, and a disdain for pleasurable pursuits—all virtues that contribute to rational and orderly business procedures and to business success—as signs of election. In effect, Weber argued, Protestantism—unlike Catholicism—gave religious approval to moneymaking and the businesspeople's way of life. Moreover, Calvin's followers seemed to believe that they had attained a special insight into their relationship with God; this conviction fostered a sense of self-assurance and righteousness. Protestantism, therefore, produced a highly individualistic attitude that valued inner strength, self-discipline, and methodical and sober behavior—necessary traits for a middle class seeking business success in a highly competitive world.

Notes

1. Giovanni Pico della Mirandola, *Oration on the Dignity of Man,* trans. A. Robert Caponigri (Chicago: Henry Regnery, 1956), p. 7.

2. François Rabelais, *Gargantua and Pantagruel,* trans. Sir Thomas Urquhart (1883), bk. 1, chap. 57.

3. John Dillenberger, ed., *Martin Luther: Selections from His Writings*

(Garden City, N.Y.: Doubleday, 1961), p. 46, taken from *The Freedom of a Christian* (1520).

4. Quoted in George H. Sabine, *A History of Political Thought* (New York: Holt, Rinehart & Winston, 1961), p. 361.

5. Quoted in Roland Bainton, *Here I Stand* (New York: Abingdon Press, 1950), p. 238.

Suggested Reading

Brucker, Gene A., *Renaissance Florence,* rev. ed. (1983). An excellent analysis of the city's physical character, its economic and social structure, its political and religious life, and its cultural achievements.

Burckhardt, Jacob, *The Civilization of the Renaissance in Italy* (1860), 2 vols. (1958). The first major interpretative synthesis of the Renaissance; still an essential resource.

Burke, Peter, *Popular Culture in Early Modern Europe* (1978). A fascinating account of the social underside from the Renaissance to the French Revolution.

Grimm, Harold J., *The Reformation Era, 1500–1650,* 2nd ed. (1973). The best and most complete narrative available.

Kelley, Donald R., *Renaissance Humanism* (1991). A recent synthesis.

Ozment, Steven E., *The Reformation in the Cities* (1975). A good survey of the Reformation in Germany.

Pullan, Brian S., *A History of Early Renaissance Italy* (1973). A solid, brief account.

Reardon, Bernard M. G., *Religious Thought in the Reformation* (1981). Doctrinal issues and disputes.

Skinner, Quentin, *The Foundations of Modern Political Thought,* 2 vols. (1978). The first volume covers the Renaissance; highly informed.

Stephens, John, *The Italian Renaissance* (1990). A recent survey.

Review Questions

1. What is the connection between the Renaissance and the Middle Ages? What special conditions gave rise to the Italian Renaissance?

2. What is humanism and how did it begin? What did the humanists contribute to education and the writing of history?

3. How can it be said that Machiavelli invented a new politics?

4. What are the general features of Renaissance art?

5. What factors encouraged the spread of the Renaissance into other lands?

6. Why is the Renaissance considered a departure from the Middle Ages and the beginning of modernity?

7. What were the medieval roots of the Reformation?

8. How did Luther's theology mark a break with the church? Why did many Germans become followers of Luther?

9. In what ways did the radical reformers differ from the other Protestants?

10. What role did the Jesuits and the Inquisition play in the Counter Reformation? What did the Counter Reformation accomplish?

11. How did the Reformation contribute to the shaping of the modern world?

Political and Economic Transformation: National States, Overseas Expansion, Commercial Revolution

$\mathcal{F}$rom the thirteenth to the seventeenth century, a new and unique form of political organization emerged in the West: the dynastic, or national, state. It harnessed the material resources of its territory, directed the energies of the nobility into national service, and increasingly centralized political authority. The national state, a product of dynastic consolidation, is the essential political institution of the modern West.

The disintegration of medieval political forms and the emergence of the modern state coincided with the gradual breakdown of the medieval socioeconomic system, based on tradition, hierarchy, and orders or estates. In the medieval system, every group—clergy, lords, serfs, guild members—occupied a particular place and performed a specific function. Society functioned best when each person fulfilled the role allotted to him or her by God and tradition. Early modern times saw the growth of a capitalist market economy whose central focus was the self-sufficient individual, striving, assertive, and motivated by self-interest. This nascent market economy, greatly boosted by the voyages of discovery and the conquest and colonization of other parts of the world, subverted the hierarchically arranged and tradition-bound medieval community. Seeking to enrich their treasuries and extend their power, states promoted commercial growth and overseas expansion. The extension of European hegemony over much of the world was well under way by the eighteenth century. ❖

Toward the Modern State

During the Middle Ages, some kings began to forge national states. However, medieval political forms differed considerably from those that developed later, in the early modern period. In the Middle Ages, kings had to share

Chronology 9.1 ❖ Economic and Political Transformations

1394–1460	Henry the Navigator, prince of Portugal, encourages expansion into Africa for gold and his anti-Muslim crusade
1469	Ferdinand and Isabella begin their rule of Castile and Aragon
1485	Henry VII begins the reign of the Tudor dynasty in England
1488	Bartholomeu Dias reaches the tip of Africa
1492	Christopher Columbus reaches the Caribbean island of Española on his first voyage; the Jews are expelled from Spain; Granada, the last Muslim kingdom in Spain, is conquered, completing the Reconquest
1497	Vasco da Gama sails around Cape of Good Hope (Africa) to India
1519	Charles V of Spain becomes Hapsburg emperor of the Holy Roman Empire
1519–1521	Hernando Cortés conquers the Aztecs in Mexico
1531–1533	Francisco Pizarro conquers the Incas in Peru
1552	Silver from the New World flows into Europe via Spain, contributing to a price revolution
1556–1598	Philip II of Spain persecutes Jews and Muslims
1562–1598	Religious wars in France

political power with feudal lords, the clergy, free cities, and representative assemblies. Central authority was tempered by overlapping jurisdictions and numerous and competing allegiances. People saw themselves as members of an estate—clergy, aristocracy, or commoners—rather than as subjects or citizens of a state. Church theorists envisioned Christian Europe as a unitary commonwealth, in which spiritual concerns prevailed over secular authority. According to this view, kings, who received their power from God, must never forget their religious obligation to rule in accordance with God's commands as interpreted by the clergy.

In the sixteenth and seventeenth centuries, kings successfully asserted their authority over competing powers, continuing a trend that had begun in the Late Middle Ages. Strong monarchs dominated or crushed the parliaments that had acted as a brake on royal power during the Middle Ages. Increasingly, too, these monarchs subjected lords and ecclesiastical authorities to royal control. They created a bureaucracy to coordinate the activities of the

---

Chronology 9.1 ❖ Continued

1572	Saint Bartholomew's Day Massacre—Queen Catherine of France orders thousands of Protestants executed
1588	English fleet defeats the Spanish Armada
1598	French Protestants are granted religious toleration by the Edict of Nantes
1624–1642	Cardinal Richelieu, Louis XIII's chief minister, determines royal policies
1640–1660	English Revolution
1648	Treaty of Westphalia ends the Thirty Years' War
1649	Charles I, Stuart king of England, is executed by an act of Parliament
1649–1660	England is co-ruled by Parliament and the army under Oliver Cromwell
1660	Charles II returns from exile and becomes king of England
1685	Louis XIV of France revokes the Edict of Nantes
1688–1689	Revolution in England: end of absolutism
1694	The Bank of England is founded
1701	Louis XIV tries to bring Spain under French control

---

central government. The old medieval political order—characterized on the one hand by feudal particularism and the strength of local authorities, and on the other, by the supranational claims and goals of a universal church—dissolved. Gradually, the national, territorial state, the hallmark of the modern world, became the essential political unit. Kings were the central figures in the creation of the national state. Strong dynastic states were formed wherever monarchs succeeded in subduing local aristocratic and ecclesiastical power systems. In their struggle to subdue the aristocracy, kings were aided by artillery; the lords' castles quickly became obsolete in the face of royal siege weapons. Where the monarchs failed, as they did in Germany and Italy, no viable states evolved until well into the nineteenth century.

By the early seventeenth century, Europeans had developed the concept of the state: an autonomous political entity to which its subjects owed duties and obligations. The essential prerequisite of the Western concept of the state, as it emerged in the early modern period, was the idea of *sovereignty*. Within its borders, the state was supreme; all other institutions, both secular and religious, had to recognize the state's authority. The art of governing entailed molding the ambitions and strength of the powerful and wealthy so that they could be harnessed to serve the state. Its power growing through war and taxation, the state had become the basic unit of political authority in the West.

Historically, the modern state has been characterized by a devotion to the nation and by feelings of national pride. A national language is used throughout the land, and the people have a sense of sharing a common culture and history, of being distinct from other peoples. There were some signs of growing national feeling during the sixteenth and seventeenth centuries, but this feature of the modern state did not become a major part of European political life until the nineteenth century. During the early modern period, devotion was largely given to a town, a province, or a noble or to the person of the king rather than to the nation, the people as a whole.

In the sixteenth and seventeenth centuries, the idea of liberty, now so basic to Western political life and thought, was only rarely discussed and then chiefly by Calvinist opponents of absolutism. Not until the mid-seventeenth century in England was there a body of political thought contending that human liberty was compatible with the new modern state. In general, despite the English (and Dutch) developments, absolutism dominated the political structure of early modern Europe. It was not until the late eighteenth and nineteenth centuries that absolutism was widely challenged by advocates of liberty.

The principle of the balance of power, an integral part of modern international relations, also emerged during early modern times. When one state threatened to dominate Europe, as did Spain under Philip II and France under Louis XIV, other states joined forces and resisted. The fear that one state would upset the balance of power and achieve European domination pervaded international relations in later centuries.

Hapsburg Spain

The Spanish political experience of the sixteenth century stands as one of the most extraordinary in the history of modern Europe. Spanish kings built a dynastic state that burst through its frontiers and encompassed Portugal, part of Italy, the Netherlands, and enormous areas in the New World. Spain became an intercontinental empire—the first in the West since Roman times.

In the eighth and ninth centuries, the Muslims controlled all of Spain except some tiny Christian kingdoms in the far north. In the ninth century, these Christian states began a five-hundred-year struggle, the Reconquest, to drive the Muslims from the Iberian Peninsula. By the middle of the thirteenth century, Granada in the south was all that remained of Muslim lands in Spain.

This long struggle for Christian hegemony in the Iberian Peninsula left the Spanish fiercely religious and strongly suspicious of foreigners. Despite centuries of intermarriage with non-Christians, by the early sixteenth century purity of blood and orthodoxy of faith became necessary for and synonymous with Spanish identity.

Ferdinand and Isabella

In 1469, Ferdinand, heir to the throne of Aragon, married Isabella, heir to the throne of Castile. Although Ferdinand and Isabella did not give Spain a single legal and tax system or a common currency, their policies did contribute decisively to Spanish unity and might. They broke the power of aristocrats, who had operated from their fortified castles like kings, waging their private wars at will; they brought the Spanish church into alliance with the state; and in 1492, they drove the Muslims from Granada, the Muslims' last territory in Spain. The crusade against the Muslim infidels accorded with the aims of the militant Spanish church. With a superior army, with the great aristocrats pacified, and with the church and the Inquisition under monarchical control, the Catholic kings expanded their interests and embarked on an imperialist foreign policy, which made Spain dominant in the New World.

The Spanish state and church persecuted both Muslims and Jews, who for centuries had contributed substantially to Spanish cultural and economic life. In 1391, thousands of Jews were massacred when anti-Jewish sentiments, fanned by popular preachers, turned to violence in major cities. Under threat of death, many Jews submitted to baptism. In succeeding years, other attacks on Jews led to more conversions. Many of these *conversos,* or new Christians, continued to practice the religion of their fathers in secret, a situation that appalled clerical authorities and the devout Ferdinand and Isabella.

In 1492, in a move to enforce religious uniformity, the crown expelled from Spain Jews unwilling to accept baptism. About 150,000 Jews (some estimates are considerably higher) were driven out, including many conversos, who opted to stay with their people. The thousands of Jews who underwent conversion and the conversos who remained were watched by the Inquisition—the church tribunal established to deal with insincere converts—for signs of backsliding. Death by fire, sometimes in elaborate public ceremonies, was the ultimate penalty for the conversos and their descendants who were suspected of practicing Judaism. Muslims also bore the pain of forced conversions and investigations, torture, and executions conducted by the Inquisition. Finally, in 1609–1614, Spain expelled them.

The Reign of Charles V: King of Spain and Holy Roman Emperor

Dynastic marriage constituted another crucial part of Ferdinand and Isabella's foreign policy. They strengthened their ties with the Austrian Hapsburg kings

Allegory of the Abdication of Charles V by Frans Francken II, 1556.   Emperor
Charles V, who ruled half of Europe and most of the Americas, abdicated in 1555,
giving his German imperial crown to his brother Ferdinand, archduke of Austria, and
the kingdoms of Spain and the Netherlands to his son Philip II. The Hapsburg dynasty
ruled Spain until the eighteenth century and Austria and Hungary until the early twentieth century. (*Rijksmuseum, Amsterdam*)

by marrying one of their children, Juana (called "the Mad" for her insanity),
to Philip the Fair, son of Maximilian of Austria, the head of the ruling Hapsburg family. Philip and Juana's son Charles inherited the kingdom of Ferdinand and Isabella in 1516 and reigned until 1556. Through his other
grandparents, he also inherited the Netherlands, Austria, Sardinia, Sicily, the
kingdom of Naples, and Franche Comté. In 1519, he was elected Holy
Roman emperor, Charles V. Charles became the most powerful ruler in Europe. But his reign saw the emergence of political, economic, and social problems that eventually led to Spain's decline.

Charles's inheritance was simply too vast to be governed effectively, but
that was only dimly perceived at the time. The Lutheran Reformation proved
to be the first successful challenge to Hapsburg power. It was the first phase
of a religious and political struggle between Catholic Spain and Protestant Europe: a struggle that would dominate the last half of the sixteenth century.

The achievements of Charles V's reign rested on the twin instruments of
army and bureaucracy. The Hapsburg Empire in the New World was vastly

extended and, on the whole, effectively administered and policed. Out of this sprawling empire, with its exploited native populations, came the greatest flow of gold and silver ever witnessed by Europeans. Constant warfare in Europe, coupled with the immensity of the Spanish administrative network, required a steady intake of capital. In the long run, however, this easy access to capital seems to have hurt the Spanish economy. There was no incentive for developing domestic industry, bourgeois entrepreneurship, or international commerce.

Moreover, constant war engendered and perpetuated a social order geared to the aggrandizement of a military class rather than to the development of a commercial class. Although war expanded Spain's power in the sixteenth century, it sowed the seeds for the financial crises of the 1590s and beyond and for the eventual decline of Spain as a world power.

Philip II

Philip II inherited the throne from his father, Charles V, who abdicated in 1556. Charles left his son with a vast empire in both the Old World and the New. Although this empire had been administered competently enough, it was facing the specters of bankruptcy and heresy. A zeal for Catholicism ruled Philip's private conduct and infused his foreign policy. In the 1560s, Philip sent the largest land army ever assembled in Europe into the Netherlands, with the intention of crushing Protestant-inspired opposition to Spanish authority. The ensuing revolt of the Netherlands lasted until 1609, and the Spanish lost their industrial heartland as a result of it.

The Dutch established a republic governed by the prosperous and progressive bourgeoisie. Rich from the fruits of manufacture and trade in everything from tulip bulbs to ships and slaves, the Dutch merchants ruled their cities and provinces with fierce pride. In the early seventeenth century, this new nation of only 1.5 million people already practiced the most innovative commercial and financial techniques in Europe.

Philip's disastrous attempt to invade England was also born of religious zeal. Philip regarded an assault on England, the main Protestant power, as a holy crusade against the "heretic and bastard," Queen Elizabeth; he particularly resented English assistance to the Protestant Dutch rebels. Sailing from Lisbon in May 1588, the Spanish Armada, carrying twenty-two thousand seamen and soldiers, met with defeat. More than half of the Spanish ships were destroyed or put out of commission. Many ships were wrecked by storms as they tried to return to Spain by rounding the coasts of Scotland and Ireland. The defeat had an enormous psychological effect on the Spanish, who saw it as divine punishment and openly pondered what they had done to incur God's displeasure.

The End of the Spanish Hapsburgs

After the defeat of the Armada, Spain gradually and reluctantly abandoned its imperial ambitions in northern Europe. The administrative structure built by

Charles V and Philip II did remain strong throughout the seventeenth century; nevertheless, by the first quarter of the century, enormous weaknesses had surfaced in Spanish economic and social life. In 1596, Philip II was bankrupt, his vast wealth depleted by the cost of foreign wars. Bankruptcy reappeared at various times in the seventeenth century, while the agricultural economy, at the heart of any early modern nation, stagnated. The Spanish in their golden age had never paid enough heed to increasing domestic production.

Despite these setbacks, Spain was still capable of taking a very aggressive posture during the Thirty Years' War (1618–1648). The Austrian branch of the Hapsburg family joined forces with their Spanish cousins, and neither the Swedes and Germans nor the Dutch could stop them. Only French participation in the Thirty Years' War on the Protestant side tipped the balance decisively against the Hapsburgs. Spanish aggression brought no victories, and with the Peace of Westphalia (1648), Spain officially recognized the independence of the Netherlands and severed its diplomatic ties with the Austrian branch of the family.

By 1660, the imperial age of the Spanish Hapsburgs had ended. The rule of the Protestant princes had been secured in the Holy Roman Empire; the largely Protestant Dutch Republic flourished; Portugal and its colony of Brazil were independent of Spain; and dominance over European affairs had passed to France. The quality of material life in Spain deteriorated rapidly, and the ever present gap between the rich and the poor widened even more drastically. The traditional aristocracy and the church retained their land and power but failed to produce effective leadership.

The Spanish experience illustrates two aspects of the history of the European state. First, the state as empire could survive and prosper only if the domestic economic base remained sound. The Spanish reliance on bullion from its colonies and its failure to cultivate industry and reform the taxation system spelled disaster. Second, states with a vital and aggressive bourgeoisie flourished at the expense of the regions where the aristocracy and the church dominated and controlled society and its mores—Spain's situation. The latter social groups tended to despise manual labor, profit taking, and technological progress. Even though they had been created by kings and dynastic families, after 1700 the major dynastic states were increasingly nurtured by the economic activities of merchants and traders—the bourgeoisie. Yet the bureaucracy of the dynastic states continued to be dominated by men drawn from the lesser aristocracy.

The Growth of French Power

Although both England and France effectively consolidated the power of their central governments, each became a model of a different form of statehood. The English model was a constitutional monarchy, in which the king's power was limited by Parliament and the rights of the English people were protected by law and tradition. The French model emphasized at every turn the glory of the king and, by implication, the sovereignty of the state and its right to stand above the interests of its subjects. France's monarchy became absolute, and French kings claimed that they had been selected by God to rule: a theory known as the divine right of kings. This theory gave monarchy a sanctity that various French kings exploited to enforce their commands on the population, including rebellious feudal lords.

The evolution of the French state was a very gradual process, completed only in the late seventeenth century. In the Middle Ages, the French monarchs recognized the rights of representative assemblies—the Estates—and consulted with them. These assemblies (whether regional or national) were composed of deputies drawn from the various elites: the clergy, the nobility, and, significantly, the leaders of cities and towns in a given region. Early modern French kings increasingly wrested power from the nobility, reduced the significance of the Estates, and eliminated interference from the church.

Religion and the French State

In every emergent state, tension existed between the monarch and the papacy. At issue was control over the church within that territory—over its personnel, its wealth, and, of course, its pulpits, from which an illiterate majority learned what their leaders wanted them to know, not only about religious issues, but also about submission to civil authority. The monarch's power to make church appointments could ensure a complacent church—a church willing to preach obedience to royal authority and to comply on matters of taxes.

For the French monarchs, centuries of tough bargaining with the papacy paid off in 1516, when Francis I (1515–1547) concluded the Concordat of Bologna. Under this agreement, Pope Leo X permitted the French king to nominate, and so in effect appoint, men of his choice to all the highest offices in the French church. The Concordat of Bologna laid the foundation for what became known as the *Gallican church*—a term signifying that the Catholic church in France was sanctioned and overseen by the French kings. Thus, in the early sixteenth century, the central government had been strengthened at the expense of papal authority and of traditional privileges enjoyed by local aristocracy.

The Protestant Reformation, however, challenged royal authority and threatened the very survival of France as a unified state. Fearful that Protestantism would undermine his power, Francis I declared Protestant beliefs and practices illegal and punishable by fines, imprisonment, and even execution. But the Protestant minority (the Huguenots) grew in strength. From 1562 to 1598, France experienced waves of religious wars, which cost the king control over vast areas of the kingdom. The great aristocratic families, the Guise for the Catholics and the Bourbons for the Protestants, drew up armies that scourged the land, killing and maiming their religious opponents and dismantling the authority of the central government.

In 1579, extreme Huguenot theorists published the *Vindiciae contra*

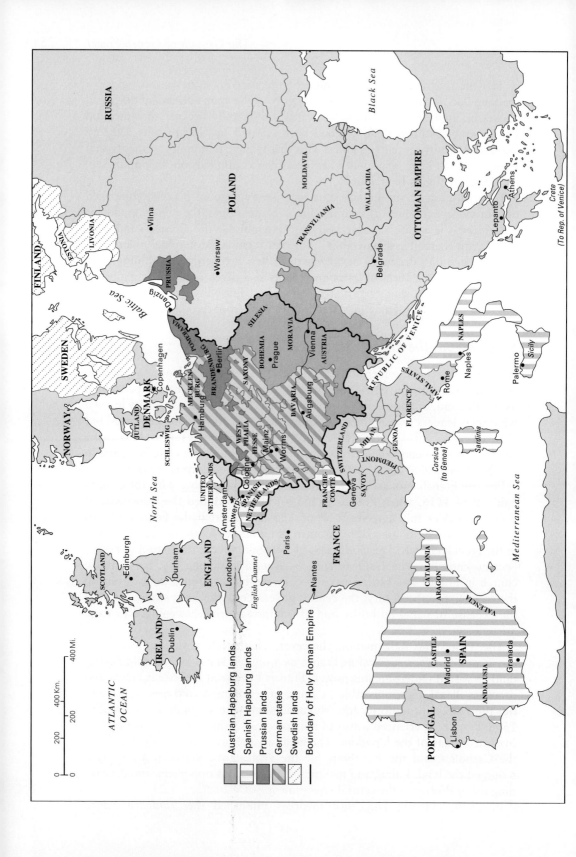

RUSSIA

Black Sea

FINLAND

SWEDEN

NORWAY

ESTONIA

LIVONIA

•Vilna

POLAND

•Warsaw

MOLDAVIA

TRANSYLVANIA

WALLACHIA

OTTOMAN EMPIRE

Lepanto•

Crete
(To Rep. of Venice)

Athens•

Baltic Sea

PRUSSIA

Danzig

POMERANIA

SILESIA

BRANDENBURG

Berlin•

MORAVIA

BOHEMIA

Prague

AUSTRIA

Vienna•

Belgrade

REPUBLIC OF VENICE

PAPAL STATES

Rome•

NAPLES

Naples•

Sicily

Palermo•

Mediterranean Sea

Sardinia

Corsica
(to Genoa)

GENOA

FLORENCE

MILAN

PIEDMONT

SAVOY

SWITZERLAND

Geneva•

FRANCHE-
COMTÉ

BAVARIA

Augsburg•

SAXONY

MECKLEN-
BURG

Hamburg

Copenhagen•

DENMARK

JUTLAND

SCHLESWIG

WEST-
PHALIA

HESSE

Cologne•

Mainz•

Worms•

UNITED
NETHERLANDS

Amsterdam•

Antwerp•

SPANISH
NETHERLANDS

North Sea

SCOTLAND

Edinburgh•

IRELAND

Dublin•

Durham•

ENGLAND

London•

English Channel

Paris•

Nantes•

FRANCE

ATLANTIC
OCEAN

PORTUGAL

Lisbon•

SPAIN

Madrid•

CASTILE

CATALONIA

ARAGON

VALENCIA

ANDALUSIA

Granada•

0   200   400 Mi.

0   200   400 Km.

Austrian Hapsburg lands

Spanish Hapsburg lands

Prussian lands

German states

Swedish lands

Boundary of Holy Roman Empire

Tyrannos. This statement, combined with a call to action, was the first of its kind in early modern times. It justified rebellion against, and even the execution of, an unjust king. European monarchs might claim power and divinely sanctioned authority, but by the late sixteenth century, their subjects had available the moral and theoretical justification to oppose their monarch's will by force, if necessary, and this justification rested on Scripture and religious conviction. Significantly, this same treatise was translated into English in 1648, a year before Parliament publicly executed Charles I, king of England.

The Valois kings floundered in the face of this kind of political and religious opposition. The era of royal supremacy instituted by Francis I came to an abrupt end during the reign of his successor, Henry II (1547–1559). Wed to Catherine de' Medici, a member of the powerful Italian banking family, Henry occupied himself not with the concerns of government, but with the pleasures of the hunt. The sons who succeeded Henry—Francis II (1559–1560), Charles IX (1560–1574), and Henry III (1574–1589)—were uniformly weak. Their mother, Catherine, who was the virtual ruler, ordered the execution of thousands of Protestants by royal troops in Paris—the beginning of the infamous Saint Bartholomew's Day Massacre (1572), which, with the bloodbath that followed, became a symbol of the excesses of religious zeal.

The civil wars begun in 1562 were renewed in the massacre's aftermath. They dragged on until the death of the last Valois king in 1589. The Valois failure to produce a male heir to the throne placed Henry, duke of Bourbon and a Protestant, in line to succeed to the French throne. Realizing that the overwhelmingly Catholic population would not accept a Protestant king, Henry (apparently without much regret) renounced his adopted religion and embraced the church. Henry IV (1589–1610) granted his Protestant subjects and former followers a degree of religious toleration through the Edict of Nantes (1598), but they were never welcomed in significant numbers into the royal bureaucracy. Throughout the seventeenth century, every French king attempted to undermine the Protestants' regional power bases and ultimately to destroy their religious liberties.

The Consolidation of French Monarchical Power

The defeat of Protestantism as a national force set the stage for the final consolidation of the French state in the seventeenth century under the great Bourbon kings, Louis XIII and Louis XIV. Louis XIII (1610–1643) realized that his rule depended on an efficient and trustworthy bureaucracy, a replenishable treasury, and constant vigilance against the localized claims to power by the great aristocracy and Protestant cities and towns. Cardinal Richelieu, who served as Louis XIII's chief minister from 1624 to 1642, became the great architect of French absolutism.

◄ **Map 9.1** Europe, 1648

Richelieu's morality rested on one sacred principle, embodied in a phrase he invented: *raison d'état,* reason of state. Richelieu sought to serve the state by bringing under the king's control the disruptive and antimonarchical elements within French society. He increased the power of the central bureaucracy, attacked the power of independent, and often Protestant, towns and cities, and persecuted the Huguenots. Above all, he humbled the great nobles by limiting their effectiveness as councilors to the king and prohibiting their traditional privileges, such as settling grievances through a duel rather than court action. Reason of state also guided Richelieu's foreign policy. It required that France turn against Catholic Spain and enter on the Protestant—and hence anti-Spanish—side of the war that was raging at the time in the Holy Roman Empire. France's entry into the Thirty Years' War produced a decisive victory for French power on the Continent.

Richelieu died in 1642, and Louis XIII the following year. Cardinal Mazarin, who took charge during the minority of Louis XIV (he was five years old when Louis XIII died), continued Richelieu's policies. Mazarin's heavy-handed actions produced a rebellious reaction, the *Fronde*: a series of street riots that eventually cost the government control over Paris and lasted from 1648 to 1653. Centered in Paris and supported by the great aristocracy, the courts, and the city's poorer classes, the Fronde threatened to develop into a full-scale uprising. It might have done so, but for one crucial factor: its leadership was divided. Court judges (lesser nobles who had often just risen from the ranks of the bourgeoisie) deeply distrusted the great aristocrats and refused in the end to make common cause with them. And both groups feared disorders among the urban masses.

When Louis XIV finally assumed responsibility for governing in 1661, he vowed that the events he had witnessed as a child during the Fronde would never be repeated. In the course of his reign, he achieved the greatest degree of monarchical power held during the early modern period. No absolute monarch in western Europe, before or at that time, had so much personal authority or commanded such a vast and effective military and administrative machine. Louis XIV's reign represents the culmination of the process of increasing monarchical authority that had been under way for centuries. Intelligent, cunning, and possessing a unique understanding of the requirements of his office, Louis XIV worked long hours at being king, and he never undertook a venture without an eye to his personal grandeur. The sumptuous royal palace at Versailles was built for that reason; similarly, etiquette and style were cultivated there on a scale never before seen in any European court.

When Mazarin died, Louis XIV did away with the office of first minister; he would rule France alone. The great nobles, "princes of the blood," enjoyed great social prestige but exercised decreasing political influence. Louis XIV treated the aristocrats to elaborate rituals, feasts, processions, displays, and banquets; amid all the clamor, however, their political power dwindled.

Louis XIV's domestic policies centered on his incessant search for new revenues. Not only the building of Versailles but also wars cost money, and Louis XIV waged them to excess. To raise capital, he used the services of Jean

The Royal Palace at Versailles by Pierre Patel, 1668.   Taking his father's royal hunting lodge as a base in 1661, the French king Louis XIV began construction of a magnificent palace at Versailles. This became the center of French royal government and kingly splendor and set the style for monarchical governments throughout Europe. (*Versailles/Cliché des Musées Nationaux*)

Baptiste Colbert, a brilliant administrator who improved the methods of tax collecting, promoted new industries, and encouraged international trade. Operating with a total bureaucracy of about a thousand officials and no longer bothering even to consult the parlements or Estates, Louis XIV ruled absolutely in accordance with the principle of divine right—that the monarch is selected to rule by God.

Yet Louis XIV's system was fatally flawed. Without any effective check on his power and on his dreams of international conquest, no limit was imposed on the state's capacity to make war or on the ensuing national debt. Louis XIV coveted vast sections of the Holy Roman Empire; he also sought to curb Dutch commercial prosperity and had designs on the Spanish Netherlands. By the 1680s, his domestic and foreign policies turned violently aggressive. In 1685, he revoked the Edict of Nantes, forcing many of the country's remaining Protestants to flee. In 1689, he embarked on a military campaign to secure territory from the Holy Roman Empire. And in 1701, he tried to bring Spain under the control of the Bourbon dynasty. Louis XIV, however, underestimated the power of his northern rivals, England and the Netherlands. Their combined power, in alliance with the Holy Roman Empire and the Austrians, defeated Louis XIV's ambitions.

Louis XIV's participation in these long wars emptied the royal treasury. By the late seventeenth century, taxes had risen intolerably, and they were levied mostly on those least able to pay—the peasants. Absolutism also meant increased surveillance of the population. Royal authorities censored books, spied on suspected heretics, Protestants, and freethinkers, and tortured and executed opponents of state policy.

In the France of Louis XIV, the dynastic state had reached maturity and had begun to display some of its classic characteristics: centralized bureaucracy; royal patronage to enforce allegiance; a system of taxation universally but inequitably applied; and suppression of political opposition either through the use of patronage or, if necessary, through force. Another important feature was the state's cultivation of the arts and sciences as a means of increasing national power and prestige. Together, these policies enabled the French monarchy to achieve political stability, enforce a uniform system of law, and channel the country's wealth and resources into the service of the state as a whole.

Yet at his death in 1715, Louis XIV left his successors a system of bureaucracy and taxation that was vastly in need of overhaul but was still locked into the traditional social privileges of the church and nobility—to an extent that made reform virtually impossible. The pattern of war, excessive taxation of the lower classes, and expenditures that surpassed revenues had severely damaged French finances. Failure to reform the system led to the French Revolution of 1789.

The Growth of Limited Monarchy and Constitutionalism in England

In 1066, William, duke of Normandy and vassal to the French king, had invaded and conquered England, acquiring at a stroke the entire kingdom. In succeeding centuries, English monarchs continued to strengthen central authority and to tighten the bonds of national unity. At the same time, however, certain institutions and traditions evolved—common law, Magna Carta, and Parliament—that checked royal power and protected the rights of the English people.

Central government in England was threatened after the Hundred Years' War (1337–1453) when English aristocrats brought back from France a taste for warfare. In the ensuing civil war—the War of the Roses (1455–1485)—

gangs of noblemen with retainers roamed the English countryside, and lawlessness prevailed for a generation. Only in 1485 did the Tudor family emerge triumphant.

The Tudor Achievement

Victory in the civil war allowed Henry VII (1485–1509) to begin the Tudor dynasty. Henry VII's goal was to check the unruly nobility. To this end, he brought commoners into the government. These commoners, unlike the great magnates, could be channeled into royal service because they craved what the king offered: financial rewards and elevated social status. Although they did not fully displace the aristocracy, commoners were brought into Henry VII's inner circle, into the Privy Council, and into the courts. The strength and efficiency of Tudor government were shown during the Reformation, when Henry VIII (1509–1547) made himself head of the English church.

The Protestant Reformation in England was a revolution in royal, as well as ecclesiastical, government. It attacked and defeated the main obstacle to monarchical authority—the power of the papacy. However, no change in religious practice could be instituted by the monarchy alone. Parliament's participation in the Reformation gave it a greater role and sense of importance than it had ever possessed in the past.

At Henry VIII's death, the Tudor bureaucracy and centralized government were strained to the utmost, yet they survived. The government weathered the reign of Henry's sickly son Edward VI (1547–1553) and the extreme Protestantism of some of his advisers; it also survived the brief and deeply troubled reign of Henry's first daughter, Mary (1553–1558), who attempted to return England to Catholicism. At Mary's death, England had come dangerously close to the religious instability and sectarian tension that undermined the French kings during the final decades of the sixteenth century.

Henry's second daughter, Elizabeth I, became queen in 1558 and reigned until her death in 1603. The Elizabethan period was characterized by a heightened sense of national identity. The English Reformation enhanced that sense, as did the increasing fear of foreign invasion by Spain. That fear was abated only by the defeat of the Spanish Armada in 1588. In the seventeenth century, the English would look back on Elizabeth's reign as a golden age. It was the calm before the storm: a time when a new commercial class was formed, which, in the seventeenth century, would demand a greater say in government operations.

Religion played a vital role in this realignment of political interests and forces. Many of the old aristocracy clung to the Anglicanism of the Henrican Reformation and in some cases to Catholicism. The newly risen gentry found in the Protestant Reformation of Switzerland and Germany a form of religious worship more suited to their independent and entrepreneurial spirit. Many of them embraced Puritanism, the English version of Calvinism.

Queen Elizabeth I (1558–1603) by Nicholas Hilliard.   In this portrait, painted after England's victory in 1588 over the Spanish Armada, the queen's prestige is enhanced by the magnificent lace, pearls, and the rich jewels of her costume and crown. (*By kind permission of the Marquess of Tavistock, and the Trustees of the Bedford Estates*)

The English Revolution, 1640–1660 and 1688–1689

The forces threatening established authority were dealt with ineffectively by the first two Stuart kings: James I (1603–1625) and Charles I (1625–1649). Like their Continental counterparts, both believed in royal absolutism, and both preached, through the established church, the doctrine of the divine right of kings. James I angered Parliament by conducting foreign policy without consulting it. The conflict between Parliament and Charles I centered on taxes and religion.

Badly needing funds to wage war, Charles I exacted "forced loans" from subjects and imprisoned without a specific charge those who would not pay. Fearing that such arbitrary behavior threatened everyone's property and person, Parliament struck back. In 1628, it refused to grant Charles I tax revenues unless he agreed to the Petition of Right, which stated that the king could not collect taxes without Parliament's consent or imprison people without a specific charge. Thus, the monarch had to acknowledge formally the long-established traditions protecting the rights of the English people.

Nevertheless, tensions between the throne and Parliament persisted, and in 1629 Charles I dissolved Parliament, which would not meet again for eleven years. What forced him to reconvene Parliament in 1640 was his need for funds to defend the realm against an invasion from Scotland. The conflict stemmed from Archbishop William Laud's attempt, approved by Charles I, to impose a common prayer book on Scottish Calvinists, or Presbyterians. Infuriated by this effort to impose Anglican liturgy on them, Scottish Presbyterians took up arms. The Long Parliament—so called because it was not disbanded until 1660—abolished extralegal courts and commissions that had been used by the king to try opponents, provided for regular meetings of Parliament, and strengthened Parliament's control over taxation. When Puritan members pressed to reduce royal authority even more and to strike at the power of the Anglican church, a deep split occurred in Parliament's ranks: Puritans and all-out supporters of parliamentary supremacy were opposed by Anglicans and supporters of the king. The ensuing civil war was directed by Parliament, financed by taxes and the merchants, and fought by the New Model Army led by Oliver Cromwell (1599–1658), a Puritan squire who gradually realized his potential for leadership.

Parliament's rich supporters financed the New Model Army, gentlemen farmers led it, and religious zealots filled its ranks, along with the usual cross section of poor artisans and day laborers. This army brought defeat to the king, his aristocratic followers, and the Anglican church's hierarchy. In January 1649, Charles I was publicly executed by order of Parliament. During the interregnum (time between kings), which lasted eleven years, one Parliament after another joined with the army to govern the country as a republic. In the distribution of power between the army and Parliament, Cromwell proved to be a key element. He had the support of the army's officers and some of its rank and file, and he had been a member of Parliament for many years. His control over the army was secured, however, only after its rank and file was purged of radicals, drawn largely from the poor. Some of these radicals wanted to level society, that is, to redistribute property and to give the vote to all male citizens.

Cromwell's death left the country without effective leadership. Parliament, having secured the interests of its constituency (gentry, merchants, and some small landowners), chose to restore court and crown and invited the exiled son of the executed king to return to the kingship. Having learned the lesson his father had spurned, Charles II (1660–1685) never instituted royal absolutism.

But Charles's brother, James II (1685–1688), was a foolishly fearless Catholic and admirer of French absolutism. He gathered at his court a coterie of Catholic advisers and supporters of royal prerogative and attempted to bend Parliament and local government to the royal will. James II's Catholicism was the crucial element in his failure. The Anglican church would not back him, and political forces similar to those that in 1640 had rallied against his father, Charles I, descended on him. The ruling elites, however, had learned their lesson back in the 1650s: civil war would produce social discontent among the masses. The upper classes wanted to avoid open warfare and preserve the monarchy as a constitutional authority, but not as an absolute one. Puritanism, with its sectarian fervor and its dangerous association with republicanism, was allowed to play no part in this second and last phase of the English Revolution.

In early 1688, Anglicans, some aristocrats, and opponents of royal prerogative formed a conspiracy against James II. Their purpose was to invite his son-in-law, William of Orange, stadholder (head) of the Netherlands and husband of James's Protestant daughter Mary, to invade England and rescue its government from James's control. Having lost the loyalty of key men in the army, powerful gentlemen in the counties, and the Anglican church, James II fled the country, and William and Mary were declared king and queen by act of Parliament.

This bloodless revolution—sometimes called the Glorious Revolution—created a new political and constitutional reality. Parliament secured its rights to assemble regularly and to vote on all matters of taxation; the rights of habeas corpus and trial by jury (for men of property and social status) were also secured. These rights were in turn legitimated in a constitutionally binding document, the Bill of Rights (1689). All Protestants, regardless of their sectarian bias, were granted toleration.

The English Revolution, in both its 1640 and its 1688 phases, secured English parliamentary government and the rule of law. Eventually, the monarchical element in that system would yield to the power and authority of parliamentary ministers and state officials. The Revolution of 1688–89 was England's last revolution. In the nineteenth and twentieth centuries, parliamentary institutions would be gradually and peacefully reformed to express a more democratic social reality. The events of 1688–89 have rightly been described as "the year one," for they fashioned a system of government that operated effectively in Britain and could also be transplanted elsewhere with modification. The British system became a model for other forms of representative government, adopted in France and in the former British colonies, beginning with the United States.

The Holy Roman Empire:
The Failure to Unify Germany

In contrast to the French, English, Spanish, and Dutch experiences in the early modern period, the Germans failed to achieve national unity. This failure is tied to the history of the Holy Roman Empire. That union of various distinct central European territories was created in the tenth century, when Otto I, in a deliberate attempt to revive Charlemagne's empire, was crowned emperor of the Romans. Later, the title was changed to Holy Roman emperor, with the kingdom consisting mainly of German-speaking principalities.

Most medieval Holy Roman emperors busied themselves not with administering their territories, but with attempting to gain control of the rich Italian peninsula and with challenging the rival authority of various popes. In the meantime, the German nobility extended and consolidated their rule over their peasants and over various towns and cities. The feudal aristocracy's power remained a constant obstacle to German unity.

In the medieval and early modern periods, the Holy Roman emperors were dependent on their most powerful noble lords—including an archbishop or two—because the office of emperor was elective rather than hereditary. German princes, some of whom were electors—for instance, the archbishops of Cologne and Mainz, the Hohenzollern elector of Brandenburg, the landgrave of Hesse, and the duke of Saxony—were fiercely independent. All belonged to the empire, yet all regarded themselves as autonomous powers. These decentralizing tendencies were highly developed by the fifteenth century. The Hapsburgs had maneuvered themselves into a position from which they could monopolize the imperial elections.

The centralizing efforts of Hapsburg Holy Roman Emperors Maximilian I (1493–1519) and Charles V (1519–1556) were impeded by the Reformation, which bolstered the Germans' already strong propensity for local independence. The German nobility were all too ready to use the Reformation as a vindication of their local power, and indeed Luther made just such an appeal to their interests. War raged in Germany between the Hapsburgs and the Protestant princes, united for mutual protection in the Schmalkaldic League. The Treaty of Augsburg (1555) conferred on every German prince the right to determine the religion of his subjects. The princes retained their power, and a unified German state was never constructed by the Hapsburgs. Religious disunity and the particularism and provinciality of the German nobility prevented its creation.

When an exhausted Emperor Charles V abdicated in 1556, he gave his kingdom to his son Philip and his brother Ferdinand. Philip inherited Spain and its colonies, as well as the Netherlands, and Ferdinand acquired the Austrian territories; two branches of the Hapsburg family were thus formed. Throughout the sixteenth century, the Austrian Hapsburgs barely managed to control the sprawling and deeply divided German territories. The Austrian Hapsburg emperors, however, never missed an opportunity to further the cause of Catholicism and to strike at the power of the German nobility.

No Hapsburg was ever more fervid in that regard than the Jesuit-trained Archduke Ferdinand II, who ascended the throne in Vienna in 1619. His policies provoked a war within the empire that engulfed the whole of Europe: the Thirty Years' War. It began when the Bohemians, whose anti-Catholic tendencies could be traced back to Jan Hus, tried to put a Protestant king on their throne. The Austrian and Spanish Hapsburgs reacted by sending an army into the kingdom of Bohemia, and suddenly the whole empire was forced to take sides along religious lines. Bohemia suffered an almost unimaginable devastation; the ravaging Hapsburg army sacked and burned three-fourths of the kingdom's towns and practically exterminated its aristocracy.

Until the 1630s, it looked as if the Hapsburgs would be able to use the war to enhance their power and promote centralization. But the intervention of Protestant Sweden, led by Gustavus Adolphus and encouraged by France, wrecked Hapsburg ambitions. The ensuing military conflict devastated vast areas of northern and central Europe. The civilian population suffered untold hardships. Partly because the French finally intervened directly, the Spanish Hapsburgs emerged from the Thirty Years' War with no benefits. The Treaty of Westphalia gave the Austrian Hapsburgs firm control of the eastern states of the kingdom, with Vienna as their capital. Austria took shape as a dynastic state, while the German territories in the empire remained fragmented by the independent interests of the feudal nobility.

European Expansion

During the period from 1450 to 1750, western Europe entered an era of overseas exploration and economic expansion that transformed society. European adventurers discovered a new way to reach the rich trading centers of India by sailing around Africa. They also conquered, colonized, and exploited a new world across the Atlantic. These discoveries and conquests brought about an extraordinary increase in business activity and the supply of money, which stimulated the growth of capitalism. People's values changed in ways that were alien and hostile to the medieval outlook. By 1750, the model Christian in northwestern Europe was no longer the selfless saint but the enterprising businessman. The era of secluded manors and walled towns was drawing to a close. A world economy was emerging, in which European economic life depended on the market in Eastern spices, African slaves, and American silver. During this age of exploration and commercial expansion, Europe generated a peculiar dynamism, unmatched by any other civilization. A process was initiated that by 1900 would give Europe mastery over most of the globe and wide-ranging influence over other civilizations.

Forces Behind the Expansion

Combined forces propelled Europeans outward and enabled them to dominate Asians, Africans, and American Indians. European monarchs, merchants, and aristocrats fostered expansion for power and profit; religion and technology played their part. As the numbers of the landed classes exceeded the supply of available land, the sons of the aristocracy looked beyond Europe for the lands and fortunes denied them at home. Nor was it unnatural for them to try to gain them by plunder and conquest; their ancestors had done the same thing for centuries.

Merchants and shippers also had reason to look abroad. Trade between Europe, Africa, and the Orient had gone on for centuries, but always through intermediaries, who increased the costs and decreased the profits on the European end. Gold had been transported by Arab nomads across the Sahara from the riverbeds of West Africa. Spices had been shipped from India and the East Indies by way of Muslim and Venetian merchants. Western European merchants now sought to break those monopolies by going directly to the source: to West Africa for gold, slaves, and pepper, and to India for pepper, spices, and silks.

The centralizing monarchical state was an important factor in the expansion. Monarchs who had successfully established royal hegemony at home, like Ferdinand and Isabella of Spain, sought opportunities to extend their control overseas. From overseas empires came gold, silver, and commerce,

Map 9.2   Overseas Exploration and Conquest, c. 1400–1600 ▶

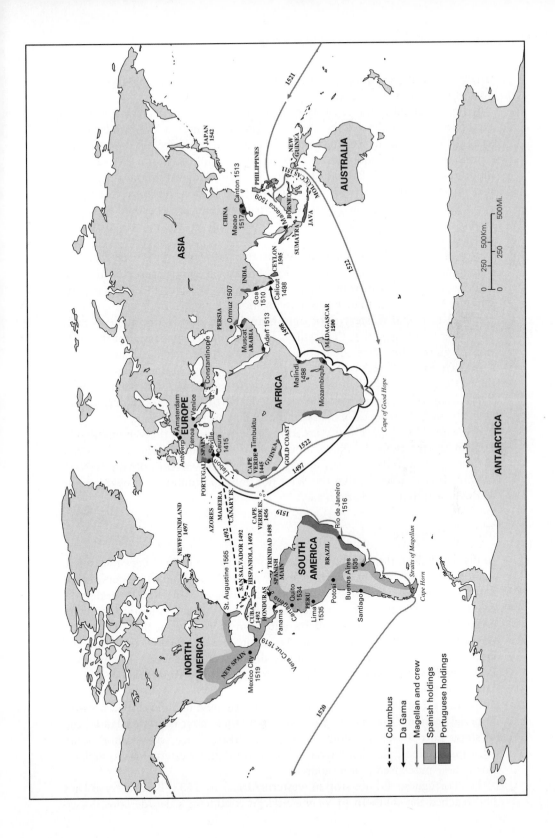

NORTH AMERICA

NEW SPAIN

Mexico City 1519

Vera Cruz 1519

Honduras

Cuba 1492

San Salvador 1492

Hispaniola 1492

St. Augustine 1565

Trinidad 1498

Spanish Main

Panama

Cartagena

Quito 1534

Lima 1535

Peru

Potosi

SOUTH AMERICA

Brazil

Rio de Janeiro 1516

Buenos Aires 1535

Santiago

Cape Horn

Straits of Magellan

Newfoundland 1497

Azores

Madeira

Canary Is.

Cape Verde Is. 1456

Portugal

Spain

Lisbon

Seville

Ceuta 1415

Cape Verde 1445

Guinea

Gold Coast

Timbuktu

Europe

Amsterdam

Antwerp

Genoa

Venice

Constantinople

Africa

Persia

Arabia

Muscat

Aden 1513

Malindi 1498

Mozambique

Madagascar 1500

Cape of Good Hope

Asia

Ormuz 1507

India

Goa 1510

Calicut 1498

Ceylon 1505

China

Macao 1517

Canton 1513

Japan 1542

Philippines

Borneo

Moluccas 1511

New Guinea

Sumatra

Java

Australia

Antarctica

1521

1522

1519

1520

1498

1497

1522

1509

Columbus

Da Gama

Magellan and crew

Spanish holdings

Portuguese holdings

0   250   500Km.
0   250   500Mi.

which paid for ever more expensive royal government at home and for war against rival dynasties abroad.

Religion helped in the expansion because the crusading tradition was well established—especially on the Iberian Peninsula, where a five-hundred-year struggle, known as the Reconquest, had taken place to drive out the Muslims. Cortés, the Spanish conqueror of Mexico, for example, saw himself as following in the footsteps of Paladin Roland, the great medieval military hero who had fought to drive back Muslims and pagans. Prince Henry the Navigator (see below) hoped that the Portuguese expansion into Africa would serve two purposes: the discovery of gold and the extension of Christianity at the expense of Islam.

Not only did the West have the will to expand; it also possessed the technology needed for successful expansion, the armed sailing vessels. This asset distinguished the West from China and the lands of Islam and helps explain why the West, rather than Eastern civilizations, launched an age of conquest resulting in global mastery. Not only were sailing ships more maneuverable and faster in the open seas than galleys (ships propelled by oars), but the addition of guns below deck that could fire and cripple or sink distant enemy ships gave them another tactical advantage. The galleys of the Arabs in the Indian Ocean and the junks of the Chinese were not armed with such guns. In battle, they relied instead on the ancient tactic of coming up alongside the enemy vessel, shearing off its oars, and boarding to fight on deck.

The gunned ship gave the West naval superiority from the beginning. The Portuguese, for example, made short work of the Muslim fleet sent to drive them out of the Indian Ocean in 1509. That victory at Diu, off the western coast of India, indicated that the West not only had found an all-water route to the Orient, but was there to stay.

The Portuguese Empire

In the first half of the fifteenth century, a younger son of the king of Portugal, named Prince Henry the Navigator (1394–1460) by English writers, sponsored voyages of exploration and the nautical studies needed to undertake them. The Portuguese first expanded into islands in the Atlantic Ocean. In 1420, they began to settle Madeira and farm there, and in the 1430s, they pushed into the Canaries and the Azores in search of new farmlands and slaves for their colonies. In the middle decades of the century, they moved down the west African coast to the mouth of the Congo River and beyond, establishing trading posts as they went.

By the end of the fifteenth century, the Portuguese had developed a viable imperial economy among the ports of West Africa, their Atlantic islands, and western Europe—an economy based on sugar, black slaves, and gold. Africans panned gold in the riverbeds of central and western Africa, and the Portuguese purchased it at its source.

The Portuguese did not stop in western Africa. By 1488, Bartholomeu Dias had reached the southern tip of the African continent; a decade later, Vasco da Gama sailed around the Cape of Good Hope and across the Indian Ocean to India. By discovering an all-water route to the Orient, Portugal broke the commercial monopoly on Eastern goods that Genoa and Venice had enjoyed. With this route to India and the East Indies, the Portuguese found the source of the spices needed to make dried and tough meat palatable. As they had done along the African coast, they established fortified trading posts—most notably at Goa on the western coast of India (Malabar) and at Malacca, on the Malay Peninsula.

The Spanish Empire

Spain stumbled onto its overseas empire, and it proved to be the biggest and richest of any until the eighteenth century. Christopher Columbus, who believed that he could reach India by sailing west, won the support of Isabella, queen of Castile. But on his first voyage (1492), he landed on a large Caribbean island, which he named Española (Little Spain). Within decades, two events revealed that Columbus had discovered not a new route to the East, but new continents: Vasco Nuñez de Balboa's discovery of the Pacific Ocean at the Isthmus of Panama in 1513, and the circumnavigation of the globe (1519–1521) by the expedition led by Ferdinand Magellan, which sailed through the strait at the tip of South America that now bears his name.

Stories of the existence of large quantities of gold and silver to the west lured the Spaniards from their initial settlements in the Caribbean to Mexico. In 1519, Hernando Cortés landed on the Mexican coast with a small army; during two years of campaigning, he managed to defeat the native rulers, the Aztecs, and to conquer Mexico for the Spanish crown. A decade later, Francisco Pizarro achieved a similar victory over the mountain empire of the Incas in Peru.

For good reasons, the Mexican and Peruvian conquests became the centers of the Spanish overseas empire. First, there were the gold hoards accumulated over the centuries by the indigenous rulers for religious and ceremonial purposes. When these supplies were exhausted, the Spanish discovered silver at Potosí in Upper Peru in 1545 and at Zacatecas in Mexico a few years later. From the middle of the century, the annual treasure fleets sailing to Spain became the financial bedrock of Philip II's war against the Muslim Turks and the Protestant Dutch and English.

Not only gold and silver lured Spaniards to the New World. The crusading spirit spurred them on as well. The will to conquer and convert the pagan peoples of the New World stemmed from the crusading tradition developed during the five previous centuries of Spanish history, in campaigns against the Muslims. The rewards were what they had always been: the propagation of the true faith, service to the crown, and handsome land grants. The land was especially attractive in the sixteenth century, for the number of *hidalgos* (lesser nobility) was increasing with the general rise in population; as a result, the amount of land available to them at home was shrinking.

In the New World, power and land gradually became concentrated in fewer

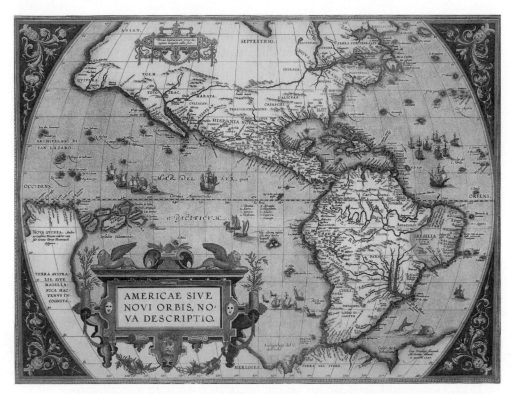

Map of the New World, Seventeenth Century.   Voyages of exploration and the exploitation of new commercial markets continued throughout the sixteenth and seventeenth centuries. The French, Dutch, and English followed the Portuguese and Spanish in planting colonies in the New World. European trading posts were established in Africa, India, and the Far East. The modern worldwide economy was being born. (*Fotomas Index, London*)

and fewer hands. Especially royal officials, their associates, and the church gained substantially in wealth and privilege. As recurrent depressions ruined smaller landowners, they were forced to sell out to their bigger neighbors. On their conversion to Christianity, the Indians were persuaded to give more and more land to the church. Thus, Spanish America became permanently divided between the privileged elite and the impoverished masses.

The effects of conquest were severe in other ways. Between 1500 and 1600, the number of Indians shrank from about twenty million to little more than two million. The major cause of this catastrophe, however, was not forced labor, but the diseases introduced from Europe—dysentery, malaria, hookworm, and smallpox—against which the Indians had little or no natural resistance. Beginning in the 1540s, the position of the natives gradually improved as the crown withdrew grants that gave authority over the native population and took increasing responsibility for controlling the Indians.

Black Slavery and the Slave Trade

One group suffered even more than the Indians: the black slaves originally brought over from West Africa. During the long period of their dominance in North Africa and the Middle East (from the seventh to the nineteenth century), the Muslim states relied on slave labor and slave soldiers from black Africa south of the Sahara. Blacks were captured and transported across the Sahara to be sold in the slave markets of North Africa. At its height in the eighteenth century, this trans-Saharan trade may have risen to some ten thousand slaves a year.

But this annual traffic was eventually dwarfed by the slave trade between West Africa and the European colonies in the New World, which began in earnest in the early sixteenth century. As Roland Oliver notes, "By the end of the seventeenth century, stimulated by the growth of plantation agriculture in Brazil and the West Indies, Atlantic shipments had increased to about thirty thousand a year, and by the end of the eighteenth century they were nearly eighty thousand."[1]

Captured in raids by African slavers, the victims were herded into specially built prisons on the West African coast. Those accepted for sale were "marked on the breast with a red-hot iron, imprinting the mark of the French, English or Dutch companies so that each nation may distinguish their own property."[2] Across the centuries, some eleven or twelve million blacks in all were exported to the New World. Of these, some 600,000 ended up in the thirteen colonies of British North America, forming the basis of the slave population of the new United States at the end of the American Revolution.

The conditions of the voyage from Africa, the so-called middle passage, were brutal. Crammed into the holds of ships, some 13 to 30 percent of blacks died on board. On arrival in the New World, slaves were greased with palm oil to improve their appearance and paraded naked into the auction hall for the benefit of prospective buyers, who paid top prices for "the strongest, youthfullest, and most beautiful."[3] The standard workload for slaves everywhere was ten or eleven hours a day six days a week. But some distinction must be made between slavery in the American South and elsewhere in the New World. In Brazil and the West Indies, slaves were worked to exhaustion and death and then replaced. Slaves formed a large majority there and were concentrated on very large plantations. Revolts were frequent but always crushed and savagely punished. In the American South, by contrast, slaves were a minority dispersed over relatively small holdings; large plantations were few. As a result, revolts and deadly epidemics were rare. After 1808, when the United States abolished the external slave trade, slaveholders could not ruthlessly exploit their slaves if they were to meet the growing need for workers caused by the increasing industrial demand for raw cotton. By 1830, the slave population of the southern states rose through natural increase to more than two million, which represented over one-third of all slaves in the New World.

The Price Revolution

Linked to overseas expansion was another phenomenon: an unprecedented inflation during the sixteenth century, known as the price revolution. For example, cereal prices multiplied by eight times or more in certain regions in the course of that century, and they continued to rise, although more slowly, during the first half of the seventeenth century. Economic historians have generally assumed that the prices of goods other than cereals increased by half as much as grain prices.

The main cause of the price revolution was the population growth during the late fifteenth and sixteenth centuries. The population of Europe almost doubled between 1460 and 1620. Until the middle of the seventeenth century, the number of mouths to feed outran the capacity of agriculture to supply basic foodstuffs, causing the vast majority of people to live close to subsistence. Until food production could catch up with the increasing population, prices, especially those of the staple food, bread, continued to rise.

The other principal cause of the price revolution was probably the silver that flowed into Europe from the New World via Spain, beginning in 1552. At some point, the influx of silver may have exceeded the necessary expansion of the money supply and may have begun contributing to the inflation. A key factor in the price revolution then was too many people with too much money chasing too few goods. The effects of the price revolution were momentous.

The Expansion of Agriculture

The price revolution had its greatest effect on farming. Food prices, rising roughly twice as much as the prices of other goods, spurred ambitious farmers to take advantage of the situation and to produce for the expanding market. The opportunity for profit drove some farmers to work harder and manage their land better.

All over Europe, landlords held their properties in the form of manors. A particular type of rural society and economy had evolved on these manors in the Late Middle Ages. By the fifteenth century, much manor land was held by peasant tenants, according to the terms of a tenure known in England as *copyhold*. The tenants had certain hereditary rights to the land in return for the performance of certain services and the payment of certain fees to the landlord. Principal among these rights was the use of the commons—the pasture, woods, and pond. For the copyholder, access to the commons often made the difference between subsistence and real want because the land tilled on the manor might not produce enough to keep a family. Arable land was worked according to ancient custom. The land was divided into strips, and each peasant of the manor was traditionally assigned a certain number of strips. This whole pattern of peasant tillage and rights in the commons was

Summer Harvest (c. 1615–1620) by Peter Brueghel the Younger (1564–1637).
England and the Netherlands underwent major agricultural changes in the early modern period. Enclosure of common fields by landlords and the abandonment of subsistence farming for specialized commercial farming transformed the agricultural economy of many parts of Europe. (*Oil on wood panel, 17¼" x 23¼", The Nelson-Atkins Museum of Art, Kansas City, Missouri: Nelson Trust*)

known as the *open-field system*. After changing little for centuries, it was met head-on by the incentives generated by the price revolution.

In England, landlords aggressively pursued the possibilities for profit resulting from the inflation of farm prices. This pursuit required far-reaching changes in ancient manorial agriculture, changes that are called *enclosure*. The open-field system was geared to providing subsistence for the local village and, as such, prevented large-scale farming for a distant market. In the open-field system, the commons could not be diverted to the production of crops for sale. Moreover, the division of the arable land into strips reserved for each peasant made it difficult to engage in profitable commercial agriculture.

English landlords in the sixteenth century launched a two-pronged attack against the open-field system in an effort to transform their holdings into market-oriented, commercial ventures. First they deprived their tenant peasantry of the use of the commons; then they changed the conditions of tenure from copyhold to leasehold. Whereas copyhold was heritable and fixed, leasehold was not. When a lease came up for renewal, the landlord could raise the rent beyond the tenant's capacity to pay. Restriction of rights to the commons deprived the poor tenant of critically needed produce. Both acts of the landlord forced peasants off the manor or into the landlord's employ as farm laborers. With tenants gone, fields could be incorporated into larger, more productive units. Landlords could hire labor at bargain prices because of the swelling population and the large supply of peasants forced off the land by enclosure. Subsistence farming gave way to commercial agriculture: the growing of a surplus for the marketplace. But rural poverty increased because of the mass evictions of tenant farmers.

In the fifteenth and sixteenth centuries, the Dutch developed a new kind of farming, known as *convertible husbandry,* which also expanded production. This farming system employed a series of innovations, including the use of soil-restoring legumes, that replaced the old three-field system of crop rotation, which had left one-third of the land unused at any given time. The new techniques used all the land every year and provided a more diversified agriculture.

The Expansion of Trade and Industry

The conditions of the price revolution also caused trade and industry to expand. Population growth that exceeded the capacity of local food supplies stimulated commerce in basic foodstuffs, for example, the Baltic trade with western Europe. Equally important as a stimulus to trade and industry was the growing income of landlords, merchants, and, in some instances, peasants. This income created a rising demand for consumer goods. Another factor in commercial and industrial expansion was the growth of the state. With increasing amounts of tax revenue to spend, the expanding monarchies of the sixteenth and seventeenth centuries bought more and more supplies—ships, weapons, uniforms, paper—and so spurred economic expansion.

Innovations in Business

Markets tended to shift from local to regional or even to international—a condition that gave rise to the merchant capitalist. The merchant capitalists' operations, unlike those of local producers, extended across local and national boundaries. An essential feature of merchant capitalism was the *putting-out system* of production. The manufacture of woolen textiles is a good example of how the system worked. The merchant capitalist would buy the raw wool from English landlords, who had enclosed their manors to take advantage of the rising price of wool. The merchant's agents collected the wool and took it (put it out) to nearby villages for spinning, dyeing, and weaving. The work was done in the cottages of peasants, many of whom had been evicted from the surrounding manors as a result of enclosure and therefore had to take what work they could get at very low wages. When the wool was processed into cloth, it was picked up and shipped to market.

A cluster of other innovations in business life accompanied the emergence of the merchant capitalist and the putting-out system. Some of these innovations had roots in the Middle Ages and were important in the evolution of the modern capitalist economy. Banking operations grew more sophisticated, making it possible for depositors to pay their debts by issuing written orders to their banks to make transfers to their creditors' accounts—the origins of the modern check. Accounting methods also improved. The widespread use of double-entry bookkeeping made errors immediately evident and gave a clear picture of the financial position of a commercial enterprise. Very important to overseas expansion was a new form of business enterprise known as the joint-stock company, which allowed small investors to buy shares in a venture. These companies made possible the accumulation of the large amounts of capital needed for large-scale operations, like the building and deployment of merchant fleets, which were quite beyond the resources of one person.

Different Patterns of Commercial Development

England and the Netherlands   In both England and the United Provinces (the Netherlands), the favorable conditions led to large-scale commercial expansion. In the 1590s, the Dutch devised a new ship, the *fluit,* or flyboat, to handle bulky grain shipments at the lowest possible cost. This innovation allowed them to capture the Baltic trade, which became a principal source of their phenomenal commercial expansion between 1560 and 1660.

Equally dramatic was their commercial penetration of the Orient. Profits from the European carrying trade built the ships that allowed the Dutch first to challenge and then to displace the Portuguese in the spice trade with the East Indies during the early seventeenth century. The Dutch chartered the United East India Company in 1602 and established trading posts in the islands, which were the beginnings of a Dutch empire, which lasted until World War II.

The English traded throughout Europe in the sixteenth and seventeenth centuries, especially with Spain and the Netherlands. The seventeenth century saw the foundation of a British colonial empire along the Atlantic seaboard in North America, from Maine to the Carolinas, and in the West Indies, where the English managed to dislodge the Spanish in some places.

In both England and the Netherlands, government promoted the interests of business. Political power in the Netherlands passed increasingly into the hands of an urban patriciate of merchants and manufacturers, based in cities like Delft, Haarlem, and especially Amsterdam. There, urban interests pursued public policies that served their pocketbooks. In England, because of the revolutionary transfer of power from the king to Parliament, economic policies also reflected the interests of big business, whether agricultural or commercial. Enclosure, for example, was abetted by parliamentary enactment. The Bank of England, founded in 1694, expanded credit and increased business confidence. The Navigation Acts, which proved troublesome to American colonists, placed restrictions on colonial trade and manufacturing to prevent competition with English merchants and manufacturers.

France and Spain   France benefited from commercial and industrial expansion, but not to the same degree as England, mainly owing to the aristocratic structure of French society. Family ties and social intercourse between the aristocracy and the merchants, like those that developed in England, were largely absent in France. Consequently, the French aristocracy remained contemptuous of commerce. Also inhibiting economic expansion were the guilds—remnants of the Middle Ages that restricted competition and production. In France, there was relatively less room than in England for the merchant capitalist operating outside the guild structures.

Spain presents an even clearer example of the failure to grasp the opportunities afforded by the price revolution. By the third quarter of the sixteenth century, Spain possessed the makings of economic expansion: unrivaled amounts of capital in the form of silver, a large and growing population, rising consumer demand, and a vast overseas empire. These factors did not bear fruit because the Spanish value system regarded business as social heresy. The Spanish held in high esteem gentlemen who possessed land gained through military service and crusading ardor, which enabled them to live on rents and privileges. So commerce and industry remained contemptible pursuits.

Numerous wars in the sixteenth century (with France, the Lutheran princes, the Ottoman Turks, the Dutch, and the English) put an increasing strain on the Spanish treasury, despite the annual shipments of silver from the New World. Spain spent its resources on maintaining and extending its imperial power and Catholicism, rather than on investing in economic expansion. In the end, the wars cost more than Spain could handle. The Dutch for a time and the English and the French for a much longer period displaced Spain as the great power. The English and the Dutch had taken advantage of the opportunities presented by the price revolution; the Spanish had not.

The Fostering of Mercantile Capitalism

The changes described—especially in England and the Netherlands—represent a crucial stage in the development of the modern economic system known as *capitalism*. This is a system of *private enterprise*: the main economic decisions (what, how much, where, and at what price to produce, buy, and sell) are made by private individuals in their capacity as owners, workers, or consumers.

From 1450 to 1600, several conditions sustained the incentive to invest and reinvest—a basic factor in the emergence of modern capitalism. One was the price revolution stemming from a supply of basic commodities that could not keep pace with rising demand. Prices continued to climb, creating the most

Spinning, Winding, and Weaving by Izaak Nicolai van Swanenburgh, Seventeenth Century.   The Netherlands had been a center of textile manufacturing since the Early Middle Ages. It continued to be a center of manufacturing in the early modern period. Traditionally, women were active in the manufacture of textiles. (*Stedelijk Museum "De Lakenhal," Leiden*)

powerful incentive of all to invest rather than to consume. Why spend now, those with surplus wealth must have asked, when investment in commercial farming, mining, shipping, and publishing (to name a few important outlets) is almost certain to yield greater wealth in the future?

Additional stimuli for investment came from governments. Governments acted as giant consumers, whose appetites throughout the early modern period were expanding. Merchants who supplied governments with everything from guns to frescoes not only prospered, but reinvested as well, because of the constancy and growth of government demand. Governments also sponsored new forms of investment, whether to supply the debauched taste for new luxuries at the king's court or to meet the requirements of the military. Moreover, private investors reaped incalculable advantages from overseas empires. Colonies supplied cheap raw materials and cheap (slave) labor and served as markets for exports. They greatly stimulated the construction of both ships and harbor facilities and the sale of insurance.

State policies, known as *mercantilism*, were also aimed at augmenting national wealth and power. According to mercantilist theory, wealth from trade was measured in gold and silver, of which there was believed to be a more or less fixed quantity. The state's goal in international trade became to sell more abroad than it bought, that is, to establish a favorable balance of payments. When the amount received for sales abroad was greater than that spent for purchases, the difference would be an influx of precious metal into the state. By this logic, mercantilists were led to argue for the goal of national sufficiency: a country should try to supply most of its own needs to keep imports to a minimum.

To fuel the national economy, governments subsidized new industries, chartered companies to engage in overseas trade, and broke down local trade barriers, such as guild regulations and internal tariffs. The price revolution, the concentration of wealth in private hands, and government activity combined to provide the foundation for sustained investment and for the emergence of mercantile capitalism. This new force in the world should not be confused with industrial capitalism. The latter evolved with the Industrial Revolution in eighteenth-century England, but mercantile capitalism paved the way for it.

Toward a Global Economy

The transformations considered in this chapter were among the most momentous in the world's history. In an unprecedented development, one small part of the world, western Europe, had become the lord of the sea-lanes, the master of many lands throughout the globe, and the banker and profit taker in an emerging world economy. Western Europe's global hegemony was to last well into the twentieth century. In conquering and settling new lands, Europeans exported Western culture around the globe, a process that accelerated in the twentieth century.

The effects of overseas expansion were profound. The native populations of the New World were decimated. As a result of the labor shortage, millions of blacks were imported from Africa to work as slaves on plantations and in mines. Black slavery would produce large-scale effects on culture, politics, and society, which have lasted to the present day.

The widespread circulation of plant and animal life also had great consequences. Horses and cattle were introduced into the New World. (So amazed were the Aztecs to see man on horseback that at first they thought horse and rider were one demonic creature.) In return, the Old World acquired such novelties as corn, the tomato, and most important, the potato, which was to become a staple of the northern European diet. Manioc, from which tapioca is made, was transplanted from the New World to Africa, where it helped sustain the population.

Western Europe was wrenched out of the subsistence economy of the Middle Ages and launched on a course of sustained economic growth. This transformation resulted from the grafting of traditional forms, such as primogeniture and holy war, onto new forces, such as global exploration, price revolution, and convertible husbandry. Out of this change emerged the beginnings of a new economic system, mercantile capitalism. This system, in large measure, paved the way for the Industrial Revolution of the eighteenth and nineteenth centuries and provided the economic thrust for European world predominance.

Notes

1. Roland Oliver, *The African Experience* (New York: HarperCollins, 1991), p. 123.
2. Quoted in Basil Davidson, *Africa in History* (New York: Collier Books, 1991), p. 215.
3. Quoted in Richard S. Dunn, *Sugar and Slaves* (Chapel Hill: University of North Carolina Press, 1972), p. 248.

Suggested Reading

Anderson, Perry, *Lineages of the Absolutist State* (1974). A useful survey, written from a Marxist perspective.

Cipolla, Carlo M., *Guns, Sails and Empires* (1965). Connections between technological innovation and overseas expansion, 1400 to 1700.

Davis, David Brion, *The Problem of Slavery in Western Culture* (1966). An authoritative study.

Davis, Ralph, *The Rise of the Atlantic Economies* (1973). A reliable survey of early modern economic history.

Dor Ner, Zvi, *Columbus and the Age of Discovery* (1991). Companion volume to the seven-part PBS series; lavishly illustrated.

Elliott, J. H., *Imperial Spain,* 1469–1716 (1963). An excellent survey of the major European power of the early modern period.

Koenigsberger, H. G., *Early Modern Europe, 1500–1789* (1987). A valuable survey of the period.

Kolchin, Peter, *American Slavery: 1619–1877* (1993). An informed synthesis.

Parry, J. H., *The Age of Reconnaissance* (1963). A short survey of exploration.

Plumb, J. H., *The Growth of Political Stability in England, 1675–1725* (1967). A basic book, clear and readable.

Shennan, J. H., *The Origins of the Modern European State* (1974). An excellent brief introduction.

Review Questions

1. In what ways did early modern kings increase their power? What relationship did they have with the commercial bourgeoisie in their countries?
2. What were the strengths and weaknesses of the Spanish state?
3. Why did England move in the direction of parliamentary government, while most countries on the Continent embraced absolutism? Describe the main factors.
4. What were the new forces for expansion operating in early modern Europe?
5. Discuss the connection between the price revolution and overseas expansion. What was the principal cause of the price revolution? Why?
6. What was enclosure? How did the price revolution encourage it?
7. What is mercantile capitalism? What fostered its development?
8. European expansion gave rise to an emerging world economy. Discuss this statement.

❖ CHAPTER 10

Intellectual Transformation: The Scientific Revolution and the Age of Enlightenment

$\mathcal{T}$he movement toward modernity initiated by the Renaissance was greatly advanced by the Scientific Revolution of the seventeenth century. The Scientific Revolution destroyed the medieval view of the universe and established the scientific method—rigorous and systematic observation and experimentation—as the essential means of unlocking nature's secrets. Increasingly, Western thinkers maintained that nature was a mechanical system governed by laws that could be expressed mathematically. The new discoveries electrified the imagination. Science displaced theology as the queen of knowledge, and reason, which had been subordinate to religion in the Middle Ages, asserted its autonomy. The great confidence in reason inspired by the Scientific Revolution helped give rise to the Enlightenment, which explicitly rejected the ideas and institutions of the medieval past and articulated the essential norms of modernity. ❖

The Medieval View of the Universe*

Medieval thinkers had constructed a coherent picture of the universe that blended the theories of two ancient Greeks, Aristotle and Ptolemy of Alexandria, with Christian teachings. To the medieval mind, the cosmos was a giant ladder, a qualitative order, ascending toward heaven. God was at the summit of this hierarchical universe and the earth, base and vile, was at the bottom just above hell. In the medieval view, the earth's central location meant that the universe centered on human beings, that by God's design human beings—the only creatures on whom God had bestowed reason and the promise of salvation—were lords of the earth. Around the earth revolved seven transparent spheres, each of which carried a "planet"—the moon, Mercury, Venus, the sun, Mars, Jupiter, and Saturn. (Since the earth did not move, it was not considered a planet.) The eighth sphere, in which the stars were embedded, also

*See also Chapter 7.

276

revolved about the earth. Beyond the stars was a heavenly sphere, the prime mover, which imparted motion to the planets and the stars, so that in one day the entire celestial system turned around the stationary earth. Enclosing the entire system was another heavenly sphere, the Empyrean, where God sat on his throne, attended by angels.

Medieval thinkers inherited Aristotle's view of a qualitative universe. Earthly objects were composed of earth, water, air, and fire, whereas celestial objects, belonging to a higher world, were composed of ether—an element too pure and perfect to be found on earth, which consisted of base matter. In contrast to earthly objects, heavenly bodies were incorruptible, that is they experienced no change. This two-world orientation blended well with the Christian outlook.

Like Aristotle, Ptolemy held that planets moved in perfect circular orbits and at uniform speeds around the earth. However, in reality the path of planets is not a circle but an ellipse, and planets do not move at uniform speed but accelerate as they approach the sun. Therefore, problems arose that required Ptolemy to incorporate into his system certain ingenious devices that earlier Greek astronomers had employed. For example, to save the appearance of circular orbits Ptolemy made use of epicycles. A planet revolved uniformly around a small circle, an epicycle, which in turn revolved about the earth in a larger circle. If one ascribed a sufficient number of epicycles to a planet, the planet could seem to move in perfectly circular orbits.

The Aristotelian-Ptolemaic model of the cosmos did appear to accord with common sense and raw perception: the earth does indeed seem and feel to be at rest. And the validity of this view seemed to be confirmed by evidence, for the model enabled thinkers to predict with considerable accuracy the movement and location of celestial bodies and the passage of time. This geocentric model and the division of the universe into higher and lower worlds also accorded with passages in Scripture. Scholastic philosophers harmonized Aristotelian and Ptolemaic science with Christian theology, producing an intellectually and emotionally satisfying picture of the universe, in which everything was arranged according to a divine plan.

A New View of Nature

In several ways, the Renaissance contributed to the Scientific Revolution. The revival of interest in antiquity during the Renaissance led to the rediscovery of some ancient scientific texts, including the works of Archimedes (287–212 B.C.), which fostered new ideas in mechanics, and to the improved translations of the medical works of Galen, a contemporary of Ptolemy, which stimulated the study of anatomy. Renaissance art, too, was a factor in the rise of modern science, for it linked an exact representation of the human body to mathematical proportions and demanded accurate observation of natural phenomena. By defining visual space and the relationship between the object

---

Chronology 10.1 ❖ The Scientific Revolution and the Enlightenment

1543	Publication of Copernicus's *On the Revolutions of the Heavenly Spheres* marks the beginning of modern astronomy
1605	Publication of Bacon's *Advancement of Learning*
1610	Publication of Galileo's *The Starry Messenger*, asserting the uniformity of nature
1632	Galileo's teachings are condemned by the church, and he is placed under house arrest
1687	Publication of Newton's *Principia Mathematica*
1690	Publication of Locke's *Two Treatises of Government*
1733	Publication of Voltaire's *Letters Concerning the English Nation*
1751–1765	Publication of the *Encyclopedia* edited by Diderot
1776	Declaration of Independence
1789	French Revolution begins

---

and the observer in mathematical terms and by delineating the natural world with unprecedented scientific precision, Renaissance art helped promote a new view of nature, which later found expression in the astronomy of Copernicus and Kepler and the physics of Galileo.

The Renaissance revival of ancient Pythagorean and Platonic ideas, which stressed mathematics as the key to comprehending reality, also contributed to the Scientific Revolution. Extending the mathematical harmony found in music to the universe at large, Pythagoras (c. 580–507 B.C.) and his followers believed that all things have form, which can be expressed numerically and that reality consists fundamentally of number relations, which the mind can grasp. Plato maintained that beyond the world of everyday objects made known to us through the senses lies a higher reality, the world of Forms, which contains an inherent mathematical order apprehended only by thought. The great thinkers of the Scientific Revolution were influenced by these ancient ideas of nature as a harmonious mathematical system knowable to the mind.

Nicolaus Copernicus: The Dethronement of the Earth

Modern astronomy begins with Nicolaus Copernicus (1473–1543), a Polish astronomer, mathematician, and church canon. He proclaimed that earth is a planet that orbits a centrally located sun together with the other planets. This heliocentric theory served as the kernel of a new world picture, which eventually supplanted the medieval view of the universe. Copernicus did not base his heliocentric theory on new observations and new data. What led him to remove the earth from the center of the universe was the complexity and cumbersomeness of the Ptolemaic system, which offended his sense of mathematical order. To Copernicus, the numerous epicycles (the number had been increased since Ptolemy, making the model even more cumbersome) violated the Platonic vision of the mathematical symmetry of the universe.

Concerned that his theories would spark a controversy, Copernicus refused to publish his work, but persuaded by his friends, he finally relented. His masterpiece, *On the Revolutions of the Heavenly Spheres,* appeared in 1543. As Copernicus had feared, his views did stir up controversy, but the new astronomy did not become a passionate issue until the early seventeenth century, more than fifty years after the publication of *On the Revolutions.* The Copernican theory frightened clerical authorities, who controlled the universities as well as the pulpits, for it seemed to conflict with Scripture. For example, Psalm 93 says: "Yea, the world is established, that it cannot be moved." And Psalm 103 says that God "fixed the earth upon its foundation not to be moved forever." In 1616, the church placed *On the Revolutions* and all other works that ascribed motion to the earth on the Index of Prohibited Books.

Galileo: Uniformity of Nature and Experimental Physics

Galileo Galilei (1564–1642) is the principal reason that the seventeenth century has been called "the century of genius." A Pisan by birth, Galileo was a talented musician and artist and a cultivated humanist; he knew and loved the Latin classics and Italian poetry. He was also an astronomer and physicist, who helped shatter the medieval conception of the cosmos and shape the modern scientific outlook. Galileo was indebted to the Platonic tradition, which tried to grasp the mathematical harmony of the universe, and to Archimedes, the Hellenistic mathematician-engineer who had sought a geometric understanding of space and motion.

Galileo rejected the medieval division of the universe into higher and lower realms and proclaimed the modern idea of nature's uniformity. Learning that a telescope had been invented in Holland, Galileo built one for himself and used it to investigate the heavens—the first person to do so. From his observations of the moon, Galileo concluded

> *that the surface of the moon is not smooth, uniform, and precisely spherical as a great number of philosophers believe it (and the other heavenly bodies) to be, but is uneven, rough, and full of cavities and prominences, being not unlike the face of the earth, relieved by chains of mountains and deep valleys.*[1]

This discovery of the moon's craters and mountains led Galileo to break with the Aristotelian notion that celestial bodies were pure, perfect, and

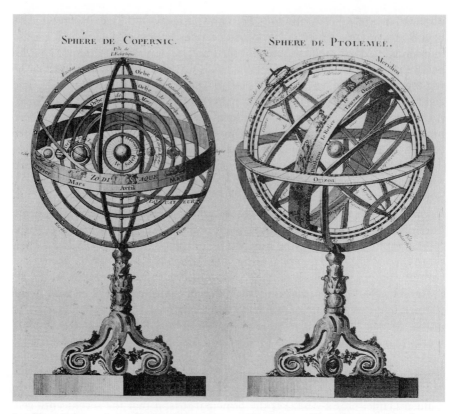

Armillary Spheres According to Copernicus and Ptolemy.   The spheres reflect the opposing views of the nature of the cosmos that confronted scholars in the sixteenth and
early seventeenth centuries. Gradually, Copernicus's heliocentric viewpoint, supported
by the discoveries of Kepler, Galileo, and Newton, overturned the Ptolemaic system.
(*Smithsonian Institution Libraries*)

unchangeable. For Galileo, there was no difference in quality between celestial and terrestrial bodies. Nature was not a hierarchical order, in which physical entities were ranked according to their possession or lack of quality;
rather, it was a homogeneous system, the same throughout.

With his telescope, Galileo discovered the four moons that orbit Jupiter, an
observation that overcame a principal objection to the Copernican system.
Galileo showed that a celestial body could indeed move around a center other
than the earth; that the earth was not the common center for all celestial bodies; and that a celestial body (the earth's moon or Jupiter's moons) could orbit
a planet at the same time that the planet revolved around another body
(the sun).

Galileo pioneered in experimental physics and advanced the modern idea
that knowledge of motion should be derived from direct observation and
from mathematics. In dealing with problems of motion, he insisted on apply-

ing mathematics to the study of moving bodies and did in fact study acceleration by performing experiments, which required careful mathematical measurement. For Aristotelian scholastics, a rock fell because it was striving to reach its proper place in the universe, thereby fulfilling its nature; it was acting in accordance with the purpose God had assigned it. Galileo completely rejected the view that motion is due to a quality inherent in an object. Rather, he said, motion is the relationship of bodies to time and distance. By holding that bodies fall according to uniform and quantifiable laws, Galileo posited an entirely different conceptual system. This system requires that we study angles and distances and search for mathematical ratios but avoid inquiring into an object's quality and purpose—the role God assigned it in a hierarchical universe.

For Galileo, the universe was a "grand book which . . . is written in the language of mathematics and its characters are triangles, circles, and other geometric figures without which it is humanly impossible to understand a single word of it."[2] In the tradition of Plato, Galileo sought to grasp the mathematical principles governing nature and ascribed to mathematics absolute authority. Like Copernicus and Kepler, he believed that mathematics expresses the harmony and beauty of God's creation.

Attack on Authority

Insisting that physical truth is arrived at through observation, experimentation, and reason, Galileo strongly denounced reliance on authority. Scholastic thinkers regarded Aristotle as the supreme authority on questions concerning nature, and university education was based on his works. These doctrinaire Aristotelians angered Galileo, who protested that they sought truth not by opening their eyes to nature and new knowledge, but by slavishly relying on ancient texts. In *Dialogue Concerning the Two Chief World Systems—Ptolemaic and Copernican* (1632), Galileo upheld the Copernican view and attacked the unquestioning acceptance of Aristotle's teachings.

Galileo also criticized Roman Catholic authorities for attempting to suppress the Copernican theory. He argued that passages from the Bible had no authority in questions involving nature.

A sincere Christian, Galileo never intended to use the new science to undermine faith. What he desired was to separate science from faith so that reason and experience alone would be the deciding factors on questions involving nature. He could not believe that "God who has endowed us with senses, reason and intellect,"[3] did not wish us to use these faculties in order to acquire knowledge. For Galileo, the aim of Scripture was to teach people the truths necessary for salvation, not to instruct them in the operations of nature, which is the task of science.

Galileo's support of Copernicus aroused the ire of both scholastic philosophers and the clergy, who feared that the brash scientist threatened a world picture that had the support of venerable ancient authorities, Holy Writ, and scholastic tradition. Already traumatized by the Protestant threat, Catholic

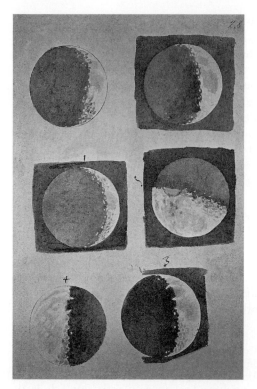

Notebook Sketches of the Phases of the Moon by Galileo Galilei, 1609–1610.   Galileo saw only shadows when he looked into his telescope. But because he was trained as an artist in the principles of light and dark coloring to emphasize or shorten distance, he knew that what he saw represented real objects, in this case mountains and valleys. Somewhat satirically, he compared the moon to Bohemia. (*Biblioteca Nazionale Centrale, Florence*)

officials cringed at ideas that might undermine traditional belief and authority.

In 1616, the Congregation of the Index, the church's censorship organ, condemned the teaching of Copernicanism. In 1633, the aging and infirm Galileo was summoned to Rome. Tried and condemned by the Inquisition, he was ordered to abjure the Copernican theory. Not wishing to bring harm to himself and certain that the truth would eventually prevail, Galileo bowed to the Inquisition. He was sentenced to life imprisonment—mostly house arrest at his own villa near Florence—the *Dialogue* was banned, and he was forbidden to write on Copernicanism. Not until 1820 did the church lift the ban on Copernicanism.

Johannes Kepler: Laws of Planetary Motion

Johannes Kepler (1571–1630), a German mathematician and astronomer, combined the Pythagorean-Platonic quest to comprehend the mathematical harmony within nature with a deep commitment to Lutheran Christianity. He contended that God gave human beings the ability to understand the laws of harmony and proportion.

As a true Pythagorean, Kepler yearned to discover the geometric harmony of the planets—what he called the "music of the spheres." Such knowledge, he believed, would provide supreme insight into God's mind. No doubt, this mystical quality sparked the creative potential of the imagination, but to be harnessed for science, it had to be disciplined by the rational faculties.

Kepler discovered the three basic laws of planetary motion, which shattered Ptolemaic cosmology. In doing so, he utilized the data collected by Tycho Brahe, a Danish astronomer, who for twenty years systematically observed the planets and stars and recorded their positions with far greater accuracy than had ever been done. Kepler sought to fit Tycho's observations into Copernicus's heliocentric model.

Kepler's first law demonstrated that planets move in elliptical orbits—not circular ones, as Aristotle and Ptolemy (and Copernicus) had believed—and that the sun is one focus of the ellipse. This discovery that a planet's path was one simple oval eliminated all the epicycles that had been used to preserve the appearance of circular motion. Kepler's second law showed that planets do not move at uniform speed, as had been believed, but accelerate as they near the sun, and he provided the rule for deciphering a planet's speed at each point in its orbit. His third law drew a mathematical relationship between the time it takes a planet to complete its orbit and its average distance from the sun. On the basis of these laws, one could calculate accurately a planet's position and velocity at a particular time—another indication that the planets were linked together in a unified mathematical system.

Derived from carefully observed facts, Kepler's laws of planetary motion buttressed Copernicanism, for they made sense only in a heliocentric universe. But why did the planets move in elliptical orbits? Why did they not fly off into space or crash into the sun? To these questions Kepler had no satisfactory answers. It was Isaac Newton (1642–1727), the great British mathematician-scientist, who arrived at a celestial mechanics that linked the astronomy of Copernicus and Kepler with the physics of Galileo and accounted for the behavior of planets.

The Newtonian Synthesis

The publication in 1687 of Isaac Newton's *Mathematical Principles of Natural Philosophy* marks the climax of the Scientific Revolution. Newton postulated three laws of motion that joined all celestial and terrestrial objects into a vast mechanical system, whose parts worked in perfect harmony and whose connections could be expressed in mathematical terms. Since Copernican astronomy was essential to his all-encompassing theory of the universe, Newton had provided mathematical proof for the heliocentric system and opposition to it dissipated.

Newton's first law is the principle of inertia: that a body at rest remains at rest unless acted on by a force and that a body in rectilinear motion continues to move in a straight line at the same velocity unless a force acts on it. A moving body does not require a force to keep it in motion, as ancient and medieval thinkers had believed. Once started, bodies continue to move; motion is as natural a condition as rest. Newton's second law states that a given force produces a measurable change in a body's velocity; a body's change of velocity is proportional to the force acting on it. Newton's third law holds that for every action or force there is an equal and opposite reaction or force. The sun pulls the earth with the same force that the earth exercises on the sun. An apple falling to the ground is being pulled by the earth, but the apple is also pulling the earth toward it. (However, since the mass of the apple is so small in comparison with the earth, the force that the apple exercises on the earth causes no visible change in the earth's motion.)

Newton asserted that the same laws of motion and gravitation that operate in the celestial world also govern the movement of earthly bodies. Ordinary mechanical laws explain both why apples fall to the ground and why planets orbit the sun. Newtonian physics ended the medieval division of the cosmos into higher and lower worlds with different laws operating in each realm. The universe is an integrated, harmonious mechanical system held together by the force of gravity. By demonstrating that the universe contains an inherent mathematical order, Newton realized the Pythagorean and Platonic visions. To his contemporaries, it seemed that Newton had unraveled all of nature's mysteries: the universe was fully explicable. It was as if Newton had penetrated God's mind.

Deeply committed to Anglican Christianity, Newton retained a central place for God in his world system. God for him was the grand architect whose wisdom and skill accounted for nature's magnificent design. Newton also believed that God could intervene in his creation and that there was no conflict between divine miracles and a clockwork universe. However, in future generations, thinkers called deists (see pages 290–291) came to regard miracles as incompatible with a universe governed by impersonal mechanical principles.

With his discovery of the composition of light, Newton also laid the foundation of the science of optics. He was a cautious experimentalist who valued experimental procedures, including drawing appropriate conclusions from accumulated data. Both Newton's mechanical universe and his championing of the experimental method were foundation blocks of the Age of Enlightenment.

Prophets of Modern Science

The accomplishments of the Scientific Revolution extended beyond the creation of a new model of the universe. They also included the formulation of a new method of inquiry into nature and the recognition that science could serve humanity. Two thinkers instrumental in articulating the implications of the Scientific Revolution were Francis Bacon and René Descartes. Both repudiated the authority of Aristotle and other ancients in scientific matters and urged the adoption of new methods for seeking and evaluating truth.

Francis Bacon: The Inductive Method

Sir Francis Bacon (1561–1626), an English statesman and philosopher, vigorously supported the advancement of science and the scientific method. Although he himself had no laboratory and made no discoveries, his advocacy of the scientific method has earned him renown as a prophet of modern science. Bacon attributed the limited progress of science over the ages to the interference of scholastic philosophers, who sought to bend theories of nature to the requirements of Scripture. Bacon also denounced scholastic thinkers for their slavish attachment to Aristotelian doctrines, which prevented independent thinking and the acquisition of new information about nature. To acquire new knowledge and improve the quality of human life, said Bacon, we should not depend on ancient texts; old authorities must be discarded. Knowledge must be pursued and organized in a new way.

The method that Bacon advocated as the way to truth and useful knowledge was the inductive approach: careful observation of nature and the systematic accumulation of data; drawing general laws from the knowledge of particulars; and testing these laws through constant experimentation. In his discovery of the circulation of blood, Bacon's contemporary, British physician William Harvey (1578–1657), successfully employed the inductive method championed by Bacon. Grasping the essential approach of modern natural science, Bacon attacked practitioners of astrology, magic, and alchemy for their errors, secretiveness, and enigmatic writings and urged instead the pursuit of cooperative and methodical scientific research that could be publicly criticized.

Bacon was among the first to appreciate the value of the new science for human life. Knowledge, he said, should help us utilize nature for human advantage; it should improve the quality of human life by advancing commerce, industry, and agriculture. Holding that knowledge is power, Bacon urged the state to found scientific institutions and praised progress in technology and the mechanical arts.

René Descartes: The Deductive Method

The scientific method encompasses two approaches to knowledge that usually complement each other: the empirical (inductive) and the rational (deductive). In the inductive approach, which is employed in such descriptive sciences as biology, anatomy, and geology, general principles are derived from analyzing data collected through observation and experiment. The essential features of the inductive method, as we have seen, were championed by Bacon, who regarded sense data as the foundation of knowledge. In the deductive approach, which is employed in mathematics and theoretical physics, truths are derived in successive steps from first principles, indubitable axioms. In the

Engraving of René Descartes (1596–1650) Tutoring Queen Christina of Sweden.   Descartes was rare among major scientists because he believed passionately in the intelligence of his female followers and correspondents. Rejecting authority, he asserted confidence in the human mind's ability to arrive at truth through its own capacities. *(Jean-Loup Charmet)*

seventeenth century, the deductive method was formulated by René Descartes (1596–1650), a French mathematician and philosopher, who is also regarded as the founder of modern philosophy.

In the *Discourse on Method* (1637), Descartes expressed his disenchantment with the learning of his day. Since much of what he had believed on the basis of authority had come to be shown as untrue, Descartes resolved to seek no other knowledge than that which he might find within himself or within nature. Rejecting as absolutely false anything about which he could have the least doubt, Descartes searched for an incontrovertible truth that could serve as the first principle of knowledge, the basis of an all-encompassing philosophical system.

Descartes found one truth to be certain and unshakable: that it was he who was doing the doubting and thinking. In his dictum "I think therefore I am," Descartes had his starting point of knowledge. Descartes is viewed as the founder of modern philosophy because he called for the individual to question and if necessary to overthrow all traditional beliefs, and he proclaimed the mind's inviolable autonomy and importance, its ability and right to understand truth. His assertions about the power of thought made people aware of their capacity to comprehend the world through their own mental powers.

Descartes saw the method used in mathematics as the most reliable avenue to certain knowledge. By applying mathematical reasoning to philosophical problems, we can achieve the same certainty and clarity evidenced in geometry. Mathematics is the key to understanding both the truths of nature and the moral order underlying human existence. The mathematical, or deductive, approach favored by Descartes consists of finding a self-evident principle, such as a geometric axiom, and then deducing other truths from it through logical reasoning. The Cartesian deductive method, with its mathematical emphasis, perfectly complements Bacon's inductive approach, which stresses observation and experimentation. The scientific achievements in modern times have stemmed from the skillful synchronization of both induction and deduction.

The Meaning of the Scientific Revolution

The radical transformation of our conception of the physical universe produced by the Scientific Revolution ultimately transformed our understanding of the individual, society, and the purpose of life. The Scientific Revolution, therefore, was a decisive factor in the shaping of the modern world. It destroyed the medieval world-view, in which the earth occupied the central position, heaven lay just beyond the fixed stars, and every object had its place in a hierarchical and qualitative order. It replaced this view with the modern conception of a homogeneous universe of unbounded space and an infinite number of celestial bodies. Gone were the barriers that separated the heavens and the earth. Gone also was the medieval notion that God had assigned an ultimate purpose to all natural objects and to all plant and animal life, that in God's plan everything had an assigned role: we have eyes because God wants us to see and rain because God wants crops to grow. Eschewing ultimate purposes, modern science examines physical nature for mathematical relationships and chemical composition.

In later centuries, further implications of the new cosmology caused great anguish. The conviction that God had created the universe for them, that the earth was fixed beneath their feet, and that God had given it the central position in his creation had brought medieval people a profound sense of security. They knew why they were here and never doubted that heaven was the final resting place for the faithful. Copernican astronomy dethroned the earth, expelled human beings from their central position, and implied an infinite universe. In the sixteenth and seventeenth centuries, few thinkers grasped the full significance of this displacement. However, in succeeding centuries, this radical cosmological transformation proved as traumatic for the modern mind as did Adam and Eve's expulsion from the Garden of Eden for the medieval mind. Today we know that the earth is one of billions and billions of celestial bodies, a tiny speck in an endless cosmic ocean, and that the universe is some twelve billion years old. Could such a universe have been created just for human beings? Could it contain a heaven that assures eternal life for the faithful and a hell with eternal fires and torments for sinners?

Few people at the time were aware of the full implications of the new cosmology. One who did understand was Blaise Pascal (1623–1662), a French scientist and mathematician. A devout Catholic, Pascal was frightened by what he called "the eternal silence of these infinite spaces" and realized that the new science could feed doubt, uncertainty, and anxiety, which threatened belief.

The conception of reason advanced by Galileo and other thinkers of the period differed fundamentally from that of medieval scholastics. Scholastic thinkers viewed reason as a useful aid for contemplating divine truth; as such, reason always had to serve theology. Influenced by the new scientific spirit, thinkers now saw the investigation of nature as reason's principal concern. What is more, they viewed this activity as autonomous and not subject to theological authority.

The Scientific Revolution fostered a rational and critical spirit among the intellectual elite. Descartes's methodical doubt, rejection of authority, and insistence on the clarity, precision, and accuracy of an idea and Francis Bacon's insistence on verification pervaded the outlook of the eighteenth-century Enlightenment thinkers; they denounced magic, spells, demons, witchcraft, alchemy, and astrology as vulgar superstitions. Phenomena attributed to occult forces, they argued, could be explained by reference to natural forces. A wide breach opened up between the intellectual elite and the masses, who remained steeped in popular superstitions and committed to traditional Christian dogma.

The creators of modern science had seen no essential conflict between traditional Christianity and the new view of the physical universe and made no war on the churches. Indeed, they believed that they were unveiling the laws of nature instituted by God at the Creation—that at last the human mind could comprehend God's magnificent handiwork. But the new cosmology and new scientific outlook ultimately weakened traditional Christianity.

The new critical spirit led the thinkers of the Enlightenment to doubt the literal truth of the Bible and to dismiss miracles as incompatible with what science teaches about the regularity of nature. So brilliantly had God crafted the universe, they said, so exquisite a mechanism was nature, that its operations did not require God's intervention. In the generations after the Scientific Revolution, theology, long considered the highest form of contemplation, was denounced as a barrier to understanding or even dismissed as irrelevant, and the clergy rapidly lost their position as the arbiters of knowledge. To many intellectuals, theology seemed sterile and profitless in comparison with the new science. Whereas science promised the certitude of mathematics, theologians seemed to quibble endlessly over unfathomable and, even worse, inconsequential issues. That much blood had been spilled over these questions discredited theology still more. In scientific academies, in salons, and in coffee houses, educated men and some women met to discuss the new ideas, and journals published the new knowledge for eager readers. European culture was undergoing a great transformation, marked by the triumph of a scientific and secular spirit among the intellectual elite.

The Scientific Revolution repudiated reliance on Aristotle, Ptolemy, and other ancient authorities in matters concerning nature and substituted in their place knowledge derived from observation, experimentation, and mathematical thinking. Citing an ancient authority was no longer sufficient to prove a point or win an argument. The new standard of knowledge derived from experience with the world, not from ancient texts or inherited views. This new outlook had far-reaching implications for the Age of Enlightenment. If the authority of ancient thinkers regarding the universe could be challenged, could not inherited political beliefs be challenged as well—for example, the divine right of kings to rule? Impressed with the achievements of science, many intellectuals started to urge the application of the scientific method to all fields of knowledge.

The new outlook generated by the Scientific Revolution served as the foundation of the Enlightenment. The Scientific Revolution gave thinkers great confidence in the power of the mind, which had discovered nature's laws, reinforcing the confidence in human abilities expressed by Renaissance humanists. In time, it was believed, the scientific method would unlock all nature's secrets, and humanity, gaining ever greater knowledge and control of nature, would progress rapidly.

The Age of Enlightenment: Affirmation of Reason and Freedom

The Enlightenment of the eighteenth century culminated the movement toward modernity initiated by the Renaissance. The thinkers of the Enlightenment, called *philosophes,* aspired to create a more rational and humane society. To attain this goal, they attacked medieval otherworldliness, rejected theology as an avenue to truth, denounced the Christian idea of people's inherent depravity, and sought to understand nature and society through reason alone, unaided by revelation or priestly authority. Adopting Descartes's method of systematic doubt, they questioned all inherited opinions and traditions. "We think that the greatest service to be done to men," said Denis Diderot, "is to teach them to use their reason, only to hold for truth what they have verified and proved."[4] The philosophes believed that they were inaugurating an enlightened age. Through the power of reason, humanity was at last liberating itself from the fetters of ignorance, superstition, and despotism with which tyrants and priests had bound it in past ages. Paris was the center of the Enlightenment, but there were philosophes and adherents of their views in virtually every leading city in western Europe and North America.

In many ways, the Enlightenment grew directly out of the Scientific Revolution. The philosophes sought to expand knowledge of nature and to apply the scientific method to the human world in order to uncover society's defects and to achieve appropriate reforms. Newton had discovered universal laws that explained the physical phenomena. Are there not general rules that also apply to human behavior and social institutions, asked the philosophes?

Could a "science of man" be created that would correspond to and comple-ment Newton's science of nature—that would provide clear and certain an-swers to the problems of the social world in the same way that Newtonian science had solved the mysteries of the physical world?

By relying on the same methodology that Newton had employed to estab-lish certain knowledge of the physical universe, the philosophes hoped to ar-rive at the irrefutable laws that operated in the realm of human society. They aspired to shape religion, government, law, morality, and economics in accor-dance with these natural laws. They believed that all things should be reevalu-ated to see if they accorded with nature, that is, if they promoted human well-being.

In championing the methodology of science, the philosophes affirmed re-spect for the mind's capacities and for human autonomy. Individuals are self-governing, they insisted. The mind is self-sufficient; rejecting appeals to clerical or princely authority, it relies on its own ability to think, and it trusts the evidence of its own experience. Rejecting the authority of tradition, the philosophes wanted people to have the courage to break with beliefs and in-stitutions that did not meet the test of reason and common sense and to seek new guideposts derived from reason. The numerous examples of injustice, in-humanity, and superstition in society outraged the philosophes. Behind their devotion to reason and worldly knowledge lay an impassioned moral indigna-tion against institutions and beliefs that degraded human beings.

Christianity Assailed: The Search for a Natural Religion

The philosophes waged an unremitting assault on traditional Christianity, de-nouncing it for harboring superstition, promulgating unreason, and fostering fanaticism and persecution. Relying on the facts of experience, as Bacon had taught, the philosophes dismissed miracles, angels, and devils as violations of nature's laws and figments of the imagination, which could not be substanti-ated by the norms of evidence. Applying the Cartesian spirit of careful reason-ing to the Bible, they pointed out flagrant discrepancies between various biblical passages and rejected as preposterous the theologians' attempts to re-solve these contradictions. With science as an ally, the philosophes challenged Christianity's claim that it possessed infallible truths, and they ridiculed the-ologians for wrangling over pointless issues and for compelling obedience to doctrines that defied reason.

Moreover, the philosophes assailed Christianity for viewing human nature as evil and human beings as helpless without God's assistance; for focusing on heaven at the expense of human happiness on earth; and for impeding the acquisition of useful knowledge by proclaiming the higher authority of dogma and revelation. Frightened and confused by religion, people have been held in subjection by clergy and tyrants, the philosophes argued. To establish an en-lightened society, clerical power must be broken, Christian dogmas repudi-ated, and the fanaticism that produced the horrors of the Crusades, the Inquisition, and the wars of the Reformation purged from the European soul.

The philosophes broke with the Christian past, even if they retained the essential elements of Christian morality.

François Marie Arouet (1694–1778), known to the world as Voltaire, was the recognized leader of the French Enlightenment. Few of the philosophes had a better mind and none had a sharper wit. Living in exile in Britain in the late 1720s, Voltaire acquired a great admiration for English liberty, commerce, science, and religious toleration. Voltaire's angriest words were directed against established Christianity, to which he attributed many of the ills of French society. He regarded Christianity as "the Christ-worshiping superstition," which someday would be destroyed "by the weapons of reason."[5] Many Christian dogmas are incomprehensible, said Voltaire, yet Christians have slaughtered one another to enforce obedience to these doctrines.

While some philosophes were atheists, most were deists, including Voltaire and Thomas Paine (1737–1809), the English-American radical. Deists sought to fashion a natural religion that accorded with reason and science, and they tried to adapt the Christian tradition to the requirements of the new science. They denied that the Bible was God's revelation, rejected clerical authority, and dismissed Christian mysteries, prophecies, and miracles—the virgin birth, Jesus walking on water, the Resurrection, and others—as violations of a lawful natural order. However, they did consider it reasonable that this magnificently structured universe, operating with clockwork precision, was designed and created at a point in time by an all-wise Creator. But in their view, once God had set the universe in motion, he refrained from interfering with its operations. Thus, deists were at odds with Newton, who allowed for divine intervention in the world.

For deists, the essence of religion was morality—a commitment to justice and humanity—and not adherence to rituals, doctrines, or clerical authority. In *The Age of Reason* (1794–95), Paine declared: "I believe in the equality of man; and I believe that religious duties consist in doing justice, loving mercy, and endeavoring to make our fellow-creatures happy."[6] Deists deemed it entirely reasonable that after death those who had fulfilled God's moral law would be rewarded, while those who had not would be punished.

Political Thought

Besides established religion, the philosophes identified another source of the evil that beset humanity: despotism. If human beings were to achieve happiness, they had to extirpate revealed religion and check the power of their rulers. "Every age has its dominant idea," wrote Diderot; "that of our age seems to be Liberty."[7] Eighteenth-century political thought is characterized by a thoroughgoing secularism; an indictment of despotism, the divine right of kings, and the special privileges of the aristocracy and the clergy; a respect for English constitutionalism because it enshrined the rule of law; and an affirmation of John Locke's theory that government had an obligation to protect the natural rights of its citizens. Central to the political outlook of the philosophes was the conviction that political solutions could be found for the ills that afflicted society.

In general, the philosophes favored constitutional government that protected citizens from the abuse of power. With the notable exception of Rousseau, the philosophes' concern for liberty did not lead them to embrace democracy, for they put little trust in the masses. Several philosophes, notably Voltaire, placed their confidence in reforming despots, like Frederick II of Prussia, who were sympathetic to enlightened ideas. However, the philosophes were less concerned with the form of government—monarchy or republic—than with preventing the authorities from abusing their power.

Seventeenth-Century Antecedents: Hobbes and Locke

The political thought of the Enlightenment was greatly affected by the writings of two seventeenth-century philosophers: Thomas Hobbes (1588–1679) and John Locke (1632–1704). Hobbes witnessed the agonies of the English civil war, including the execution of Charles I in 1649. These developments fortified his conviction that absolutism was the most desirable and logical form of government. Only the unlimited power of a sovereign, Hobbes wrote in his major work, *Leviathan* (1651), could contain human passions that disrupt the social order and threaten civilized life; only absolute rule could provide an environment secure enough for people to pursue their individual interests.

Influenced by the new scientific thought that saw mathematical knowledge as the avenue to truth, Hobbes aimed at constructing political philosophy on a scientific foundation and rejected the authority of tradition and religion as inconsistent with a science of politics. Thus, although Hobbes supported absolutism, he dismissed the idea advanced by other theorists of absolutism that the monarch's power derived from God. He also rejected the idea that the state should not be obeyed when it violated God's law. Like Machiavelli, Hobbes made no attempt to fashion the earthly city in accordance with Christian teachings. *Leviathan* is a rational and secular political statement; its significance lies in its modern approach, rather than in Hobbes's justification of absolutism.

Hobbes had a pessimistic view of human nature. Believing that people are innately selfish and grasping, he maintained that competition and dissension, rather than cooperation, characterize human relations. Without a stringent authority to make and enforce law, life would be miserable, a war of every man against every man, he said. Therefore, he prescribed a state with unlimited power since only in this way could people be protected from each other and civilized life preserved. Although the philosophes generally rejected Hobbes's gloomy view of human nature, they embraced his secular approach to politics, particularly his denunciation of the theory of the divine right of kings.

In contrast to Hobbes, John Locke saw people as essentially good and humane and developed a conception of the state fundamentally different from Hobbes's. In the *Two Treatises of Government* (1690), Locke maintained that human beings are born with natural rights to life, liberty, and property, and they establish the state to protect these rights. Consequently, neither executive nor legislature—neither king nor assembly—has the authority to deprive individuals of their natural rights. Whereas Hobbes justified absolute monarchy, Locke explicitly endorsed constitutional government, in which the power to govern derives from the consent of the governed and the state's authority is limited by agreement. Rulers hold their authority under the law; when they act outside the law, they forfeit their right to govern. Thus, if government fails to fulfill the end for which it was established—the preservation of the individual's right to life, liberty, and property—the people have a right to dissolve that government.

The value that Locke gave to reason and freedom and his theories of natural rights and the right of rebellion against unjust authority had a profound effect on the Enlightenment and the liberal revolutions of the late eighteenth and early nineteenth centuries. Thus, in the Declaration of Independence, Thomas Jefferson restated Locke's principles to justify the American Revolution.

Montesquieu

The contribution of Charles Louis de Secondat, baron de la Brède et de Montesquieu (1689–1755), to political theory rests essentially on his *The Spirit of the Laws* (1748), a work of immense erudition, covering many topics. Montesquieu held that the study of political and social behavior is not an exercise in abstract thought, but must be undertaken in relation to geographic, economic, and historic conditions. To this end, Montesquieu accumulated and classified a wide diversity of facts, from which he tried to draw general rules governing society. He concluded that different climactic and geographic conditions and different national customs, habits, religions, and institutions give each nation a particular character; each society requires constitutional forms and laws that pay heed to the character of its people. Montesquieu's effort to explain social and political behavior empirically—to found a science of society based on the model of natural science—makes him a forerunner of modern sociology.

Montesquieu regarded despotism as a pernicious form of government, corrupt by its very nature. Ruling as he wishes and unchecked by law, the despot knows nothing of moderation and institutionalizes cruelty and violence. The slavelike subjects, wrote Montesquieu, know only servitude, fear, and misery. Driven by predatory instincts, the despotic ruler involves his state in wars of conquest, caring not at all about the suffering this causes his people. In a despotic society, economic activity stagnates, for merchants, fearful that their goods will be confiscated by the state, lose their initiative.

To safeguard liberty from despotism, Montesquieu advocated the principle of separation of powers. In every government, said Montesquieu, there are three sorts of powers: legislative, executive, and judiciary. When one person or one body exercises all three powers—if the same body both prosecutes and judges, for example—liberty cannot be preserved. Where sovereignty is monopolized by one person or body, power is abused and political liberty is denied. In a good government, one power balances and checks another power, an argument that impressed the framers of the U.S. Constitution.

Voltaire

Unlike Hobbes and Locke, Voltaire was not a systematic political theorist, but a propagandist and polemicist, who hurled pointed barbs at all the abuses of the Old Regime. Nevertheless, Voltaire's writings do contain ideas that form a coherent political theory, which in many ways expresses the outlook of the Enlightenment.

Voltaire disdained arbitrary power since it is based on human whim rather than on established law. He described a prince who imprisons or executes his subjects unjustly and without due process as "nothing but a highway robber who is called 'Your Majesty.'" For Voltaire, freedom consisted in being governed by an established and standard code of law that applies equally to all. Without the rule of law, wrote Voltaire, there is no liberty of person, no freedom of thought or of religion, no protection of personal property, no impartial judiciary, and no protection from arbitrary arrest. Underlying Voltaire's commitment to the rule of law was his conviction that power should be used rationally and beneficially.

Voltaire's respect for the rule of law was strengthened by his stay in England between 1726 and 1729, which led to the publication of *The English Letters* in 1733. In this work, Voltaire presents an idealized and, at times, inaccurate picture of English politics and society. More important, however, is the fact that his experience with English liberty gave him hope that a just and tolerant society was not a utopian dream, thereby strengthening his resolve to attack the abuses of French society.

As noted earlier, Voltaire was no democrat. He had little confidence in the capacities of the common people, whom he saw as prone to superstition and fanaticism. Nor did he advocate revolution. What he did favor was reforming society through the advancement of reason and the promotion of science and technology. Voltaire himself fought to introduce several reforms into France, including freedom of the press, religious toleration, a fair system of criminal justice, proportional taxation, and curtailment of the privileges of the clergy and nobility.

Rousseau

"Man is born free and everywhere he is in chains."[8] With these stirring words, the Geneva-born French thinker Jean Jacques Rousseau (1712–1778)

Marble Bust of Voltaire by Jean Antoine Houdon, 1781. François Marie Arouet (1694–1778), better known as Voltaire, was the most celebrated mind and wit in Europe. A relentless critic of religious dogmatism and intolerance, he denounced censorship and advised and urged the enlightened despots of Russia and Prussia to use their absolute power to reform society. He attacked his own country's institutions and praised those of England. His literary brilliance was acknowledged even by his enemies; he was the single most effective leader of the French philosophes. (*Musée Fabre, Montpellier*)

began *The Social Contract* (1762). Rousseau considered the state as it was then constituted to be unjust and corrupt. It was dominated by the rich and the powerful, who used it to further their interests, whereas the weak knew only oppression and misery. In Rousseau's view, the modern state deprived human beings of their natural freedom and fostered a selfish individualism, which undermined feelings of mutuality and concern for the common good.

Rousseau wanted the state to be a genuine democracy, a moral association that bound people together in freedom, equality, and civic devotion. For Rousseau, individuals fulfilled their moral potential not in isolation, but as committed members of the community; human character was ennobled when people cooperated with each other and cared for one another. Rousseau admired the ancient Greek city-state, the polis, for it was an organic community in which citizens set aside private interests in order to attain the common good. In *The Social Contract*, he sought to recreate the community spirit and the political freedom that characterized the Greek city-state.

What Rousseau proposed was that each person surrender unconditionally all his rights to the community as a whole and submit to its authority. To prevent the assertion of private interests over the common good, Rousseau wanted the state to be governed in accordance with the general will—an underlying principle that expressed what was best for the community. He did not conceive of the general will as a majority or even a unanimous vote, both of which could be wrong. Rather, it was a plainly visible truth, easily discerned by common sense and by reason and by listening to our hearts. In Rousseau's view, just and enlightened citizens imbued with public spirit would have the good sense and moral awareness to legislate in accordance with the general will.

Like ancient Athens, the state that Rousseau envisioned was a direct democracy, in which the citizens themselves, not their representatives, constituted the lawmaking body. Consequently, the governed and the government were one and the same. Rousseau condemned arbitrary and despotic monarchy, the divine-right theory of kings, and the traditional view that people should be governed by their betters, lords and clergy, who were entitled to special privileges. He granted sovereignty to the people as a whole and affirmed the principle of equality.

Rousseau remains a leading theorist of democratic thought. His critics assert that his political thought, whose goal is a body of citizens who think alike, buttresses a dangerous collectivism and even totalitarianism. These critics argue that Rousseau did not place constitutional limitations on sovereignty or erect safeguards to protect individual and minority rights from a potentially tyrannical majority. They note, too, that Rousseau rejected entirely the Lockean principle that citizens possess rights independently of the state, as well as the right to act against the state.

Social and Economic Thought

The philosophes rejected the Christian belief that human beings are endowed with a sinful nature, a consequence of Adam and Eve's disobedience of God. They knew from experience, of course, that human beings behave wickedly and seem hopelessly attached to nonrational modes of thinking. While they retained a certain pessimism about human nature, the philosophes generally believed in individuals' essential goodness and in their capacity for moral improvement. "Nature has not made us evil," wrote Diderot, "it is bad education, bad models, bad legislation that corrupt us."[9] And Voltaire declared that a person is "born neither good nor wicked; education, example, the government into which he is thrown—in short, occasion of every kind—determines him to virtue or vice."[10] The philosophes' conception of human nature rested heavily on John Locke's epistemology, or theory of knowledge. To the philosophes, it seemed that Locke had discovered the fundamental principles governing the human mind, an achievement comparable to Newton's discovery of the laws governing physical bodies.

Epistemology, Psychology, and Education

In his *Essay Concerning Human Understanding* (1690), a work of immense significance in the history of philosophy, Locke argued that human beings are not born with innate ideas (the idea of God, principles of good and evil, and rules of logic, for example), divinely implanted in their minds as Descartes had maintained. Rather, said Locke, the human mind is a blank slate upon which are imprinted sensations derived from contact with the phenomenal world. Knowledge is derived from experience.

Locke's theory of knowledge had profound implications. If there are no innate ideas, said the philosophes, then human beings, contrary to Christian doctrine, are not born with original sin, are not depraved by nature. All that individuals are derives from their particular experiences. If people are provided with a proper environment and education, they will behave morally; they will become intelligent and productive citizens. By the proper use of their reason, people could bring their beliefs, their conduct, and their institutions into harmony with natural law. This was how the reform-minded philosophes interpreted Locke. They preferred to believe that evil stemmed from faulty institutions and poor education, both of which could be remedied, rather than from a defective human nature.

The most important work of Enlightenment educational thought was Rousseau's *Émile* (1762), in which he suggested educational reforms that would instill in children self-confidence, self-reliance, and emotional security—necessary qualities if they were to become productive adults and responsible citizens. If the young are taught to think for themselves, said Rousseau, they will learn to cherish personal freedom. A strong faith in the essential goodness of human nature underlay Rousseau's educational philosophy. He also assumed that youngsters have an equal capacity to learn and that differences in intelligence are due largely to environmental factors.

Rousseau understood that children should not be treated like little adults, for children have their own ways of thinking and feeling. He railed against those who robbed children of the joys and innocence of childhood by chaining them to desks, ordering them about, and filling their heads with rote learning. Instead, he urged that children experience direct contact with the world to develop their body and senses and their curiosity, ingenuity, resourcefulness, and imagination. It is the whole child that concerns Rousseau.

Freedom of Conscience and Thought

The philosophes regarded religious persecution—whose long and blood-stained history included the burning of heretics in the Middle Ages, the slaughter of Jews and Muslims during the First Crusade, and the massacres of the wars of the Reformation—as humanity's most depraved offense against reason. While the worst excesses of religious fanaticism had dissipated by the eighteenth century, examples of religious persecution still abounded, particularly in Catholic lands. In his pleas for tolerance, Voltaire spoke for all the philosophes:

> *I shall never cease . . . to preach tolerance from the housetops . . .*
> *until persecution is no more. The progress of reason is slow, the roots*
> *of prejudice lie deep. Doubtless, I shall never see the fruits of my ef-*
> *forts, but they are seeds which may one day germinate.*[11]

Censorship was a serious and ever present problem for the philosophes. After the publication of Voltaire's *English Letters*, his printer was arrested and the book confiscated and publicly burned as irreligious. On another occasion, when Voltaire was harassed by the authorities, he commented that "It is easier for me to write books than to get them published."[12] Denounced by ecclesiastical and ministerial authorities as a threat to religion and constituted authority, *On the Mind* (1758), by Claude-Adrien Helvetius (1715–1771), was burned by the public executioner. Denis Diderot (1713–1784), the principal editor of the thirty-eight-volume *Encyclopedia*, whose 150 or more contributors included the leading Enlightenment thinkers, had to contend with French authorities, who, at times, suspended publication. After the first two volumes appeared, the authorities condemned the work for containing "maxims that would tend to destroy royal authority, foment a spirit of independence and revolt . . . and lay the foundations for the corruption of morals and religion."[13] In 1759, Pope Clement XIII condemned the *Encyclopedia* for having "scandalous doctrines [and] inducing scorn for religion."[14] It required careful diplomacy and clever ruses to finish the project and still incorporate ideas considered dangerous by religious and governmental authorities. The *Encyclopedia* had been undertaken in Paris during the 1740s as a monumental effort to bring together all human knowledge and to propagate Enlightenment ideas. Its numerous articles on science and technology and its limited coverage of theological questions attest to the new interests of eighteenth-century intellectuals. With the project's completion in 1772, Diderot and Enlightenment opinion triumphed over clerical, royal, and aristocratic censors.

An article in the *Encyclopedia*, "The Press,"conveys the philosophes' yearning for freedom of thought and expression. For them, the term *press* designated more than newspapers and journals; it encompassed everything in print, particularly books.

> *People ask if freedom of the* press *is advantageous or prejudicial to a*
> *state. The answer is not difficult. It is of the greatest importance to*
> *conserve this practice in all states founded on liberty. I would even*
> *say that the disadvantages of this liberty are so inconsiderable com-*
> *pared to the advantages that this ought to be the common right of the*
> *universe, and it is certainly advisable to authorize its practices in all*
> *governments.*[15]

Humanitarianism

A humanitarian spirit, which no doubt owed something to Christian compassion, pervaded the outlook of the philosophes. It expressed itself in attacks on torture, which was commonly used to obtain confessions in many European lands, on cruel punishments for criminals, on slavery, and on war. The philosophes' humanitarianism rested on the conviction that human nature was essentially virtuous and that human beings were capable of benevolent feelings toward each other.

In *On Crimes and Punishments* (1764), Cesare Beccaria (1738–1794), an Italian economist and criminologist inspired in part by Montesquieu, condemned torture as inhuman, "a criterion fit for a cannibal."[16] He saw it as an irrational way of determining guilt or innocence, for an innocent person, unable to withstand the agonies of torture, will confess to anything and a criminal with a high threshold for pain will be exonerated. Influenced by Beccaria's work, reform-minded jurists, legislators, and ministers called for the elimination of torture from codes of criminal justice, and several European lands abolished torture in the eighteenth century.

Though not pacifists, the philosophes denounced war as barbaric and an affront to reason. They deemed it to be a scourge promoted by power-hungry monarchs and supported by fanatical clergy, wicked army leaders, and ignorant commoners. In his literary masterpiece, *Candide* (1759), Voltaire ridiculed the rituals of war. The article "Peace" in the *Encyclopedia* described war as

> *the fruit of man's depravity; it is a convulsive and violent sickness of the body politic. . . . [It] depopulates the nation, causes the reign of disorder. . . . makes the freedom and property of citizens uncertain . . . disturbs and causes the neglect of commerce; land becomes uncultivated and abandoned. . . . If reason governed men and had the influence over the heads of nations that it deserves, we would never see them inconsiderately surrender themselves to the fury of war; they would not show that ferocity that characterizes wild beasts.*[17]

Montesquieu, Voltaire, Hume, Benjamin Franklin, Thomas Paine, and other philosophes condemned slavery and the slave trade. In Book 15 of *The Spirit of the Laws*, Montesquieu scornfully refuted all justifications for slavery. Ultimately, he said, slavery, which violates the fundamental principle of justice underlying the universe, derived from base human desires to dominate and exploit other human beings. Adam Smith (see next section), the Enlightenment's leading economic theorist, demonstrated that slave labor was inefficient and wasteful. In 1780, Paine helped draft the act abolishing slavery in Pennsylvania. An article in the *Encyclopedia*, "The Slave Trade," denounced slavery as a violation of the individual's natural rights:

Engraving, Newgate Prison, Eighteenth Century.   Prison conditions during the Age of Enlightenment were appalling. Here, a manacled man struggles with a wheelbarrow, and two others are led off to the gallows. Meanwhile, a guard watches over the dungeon filled with bound prisoners, who were as often debtors as criminals.

> *If commerce of this kind can be justified by a moral principle, there is no crime, however atrocious it may be, that cannot be made legitimate. . . . Men and their liberty are not objects of commerce; they can be neither sold nor bought. . . . There is not, therefore, a single one of these unfortunate people regarded only as slaves who does not have the right to be declared free.*[18]

The philosophes, who often enjoyed the company of intelligent and sophisticated women in the famous salons, continued to view women as intellectually and morally inferior to men. Although some philosophes, notably Condorcet, who wrote *Plea for the Citizenship of Women* (1791), did argue for female emancipation, they were the exception. Most concurred with David Hume (1711–1776), a Scottish sceptic, who held that "nature has subjected" women to men and that their "inferiority and infirmities are absolutely incurable."[19] Rousseau, who also believed that nature had granted men power over women, regarded traditional domesticity as a woman's proper role.

> *I would a thousand times rather have a homely girl, simply brought up, than a learned lady and a wit who would make a literary circle of my house and install herself as its president. A female wit is a scourge to her husband, her children, her friends, her servants, to everybody. From the lofty height of her genius, she scorns every womanly duty, and she is always trying to make a man of herself.*[20]

Nevertheless, by clearly articulating the ideals of liberty and equality, the philosophes made a women's movement possible. The growing popularity of these ideals could not escape women, who measured their own position by them. Moreover, by their very nature, these ideals were expansive. Denying them to women would ultimately be seen as an indefensible contradiction.

Thus, Mary Wollstonecraft's *Vindication of the Rights of Woman*, written under the influence of the French Revolution, protested against the prevailing subordination and submissiveness of women and the limited opportunities afforded them to cultivate their minds. She considered it an act of tyranny for women "to be excluded from a participation of the natural rights of mankind."[21]

Laissez-Faire Economics

In *The Wealth of Nations* (1776), Adam Smith (1732–1790), professor of moral philosophy in Scotland, attacked the theory of mercantilism, which held that a state's wealth was determined by the amount of gold and silver it possessed. According to this theory, to build up its reserves of precious metals, the state should promote domestic industries, encourage exports, and discourage imports. Mercantilist theory called for government regulation of the economy so that the state could compete successfully with other nations for a share of the world's scarce resources. Smith argued that the real basis of a country's wealth was measured by the quantity and quality of its goods and services and not by its storehouse of precious metals. Government intervention, he said, retards economic progress; it reduces the real value of the annual produce of the nation's land and labor. On the other hand, when people pursue their own interests—when they seek to better their condition—they foster economic expansion, which benefits the whole society.

Smith limited the state's authority to maintaining law and order, administering justice, and defending the nation. The concept of *laissez faire*—that government should not interfere with the market—became a core principle of nineteenth-century liberal thought.

The Idea of Progress

The philosophes were generally optimistic about humanity's future progress. Two main assumptions contributed to this optimism. First, accepting Locke's theory of knowledge, the philosophes attributed evil to a flawed but remediable environment, not to an inherently wicked human nature. Hopeful that a reformed environment would bring out the best in people, they looked forward to a day when reason would prevail over superstition, prejudice, intolerance, and tyranny. Second, the philosophes' veneration of science led them to believe that the progressive advancement of knowledge would promote material and moral progress.

A work written near the end of the century epitomized the philosophes' vision of the future: *Sketch for a Historical Picture of the Progress of the Human Mind* (1794) by Marie Jean Antoine Nicolas Caritat, marquis de Condorcet (1743–1794). A mathematician and historian of science and a contributor to the *Encyclopedia,* Condorcet campaigned for religious toleration and the abolition of slavery. During the French Revolution, he attracted the enmity of the dominant Jacobin party and in 1793 was forced to go into hiding. Secluded in Paris, he wrote *Sketch.* Arrested in 1794, Condorcet died during his first night in prison either from exhaustion or from self-administered poison. In *Sketch,* Condorcet lauded recent advances in knowledge that enabled reason to "lift her chains (and) shake herself free"[22] from superstition and tyranny. Passionately affirming the Enlightenment's confidence in reason and science, Condorcet expounded a theory of continuous and indefinite human improvement. He pointed toward a future golden age, characterized by the triumph of reason and freedom.

> *Our hopes for the future condition of the human race can be subsumed under three important heads: the abolition of inequality between nations, the progress of equality within each nation, and the true perfection of mankind. . . .*
>
> *The time will therefore come when the sun will shine only on free men who know no other master but their reason; when tyrants and slaves, priests and their stupid or hypocritical instruments will exist only in works of history and on the stage; and we shall think of them only to pity their victims and their dupes; to maintain ourselves in a state of vigilance by thinking on their excesses; and to learn how to recognize and so to destroy, by force of reason, the first seeds of tyranny and superstition, should they ever dare to reappear amongst us.*[23]

But the philosophes were not starry-eyed dreamers. They knew that progress was painful, slow, and reversible. Voltaire's *Candide* was a protest against a naive optimism that ignored the granite might of human meanness, ignorance, and irrationality. "Let us weep and wail over the lot of philosophy," wrote Diderot. "We preach wisdom to the deaf and we are still far indeed from the age of reason."[24]

War, Revolution, and Politics

The major conflicts of the eighteenth century were between Britain and France for control of territory in the New World and between Austria and Prussia for dominance in central Europe. Then, in the late 1700s, the American and French Revolutions broke out; they helped shape the liberal-democratic tradition.

Warfare and Revolution

In 1740, Prussia, ruled by the aggressive Frederick the Great, launched a successful war against Austria and was rewarded with Silesia, which increased the Prussian population by 50 percent. Maria Theresa, the Austrian queen, never forgave Frederick and in 1756 formed an alliance with France against Prussia. The ensuing Seven Years' War (1756–1763), which involved every major European power, did not significantly change Europe, but it did reveal Prussia's growing might.

At the same time, the French and the English fought over their claims in the New World. England's victory in the conflict (known in American history as the French and Indian War) deprived France of virtually all of its North American possessions and set in motion a train of events that culminated in the American Revolution. The war drained the British treasury, and now Britain had the additional expense of paying for troops to guard the new North American territories that it had gained in the war. As strapped British taxpayers could not shoulder the whole burden, the members of Parliament thought it quite reasonable that American colonists should help pay the bill; after all, Britain had protected the colonists from the French and was still protecting them in their conflicts with Indians. New colonial taxes and import duties imposed by Parliament produced vigorous protests from the Americans.

The quarrel turned to bloodshed in April and June 1775, and on July 4, 1776, delegates from the various colonies adopted the Declaration of Independence, written mainly by Thomas Jefferson. Applying Locke's theory of natural rights, this document declared that government derives its power from the consent of the governed, that it is the duty of a government to protect the rights of its citizens, and that people have the right to "alter or abolish" a government that deprives them of their "unalienable rights."

Why were the American colonists so ready to revolt? For one thing, they had brought with them a highly idealized understanding of English liberties; long before 1776, they had extended representative institutions to include small property owners, who probably could not have voted in England. The colonists had come to expect representative government, trial by jury, and protection from unlawful imprisonment. Each of the thirteen colonies had an elected assembly, which acted like a miniature parliament. In these

The Signing of the Declaration of Independence, Philadelphia, July 4, 1776, by John Trumbull (Detail).   The success of the American Revolution was hailed as a victory of liberty over tyranny. French military and financial support of the Americans led to the bankruptcy of the French monarchy by 1788, a factor that contributed to the French Revolution. The American founding fathers were familiar with the ideas of the Enlightenment, particularly John Locke's theory of natural rights. (*Copyright Yale University Art Gallery*)

assemblies, Americans gained political experience and quickly learned to be self-governing.

Familiarity with the thought of the Enlightenment and the republican writers of the English Revolution also contributed to the Americans' awareness of liberty. The ideas of the philosophes traversed the Atlantic and influenced educated Americans, particularly Thomas Jefferson and Benjamin Franklin. Like the philosophes, American thinkers expressed a growing confidence in reason, valued freedom of religion and of thought, and championed the principle of natural rights.

Another source of hostility toward established authority among the American colonists was their religious traditions, particularly those of the Puritans, who believed that the Bible was infallible and its teachings a higher law than the law of the state. Like their counterparts in England, American Puritans challenged political and religious authorities who, in their view, contravened God's law. Thus, Puritans acquired two habits that were crucial to the development of political liberty: dissent and resistance. When transferred to the realm of politics, these Puritan tendencies led Americans to resist authority that they considered unjust.

American victory came in 1783 as a result of several factors. George Washington proved to be a superior leader, able to organize and retain the loyalty of his troops. France, seeking to avenge its defeat in the Seven Years' War, helped the Americans with money and provisions and then, in 1778, entered the conflict. Britain had difficulty shipping supplies across three thousand miles of ocean, was fighting the French in the West Indies and elsewhere at the same time, and ultimately lacked commitment to the struggle.

Reformers in other lands quickly interpreted the American victory as a successful struggle of liberty against tyranny. During the Revolution, the various American states drew up constitutions based on the principle of popular sovereignty and included bills of rights that protected individual liberty. They also managed, somewhat reluctantly, to forge a nation. Rejecting both monarchy and hereditary aristocracy, the Constitution of the United States created a republic in which power derived from the people. A system of separation of powers and checks and balances set safeguards against the abuse of power, and the Bill of Rights provided for protection of individual rights. To be sure, the ideals of liberty and equality were not extended to all people— slaves knew nothing of the freedom that white Americans cherished, and women were denied the vote and equal opportunity. But to reform-minded Europeans, it seemed that Americans were fulfilling the promise of the Enlightenment; they were creating a freer and better society.

Enlightened Despotism

The philosophes used the term *enlightened despotism* to refer to an ideal shared by many of them: rule by a strong monarch who would implement rational reforms and remove obstacles to freedom. Some eighteenth-century monarchs and their ministers—Frederick the Great in Prussia, Catherine the Great in Russia, Charles III in Spain, Maria Theresa and, to a greater extent, her son Joseph II in Austria, and Louis XV in France—did institute educational, commercial, and religious reforms.

Behind the reforms of enlightened despots lay the realization that the struggle for power in Europe called for efficient government administration and ample funds. Enlightened despots appointed capable officials to oversee the administration of their kingdoms, eliminate costly corruption, and collect taxes properly. Rulers strengthened the economy by encouraging the expansion of commerce through reduced taxes on goods and through agricultural reforms. In central and eastern Europe, some rulers moved toward abolishing serfdom or at least improving conditions for serfs. (In western Europe, serfdom had virtually died out.) Provisions were made to care for widows, orphans, and invalids. Censorship was eased, greater religious freedom was granted to minorities, criminal codes were made less harsh, and there were some attempts at prison reform. By these measures, enlightened despots hoped to inspire greater popular support for the state, an important factor in the European power struggle.

The Enlightenment and the Modern Mentality

The philosophes articulated core principles of the modern outlook. Asserting that human beings are capable of thinking independently of authority, they insisted on a thoroughgoing rational and secular interpretation of nature and society. They critically scrutinized authority and tradition and valued science and technology as a means for promoting human betterment. Above all, they sought to emancipate the mind from the bonds of ignorance and superstition and to rescue people from intolerance, cruelty, and oppression. Because of their efforts, torture (which states and Christian churches had endorsed and practiced) was eventually abolished in Western lands, and religious toleration and freedom of speech and of the press became the accepted norms. The arguments that the philosophes marshaled against slavery were utilized by those who fought against the slave trade and called for emancipation. Enlightenment economic thought, particularly Adam Smith's *Wealth of Nations,* gave theoretical support to a market economy based on supply and demand—an outlook that fostered commercial and industrial expansion. The philosophes' denunciation of despotism and championing of natural rights, equality under the law, and constitutional government are the chief foundations of modern liberal government.

The ideals of the Enlightenment spread from Europe to America and helped shape the political thought of the Founding Fathers. The Declaration of Independence clearly articulated Locke's basic principles: that government derives its authority from the governed, that human beings are born with natural rights, which government has a responsibility to protect, and that citizens have the right to resist a government that deprives them of their rights. The Constitution asserted that the people are sovereign: "We the People of the United States . . . do ordain and establish this Constitution for the United States of America." And it contained several safeguards against despotic power, including Montesquieu's principle of separation of powers, which was also written into several state constitutions. Both the bills of rights drawn up by the various states and the federal Bill of Rights gave recognition to the individual's inherent rights and explicitly barred government from tampering with them—a principal concern of the philosophes.

The philosophes broke with the traditional Christian view of human nature and the purpose of life. In that view, men and women were born in sin; suffering and misery were their lot, and relief could come only from God; and for many, eternal damnation was a deserved final consequence. In contrast, the philosophes expressed confidence in people's ability to attain happiness by improving the conditions of their earthly existence and articulated a theory of human progress that did not require divine assistance.

To be sure, the promise of the Enlightenment has not been achieved. More education for more people and the spread of constitutional government have not eliminated fanaticism and superstition, violence and war, or evil and injustice. In the light of twentieth-century events, it is difficult to subscribe to Condorcet's belief in linear progress. As Peter Gay observes,

> *The world has not turned out the way the philosophes wished and half expected that it would. Old fanaticisms have been more intractable, irrational forces more inventive than the philosophes were ready to conjecture in their darkest moments. Problems of race, of class, of nationalism, of boredom and despair in the midst of plenty have emerged almost in defiance of the philosophes' philosophy. We have known horrors, and may know horrors, that the men of the Enlightenment did not see in their nightmares.[25]*

Nevertheless, the philosophes' achievement should not be diminished. Their ideals became an intrinsic part of the liberal-democratic tradition and inspired nineteenth- and twentieth-century reformers. The spirit of the Enlightenment will always remain indispensable to all those who cherish the traditions of reason and freedom.

Notes

1. Galileo Galilei, *The Starry Messenger,* in *Discoveries and Opinions of Galileo,* trans. and ed. Stillman Drake (Garden City, N.Y.: Doubleday Anchor Books, 1957), p. 31.
2. Galileo Galilei, *The Assayer,* in *Discoveries and Opinions,* pp. 237–238.
3. Galileo Galilei, "Letter to the Grand Duchess Christina," in *Discoveries and Opinions,* p. 183.
4. Quoted in Frank E. Manuel, *Age of Reason* (Ithaca, N.Y.: Cornell University Press, 1951), p. 28.
5. Quoted in Ben Ray Redman, ed., *The Portable Voltaire* (New York: Viking Press, 1949), p. 26.
6. Thomas Paine, *The Age of Reason* (New York: Eckler, 1892), p. 5.
7. Quoted in Paul Hazard, *European Thought in the Eighteenth Century* (New Haven: Yale University Press, 1954), p 174.
8. Jean Jacques Rousseau, *The Social Contract,* in *The Social Contract and Discourses,* ed. and trans. G. D. H. Cole (New York: Dutton, 1950), bk. 1, chap. 1, p. 3.
9. Quoted in Peter Gay, *The Enlightenment: An Interpretation,* vol. 2, *The Science of Freedom* (New York: Vintage Books, 1966), p. 170.
10. Quoted in Steven Seidman, *Liberalism and the Origins of European Social Theory* (Berkeley: University of California Press, 1983), p. 30.
11. Voltaire, "Letter to M. Bertrand," in *Candide and Other Writings,* ed. Haskell M. Block (New York: Modern Library, 1956), p. 525.
12. Quoted in Peter Gay, *Voltaire's*

Politics (New York: Random House, Vintage Books, 1965), p. 71.

13. Quoted in Stephen J. Gendzier, ed. and trans., *Denis Diderot's The Encyclopedia Selections* (New York: Harper Torchbooks, 1967), p. xxv.

14. Ibid., p. xxvi.

15. Excerpted in Gendzier, *Diderot's Encyclopedia Selections,* p. 199.

16. Cesare Beccaria, *On Crimes and Punishments,* trans. Henry Paolucci (Indianapolis: Library of Liberal Arts, 1963), p. 32.

17. Excerpted in Gendzier, *Diderot's Encyclopedia Selections,* pp. 183–184.

18. Excerpted in ibid., pp. 229–230.

19. Quoted in Bonnie S. Anderson and

Judith P. Zinsser, *A History of Their Own* (New York: Harper & Row, 1988), 2:113.

20. Jean Jacques Rousseau, *Emile,* trans. Barbara Foxley (London: Dent, Everyman's Library, 1974), p. 370.

21. Mary Wollstonecraft, *Vindication of the Rights of Woman* (London: Dent, 1929), pp. 11–12.

22. Antoine Nicolas de Condorcet, *Sketch for a Historical Picture of the Progress of the Human Mind,* trans. June Barraclough (London: Weidenfeld & Nicholas, 1955), p. 124.

23. Ibid., pp. 173–179.

24. Quoted in Gay, *The Enlightenment,* 1:20.

25. Ibid., 2:567.

Suggested Reading

Anchor, Robert, *The Enlightenment Tradition* (1967). A useful survey.

Andrade, da C. E. N., *Sir Isaac Newton* (1954). Brief and clear.

Armitage, Angus, *The World of Copernicus* (1951). Good discussion of the old astronomy and the birth of the new.

Brumfit, J. H., *The French Enlightenment* (1972). A useful survey.

Cohen, I. B., *The Birth of a New Physics* (1960). A classic study.

Commager, Henry Steele, *The Empire of Reason* (1977). The Enlightenment in the United States.

Drake, Stillman, *Galileo* (1980). By a leading authority.

Gay, Peter, *The Enlightenment: An Interpretation,* 2 vols. (1966). An exhaustive study.

Hampson, Norman, *The Enlightenment* (1968). A useful survey.

Rosen, Edward, *Copernicus and the Scientific Revolution* (1984). By a recognized authority.

Review Questions

1. How did the Scientific Revolution transform the medieval view of the universe?

2. Describe the major achievements of Copernicus, Kepler, Galileo, and Newton.

3. How did the Scientific Revolution contribute to the shaping of the modern mentality?

4. Why is the eighteenth century referred to as the Age of

Enlightenment? What are the antecedents of the Enlightenment?

5. Why did the philosophes attack Christianity?

6. How did Voltaire exemplify the philosophes?

7. Compare and contrast the political thought of Hobbes and Locke. Why is Locke considered a forerunner of liberalism?

8. Why is Rousseau considered a

theorist of democracy? Why has his political thought come under attack?

9. What was the significance of Locke's theory of knowledge for the Enlightenment?

10. How did the ideals of the Enlightenment contribute to feminism and the movement to abolish slavery?

11. What ideals of the Enlightenment found expression during the period of the American Revolution?

12. How did the Enlightenment contribute to the shaping of the modern mentality?

PART FOUR

The Modern West: Progress and Breakdown

1789–1914

Drawing by Gerald of the French Royal Family's Refuge in the Assembly Hall After the 1792 Sacking of the Tuileries. (*Jean-Loup Charmet*)

	POLITICS AND SOCIETY	THOUGHT AND CULTURE
1790	French Revolution begins (1789) Declaration of the Rights of Man and of the Citizen (1789) Reign of Terror (1793–1794) Napoleon seizes power (1799)	Kant, *Critique of Pure Reason* (1781) Burke, *Reflections on the Revolution in France* (1790) Wollstonecraft, *Vindication of the Rights of Woman* (1792) Wordsworth, *The Lyrical Ballads* (1798) Beethoven, Fifth Symphony (1807–1808) Goethe, *Faust* (1808, 1832)
1810	Napoleon invades Russia (1812) Napoleon defeated at Waterloo (1815) Congress of Vienna (1814–1815) Revolutions in Spain, Italy, Russia, and Greece (1820–1829)	Byron, *Childe Harold* (1812) Shelley, *Prometheus Unbound* (1820) Hegel, *The Philosophy of History* (1822–1831)
1830	Revolutions in France, Belgium, Poland, and Italy (1830–1832) Reform Act of 1832 in Britain Irish famine (1845–1849) Revolutions in France, Germany, Austria, and Italy (1848)	Comte, *Course in Positive Philosophy* (1830–1842) De Tocqueville, *Democracy in America* (1835–1840) Marx, *Communist Manifesto* (1848)
1850	Second Empire in France (1852–1870) Commodore Perry opens Japan to trade (1853) Unification of Italy (1859–1870) Civil War in the United States (1861–1865) Unification of Germany (1866–1871) Opening of Suez Canal (1869)	Dickens, *Hard Times* (1854) Flaubert, *Madame Bovary* (1856) Darwin, *Origin of Species* (1859) Mill, *On Liberty* (1859) Marx, *Capital* (1867) Dostoevski, *The Idiot* (1868) Mill, *The Subjection of Women* (1869)
1870	Franco-Prussian War (1870–1871) Third Republic in France (1870–1940) Berlin Conference on Africa (1884) Reform Bill of 1884 in Great Britain	Darwin, *Descent of Man* (1871) Nietzsche, *The Birth of Tragedy* (1872) Ibsen, *A Doll's House* (1879) Zola, *The Experimental Novel* (1880) Nietzsche, *The Anti-Christ* (1888)
1890	Dreyfus affair in France (1894–1899) Sino-Japanese War (1894–1895) Boer War in South Africa (1899–1902)	Chamberlain, *The Foundations of the Nineteenth Century* (1899) Durkheim, *Suicide* (1899)
1900	Russo-Japanese War (1904–1905) Anglo-French Entente Cordiale (1904) Anglo-Russian Entente (1907)	Freud, *The Interpretation of Dreams* (1900) Cubism in art: Picasso, Braque Planck's quantum theory (1900) Lenin, *What Is to be Done?* (1902) Einstein's theory of relativity (1905) Sorel, *Reflections on Violence* (1908)

CHAPTER II

The Era of the French Revolution: Affirmation of Liberty and Equality

*T*he outbreak of the French Revolution in 1789 stirred the imagination of Europeans. Both participants and observers sensed that they were living in a pivotal age. On the ruins of the Old Order founded on privilege and despotism, a new era was forming, which promised to realize the ideals of the Enlightenment. These ideals included the emancipation of the human person from superstition and tradition, the triumph of liberty over tyranny, the refashioning of institutions in accordance with reason and justice, and the tearing down of barriers to equality. It seemed that the natural rights of the individual, hitherto a distant ideal, would now reign on earth, ending centuries of oppression and misery. Never before had people shown such confidence in the power of human intelligence to shape the conditions of existence. Never before had the future seemed so full of hope. ❖

The Old Regime

Eighteenth-century French society was divided into three orders, or Estates, which were legally defined groupings. The clergy constituted the First Estate, the nobility the Second Estate, and everyone else the Third Estate. The clergy and nobility, totaling about 500,000 out of a population of 26 million, enjoyed special privileges. The social structure of the Old Regime, based on privileges and inequalities sanctioned by law, produced tensions that contributed to the Revolution.

The First Estate

The powers and privileges of the French Catholic church made it a state within a state. As it had done for centuries, the church registered births, marriages, and deaths; collected tithes (a tax on products from the soil); censored books considered dangerous to religion and morals; operated schools; and distributed relief to the poor. Although its land brought in an immense revenue, the church paid no taxes. Instead, it made a "free gift" to the state—the church determined the amount—which was always smaller than direct taxes would have been.

The clergy reflected the social divisions in France. The upper clergy shared the attitudes and way of life of the nobility from which they sprang. The parish priests, commoners by birth, resented the haughtiness and luxurious living of the upper clergy. In 1789, when the Revolution began, many priests sympathized with the reform-minded people of the Third Estate.

The Second Estate

Like the clergy, the nobility was a privileged order. Nobles held the highest positions in the church, army, and government. They were exempt from most taxes (or used their influence to evade paying taxes), collected manorial dues from peasants, and owned between one-quarter and one-third of the land. In addition to the income that they drew from their estates, nobles were becoming increasingly involved in such nonaristocratic enterprises as banking and finance. Nobles were the leading patrons of the arts. Many key philosophes—Montesquieu, Condorcet, d'Holbach—were nobles. Most nobles, however, were suspicious and intolerant of the liberal ideas advanced by the philosophes.

All nobles were not equal; there were gradations of dignity among the 350,000 members of the nobility. Enjoying the most prestige were *nobles of the sword*: families that could trace back their aristocratic status several centuries. The highest of the ancient nobles were engaged in the social whirl at Versailles and Paris, receiving pensions and sinecures from the king but performing few useful services for the state. Most nobles of the sword, unable to afford the gilded life at court, remained on their provincial estates, the poorest of them barely distinguishable from prosperous peasants.

Alongside this ancient nobility, a new nobility had arisen, created by the monarchy. To obtain money, reward favorites, and weaken the old nobility, French kings had sold titles of nobility to members of the bourgeoisie and had conferred noble status on certain government offices bought by wealthy bourgeois. Particularly significant were the *nobles of the robe*, whose ranks included many former bourgeois who had purchased judicial offices in the parlements—the high law courts.

Opinion among the aristocrats was divided. Influenced by the liberal ideals of the philosophes, some nobles sought to reform France; they wanted to end royal despotism and establish a constitutional government. To this extent, the liberal nobility had a great deal in common with the bourgeoisie. These liberal nobles saw the king's difficulties in 1788 as an opportunity to regenerate the nation under enlightened leadership. When they resisted the king's policies, they claimed that they were opposing royal despotism. But many nobles, concerned with preserving their privileges and honorific status, were hostile to liberal ideals and opposed reform.

Chronology 11.1 ❖ The French Revolution

July 1788	Calling of the Estates General
June 17, 1789	Third Estate declares itself the National Assembly
July 14, 1789	Storming of the Bastille
Late July 1789	The Great Fear
August 4, 1789	Nobles surrender their special privileges
April 20, 1792	Legislative Assembly declares war on Austria
Sept. 21–22, 1792	Abolition of the monarchy
June 1793	Jacobins replace the Girondins as the dominant group in the National Convention
July 28, 1794	Robespierre is guillotined

The Third Estate

The Third Estate comprised the bourgeoisie, the peasants, and the urban workers. Although the bourgeoisie provided the leadership for the Revolution, its success depended on the support given by the rest of the Third Estate.

The Bourgeoisie   The bourgeoisie consisted of merchant manufacturers, wholesale merchants, bankers, master craftsmen, doctors, lawyers, intellectuals, and government officials below the top ranks. Although the bourgeoisie had wealth, it lacked social prestige. A merchant, despite his worldly success, felt that his occupation denied him the esteem enjoyed by the nobility.

Influenced by the aristocratic values of the day and envious of the nobility's lifestyle, the bourgeoisie sought to erase the stigma of common birth and to rise socially by becoming landowners. By 1789, the bourgeoisie owned about 20 percent of the land. Traditionally, some of its members had risen socially either by purchasing a judicial or political office that carried with it a title of nobility or by gaining admission to the upper clergy and the officer ranks of the army. Access to the nobility remained open throughout the eighteenth century. Nevertheless, since the highest and most desired positions in the land were reserved for the nobility, able bourgeois were often excluded for a variety of reasons: the high cost of purchasing an office, the limited number of new offices created, the resistance of nobles to their advancement, or the hostility of the older nobility toward those recently ennobled. No doubt these men felt frustrated and came to resent a social system that valued birth more than talent. For most of the century, however, the bourgeoisie did not challenge the existing social structure, including the special privileges of the nobility.

By 1789, the bourgeois had many grievances. They wanted all positions in church, army, and state to be open to men of talent regardless of birth. They sought a parliament that would make laws for the nation; a constitution that would limit the king's power and guarantee freedom of thought, a fair trial, and religious toleration; and administrative reforms that would eliminate waste, inefficiency, and interference with business.

The Peasantry   The condition of the more than twenty-one million French peasants was a paradox. On the one hand, they were better off than peasants in Austria, Prussia, Poland, and Russia, where serfdom still predominated. In France, serfdom had largely disappeared; many peasants owned their land, and some were even prosperous. On the other hand, most French peasants lived in poverty, which worsened in the closing years of the Old Regime.

The typical peasant holding was barely large enough to eke out a living. The rising birthrate (between 1715 and 1789, the population may have increased from eighteen million to twenty-six million) led to the continual subdivision of farms among heirs. Moreover, many peasants did not own land but rented it from a nobleman or a prosperous neighbor. Others worked as sharecroppers, turning over a considerable share of the harvest to their creditors.

An unjust and corrupt system of taxation weighed heavily on the peasantry. Louis XIV had maintained his grandeur and financed his wars by milking ever more taxes from the peasants, a practice that continued throughout the eighteenth century. An army of tax collectors victimized the peasantry. In addition to royal taxes, peasants paid the tithe to the church and manorial dues to lords.

Although serfdom had ended in most parts of France, lords continued to demand obligations from peasants, as they had done in the Middle Ages. Besides performing labor services on the lord's estate, peasants still had to grind their grain in the lord's mill, bake their bread in his oven, press their grapes in his winepress, and give him part of their produce in payment. (These fees were called *banalities*.) In addition, the lord exercised exclusive hunting rights on lands tilled by peasants. Those rights were particularly onerous, for the lord's hunting parties damaged crops. Lords were determined to hold on to these privileges not only because of the income they brought, but because they were symbols of authority and social esteem.

Urban Laborers   The urban laboring class in this preindustrial age consisted of journeymen working for master craftsmen, factory workers in small-scale industries, and wage earners such as day laborers, gardeners, handymen, and deliverymen, who were paid by those whom they served. Conditions for the urban poor, like those for the peasant wage earners, worsened in the late eighteenth century. From 1785 to 1789, the cost of living increased by 62 percent, while wages rose only by 22 percent. For virtually the entire decade of the Revolution, urban workers struggled to keep body and soul together in the face of food shortages and rising prices, particularly the price of their staple food, bread. Material want drove the urban poor to acts of violence that affected the course of the Revolution.

Inefficient Administration and Financial Disorder

The administration of France was complex, confusing, and ineffective. The practice of buying state offices from the king, introduced as a means of raising money, resulted in many incompetent officeholders. Tariffs on goods shipped from one province to another and differing systems of weights and measures hampered trade. No single law code applied to all the provinces; instead, there were overlapping and conflicting law systems, based on old Roman law or customary feudal law, which made the administration of justice slow, arbitrary, and unfair. To admirers of the philosophes, the administrative system was an insult to reason. The Revolution would sweep the system away.

Financial disorders also contributed to the weakness of the Old Regime. In the regime's last years, the government could not raise sufficient funds to cover expenses. By 1787, it still had not paid off the enormous debt incurred during the wars of Louis XIV, let alone the costs of succeeding wars during the eighteenth century, particularly France's aid to the colonists in the American Revolution. The king's gifts and pensions to court nobles and the extravagant court life further drained the treasury.

Finances were in a shambles not because France was impoverished, but because of an inefficient and unjust tax system. Although serious, the financial crisis could have been solved if the clergy, nobility, and bourgeoisie paid their fair share of taxes. With France on the brink of bankruptcy, some of the king's ministers proposed that the nobility and church surrender some of their tax exemptions, but the privileged orders resisted. Some nobles resisted because they were steadfast defenders of noble prerogatives; the more liberal nobles resisted because they saw an opportunity to check absolutism and introduce fundamental reforms that would regenerate the nation.

The resistance of the nobility forced the government, in July 1788, to call for a meeting of the Estates General—a medieval representative assembly, which had last met in 1614—to deal with the financial crisis. The body was to convene in May 1789. Certain that they would dominate the Estates General, the nobles intended to weaken the power of the throne. Once in control of the government, they would introduce financial reforms. But the revolt of the nobility against the crown had unexpected consequences. It opened the way for revolutions by the Third Estate, which destroyed the Old Regime and with it the aristocracy and its privileges.

The Roles of the Enlightenment and the American Revolution

Revolutions are born in the realm of the spirit. Revolutionary movements, says George Rudé, a historian of the French Revolution, require "some unifying body of ideas, a common vocabulary of hope and protest, something, in short, like a common 'revolutionary psychology.'"[1] For this reason, many historians see a relationship between the Enlightenment and the French Revolution. The philosophes were not revolutionaries themselves, but their attacks on the pillars of the established order helped to create revolutionary psychology. As Henri Peyre observes,

> *Eighteenth-century philosophy taught the Frenchman to find his condition wretched, or in any case, unjust and illogical and made him disinclined to the patient resignation to his troubles that had long characterized his ancestors. . . . The propaganda of the "Philosophes" perhaps more than any other factor accounted for the fulfillment of the preliminary condition of the French Revolution, namely discontent with the existing state of things.*[2]

As the Revolution progressed, its leaders utilized the philosophes' ideas and language to justify their own reform program.

The American Revolution, which gave practical expression to the liberal philosophy of the philosophes, also helped to pave the way for the French Revolution. The Declaration of Independence, which proclaimed the natural rights of man and sanctioned resistance against a government that deprived men of these rights, influenced the framers of the Declaration of the Rights of Man and of the Citizen (see page 323). The United States showed that a nation could be established on the principle that sovereign power derived from the people. The Americans set an example of social equality unparalleled in Europe. In the United States, there was no hereditary aristocracy, no serfdom, and no state church. Liberal French aristocrats, such as the Marquis de Lafayette, who had fought in the American Revolution, returned to France more optimistic about the possibilities of reforming French society.

A Bourgeois Revolution?

Because the bourgeois were the principal leaders and chief beneficiaries of the French Revolution, many historians have viewed it, along with the English revolutions of the seventeenth century and the growth of capitalism, as "an episode in the general rise of the bourgeoisie."[3] Those who regard the Revolution as a "bourgeois revolution" argue that in the last part of the eighteenth century it became increasingly difficult for the bourgeoisie to gain the most honored offices in the land. According to this view, in the eighteenth century, a decadent and reactionary aristocracy sought to regain the powers that it had lost under Louis XIV. Through parlements, aristocrats blocked reforms proposed by the king that threatened their privileges, and they united to prevent commoners from entering their ranks.

The nobility's determination to safeguard its power and social exclusiveness collided head-on with the aspirations of a wealthy, talented, and progressive bourgeoisie. Finding the path to upward mobility and social dignity barred, the bourgeoisie, imbued with the rational outlook of the Enlightenment, came to perceive nobles as an obstacle to its advancement and the nation's progress. "The essential cause of the Revolution," concludes French historian Albert Soboul, "was the power of a bourgeoisie arrived at its maturity and confronted by a decadent aristocracy holding tenaciously to its privileges."[4] Thus, when the bourgeois found the opportunity during the Revolution, they ended the legal division of France into separate orders.

Recently, some historians have challenged this interpretation. These revisionists argue that before 1789 the nobles and the bourgeoisie did not represent antagonistic classes divided by sharp differences. On the contrary, they were not clearly distinguishable from each other. The bourgeois aspired to noble status, and many nobles were involved in business enterprises—mining, metallurgy, textiles, and overseas trading companies—traditionally considered the province of the bourgeoisie. Abandoning a traditional aristocratic disdain for business, many nobles had acquired the capitalist mentality associated with the middle class. Some nobles also shared with the bourgeois the liberal values of the philosophes and a desire to do away with monarchical despotism and reform France according to rational standards. Thus, French nobles, particularly those who lived in urban centers or had traveled to Britain and the American colonies, were receptive both to new means of livelihood and to progressive ideas.

Moreover, the French nobility was constantly infused with new blood from below. During the eighteenth century, thousands of bourgeois, through marriage, the purchase of an office, or service as local officials—mayors, for example—had some entitlement of nobility. As British historian William Doyle puts it, "the nobility was an open elite, not a hereditary class apart. Nor is it now possible to maintain that this elite grew less open as the eighteenth century went on thanks to some exclusive 'aristocratic reaction.'"[5]

Just prior to 1789, revisionists contend, nobles and prosperous bourgeois were no longer clearly differentiated; the traditional distinctions that had set them apart were now obsolete. France's social elite actually consisted not of a hereditary nobility, but of *notables*—both nobles and bourgeois—distinguished more by wealth than by birth. Bourgeois notables were essentially moderate; they did not seek the destruction of the aristocracy that was accomplished in the opening stage of the Revolution. The elimination of aristocratic privileges was not part of a preconceived bourgeois program, revisionists maintain, but an improvised response to the violent upheavals in the countryside in July and August 1789. Moreover, not until early 1789, when a struggle erupted over the composition of the Estates General (see the next section), did the bourgeoisie start to become conscious of itself as a class with interests that clashed with those of the aristocracy. Until then, both the bourgeoisie and many aristocrats were united around a common and moderate reform program.

Finally, revisionists argue that the feudal nobility was not as decadent or reactionary as traditional accounts would have it. The nobles resisted the king's reforming ministers because they doubted the ability of a despotic and incompetent state to solve the financial crisis. To be sure, there were aristocrats who selfishly wanted to cling to their privileges, but many also aspired to serve the public good by instituting structural changes that would liberate the nation from despotic and inefficient rule and reform its financial and administrative system. It was this desire to institute crucial changes in French political life, say revisionists, that led nobles to press for the convening of the Estates General.

The Moderate Stage, 1789–1791

Since a significant number of nobles were sympathetic to reform, there was no insuperable gulf between the Second and Third Estates as the Estates General prepared to meet. However, it soon became clear that the hopes of reformers clashed with the intentions of many aristocrats.

What had started as a struggle between the crown and the aristocracy was turning into something far more significant: a conflict between the two privileged orders on one side and the Third Estate on the other. One pamphleteer, Abbé Sieyès (1748–1836), expressed the hatred that members of the bourgeoisie felt for the aristocracy. "The privileged order has said to the Third Estate: 'Whatever be your services, whatever be your talents, you shall go thus far and no farther. It is not fitting that you be honored.'" The higher positions in the land, said Sieyès, should be the "reward for talents," not the prerogative of birth. Without the Third Estate, "nothing can progress"; without the nobility, "everything would proceed infinitely better."[6]

Formation of the National Assembly

The Estates General convened at Versailles on May 5, 1789, but was stalemated by the question of procedure. Seeking to control the assembly, the nobility insisted that the three Estates follow the traditional practice of meeting separately and voting as individual bodies. Since the two privileged orders were likely to stand together, the Third Estate would always be outvoted, two to one. But the delegates from the Third Estate, unwilling to allow the nobility and the higher clergy to dominate the Estates General, proposed instead that the three Estates meet as one body and vote by head. There were some 610 delegates from the Third Estate; the nobility and clergy together had an equivalent number. Since the Third Estate could rely on the support of sympathetic parish priests and liberal nobles, it would be assured a majority if all the orders met together. As aristocrats and bourgeois became more polarized, anti-noble rhetoric gained a growing audience among all segments of the Third Estate. Many commoners now saw the aristocracy as the chief obstacle to reform.

On June 17, the Third Estate made a revolutionary move. It declared itself the National Assembly. On June 20, locked out of their customary meeting hall (apparently by accident), the Third Estate delegates moved to a nearby

Formation of the National Assembly by Jacques Louis David (Detail).   By forming the National Assembly in June 1789, the Third Estate successfully challenged the nobility and defied the king. In this painting glorifying the event, aristocrat, clergyman, and commoner embrace before a cheering National Assembly. (*Versailles/Cliche des Musèes Nationaux*)

tennis court and took a solemn oath not to disband until a constitution had been drawn up for France. Louis XVI commanded the National Assembly to separate into orders, but the Third Estate held firm. The steadfastness of the delegates and the menacing actions of Parisians who supported the National Assembly forced Louis XVI to yield. On June 27, he ordered the nobility (some had already done so) and the clergy (a majority had already done so) to join with the Third Estate in the National Assembly.

But the victory of the bourgeoisie was not yet secure, for most nobles had not resigned themselves to a bourgeois-dominated National Assembly. It appeared that Louis XVI, influenced by court aristocrats, had resolved to use force against the National Assembly and stop the incipient revolution. At this point, uprisings by the common people of Paris and peasants in the countryside saved the National Assembly, exacerbated hostilities between the Third Estate and the nobility, and ensured the victory of the forces of reform.

Storming of the Bastille

In July 1789, the level of tension in Paris was high for three reasons. First, the calling of the Estates General had aroused hopes for reform. Second, the price of bread was soaring: in August 1788, a Parisian laborer had spent 50 percent of his income on bread; by July 1789, he was spending 80 percent. A third element in the tension was the fear of an aristocratic plot to crush the National Assembly. Afraid that royal troops would bombard and pillage the city, Parisians searched for weapons.

On July 14, eight hundred to nine hundred Parisians gathered in front of the Bastille, a fortress used as a prison and a scorned symbol of royal despotism. They gathered primarily to obtain gunpowder and to remove the cannon that threatened a heavily populated working-class district. As the tension mounted, the Parisians stormed and captured the Bastille. The fall of the Bastille had far-reaching consequences: a symbol of the Old Regime had fallen; some court nobles hostile to the Revolution decided to flee the country; the frightened king told the National Assembly that he would withdraw the troops ringing Paris. The revolutionary act of the Parisians had indirectly saved the National Assembly and with it the bourgeois revolution.

The Great Fear

Revolution in the countryside also served the interests of the reformers. Inflamed by economic misery and stirred by the uprisings of the Parisians, peasants began to burn manor houses and destroy the registers on which their obligations to the lords were inscribed. The flames of the peasants' insurrection were fanned by rumors that aristocrats were organizing bands of brigands to attack the peasants. The mythical army of brigands never materialized, but the Great Fear, as this episode is called, led more peasants to take up arms. Suspicious of an aristocratic plot to thwart efforts at reform and releasing years of stored-up hatred for the nobles, the peasants attacked the lords' chateaux with great fury.

Like the insurrection in Paris, the peasant upheavals in late July and early August worked to the advantage of the reformers. The attacks provided the National Assembly with an opportunity to strike at noble privileges by putting into law what the peasants had accomplished with the torch—the destruction of feudal remnants. On the night of August 4, 1789, aristocrats seeking to restore calm in the countryside surrendered their special privileges: exclusive hunting rights, tax exemptions, monopoly of highest offices, manorial courts, and the right to demand labor services from peasants.

In the decrees of August 5 and 11, the National Assembly implemented the resolutions of August 4. The Assembly also declared that the planned constitution should be prefaced by a declaration of rights. On August 26, it adopted the Declaration of the Rights of Man and of the Citizen.

October Days

Louis XVI, cool to these reforms, postponed his approval of the August Decrees and the Declaration of Rights. It would require a second uprising by the

Storming of the Bastille, July 14, 1789.   A Parisian crowd stormed the dreaded fortress of the Bastille, long identified with the abuses of the Old Regime. (*Brown Brothers*)

Parisians to force the king to agree to the reforms and to nail down the victory of the reformers.

On October 5, 1789, Parisian women and men marched twelve miles to Versailles to protest the lack of bread to the National Assembly and the king. A few hours later, twenty thousand Paris Guards, a citizen militia sympathetic to the Revolution, also set out for Versailles in support of the protesters. The king had no choice but to promise bread and to return with the demonstrators to Paris. Aware that he had no control over the Parisians and fearful of further violence, Louis XVI approved the August Decrees and the Declaration of Rights. Nobles who had urged the king to use force against the Assembly and had tried to block reforms fled the country in large numbers.

Reforms of the National Assembly

With resistance weakened, the National Assembly continued the work of reform begun in the summer of 1789. Its reforms, which are summarized below, destroyed the Old Regime.

1.   *Abolition of special privileges.* By ending the special privileges of the nobility and the clergy in the August Decrees, the National Assembly legalized

the equality that the bourgeoisie had demanded. The aristocratic structure of the Old Regime, a remnant of the Middle Ages that had hindered the progressive bourgeoisie, was eliminated.

2. *Statement of human rights.* The Declaration of the Rights of Man and of the Citizen expressed the liberal and universal goals of the philosophes. In proclaiming the inalienable right to liberty of person, freedom of religion and thought, and equal treatment under the law, the declaration affirmed the dignity of the individual. It asserted that government belonged not to any ruler, but to the people as a whole, and that its aim was the preservation of the natural rights of the individual. Because the declaration contrasted sharply with the principles espoused by an intolerant clergy, a privileged aristocracy, and a despotic monarch, it has been called the death warrant of the Old Regime.

3. *Subordination of church to state.* The National Assembly also struck at the privileges of the Roman Catholic church. The August Decrees declared the end of tithes. To obtain badly needed funds, the Assembly in November 1789 confiscated church lands and put them up for sale. In 1790, the Assembly passed the Civil Constitution of the Clergy, which altered the boundaries of the dioceses, reducing the number of bishops and priests, and transformed the clergy into government officials elected by the people and paid by the state.

Almost all bishops and many priests opposed the Civil Constitution. It divided the French and gave opponents of the Revolution an emotional issue around which to rally supporters.

4. *A constitution for France.* In September 1791, the National Assembly issued a constitution limiting the power of the king and guaranteeing all French citizens equal treatment under the law. Citizens paying less than a specified amount in taxes could not vote. Probably about 30 percent of the males over the age of twenty-five were excluded by this stipulation, and only the more well-to-do citizens qualified to sit in the Legislative Assembly, a unicameral parliament created to succeed the National Assembly. Despite this restriction, suffrage requirements under the constitution of 1791 were far more generous than in Britain.

5. *Administrative and judicial reforms.* The National Assembly replaced the patchwork of provincial units with eighty-three new administrative units, or departments, approximately equal in size. Judicial reforms complemented the administrative changes. A standardized system of courts replaced the innumerable jurisdictions of the Old Regime, and the sale of judicial offices was ended. The penal code completed by the National Assembly abolished torture and barbarous punishments.

6. *Aid for business.* The National Assembly abolished all tolls and duties on goods transported within the country, established a uniform system of weights and measures, eliminated the guilds (medieval survivals, which blocked business expansion), and forbade workers to form unions or to strike.

By ending absolutism, striking at the privileges of the nobility, and preventing the mass of people from gaining control over the government, the

National Assembly consolidated the rule of the bourgeoisie. With one arm, it broke the power of aristocracy and throne; with the other, it held back the common people. Although the reforms benefited the bourgeoisie, it would be a mistake to view them merely as a selfish expression of bourgeois interests. The Declaration of the Rights of Man and of the Citizen was addressed to all; it proclaimed liberty and equality as the right of all and called on citizens to treat each other with respect.

The Radical Stage, 1792–1794

Pleased with their accomplishments—equality before the law, careers open to talent, a written constitution, parliamentary government—the men of 1789 wished the Revolution to go no further. But revolutionary times are unpredictable. Soon the Revolution moved in a direction neither anticipated nor desired by the reformers. A counterrevolution, led by irreconcilable nobles and alienated churchmen, gained the support of the strongly Catholic peasants. It threatened the Revolution, forcing the revolutionary leadership to resort to extreme measures.

The Sans-Culottes

The discontent of the *sans-culottes**—small shopkeepers, artisans, and wage earners—also propelled the Revolution toward radicalism. Although they had played a significant role in the Revolution, particularly in the storming of the Bastille and in the October Days, they had gained little. The sans-culottes, says French historian Albert Soboul, "began to realize that a privilege of wealth was taking the place of a privilege of birth. They foresaw that the bourgeoisie would succeed the fallen aristocracy as the ruling class."[7] Inflamed by poverty and their hatred of the rich, the sans-culottes insisted that it was the government's duty to guarantee them the "right of existence"—a policy that ran counter to the economic individualism of the bourgeoisie.

The sans-culottes demanded that the government increase wages, set price controls on food supplies, end food shortages, and pass laws to prevent extremes of wealth and poverty. Whereas the men of 1789 sought equality of rights, liberties, and opportunities, the sans-culottes expanded the principle of equality to include narrowing the gap between the rich and the poor. To reduce economic inequality, they called for higher taxes for the wealthy and the redistribution of land. Politically, they favored a democratic republic in which the common man had a voice.

In 1789, the bourgeoisie had demanded equality with the aristocrats: the right to hold the most honored positions in the nation and an end to the spe-

---

*Literally, *sans-culottes* means "without culottes" and refers to the people who did not wear the knee breeches that aristocrats wore before the revolution.

cial privileges of the nobility. By the close of 1792, the sans-culottes were demanding equality with the bourgeois. They wanted political reforms that would give the poor a voice in the government and social reforms that would improve their lot.

Despite the pressures exerted by reactionary nobles and clergy on the one hand and discontented sans-culottes on the other, the Revolution might not have taken a radical turn if France had remained at peace. The war that broke out with Austria and Prussia in April 1792 exacerbated internal dissensions, worsened economic conditions, and threatened to undo the reforms of the Revolution. It was under these circumstances that the Revolution moved from its moderate stage into a radical one, which historians refer to as the Second French Revolution.

Foreign Invasion

In June 1791, Louis XVI and the royal family, traveling in disguise, fled Paris for northeastern France to join with *émigrés* (nobles who had left revolutionary France and were organizing a counterrevolutionary army) and to rally foreign support against the Revolution. Discovered at Varennes by a village postmaster, they were brought back to Paris as virtual prisoners. The flight of the king turned many French people against the monarchy, strengthening the position of the radicals who wanted to do away with kingship altogether and establish a republic. But it was foreign invasion that ultimately led to the destruction of the monarchy.

On April 20, 1792, fearful that Austria intended to overthrow the Revolution and eager to spread revolutionary ideals, France declared war on Austria. Commanded by the duke of Brunswick, a combined Austrian and Prussian army crossed into France. In an atmosphere already charged with tension, the duke of Brunswick issued a manifesto declaring that if the royal family were harmed he would exact a terrible vengeance on the Parisians. On August 10, enraged Parisians and militia from other cities attacked the king's palace, killing several hundred Swiss guards.

In early September, as foreign troops advanced deeper into France, rumors spread that jailed priests and aristocrats were planning to break out of their cells to support the duke of Brunswick. The Parisians panicked. Driven by fear, patriotism, and murderous impulses, they raided the prisons and massacred eleven hundred to twelve hundred prisoners. Most of the victims were not political prisoners but ordinary criminals.

On September 21 and 22, the National Convention (the new lawmaking body) abolished the monarchy and established a republic. In December, Louis XVI was placed on trial, and in January 1793 he was executed for conspiring against the liberty of the French people. The uprising of August 10, the September massacres, the creation of a republic, and the execution of Louis XVI all confirmed that the Revolution was taking a radical turn.

Meanwhile, the war continued. Short of supplies, hampered by bad weather, and lacking sufficient manpower, the duke of Brunswick never did

The Execution of Louis XVI.   The king died with dignity. His last words were, "I forgive my enemies; I trust that my death will be for the happiness of my people, but I grieve for France, and I fear that she may suffer the anger of the Lord." (*Giraudon/Art Resource, NY*)

reach Paris. Outmaneuvered at Valmy on September 20, 1792, the foreign forces retreated to the frontier, and the armies of the republic took the offensive. By the beginning of 1793, French forces had overrun Belgium (then a part of the Austrian Empire), the German Rhineland, and the Sardinian provinces of Nice and Savoy. To the peoples of Europe, the National Convention had solemnly announced that it was waging a popular crusade against privilege and tyranny, against aristocrats and princes.

These revolutionary social ideas, the execution of Louis XVI, and, most important, French expansion, which threatened the balance of power, frightened the rulers of Europe. Urged on by Britain, by the spring of 1793 they formed an anti-French alliance. The allies' forces pressed toward the French borders, endangering the republic.

Counterrevolutionary insurrections further undermined the fledgling republic. In the Vendée, in western France, peasants who were protesting against taxation and conscription and were still loyal to their priests and Catholic tradition, which the Revolution had attacked, took up arms against the republic.

Led by local nobles, the peasants of the Vendée waged a guerrilla war for religion, royalism, and their traditional way of life. In other quarters, federalists revolted in the provinces, objecting to the power wielded by the centralized government in Paris. The republic was unable to exercise control over much of the country.

The Jacobins

As the republic tottered under the weight of foreign invasion, internal insurrection, and economic crisis, the revolutionary leadership grew still more radical. In June 1793, the Jacobins replaced the Girondins as the dominant group in the National Convention. The Girondins favored a government in which the departments would exercise control over their own affairs. The Jacobins, on the other hand, wanted a strong central government, with Paris as the seat of power. Both Girondins and Jacobins came from the bourgeoisie, but the Girondins opposed government interference in business, whereas the Jacobins supported temporary government controls to deal with the needs of war and economic crisis. This last point was crucial; it won the Jacobins the support of the sans-culottes. On June 2, 1793, some eighty thousand armed sans-culottes surrounded the Convention and demanded the arrest of Girondin delegates— an act that enabled the Jacobins to gain control of the government.

The problems confronting the Jacobins were staggering. They had to cope with civil war, particularly in the Vendée, economic distress, blockaded ports, and foreign invasion. They lived with the terrible dread that, if they failed, the Revolution for liberty and equality would perish. Only strong leadership could save the republic. It was provided by the Committee of Public Safety, which organized the nation's defenses, supervised ministers, ordered arrests, and imposed the central government's authority throughout the nation.

The Jacobins continued the work of reform. In 1793, a new constitution expressed Jacobin enthusiasm for political democracy. It contained a new Declaration of Rights, which affirmed and amplified the principles of 1789. By giving all adult males the right to vote, it overcame sans-culotte objections to the constitution of 1791. However, the threat of invasion and the revolts caused the implementation of the new constitution to be postponed, and it was never put into effect. By abolishing both slavery in the French colonies and imprisonment for debt and by making plans for free public education, the Jacobins revealed their humanitarianism and their debt to the philosophes. To halt inflation and gain the support of the poor—both necessary for the war effort—the Jacobins decreed the *law of the maximum,* which fixed prices on bread and other essential goods and raised wages.

The Nation in Arms

To fight the war against foreign invaders, the Jacobins, in an act that anticipated modern conscription, drafted unmarried men between eighteen and twenty-five years of age. They mobilized all the resources of the country,

Liberty Armed with the Scepter of Reason Strikes Down Ignorance and Fanaticism, an Engraving by Jean-Baptiste Chapuy, c. 1793. Using a scepter given to her by Reason standing at the left, Liberty strikes down ignorance and fanaticism, usually identified with religion. Many of these prints were produced in 1793 and 1794 when there was a concerted effort to replace traditional Christianity with a civic religion, the Cult of Reason. (*Bibliothèque Nationale, Paris*)

infused the army with a love for *la patrie* (the nation), and, in a remarkable demonstration of administrative skill, equipped an army of more than 800,000 men. In creating the nation in arms, the Jacobins heralded the emergence of modern warfare. Inspired by the ideals of liberty, equality, and fraternity and commanded by officers who had proved their skill on the battlefield, the citizen soldiers of the republic won decisive victories. In May and June 1794, the French routed the allied forces on the vital northern frontier, and by the end of July, France had become the triumphant master of Belgium.

By demanding complete devotion to the nation, the Jacobin phase of the Revolution also heralded the rise of modern nationalism. In the schools, in newspapers, speeches, and poems, on the stage, and at rallies and meetings of patriotic societies, the French people were told of the glory won by republican soldiers on the battlefield and were reminded of their duties to *la patrie*. "The citizen is born, lives, and dies for the fatherland"—these words were written in public places for all citizens to read and ponder. The soldiers of the Revolution fought not for money or for a king, but for the nation. Could this heightened sense of nationality, which concentrated on the special interests of the French people, be reconciled with the Declaration of the Rights of Man, whose principles were addressed to all humanity? The revolutionaries themselves did not understand the implications of the new force that they had unleashed.

The Republic of Virtue and the Reign of Terror

While forging a revolutionary army to deal with external enemies, the Jacobins were also waging war against internal opposition. The pivotal personality in this struggle was Maximilién Robespierre (1758–1794), who had a fervent faith in the rightness of his beliefs and a total commitment to republican democracy. Robespierre wanted to create a better society founded on reason, good citizenship, and patriotism. In his Republic of Virtue, there would be no kings or nobles, men would be free, equal, and educated, reason would be glorified, and superstition would be ridiculed. There would be no extremes of wealth or poverty; man's natural goodness would prevail over vice and greed; and laws would preserve, not violate, inalienable rights. Robespierre pursued his ideal society with religious zeal. Knowing that the Republic of Virtue could not be established while France was threatened by foreign and civil war, Robespierre urged harsh treatment for enemies of the republic, who "must be prosecuted by all not as ordinary enemies, but as rebels, brigands, and assassins."[8]

With Robespierre playing a key role, the Jacobin leadership attacked those they considered enemies of the republic: Girondins who challenged Jacobin authority; federalists who opposed a strong central government emanating from Paris; counterrevolutionary priests and nobles and their peasant supporters; and profiteers who hoarded food. The Jacobins even sought to discipline the ardor of the sans-culottes, who had given them power. Fearful that sans-culotte spontaneity would undermine central authority and promote anarchy, Robespierrists brought about the dissolution of sans-culotte societies. They also executed sans-culotte leaders known as the *enragés* (literally, madmen), who threatened insurrection against Jacobin rule and pushed for more social reforms than the Jacobins would allow. The *enragés* wanted to set limits on income and on the size of farms and businesses—policies considered far too extreme by the supporters of Robespierre.

Robespierre and his fellow Jacobins did not make terror a deliberate government policy because they were bloodthirsty or power mad. Instead, they sought to establish a temporary dictatorship in a desperate attempt to save the republic and the Revolution. Deeply devoted to republican democracy, the Jacobins viewed themselves as bearers of a higher faith. Like all visionaries, Robespierre was convinced that he knew the right way and that the new society he envisaged would benefit all humanity. He saw those who impeded its implementation as not just opponents, but sinners who had to be liquidated for the general good.

Special courts were established in Paris and other cities to try suspects. The proceedings were carried on in haste, and most judgments called for either acquittal or execution. In the Vendée, where civil war raged, many of the arrested were executed by firing squads, without trial; some five thousand were loaded onto barges, which were then sunk in the middle of the Loire River. Ironically, most of the executions took place after the frontiers had been secured and the civil war crushed. In many respects, the Terror was less a means of saving the beleaguered Republic and more a way of shaping the new republican society and the new individual in accordance with the radical Jacobin ideology. Perhaps as many as forty thousand people from all segments of society perished during the Terror.

The Jacobins did save the republic. Their regime expelled foreign armies, crushed the federalist uprisings, contained the counterrevolutionaries in the Vendée, and prevented anarchy. Without the discipline, order, and unity imposed on France by the Robespierrists, it is likely that the republic would have collapsed under the twin blows of foreign invasion and domestic anarchy.

Nonetheless, the Reign of Terror poses fundamental questions about the meaning of the French Revolution and the validity of the Enlightenment conception of the individual. To what extent was the Terror a reversal of the ideals of the Revolution as formulated in the Declaration of the Rights of Man? To what extent did the feverish passions and fascination with violence demonstrated in the mass executions in the provinces and in the public spectacles in Paris indicate a darker side of human nature, beyond the control of reason? Did Robespierre's religion of humanity revive the fanaticism and cruelty of the wars of religion, which had so disgusted the philosophes? Did the Robespierrists, who considered themselves the staunchest defenders of the Revolution's ideals, soil and subvert these ideals by their zeal? The Jacobins mobilized the might of the nation, created the mystique of *la patrie*, imposed dictatorial rule in defense of liberty and equality, and legalized and justified terror committed in the people's name. In so doing, were they unwittingly unleashing new forces that in later years would be harnessed by totalitarian regimes—regimes consciously resolved to stamp out the liberal heritage of the Revolution?

The Fall of Robespierre

Feeling the chill of the guillotine blade on their own necks, Robespierre's opponents in the Convention ordered his arrest and the arrest of some of his supporters. On July 28, 1794, the tenth of Thermidor according to the new republican calendar, Robespierre was guillotined. After the fall of Robespierre, the machinery of the Jacobin republic was dismantled.

Leadership passed to the property-owning bourgeois who had endorsed the constitutional ideas of 1789–91, the moderate stage of the Revolution. The new leadership, known as Thermidoreans until the end of 1795, wanted no more of the Jacobins or of Robespierre's society. They had viewed Robespierre as a threat to their political power because he would have allowed the common people a considerable voice in the government. They had also deemed him a threat to their property because he would have introduced some state regulation of the economy to aid the poor.

The Thermidorean reaction was a counterrevolution. The new government purged the army of the officers who were suspected of Jacobin leanings, abolished the law of the maximum, and declared void the constitution of 1793. A new constitution, approved in 1795, reestablished property requirements for voting. The counterrevolution also produced a counterterror, as royalists and Catholics massacred Jacobins in the provinces.

At the end of 1795, the new republican government, the Directory, was burdened by war, a sagging economy, and internal unrest. The Directory crushed insurrections by Parisian sans-culottes, maddened by hunger and hatred of the rich (1795, 1796), and by royalists seeking to restore the monarchy (1797). As military and domestic pressures increased, power began to pass into the hands of generals. One of them, Napoleon Bonaparte, seized control of the government in November 1799, pushing the Revolution into yet another stage.

Napoleon and France: Return to Autocratic Rule

Napoleon was born on August 15, 1769, on the island of Corsica, the son of a petty noble. After finishing military school in France, he became an artillery officer. The wars of the French Revolution afforded him an opportunity to advance his career; in 1796, he was given command of the French Army of Italy. In Italy, against the Austrians, Napoleon demonstrated a dazzling talent for military planning and leadership, which earned him an instant reputation. Having tasted glory, he could never do without it. Since he had experienced only success, nothing seemed impossible; he sensed that he was headed for greatness.

In 1799, Napoleon was leading a French army in Egypt when he decided to return to France and make his bid for power. He joined a conspiracy that overthrew the Directory and created an executive office of three consuls. As first consul, Napoleon monopolized power. In 1802, he was made first consul for life, with the right to name his successor. And on December 2, 1804, in a magnificent ceremony at the Cathedral of Notre Dame in Paris, Napoleon crowned himself emperor of the French. General, first consul, and then emperor—it was a breathless climb to the heights of power. Napoleon, who once said that he loved "power as a musician loves his violin," was determined never to lose it.

An Enlightened Despot

Napoleon did not identify with the republicanism and democracy of the Jacobins; rather, he belonged to the tradition of eighteenth-century enlightened despotism. Like the reforming despots, he admired administrative uniformity and efficiency, disliked feudalism, religious persecution, and civil inequality, and favored government regulation of trade and industry. He saw in enlightened despotism a means of ensuring political stability and strengthening the state. Napoleon did preserve several gains of the Revolution: equality under the law, careers open to men of talent, promotion of secular education, and the weakening of clerical power. But he suppressed political liberty.

Napoleon succeeded in giving France a strong central government and administrative uniformity. An army of officials, subject to the emperor's will, reached into every village, linking together the entire nation. This centralized state suited Napoleon's desire for orderly government and rational administration, enabled him to concentrate power in his own hands, and provided him with the taxes and soldiers needed to fight his wars. To suppress irreconcilable opponents, primarily diehard royalists and republicans, Napoleon

---

Chronology 11.2 ❖ Napoleon's Career

1796	Napoleon gets command of the French Army of Italy
November 10, 1799	He helps to overthrow the Directory's rule, establishing a strong executive in France
December 2, 1804	He crowns himself emperor of the French
October 21, 1805	Battle of Trafalgar—French and Spanish fleets are defeated by the British
October 1806	Napoleon defeats the Prussians at Jena, and French forces occupy Berlin
1808–1813	Peninsular War—Spaniards, aided by the British, fight against French occupation
October–December 1812	Grand Army retreats from Russia
October 1813	Allied forces defeat Napoleon at Leipzig
1814	Paris is captured and Napoleon is exiled to Elba
March 20, 1815	Escaping, he enters Paris and begins "hundred days" rule
June 1815	Defeated at Waterloo, Napoleon is exiled to St. Helena

---

used the instruments of the police state—secret agents, arbitrary arrest, summary trials, and executions.

To prevent hostile criticism of his rule and promote popular support for his policies and person, Napoleon also shaped public opinion. He was thus a precursor of twentieth century dictators. Liberty of the press came to an end. Printers swore an oath of obedience to the emperor, and newspapers were converted into government mouthpieces.

Napoleon tried to close the breach between the state and the Catholic church that had opened during the Revolution. Such a reconciliation would gain the approval of the mass of the French people, who still remained devoted to their faith, and would also reassure the peasants and bourgeois who had bought confiscated church lands. For these reasons, Napoleon negotiated an agreement with the pope. The Concordat of 1801 recognized Catholicism as the religion of the great majority of the French, rather than as the official state religion (the proposal that the pope desired). Napoleon had achieved his aim. The Concordat made his regime acceptable to Catholics and to owners of former church lands.

Coronation of Napoleon and Josephine by Jacques Louis David.   Napoleon crowned himself emperor in a magnificent ceremony. To French émigrés and nobles throughout Europe, he was the "crowned Jacobin" who threatened aristocratic privileges and European stability. (*Louvre* © *R.M.N.*)

Legal, Educational, and Financial Policies

Under the Old Regime, France was plagued by numerous and conflicting law codes. Reflecting local interests and feudal traditions, these codes obstructed national unity and administrative efficiency. Efforts by the revolutionaries to draw up a unified code of laws bogged down. Recognizing the value of such a code in promoting effective administration throughout France, Napoleon pressed for the completion of the project. The Code Napoléon incorporated many principles of the Revolution: equality before the law, the right to choose one's profession, freedom of conscience, protection of property rights, the abolition of serfdom, and the secular character of the state.

The code also had its less liberal side, denying equal treatment to workers in their dealings with employers, to women in their relations with their husbands, and to children in their relations with their fathers. In making wives inferior to their husbands in matters of property, adultery, and divorce, the code reflected both Napoleon's personal attitude and the general view of the times toward women and family stability. The restoration of slavery in the French colonies—which the Jacobins had abolished—was another violation of equality.

Napoleon's educational policy was in many ways an elaboration of the school reforms initiated during the Revolution. Like the revolutionaries, Napoleon favored a system of public education with a secular curriculum and a minimum of church involvement. For Napoleon, education served a dual purpose: it would provide him with capable officials to administer his laws and trained officers to lead his armies, and it would indoctrinate the young in obedience and loyalty. He established the University of France, a giant board of education that placed education under state control. To this day, the French school system, unlike that in the United States, is strictly centralized, with curriculum and standards set for the entire country.

Napoleon's financial and economic policies were designed to strengthen France and enhance his popularity. To stimulate the economy and to retain the favor of the bourgeois who supported his seizure of power, Napoleon aided industry through tariffs and loans, and he fostered commerce (while also speeding up troop movements) by building or repairing roads, bridges, and canals. To protect the currency from inflation, he established the Bank of France, which was controlled by the nation's leading financiers. By keeping careers open to talent, he endorsed one of the key demands of the bourgeoisie during the Revolution. Fearing a revolution based on lack of bread, he provided food at low prices and stimulated employment for the laboring poor. He endeared himself to the peasants by not restoring feudal privileges and by allowing them to keep the land they had obtained during the Revolution.

Napoleon and Europe: Diffusion of Revolutionary Institutions

Napoleon, the Corsican adventurer, realized Louis XIV's dream of French mastery of Europe. Between 1805 and 1807, he decisively defeated Austria, Prussia, and Russia, becoming the virtual ruler of Europe. In these campaigns, as in his earlier successes in Italy, Napoleon demonstrated his greatness as a military commander.

By 1810, Napoleon dominated the Continent, except for the Balkan Peninsula. The Grand Empire comprised lands annexed to France, vassal states, and cowed allies. The French Republic had already annexed Belgium and the German Left Bank of the Rhine. Napoleon incorporated several other areas into France: German coastal regions as far as the western Baltic and large areas of Italy, including Rome, Geneva and its environs, Trieste, and the Dalmatian coast. Vassal states in the Grand Empire included five kingdoms ruled by Napoleon's relatives: two kingdoms in Italy, and the kingdoms of Holland, Westphalia, and Spain.

Besides the five satellite kingdoms, the Grand Empire contained several other vassal states. Napoleon formed the Confederation of the Rhine in 1806.

Map 11.1   Napoleon's Europe, 1810   ▶

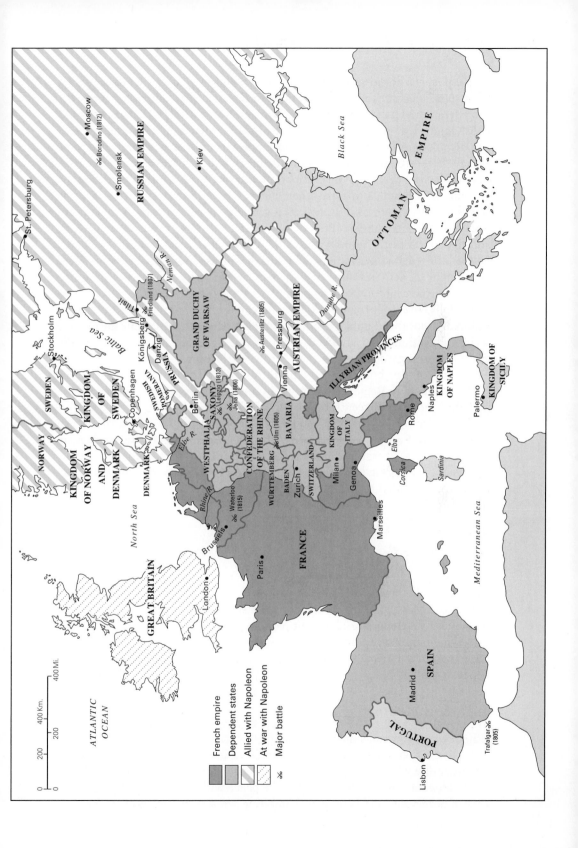

ATLANTIC
OCEAN

400 Mi.

400 Km.

GREAT BRITAIN

London ●

Brussels ●

Waterloo
(1815)

North Sea

NORWAY

KINGDOM
OF
NORWAY
AND
DENMARK

DENMARK

Copenhagen ●

Stockholm ●

SWEDEN

KINGDOM
OF
SWEDEN

Baltic Sea

St. Petersburg ●

SWEDISH POMERANIA

Königsberg ●

Danzig ●

Tilsit ●
Friedland (1807)

Neman R.

PRUSSIA

Berlin ●

Elbe R.

WESTPHALIA

SAXONY

Leipzig (1813)

Jena (1806)

CONFEDERATION
OF THE RHINE

WÜRTTEMBERG

BADEN

Zurich ●

SWITZERLAND

Rhine R.

Paris ●

FRANCE

Marseilles ●

BAVARIA

Ulm (1805)

KINGDOM
OF
ITALY

Milan ●

Genoa ●

Corsica

Elba

Sardinia

Mediterranean Sea

GRAND DUCHY
OF WARSAW

RUSSIAN EMPIRE

Moscow ● (1812)

Borodino (1812)

Smolensk ●

Kiev ●

Austerlitz (1805)

Pressburg ●

Vienna ●

AUSTRIAN EMPIRE

Danube R.

ILLYRIAN PROVINCES

Black Sea

OTTOMAN
EMPIRE

Rome ●

Naples ●

KINGDOM
OF NAPLES

Palermo ●

KINGDOM OF
SICILY

SPAIN

Madrid ●

PORTUGAL

Lisbon ●

Trafalgar
(1805)

French empire
Dependent states
Allied with Napoleon
At war with Napoleon
Major battle

Its members, a loose association of sixteen (later eighteen) German states, were subservient to the emperor, as were the nineteen cantons of the Swiss confederation. The Grand Duchy of Warsaw, formed in 1807 from Prussia's Polish lands, was placed under the rule of the German king of Saxony, one of Napoleon's vassals. Finally, the Grand Empire included states compelled to be French allies—Austria, Prussia, and Russia, as well as Sweden and Denmark.

With varying degrees of determination and success, Napoleon extended the reforms of the Revolution to other lands. His officials instituted the Code Napoléon, organized an effective civil service, opened careers to talent, and equalized the tax burden. Besides abolishing serfdom, manorial payments, and the courts of the nobility, they did away with clerical courts, promoted freedom of religion, permitted civil marriage, pressed for civil rights for Jews, and fought clerical interference with secular authority. They also abolished guilds, introduced a uniform system of weights and measures, eliminated internal tolls, and built roads, bridges, and canals. They promoted secular education and improved public health. Napoleon had launched a European-wide social revolution that attacked the privileges of the aristocracy and the clergy—who regarded him as that "crowned Jacobin"—and worked to the advantage of the bourgeoisie. This diffusion of revolutionary institutions weakened the Old Regime irreparably in much of Europe and speeded up the modernization of nineteenth-century Europe.

Pleased by the overhaul of feudal practices and the reduction of clerical power, many Europeans, particularly the progressive bourgeoisie, welcomed Napoleon as a liberator. But there was another side to Napoleon's rule. Napoleon, the tyrant of Europe, turned conquered lands into satellite kingdoms and exploited them for the benefit of France: a policy that gained him the enmity of many Europeans.

The Fall of Napoleon

Aside from the hostility of subject nationals, Napoleon had to cope with the determined opposition of Great Britain. Its subsidies and encouragement kept resistance to the emperor alive. But perhaps Napoleon's greatest obstacle was his own boundless ambition, which warped his judgment. From its peak, the emperor's career soon slid downhill to defeat, dethronement, and deportation.

Failure to Subdue England

Britain was Napoleon's most resolute opponent. It could not be otherwise, for any power that dominated the Continent could organize sufficient naval might to threaten British commerce, challenge its sea power, and invade the island kingdom. Britain would not make peace with any state that sought European hegemony, and Napoleon's ambition would settle for nothing less.

Unable to invade Britain while British warships commanded the English Channel, Napoleon decided to bring what he called "the nation of shopkeepers" to its knees by damaging the British economy. His plan, called the *Continental System,* was to bar all countries under France's control from buying British goods. However, by smuggling goods onto the Continent and increasing trade with the New World, Britain, although hurt, escaped economic ruin. Besides, the Continental System punished European lands dependent on British imports; the bourgeoisie, generally supportive of Napoleon's social and administrative reforms, turned against him because of the economic distress it caused. Furthermore, Napoleon's efforts to enforce the system enmeshed him in two catastrophic blunders: the occupation of Spain and the invasion of Russia.

The Spanish Ulcer

An ally of France since 1796, Spain proved a disappointment to Napoleon. It failed to prevent the Portuguese from trading with Britain and contributed little military or financial aid to France's war effort. Napoleon decided to incorporate Spain into his empire; in 1808, he deposed the Spanish ruler and designated his own brother Joseph as king of Spain.

Napoleon believed that the Spanish would rally round the gentle Joseph and welcome his liberal reforms. This confidence was a fatal illusion. Spanish nobles and clergy feared French liberalism; the overwhelmingly peasant population, illiterate and credulous, intensely proud, fanatically religious, and easily aroused by the clergy, viewed Napoleon as the Devil's agent. Loyal to the Spanish monarchy and faithful to the church, the Spanish fought a "War to the Knife" against the invaders.

Seeking to keep the struggle against Napoleon alive, Britain came to the aid of the Spanish insurgents. The intervention of British troops, commanded by Sir Arthur Wellesley, the future duke of Wellington, led to the ultimate defeat of Joseph in 1813. The "Spanish ulcer" drained Napoleon's treasury, tied down hundreds of thousands of French troops, enabled Britain to gain a foothold on the Continent from which to invade southern France, and inspired patriots in other lands to resist the French emperor.

The German War of Liberation

Anti-French feeling also broke out in the German states. Hatred of the French invaders evoked a feeling of national outrage among some Germans, who up to this time had thought only in terms of their own particular state and prince. Some German intellectuals, using the emotional language of nationalism, called for a war of liberation against Napoleon and, in some instances, for the creation of a unified Germany.

Besides kindling a desire for national independence and unity, the disastrous defeat of the Prussians at Jena (1806) and French domination of Germany stimulated a movement for reform among members of the Prussian high bureaucracy and officer corps. To survive in a world altered by the French Revolution, Prussia would have to learn the principal lessons of the Revolution: that aroused citizens fighting for a cause make better soldiers than mercenaries and oppressed serfs and that officers selected for daring and intelligence command better than nobles possessing only a gilded birthright. The reformers believed that the elimination of social abuses would overcome defeatism and apathy and encourage Prussians to serve the state willingly and to fight bravely for national honor. A revitalized Prussia could then deal with the French.

Among the important reforms introduced in Prussia between 1807 and 1813 were the abolition of serfdom, the granting to towns of a large measure of self-administration, the awarding of army commissions on the basis of merit instead of birth, the elimination of cruel punishment in the ranks, and the establishment of national conscription. In 1813, the reform party forced King Frederick William III to declare war on France. The military reforms did improve the quality of the Prussian army. In the War of Liberation (1813), Prussian soldiers demonstrated far more enthusiasm and patriotism than they had at Jena in 1806, and the French were driven from Germany. The German War of Liberation came on the heels of Napoleon's disastrous Russian campaign.

Disaster in Russia

Deteriorating relations between Russia and France led Napoleon to his fatal decision to attack the Eastern giant. His creation of the Grand Duchy of Warsaw irritated the tsar, who feared a revival of Polish power and resented French influence on Russia's border. Another source of friction between the tsar and Napoleon was Russia's illicit trade with Britain, in violation of the Continental System. No doubt Napoleon's inexhaustible craving for power also compelled him to strike at Russia.

In June 1812, the Grand Army, 614,000 men strong, crossed the Neman River into Russia. Fighting mainly rear-guard battles and retreating according to plan, the tsar's forces lured the invaders into the vastness of Russia, far from their lines of supply. On September 14, the Grand Army, its numbers greatly reduced by disease, hunger, exhaustion, desertion, and battle, entered Moscow, which the Russians had virtually evacuated. To show their contempt for the French conquerors and to deny the French shelter, the Russians set fire to the city, which burned for five days. Taking up headquarters in Moscow, Napoleon waited for Alexander I to admit defeat and come to terms. But the tsar remained intransigent.

Napoleon was in a dilemma: to penetrate deeper into Russia was certain death; to stay in Moscow with winter approaching meant possible starvation. Faced with these alternatives, Napoleon decided to retreat westward. On October 19, 1812, ninety-five thousand troops and thousands of wagons loaded with loot left Moscow for the long trek back. In early November came the first snow and frost. Army stragglers were slaughtered by Russian Cossacks

Disaster in Russia.   Lacking winter provisions, Napoleon's Grand Army abandoned Moscow in October 1812. The retreating French were decimated by hunger, winter, and Russian attacks. (*Musée de l'Armee*)

and peasant partisans. In the middle of December, with the Russians in pursuit, the remnants of the Grand Army staggered across the Neman River into East Prussia.

Final Defeat

After the destruction of the Grand Army, the empire crumbled. Although Napoleon raised a new army, he could not replace the equipment, cavalry horses, and experienced soldiers squandered in Russia. Now he had to rely on schoolboys and overage veterans. Most of Europe joined in a final coalition against France. In October 1813, allied forces from Austria, Prussia, Russia, and Sweden defeated Napoleon at Leipzig; in November, Anglo-Spanish forces crossed the Pyrenees into France. Finally, in the spring of 1814, the allies captured Paris. Napoleon abdicated and was exiled to the tiny island of Elba, off the coast of Italy. The Bourbon dynasty was restored to the throne of France in the person of Louis XVIII, younger brother of the executed Louis XVI and the acknowledged leader of the émigrés.

Only forty-four years of age, Napoleon did not believe that it was his destiny to die on Elba. On March 1, 1815, he landed on the French coast with a thousand soldiers, and three weeks later he entered Paris to a hero's welcome. Raising a new army, Napoleon moved against the allied forces in Belgium. There, the Prussians, led by Field Marshal Gebhard von Blücher, and the

British, led by the duke of Wellington, defeated Napoleon at Waterloo in June 1815. Napoleon's desperate gamble to regain power—the famous "hundred days"—had failed. This time the allies sent Napoleon to Saint Helena, a lonely island in the South Atlantic a thousand miles off the coast of southern Africa. On this gloomy and rugged rock, Napoleon Bonaparte, emperor of France and would-be conqueror of Europe, spent the last six years of his life.

The Meaning of the French Revolution

The French Revolution was a decisive period in the shaping of the modern West. It implemented the thought of the philosophes, destroyed the hierarchical and corporate society of the Old Regime, which was a legacy of the Middle Ages, promoted the interests of the bourgeoisie, and quickened the growth of the modern state.

The French Revolution weakened the aristocracy. With their feudal rights and privileges eliminated, the nobles became simply ordinary citizens. Throughout the nineteenth century, France would be governed by both the aristocracy and the bourgeoisie; property, not noble birth, determined the composition of the new ruling elite.

The principle of careers open to talent gave the bourgeois access to the highest positions in the state. Having wealth, talent, ambition, and now opportunity, the bourgeoisie would play an ever more important role in French political life. Throughout the Continent, the reforms of the French Revolution served as a model for progressive bourgeois, who sooner or later would challenge the Old Regime in their own lands.

The French Revolution transformed the dynastic state, on which the Old Regime was based, into the modern state: national, liberal, secular, and rational. When the Declaration of the Rights of Man and of the Citizen stated that "the source of all sovereignty resides essentially in the nation," the concept of the state took on a new meaning. The state was no longer merely a territory or a federation of provinces; it was not the private possession of the king claiming to be God's lieutenant on earth. In the new conception, the state belonged to the people as a whole, and the individual, formerly a subject, was now a citizen with both rights and duties and was governed by laws that drew no distinction on the basis of birth.

The liberal thought of the Enlightenment found practical expression in the reforms of the Revolution. Absolutism and divine right of monarchy, repudiated in theory by the philosophes, were invalidated by constitutions that set limits to the powers of government and by elected parliaments that represented the governed. By providing for equality before the law and the protection of human rights—habeas corpus, trial by jury, and freedom of religion, speech, and the press—the Revolution struck at the abuses of the Old Regime. Because of violations and interruptions, these gains seemed at times more theoretical than actual. Nevertheless, these liberal ideals reverberated throughout the Continent. During the nineteenth century, the pace of reform would quicken.

By disavowing any divine justification for the monarch's power and by depriving the church of its special position, the Revolution accelerated the secularization of European political life. Sweeping aside the administrative chaos of the Old Regime, the Revolution attempted to impose rational norms on the state. The sale of public offices, which had produced ineffective and corrupt administrators, was eliminated, and the highest positions in the land were opened to men of talent, regardless of birth. The Revolution abolished the peasantry's manorial obligations, which had hampered agriculture, and swept away barriers to economic expansion. It based taxes on income and streamlined their collection. The destruction of feudal remnants, internal tolls, and the guilds speeded up the expansion of a competitive market economy. In the nineteenth century, reformers in the rest of Europe would follow the lead set by France.

By spreading revolutionary ideals and institutions, Napoleon made it impossible for the traditional rulers to restore the Old Regime intact after his downfall. The secularization of society, the transformation of the dynastic state into the modern national state, and the prominence of the bourgeoisie were assured.

The French Revolution also unleashed two potentially destructive forces identified with the modern state: total war and nationalism. These contradicted the rational and universal aims of the reformers as stated in the Declaration of the Rights of Man and of the Citizen. Whereas eighteenth-century wars were fought by professional soldiers for limited aims, the French Revolution brought conscription and the mobilization of all the state's resources for armed conflict. The world wars of the twentieth century were the terrible fulfillment of this new development in warfare. The French Revolution also gave birth to modern nationalism. During the Revolution, loyalty was directed to the entire nation, not to a village or province or to the person of the king. The whole of France became the fatherland. Under the Jacobins, the French became converts to a secular faith preaching total reverence for the nation.

The Revolution attempted to reconstruct society on the basis of Enlightenment thought. The Declaration of the Rights of Man, whose spirit permeated the reforms of the Revolution, upheld the dignity of the individual, demanded respect for the individual, attributed to each person natural rights, and barred the state from denying those rights. It insisted that society and the state have no higher duty than to promote the freedom and autonomy of the individual. The tragedy of the Western experience is that this humanist vision, brilliantly expressed by the Enlightenment and given recognition in the reforms of the French Revolution, would be undermined in later generations. Ironically, by spawning total war, nationalism, terror as government policy, and a revolutionary mentality that sought to change the world through coercion and violence, the French Revolution itself contributed to the shattering of this vision.

Notes

1. George Rudé, *Revolutionary Europe, 1783–1815* (New York: Harper Torchbooks, 1966), p. 74.
2. Henri Peyre, "The Influence of Eighteenth-Century Ideas on the French Revolution," *Journal of the History of Ideas,* 10 (1949):73.
3. George Lefebvre, *The French Revolution from 1793 to 1799,* trans. John Hall Stewart and James Friguglietti (New York: Columbia University Press, 1964) 2:360.
4. Quoted in T. C. W. Blanning, *The French Revolution: Aristocrats Versus Bourgeois?* (Atlantic Highlands, N.J.: Humanities Press, 1987), p. 9.
5. William Doyle, *Origins of the French Revolution* (London: Oxford University Press, 1980), p. 21.
6. Excerpted in John Hall Stewart, ed., *A Documentary Survey of the French Revolution* (New York: Macmillan, 1951), pp. 43–44.
7. Albert Soboul, *The Parisian Sans-Culottes and the French Revolution, 1793–94,* trans. Gwynne Lewis (London: Oxford University Press, 1964), pp. 28–29.
8. Excerpted in George Rudé, ed., *Robespierre* (Englewood Cliffs, N.J.: Prentice-Hall, 1976), p. 57.

Suggested Reading

Blanning, T. C. W., *The French Revolution: Aristocrats Versus Bourgeois?* (1987). Summarizes recent scholarship on the question; a volume in Studies of European History series.

Chandler, David, *The Campaigns of Napoleon* (1966). An exhaustive analysis of Napoleon's art of war.

Connelley, Owen, *Napoleon's Satellite Kingdoms* (1965). Focuses on the kingdoms in Naples, Italy, Holland, Spain, and Westphalia, which were created by Napoleon and ruled by his relatives.

Cronin, Vincent, *Napoleon Bonaparte* (1972). A highly acclaimed biography.

Doyle, William, *Origins of the French Revolution* (1980). In recent decades, several historians have challenged the traditional view that the French Revolution was an attempt by the bourgeoisie to overthrow the remnants of aristocratic power and privilege and that it was a victory of a capitalist bourgeois order over feudalism. This book summarizes the new scholarship and argues that the nobility and bourgeoisie had much in common before the Revolution.

Forrest, Alan, *The French Revolution* (1995). Social, political, and ideological changes wrought by the Revolution.

Furet, François, and Mona Ozouf, eds., *A Critical Dictionary of the French Revolution* (1989). Articles on many topics; highly recommended.

Gershoy, Leo, *The Era of the French Revolution* (1957). A brief survey, with useful documents.

Gottschalk, Louis, and Donald Lach, *Toward the French Revolution* (1973). A survey of the eighteenth-century background of the French Revolution.

Herold, J. Christopher, ed., *The Mind of Napoleon* (1955). A valuable selection from the written and spoken words of Napoleon.

———, *The Horizon Book of the Age of Napoleon* (1965). Napoleon and his time.

Higgins, E. L., ed., *The French Revolution* (1938). Excerpts from contemporaries.

Holtman, Robert B., *The Napoleonic Revolution* (1967). A portrait of Napoleon as revolutionary innovator who influenced every aspect of European life; particularly good on Napoleon the propagandist.

Lefebvre, Georges, *The French*

Revolution, 2 vols. (1962, 1964). A detailed analysis by a master historian.

———, *The Coming of the French Revolution* (1967). A brilliant analysis of the social structure of the Old Regime and the opening phase of the Revolution.

Markham, Felix, *Napoleon* (1963). A first-rate short biography.

———, *Napoleon and the Awakening of Europe* (1965). An exploration of Napoleon's influence on other lands.

Palmer, R. R., *The Age of the Democratic Revolution,* 2 vols. (1959, 1964). The French Revolution as part of a revolutionary movement that spread on both sides of the Atlantic.

———, *Twelve Who Ruled* (1965). An admirable treatment of the Terror.

Rudé, George, *The Crowd in the French Revolution* (1959). An analysis of the composition of the crowds that stormed the Bastille, marched to Versailles, and attacked the king's palace.

———, *Robespierre: Portrait of a Revolutionary Democrat* (1976). A biography of the revolutionary leader.

Stewart, J. H., *A Documentary Survey of the French Revolution* (1951). A valuable collection of documents.

Sutherland, D. M. G., *France 1789–1815* (1986). Like Doyle, Sutherland departs from the classic theory of the bourgeois revolution.

Review Questions

1. Analyze the causes of the French Revolution.
2. Identify and explain the significance of the following: the formation of the National Assembly, the storming of the Bastille, the Great Fear, and the October Days.
3. Analyze the nature and significance of the reforms of the National Assembly.
4. What were the grievances of the sans-culottes?
5. What were the accomplishments of the Jacobins?
6. Describe Robespierre's basic philosophy.
7. Napoleon both preserved and destroyed the ideals of the French Revolution. Discuss this statement.
8. Account for Napoleon's downfall. What were Napoleon's greatest achievements? What were his greatest failures?
9. Why was the era of the French Revolution a decisive period in the shaping of the West?

❖ CHAPTER 12

The Industrial Revolution: The Transformation of Society

*I*n the last part of the eighteenth century, as a revolution for liberty and equality swept across France and sent shock waves through Europe, a different kind of revolution, a revolution in industry, was transforming life in Great Britain. In the nineteenth century, the Industrial Revolution spread to the United States and to the European continent. Today, it encompasses virtually the entire world; everywhere the drive to substitute machines for human labor continues at a rapid pace.

After 1760, dramatic changes occurred in Britain in the way goods were produced and labor organized. New forms of power, particularly steam, replaced animal strength and human muscle. Better ways of obtaining and using raw materials were discovered, and a new form of organizing production and workers—the factory—came into use. In the nineteenth century, technology moved from triumph to triumph with a momentum unprecedented in human history. The resulting explosion in economic production and productivity transformed society with breathtaking speed. ❖

The Rise of the Industrial Age

The process of industrialization began in western Europe for a number of reasons. Western Europe was wealthier than much of the world, and its wealth was spread across more classes of people. Contributing to the accumulation of capital was the rapid expansion of trade, both overseas and on the Continent, during the sixteenth and seventeenth centuries (the commercial revolution). This expansion resulted from an aggressive search for new markets and tapped the wealth of a much larger area of the world than the Mediterranean lands accessible to earlier generations. Thus, the resources, both human and material, of the New World and of Africa fueled Europe's accumulation of wealth.

Engaged in fierce military and commercial rivalries, early modern states, with varying degrees of success, actively promoted industries to manufacture weaponry, uniforms, and ships; they also encouraged commerce for the sake

---

Chronology 12.1 ❖ The Industrial Revolution

1764–1767	Hargreaves invents the spinning jenny
1769	Watt invents modern steam engine
1785	Cartwright develops power loom
1825	Workers are allowed to unionize but not to strike
1830	First railway line is built in England
1832	Reform Bill of 1832 expands British voting rights

---

of tax revenues. The ensuing growth in commerce nurtured a greatly expanded economy, in which many levels of society participated: owners of large estates, merchant princes, innovative entrepreneurs, sugar plantation colonials, slave traders, sailors, and peasants.

The rise in population and agricultural productivity also helped to spur industrialization. The enormous European population growth of the eighteenth century provided industry with both consumers and labor. The population expanded rapidly partly because the number of deaths from war, famine, and disease declined. More efficient agriculture and better food distribution reduced malnutrition, which meant better health, more births, and fewer deaths. Developments in agriculture contributed greatly to the coming of the industrial age in Europe. Over the centuries, the decline of serfdom and manorial obligations and the increasing efficiency of agriculture freed people for new forms of labor. By the eighteenth century, traditional patterns of farming were breaking up in western Europe. Agriculture became more and more a capitalist enterprise; production was undertaken for the market, not for family or village consumption.

Land formerly used in common by villagers for grazing animals was claimed as private property, generally by great landowners, whose political power gave them an advantage. This process of enclosure, or fencing off formerly communal land for private use, took place over much of Europe. Once the peasants were gone, landlords could bring these lands under cultivation and produce a surplus for the marketplace. Consequently, land use grew more efficient. Through convertible husbandry, which cycled land from grain production through soil-restoring crops of legumes and then pasturage, farmers could keep cultivating all their fields, rather than leave some fallow, as had been the practice for centuries.

Finally, two European cultural traditions played crucial roles in the rise of industrialism. One was individualism, which had its roots in both the Renaissance and the Reformation; during the era of the commercial revolution, it manifested itself in hard-driving, ambitious merchants and bankers. This spirit of individualism, combined with the wide latitude states gave to private

The Agricultural Revolution: The McCormick Reaper.   Harvesting grain by machine released great numbers of laborers from farms to labor in factories and cities. The great demand for labor may explain, in part, the constant search for and investment in mechanical devices for farm and factory in America, a major food exporter even today. (*State Historical Society of Wisconsin*)

economic activity, fostered the development of dynamic capitalist entrepreneurs. The second cultural tradition promoting industrialization was the high value westerners placed on the rational understanding and control of nature. Both individualism and the tradition of reason, concludes historian David S. Landes, "gave Europe a tremendous advantage in the invention and adoption of new technology. The will to mastery, the rational approach to problems that we call scientific method, the competition for wealth and power—together these broke down the resistance of inherited ways and made change a positive good."[1]

Britain First

Britain possessed several advantages that enabled it to take the lead. Large and easily developed supplies of coal and iron had given the British a long tradition of metallurgy and mining. In the early stages of industrialization, Britain's river transportation system was supplemented by canals and toll roads (turnpikes), which private entrepreneurs financed and built for profit. In addition, Britain had a labor pool of farmers who could no longer earn a living on the land for themselves and their families.

Britain also had capital available for investment in new industries. These funds came from wealthy landowners and merchants who had grown rich through commerce, including the slave trade. Interest rates on loans fell in the eighteenth century, stimulating investment. Britain's expanding middle class provided a home market for emerging industries. So, too, did its overseas colonies, which also supplied raw materials—particularly cotton, needed for the developing textile industry. A vigorous spirit of enterprise and the opportunity for men of ability to rise from common origins to riches and fame also help explain the growth of industrialization.

Changes in Technology

The Cotton Industry   Long the home of an important wool trade, Britain in the eighteenth century jumped ahead in the production of cotton, the industry that first showed the possibility of unprecedented growth rates. British cotton production expanded tenfold between 1760 and 1785, and another tenfold between 1785 and 1825. A series of inventions revolutionized the industry and drastically altered the social conditions of the work.

In 1733, long before expansion started, a simple invention—John Kay's flying shuttle—made it possible for weavers to double their output. The flying shuttle enabled weavers to produce faster than spinners could spin—until James Hargreaves's spinning jenny, perfected by 1768, allowed an operator to work several spindles at once, powered only by human energy. Within five years, Richard Arkwright's water frame spinning machine could be powered by water or animals, and Samuel Crompton's spinning mule (1779) powered many spindles, first by human and later by animal and water energy. These changes improved spinning productivity so much that it caused bottlenecks in weaving, until Edmund Cartwright developed a power loom in 1785.* To the end of the century, there was a race to speed up the spinning part of the process and then the weaving part by applying water power to looms or new, larger devices to the jenny.

Arkwright's water frame made it more efficient to bring many workers together, rather than sending work out to individuals in their own homes. This development was the beginning of the factory system, which within a generation would revolutionize the conditions of labor. Because water power drove these early machines, mills were located near rivers and streams. Towns thus grew up where machinery could be powered by water; the factory system concentrated laborers and their families near the factories.

The Steam Engine   James Watt, a Scottish engineer, developed the steam engine in the 1760s. Because steam engines ran on coal or wood, not water power, they allowed greater flexibility in locating textile mills. Factories were

---

*Technological developments in America helped to meet the growing demand for raw cotton. Eli Whitney's cotton gin (1793) removed the seeds from raw cotton quickly and cheaply, leading farmers and plantation owners to devote more land to cotton. Within a generation, more laborers were required for the fields and fewer to process the cotton. The increased demand for slave labor brought far-reaching repercussions.

Woman at Hargreaves's Spinning Jenny.   The cotton textile trade was one of the first to be mechanized. In cottage industries, the whole family contributed to the thread and cloth. Many early inventions were made by the workers themselves, such as Hargreaves's adjustment of his wife's thread-spinning tool. (*Mary Evans Picture Library*)

no longer restricted to the power supplied by a river or a stream or to the space available beside flowing water; they could be built anywhere. With steam, the whole pattern of work changed because weaker, younger, and less skilled workers could be taught the few simple tasks necessary to mind the machine. The shift from male to female and child labor was a major social change.

The Iron Industry   Although steam power allowed employers to hire weaker people to operate machinery, it required machines made of stronger metal to withstand the forces generated by a stronger power source. By the 1780s, trial and error had perfected the production of wrought iron, which became the most widely used metal until steel began to be cheaply produced in the 1860s.

The iron industry made great demands on the coal mines to fuel its furnaces. Because steam engines enabled miners to pump water from the mines more efficiently and at a much deeper level, rich veins in existing mines became accessible for the first time. The greater productivity in coal allowed the continued improvement of iron smelting. Then, in 1856, Henry Bessemer developed a process for converting pig iron into steel by speedily removing the impurities in the iron. In the 1860s, William Siemens and the brothers Pierre

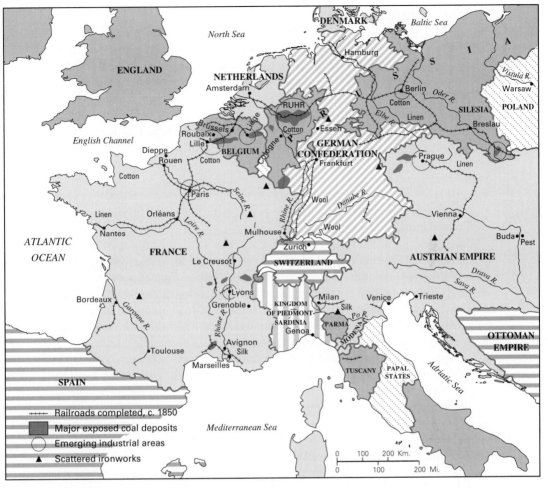

Map 12.1   Industrial Growth on the Continent, Mid-1800s

and Émile Martin developed the open-hearth process, which could handle much greater amounts of metal than Bessemer's converter. Steel became so cheap to produce that it quickly replaced iron in industry because of its greater tensile strength and durability.

Transportation   The steam engine and iron and steel brought a new era in transport. As machines speeded up factory production, methods of transportation also improved. In 1830, the first railway line was built in England, connecting Manchester and Liverpool; this sparked an age of railway building throughout much of the world. Shipping changed radically with the use of vessels without sails, which had greater tonnage capacity.

Society Transformed

The innovations in agricultural production, business organization, and technology had revolutionary consequences for society, economics, and politics. People were drawn from the countryside into cities, and traditional ways of life changed. Much of the old life persisted, however, particularly during the first half of the nineteenth century. Landed property was still the principal form of wealth, and large landowners continued to exercise political power. From England to Russia, families of landed wealth (often the old noble families) still constituted the social elite. European society remained overwhelmingly rural; as late as the midcentury, only England was half urban. Nevertheless, contemporaries were so overwhelmed by industrialization that they saw it as a sudden and complete break with the past: the shattering of traditional moral and social patterns.

Cities grew in number, size, and population as a result of industrialization. For example, between 1801 and 1851, the population of Birmingham rose from 73,000 to 250,000 and that of Liverpool from 77,000 to 400,000. Industrial cities expanded rapidly, without planning or much regulation by local or national government. So much growth with so little planning or control led to cities with little sanitation, no lighting, wretched housing, poor transportation, and little security.

Rich and poor alike suffered in this environment of disease, crime, and ugliness, although the poor obviously bore the brunt of these evils. They lived in houses located as close to the factories as possible. The houses were several stories high and built so close to each other that only courtyards separated them. Sometimes, a whole family huddled together in one room or even shared a room with another family. Open sewers, polluted rivers, factory smoke, and filthy streets allowed disease to spread. In Britain, about twenty-six out of every one hundred children died before the age of five. Almost universally, those who wrote about industrial cities—England's Manchester, Leeds, and Liverpool, and France's Lyons—described the stench, the filth, the inhumane crowding, the poverty, and the immorality.

Changes in Social Structure

The Industrial Revolution destroyed forever the old division of society into clergy, nobility, and commoners. The development of industry and commerce caused a corresponding development of a bourgeoisie: a middle class, comprising people of common birth who engaged in trade and other capitalist ventures. The wealthiest bourgeois were bankers, factory and mine owners, and merchants, but the middle class also included shopkeepers, managers, lawyers, and doctors. The virtues of work, thrift, ambition, and prudence characterized the middle class as a whole, as did the perversion of these virtues into materialism, selfishness, callousness, harsh individualism, and smugness.

Urbanization: View of Sheffield by William Ibbit, 1815. Unlike Manchester, which was a new factory town, springing up from the fields without plan or government at first, Sheffield was an old cutlery manufacturing center which expanded enormously when the introduction of mass production technology brought a new wave of workers. (*Sheffield City Museum*)

From the eighteenth century on, as industry and commerce developed, the middle class grew in size, first in England and then throughout western Europe. During the eighteenth and nineteenth centuries, the middle class struggled against the entrenched aristocracy to end political, economic, and social discrimination. By the end of the nineteenth century, bourgeois politicians held the highest offices in much of western Europe and shared authority with aristocrats, whose birth no longer guaranteed them the only political and social power in the nation. As industrial wealth grew more important, the middle class became more influential. Its wealthy members also tended to imitate the aristocracy: it was common throughout Europe for rich bourgeois to spend fortunes buying great estates and emulating aristocratic manners and pleasures. Likewise, the middle class valued respectability. In these and many other ways, the bourgeois copied the aristocracy for most of the century.

Industrialization may have reduced some barriers between the landed elites and the middle class, but it sharpened the distinctions between the middle class and the laboring class. Like the middle class, the proletariat encompassed different economic levels: rural laborers, miners, and city workers. Many gradations existed among city workers, from artisans to factory workers and servants. Factory workers were the newest and most rapidly growing social group; at midcentury, however, they did not constitute most of laboring people in any major city. For example, as late as 1890, they made up only one-sixth of London's population.

The artisans were the largest group of workers in the cities for the first half of the nineteenth century, and in some places for much longer than that. They worked in construction, printing, small tailoring or dressmaking establishments, food preparation and processing, and crafts producing such luxury items as furniture, jewelry, lace, and velvet. Artisans were distinct from factory workers; their technical skills were difficult to learn, and traditionally their crafts were acquired in guilds, which still functioned as both social and economic organizations. Artisans were usually educated (they could read and write), lived in one city or village for generations, and maintained stable families, often securing places for their children in their craft. As the Industrial Revolution progressed, however, they found it hard to compete with cheap, factory-produced goods, and their livelihoods were threatened.

Servants were especially numerous in capital cities. In the first half of the nineteenth century, in cities like Paris and London, where the number of factories was not great, there were more servants than factory workers. Servants usually had some education. If they married and had a family, they taught their children to read and write and sometimes to observe the manners and values of the household in which the parent had worked. Many historians believe that these servants passed on to their children their own deference to authority and their aspirations to bourgeois status, which may have limited social discontent and radical political activity.

Working-Class Life

Life was not easy for those whose labor contributed to the industrializing process. Usually, factory workers were recent arrivals from agricultural areas, where they had been driven off the land. They frequently moved to the city without their families, leaving them behind until they could afford to support them in town. These people entered rapidly growing industries, where long hours—sometimes fifteen a day—were not unusual. Farming had meant long hours, too, as had the various forms of labor for piecework rates in the home, but the pace of the machine, the dull routine, and dangerous conditions in factories and mines made work even more oppressive. Miners, for example, labored under the hazards of cave-ins, explosions, and deadly gas fumes. Deep beneath the earth's surface, life was dark, cold, wet, and tenuous. Their bodies stunted and twisted, their lungs wrecked, miners toiled their lives away in "the pits."

Sometimes, compared with their lives in the country, the workers' standard of living rose, particularly if they were part of a whole family that found work; the pay for a family might be better than they could have earned for agricultural labor. But working conditions were terrible, as were living conditions. The factories were dirty, hot, unventilated, and frequently dangerous. Workers toiled long hours, were fined for mistakes and even for accidents, were fired at the will of the employer or foreman, and suffered from job insecurity. They often lived in overcrowded and dirty housing. If they were unmarried or had left their family in the country, they often lived in barracks

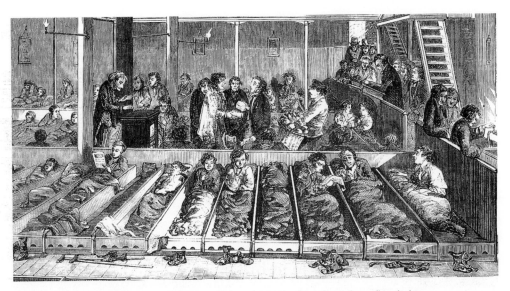

Engraving from the *Illustrated Times*, 1859.   As unemployed workers flooded into the great cities of Europe, homelessness became a pressing social problem. Here to keep dry and warm, homeless men sleep in coffins for the living in a factory or prison-like building. These facilities were charitable institutions—not the poor-law workhouses—but they too reflected the common morality of the day that poverty was the fault of the poor, who should learn to help themselves. (*Mansell Collection*)

with other members of their sex. If they lost their jobs, they also lost their shelter.

In the villages they had left, they had been poor but were socially connected to family, church, and even to local landlords. But in the cities, factory workers labored in plants with twenty to a hundred workers and had little contact with their employers. Instead, they were pushed by foremen to work hard and efficiently for long hours to keep up with the machines. Workers had little time on the job to socialize with others; they were fined for talking to one another, for lateness, and for many petty infringements. They often became competitors in order to keep their jobs. Lacking organization, a sense of comradeship, education, and experience of city life, factory workers found little comfort when times were bad.

Workers often developed a life around the pub, the café, or some similar gathering place, where there were drinks and games and the gossip and news of the day. On Sundays, their one day off, workers drank and danced; absenteeism was so great on Monday that the day was called "holy Monday." Gin drinking was denounced on all sides; workers and reformers alike urged temperance. Many workers played sports, and some social organizations grew up around their sporting games. In these and other ways, workers developed a culture of their own—a culture that was misunderstood and often deplored by middle-class reformers.

Many contemporaries felt that the poor—those who were so unfortunate that they needed the assistance of others—were growing in numbers, that their condition was woeful, and that it had actually deteriorated in the midst of increased wealth. If machines could produce so much wealth and so many products, then why, social observers wondered, were there so many poor people? Parliamentary reports and investigations of civic-minded citizens documented the suffering for all to read.

Historians still debate how bad workers' conditions were in the early stages of industrialization. Most workers experienced periods of acute distress, but historians generally conclude that the standard of living slowly improved during the eighteenth and nineteenth centuries. Although historians take an optimistic view of the long-range effects of industrialization, the rapidity of change wreaked great hardships on the workers of all countries, who endured cruel conditions in factories and slums.

The Rise of Reform in Britain

Although it was the freest state in Europe in the early decades of the nineteenth century, Britain was far from democratic. A constitutional monarchy, with many limits on the powers of king and state, Britain was nonetheless dominated by aristocrats. Landed aristocrats controlled both the House of Lords and the House of Commons—the House of Lords because they constituted its membership and the House of Commons because they patronized or sponsored men favorable to their interests. The vast majority of people, from the middle class as well as from the working class, could not vote. Many towns continued to be governed by corrupt groups. New industrial towns were not allowed to elect representatives to Parliament; often lacking a town organization, they could not even govern themselves effectively.

The social separation of noble and commoner was not as rigid in Britain as on the Continent. Younger sons of aristocrats did not inherit titles and were therefore obliged to make careers in law, business, the military, and the church. The upper and middle classes mingled much more freely than on the Continent, and the wealthiest merchants tended to buy lands, titles, and husbands for their daughters. However, Parliament, the courts, local government, the established Anglican church, and the monarch were all part of a social and political system dominated by aristocratic interests and values. This domination persisted despite the vast changes in social and economic structure that had taken place in the process of industrialization during the second half of the eighteenth century.

Some members of Parliament urged timely reforms. In 1828, Parliament repealed a seventeenth-century act that in effect barred Nonconformists (non-Anglican Protestants) from government positions and from universities; the following year, Catholics gained the right to sit in Parliament. In 1833, slavery was abolished within the British Empire. (The British slave trade had been abolished earlier.) The Municipal Corporations Act (1835) granted towns and cities greater authority over their affairs. This measure created town and city governments that could, if they wished, begin to solve some problems of urbanization and industrialization. These municipal corporations could institute reforms such as sanitation, which Parliament encouraged by passing the first Public Health Act in 1848.

Increasingly, reform centered on extending suffrage and enfranchising the new industrial towns. Middle-class men, and even workers, hoped to gain the right to vote. Because of population shifts, some sparsely populated regions—called rotten boroughs—sent representatives to the House of Commons, while many densely populated factory towns had little or no representation. Often a single important landowner controlled many seats in the Commons. Voting was public, which allowed intimidation, and candidates frequently tried to influence voters with drinks, food, and even money.

Intense and bitter feelings built up during the campaign for the Reform Bill of 1832. The House of Commons passed the bill to extend the suffrage by some 200,000, almost double the number who were then entitled to vote. The House of Lords, however, refused to pass the bill. There were riots and strikes in many cities, and mass meetings, both of workers and of middle-class people, took place all over the country. King William IV (1830–1837) became convinced, along with many politicians, that the situation was potentially revolutionary. To defuse it, he threatened to increase the number of the bill's supporters in the House of Lords by creating new peers. This threat brought reluctant peers into line, and the bill was passed. The Reform Act of 1832 extended the suffrage to the middle class and made the House of Commons more representative. The rotten boroughs lost their seats, which were granted to towns. However, because there were high property qualifications, workers did not gain the right to vote.

Workers did obtain some relief when humanitarians pressured Parliament to pass the Factory Act (1833), which legislated that no child under thirteen could work more than nine hours a day and that no one aged thirteen to eighteen could work more than sixty-nine hours a week. The act also provided some inspectors to investigate infractions and punish offenders. That same year, Parliament also banned children under ten from the mines. The Factory Act of 1847 stipulated that boys under eighteen and women could work no more than ten hours a day in factories. At first, workers resented the prohibition of child labor since their family income would be greatly reduced if their children could not work, but they gradually came to approve of this law. The ten-hour day for adult male workers was not enacted until 1874.

The Chartist reform movement, whose adherents came from the ranks of both intellectual radicals and workers, pressed for political, not economic, reforms. During the 1830s and 1840s, the Chartists agitated for democratic measures, such as universal manhood suffrage, the secret ballot, salaries and the abolition of property qualifications for members of Parliament, and annual meetings of Parliament. The Chartist platform remained the democratic

Cartoon Showing the Controversy Surrounding Grey's Reform Act.   Depicted here are supporters of the Reform Bill of 1832, hacking away at the rotten system. On the right, opponents of reform seek to preserve the status quo. (*Hulton Deutsch Collection*)

reform program for the rest of the century, long after the death of Chartism itself at midcentury. All of the Chartists' demands, except for annual elections for members of Parliament, were eventually realized.

The last political effort by the Chartists was led by Feargus O'Connor, a charismatic Irishman, who organized a mass demonstration to present a huge petition of its demands to Parliament in 1848. The cabinet ignored the great "People's Charter," which had signatures of at least two million names. The movement died out just as most of Europe burst into revolution. The working-class leadership of Chartism turned away from political programs almost exclusively to economic activity, such as trade unions, which could bring immediate benefits to workers.

At the beginning of the nineteenth century, elementary education in Britain was managed by private individuals and church organizations. Schools were financed by contributions, grants, and fees paid by students. The government neither financed nor promoted education. As a result, very few poor children attended school. Indeed, many government officials feared that educating the poor would incite unrest. If the lower classes read publications attacking Christianity and challenging authority, they would become insolent to their superiors. One member of Parliament declared that schooling would teach the poor "to despise their lot in life, instead of making them good servants in agriculture and other laborious employments to which their rank in society had destined them." However, many Britons, inheriting the Enlightenment's confidence in education, favored schooling for the poor. In 1833, Parliament began to allocate small sums for elementary education. These funds were inadequate; in 1869, only about half of all children of school age attended school. The Education Act of 1870 gave local governments the power to establish elementary schools. By 1891, these schools were free and attendance was required.

Many workers and radicals believed that the only hope for their class lay in unified action through trade unions. At first, Parliament fought the unions, passing the Combination Acts (1799–1800), which made unions illegal. In 1825, Parliament allowed workers to unionize but forbade them to strike. Unions made some headway in protecting their members from unemployment and dangerous working conditions, but strikes (which remained officially illegal until 1875) were rarely successful and were often suppressed by force.

Unlike the Continental states, England avoided revolution. British politicians thought that it was because they had made timely reforms in the 1830s and 1840s. This belief itself became a force in political life. Whenever times were hard, there were always political leaders who would say that the remedy was reform and that reform would prevent revolution. The political experience of the first half of the nineteenth century laid the foundation for British parliamentary practices, which came to be the model of liberal, progressive, and stable politics. Britain was the symbol for all those who argued for reform rather than revolution. In the rest of Europe in 1848, however, such arguments were meeting with little success.

Responses to Industrialization

The problems created by rapid industrialization profoundly influenced political and social thought. Liberalism, which began as an attempt to safeguard individual rights from oppressive state authority, now had to confront an unanticipated problem: the distress caused by rapid industrialization and urbanization. Also responding to this ordeal was a new group of thinkers, called socialists.

Liberalism*

Adopting the laissez-faire theory of Adam Smith, liberals maintained that a free economy, in which private enterprise would be unimpeded by government regulations, was as important as political freedom to the well-being of the individual and the community. When people acted from self-interest, liberals said, they worked harder and achieved more; self-interest and natural competitive impulses spurred economic activity and ensured the production of more and better goods at the lowest possible price, benefiting the entire

*See also Chapter 13.

nation. For this reason, the government must neither block free competition nor deprive individuals of their property, which was their incentive to work hard and efficiently.

Convinced that individuals were responsible for their own misfortunes, liberals were often unmoved by the misery of the poor. Indeed, they used the principle of laissez faire—that government should not interfere with the natural laws of supply and demand—to justify their opposition to humanitarian legislation intended to alleviate the misery of the factory workers. Liberals regarded such social reforms as unwarranted and dangerous meddling with the natural law of supply and demand.

They drew comfort from the theory advanced by Thomas Malthus (1766–1834) in his *Essay on the Principle of Population* (1798), which supported laissez-faire economics. Malthus asserted that population always grows at a faster rate than the food supply; consequently, government programs to aid the poor and provide higher wages would only encourage larger families and thus perpetuate poverty. Malthus seemed to supply "scientific" justification for opposing state action to help the poor. Poverty, argued Malthusians, was not the fault of factory owners. It was an iron law of nature—the result of population pressure on resources—and could not be eliminated by state policies. According to Malthus, the state could not ameliorate the poor's misery; "the means of redress," he said, "are in their own hands, and in the hands of no other persons whatever." This "means of redress" would be a lowering of the birthrate through late marriages and chastity, but Malthus believed that the poor lacked the self-discipline to refrain from sexual activity. When they receive higher wages, they have more children, thereby upsetting the population-resource balance and bringing misery to themselves and others.

A fellow economist, David Ricardo (1772–1823), gave support to Malthus's gloomy outlook. Wages, he said, tended to remain at the minimum needed to maintain workers. Higher wages encouraged workers to have more children, causing an increase in the labor supply, and greater competition for jobs would then force down wages. Ricardo's disciples made his law inflexible. This "iron law of wages" meant bleak prospects for the working poor. Many workers felt that the new science of economics offered them little hope. They argued that the liberals were concerned only with their class and national interests and that they were callous and apathetic toward the sufferings of the poor.

Liberals of the early nineteenth century saw poverty and suffering as part of the natural order and beyond the scope of government. They feared that state intervention in the economy to redress social ills would disrupt the free market, threatening personal liberty and hindering social well-being. In time, however, the liberals modified their position. First, they supported government action to provide education or opportunity for all, and then they accepted the principle of state aid to the poor. They came to believe that justice required some protection against the economy's ravages for those who were powerless. Reform, they concluded, was possible without losing the advantages of capitalism or sacrificing personal liberty.

Early Socialism

The socialists went further than the liberals. They argued that the liberals' concern for individual freedom and equality had little impact on the poverty, oppression, and gross inequality of wealth plaguing modern society. Liberal ideals, socialists claimed, protected the person and property of the wealthy while the majority were mired in poverty and helplessness. Asserting that the liberals' doctrine of individualism degenerated into selfish egoism, which harmed community life, socialists demanded the creation of a new society, based on cooperation rather than competition. Reflecting the spirit of the Enlightenment and the French Revolution, socialists, like liberals, denounced the status quo for perpetuating injustice and held that people could create a better world. Like liberals, too, they placed the highest value on a rational analysis of society and on transforming society in line with scientifically valid premises, whose truth rational people could grasp. Socialists believed that they had discerned a pattern in human society, which, if properly understood and acted upon, would lead men and women to an earthly salvation. Thus, socialists were also romantics, for they dreamed of a new social order, a future utopia, where each individual could find happiness and fulfillment.

Saint-Simon   Henri Comte de Saint-Simon (1760–1825) renounced his title during the French Revolution and enthusiastically preached the opportunity for a new society. His mission, he believed, was to set society right by instilling an understanding of the new age that science and industry were shaping. He argued that just as Christianity had provided social unity and stability during the Middle Ages, so scientific knowledge would bind the society of his time. The scientists, industrialists, bankers, artists, and writers would replace the clergy and the aristocracy as the social elite and harness technology for the betterment of humanity. Saint-Simon's disciples championed efforts to build great railway and canal systems, including the Suez and Panama Canals. His vision of a scientifically organized society led by trained experts was a powerful force among intellectuals in the nineteenth century and is very much alive today among those who believe in a technocratic society.

Fourier   Another early French socialist, Charles Fourier (1772–1837), believed—like the romantics—that society conflicted with the natural needs of human beings and that this tension was responsible for human misery. Only the reorganization of society so that it would satisfy people's desire for pleasure and contentment would end that misery. Whereas Saint-Simon and his followers had elaborate plans to reorganize society on the grand scale of large industries and giant railway and canal systems, Fourier sought to create small communities to let men and women enjoy life's simple pleasures.

These communities of about sixteen hundred people, called *phalansteries,* would be organized according to the unchanging needs of human nature. All the people would work at tasks that interested them and would produce things that brought them and others pleasure. Like Adam Smith, Fourier understood that specialization bred boredom and alienation from work and

Saint-Simonian Community at Ménilmontant.   Followers of Saint-Simon established this community in a suburb of Paris. It was headed by Father Enfantin, whose iconoclastic theories of love and marriage outraged many people. (*Bibliothèque Nationale, Paris*)

life. Unlike Smith, he did not believe that vastly increased productivity compensated for the evils of specialization. In the phalansteries, money and goods would not be equally distributed; those with special skills and responsibilities would be rewarded accordingly. This system of rewards conformed to nature because people have a natural desire to be rewarded.

Fourier thought that marriage distorted the natures of both men and women since monogamy restricted their sexual needs and narrowed the scope of their lives to just the family. Instead, people should think of themselves as part of the family of all humanity. Because married women had to devote all their strength and time to household and children, they had no time or energy left to enjoy life's pleasures. Fourier did not call for the abolition of the family, but he did hope that it would disappear of its own accord as society adjusted to his theories. Men and women would find new ways of fulfilling themselves sexually, and the community would be organized so that it could care for the children. Fourier's ideas found some acceptance in the United States, where in the 1840s at least twenty-nine communities were founded on Fourierist principles. None, however, lasted more than five or six years.

Owen   In 1799, Robert Owen (1771–1858) became part owner and manager of the New Lanark cotton mills in Scotland. Distressed by the widespread mistreatment of workers, Owen resolved to improve the lives of his employees and show that it was possible to do so without destroying profits. He raised wages, upgraded working conditions, refused to hire children under ten, and provided workers with neat homes, food, and clothing, all at reasonable prices. He set up schools for children and for adults. In every way, he demonstrated his belief that healthier, happier workers produced more than the less fortunate ones. Like Saint-Simon, Owen believed that industry and technology could and would enrich humankind, if organized according to the proper principles. Visitors came from all over Europe to see Owen's factories.

Just like many philosophes, Owen was convinced that the environment was the principal shaper of character—that the ignorance, alcoholism, and crime of the poor derived from bad living conditions. Public education and factory reform, said Owen, would make better citizens of the poor. Owen came to believe that the entire social and economic order must be replaced by a new system, based on harmonious group living rather than on competition. He established a model community at New Harmony, Indiana, but it was short-lived.

Industrialism in Perspective

Like the French Revolution, the Industrial Revolution helped to modernize Europe. Eventually, it transformed every facet of society. In preindustrial society—Europe in the mid-eighteenth century—agriculture was the dominant economic activity and peasants were the most numerous class. Peasant life centered on the family and the village, which country folk rarely left. The new rational and critical spirit associated with the Enlightenment hardly penetrated rural Europe; there, religious faith, clerical authority, and ancient superstition remained firmly entrenched.

The richest and most powerful class was the aristocracy, whose wealth stemmed from land. Nobles dominated the countryside and enjoyed privileges protected by custom and law. Eighteenth-century aristocrats, like their medieval forebears, viewed society as a hierarchy, in which a person's position in life was determined by his or her inherited status. By championing the ideals of liberty and equality, the French Revolution undermined the traditional power structure: king, aristocracy, and clergy. By advocating the rational and secular outlook of the Enlightenment, the French reformers further dismantled the religious and political pillars of traditional society.

Traditional society was predominantly rural. By the start of the nineteenth century, 20 percent of the population of Britain, France, and Holland lived in cities; in Russia, the figure was only 5 percent. Artisan manufacturing in small shops and trade for local markets were the foundations of the urban economy, although some cities did produce luxury goods for wider markets. Textile manufacturing was conducted through the putting-out system, in which wool was turned into cloth in private dwellings, usually the homes of peasants.

The Industrial Revolution transformed all areas of society. Eventually, agricultural villages and handicraft manufacturing were eclipsed in importance by cities and factories. In the society fashioned by industrialization and urbanization, aristocratic power and values declined; at the same time, the bourgeoisie increased in number, wealth, importance, and power. More and more, a person was judged by talent rather than by birth, and opportunities for upward social mobility expanded. The Industrial Revolution became a great force for democratization: during the nineteenth century, first the middle class and then the working class gained the vote. The Industrial Revolution also hastened the secularization of European life. In the cities, former villagers, separated from traditional communal ties, drifted away from their ancestral religion. In a world being reshaped by technology, industry, and science, Christian mysteries lost their force, and for many, salvation became a remote concern. Modernization did not proceed everywhere at the same pace and with the same thoroughness. Generally, premodern social and institutional forms remained deeply entrenched in eastern and southern Europe, persisting well into the twentieth century.

Although the Industrial Revolution created many problems, some of which still endure, it was a great triumph. Ultimately, it made possible the highest standard of living in human history and created new opportunities for social advancement, political participation, and educational and cultural development. It also widened the gap between the West and the rest of the world in terms of science and technology. By 1900, Western states, aided by superior technology, extended their power over virtually the entire globe, completing the trend that had begun with the Age of Exploration.

Note

1. David S. Landes, *The Unbound Prometheus: Technological Change and Industrial Development in* *Western Europe from 1750 to the Present* (Cambridge, Mass.: Harvard University Press, 1969), p. 33.

Suggested Reading

Ashton, T. S., *The Industrial Revolution, 1700–1830* (1962). A still useful account.

Deane, Phyllis, *The First Industrial Revolution, 1750–1850* (1965). An excellent introduction.

Floud, Roderick, and Donald McCloskey, *The Economic History of Britain Since 1900,* 2 vols. (1981). Incorporates the latest scholarship on British industrialization.

Heilbroner, Robert, *The Worldly Philosophers* (1953). Good discussions of early economic thinkers.

Himmelfarb, Gertrude, *The Idea of Poverty: England in the Early Industrial Age* (1983). A brilliant

history of English social thought, focused on the condition of the poor.

Hobsbawm, Eric, *The Age of Revolution: 1789–1848* (1964). A survey of this tumultuous period, stressing the connections between economic, social, and political revolution.

Landes, David S., *The Unbound Prometheus: Technological Change and Industrial Development in Western Europe from 1750 to the Present* (1969). A classic treatment of a complex subject.

Langer, William L., *Political and Social Upheaval: 1832–1852* (1969). An excellent source, with good references and bibliography.

Thompson, E. P., *The Making of the English Working Class* (1966). A very readable, dramatic, enormously influential, and controversial book.

Webb, R. K., *Modern England from the Eighteenth Century* (1967 and 1980). A balanced, well-written, and well-informed text, up-to-date on historical controversies.

Review Questions

1. What were the causes of the Industrial Revolution? Why did it begin in Britain?
2. How did the Industrial Revolution transform the social structure?
3. What problems did the Industrial Revolution create for the working class?
4. How did Parliament respond to demands for reform from 1815 to 1848?
5. Why are Saint-Simon, Fourier, and Owen regarded as early socialists?
6. The Industrial Revolution was a principal force in the shaping of the modern world. Discuss this statement.

❖ CHAPTER **13**

Thought and Culture in the Early Nineteenth Century

*A*fter the defeat of Napoleon, the traditional rulers of Europe, some of them just restored to power, were determined to protect themselves and society from future revolutions. As defenders of the status quo, they attacked the reformist spirit of the philosophes, which had produced the French Revolution. In conservatism, which championed tradition over reason, hierarchy over equality, and the community over the individual, they found a philosophy to justify their assault on the Enlightenment and the Revolution.

But the forces unleashed by the Revolution had penetrated European consciousness too deeply to be eradicated. One of them was liberalism, which aimed to secure the liberty and equality proclaimed by the Revolution. Another was nationalism, which sought to free subject peoples and unify fragmented nations.

The postrevolutionary period also witnessed the flowering of a new cultural orientation. *Romanticism,* with its plea for the liberation of human emotions and the free expression of personality, challenged the Enlightenment stress on rationalism. Although primarily a literary and artistic movement, romanticism also permeated philosophy and political thought, particularly conservatism. ❖

Romanticism: A New Cultural Orientation

The Romantic Movement, which began in the closing decades of the eighteenth century, dominated European cultural life in the first half of the nineteenth. Most of Europe's leading cultural figures came under its influence. Among the exponents of romanticism were the poets Shelley, Wordsworth, Keats, and Byron in England; the novelist Victor Hugo and the Catholic novelist and essayist Chateaubriand in France; and the writers A. W. and Friedrich Schlegel, the dramatist and poet Schiller, and the philosopher Schelling in Germany. Caspar David Friedrich in Germany and John Constable in England expressed the romantic mood in art, and later Beethoven, Schubert, Chopin, and Wagner expressed it in music.

Exalting Imagination and Feelings

Perhaps the central message of the romantics was that the imagination of the individual should determine the form and content of an artistic creation. This outlook ran counter to the rationalism of the Enlightenment, which itself had been a reaction against the otherworldly Christian orientation of the Middle Ages. The philosophes had attacked faith because it thwarted and distorted reason; romantic poets, philosophers, and artists now denounced the rationalism of the philosophes because it crushed the emotions and impeded creativity.

The philosophes, said the romantics, had turned flesh-and-blood human beings into soulless thinking machines. For human beings to be restored to their true nature, to become whole again, they must be emancipated from the tyranny of excessive intellectualizing; the feelings must be nurtured and expressed. Taking up one of Rousseau's ideas, romantics yearned to rediscover in the human soul the pristine freedom and creativity that had been squashed by habits, values, rules, and standards imposed by civilization. The philosophes had concentrated on people in general, focusing on the elements of human nature shared by all people. Romantics, on the other hand, emphasized human diversity and uniqueness—those traits that set one human being apart from others. Discover and express your true self, the romantics urged: play your own music; write your own poetry; paint your own vision of nature; live, love, and suffer in your own way.

Whereas the philosophes had asserted the mind's autonomy—its capacity to think for itself independent of authority—romantics gave primary importance to the autonomy of the personality—the individual's need and right to find and fulfill an inner self. To the philosophes, feelings were an obstacle to clear thinking, but to the romantics they were the essence of being human. People could not live by reason alone, said the romantics. They agreed with Rousseau, who wrote: "For us, to exist is to feel and our sensibility is incontestably prior to our reason."[1] For the romantics, reason was cold and dreary, and its understanding of people and life meager and inadequate. Reason could not grasp or express the complexities of human nature or the richness of human experience. By always dissecting and analyzing, by imposing deadening structure and form, and by demanding adherence to strict rules, reason crushed inspiration and creativity and barred true understanding. "The Reasoning Power in Man," wrote William Blake, the British poet, artist, and mystic, is "an Incrustation over my Immortal / Spirit."[2]

The romantics saw spontaneous, unbounded feelings, rather than the constricted intellect, as the avenue to truth. By cultivating their instincts and imagination, individuals could experience reality and discover their authentic selves. The romantics wanted people to feel and to experience—"To bathe in the Waters of Life," said Blake.[3] Consequently, they insisted that imaginative poets had a greater insight into life than analytical philosophers. "I am certain of nothing but of the holiness of the Heart's affections and the truth of

Dante's Inferno: The Whirlwind of Lovers by William Blake (1757–1827).   Blake
was a radical Romantic painter and poet who totally rejected the aristic conventions
of the past. His religious and political beliefs were as unique as his art; he spent his life
trying to convey tormented inward visions. A prolific illustrator, his imaginative genius was stimulated by great literature such as Dante's *Divine Comedy*. (*National
Gallery of Art, Washington, D.C. Gift of W. G. Allen*)

Imagination," wrote John Keats. "O for a Life of Sensations rather than of
Thoughts."[4]

The Enlightenment mind had been clear, critical, and controlled. It had adhered to standards of esthetics, thought to be universal, that had dominated
European cultural life since the Renaissance. Romantic poets, artists, and musicians broke with these traditional styles and uniform rules and created new
cultural forms and techniques. "We do not want either Greek or Roman
Models," Blake declared, "but [should be] just & true to our own Imaginations."[5] Victor Hugo (1802–1885), the dominant figure among French romantics, urged in the Preface to his play *Cromwell:* "Freedom in art! . . . Let
us take the hammer to the theories, the poetics [the analysis of poetry] and the
systems."[6] The romantics felt deeply that one did not learn how to write poetry or paint pictures by following textbook rules; nor could one grasp the
poet's or artist's intent by judging works according to fixed standards. The
romantics also explored the inner life of the mind, which Freud would later
call *the unconscious.* It was this layer of the mind—the wellspring of creativ-

ity, mysterious, primitive, more elemental and more powerful than reason—that the romantics yearned to revitalize and release.

Nature, God, History

The philosophes had viewed nature as a lifeless machine: a giant clock, all of whose parts worked together with precision and in perfect harmony. Nature's laws, operating with mathematical certainty, were uncovered by the methodology of science. To the romantics, nature was alive and suffused with God's presence. Nature stimulated the creative energies of the imagination; it taught human beings a higher form of knowledge. As William Wordsworth wrote in his poem "The Tables Turned,"

> *One impulse from a vernal wood*
> *May teach you more of man,*
> *Of moral evil and of good,*
> *Than all the sages can.*[7]

Regarding God as a great watchmaker—a detached observer of a self-operating mechanical universe—the philosophes tried to reduce religion to a series of scientific propositions. Many romantics, on the contrary, viewed God as an inspiring spiritual force and condemned the philosophes for weakening Christianity by submitting its dogmas to the test of reason. For the romantics, religion was not science and syllogism, but a passionate and authentic expression of human nature. They called for acknowledgment of the individual as a spiritual being and for cultivation of the religious side of human nature. This appeal accorded with their goal of restoring the whole personality, which, they were convinced, had been fragmented and distorted by the philosophes' excessive emphasis on the intellect.

The philosophes and the romantics viewed the Middle Ages very differently as well. To the former, that period was a time of darkness, superstition, and fanaticism; surviving medieval institutions and traditions only barred progress. The romantics, on the other hand, revered the Middle Ages. To the romantic imagination, the Middle Ages abounded with Christian mysteries, heroic deeds, and social harmony.

The romantics also disagreed with the philosophes on their conception of history. For the philosophes, history served a didactic purpose by providing examples of human folly. Such knowledge helped people to prepare for a better future, and for that reason alone history was worth studying. To the romantics, a historical period, like an individual, was a unique entity with its own soul. They wanted the historian to portray and analyze the variety of nations, traditions, and institutions that constituted the historical experience, always recognizing what is particular and unique to a given time and place. The romantics' insistence on comprehending the specific details of history and culture within the context of the times is the foundation of modern historical scholarship.

Searching for universal principles, the philosophes had dismissed folk

Lord Byron (1788–1824). One of the leading romantic poets, Byron created the "Byronic hero," a lonely and mysterious figure. His own short life exalted the emotions and the senses. He went to Greece in 1824 to aid the revolutionaries and died there from poor health. (*Stock Montage*)

traditions as peasant superstitions and impediments to progress. The romantics, on the other hand, rebelling against the standardization of culture, saw native languages, songs, and legends as the unique creations of a people and the deepest expression of national feeling. The romantics regarded the legends, myths, and folk traditions of a people as the fount of poetry and art and the spiritual source of a people's cultural vitality, creativity, and identity. Consequently, they examined these earliest cultural expressions with awe and reverence. In this way, romanticism played a part in shaping modern nationalism.

The Impact of the Romantic Movement

The romantic revolt against the Enlightenment had an important and enduring impact on European history. By focusing on the creative capacities inherent in the emotions—intuition, instinct, passion, will, empathy—the romantics shed light on a side of human nature that the philosophes had often overlooked or undervalued. By encouraging personal freedom and diversity in art, music, and literature, they greatly enriched European cultural life. Future artists, writers, and musicians would proceed along the path opened by the romantics. Modern art, for example, owes much to the Romantic Movement's emphasis on the legitimacy of human feeling and its exploration of the hidden world of dreams and fantasies. Romantics were among the first to attack the emerging industrial capitalism for subordinating individuals to the requirements of the industrial process and treating them as mere things. Furthermore, by recognizing the distinctive qualities of historical periods, peoples, and cultures, they helped create the modern historical outlook. Because it valued a nation's past, romanticism also contributed to modern nationalism and conservatism.

However, the Romantic Movement had a potentially dangerous side: it serves as background to the extreme nationalism of the twentieth century. As Ernst Cassirer has pointed out, the romantics "never meant to politicize but to 'poeticize' the world," and their deep respect for human individuality and national diversity was not compatible with Hitler's racial nationalism. Yet by waging their attack on reason with excessive zeal, the romantics undermined respect for the rational tradition of the Enlightenment and thus set up a precondition for the rise and triumph of fascist movements. Although their intention was cultural and not political, by idealizing the past and glorifying ancient folkways, legends, native soil, and native language, the romantics introduced a highly charged nonrational component into political life. In later generations, romanticism, particularly in Germany, fused with political nationalism to produce, says Horst von Maltitz, "a general climate of inexact thinking, an intellectual . . . dream world and an emotional approach to problems of political action to which sober reasoning should have been applied."[8]

The romantics' veneration of a people's history and traditions and their search for a nation's soul in an archaic culture would have struck the philosophes as barbarous—a regression to superstition and a triumph of myth over reason. Indeed, when transferred to the realm of politics, the romantics' idealization of the past and fascination with inherited national myths as the source of wisdom did reawaken a way of thinking about the world that rested more on feeling than on reason. In the process, people became committed to nationalist and political ideas that were fraught with danger. The glorification of myth and the folk community constitutes a link, however unintended, between romanticism and extreme nationalism, which culminated in the world wars of the twentieth century.

German Idealism

The romantics' stress on the inner person also found expression in the school of German philosophy called *idealism.* Idealists held that the world is not something objective that exists independently of individual consciousness. Rather, it is human consciousness, the knowing subject, that builds the world and determines its form. German idealism was partly a response to the challenge posed by David Hume, the great Scottish empiricist and skeptic.

The Challenge Posed by Hume's Empiricism

In his *Treatise of Human Nature* (1739–40) and *Enquiry Concerning Human Understanding* (1748), Hume cast doubt on the view that scientific certainty was possible. Science rests on the conviction that regularities observed in the past and the present will be repeated in the future: that there does exist an objective reality, which rational creatures can comprehend. Hume, however, argued that science cannot demonstrate a *necessary connection* between cause and effect. Because we repeatedly experience a burning sensation when our fingers have contact with a flame, we assume a cause and effect relationship. This is unwarranted, said Hume. All we can acknowledge is that there is a constant conjunction between the flame and the burning sensation.

According to Hume, we cannot prove that there is a law at work in nature guaranteeing that a specific cause will produce a specific effect. What we mean by cause and effect is simply something that the mind, through habit, imposes on our sense perceptions. For practical purposes, we can say that two events are in association with each other, but we cannot conclude with certainty that the second was caused by the first—that natural law is operating within the physical universe. Such a radical empiricism undermines the very foundations of science, so revered by progressive thinkers.

Immanuel Kant

In the *Critique of Pure Reason* (1781), Immanuel Kant (1724–1804), the great German philosopher and proponent of Newtonianism and the scientific method, undertook the challenge of rescuing reason and science from Hume's empiricism. The mind—the knowing subject—said Kant, is not a *tabula rasa,* a blank slate, which passively receives sense impressions, but an active instrument, which structures, organizes, and interprets the multiplicity of sensations coming to it. The mind can coordinate a chaotic stream of sensations because it contains its own inherent logic; it is equipped with several categories of understanding, including cause and effect.

Because of the way our mind is constituted, we presuppose a relationship of cause and effect in all our experiences with the objects of this world. The mind imposes structure and order on our sense experiences. Cause and effect and the other categories of the mind permit us to attribute certainty to scientific knowledge. The physical world must possess certain definite characteristics because these characteristics conform to the categories of the mind. The object, said Kant, must "accommodate itself to the subject."

Kant rescued science from Hume's assault: the laws of science are universally valid. But in the process, Kant made scientific law dependent on the mind and its a priori categories. We see nature in a certain way because of the mental apparatus that we bring to it. The mind imposes its own laws on nature—on the raw impressions received by the senses—giving the physical world form, structure, and order. By holding that objects must conform to the rules of the human mind, that it is the knowing subject that creates order within nature, Kant gave primacy to the knower rather than to the objects of knowledge. He saw the mind as an active agent, not a passive recipient of sensations. This "turn in philosophy," which Kant considered as revolutionary as the Copernican theory had been for astronomy, gave unprecedented importance to the power of the mind—to the active and creative knower.

It is a fundamental principle of Kant's thought that we cannot know ultimate reality. Our knowledge is limited to the phenomenal world, the realm of natural occurrences. We can only know things that we experience, that is, things as they appear to us through the active intervention of the mind's categories. We can have no knowledge of a thing-in-itself, that is, of an object's ultimate or real nature—its nature as it is independently of the way we experience it, apart from the way our senses receive it. The human mind can only acquire knowledge of that portion of reality revealed through sense experience. We can say nothing about the sun's true nature but only describe the way the sun appears to us: that is, our impression of the sun formed by the mind's ordering of our sense experiences of it. Thus, at the same time that Kant reaffirmed the validity of scientific law, he also limited the range of science and reason.

G.W. F. Hegel

Kant had insisted that knowledge of what lies beyond phenomena—knowledge of ultimate or absolute reality itself—is forever denied us. Georg Wilhelm Friedrich Hegel (1770–1831), another German philosopher, could not accept this. He constructed an all-embracing metaphysical system, which attempted to explain all reality and uncover the fundamental nature and meaning of the universe and human history.

Adopting Kant's notion that the mind imposes its categories on the world, Hegel emphasized the importance of the thinking subject in the quest for truth. However, Kant held that we can have knowledge only of how a thing appears to us, not of the thing-in-itself. Hegel, in contrast, maintained that ultimate reality, total truth, is knowable to the human mind: the mind can comprehend the truths underlying all existence and can grasp the essential meaning of human experience.

Kant had asserted the essential idealist position that the knowing subject organizes our experiences of the phenomenal world. Hegel took a giant step beyond that view by contending that there exists a universal Mind—Absolute Spirit, the thing-in-itself—whose nature can be apprehended through thought.

Because Hegel viewed Absolute Spirit not as fixed and static, but as evolving and developing, history plays a central role in his philosophical system. History is the development of Spirit in time. In the arena of world history, truth unfolds and makes itself known to the human mind. Like the Romantics, Hegel said that each historical period has a distinctive character, which separates it from every preceding age. The art, science, philosophy, religion, politics, and leading events are so interconnected that the period may be seen to possess an organic unity, a historical coherence.

Hegel believed that world history reveals a rational process; an internal principle of order underlies historical change. There is a purpose and an end to history: the unfolding of Absolute Spirit. In the course of history, an

Hegel in His Study.   Georg Wilhelm Friedrich Hegel (1770–1831) constructed a comprehensive philosophical system that sought to explain all reality. His philosophy of history, particularly the theories of dialectical conflict and of progression toward an ultimate end, greatly influenced Karl Marx. (*Bildarchiv Preussischer Kulturbesitz, Berlin*)

immanent Spirit manifests itself. Gradually, progressively, and nonrepetitively, it actualizes itself, becoming itself fully. Nations and exceptional human beings, "World Historical" individuals—Alexander the Great, Caesar, Napoleon—are the mediums through which Spirit realizes its potentialities and achieves self-consciousness. Hegel's philosophy of history gives meaning, purpose, and direction to historical events. Where is history taking us? What is its ultimate meaning? For Hegel, history is humanity's progress from lesser to greater freedom: "The History of the World is none other than the progress of the consciousness of Freedom . . . [It is] the absolute goal of history."[9]

According to Hegel, Spirit manifests itself in history through a dialectical confrontation between opposing ideas or forces; the struggle between one idea (thesis) and its adversary (antithesis) is evident in all spheres of human activity. This clash of opposites gains in intensity, ending in a resolution (synthesis) that unifies both opposing views. Thought and history thus enter a new and higher stage, that of synthesis, which, by absorbing the truths within both the thesis and the antithesis, achieves a higher level of truth and a higher stage of history. Soon this synthesis itself becomes a thesis that enters into another conflict with another set of opposing ideas; this conflict, too, is resolved by a still higher synthesis. Thus, the dynamic struggle between thesis and antithesis—sometimes expressed in revolutions and war, sometimes in art, religion, and philosophy—and its resolution into a synthesis accounts for movement in history. Or, in Hegelian language, Spirit is closer to realization: its rational essence is progressing from potentiality to actuality. The dialectic is the march of Spirit through human affairs. Since Hegel held that freedom is the essence of Spirit, it is through history that human beings progress toward consciousness of their own freedom. They become self-consciously aware of their own self-determination—their ability to regulate their lives rationally according to their own consciousness.

But for individual freedom to be realized, said Hegel, social and political institutions must be rationally determined and organized: that is, the will of the individual must be harmonized with the needs of the community. For Hegel, freedom is not a matter of securing abstract natural rights for the individual, the goal of the French Revolution. Rather, true freedom is attained only within the social group. Thus, in Hegel's view, human beings discover their essential character—their moral and spiritual potential—only as citizens of a cohesive political community. This view goes back to the city-states of ancient Greece, which Hegel admired. In the state's laws and institutions, which are manifestations of reason and the objectivization of Spirit, individuals find a basis for rationally determining their own lives. In this way, the private interests of citizens become one with the interests of the community.

For Hegel, Absolute Spirit, which is also Ultimate Reason, realizes itself in the state, the highest form of human association. The state joins fragmented individuals together into a community and substitutes a rule of justice for the rule of instincts. It permits individuals to live the ethical life and to develop their human potential. An individual cannot achieve these goals in isolation. Hegel's thought reveals a powerful undercurrent of statism: the exaltation of the state and the subordination of the individual to it. For Hegel, the national state was the embodiment of Universal Reason and the supreme achievement of Absolute Spirit.

German conservatives used Hegel's idea that existing institutions have a rational legitimacy to support their opposition to rapid change. Existing reality, even if it appears cruel and hateful, is the actualization of Absolute Spirit. Therefore, it is inherently necessary and rational and should not be altered.

Some of Hegel's followers, known as Young Hegelians, interpreted Hegel in a radical sense. They rejected his view that the Prussian state, or any German state, was the goal of world history, the realization of freedom. The Germany of their day, held the Young Hegelians, had not attained a harmony between the individual and society: it was not rationally organized and did not foster freedom. These Young Hegelians saw Hegel's philosophy as a means of radically altering the world to make existing society truly rational. The most important of the radical Young Hegelians was Karl Marx. Marx retained Hegel's overarching principle that history contains an inner logic, that it is an intelligible process, and that a dialectical struggle propels history from a lower to a higher stage (see Chapter 15).

Conservatism: The Value of Tradition

To the traditional rulers of Europe—kings, aristocrats, and clergy—the French Revolution was a great evil, which had inflicted a near-fatal wound on civilization. Disgusted and frightened by the revolutionary violence, terror, and warfare, the traditional rulers sought to refute the philosophes' worldview, which had spawned the Revolution. To them, natural rights, equality, the goodness of man, and perpetual progress were perverse doctrines that had produced the Jacobin "assassins." In conservatism, they found a political philosophy to counter the Enlightenment ideology.

Edmund Burke's *Reflections on the Revolution in France* (1790) was instrumental in shaping conservative thought. Burke (1729–1797), an Anglo-Irish statesman and political theorist, wanted to warn his countrymen of the dangers inherent in the ideology of the revolutionaries. Although writing in 1790, he astutely predicted that the Revolution would lead to terror and military dictatorship. To Burke, fanatics armed with pernicious principles—abstract ideas divorced from historical experience—had dragged France through the mire of revolution. Burke developed a coherent political philosophy, which served as a counterweight to the ideology of the Enlightenment and the Revolution.

Hostility to the French Revolution

Entranced by the great discoveries in science, the philosophes and French reformers had believed that the human mind could also transform social institutions and ancient traditions according to rational models. Progress through reason became their faith. Dedicated to creating a new future, the revolutionaries abruptly dispensed with old habits, traditional authority, and familiar ways of thought.

To conservatives, who, like the romantics, venerated the past, this was supreme arrogance and wickedness. They regarded the revolutionaries as presumptuous men who recklessly severed society's links with ancient institutions and traditions and condemned venerable religious and moral beliefs as ignorance. By attacking time-honored ways, the revolutionaries had deprived French society of moral leadership and had opened the door to anarchy and terror. "You began ill," wrote Burke of the revolutionaries, "because you began by despising everything that belonged to you. . . . When ancient opinions and rules of life are taken away, the loss cannot possibly be estimated. From that moment we have no compass to govern us; nor can we know distinctly to what port we steer."[10]

The philosophes and French reformers had expressed unlimited confidence in the power of human reason to understand and to change society. While appreciating human rational capacities, conservatives also recognized the limitations of reason. They saw the Revolution as a natural outgrowth of an arrogant Enlightenment philosophy, which overvalued reason and sought to reshape society according to abstract principles.

Conservatives did not view human beings as good by nature. Human wickedness was not caused by a faulty environment, as the philosophes had proclaimed, but lay at the core of human nature, as Christianity taught. Evil was held in check not by reason, but by tried and tested institutions, traditions, and beliefs. Without these habits inherited from ancestors, said conservatives, sinful human nature threatened the social order.

Because monarchy, aristocracy, and the church had endured for centuries, argued the conservatives, they had worth. By despising and uprooting these ancient institutions, revolutionaries had hardened the people's hearts, perverted their morals, and caused them to commit terrible outrages upon each other and society. As conservatives saw it, revolutionaries had divorced people and society from their historical settings and reduced them to abstractions; they had drawn up constitutions based on the unacceptable principle that government derives its power from the consent of the governed.

For conservatives, God and history were the only legitimate sources of political authority. States were not made; rather, they were an expression of the nation's moral, religious, and historical experience. No legitimate or sound constitution could be drawn up by a group assembled for that purpose. Scraps of paper with legal terminology and philosophical visions could not produce an effective government. Instead, a sound political system evolved gradually and inexplicably in response to circumstances.

The Quest for Social Stability

The liberal philosophy of the Enlightenment and the French Revolution started with the individual. The philosophes and the revolutionaries envisioned a society in which the individual was free and autonomous. Conservatives, on the other hand, believed that society was not a mechanical arrangement of disconnected individuals, but a living organism, held together by centuries-old bonds. Individualism would imperil social stability, destroy obedience to law, and fragment society into self-seeking isolated atoms. Conservatives held that the community was more important than the individual. Whereas the philosophes had attacked Christianity for promoting superstition and fanaticism, conservatives saw religion as the basis of civil society. Catholic conservatives, in particular, held that God had constituted the church and monarchy to check sinful human nature.

Conservatives viewed equality as another pernicious abstraction that contradicted all historical experience. For conservatives, society was naturally hierarchical, and they believed that some men, by virtue of their intelligence, education, wealth, and birth, were best qualified to rule and instruct the less able. They said that by denying the existence of a natural elite and uprooting the long-established ruling elite, which had learned its art through experience, the revolutionaries had deprived society of effective leaders, brought internal disorder, and prepared the way for a military dictatorship.

Conservatism pointed to a limitation of the Enlightenment. It showed that human beings and social relationships are far more complex than the philosophes had imagined. People do not always accept the rigorous logic of the philosopher and are not eager to break with ancient ways, however illogical they appear. They often find familiar customs and ancestral religions more satisfying guides to life than the blueprints of philosophers. The granite might of tradition remains an obstacle to all the visions of reformers. Conservative theorists warned that revolutionary violence in the pursuit of utopian dreams transforms politics into an ideological crusade that ends in terror and despotism. These warnings bore bitter fruit in the twentieth century.

Liberalism: The Value of the Individual

The decades after 1815 saw a spectacular rise of the bourgeoisie. Talented and ambitious bankers, merchants, manufacturers, professionals, and office-holders wanted to break the stranglehold of the landed nobility—the traditional elite—on political power and social prestige. They also wanted to eliminate restrictions on the free pursuit of profits. The political philosophy of the bourgeoisie was most commonly liberalism. While conservatives sought to strengthen the foundations of traditional society, which had been severely shaken in the period of the French Revolution and Napoleon, liberals strove to alter the status quo and to realize the promise of the Enlightenment and the French Revolution.

The Sources of Liberalism

In the long view of Western civilization, liberalism is an extension and development of the democratic practices and rational outlook that originated in ancient Greece. Also flowing into the liberal tradition is Judeo-Christian respect for the worth and dignity of the individual endowed by God with freedom to make moral choices. But nineteenth-century liberalism had its immediate historical roots in seventeenth-century England. At that time, the struggle for religious toleration by English Protestant dissenters established the principle of freedom of conscience, which is easily translated into freedom of opinion and expression in all matters. The Glorious Revolution of 1688 set limits on the power of the English monarchy. At the same time, John Locke's natural rights philosophy declared that the individual was by nature entitled to freedom, and it justified revolutions against rulers who deprived citizens of their lives, liberty, or property.

The French philosophes helped shape liberalism. From Montesquieu, liberals derived the theory of the separation of powers and of checks and balances—principles intended to guard against despotic government. The philosophes supported religious toleration and freedom of thought, expressed confidence in the capacity of the human mind to reform society, maintained that human beings are essentially good, and believed in the future progress of humanity—all fundamental principles of liberalism.

The American and French Revolutions were crucial phases in the history of liberalism. The Declaration of Independence gave expression to Locke's theory of natural rights; the Constitution of the United States incorporated Montesquieu's principles and demonstrated that people could create an effective government; and the Bill of Rights protected the person and rights of the individual. In destroying the special privileges of the aristocracy and opening careers to talent, the French National Assembly of 1789 had implemented the liberal ideal of equality under the law. It also drew up the Declaration of the Rights of Man and of the Citizen, which affirmed the dignity and rights of the individual, and a constitution that limited the king's power. Both revolutions explicitly called for the protection of property rights, another basic premise of liberalism.

Individual Liberty

The liberals' primary concern was the enhancement of individual liberty. They agreed with Kant that every person exists as an end in himself or herself and not as an object to be used arbitrarily by others. If uncoerced by government and churches and properly educated, a person could develop into a good, productive, and self-directed human being.

Liberals rejected a legacy of the Middle Ages, the classification of an individual as a commoner or aristocrat on the basis of birth. They held that a man was not born into a certain station in life but made his way through his own efforts. Taking their cue from the French Revolution, liberals called for an end to all privileges of the aristocracy.

In the tradition of the philosophes, liberals stressed the preeminence of reason as the basis of political life. Unfettered by ignorance and tyranny, the mind could eradicate evils that had burdened people for centuries and begin an age of free institutions and responsible citizens. For this reason, liberals supported the advancement of education.

Liberals attacked the state and other authorities that prevented the individual from exercising the right of free choice, interfered with the right of free expression, and blocked the individual's self-determination and self-development. They agreed with John Stuart Mill, the British philosopher, who declared that "over his own body and mind, the individual is sovereign. . . . that the only purpose for which power can be rightfully exercised over any member of a civilized community, against his will, is to prevent harm to others."[11]

To guard against the absolute and arbitrary authority of kings, liberals demanded written constitutions that granted freedom of speech, the press, and religion; freedom from arbitrary arrest; and the protection of property rights. To prevent the abuse of political authority, they called for a freely elected parliament and the distribution of power among the various branches of government. Liberals held that a government that derived its authority from the consent of the governed, as given in free elections, was least likely to violate individual freedom. A corollary of this principle was that the best government is one that governs least—that is, one that interferes as little as possible with the economic activities of its citizens and does not involve itself in their private lives or their beliefs.

Liberalism and Democracy

Many bourgeois liberals viewed with horror the democratic creed that all people should share in political power. To them, the participation of commoners in politics meant a vulgar form of despotism and the end of individual liberty. They saw the masses—uneducated, unpropertied, inexperienced, and impatient—as lacking both the ability and the temperament to maintain liberty and protect property.

Because bourgeois liberals feared that democracy could crush personal freedom as ruthlessly as any absolute monarch, they called for property requirements for voting and officeholding. They wanted political power to be concentrated in the hands of a safe and reliable—that is, a propertied and educated—middle class. Such a government would prevent revolution from below, a prospect that caused anxiety among bourgeois liberals.

To be sure, early-nineteenth-century liberals engaged in revolutions, but their aims were always limited. Once they had destroyed absolute monarchy and gained a constitution and a parliament or a change of government, they quickly tried to end the revolution. When the fever of revolution spread to the masses, liberals either withdrew or turned counterrevolutionary, for they feared the stirrings of the multitude.

Although liberalism was the political philosophy of a middle class generally hostile to democracy, the essential ideals of democracy flowed logically from liberalism. Eventually, democracy became a later stage in the evolution of liberalism because the masses, their political power enhanced by the Industrial Revolution, would press for greater social, political, and economic equality. Thus, by the early twentieth century, many European states had introduced universal suffrage, abandoned property requirements for officeholding, and improved conditions for workers.

But the fears of nineteenth-century liberals were not unfounded. In the twentieth century, the participation of common people in politics has indeed threatened freedom. Impatient with parliamentary procedures, the masses, particularly when troubled by economic problems, have in some instances given their support to demagogues who promised swift and decisive action. The granting of political participation to the masses has not always made people freer. The confidence of democrats has been shaken in the twentieth century by the seeming willingness of the masses to trade freedom for authority, order, economic security, and national power. Liberalism is based on the assumption that human beings can and do respond to rational argument and that reason will prevail over base human feelings. The history of our century shows that this may be an overly optimistic assessment of human nature.

Nationalism: The Sacredness of the Nation

Nationalism is a conscious bond shared by a group of people who feel strongly attached to a particular land and who possess a common language, culture, and history, marked by shared glories and sufferings. Nationalists contend that one's highest loyalty and devotion should be given to the nation. They exhibit great pride in their people's history and traditions and often feel that their nation has been specially chosen by God or history. They assert that the nation—its culture and history—gives meaning to an individual's life and actions. Like a religion, nationalism provides the individual with a sense of community and with a cause worthy of self-sacrifice. Identifying with the nation's collective achievements enhances feelings of self-worth.

In an age when Christianity was in retreat, nationalism became the dominant spiritual force in nineteenth-century European life. Nationalism provided new beliefs, martyrs, and "holy" days that stimulated reverence; it offered membership in a community, which satisfied the overwhelming psychological need of human beings for fellowship and identity. And nationalism gave a mission—the advancement of the nation—to which people could dedicate themselves.

The Emergence of Modern Nationalism

The essential components of modern nationalism emerged at the time of the French Revolution. The Revolution asserted the principle that sovereignty derived from the nation, from the people as a whole: the state was not the private possession of the ruler but the embodiment of the people's will. The nation state was above king, church, estate, guild, or province; it superseded all other loyalties. The French people must view themselves not as subjects of the king, not as Bretons or Normans, not as nobles or bourgeois, but as citizens of a united fatherland, *la patrie.* These two ideas—that the people possess unlimited sovereignty and that they are united in a nation—were crucial in fashioning a nationalist outlook.

As the Revolution moved from the moderate to the radical stage, French nationalism intensified. In 1793–94, when foreign invasion threatened the republic, the Jacobins created a national army, demanded ever greater allegiance to and sacrifice for the nation, and called for the expansion of France's borders to the Alps and the Rhine. With unprecedented success, the Jacobins used every means—press, schoolroom, and rostrum—to instill a love of country.

The Romantic Movement also awakened nationalist feelings. By examining the language, literature, and folkways of their people, romantic thinkers instilled a sense of national pride in their compatriots. Johann Gottfried Herder (1744–1803), a prominent German writer, conceived the idea of the *Volksgeist*—the soul of the people. For Herder, each people was unique and creative; each expressed its genius in language, literature, monuments, and folk traditions. Herder did not make the theoretical jump from a spiritual or cultural nationalism to political nationalism; he did not call for the formation of states based on nationality. But his emphasis on the unique culture of a people stimulated a national consciousness among Germans and the various Slavic peoples who lived under foreign rule. Fascination with the Volksgeist prompted intellectuals to investigate the past of their own people, to rediscover their ancient traditions, and to extol their historic language and culture. From this cultural nationalism, it was only a short step to a political nationalism, calling for national liberation, unification, and statehood.

The romantics were the earliest apostles of German nationalism. They restored to consciousness memories of the German past, and they emphasized the peculiar qualities of the German folk and the special destiny of the German nation. The romantics glorified medieval Germany and valued hereditary monarchy and aristocracy as vital links to the nation's past. They saw the existence of each individual as inextricably bound up with folk and fatherland, and they found the self-realization for which they yearned in the uniting of their own egos with the national soul. To these romantics, the national community was a vital force, giving the individual both an identity and a purpose in life. The nation stood above the individual; the national spirit linked isolated souls into a community of brethren.

Nationalism and Liberalism

In the early 1800s, liberals were the principal leaders and supporters of nationalist movements. They viewed the struggle for national rights—the freedom of a people from foreign rule—as an extension of the struggle for the rights of the individual. There could be no liberty, said nationalists, if people were not free to rule themselves in their own land.

Liberals called for the unification of Germany and Italy, the rebirth of Poland, the liberation of Greece from Turkish rule, and the granting of autonomy to the Hungarians of the Austrian Empire. Liberal nationalists envisioned a Europe of independent states, based on nationality and popular sovereignty. Free of foreign domination and tyrant princes, these newly risen states would protect the rights of the individual and strive to create a brotherhood of nationalities in Europe.

In the first half of the nineteenth century, few intellectuals recognized the dangers inherent in nationalism or understood the fundamental contradiction between liberalism and nationalism. For the liberal, the idea of universal natural rights transcended all national boundaries. Inheriting the cosmopolitanism of the Enlightenment, liberalism emphasized what all people had in common, demanded that all individuals be treated equally under the law, and preached toleration. Nationalists, manifesting the particularist attitude of the in-group and the tribe, regarded the nation as the essential fact of existence. Consequently, they often willingly subverted individual liberty for the sake of national grandeur. Whereas the liberal sought to protect the rights of all within the state, the nationalist often ignored or trampled on the rights of individuals and national minorities.

Liberalism grew out of the rational tradition of the West, but nationalism derived from an emotional attachment to ancient customs and bonds. Because it fulfilled an elemental yearning for community and kinship, nationalism exerted a powerful hold over human hearts, often driving people to political extremism. Liberalism demanded objectivity in analyzing tradition, society, and history; nationalism, however, evoked a mythic and romantic past, which often distorted history.

In the last part of the nineteenth century, the irrational and mythic quality of nationalism intensified. By stressing the unique qualities and history of a particular people, nationalism promoted hatred between nationalities. By kindling deep love for the past, including a longing for ancient borders, glories, and power, nationalism led to wars of expansion. When it roused the emotions to fever pitch, nationalism shattered rational thinking, dragged the mind into a world of fantasy and myth, and introduced extremism into politics. Love of nation became an overriding passion, threatening to extinguish the liberal ideals of reason, freedom, and equality.

Notes

1. Quoted in H. G. Schenk, *The Mind of the European Romantics* (Garden City, N.Y.: Doubleday, 1969), p. 4.
2. William Blake, *Milton*, in *The Poetry and Prose of William Blake*, ed. David V. Erdman (Garden City, N.Y.: Doubleday, 1965), plate 40, lines 34–36.
3. Ibid., plate 41, line 1.
4. Letter of John Keats, November 22, 1817, in *The Letters of John Keats*, ed. Hyder E. Rollins (Cambridge, Mass.: Harvard University Press, 1958), 1:184–185.
5. Blake, *Milton*, Preface.
6. Quoted in Robert T. Denommé, *Nineteenth-Century French Romantic Poets* (Carbondale: Southern Illinois University Press, 1969), p. 28.
7. From "The Tables Turned," in *The Complete Poetical Works of Wordsworth*, ed. Andrew J. George (Boston: Houghton Mifflin, 1904, rev. ed., 1982), p. 83.
8. Horst von Maltitz, *The Evolution of Hitler's Germany* (New York: McGraw-Hill, 1973), p. 217.
9. G. W. F. Hegel, *The Philosophy of History*, trans. J. Sibree (New York: Dover, 1956), pp. 19, 23.
10. Edmund Burke, *Reflections on the Revolution in France* (New York: Liberal Arts Press, 1955), pp. 40, 89.
11. John Stuart Mill, *On Liberty*, ed. Currin V. Shields (Indianapolis: Bobbs-Merrill, 1956), chap. 1.

Suggested Reading

Arblaster, Anthony, *The Rise and Decline of Western Liberalism* (1984). A critical analysis of liberalism, its evolution and characteristics.

Bullock, Alan, and Maurice Shock,

eds., *The Liberal Tradition from Fox to Keynes* (1956). Selections from the works of British liberals, preceded by an essay on the liberal tradition.

de Ruggiero, Guido, *The History of European Liberalism* (1927). A classic study.

Epstein, Klaus, *The Genesis of German Conservatism* (1966). An analysis of German conservative thought as a response to the Enlightenment and the French Revolution.

Harris, R. W., *Romanticism and the Social Order, 1780–1830* (1969). Involvement of English romantics in social and political questions.

Hayes, Carlton J. H., *Historical Evolution of Modern Nationalism* (1931). A pioneering work in the study of nationalism.

Honour, Hugh, *Romanticism* (1979). A study of the influence of romanticism on the visual arts.

Kohn, Hans, *The Idea of Nationalism* (1961). A comprehensive study of

nationalism from the ancient world through the eighteenth century by a leading student of the subject.

————, *Prelude to Nation-States* (1967). The emergence of nationalism in France and Germany.

Schapiro, J. S., *Liberalism: Its Meaning and History* (1958). A useful survey with readings.

Schenk, H. G., *The Mind of the European Romantics* (1966). A comprehensive analysis of the Romantic Movement.

Shafer, B. C., *Faces of Nationalism* (1972). The evolution of modern nationalism in Europe and the non-European world; contains a good bibliography.

Smith, A. D., *Theories of Nationalism* (1972). The relationship between nationalism and modernization.

Weiss, John, *Conservatism in Europe, 1770–1945* (1977). Conservatism as a reaction to social modernization.

Review Questions

1. The Romantic Movement was a reaction against the dominant ideas of the Enlightenment. Discuss this statement.
2. What was the significance of the Romantic Movement?
3. How did Kant try to resolve the problem posed by Hume's empiricism? What was the significance of his thought?
4. What was Hegel's view of history? What influence did it have?
5. What were the attitudes of the conservatives toward the

philosophes and the French Revolution?
6. What were the sources of liberalism?
7. The central concern of liberals was the enhancement of individual liberty. Discuss this statement.
8. How did the French Revolution and romanticism contribute to the rise of modern nationalism?
9. What is the relationship between nationalism and liberalism?
10. Account for the great appeal of nationalism.

❖ CHAPTER 14

Surge of Liberalism and Nationalism: Revolution, Counterrevolution, and Unification

*D*uring the years 1815 through 1848, the forces unleashed by the French Revolution clashed with the traditional outlook of the Old Regime. The period opened with the Congress of Vienna, which drew up a peace settlement after the defeat of Napoleon, and closed with the revolutions that swept across most of Europe in 1848. Outside France, much of the Old Regime had survived the stormy decades of the French Revolution and Napoleon. Monarchs still held the reins of political power. Aristocrats, particularly in central and eastern Europe, retained their traditional hold on the army and administration, controlled the peasantry and local government, and enjoyed tax exemptions. Determined to enforce respect for traditional authority and to smother liberal ideals, the conservative ruling elites resorted to censorship, secret police, and armed force. But the liberals and nationalists, inspired by the revolutionary principles of liberty, equality, and fraternity, continued to engage in revolutionary action. ❖

The Congress of Vienna

After the defeat of Napoleon, a congress of European powers met at Vienna (1814–1815) to draw up a peace settlement. The delegates wanted to restore stability to a continent torn by revolution and war and to reestablish the balance of power shattered by Napoleonic France.

Statesmen and Issues

The pivotal figure at the Congress of Vienna was Prince Klemens von Metternich (1773–1859) of Austria. A man of the Old Order, Metternich believed that both domestic and international stability depended on rule by monarchs

---

Chronology 14.1 ❖ The Surge of Nationalism

1821	Austria crushes revolts in Italy
1823	French troops crush revolt in Spain
1825	Uprising in Russia crushed by Nicholas I
1829	Greece gains its independence from Ottoman Empire
1830	The July Ordinances in France are followed by a revolution, which forces Charles X to abdicate
1831	The Polish revolution fails
1831–1832	Austrian forces crush a revolution in Italy
1848	The year of revolution
1862	Bismarck becomes chancellor of Prussia
1864	Austria and Prussia defeat Denmark in a war over Schleswig-Holstein
1866	Seven Weeks' War between Austria and Prussia: Prussia emerges as the dominant power in Germany
1870–1871	Franco-Prussian War: German unification completed
January 18, 1871	William I becomes German Kaiser

---

and respect for the aristocracy. The misguided liberal belief that society could be reshaped according to the ideals of liberty and equality, said Metternich, had led to twenty-five years of revolution, terror, and war. To restore stability and peace, the old Europe must suppress liberal ideas and quash the first signs of revolution.

Metternich also feared the new spirit of nationalism. As a multinational empire, Austria was particularly vulnerable to nationalist unrest. If its ethnic groups—Poles, Czechs, Magyars, Italians, South Slavs, and Romanians—became infected with the nationalist virus, they would destroy the Hapsburg Empire. Moreover, by arousing the masses and setting people against people, nationalism could undermine the foundations of the European civilization that he cherished.

Determined to end the chaos of the Napoleonic period and restore stability to Europe, Metternich wanted to return to power the ruling families deposed by more than two decades of revolutionary warfare. He also sought to reestablish the balance of power in Europe so that no one country could be in a position to dominate the Continent as Napoleon had done. There must be no more Napoleons who obliterate states, topple kings, and dream of European hegemony.

Other nations at the Congress of Vienna included Britain, Russia, France, and Prussia. Representing Britain was Robert Stewart, Viscount Castlereagh (1769–1822), the British foreign secretary, who was realistic and empirically minded. Although an implacable enemy of Napoleon, Castlereagh demonstrated mature statesmanship by not seeking to punish France severely. Tsar Alexander I (1777–1825) attended the Congress himself. Steeped in Christian mysticism, the tsar wanted to create a European community based on Christian teachings. Alexander regarded himself as the savior of Europe, an attitude that caused other diplomats to view him with distrust. Representing France was Prince Charles Maurice de Talleyrand-Périgord (1754–1838). A devoted patriot, Talleyrand sought to remove from France the stigma of the Revolution and Napoleon. Prince Karl von Hardenberg (1750–1822) represented Prussia. Like Metternich, Castlereagh, and Talleyrand, the Prussian statesman believed that the various European states, besides pursuing their own national interests, should concern themselves with the well-being of the European community as a whole.

Two interrelated issues threatened to disrupt the conference and enmesh the Great Powers in another war. One was Prussia's intention to annex the German kingdom of Saxony; the other was Russia's demand for Polish territories. The tsar wanted to combine the Polish holdings of Russia, Austria, and Prussia into a new Polish kingdom under Russian control. Both Britain and Austria regarded such an extension of Russian domination into central Europe as a threat to the balance of power.

Talleyrand suggested that Britain, Austria, and France join in an alliance to oppose Prussia and Russia. This clever move restored France to the family of nations. Now France was no longer the hated enemy but a necessary counterweight to Russia and Prussia. Threatened with war, Russia and Prussia moderated their demands and the crisis ended.

The Settlement

After months of discussion, quarrels, and threats, the delegates to the Congress of Vienna finished their work. Resisting Prussia's demands for a punitive peace, the allies did not punish France severely. They feared that a humiliated France would only prepare for a war of revenge. Besides, Metternich continued to need France to balance the power of both Prussia and Russia. France had to pay a large indemnity over a five-year period and submit to allied occupation until the obligation was met.

Although it lost most of its conquests, France emerged with somewhat more land than it possessed before the Revolution. To guard against a resurgent France, both Prussia and Holland received territories on the French border. Holland obtained the southern Netherlands (Belgium); Prussia gained the Rhineland and part of Saxony, but not as much as the Prussians had desired.

Congress of Vienna, 1815, by Jean Baptiste Isabey (1767–1855).   The delegates to the Congress of Vienna sought to re-establish many features of Europe that existed before the French Revolution and Napoleon. They can be accused of shortsightedness; nevertheless, the balance of power that they formulated preserved international peace. Metternich is standing before a chair at the left. (*The New York Public Library*)

Nevertheless, Prussia emerged from the settlement significantly larger and stronger. Russia obtained Finland and a considerable part of the Polish territories, but not as much as the tsar had anticipated; the Congress prevented further Russian expansion into central Europe. The northern Italian province of Lombardy was restored to Austria, which also received adjacent Venetia. England obtained strategic naval bases: Helgoland in the North Sea, Malta and the Ionian Islands in the Mediterranean, the Cape Colony in South Africa, and Ceylon in the Indian Ocean. Germany was organized into a confederation of thirty-eight (later thirty-nine) states. Norway was given to Sweden. The legitimate rulers, who had been displaced by the Revolution and the wars of Napoleon, were restored to their thrones in France, Spain, Portugal, the Kingdom of the Two Sicilies, the Papal States, and many German states.

The conservative delegates at the Congress of Vienna have often been criticized for ignoring the liberal and nationalist aspirations of the different peoples and turning the clock back to the Old Regime. Critics have castigated the Congress for dealing only with the rights of thrones and not the rights of peoples. But after the experience of two world wars in the twentieth century, some historians today are impressed by the peacemakers' success in restoring a balance of power that effectively stabilized international relations. No one country was strong enough to dominate the Continent, and no Great Power was so unhappy that it resorted to war to undo the settlement. Not until the unification of Germany in 1870–71 was the balance of power upset; not until World War I in 1914 did Europe have another general war of the magnitude of the Napoleonic wars.

Revolutions, 1820–1829

Russia, Austria, Prussia, and Great Britain agreed to act together to preserve the territorial settlement of the Congress of Vienna and the balance of power. After paying its indemnity, France was admitted into this Quadruple Alliance, also known as the Concert of Europe. Metternich intended to use the Concert of Europe to maintain harmony between nations and internal stability within nations. Toward this end, conservatives in their respective countries censored books and newspapers and imprisoned liberal and nationalist activists.

But repression could not contain the liberal and nationalist ideals unleashed by the French Revolution. The first revolution after the restorations of legitimate rulers occurred in Spain in 1820. Fearing that the Spanish uprising, with its quasi-liberal overtones, would inspire revolutions in other lands, the Concert of Europe empowered France to intervene. In 1823, a hundred thousand French troops crushed the revolution.

Revolutionary activity in Italy also frightened the Concert of Europe. In 1815, Italy consisted of several separate states. In the south, a Bourbon king ruled the Kingdom of the Two Sicilies; the pope governed the Papal States in central Italy; and Hapsburg Austria ruled Lombardy and Venetia in the north. Hapsburg princes subservient to Austria ruled the duchies of Tuscany, Parma, and Modena. Piedmont in the northwest and the island of Sardinia were governed by an Italian dynasty, the House of Savoy.

Besides all these political divisions, Italy was split economically and culturally. Throughout the peninsula, attachment to the local region was stronger than devotion to national unity. Economic ties between north and south were weak; inhabitants of the northern Italian cities felt little closeness to Sicilian peasants. Except for the middle class, most Italians clung to the values of the Old Regime.

Through novels, poetry, and works of history, an expanding intellectual elite awakened interest in Italy's glorious past. They insisted that a people who had built the Roman Empire and had produced the Renaissance must not remain weak and divided, their land occupied by Austrians. These sentiments appealed particularly to university students and the middle class. But the rural masses, illiterate and preoccupied with the hardships of daily life, showed little interest in this struggle for national revival.

Secret societies kept alive the hopes for liberty and independence from foreign rule in the period after 1815. The most important of these societies was

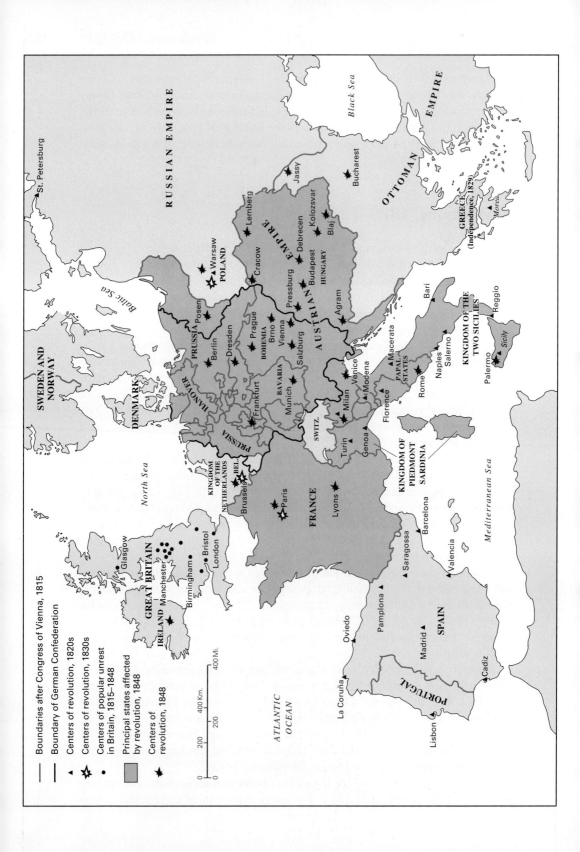

Boundaries after Congress of Vienna, 1815

Boundary of German Confederation

▲ Centers of revolution, 1820s

☆ Centers of revolutions, 1830s

• Centers of popular unrest in Britain, 1815–1848

Principal states affected by revolution, 1848

★ Centers of revolution, 1848

400 Mi.
200   400 Km.
0   200

SWEDEN AND NORWAY

RUSSIAN EMPIRE

→ St. Petersburg

Baltic Sea

DENMARK

North Sea

GREAT BRITAIN

Glasgow

Manchester

Birmingham

IRELAND

Bristol

London

ATLANTIC OCEAN

HANOVER

PRUSSIA

☆ Posen

★ Berlin

★ Dresden

BOHEMIA

★ Prague

★ Brno

Frankfurt

PRUSSIA

KINGDOM OF THE NETHERLANDS

BEL.
☆☆ Brussels

FRANCE

☆☆ Paris

★ Lyons

BAVARIA

Munich

Vienna ★

Salzburg ★

☆ Cracow

★ Warsaw
▲ POLAND

Lemberg ★

★ Pressburg

Budapest ★

HUNGARY

Debrecen ★

Kolozsvar ★

Blaj ★

AUSTRIAN EMPIRE

Agram ★

Jassy ▲

Bucharest ▲

OTTOMAN EMPIRE

Black Sea

GREECE
(Independence, 1829)

Morea

SWITZ.

Turin ▲

Genoa ▲

KINGDOM OF PIEDMONT SARDINIA

Milan ▲

Modena ▲

Venice

Florence

PAPAL STATES

Macerata ▲

Rome

Naples ▲

Salerno ▲

Bari ▲

KINGDOM OF THE TWO SICILIES

Palermo ★

Sicily

Reggio ▲

Mediterranean Sea

Barcelona ▲

Saragossa ▲

Valencia ▲

Pamplona ▲

SPAIN

Madrid ▲

Oviedo ▲

La Coruña ▲

PORTUGAL

Lisbon ▲

Cadiz ▲

the Carbonari, which had clubs in every state in Italy and a membership drawn largely from the middle class and the army. In 1820, the Carbonari enjoyed a few months of triumph in the Kingdom of the Two Sicilies. Supported by the army and militia, they forced King Ferdinand I to grant a constitution and a parliamentary government. But Metternich feared that the germ of revolution would spread to other countries. Supported by Prussia and Russia, Austria suppressed the constitutional government in Naples and another revolution that broke out in Piedmont. In both cases, Austria firmly fixed an absolute ruler on the throne.

A revolution also failed in Russia. During the Napoleonic wars and the occupation of France, Russian officers were introduced to French ideas. Contrasting French liberal attitudes with Russian autocracy, some officers resolved to change conditions in Russia. Like their Western counterparts, they organized secret societies and disseminated liberal ideas within Russia. When Alexander I died, these liberal officers struck. Their uprising in December 1825 was easily smashed by the new tsar, Nicholas I, and the leaders were severely punished.

The revolutions in Spain, Italy, and Russia were suppressed, but the Concert of Europe also suffered setbacks. Stimulated by the ideals of the French Revolution, the Greeks revolted against their Turkish rulers in 1821. Although the Turkish sultan was the legitimate ruler, Russia, France, and Britain aided the Greek revolutionaries, for they were Christians, whereas the Turks were Muslims; moreover, pro-Greek sentiments were very strong among educated western Europeans, who had studied the literature and history of ancient Greece. To them, the Greeks were struggling to regain the freedom of their ancient forebears. Not only the pressure of public opinion but also fear of Russian motives led Britain to join in intervention. If Russia carried out its intention of aiding the Greeks on its own, no doubt it would never surrender control. Britain could not permit this extension of Russian power in the eastern Mediterranean. Despite Metternich's objections, Britain, France, and Russia took joint action against the Turks, and in 1829 Greece gained its independence.

Revolutions, 1830–1832

After Napoleon's defeat, a Bourbon king, Louis XVIII (1814–1824), ascended the throne of France. Recognizing that the French people would not accept a return to the Old Order, Louis pursued a moderate course. Although his pseudoconstitution, the Charter, declared that the king's power rested on divine right, it acknowledged that citizens possessed fundamental rights: freedom of thought and religion and equal treatment under the law. It also set up a two-house parliament. But peasants, urban workers, and most bourgeois

◄ **Map 14.1**   Europe's Age of Revolutions

Liberty Leading the People, 1830, by Eugene Delacroix (1799–1863).   Early nineteenth-century reformers found their rallying cry in liberty, a legacy of the French Revolution. In this painting, Delacroix, the leader of French romantic artists, glorifies liberty. (*Louvre/Cliche des Musées Nationaux*)

could not meet the property requirements for voting. Louis XVIII was resisted by diehard aristocrats, called *ultras*, who wanted to erase the past twenty-five years of French history and restore the power and privileges of church and aristocracy. Their leader was the king's younger brother, the comte d'Artois, who after Louis's death in 1824 ascended the throne as Charles X (1824–1830).

The new government aroused the hostility of the bourgeoisie by indemnifying the émigrés for the property they had lost during the Revolution, censoring the press, and giving the church greater control over education. In the election of 1830, the liberal opposition to Charles X won a decisive victory. Charles responded with the July Ordinances, which dissolved the newly elected chamber; the Ordinances also deprived rich bourgeois of the vote and severely curbed the press.

The bourgeois, students, and workers rebelled. They hoped to establish a republic, but the wealthy bourgeois who took control of the revolution feared republican radicalism. They offered the throne to the duc d'Orléans; Charles X abdicated and went into exile in Britain. The new king, Louis Philippe (1830–1848), never forgot that he owed his throne to the rich bourgeois. And the Parisian workers who had fought for a republic and economic reforms to alleviate poverty felt betrayed by the outcome, as did the still disenfranchised petty bourgeois.

   The Revolution of 1830 in France set off shock waves in Belgium, Poland, and Italy. The Congress of Vienna had assigned Catholic Belgium to Protestant Holland; from the outset, the Belgians had protested. Stirred by the events in Paris, Belgian patriots proclaimed their independence from Holland and established a liberal government. Inspired by the uprisings in France and Belgium, Polish students, intellectuals, and army officers took up arms against their Russian overlords. The revolutionaries wanted to restore Polish independence, a dream that poets, musicians, and intellectuals had kept alive. Polish courage, however, was no match for Russian might, and Warsaw fell in 1831. The tsar took savage revenge on the revolutionaries. In 1831–32, the Austrians suppressed another insurrection by the Carbonari in the Papal States. During these uprisings, the peasants gave the Carbonari little support; indeed, they seemed to side with the traditional rulers.

The Revolutions of 1848: France

In 1848, often called *the year of revolution,* uprisings for political liberty and nationhood erupted throughout Europe. The economic crisis of the previous two years aggravated discontent with the existing regimes, but "it was the absence of liberty," concludes historian Jacques Droz, "which . . . was most deeply resented by the peoples of Europe and led them to take up arms."[1]

The February Revolution

An uprising in Paris set in motion the revolutionary tidal wave that was to engulf much of Europe in 1848. The Revolution of 1830 had broken the back of the ultras in France. There would be no going back to the Old Regime. But King Louis Philippe and his ministers, moderates by temperament and philosophy, had no intention of going forward to democracy.

   The government of Louis Philippe was run by a small elite, consisting of bourgeois bankers, merchants, and lawyers, as well as aristocrats who had abandoned the hope of restoring the Old Regime. This ruling elite championed the revolutionary ideas of equal treatment under the law and of careers open to talent but feared democracy and blocked efforts to broaden the franchise. (Only about 3 percent of adult French males were qualified to vote.) The opposition—radical republicans, or democrats—wanted to abolish the monarchy and grant all men the vote. The situation reached a climax in

February 1848, when the bourgeoisie, as well as students and workers, took to the streets to demand reforms; this led to a violent confrontation with soldiers. Unable to pacify the enraged Parisians, Louis Philippe abdicated, and France became a republic.

The June Days: Revolution of the Oppressed

The new bourgeois leaders were committed to political democracy, but only a few favored the social reforms demanded by the laboring poor. A meager harvest in 1846 and an international financial crisis in 1847, which drastically curtailed French factory production, aggravated the misery of the working class. Workers who could find jobs labored twelve to fourteen hours a day under brutalizing conditions. In some districts, one out of three children died before the age of five, and everywhere in France, beggars, paupers, prostitutes, and criminals were evidence of the struggle to survive. Prevented by law from striking, unable to meet the financial requirements for voting, and afflicted with unemployment, the urban workers wanted relief.

The middle-class leaders of the new republic, however, had little understanding of the workers' plight and little sympathy for it. By reason of occupation and wealth, the middle class saw itself as separate from the working class. To the bourgeoisie, the workers were dangerous creatures, "the wild ones," "the vile mob." But the inhabitants of the urban slums could no longer be ignored. They felt, as Alexis de Tocqueville, the astute statesman and political theorist, stated, "that all that is above them is incapable and unworthy of governing them; that the present distribution of goods [prevalent until now] . . . is unjust; that property rests on a foundation which is not an equitable foundation."[2]

Although the new leaders gave all adult males the vote and abolished censorship, they made only insincere and halfhearted attempts to ease the distress of the urban poor. The government limited the workday to ten hours, legalized labor unions, and established national workshops, which provided food, medical benefits, and employment on public works projects. But to the workers, this was a feeble effort to deal with their monumental hardships. To the property-owning peasantry and bourgeoisie, the national workshops were a hateful concession to socialist radicalism and a waste of government funds. When the government closed the workshops, working-class hostility and despair turned to open rebellion. Again barricades went up in the streets of Paris.

The June revolution in Paris was a revolt against poverty and a cry for the redistribution of property. The workers stood alone. To the rest of the nation, they were barbarians attacking civilized society. Aristocrats, bourgeois, and peasants feared that no one's property would be safe if the revolution succeeded. From hundreds of miles away, Frenchmen flocked to Paris to crush what they considered to be the madness within their midst. After three days of vicious street fighting and atrocities on both sides, the army extinguished the revolt. Some 1,460 lives had been lost, including four generals. The June Days left deep scars on French society. For many years, workers would never forget that the rest of France had united against them; the rest of France would remain terrified of working-class radicalism.

In December 1848, the French people, in overwhelming numbers, elected Louis Napoleon—nephew of the great emperor—president of the Second Republic. They were attracted by the magic of Louis Napoleon's name, and they expected him to prevent future working-class disorders. The election, in which all adult males could vote, demonstrated that most Frenchmen were socially conservative; they were unsympathetic to working-class poverty and deeply suspicious of socialist programs.

The Revolutions of 1848: Germany, Austria, and Italy

Like an epidemic, the fever of revolution that broke out in Paris in February raced across the Continent. Liberals, excluded from participation in political life, fought for parliaments and constitutions; many liberals were also nationalists who wanted unity or independence for their nations.

The German States: Liberalism Discredited

After the Congress of Vienna, Germany consisted of a loose confederation of thirty-nine independent states, of which Austria and Prussia were the most powerful. Jealous of the states' independence and determined to preserve their own absolute authority, the ruling princes detested liberal and nationalist ideals.

The German nationalism that had emerged during the French occupation intensified during the restoration (the post-Napoleonic period). Inspired in part by the ideas of the romantics, intellectuals insisted that Germans, who shared a common language and culture, should also be united politically. During the restoration, the struggle for German unity and liberal reforms continued to be waged primarily by students, professors, writers, lawyers, and other educated people. The great mass of people, knowing only loyalty to their local prince, remained unmoved by appeals for national unity.

The successful revolt against Louis Philippe, hostility against absolute princes, and the general economic crisis combined to produce uprisings in the capital cities of the German states in March 1848. Throughout Germany, liberals clamored for constitutions, parliamentary government, freedom of thought, and an end to police intimidation. Some called for the creation of a unified Germany governed by a national parliament and headed by a constitutional monarch. The poor of town and countryside, their plight worsened by the great depression of the 1840s, joined the struggle.

Terrified that these disturbances would lead to anarchy, the princes made concessions to the liberals, whom they had previously censored, jailed, and exiled. During March and April 1848, the traditional rulers in Prussia and other German states replaced reactionary ministers with liberals, eased censorship, established jury systems, framed constitutions, formed parliaments, and ended peasant obligations to lords.

Liberals took advantage of their successes to form a national assembly charged with the task of creating a unified and liberal Germany. Representatives from all the German states attended the assembly, which met at Frankfurt. After many long debates, the Frankfurt Assembly approved a federation of German states. The German union would have a parliament and would be headed by the Prussian king. Austria, with its many non-German nationalities, would be excluded from the federal union. The deputies selected Frederick William IV as emperor of the new Germany, but the Prussian king refused; he would never wear a crown given to him by common people during a period of revolutionary agitation. While the delegates debated, the ruling princes recovered from the first shock of revolution and ordered their armies to crush the revolutionaries. One by one the liberal governments fell.

German liberalism had failed to unite Germany or to create a constitutional government dominated by the middle class. Liberalism, never securely rooted in Germany, was discredited. In the following decades, many Germans, identifying liberalism with failure, abandoned liberal values and turned to authoritarian Prussia for leadership in the struggle for unification. The fact that authoritarians hostile to the spirit of parliamentary government eventually united Germany had deep implications for future German and European history.

Austria: Hapsburg Dominance

The Hapsburg (Austrian) Empire, the product of dynastic marriage and inheritance, had no common nationality or language; it was held together only by the reigning Hapsburg dynasty, its army, and its bureaucracy. The ethnic composition of the empire was enormously complex. The Germans dominated; concentrated principally in Austria, they constituted about 25 percent of the empire's population. The Magyars predominated in the Hungarian lands of the empire. The great bulk of the population consisted of Slavs: Czechs, Poles, Slovaks, Slovenes, Croats, Serbs, and Ruthenians. In addition, there were Italians in northern Italy and Romanians in Transylvania. The Hapsburg dynasty, aided by the army and the German-dominated civil service, prevented the multinational empire from collapsing into anarchy.

Metternich, it is often said, suffered from a "dissolution complex": he understood that the new forces of nationalism and liberalism could break up the Austrian Empire. Liberal ideas could lead Hapsburg subjects to challenge the authority of the emperor, and nationalist feelings could cause the different peoples of the empire to rebel against German domination and Hapsburg rule. To keep these ideas from infecting Austrian subjects, Metternich's police imposed strict censorship, spied on professors, and expelled from the universities students caught reading forbidden books. Despite Metternich's political police, the universities still remained hotbeds of liberalism.

In 1848, revolutions spread throughout the Austrian Empire, starting in Vienna. Aroused by the abdication of Louis Philippe, Viennese liberals denounced Hapsburg absolutism and demanded a constitution, relaxation of censorship, and restrictions on the police. Intimidated by the revolutionaries, the government allowed freedom of the press, accepted Metternich's resignation, and promised a constitution. The Constitutional Assembly was convened and in August voted the abolition of serfdom. At the same time that the Viennese insurgents were tasting the heady wine of reform, revolts in other parts of the empire—Bohemia, Hungary, and northern Italy—added to the distress of the monarchy.

But the revolutionaries' victory was only temporary, and the defeat of the Old Order only illusory. The Hapsburg government soon began to recover its balance. The first government victory came with the crushing of the Czechs in Bohemia. In 1848, Czech nationalists wanted the Austrian Empire reconstructed along federal lines that would give the Czechs equal standing with Germans. General Alfred zu Windischgrätz bombarded Prague, the capital of Bohemia, into submission and reestablished Hapsburg control.

In October 1848, the Hapsburg authorities ordered the army to bombard Vienna. Against the regular army, the courageous but disorganized and divided students and workers had little hope. In March 1849, the Hapsburg rulers replaced the liberal constitution drafted by the popularly elected Constitutional Assembly with a more conservative one drawn up by their own ministers.

The most serious threat to the Hapsburg realm came from the Magyars in Hungary. Some twelve million people lived in Hungary, five million of whom were Magyars. The other nationalities consisted of South Slavs (Croats and Serbs) and Romanians. Louis Kossuth (1802–1894), a member of the lower nobility, called for both social reform and a deepening of national consciousness in Hungary. Led by Kossuth, the Magyars demanded local autonomy. Hungary would remain within the Hapsburg Empire but have its own constitution and national army and control its own finances. The Hungarian leadership introduced liberal reforms: suffrage for all males who could speak Magyar and owned some property, freedom of religion, freedom of the press, the abolition of serfdom, and the end of the privileges of the nobles and the church. Within a few weeks, the Hungarian parliament changed Hungary from a feudal to a modern liberal state.

But the Hungarian leaders' nationalist dreams towered above their liberal ideals. The Magyars intended to incorporate lands inhabited by Croats, Slovaks, and Romanians into their state (Magyars considered these lands an integral part of historic Hungary) and to transform these peoples into Hungarians. In the spring of 1849, the Hungarians renounced their allegiance to the Hapsburgs and proclaimed Hungary an independent state, with Kossuth as president.

The Hapsburg rulers took advantage of the ethnic animosities inside and outside Hungary. They encouraged Romanians and Croats to resist the new Hungarian government. When Hapsburg forces moved against the Magyars, they were joined by an army of Croats, whose nationalist aspirations had been flouted by the Magyars. The Emperor Francis Joseph, who had recently ascended the Hapsburg throne, also appealed to Tsar Nicholas I for help. The tsar complied, fearing that a successful revolt by the Hungarians might lead the Poles to rise up against their Russian overlords. The Hungarians fought with extraordinary courage but were overcome by superior might.

Italy: Continued Fragmentation

Eager to end the humiliating Hapsburg occupation and domination and to link the disparate states into a unified and liberal nation, Italian nationalists, too, rose in rebellion in 1848. Revolution broke out in Sicily six weeks before the February revolution in Paris. Bowing to the revolutionaries' demands, King Ferdinand II of Naples granted a liberal constitution. The grand duke of Tuscany, King Charles Albert of Piedmont-Sardinia, and Pope Pius IX, ruler of the Papal States, also felt compelled to introduce liberal reforms.

Then the revolution spread to the Hapsburg lands in the north. After "Five Glorious Days" (March 18–22) of street fighting, the citizens of Milan forced the Austrians to withdraw. The people had liberated their city. On March 22, the citizens of Venice declared their city free from Austrian rule and set up a republic. King Charles Albert, who hoped to acquire Lombardy and Venetia, declared war on Austria. Intimidated by the insurrections, the ruling princes of the Italian states and Hapsburg Austria had lost the first round.

But soon everywhere in Italy the forces of reaction recovered and reasserted their authority. The Austrians defeated the Sardinians and reoccupied Milan, and Ferdinand II crushed the revolutionaries in the south. Revolutionary disorders in Rome had forced Pope Pius IX to flee in November 1848; in February 1849, the revolutionaries proclaimed Rome "a pure democracy with the glorious title of the Roman Republic." Heeding the pope's call for assistance, Louis Napoleon, the newly elected French president, attacked Rome, destroyed the infant republic, and allowed Pope Pius to return. The last city to fall to the reactionaries was Venice, which the Austrians subjected to a merciless bombardment. Italy was still a fragmented nation.

The Revolutions of 1848: An Assessment

The revolutions of 1848 began with much promise, but they all ended in defeat. The revolutionaries' initial success was due less to their strength than to the governments' hesitancy to use their superior force. However, the reactionary leaders of Europe overcame their paralysis and moved decisively to smash the revolutions. The courage of the revolutionaries was no match for the sheer power of regular armies. Thousands were killed and imprisoned; many fled to America.

Class divisions weakened the revolutionaries. The union between middle-class liberals and workers, which brought success in the opening stages of the revolutions, was only temporary. Bourgeois liberals favoring political reforms—constitution, parliament, and protection of basic rights—grew fearful of the laboring poor, who demanded social reforms, that is, jobs and bread. To the bourgeois, the workers were an uneducated mob driven by dark instincts. When the working class engaged in revolutionary action, a terrified middle class deserted the cause of revolution or joined the old elites in subduing the workers.

Intractable nationalist animosities helped to destroy all the revolutionary movements against absolutism in central Europe. In many cases, the different nationalities hated each other more than they hated the reactionary rulers. Hungarian revolutionaries dismissed the nationalist yearnings of the Croats and Romanians living in Hungary, who in turn helped the Hapsburg dynasty extinguish the nascent Hungarian state. The Germans of Bohemia resisted Czech demands for self-government and the equality of the Czech language with German. When German liberals at the Frankfurt Assembly debated the boundary lines of a united Germany, the problem of Prussia's Polish territories emerged. In 1848, Polish patriots wanted to recreate the Polish nation, but German delegates at the convention, by an overwhelming majority, opposed returning the Polish lands seized by Prussia in the late eighteenth century.

Before 1848, democratic idealists envisioned the birth of a new Europe of free people and liberated nations. The revolutions in central Europe showed that nationalism and liberalism were not natural allies and that nationalists were often indifferent to the rights of other peoples. Disheartened by these nationalist antagonisms, John Stuart Mill, the English liberal statesman and philosopher, lamented that "the sentiment of nationality so far outweighs the love of liberty that the people are willing to abet their rulers in crushing the liberty and independence of any people not of their race or language."[3]

Even though the revolutionaries failed to achieve their liberal and nationalist aims, the liberal gains were not insignificant. All French men obtained the right to vote; the labor services of peasants were abolished in Austria and the German states; and parliaments, dominated, to be sure, by princes and aristocrats, were established in Prussia and other German states. In later decades, liberal reforms would become more widespread. These reforms would be introduced peacefully, for the failure of the revolutions of 1848 convinced many people, including liberals, that popular uprisings were ineffective ways of changing society. The age of revolution, initiated by the French Revolution of 1789, had ended.

The Unification of Italy

In 1848, liberals had failed to drive the Austrians out of Italy and unite the Italian nation. By 1870, however, Italian unification had been achieved, mainly through the efforts of three men: Mazzini, Cavour, and Garibaldi.

Mazzini: The Soul of the Risorgimento

Giuseppe Mazzini (1805–1872) dedicated his life to the creation of a united and republican Italy—a goal he pursued with extraordinary moral intensity and determination. Mazzini was both a romantic and a liberal. As a liberal, he fought for republican and constitutional government and held that national unity would enhance individual liberty. As a romantic, he believed that an awakened Italy would lead to the regeneration of humanity. Mazzini was convinced that, just as Rome had provided law and unity in the ancient world and the Roman pope had led Latin Christendom during the Middle Ages, so a third Rome, a newly united Italy, would usher in a new age of free nations, personal liberty, and equality.

Mazzini had great charisma, determination, courage, and eloquence; he was also a prolific writer. His idealism attracted the intelligentsia and youth and kept alive the spirit of national unity. He infused the *Risorgimento,* the movement for Italian unity, with spiritual intensity. After his release from prison for participating in the insurrection of 1831, Mazzini went into exile and founded a new organization—Young Italy. Consisting of dedicated revolutionaries, many of them students, Young Italy was intended to serve as the instrument for the awakening of Italy and the transformation of Europe into a brotherhood of free peoples. Mazzini believed that a successful revolution must come from below—from the people, moved by a profound love for their nation. They must overthrow the Hapsburg princes and create a democratic republic.

Cavour and Victory over Austria

The failure of the revolutions of 1848 contained an obvious lesson: that Mazzini's approach, an armed uprising by aroused masses, did not work. The masses were not deeply committed to the nationalist cause, and the revolutionaries were no match for the Austrian army. Italian nationalists now hoped that the kingdom of Piedmont-Sardinia, ruled by an Italian dynasty, would expel the Austrians and lead the drive for unity. Count Camillo Benso di Cavour (1810–1861), the chief minister of Piedmont-Sardinia, became the architect of Italian unity.

Unlike Mazzini, Cavour was neither a dreamer nor a speechmaker but a tough-minded practitioner of *realpolitik,* "the politics of reality." Focusing on the world as it actually was, he dismissed ideals as illusions. A cautious and practical politician, Cavour realized that mass uprisings could not succeed against Austrian might. Moreover, mistrusting the common people, he did not favor Mazzini's goal of a democratic republic. Cavour had no precise blueprint for unifying Italy. His immediate aim was to increase the territory of Piedmont by driving the Austrians from northern Italy and incorporating Lombardy and Venetia into Piedmont-Sardinia.

To improve Piedmont's image in foreign affairs, Cavour launched a reform program to strengthen the economy. He reorganized the currency, taxes, and the national debt; in addition, he had railways and steamships built, fostered improved agricultural methods, and encouraged new businesses. Within a few years, Piedmont had become a progressive modern state.

In 1855, Piedmont joined England and France in the Crimean War against Russia. Cavour had no quarrel with Russia but sought the friendship of Britain and France and a chance to be heard in world affairs. At the peace conference, Cavour was granted an opportunity to denounce Austria for occupying Italian lands. He soon found a supporter in Napoleon III (the former Louis Napoleon), the French emperor, who hoped that a unified northern Italy would become an ally and client of France.

In 1858, Cavour and Napoleon III reached a secret agreement. If Austria attacked Piedmont, France would aid the Italian state. Piedmont would annex Lombardy and Venetia and parts of the Papal States. For its assistance, France would obtain Nice and Savoy from Piedmont. With this agreement in his pocket, Cavour cleverly maneuvered Austria into declaring war. He did so by strengthening Piedmont's army and encouraging volunteers from Austrian-controlled Lombardy to join it, for it had to appear that Austria was the aggressor.

Supported by French forces and taking advantage of poor Austrian planning, Piedmont conquered Lombardy and occupied Milan. But Napoleon III quickly had second thoughts. If Piedmont took any of the pope's territory, French Catholics would blame their own leader. Even more serious was the fear that Prussia, suspicious of French arms, would aid Austria. For these reasons, Napoleon III, without consulting Cavour, signed an armistice with Austria. Piedmont would acquire Lombardy, but no more. An outraged Cavour demanded that his state continue the war until all northern Italy was liberated, but King Victor Emmanuel of Piedmont accepted the Austrian peace terms. The victory of Piedmont-Sardinia, however, proved greater than Cavour had anticipated. During the conflict, patriots in Parma, Modena, Tuscany, and Romagna (one of the Papal States) had seized power. These new revolutionary governments voted to join with Piedmont.

Garibaldi and Victory in the South

Piedmont's success spurred revolutionary activity in the Kingdom of the Two Sicilies. In the spring of 1860, some one thousand red-shirted adventurers and patriots, led by Giuseppe Garibaldi (1807–1882), landed in Sicily, determined to liberate the land from its Bourbon ruler. After the liberation, Garibaldi that same year invaded the mainland. He occupied Naples without a fight and prepared to advance on Rome.

Cavour, however, feared that an assault on Rome by Garibaldi would lead to French intervention. Napoleon III had pledged to defend the pope's lands, and a French garrison had been stationed in Rome since 1849. Besides, Cavour considered Garibaldi too impulsive and rash, too attracted to republican ideals, and too popular to lead the struggle for unification. Garibaldi held exceptional views for his day. He supported the liberation of all subject

Victor Emmanuel and Garibaldi at the Bridge of Teano, 1860.   The unification of
Italy was the work of the romantic liberal Giuseppe Mazzini, the practical politician
Count Cavour, and the seasoned revolutionary Giuseppe Garibaldi. Selflessly,
Garibaldi turned over his conquests in the south to Victor Emmanuel in 1861.
(*Scala/Art Resource, NY*)

nationalities, female emancipation, the right of workers to organize, racial
equality, and the abolition of capital punishment. But the cause of Italian national unity was his true religion.

To head off Garibaldi, Cavour persuaded Napoleon III to approve an invasion of the Papal States by Piedmont. A papal force offered only token opposition, and the Papal States of Umbria and the Marches soon voted for union
with Piedmont, as did Naples and Sicily. Refusing to trade on his prestige
with the masses to fulfill personal ambition, Garibaldi turned over his conquests to Piedmont's King Victor Emmanuel, who was declared king of Italy
in 1861.

Italian Unification Completed

Two regions still remained outside the control of the new Italy: the city of
Rome, ruled by the pope and protected by French troops; and Venetia, occu-

pied by Austria. Cavour died in 1861, but the march toward unification continued. During the conflict between Prussia and Austria in 1866, Italy sided with the victorious Prussians and was rewarded with Venetia. During the Franco-Prussian War of 1870, France withdrew its garrisons from Rome; much to the anger of the pope, Italian troops marched in, and Rome was declared the capital of Italy.

The Unification of Germany

In 1848, German liberals and nationalists, believing in the strength of their ideals, had naively underestimated the power of the conservative Old Order. After the failed revolution, some disenchanted revolutionaries retained only a halfhearted commitment to liberalism or embraced conservatism. Others fled the country, weakening the liberal leadership. All liberals came to doubt the effectiveness of revolution as a way to transform Germany into a unified state; all gained a new respect for the realities of power. Abandoning idealism for realism, liberals now thought that German unity would be achieved through Prussian arms, not liberal ideals.

Prussia, Agent of Unification

During the late seventeenth and eighteenth centuries, Prussian kings had fashioned a rigorously trained and disciplined army. The state bureaucracy, often staffed by ex-soldiers, perpetuated the military mentality. As the chief organizations in the state, the army and the bureaucracy drilled into the Prussian people a respect for discipline and authority.

The Prussian throne was supported by the Junkers. These powerful aristocrats, who owned vast estates farmed by serfs, were exempt from most taxes and dominated local government in their territories. The Junkers' commanding position made them officers in the royal army, diplomats, and leading officials in the state bureaucracy. The Junkers knew that a weakening of the king's power would lead to the loss of their own aristocratic prerogatives.

In France in the late 1700s, a powerful and politically conscious middle class had challenged aristocratic privileges. The Prussian monarchy and the Junkers had faced no such challenge, for the Prussian middle class at that time was small and without influence. The idea of the rights of the individual did not deeply penetrate Prussian consciousness or undermine the Prussian tradition of obedience to military and state authority. Liberalism did not take firm root in Germany.

In 1834, under Prussian leadership, the German states, with the notable exception of Austria, established the *Zollverein,* a customs union that abolished tariffs between the states. The customs union stimulated economic activity and promoted a desire for greater unity. The Zollverein led many Germans to view Prussia, not Austria, as the leader of the unification movement.

Bismarck and the Road to Unity

Austria was the chief barrier to the extension of Prussian power in Germany. This was one reason why William I (1861–1888) called for a drastic reorganization of the Prussian army. But the liberals in the lower chamber of the Prussian parliament blocked passage of the army reforms, for they feared that the reforms would greatly increase the power of the monarchy and the military establishment. Unable to secure passage, William withdrew the reform bill and asked the lower chamber for additional funds to cover government expenses. When parliament granted these funds, he used the money to institute the army reforms. Learning from its mistake, the lower chamber would not approve the new budget in 1862 without an itemized breakdown. If the liberals won this conflict between the liberal majority in the lower chamber and the crown, they would, in effect, establish parliamentary control over the king and the army.

At this critical hour, King William asked Otto von Bismarck (1815–1898) to lead the battle against parliament. Descended on his father's side from an old aristocratic family, Bismarck was a staunch supporter of the Prussian monarchy and the Junker class and a devout patriot. He yearned to increase the territory and prestige of his beloved Prussia and to protect the authority of the Prussian king, who, Bismarck believed, ruled by the grace of God. Like Cavour, Bismarck was a shrewd and calculating practitioner of realpolitik.

Liberals were outraged by Bismarck's domineering and authoritarian manner and his determination to preserve monarchical power and the aristocratic order. Set on continuing the reorganization of the army and not bowing to parliamentary pressure, Bismarck ordered the collection of taxes without parliament's approval—an action that would have been unthinkable in Britain or the United States. He dismissed the lower chamber, imposed strict censorship on the press, arrested outspoken liberals, and fired liberals from the civil service. The liberals protested against these arbitrary and unconstitutional moves. What led to a resolution of the conflict was Bismarck's extraordinary success in foreign affairs.

Wars with Denmark and Austria   To Bismarck, a war between Austria and Prussia seemed inevitable, for only by removing Austria from German affairs could Prussia extend its dominion over the other German states. Bismarck's first move, however, was not against Austria but against Denmark—in 1864, over the disputed duchies of Schleswig and Holstein. Austria joined as Prussia's ally because it hoped to prevent Prussia from annexing the territories. After Denmark's defeat, Austria and Prussia quarreled over the ultimate disposition of these lands. Bismarck used the dispute to goad Austria into war. The Austrians, on their side, were convinced that Prussia must be defeated if Austria wanted to retain its influence over German affairs.

In the Austro-Prussian war of 1866, Prussia, with astonishing speed, assembled its forces and overran Austrian territory. At the battle of Sadowa (or Königgrätz), Prussia decisively defeated the main Austrian forces, and the

Otto von Bismarck.   Bismarck (1815–1898), the Iron Chancellor, was instrumental in unifying Germany. A conservative, he resisted parliament's efforts to weaken the monarch's power. Here he is portrayed in his youth before becoming chancellor. (*Photo AKG London*)

Seven Weeks' War ended. Prussia took no territory from Austria, but the latter agreed to Prussia's annexation of Schleswig and Holstein and a number of small German states. Prussia, moreover, organized a confederation of North German states, from which Austria was excluded. In effect, Austria was removed from German affairs, and Prussia became the dominant power in Germany.

The Triumph of Nationalism and Conservatism over Liberalism   The Prussian victory had a profound impact on political life within Prussia. Bismarck was the man of the hour, the great hero who had extended Prussia's power. Most liberals forgave Bismarck for his authoritarian handling of parliament. The liberal press that had previously denounced Bismarck for running roughshod over the constitution embraced him as a hero. Prussians were urged to concentrate on the glorious tasks ahead and put aside the constitutional struggle, which seemed petty by contrast.

Bismarck recognized the great appeal of nationalism and used it to expand Prussia's power over other German states and strengthen Prussia's voice in European affairs. By heralding his state as the champion of unification, he gained the support of nationalists throughout Germany. In the past, the nationalist cause had belonged to the liberals, but Bismarck appropriated it to promote Prussian expansion and conservative rule.

Prussia's victory over Austria, therefore, was a triumph for conservatism

404 Chapter 14 Surge of Liberalism and Nationalism

and nationalism and a defeat for liberalism. The liberal struggle for constitutional government in Prussia collapsed. The Prussian monarch retained the right to override parliamentary opposition and act on his own initiative. In 1848, Prussian might had suppressed a liberal revolution; in 1866, many liberals, beguiled by Bismarck's military triumphs, gave up the struggle for responsible parliamentary government. They had traded political freedom for Prussian military glory and power.

The capitulation of Prussian liberals demonstrated the essential weakness of the German liberal tradition. German liberals displayed a diminishing commitment to the principles of parliamentary government and a growing fascination with force, military triumph, and territorial expansion. Enthralled by Bismarck's achievement, many liberals abandoned liberalism and threw their support behind the authoritarian Prussian state. Germans of all classes acquired an adoration for Prussian militarism and for the power state, with its Machiavellian guideline that all means are justified if they result in the expansion of German power. In 1848, German liberals had called for "Unity and Freedom." What Bismarck gave them was unity and authoritarianism.

War with France Prussia emerged from the war with Austria as the leading power in the North German Confederation; the Prussian king controlled the armies and foreign affairs of the states within the confederation. To complete the unification of Germany, Bismarck would have to draw the South German states into the new German confederation. But the South German states, Catholic and hostile to Prussian authoritarianism, feared being absorbed by Prussia.

Bismarck hoped that a war between Prussia and France would ignite the nationalist feelings of the South Germans, causing them to overlook the differences that separated them from Prussia. If war with France would serve Bismarck's purpose, it was also not unthinkable to Napoleon III, the emperor of France. The creation of a powerful North German Confederation had frightened the French, and the prospect that the South German states might one day add their strength to the new Germany was terrifying. Both France and Prussia had parties that advocated war.

A cause for war arose over the succession to the vacated Spanish throne. King William of Prussia discussed the issue with the French ambassador and sent Bismarck a telegram informing him of what had ensued. With the support of high military leaders, Bismarck edited the telegram. The revised version gave the impression that the Prussian king and the French ambassador had insulted each other. Bismarck wanted to inflame French feeling against Prussia and arouse German opinion against France. He succeeded. In both Paris and Berlin, crowds of people, gripped by war fever, demanded satisfaction. When France declared a general mobilization, Prussia followed suit; Bismarck had his war.

As Bismarck had anticipated, the South German states came to the aid of Prussia. Quickly and decisively routing the French forces and capturing Napoleon III, the Prussians went on to besiege Paris. Faced with starvation,

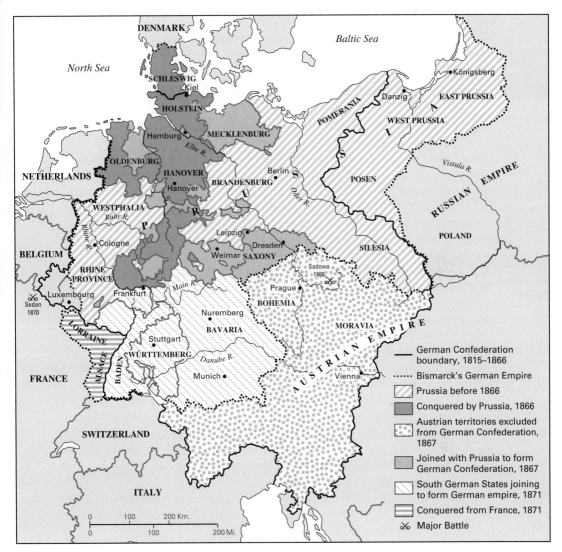

Map 14.2   Unification of Germany, 1866–1871

Paris surrendered in January 1871. France was compelled to pay a large indemnity and to cede to Germany the border provinces of Alsace and Lorraine—a loss that French patriots could never accept.

The Franco-Prussian War completed the unification of Germany. On January 18, 1871, at Versailles, the German princes granted the title of German kaiser (emperor) to William I. A powerful nation had arisen in central Europe. Its people were educated, disciplined, and efficient; its industries and commerce were rapidly expanding; its army was the finest in Europe. Vigorous, confident, and intensely nationalistic, the new German Empire would be eager to play a greater role in world affairs. No nation in Europe was a match for the new Germany. Metternich's fears had been realized: a Germany dominated by Prussia had upset the balance of power. The unification of Germany created fears, tensions, and rivalries that would culminate in a world war.

Nationality Problems in the Hapsburg Empire

In Italy and Germany, nationalism had led to the creation of unified states; in Austria, nationalism eventually caused the destruction of the centuries-old Hapsburg dynasty. A mosaic of different peoples, each with its own history and traditions, the Austrian Empire could not weld together and reconcile antagonistic nationalities when nationalistic consciousness was high. The empire's collapse in the final stages of World War I marked the end of years of hostility among its various subjects.

In the first half of the nineteenth century, the Germans, constituting less than one-quarter of the population, were the dominant national group in the empire. But Magyars, Poles, Czechs, Slovaks, Croats, Romanians, Ruthenians, and Italians were experiencing national self-awareness. Poets and writers, who had been educated in Latin, French, and German, began to write in their mother tongue and extol its splendor. By searching their past for glorious ancestors and glorious deeds, writers kindled pride in their native history and folklore and aroused anger against past and present injustices.

In 1848–49, the Hapsburg monarchy had extinguished the Magyar bid for independence, the Czech revolution in Prague, and the uprisings in the Italian provinces of Lombardy and Venetia. Greatly alarmed by these revolutions, the Austrian power structure resolved to resist pressures for political rights by strengthening autocracy and tightening the central bureaucracy. German and Germanized officials took over administrative and judicial duties formerly handled on a local level. An expanded secret police stifled liberal and nationalist expressions. The various nationalities, of course, resented these efforts at centralization and repression.

The defeats by France and Piedmont in 1859 and by Prussia in 1866 cost Austria its two Italian provinces. The defeat by Prussia also forced the Hapsburg monarchy to make concessions to the Magyars, the strongest of the non-German nationalities; without a loyal Hungary, the Hapsburg monarchy could suffer other humiliations. The Settlement of 1867 split the Hapsburg territories into Austria and Hungary. The two countries retained a common ruler, Francis Joseph (1848–1916), who was emperor of Austria and king of Hungary. Hungary gained complete control over its internal affairs: the administration of justice and education. A ministry composed of delegates from both lands conducted foreign and military affairs and dealt with common financial concerns.

With the Settlement of 1867, Magyars and Germans became the dominant nationalities in the empire. The other nationalities felt that the German-Magyar political, economic, and cultural domination blocked their own na-

The Young Czech Party Demonstrating in the Austrian Parliament, 1900. The Hapsburg Empire was burdened by conflicts between its different nationalities. In Bohemia, Czechs and Germans often engaged in violent confrontations as Czechs pressed for recognition of their language and rights. (*Osterreichische Nationalbibliothek*)

tional aspirations. Nationality struggles in the half-century following the Settlement of 1867 consumed the energies of the Austrians and Hungarians. In both lands, however, the leaders failed to solve the problem of minorities—a failure that ultimately led to the dissolution of the empire during the last weeks of World War I.

Notes

1. Jacques Droz, *Europe Between Revolutions, 1815–1848* (New York: Harper Torchbooks, 1967), p. 248.
2. *The Recollections of Alexis de Tocqueville*, trans. Alexander Teixeira de Mattos (Cleveland, Ohio: Meridian Books, 1969), pp. 11–12.
3. Quoted in Hans Kohn, *Nationalism: Its Meaning and History* (Princeton, N.J.: Van Nostrand, 1965), pp. 51–52.

Suggested Reading

Beales, Derek, *The Risorgimento and the Unification of Italy* (1971). A comprehensive overview, followed by documents.

Droz, Jacques, *Europe Between Revolutions, 1815–1848* (1967). A fine survey of the period.

Fasel, George, *Europe in Upheaval: The*

Chapter 14   Surge of Liberalism and Nationalism

Revolutions of 1848 (1970). A good
introduction.

Fejtö, François, ed., *The Opening of an
Era: 1848* (1973). Contributions by
nineteen eminent European
historians.

Hibbert, Christopher, *Garibaldi and
His Enemies* (1965). A vivid portrait
of the Italian hero.

Holborn, Hajo, *A History of Modern
Germany, 1840–1945* (1969). A
standard reference work.

Kohn, Hans, *Nationalism: Its Meaning
and History* (1965). A concise history
of modern nationalism by a leading
student of the subject.

Langer, W. L., *Political and Social
Upheaval, 1832–1852* (1969).
Another volume in The Rise of
Modern Europe series by its editor.
Rich in data and interpretation;

contains a valuable bibliographical
essay.

Pauley, B. F., *The Habsburg Legacy,
1867–1939* (1972). A good brief
work on a complex subject.

Robertson, Priscilla, *Revolutions of
1848* (1960). Vividly portrays the
events and the personalities involved.

Rodes, John E., *The Quest for Unity:
Modern Germany, 1848–1970*
(1971). A good survey of German
history.

Sperber, Jonathan, *The European
Revolution, 1848–1851* (1994). A
recent comprehensive overview.

Stearns, Peter N., *1848: The
Revolutionary Tide in Europe*
(1974). Strong on social factors.

Talmon, J. L., *Romanticism and Revolt*
(1967). The forces shaping European
history from 1815 to 1848.

Review Questions

1. How did the Congress of Vienna violate the principle of nationalism? What was the chief accomplishment of the Congress?
2. Between 1820 and 1832, where were revolutions suppressed, and how? Where were revolutions successful, and why?
3. What were the complaints of the urban poor to the new French government after the February revolution in 1848? What was the significance of the June Days in French history?
4. Why did the revolutions of 1848 fail in the German states, the Austrian Empire, and Italy?
5. What were the liberal gains of the revolutions of 1848? Why were

liberals and nationalists disappointed with the results of these revolutions?
6. Mazzini was the soul, Cavour the brains, and Garibaldi the sword in the struggle for the unification of Italy. Discuss their participation in and contributions to the struggle.
7. Prussia's victory over Austria was a triumph for conservatism and a defeat for liberalism. Discuss this statement.
8. What was the significance of the Franco-Prussian War for European history?
9. In the Hapsburg Empire, nationalism was a force for disunity. Discuss this statement.

❖ CHAPTER 15

Thought and Culture in the Mid-Nineteenth Century: Realism and Social Criticism

*T*he second half of the nineteenth century was marked by great progress in science, a surge in industrialism, and a continuing secularization of life and thought. The main intellectual currents of the century's middle decades reflected these trends. Realism, positivism, Darwinism, Marxism, and liberalism all reacted against romantic, religious, and metaphysical interpretations of nature and society, focusing instead on the empirical world. Adherents of these movements relied on careful observation and strove for scientific accuracy. This emphasis on objective reality helped to stimulate a growing criticism of social ills; for despite unprecedented material progress, reality was often sordid, somber, and dehumanizing.   ❖

Realism and Naturalism

Realism, the dominant movement in art and literature in the mid-nineteenth century, opposed the romantic veneration of the inner life and romantic sentimentality. The romantics exalted passion and intuition, let their imaginations transport them to a presumed idyllic medieval past, and sought inner solitude amid nature's wonders. Realists, on the other hand, concentrated on the actual world: social conditions, contemporary manners, and the familiar details of everyday life. With clinical detachment and meticulous care, they analyzed how people looked, worked, and behaved.

Like scientists, realist writers and artists carefully investigated the empirical world. For example, Gustave Courbet (1819–1877), who exemplified realism in painting, sought to practice what he called a "living art." He painted common people and commonplace scenes: laborers breaking stones, peasants tilling the soil or returning from a fair, a country burial, wrestlers, bathers, family groups. In a matter-of-fact style, without any attempt at glorification, realist artists also depicted floor scrapers, rag pickers, prostitutes, and beggars.

Seeking to portray life as it is, realist writers frequently dealt with social abuses and the sordid aspects of human behavior and social life. In his novels,

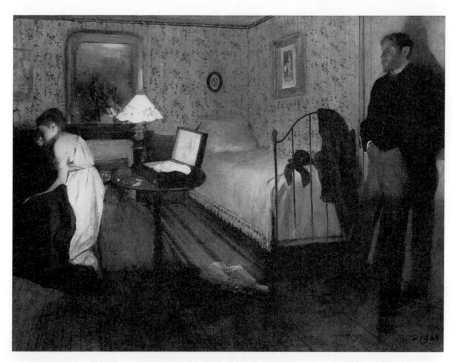

Interior by Edgar Degas, 1868–1869.   Set in a world of poor shopkeepers and clerks, *Thérèse Raquin* (1867) was Émile Zola's first great success as a naturalist novelist. This Degas painting depicts the sexual tension and violent emotions which Zola sought to uncover in his work. (*Philadelphia Museum of Art, The Henry P. McIlhenny Collection in Memory of Francis P. McIlhenny*)

Honoré de Balzac (1799–1850) described how social and economic forces affected people's behavior. Ivan Turgenev's *Sketches* (1852) portrayed rural conditions in Russia and expressed compassion for the brutally difficult life of serfs. In *War and Peace* (1863–1869), Leo Tolstoy vividly described the manners and outlook of the Russian nobility and the tragedies that attended Napoleon's invasion of Russia. In *Anna Karenina* (1873–1877), he treated the reality of class divisions and the complexities of marital relationships. The novels of Charles Dickens—*Bleak House* (1853), *Hard Times* (1854), and several others—depicted the squalor of life, the hypocrisy of society, and the drudgery of labor in British industrial cities.

Many regard Gustave Flaubert's *Madame Bovary* (1857) as the quintessential realistic novel; it tells the story of a self-centered wife who shows her hatred for her devoted, hardworking, but dull husband by committing adultery. Commenting on the realism of *Madame Bovary*, one critic noted that it "represents an obsession with description. Details are counted one by one, all are given equal value, every street, every house, every book, every blade of grass is described in full."[1]

Literary realism evolved into naturalism when writers tried to demonstrate a causal relationship between human character and the social environment: that certain conditions of life produced predictable character traits in human beings. The belief that the law of cause and effect governed human behavior reflected the immense prestige attached to science in the closing decades of the nineteenth century. The leading naturalist novelist, Émile Zola (1840–1902), probed the slums, brothels, mining villages, and cabarets of France, examining how people were conditioned by the squalor of their environment. Henrik Ibsen (1828–1906), a Norwegian and the leading naturalist playwright, examined with clinical precision the commercial and professional classes, their personal ambitions and family relationships. His *Pillars of Society* (1877) scrutinized bourgeois social pretensions and hypocrisy. In *A Doll's House* (1879), he took up a theme that shocked the late nineteenth century bourgeois audience: a woman leaving her husband to seek a more fulfilling life.

In striving for a true-to-life portrayal of human behavior and the social environment, realism and naturalism reflected attitudes shaped by science, industrialism, and secularism, which stressed the importance of the external world. The same outlook also gave rise to positivism in philosophy.

Positivism

Positivists viewed science as the highest achievement of the mind and sought to apply a strict empirical approach to the study of society. They believed that the philosopher must proceed like a scientist, carefully assembling and classifying data and formulating general rules that demonstrate regularities in the social experience. Such knowledge, based on concrete facts, would provide the social planner with useful insights. Positivists rejected metaphysics, which, in the tradition of Plato, tried to discover ultimate principles through reason alone, rather than through observation of the empirical world. For positivists, any effort to go beyond the realm of experience to a deeper reality would be a mistaken and fruitless endeavor.

Auguste Comte (1798–1857), the father of positivism, called for a purely scientific approach to history and society: only through a proper understanding of the laws governing human affairs could society, which was in a state of intellectual anarchy, be rationally reorganized. Comte named his system *positivism* because he believed that it rested on sure knowledge derived from observed facts and was therefore empirically verifiable. Like others of his generation, Comte believed that scientific laws underlay human affairs and could be discovered through the methods of the empirical scientist—that is, through recording and systematizing observable data. "I shall bring factual proof," he said, "that there are just as definite laws for the development of the human race as there are for the fall of a stone."[2]

One of the laws that Comte believed he had discovered was the "law of the three stages." The human mind, he asserted, had progressed through three broad historical stages: the theological, the metaphysical, and the scientific. In the theological stage, the most primitive of the three, the mind found a supernatural explanation for the origins and purpose of things, and society was ruled by priests. In the metaphysical stage, which included the Enlightenment, the mind tried to explain things through abstractions—such as "nature," "equality," "natural rights," or "popular sovereignty"—that rested on hope and belief rather than on empirical investigation. The metaphysical stage was a transitional period between the infantile theological stage and the highest stage of society, the scientific, or positive, stage. In this culminating stage, the mind breaks with all illusions inherited from the past, formulates laws based on careful observation of the empirical world, and reconstructs society in accordance with these laws. People remove all mystery from nature and base their social legislation on laws of society similar to the laws of nature discovered by Newton.

Although Comte attacked the philosophes for delving into abstractions instead of fashioning laws based on empirical knowledge, he was also influenced by the spirit of eighteenth-century philosophy. Like the philosophes, he valued science, criticized supernatural religion, and believed in progress. In this way, he accepted the Enlightenment's legacy, including the empirical and antitheological spirit of Diderot's *Encyclopedia,* Montesquieu's quest for historical laws governing society, and Condorcet's vision of intellectual and social progress as an inevitable condition of humanity. Because Comte advocated the scientific study of society, he is regarded as a principal founder of modern sociology.

Darwinism

In a century distinguished by scientific discoveries, perhaps the most important scientific advance was the theory of evolution formulated by Charles Darwin (1809–1882), an English naturalist. Darwin did for his discipline what Newton had done for physics; he made biology an objective science based on general principles. The Scientific Revolution of the seventeenth century had given people a new conception of space; Darwin radically altered our conception of time and biological life, including human origins.

Natural Selection

During the eighteenth century, almost all people had adhered to the biblical account of creation contained in Genesis: God had instantaneously created the universe and the various species of animal and plant life, and he had given every river and mountain and each species of animal and plant a finished and permanent form distinct from every other species. God had designed the bird's wings so that it could fly, the fish's eyes so that it could see under water, and the human's legs so that people could walk. All this, it was believed, had occurred some six thousand years ago.

Gradually, this view was questioned. In 1794, Erasmus Darwin, the grandfather of Charles Darwin, published *Zoonomia, or the Laws of Organic Life,* which offered evidence that the earth had existed for millions of years before the appearance of people and that animals experienced modifications, which they passed on to their offspring. Nearly forty years later, Sir Charles Lyell published his three-volume *Principles of Geology* (1830–1833), which showed that the planet had evolved slowly over many ages.

In December 1831, Charles Darwin sailed as a naturalist on the H.M.S. *Beagle,* which surveyed the shores of South America and some Pacific islands. During the five-year expedition, Darwin collected and examined specimens of plant and animal life; he concluded that many animal species had perished, that new species had emerged, and that there were links between extinct and living species. In the *Origin of Species* (1859) and the *Descent of Man* (1871), Darwin used empirical evidence to show that the wide variety of animal species was due to a process of development over many millennia, and he supplied a convincing theory that explained how evolution operates.

Darwin adopted the Malthusian idea (see page 358) that the population reproduces faster than the food supply, causing a struggle for existence. Not all infant organisms grow to adulthood; not all adult organisms live to old age. The principle of *natural selection* determines which members of the species have a better chance of survival. The offspring of lions, giraffes, or insects are not exact duplications of their parents. A baby lion might have the potential for being slightly faster or stronger than its parents; a baby giraffe might grow up to have a longer neck than its parents; an insect might have a slightly different color.

These small and random variations give the organism a crucial advantage in the struggle for food and against natural enemies. The organism favored by nature is more likely to reach maturity, to mate, and to pass on its superior qualities to its offspring, some of which will acquire the advantageous trait to an even greater degree than the parent. Over many generations, the favorable characteristic becomes more pronounced and more widespread within the species. Over millennia, natural selection causes the death of old, less adaptable species and the creation of new ones. Very few of the species that dwelt on earth ten million years ago still survive, and many new ones, including human beings, have emerged. People themselves are products of natural selection, evolving from earlier, lower, nonhuman forms of life.

Darwinism and Christianity

Like Newton's law of universal gravitation, Darwin's theory of evolution had revolutionary consequences in areas other than science. Evolution challenged traditional Christian belief. To some, it undermined the infallibility of Scripture and the conviction that the Bible was indeed the Word of God.

Darwin's theory touched off a great religious controversy between fundamentalists, who defended a literal interpretation of Genesis, and advocates of the new biology. A Methodist publication contended: "We regard this theory,

A Caricature of Darwin.   Darwin's theory of evolution created much controversy and aroused considerable bitterness. In this caricature, the apelike Darwin, holding a mirror, is explaining his theory of evolution to a fellow ape. (*Hulton Picture Company/Bettmann Archive*)

which seeks to eliminate from the universe the immediate, ever-present, all pervasive action of a living and personal God, which excludes the possibility of the supernatural and the miraculous . . . as practically destructive of the authority of divine revelation, and subversive of the foundation of religion and morality."[3] In time, most religious thinkers tried to reconcile evolution with the Christian view that there was a Creation and that it had a purpose. These Christian thinkers held that modifications within a species were made by an intelligent creator—that God had created and then directed the evolutionary process.

Darwinism ultimately helped end the practice of relying on the Bible as an authority in questions of science, completing a trend initiated earlier by Galileo. Darwinism contributed to the waning of religious belief and to a growing secular attitude, which dismissed or paid scant attention to the Christian view of a universe designed by God and a soul that rises to heaven.

For many, the conclusion seemed inescapable: nature contained no divine design or purpose, and the human species itself was a chance product of impersonal forces. The core idea of Christianity—that people were children of God participating in a drama of salvation—rested more than ever on faith rather than reason. Some even talked openly about the death of God. The notion that people are sheer accidents of nature was shocking. Copernicus had deprived people of the comforting belief that the earth had been placed in the center of the universe just for them; Darwin deprived people of the privilege of being God's special creation, thereby contributing to the feeling of anxiety that characterizes the twentieth century.

Social Darwinism

Darwin's theories were extended by others beyond the realm in which he had worked. Social thinkers, who recklessly applied Darwin's conclusions to the social order, produced theories that had dangerous consequences for society. Social Darwinists—those who transferred Darwin's scientific theories to social and economic issues—used the terms "struggle for existence" and "survival of the fittest" to buttress an often brutal economic individualism and political conservatism. Successful businessmen, they said, had demonstrated their fitness to prevail in the competitive world of business. Their success accorded with nature's laws and therefore was beneficial to society; those who lost out in the socioeconomic struggle demonstrated their unfitness. Traditionally, failure had been ascribed to human wickedness or to God's plan. Now it was being attributed to an inferior hereditary endowment.

Using Darwin's model of organisms evolving and changing slowly over tens of thousands of years, conservatives insisted that society, too, should experience change at an unhurried pace. Instant reforms conflicted with nature's laws and wisdom and resulted in a deterioration of the social body.

The application of Darwin's biological concepts to the social world, where they did not apply, also buttressed imperialism, racism, nationalism, and militarism: doctrines that preached relentless conflict. Social Darwinists insisted that nations and races were engaged in a struggle for survival in which only the fittest survive and deserve to survive. Karl Pearson, a British professor of mathematics, wrote in *National Life from the Standpoint of Science* (1900): "History shows me only one way, and one way only in which a higher state of civilization has been produced, namely the struggle of race with race, and the survival of the physically and mentally fitter race."[4] "We are a conquering race," said U.S. Senator Albert J. Beveridge. "We must obey our blood and occupy new markets, and if necessary, new lands."[5] "War is a biological necessity of the first importance,"[6] asserted the Prussian general Friedrich von Bernhardi in *Germany and the Next War* (1911).

Darwinian biology was used to promote the belief in Anglo-Saxon (British and American) and Teutonic (German) racial superiority. Social Darwinists attributed to racial qualities the growth of the British Empire, the expansion of the United States to the Pacific, and the extension of German power. The domination of other peoples—American Indians, Africans, Asians, Poles— was regarded as the natural right of the superior race.

The theory of evolution was a great achievement of the rational mind, but in the hands of the Social Darwinists it served to undermine the

Enlightenment tradition. Whereas the philosophes emphasized human equality, Social Darwinists divided humanity into racial superiors and inferiors. The philosophes believed that states would increasingly submit to the rule of law to reduce violent conflicts; Social Darwinists, on the other hand, regarded racial and national conflict as a biological necessity, a law of history, and a means to progress. In propagating a tooth-and-claw version of human and international relations, Social Darwinists dispensed with the humanitarian and cosmopolitan sentiments of the philosophes and distorted the image of progress. Their views promoted territorial aggrandizement and military buildup and led many to welcome World War I. The Social Darwinist notion of the struggle of races for survival became a core doctrine of the Nazi party after World War I and helped to provide the "scientific" and "ethical" justification for genocide.

Marxism

The failure of the revolutions of 1848 and a growing fear of working-class violence led liberals to abandon revolution and to press for reforms through the political process. In the last part of the nineteenth century, socialists and anarchists became the chief proponents of revolution. Both liberalism and Marxism shared common principles derived from the Enlightenment. Their adherents believed in the essential goodness and perfectibility of human nature and claimed that their doctrines rested on rational foundations. They wanted to free individuals from accumulated superstition, ignorance, and prejudices of the past and to fashion a more harmonious and rational society. Both liberals and Marxists believed in social progress and valued the full realization of human talents.

Despite these similarities, liberalism and Marxism differed profoundly. The goal of Marxism—the seizure of power by the working class and the destruction of capitalism—was inimical to bourgeois liberals. So, too, was the Marxist belief that violence and struggle were the essence of history, the instruments of progress, and the vehicle to a higher stage of humanity. Liberals, who placed the highest value on the individual, held that through education and self-discipline people could overcome inequality and poverty. Marxists, however, insisted that without a transformation of the economic system individual effort by the downtrodden would amount to very little.

Karl Marx (1818–1883) was born of German-Jewish parents (both descendants of prominent rabbis). To save his job as a lawyer, Marx's father converted to Protestantism. Enrolled at a university to study law, Marx switched to philosophy. In 1842, he was editing a newspaper, which was soon suppressed by the Prussian authorities for its outspoken ideas. Leaving his native Rhineland, Marx went to Paris, where he met another German, Friedrich Engels (1820–1895), who was the son of a prosperous textile manufacturer. Marx and Engels entered into a lifelong collaboration and became members

Karl Marx with His Daughter. Interpreting history in economic terms, Marx predicted that socialism would replace capitalism. He called for the proletariat to overthrow capitalism and to establish a classless society. (*Culver Pictures*)

of socialist groups. In February 1848, they published the *Communist Manifesto,* which called for a working-class revolution to overthrow the capitalist system. Forced to leave France in 1849 because of his political views, Marx moved to London, where he remained to the end of his life. There he spent years writing *Capital*—a study and critique of the modern capitalistic economic system, which, he predicted, would be destroyed by a socialist revolution.

A Science of History

As did other thinkers influenced by the Enlightenment, Marx believed that human history, like the operations of nature, was governed by scientific law. Marx was a strict materialist: rejecting all religious and metaphysical interpretations of both nature and history, he sought to fashion an empirical science of society. He viewed religion as a human creation—a product of people's imagination and feelings, a consolation for the oppressed—and the happiness it brought as an illusion. Real happiness would come, said Marx, not by transcending the natural world but by improving it. Rather than deluding oneself by seeking refuge from life's misfortunes in an imaginary world, one must confront the ills of society and reform them. This last point was crucial: "The philosophers have only *interpreted* the world in different ways; the point is to *change* it."[7]

The world could be rationally understood and changed, said Marx. People were free to make their own history, but to do so effectively, they must grasp the inner meaning of history: the laws governing human affairs in the past and operating in the present. Marx adopted Hegel's view that history was not an assortment of unrelated and disconnected events, but a progressive development, which, like the growth of a plant, proceeded ineluctably according to its own inner laws (see pages 371–373). For both Hegel and Marx, the historical process was governed by objective and rational principles. Marx also adopted Hegel's view that history advanced dialectically: that the clash of opposing forces propelled history into higher stages.

However, Marx also broke with Hegel in crucial ways. For Hegel, it was the dialectical clash of opposing ideas that moved history into the next stage; for Marx, it was the clash of classes representing conflicting economic interests—what is called dialectical materialism—that accounted for historical change and progress. In Hegel's view, history was the unfolding of the metaphysical Spirit, and a higher stage of development was produced by the synthesis of opposing ideas. According to Marx, Hegel's system suffered from mystification. It transcended the realities of the known world; it downgraded the real world, which became a mere attribute of Spirit. Marx saw Hegel's abstract philosophy as diverting attention from the real world and its problems, which cried out for understanding and solution; it was a negation of life.

For Marx, history was explainable solely in terms of natural processes—empirically verifiable developments. Marx valued Hegel's insight that history is a progressive and purposeful process, but he criticized Hegel for embedding his insights in metaphysical theological fantasy. Hegel, said Marx, had made a mystical principle the real subject of history and thought. But, in truth, it is the "real man," the person living in and conditioned by the objective world—the only true reality—who is the center of history. History is not Spirit aspiring to self-actualization but people becoming fully human, fulfilling their human potential.

For Marx, the moving forces in history were economic and technological factors: the ways in which goods are produced and wealth distributed. They accounted for historical change and were the basis of all culture—politics, law, religion, morals, and philosophy. "The history of humanity," he concluded, "must therefore always be studied and treated in relation to the history of industry and exchange."[8] Marx said that material technology—the methods of cultivating land and the tools for manufacturing goods—determined society's social and political arrangements and its intellectual outlooks. For example, the hand mill, the loose yoke, and the wooden plow had given rise to feudal lords, whereas power-driven machines had spawned the industrial capitalists.

Class Conflict

Throughout history, said Marx, there has been a class struggle between those who own the means of production and those whose labor has been exploited to provide wealth for this upper class. The opposing tension between classes has pushed history forward into higher stages. In the ancient world, when wealth was based on land, the struggle was between master and slave, patrician and plebeian; during the Middle Ages, when land was still the predominant mode of production, the struggle was between lord and serf. In the modern industrial world, two sharply opposed classes were confronting each other: the capitalists owning the factories, mines, banks, and transportation systems, and the exploited wage earners (the proletariat).

According to Marx and Engels, the class with economic power also controlled the state. That class used political power to protect and increase its property and to hold down the laboring class. "Thus the ancient State was above all the slaveowners' state for holding down the slaves," said Engels, "as a feudal State was the organ of the nobles for holding down the . . . serfs, and the modern representative State is the instrument of the exploitation of wage-labor by capital."[9]

Furthermore, Marx and Engels asserted, the class that controlled material production also controlled mental production: that is, the ideas held by the ruling class became the dominant ideas of society. These ideas, presented as laws of nature or moral and religious standards, were regarded as the truth by oppressor and oppressed alike. In reality, however, these ideas merely reflected the special economic interests of the ruling class. Thus, said Marx, bourgeois ideologists would insist that natural rights and laissez-faire economics were laws of nature having universal validity. But these "laws" were born of the needs of the bourgeoisie in its struggle to wrest power from an obsolete feudal regime and to protect its property from the state. Similarly, nineteenth-century slave owners convinced themselves that slavery was morally right—that it had God's approval and was good for the slave. Slave owners and capitalist employers alike may have defended their labor systems by citing universal principles that they thought were true, but in reality their systems rested on a simple economic consideration: slave labor was good for the pocketbook of the slave owner, and wage labor was good in the same way for the capitalist.

The Destruction of Capitalism

Under capitalism, said Marx, workers knew only poverty. They worked long hours for low wages, suffered from periodic unemployment, and lived in squalid, overcrowded dwellings. Most monstrous of all, they were forced to send their young children into the factories.

Capitalism, as Marx saw it, also produced another kind of poverty: poverty of the human spirit. Under capitalism, the factory worker was reduced to a laboring beast, performing tedious and repetitive tasks in a dark, dreary, dirty cave—an altogether inhuman environment, which deprived people of their human sensibilities. Unlike the artisans in their own shops, factory workers found no pleasure and took no pride in their work; they did not have the satisfaction of creating a finished product that expressed their skills. Work, said

Marx, should be a source of fulfillment for people. It should enable people to affirm their personalities and develop their potential. By treating people not as human beings but as cogs in the production process, capitalism alienated people from their work, themselves, and one another.

Marx believed that capitalist control of the economy and the government would not endure forever. The capitalist system would perish just as the feudal society of the Middle Ages and the slave society of the ancient world had perished. From the ruins of a dead capitalist society, a new socioeconomic system, socialism, would emerge.

Marx predicted how capitalism would be destroyed. Periodic unemployment would increase the misery of the workers and intensify their hatred of capitalists. Owners of small businesses and shopkeepers, unable to compete with the great capitalists, would sink into the ranks of the working class, greatly expanding its numbers. Society would become polarized into a small group of immensely wealthy capitalists and a vast proletariat, poor, embittered, and desperate. This monopoly of capital by the few would become a brake on the productive process.

Growing increasingly conscious of their misery, the workers—aroused, educated, and organized by communist intellectuals—would revolt. "Revolution is necessary," said Marx, "not only because the *ruling class* cannot be overthrown in any other way, but also because only in a revolution *can the class which overthrows it* rid itself of the accumulated rubbish of the past and become capable of reconstructing society."[10] The working-class revolutionaries would smash the government that helped the capitalists maintain their dominance. Then they would confiscate the property of the capitalists, abolish private property, place the means of production in the workers' hands, and organize a new society. The *Communist Manifesto* ends with a ringing call for revolution: "The Communists . . . openly declare that their ends can be attained only by the forcible overthrow of all existing social conditions. Let the ruling classes tremble at a Communist revolution. The proletarians have nothing to lose but their chains. They have a world to win. Workingmen of all countries, unite!"[11]

Marx did not say a great deal about the new society that would be ushered in by the socialist revolution. With the destruction of capitalism, the distinction between capitalist and worker would cease and with it the class conflict. No longer would society be divided into haves and have-nots, oppressor and oppressed. Since this classless society would contain no exploiters, there would be no need for a state, which was merely an instrument for maintaining and protecting the power of the exploiting class. Thus, the state would eventually wither away. The production and distribution of goods would be carried out through community planning and communal sharing, which would replace the capitalist system of competition. People would work at varied tasks, just as Fourier (see page 359) had advocated, rather than being confined to one form of employment. No longer factory slaves, people would be free to fulfill their human potential, to improve their relationships on a basis of equality with others, and to work together for the common good.

Marx's Influence

Marxism had immense appeal both for the downtrodden and for intellectuals. It promised to end the injustices of industrial society; it claimed the certainty of science; and it assured adherents that the triumph of their cause was guaranteed by history. In many ways, Marxism was a secular religion: the proletariat became a chosen class, endowed with a mission to achieve worldly salvation for humanity.

Marx's influence grew during the second wave of industrialization, in the closing decades of the nineteenth century, when class bitterness between the proletariat and the bourgeoisie seemed to worsen. Many workers thought that liberals and conservatives had no sympathy for their plight and that the only way to improve their lot was through socialist parties.

The emphasis Marx gave to economic forces has immeasurably broadened the perception of historians, who now explore the economic factors in historical developments. This approach has greatly expanded our understanding of Rome's decline, the outbreak of the French Revolution and the American Civil War, and other crucial developments. Marx's theory of class conflict has provided social scientists with a useful tool for analyzing social process. His theory of alienation has been adapted by sociologists and psychologists. Of particular value to social scientists is Marx's insight that the ideas people hold to be true and the values they consider valid often veil economic interests. On the political level, both the socialist parties of western Europe, which pressed for reform through parliamentary methods, and the communist regimes in Russia and China, which came to power through revolution, claimed to be heirs of Marx.

Critics of Marx

Critics point out serious weaknesses in Marxism. The rigid Marxist who tries to squeeze all historical events into an economic framework is at a disadvantage. Economic forces alone will not explain the triumph of Christianity in the Roman Empire, the fall of Rome, the Crusades, the French Revolution, modern imperialism, World War I, or the rise of Hitler. Economic explanations fall particularly flat in trying to account for the emergence of modern nationalism, whose appeal, resting on deeply ingrained emotional needs, crosses class lines. The greatest struggles of the twentieth century have been not between classes but between nations.

Many of Marx's predictions or expectations failed to materialize. Workers in Western lands did not become the oppressed and impoverished working class that Marx had described in the mid-nineteenth century. Because of increased productivity and the efforts of labor unions and reform-minded governments, Western workers improved their lives considerably, so that they now enjoy the highest standard of living in history. The tremendous growth of a middle class of professionals, civil service employees, and small-business people belies Marx's prediction that capitalist society would be polarized into a small group of very rich capitalists and a great mass of destitute workers.

Marx believed that socialist revolutions would break out in the advanced industrialized lands. But the socialist revolutions of the twentieth century have occurred in underdeveloped, predominantly agricultural countries. The state in communist lands, far from withering away, grew more centralized, powerful, and oppressive. In no country where communist revolutionaries have seized power have people achieved the liberty that Marx desired. Nor, indeed, have communists been able to sustain a viable economic system. The phenomenal collapse of communist regimes in the former Soviet Union and Eastern Europe in recent years testifies to Marxism's failure. All these failed predictions and expectations seem to contradict Marx's claim that his theories rested on an unassailable scientific foundation.

Liberalism in Transition

In the early part of the nineteenth century, European liberals were preoccupied with protecting the rights of the individual against the demands of the state. They championed laissez faire because they feared that state interference in the economy to redress social evils would threaten individual rights and the free market, which they thought were essential to personal liberty. They favored property requirements for voting and officeholding because they were certain that the unpropertied and uneducated masses lacked the wisdom and experience to exercise political responsibility.

In the last part of the century, liberals began to support—though not without reservation and qualification—both extended suffrage and government action to remedy the abuses of unregulated industrialization. This growing concern for the welfare of the laboring poor coincided with and was influenced by an unprecedented proliferation of humanitarian movements on both sides of the Atlantic. Nurtured by both the Enlightenment, as well as Christian teachings, reform movements called for the prohibition of child labor, schooling for the masses, humane treatment for prisoners and the mentally ill, equality for women, the abolition of slavery, and an end to war. By the beginning of the twentieth century, liberalism had evolved into liberal democracy, and laissez faire had been superseded by a reluctant acceptance of social legislation and government regulation. But from beginning to end, the central concern of liberals remained the protection of individual rights.

John Stuart Mill

The transition from laissez-faire liberalism to a more socially conscious and democratic liberalism is seen in the thought of John Stuart Mill (1806–1873), a British philosopher and statesman. Mill's *On Liberty* (1859) is the classic statement of individual freedom: that the government and the majority have no right to interfere with the liberty of another human being whose actions do no injury to others.

Mill regarded freedom of thought and expression and the toleration of opposing and unpopular viewpoints as necessary preconditions for the shaping of a rational, moral, and civilized citizen. When we silence an opinion, said Mill, we hurt present and future generations. If the opinion is correct, "we are deprived of the opportunity of exchanging error for truth." If the opinion is wrong—and of this we can never be entirely certain—we "lose the clearer perception and livelier impression of truth produced by its collision with error."[12] Therefore, government has no right to force an individual to hold a view "because it will be better for him to do so, or because it will make him happier, or because in the opinions of others, to do so would be wise, or even right. These are good reasons for remonstrating with him, or reasoning with him, or persuading him, or entreating him, but not for compelling him or visiting him with any evil in case he do otherwise."[13]

Mill would place limits on the power of government, for in an authoritarian state citizens cannot develop their moral and intellectual potential. Although he feared the state as a threat to individual liberty, Mill also recognized the necessity for state intervention to promote individual self-development: the expansion of individual moral, intellectual, and esthetic capacities. For example, he maintained that it was permissible for the state to require children to attend school against the wishes of their parents, to regulate hours of labor, to promote health, and to provide workers' compensation and old-age insurance.

In *Considerations on Representative Government* (1861), Mill endorsed the active participation of all citizens, including the lower classes, in the political life of the state. However, he also proposed a system of plural voting, in which education and character would determine the number of votes each person was entitled to cast. In this way, Mill, a cautious democrat, sought to protect the individual from the tyranny of a politically unprepared majority.

Thomas Hill Green

Four thinkers stood out in the late 1800s as the leading figures in the shaping of a new liberal position in Britain: Thomas Hill Green (1836–1882), an Oxford University professor; D. G. Ritchie (1853–1903), who taught philosophy at Oxford and Saint Andrews; J. A. Hobson (1858–1940), a social theorist; and L. T. Hobhouse (1864–1929), an academic who also wrote for the *Manchester Guardian*. In general, they argued that laissez faire protected the interests of the economically powerful class and ignored the welfare of the nation. For example, Green valued private property but could not see how this principle helped the poor. "A man who possesses nothing but his powers of labor and who has to sell these to a capitalist for bare daily maintenance, might as well . . . be denied rights of property altogether."[14]

Green argued that the do-nothing state advocated by traditional laissez-faire liberalism condemned many citizens to destitution, ignorance, and despair. The state must preserve individual liberty and at the same time secure the common good by promoting conditions favorable for the self-development of the majority of the population.

Liberalism, for Green, encompassed more than the protection of individual rights from an oppressive government. A truly liberal society, he said, gives people the opportunity to fulfill their moral potential and human capacities. And social reforms initiated by the state assisted in the realization of this broader conception of liberty. Green and other advocates of state intervention contended that the government has a moral obligation to create social conditions that permit individuals to make the best of themselves. Toward that end, the state should promote public health, ensure decent housing, and provide for education. The uneducated and destitute person cannot be morally self-sufficient or a good citizen, Green and other progressives argued.

Green and his colleagues remained advocates of capitalism but rejected strict laissez faire, which, they said, benefited only a particular class at the expense of the common good. Overcoming a traditional liberal mistrust of state power, they assigned the state a positive role in improving social conditions and insisted that state actions need not threaten individual freedom.

In general, by the beginning of the twentieth century, liberals in Britain increasingly acknowledged the need for social legislation; the foundations for the British welfare state were being laid. On the Continent, too, social welfare laws were enacted. To be sure, the motives behind such legislation were quite diverse and often had little to do with liberal sentiments. Nevertheless, in several countries, liberalism was expanding into political and social democracy, a trend that would continue in the twentieth century.

Feminism: Extending the Principle of Equality

Another example of the expansion of liberalism was the emergence of feminist movements in western Europe and the United States. Feminists insisted that the principles of liberty and equality expressed by the philosophes and embodied in the French Declaration of the Rights of Man and of the Citizen and the American Declaration of Independence be applied to women. Thus, Olympe de Gouges's *Declaration of the Rights of Women* (1791), modeled after the Declaration of the Rights of Man and of the Citizen, the French Revolution's tribute to Enlightenment ideals, stated: "Woman is born free and remains equal to man in rights. . . . The aim of every political association is the preservation of the natural . . . rights of man and woman."[15] And in 1837, English novelist and economist Harriet Martineau observed: "One of the fundamental principles announced in the Declaration of Independence is that governments derive their just power from the consent of the governed. How can the political condition of women be reconciled with this?"[16]

In the United States, in the 1830s, Angelina and Sarah Grimké spoke in public—something women rarely did—against slavery and for women's

Child Mine Labor, Report of a Parliamentary Commission of Inquiry, 1842.   In 1842 the British Parliament passed the Mines Act, prohibiting employment of girls and boys under the age of ten in coal mines. This report, detailing children being forced to drag sledge tubs though narrow tunnels, among other abuses, convinced Parliament to act. Further legislation regulating safety and labor practices in the coal industry followed after 1850. (*Hulton Deutsch Collection*)

rights. In 1838, Sarah Grimké published *Letters on the Equality of the Sexes and the Condition of Women,* where she stated emphatically: "Men and women were Created Equal: they are both moral and accountable beings, and whatever is *right* for man to do is *right* for women. . . . How monstrous, how anti-Christian, is the doctrine that woman is to be dependent on man!"[17] The Woman's Suffrage Movement, holding its first convention in 1848 in Seneca Falls, New York, drew up a Declaration of Statements and Principles, which broadened the Declaration of Independence: "We hold these truths to be self-evident: that all men and women are created equal." The document protested "that woman has too long rested satisfied in the circumscribed limits which corrupt customs and a perverted application of the Scriptures have marked out for her" and called for the untiring effort of both men and women to secure for women "an equal participation with men in the various trades, professions, and commerce."[18]

In their struggle for equality, feminists had to overcome deeply ingrained premises about female inferiority and deficiencies. Opponents of women's rights argued that feminist demands would threaten society by undermining marriage and the family. An article in the *Saturday Review,* an English periodical, declared that "It is not the interest of States . . . to encourage the existence of women who are other than entirely dependent on man as well for subsistence as for protection and love. . . . Married life is a woman's profession."[19] In 1870, a member of the House of Commons wondered "what would become, not merely of woman's influence, but of her duties at home, her care of the household, her supervision of all those duties and surroundings which make a happy home . . . if we are to see women coming forward and taking part in the government of the country."[20] This concern for the family combined with the traditional, biased view of woman's nature, as one writer for the *Saturday Review* revealed:

> *The power of reasoning is so small in women that they need adventitious help, and if they have not the guidance and check of a religious conscience, it is useless to expect from them self-control on abstract principles. They do not calculate consequences, and they are reckless when they once give way, hence they are to be kept straight only through their affections, the religious sentiment and a well-educated moral sense.*[21]

In contrast to most of their contemporaries, some prominent men did support equal rights for women. "Can man be free if woman be slave?"[22] asked Shelley, who favored female suffrage. So, too, did social theorist Jeremy Bentham and political economist William Thompson, who wrote *Appeal of One Half of the Human Race* (1825). John Stuart Mill thought that differences between the sexes (and between the classes) were due far more to education than to inherited inequalities. Believing that all people—women as well as men—should be able to develop their talents and intellects as fully as possible, Mill was an early champion of female equality, including women's suffrage. In 1867, Mill, as a member of Parliament, proposed that the suffrage be extended to women (the proposal was rejected by a vote of 194 to 74).

In 1851, Mill had married Harriet Taylor, a long-time friend and a recent widow. An ardent feminist, Harriet Mill influenced her husband's thought. In *The Subjection of Women* (1869), Mill argued that male dominance of women constituted a flagrant abuse of power. He described female inequality as a single relic of an old outlook, which had been exploded in everything else. It violated the principle of individual rights and hindered the progress of humanity:

> *. . . the principle which regulates the existing social relations between the two sexes—the legal subordination of one sex to the other—is wrong in itself, and now one of the chief hindrances to human improvement . . . it ought to be replaced by a principle of perfect equality, admitting no power or privilege on the one side, nor disability on the other.*[23]

Mill considered it only just that women be free to take on all the functions and enter all the occupations until then reserved for men. The struggle for female rights became a major issue in several lands at the end of the nineteenth century and the beginning of the twentieth.

Notes

1. Quoted in Leonard J. Davis, "Gustave Flaubert," in *The* *Romantic Century*, vol. 7 of *European Writers*, ed. Jacques

Barzun and George Stade (New York: Charles Scribner's Sons, 1985), p. 1382.

2. Quoted in Ernst Cassirer, *The Problem of Knowledge*, trans. William H. Woglom and Charles W. Hendel (New Haven, Conn.: Yale University Press, 1950), p. 244.

3. Excerpted in Richard Olson, ed., *Science as Metaphor* (Belmont, Calif.: Wadsworth, 1971), p. 124.

4. Karl Pearson, *National Life from the Standpoint of Science* (London: Adam & Charles Black, 1905), p. 21.

5. Quoted in H. W. Koch, "Social Darwinism in the 'New Imperialism,'" in *The Origins of the First World War*, ed. H. W. Koch (New York: Taplinger, 1972), p. 345.

6. Friedrich von Bernhardi, *Germany and the Next War*, trans. Allen H. Powles (New York: Longman, Green, 1914), p. 18.

7. Karl Marx, *Theses on Feuerbach*, excerpted in *Karl Marx: Selected Writings in Sociology and Social Philosophy*, ed. T. B. Bottomore and Maximilien Rubel (London: Watts, 1956), p. 69.

8. Karl Marx, *The German Ideology* (New York: International Publishers, 1939), p. 18.

9. Friedrich Engels, *The Origin of the Family, Private Property & the State*, in *A Handbook of Marxism*, ed. Emile Burns (New York: Random House, 1935), p. 330.

10. Marx, *German Ideology*, p. 69.

11. Karl Marx, *Communist Manifesto*, trans. Samuel Moore (Chicago: Henry Regnery, 1954), pp. 81–82.

12. John Stuart Mill, *On Liberty* (Boston: Ticknor & Fields, 1863), p. 36.

13. Ibid., p. 22.

14. Thomas Hill Green, *Lectures on the Principles of Political Obligation* (Ann Arbor: University of Michigan Press, 1967), p. 219.

15. Excerpted in Eleanor S. Riemer and John C. Fout, eds., *European Women: A Documentary History, 1789–1945* (New York: Schocken Books, 1980), pp. 63–64.

16. Excerpted in Gayle Graham Yates, ed., *Harriet Martineau on Women* (New Brunswick, N.J.: Rutgers University Press, 1985), p. 134.

17. Excerpted in Miriam Schneir, ed., *Feminism: The Essential Historical Writings* (New York: Vintage Books, 1972), pp. 40–41.

18. Ibid., pp. 76, 82.

19. Quoted in J. A. and Olive Banks, *Feminism and Family Planning in Victorian England* (Liverpool: Liverpool University Press, 1965), p. 43.

20. Ibid., p. 46.

21. Ibid., p. 47.

22. Percy Bysshe Shelly, "The Revolt of Islam," canto 2, stanza 43, in *The Complete Poetical Works of Percy Bysshe Shelley*, ed. Thomas Hutchinson (London: Oxford University Press, 1929), p. 63.

23. John Stuart Mill, *The Subjection of Women*, in *On Liberty, Etc.* (London: Oxford University Press, 1924), p. 427.

Suggested Reading

Andreski, Stanislav, ed., *The Essential Comte* (1974). An excellent collection of excerpts from Comte's works.

Becker, George J., *Master European Realists of the Nineteenth Century* (1982). Discussions of Flaubert, Zola, Chekhov, and other realists.

Bullock, Alan, and Maurice Shock, eds., *The Liberal Tradition* (1956). Well-chosen selections from the writings of British liberals; the introduction is an excellent survey of liberal thought.

Farrington, Benjamin, *What Darwin Really Said* (1966). A brief study of Darwin's work.

Grant, Damian, *Realism* (1970). A very good short survey.

Greene, J. C., *The Death of Adam* (1961). The impact of evolution on Western thought.

Hemmings, F. W. J., ed., *The Age of Realism* (1978). A series of essays exploring realism in various countries.

Hofstadter, Richard, *Social Darwinism in American Thought* (1955). A classic treatment of the impact of evolution on American conservatism, imperialism, and racism.

McLellan, David, *Karl Marx: His Life and Thought* (1977). A highly regarded biography.

————, ed., *Karl Marx: Selected Writings* (1977). A balanced selection of Marx's writings.

Manuel, Frank E., *The Prophets of Paris* (1965). Contains a valuable chapter on Comte.

Tucker, Robert, *The Marxian Revolutionary Idea* (1969). Marxism as a radical social philosophy.

————, *Philosophy and Myth in Karl Marx* (1972). Relationship of Marxist thought to German philosophy; good treatment of Marx's early writings.

————, ed., *The Marx-Engels Reader* (1972). An anthology of Marx's essential writings.

Review Questions

1. How did realism differ from romanticism?
2. Realism and naturalism reflected attitudes shaped by science, industrialism, and secularism. Discuss this statement.
3. What was the relationship between positivism and science?
4. What was Comte's "law of the three stages"?
5. The theory of evolution had revolutionary consequences in areas other than science. Discuss this statement.
6. Why were Social Darwinist theories so popular?
7. What did Marx have in common with the philosophes of the Enlightenment?
8. What did Marx's philosophy of history owe to Hegel? How did it diverge from Hegel?
9. What relationship did Marx see between economics and politics?
10. What relationship did Marx see between economics and ideas?
11. Why did Marxism attract followers?
12. Discuss Marx's historical influence.
13. Why was Marx convinced that capitalism was doomed? How would its destruction come about?
14. What weaknesses in Marxism have critics pointed out?
15. Relate the theories of Mill and Green to the evolution of liberalism. Draw relevant comparisons and contrasts regarding their theories.
16. The feminist movement was an outgrowth of certain ideals that emerged during the course of Western history. Discuss this statement.
17. What arguments were used by opponents of equal rights for women?

❖ CHAPTER 16

Europe in the Late Nineteenth Century: Modernization, Nationalism, Imperialism

*I*n the last part of the nineteenth century, the accelerated pace of industrialization and urbanization continued the process of modernization, which had begun earlier with the Industrial Revolution and transformed European and American societies. Simultaneously, Western nations built governmental machinery for including and controlling great numbers of citizens. This strengthening and centralizing process—*state building* in modern terminology—became the major activity of Western governments. State building meant not only strengthening central authority, but also absorbing previously excluded classes into the community, primarily through the power of nationalism, which governments fostered. A state's power grew enormously as its government affected the lives of ordinary citizens through military conscription, public education, and broad taxation.

Industrialization facilitated the trends toward centralization by concentrating factory workers in cities and loosening traditional rural ties. It greatly affected international relations as well. The amount of coal and iron produced, the mileage and tonnage of railways and navies, the mechanization of industry, and the skill of the populace became important components of national power.

Nationalism, which intensified during the last part of the nineteenth century, was to turn into the dominant spiritual force of European life. It grew increasingly belligerent, intolerant, and irrational, threatening both the peace of Europe and the liberal humanist tradition of the Enlightenment. Nationalism and industrialization were the principal forces behind imperialism, leading European nations and the United States to extend their power over Asian, African, and Latin American lands. ❖

Chronology 16.1 ❖ Expansion of Western Power

1839–1842	Opium War: the British defeat the Chinese, annexing treaty ports in China and opening them to Western trade
1851–1852	Louis Napoleon Bonaparte overthrows Second Republic, becoming Emperor Napoleon III
1853	Commodore Perry, with U.S. naval forces, opens Japan to trade
1857–1858	Sepoy Mutiny; Britain replaces the East India Company and begins ruling India through a viceroy
1867	Second Reform Bill doubles the English electorate
1869	Opening of the Suez Canal
1870	Third French Republic is established
1870–1871	Franco-Prussian War; Paris Commune; creation of German Empire, with William I as Kaiser and Bismarck as chancellor
1876	Stanley sets up posts in the Congo for Leopold II of Belgium
1882	Britain occupies Egypt
1884	Berlin Conference on Africa; Reform Bill grants suffrage to most English men
1894–1906	Dreyfus affair in France
1898	Spanish-American War: United States acquires the Philippines and Puerto Rico and occupies Cuba; battle of Omdurman
1899–1902	Boer War between the British and the Afrikaners
1900	Boxers rebel against foreign presence in China
1904–1905	Russo-Japanese War: the Japanese defeat the Russians
1911	Parliament Act limits power of the House of Lords
1919	Britain grants a legislative assembly in India; Gandhi's passive resistance movement broadens with the Amritsar Massacre

The Advance of Industry

Historians call the second half of the nineteenth century the Second Industrial Revolution because of the great increase in the speed and scale of economic and social transformation. This changed world was defined by technological advances and new forms of business and labor organization. It was also characterized by the rise of the middle class to political and social power corresponding to its economic power; the decline of traditional groups, or classes; and dramatic changes in the role of women and children in the family.

At the midcentury, farming was still the main occupation of people everywhere, including Britain, where industrialization was most advanced. Even Britain had more domestic servants than factory workers and twice as many agricultural laborers as textile and clothing workers. Large factories were few, and handicrafts still flourished. Sailing ships still outnumbered steamships, and horses carried more freight than trains. This situation, however, changed radically in two spurts: the first between 1850 and 1870, and the second from the 1890s until World War I.

During the first spurt, in Europe and America the shift from hand to machine production accelerated, leading to the concentration of factory workers in industrial cities and to the growth of unions. The standard of living for most workers rose. New machines and processes, legislation, and trade union bargaining relieved the worst conditions of early industrialization. At the same time, the first regulations of urban development and sanitation began to improve living conditions. In the more advanced industrial areas, the social organization of the workplace changed: the introduction of heavy equipment resulted in men replacing women and children in the factories. The somewhat higher wages for skilled male laborers meant that women with families were no longer compelled by dire necessity to work in factories. However, women forced out of factories (they would return during World War I) were not freed for a life of leisure. They took on jobs as domestics, pieceworkers, seamstresses, or laundresses. Children became students as the state and the economy demanded that they acquire at least a minimal education.

The scale of development changed markedly during the second spurt. Giant firms run by boards of directors, including financiers, operated far-flung enterprises of enormous, mechanized factories, which were manned by unskilled, low-paid, and often seasonal workers. These industrial giants were able to control the output, price, and distribution of commodities. They dominated smaller firms, financed and controlled research and development, and expanded far beyond their national frontiers. The "captains of industry"—the owners or managers of these large firms—possessed such extraordinary economic power that they often commanded political power as well. The emergence and concentration of heavy industry in large firms, capitalized by specialist banks, characterized the post-1890 period all over Europe. Such rapid growth caught the imagination of businessmen, as well as of socialist critics.

Revolutionary technological changes furthered the growth of industry. At the midcentury, all of Europe caught the railroad mania that had seized Britain in the 1840s. This epic expansion of railroads was paralleled in shipping. In 1850, steam-powered ships constituted only 5 percent of the world's tonnage; by 1893, the figure had risen to half of all tonnage. At the turn of the century, two German engineers, Gottlieb Daimler and Karl Benz, joined to perfect the internal combustion engine. Then an American, Henry Ford, using mass-production assembly-line techniques, brought out his Model T for "the ordinary man," and the automobile age was born. The invention of the diesel engine by another German in 1897 meant that cheaper, more efficient fuel could be used. Diesel engines soon replaced steam engines on giant cargo ships, warships, and luxury liners. In communications, the advent of the telegraph, telephone, and later radio also revolutionized people's lives.

However, economic development was extremely uneven. Central, southern, and eastern Europe remained backward in many respects and stayed so until World War I and after. In these overwhelmingly agricultural societies, manufacturing consisted for the most part of consumer-oriented, small-scale operations in textiles and food processing, in which artisans maintained their place.

Accelerated Urbanization

More rapid industrialization increased the numbers of northwestern Europeans and Americans who lived in cities, which became more numerous, larger, and more densely populated. Although not an industrial city, London had become a megalopolis of five million people by 1880 and was home to seven million by 1914. Paris increased from two million to three million between 1850 and World War I. Berlin, a city of only half a million in 1866, reached two million by World War I. There were only three German cities of more than a hundred thousand on the eve of unification, but by 1903 there were fifteen.

In the cities, the middle class rose to political, economic, and social prominence, often expressing its newfound importance and prosperity through civic activity. As machinery replaced handicraft, the artisan working class experienced a sharp decline. Factory workers, their ranks swelled by peasants and artisans, emerged as an important social group in cities. Cut off from the regions of their birth, the peasants and artisans who worked in factories shed their old loyalties; in the cities, some found a place for themselves in their neighborhoods, some in union and party activities, and some none at all. Industrialization also created a new, "white-collar" group of clerks, who tried to differentiate themselves from factory workers.

The Rise of Socialist Parties

Between 1850 and 1914, workers' lives improved because of trade union organization, government intervention in the economy, and the general increase in productivity brought about by industrialization. Still, members of the working class faced problems and inequities that drew them to socialist parties, which strove for government control of industry and worker control of government and workplace. Most workers and their families lived in bleak, overcrowded tenements, without central heating or running water. They worked long hours—as much as fifty-five per week in the trades where governments restricted the length of the workweek, and from seventy to seventy-five in unregulated trades. Their jobs were exhausting and monotonous. They

Painting of the Bowery by Louis Sontag, 1895.   New York City street scene bursting with commerical energies and activity as the night is lighted by blazing electricity. The painting puts pushcarts, trolleys, horse-drawn cabs, and trains side by side, as it does the classic architecture of the theater and the four-story buildings housing shops and families on the Bowery. The life of the city throbs with the energy of modern technology. (*Museum of the City of New York #32.275.2. Gift of William B. Miles*)

also suffered from malnutrition. The English men and boys who appeared for medical exams to serve in the Boer War were found to be so physically unfit that their condition prompted reforms to improve the health and education of the laboring class. The working class as a whole suffered from diseases, particularly tuberculosis, and from lack of medical care. Women often died in childbirth owing to inadequate treatment, and men, particularly miners and dockworkers, commonly experienced job accidents that maimed and killed. Socialists argued that these conditions were due to the capitalist profit system, which exploited and impoverished workers and enriched the owners.

Socialist parties grew phenomenally in Germany and rapidly in much of the rest of Europe. Even Russia, which was scarcely industrial, had a Marxist socialist party. The growth of socialism reflected the workers' increased consciousness that they had special needs, which other political parties did not fulfill. However, socialists were divided about tactics. "Orthodox" Marxists believed that socialist-led revolution was the necessary first step for change; this group included Wilhelm Liebknecht and August Bebel of Germany and Jules Guesde of France. Others—"revisionist" Marxists—who were influenced by the German theoretician Eduard Bernstein, urged socialists to use the political and economic systems to build a socialist society without revolution.

Great Britain: Reform and Unrest

The process of reform, begun with the Reform Bill of 1832 and the Factory Acts, continued in the era of the Second Industrial Revolution. The Reform Bill of 1867, skillfully maneuvered through Parliament by Benjamin Disraeli (1804–1881), gave the vote to urban workers, doubling the electorate. Some of Disraeli's fellow members in the Conservative party feared that extending the vote to the largely uneducated masses would ruin the nation, but Disraeli maintained that this democratic advance would strengthen the bonds between the people and the state. Moreover, he believed that the Conservatives' social program and imperialist foreign policy would win the newly enfranchised poor to the party.

The work of electoral reform was continued by the Liberal party under the leadership of William Gladstone (1809–1898), who served four terms as prime minister. The Ballot Act (1872) provided for the secret ballot, which enabled working-class voters to avoid intimidation by their employers. Next, the Reform Bill of 1884 enfranchised rural laborers; now almost all English males could vote.

Social Reform

Unlike their continental brothers, British workers on the whole had never been attracted to socialism, particularly not to Marxism. In the 1880s, however, widespread poverty and new trends in industry—especially monopolies, cartels, and foreign competition—led some labor leaders to urge greater militancy. These conditions brought about the creation of the Labour party.

The Labour party might never have grown without the Taff Vale decision (1901), which awarded damages to an employer picketed by a union. If workers could be fined for picketing or other actions restraining trade, their unions could be broken and they would lose the economic gains of half a century. Galvanized by the Taff Vale decision and eager to win reforms for the working class, labor took to politics. In the elections of 1906, the new Labour party gained twenty-nine members in the House of Commons; it would become an important faction in British politics.

Between 1906 and 1911, the Liberals, led by David Lloyd George (1863–1945) and the then Liberal Winston Churchill (1874–1965), introduced a series of important social measures. Aided by the Labour party, they enacted a program of old-age pensions, labor exchanges to help the unemployed find work, unemployment and health insurance (a program deeply influenced by Bismarckian social legislation), and minimum wages for certain industries. Parliament also repealed the Taff Vale decision. In the process, however, a constitutional crisis developed between the Liberals, who had Labour support, and the Conservatives, who dominated the House of Lords. The crisis ended with the Parliament Act of 1911, which decreed that the House of Lords could only delay, not prevent, the passage of a bill that the House of Commons had approved.

Feminist Agitation

On the issue of women's suffrage, British democracy was lagging. Influenced by the ideals of the American and French revolutions, women had begun to protest their unequal status. In 1867, John Stuart Mill proposed extending the vote to women but his colleagues in Parliament rejected the proposal. The following year, Lydia Becker became the first Englishwoman to speak in public for women's suffrage. Many people, both men and women, viewed female suffrage as too radical a break with tradition. Some asserted that women were represented by their husbands or male relatives and therefore did not need the right to vote. Others protested that women lacked the ability to participate responsibly in political life. Queen Victoria, who supported other reforms, called women's suffrage "that mad, wicked folly."

Although many Liberals and some Labourites favored women's suffrage, women were advised by the leader of the Liberals "to keep on pestering . . . but exercise the virtue of patience." For the women who deemed this advice patronizing and whose patience was running out, a family of feminists advocated a more militant course of action. Emmeline Pankhurst and her daughters Sylvia and Christabel urged demonstrations, invasions of the House of Commons, destruction of property, and hunger strikes. They did not urge these dramatic actions all at once, but when their petitions and demands were ignored, they moved to more and more shocking deeds. Suffragettes began a campaign of breaking windows, starting fires in mailboxes, and chaining themselves to the gates at Parliament. As a gesture of protest, in 1913 one militant threw herself to her death under King Edward VII's horse at the races.

When feminists were arrested for violating the law, they staged hunger strikes. Ugly situations resulted, with the police force feeding the demonstrators and subjecting them to ridicule and rough treatment. Often the police would release half-starved feminists and, when they had recovered their

Poster Published by the Artists' Suffrage League, Designed by Emily Harding Andrews, c. 1908. This suffragette poster illustrates the fact that British women could not vote in the early twentieth century. The cap and gown of the woman college graduate does not help her find the key which will release her from the imprisoning categorization with felons and the mentally ill, who couldn't vote for Parliament either. Women played an important role in local government, where they were in charge of schools, orphanages, and hospitals, but were unable to vote for members of the House of Commons until after World War I. (*Library of Congress*)

health, would reimprison them. Ridiculed, humiliated, and punished—but above all legally ignored—the feminists refused to accept the passive role that a male-dominated society had assigned them. When women played a major part on the home front in World War I, many of the elite changed their minds, and in 1918, British women over the age of thirty gained the vote. In 1928, Parliament lowered the voting age for women to twenty-one, the same qualifying age as that for male voters.

The Irish Question

Feminist agitation was one explosive issue confronting prewar Britain. Another was the Irish question. While moderate Irish nationalists called for *home rule* (self-government within the British Empire), something favored by many members of Parliament, Irish Catholic extremists, such as the Irish Republican Brotherhood and the Gaelic League, pressed for full independence. Fearing Catholic domination, the Protestant Irish (Ulstermen) in the northern counties of Ulster strongly opposed independence for Ireland.

The Ulster Volunteers recruited a large private army and openly trained it for revolution in the event that home rule was enacted. Gangs smuggled guns, soldiers fired on demonstrators, violence bred violence, and civil war seemed close. In 1916, the Easter Rebellion, an Irish insurrection, was suppressed and its leaders executed. But the English cabinet was moved to proceed with home rule at once. The Irish revolt of 1919–20 brought matters to a head: Ireland was divided, the overwhelmingly Catholic south gaining independence and the six predominantly Protestant counties of Ulster remaining part of the United Kingdom.

At the beginning of the twentieth century, labor, Irish, and female militancy marred Britain's image of a stable, liberal, constitutional regime. Nevertheless, British parliamentary government survived every crisis and proved itself able to carry the nation successfully through a grueling world war.

France: A Troubled Nation

In 1852, Louis Napoleon Bonaparte (1808–1873), who had been elected president of the Second French Republic in 1848, took the title of emperor in the tradition of his illustrious uncle. Napoleon III ruled in an authoritarian manner, permitting no opposition, censoring the press, and allowing the legislature little power. But in the 1860s, in a drastic shift, he introduced liberal reforms, pardoning political prisoners, removing press censorship, allowing workers the right to form unions, and approving a new constitution, with safeguards for individual liberty. His reforms have perplexed historians. Was Napoleon III a sincere believer in liberal ideals who waited until his power was firmly established before implementing these ideals, or did he introduce reforms only because he feared unrest?

Defeat in the Franco-Prussian War brought down the empire of Napoleon III. Bitter frustration with defeat and hatred of the Prussian invaders led the people of Paris to rise against the armistice signed by the provisional government—the politicians who had replaced Napoleon. The Paris Commune (1871) began as a patriotic refusal to accept defeat and as a rejection of Napoleon's rule, but it became a rejection of the provisional government as well. Ultimately, the Communards (as those who resisted the Prussians and the provisional government were called) also challenged property owners.

The Communards included followers of the anarchist Joseph Proudhon and groups of republican and socialist veterans of the revolution of 1848, gathered from prisons, from hiding, and from exile. For two months in the spring of 1871, these revolutionaries ruled Paris. Then Adolphe Thiers, head of the provisional government that still governed the rest of France, ordered an attack on Paris. The fighting was bitter and desperate, with many acts of terrorism and violence. Both sides in this civil war set fires that destroyed large parts of the city they loved. The Communards were defeated and treated as traitors: twenty thousand of them were executed without trial, and those who were tried received harsh sentences (death, life imprisonment, and deportation to prison colonies). Governing classes across Europe viewed the Paris Commune as a sign that the people should be ruled with an iron fist.

At first it seemed that a monarchy would succeed the empire of Napoleon III. But disunity among the monarchists enabled France to become a republic by default. Unlike Britain with its two-party system, the Third French Republic had many political parties, which contributed to instability. No one party had sufficient weight in parliament to provide strong leadership. Prime ministers resigned in rapid succession; cabinets rose and fell frequently, giving the impression of a state without direction. Political life seemed to consist of wheeling and dealing. Yet in the process, legislation was enacted that made elementary education free and compulsory and legalized trade unions. The Third Republic survived, though not without major crises; the principal one was the Dreyfus affair.

In 1894, Captain Alfred Dreyfus, an Alsatian-Jewish artillery officer, was wrongly accused of having sold secrets to the Germans. After a court martial, he was condemned to life imprisonment on Devil's Island. Anti-Semitic elements joined with the Republic's opponents—monarchists, army leaders, clerics, and nationalists—to denounce and block every attempt to clear Dreyfus of the charges against him. In the beginning, few people defended Dreyfus; the vast majority felt that the honor of France and the army was at stake. Then individuals, mainly radical republicans, came to his defense, including the writers Anatole France and Émile Zola and the future republican leader Georges Clemenceau, along with university students. They protested and demonstrated, insisting on a retrial and a revision of the verdict. After many humiliations, Dreyfus was finally cleared in 1906.

The result of the victory of the radical republicans, however, was a fierce campaign to root out those opposing the Republic. The radicals attacked the church, expelled religious orders, confiscated their property, and waged a vigorous campaign to replace the influence of the parish priest with that of the district schoolmaster. Complete separation of church and state was ordered; taxes no longer supported the parishes and religious schools.

Despite progress in the middle of the nineteenth century, French economic development lagged. France had fewer and smaller industries than Britain or Germany, and more French people lived in rural areas and small communities. In the 1880s, both trade unionism and political parties with a socialist program began to make headway and to press for social reform through the democratic parliamentary institutions of the Republic. However, France was very slow to enact social measures such as pensions and regulations governing working conditions, wages, and hours. These measures, which might have improved the lives of ordinary people, were regarded by the ruling elite as socialism and by socialists as token offerings to buy off workers.

France was a troubled country, and the Third Republic was not a popular regime. The church, the army, socialism, and even memories of the monarchy and the empire inspired deeper passions than the Republic, which survived only because the dissension among its enemies allowed it to survive. France approached World War I as a deeply divided country. Yet when World War I broke out, the French people rallied to defend the nation.

Germany: The Power-State

Prussia's victory over France in the Franco-Prussian War of 1870–71 completed the struggle for German unification. The new government, the German Reich (empire), was headed by the king of Prussia. Though the Reichstag (lower house) was elected by universal suffrage, the real power lay in the hands of the emperor and Bismarck, the "Iron Chancellor," who was responsible only to the emperor. The German kaiser (emperor), unlike the British monarch, had considerable control over lawmaking and foreign affairs and commanded the army and navy. The emperor alone could remove the chancellor or the cabinet members from office. The sole control over Bismarck was the Reichstag's refusal to pass the budget, an extreme measure that politicians were usually unwilling to take.

German liberals did not vigorously struggle for basic political and civil liberties; they tolerated evasions of principle and practices that British politicians would never have allowed. While Britain, France, the United States, and other Western states were becoming more democratic, Germany remained a semi-autocratic state. The failure of democratic attitudes and procedures to take root in Germany was to have dangerous consequences for the future.

Bismarck's political practices weakened liberal and democratic elements, and he regarded parties as incapable of making policy for the country. In Bismarck's mind, the Catholics and the socialists were internationalists who did not place the interests of Germany first. He began to persecute Catholics, who made up about 40 percent of the population. The *Kulturkampf* (struggle for culture) was a series of laws passed in 1873 to subject the church to the state. The laws discriminated against the Jesuits and required state supervision of the church and training of priests in state schools. Catholics had to be married by the state. Churchmen who refused to accept these laws were imprisoned or exiled. German liberals did not defend the civil liberties of the Catholics against these laws. Persecution only strengthened the German Catholics' loyalty to their church, however, and the Catholic Center party gained support. Prussian conservatives, though Protestant, resented Bismarck's anticlerical policy, which could hurt Lutherans as well as Catholics. With the succession of Leo XIII to the papacy in 1878, Bismarck quietly opened negotiations for peace with the church.

When two attempts were made on William I's life in 1878, Bismarck demanded that the socialists be suppressed. In reality, the socialists, few in number, were not a threat; their immediate practical program was a demand for civil liberties and democracy in Germany. Only the narrowest of conservative views would have labeled the socialists as dangerous, but many in Germany, particularly the Prussian Junker class, held such a narrow view. The liberals once again did not oppose Bismarck's special legislation outlawing subversive organizations and authorizing the police to ban meetings and newspapers. The Social Democratic party, like the Catholic Center party before, survived the persecution. It grew stronger and better disciplined as the liberals grew weaker, discredited by their unwillingness to act.

Bismarck's policy was not merely repressive. He tried to win the workers by paternalistic social legislation. Like many conservatives, he was disturbed by the effects of industrialization, which had developed at a rapid pace in the 1850s and 1860s. Germany was the first state to enact a program of social legislation for the proletariat; it included insurance against sickness, disability, accidents, and old age. The employer, the state, and the worker each contributed small amounts to an insurance fund. Many people called the legislation state socialism.

Despite Bismarck's attempts to woo the workers away from socialism, the German working class continued to support the Social Democratic party in elections. On the eve of World War I, union membership was roughly three million, and the Social Democratic party was the largest single party in Germany. The socialists talked revolution, but the unions—the largest and most powerful in Europe—and many party members favored policies of gradual reform. Great numbers of German workers were patriotic, even imperialistic, and thought that their government deserved their loyalty.

By 1900, Germany had caught up with, and in some areas surpassed, Britain in economic growth. Aided by the skill of its scientists and inventors, Germany became a leader in the chemical and electrical industries. It possessed the most extensive sector of large-scale, concentrated industrial and corporate capitalism of any Great Power. Within a short period, Germany had become a strong, industrialized state, ready and eager to play an important role in world affairs. Its growing industrial and military might, linked with an aggressive nationalism, alarmed other countries. This combination of German vitality, aggressiveness, and the fears of its rivals helped lead to World War I.

Italy: Unfulfilled Expectations

Italian nationalists expected greatness from the unification of their country, so long conquered, plundered, divided, and ruled by absolute princes. But the newly unified Italy faced serious problems. An overwhelmingly Roman Catholic country, it was split by religious controversy. Liberals and republicans wanted a secular state, with civil marriage and public education, which was anathema to the church.

Another divisive factor was Italy's long tradition of separate and rival states. Many Italians doubted that the central government would deal justly with every region. Furthermore, few Italians could participate in the constitutional monarchy. Of the twenty-seven million citizens, only about two million could vote—even after the reforms of 1881, which tripled the electorate. Liberals could point out that almost every literate male could vote, but this achievement was small consolation to those who had fought for unification but now were denied voting privileges because they did not pass a literacy test.

Among Italian workers, cynicism about the government was so deep that many turned to radical movements, which advocated the rejection of authority and the tactics of terrorism, assassination, and general strikes. Disgust with parliamentary government led the workers to believe that direct action would gain more than elections and parties. Other alienated Italians included peasants in some rural areas, particularly in the south. They were so isolated from the national political and economic life that traditional patterns of loyalty to the local landowner, now also a political leader, persisted. Catholic, loyal to their landlord, and bitterly unhappy with their economic situation, they saw few signs of the new state other than taxation and conscription.

The ruling elite brushed aside Italy's difficult social and economic problems and concentrated instead on issues more easily expressed to an inexperienced political nation: nationalism, foreign policy, and military glory. The politicians trumpeted Italy's ambitions for Great Power status to justify military expenditures beyond the means of such a poor state. They presented Italy's scramble for African and Mediterranean territories as the solution to all its social ills. The profits from exploiting others would pay for badly needed social reforms, and the raw materials gained would fuel industrialization. None of these promises came true, which deepened the cynicism of a disillusioned people. As a foreign and as a domestic policy, this pursuit of glory was too costly for the fragile nation.

Before World War I, Italy was deeply divided politically. A wave of strikes and rural discontent gave sufficient warning to political leaders so that they declared neutrality, deciding, unlike Russia, not to risk the shaky regime by entering the war. But the appeals of expansionism were too great for them to maintain this policy.

The United States, 1865–1914

Within a generation after its bloody Civil War (1861–1865), fought to prevent the dissolution of the union, the United States moved into the rank of giant industrial powers, then to the status of a Great Power, and by the end of World War I, to world leadership.

In many ways, the early industrialization of the United States resembled that of Britain. Unskilled European and rural laborers furnished the manpower for New England textile mills, just as Irish and rural laborers had done for England. Government provided a stable framework for commerce, maintained tariffs to keep out foreign (mainly British) competition and, like Britain, did not aspire to regulate private enterprise. As in Britain, it was the growth of a large internal market for cheap, standardized goods that encouraged entrepreneurs to take the risks of investment and production on a large scale. Even more than the British—perhaps because of the much larger market for cheap goods—Americans took to machines, with standardized and interchangeable parts, which could produce cheap goods. (Eli Whitney, who invented the cotton gin, got his start in the production of interchangeable parts for handguns.) Unlike Britain, however, the United States was dependent on an influx of capital (most of it from Britain). This influx continued even after the Civil War, when great sectors of the American economy moved from the work of artisans to modern concentrated industry.

After the Civil War, American industrialization gained momentum. American industrial power rested on the exploitation of the continent's resources and on the extension of agriculture and transportation across the continent. The other crucial factors were a cheap labor force and substantial foreign investment in large-scale corporations in heavy industries, such as coal mining and iron and steel manufacture. The government fostered railroad building, tariff regulation, and free immigration—all of which contributed to the construction of an industrial giant in the northeastern segment of the country. Otherwise, however, the government took a laissez-faire stance.

Urbanization, with its concomitant social problems, accompanied industrialization. American politicians were much less inclined to support social legislation, including pensions and minimum wages, than their European counterparts. Yet the United States had less labor strife until the end of the century. For one thing, its workers shared the dream of entrepreneurial success much more than European workers. For another, class solidarity was difficult to develop among varied ethnic groups of different cultures and languages. Each new immigrant group (and later the rural blacks) entered at the bottom, supplying cheap and competitive labor and experiencing the violent reactions of their fellow workers from other ethnic groups. Established workers, already assimilated, were able to prohibit Asian immigration at the end of the century, after Chinese workers had built the transcontinental railroad.

Labor conflict did flare up, however, in the decade before World War I. Generally, workers voted for one of the two major parties, but in the election of 1912 more than a million voted for the Socialist candidate. Not all of these voters were the "foreigners," or recent immigrants, that contemporaries pretended made up the ranks of those who were critical of the money power of giant cartels and monopolies. Theodore Roosevelt of the Republicans and Woodrow Wilson of the Democrats both called for curbing monopolies, or trusts. Unrestrained competition, which made some people millionaires and others paupers, also upset many Americans, as did the restrictions on labor union organizing.

By 1914, the American market was the largest, most homogeneous, and most rapidly growing in the world. The United States was the largest industrial nation, producing more steel and coal than any other country. It was also the world's leader in automobiles, farming technology, and the production of electricity and petroleum. Its labor was the most productive and had the highest standard of living. The United States had achieved this position in little more than a generation.

The Rise of Racial Nationalism

In the first half of the nineteenth century, European nationalism and liberalism went hand in hand. Liberals sought both the rights of the individual and national independence and unification. Liberal nationalists believed that a unified state free of foreign subjugation was in harmony with the principle of natural rights, and they insisted that love of country led to love of humanity. As nationalism grew more extreme, however, its profound difference from liberalism became more apparent. The extreme nationalism of the late nineteenth and early twentieth centuries contributed to World War I and to the rise of fascism after the war; it was the seedbed of totalitarian nationalism.

Concerned exclusively with the greatness of the nation, extreme nationalists rejected the liberal emphasis on political liberty. They attacked parliamentary government as an obstacle to national power and greatness and maintained that authoritarian leadership was needed to meet national emergencies. The needs of the nation, they said, transcended the rights of the individual.

Extreme nationalists also rejected the liberal ideal of equality. Placing the nation above everything, nationalists accused national minorities of corrupting the nation's spirit; and they glorified war as a symbol of the nation's resolve and will. In the name of national power and unity, they persecuted minorities at home and stirred up hatred against other nations. Increasingly, they embraced militaristic, imperialistic, and racist doctrines. At the founding of the Nationalist Association in Italy in 1910, one leader declared: "Just as socialism teaches the proletariat the value of class struggle, so we must teach Italy the value of international struggle. But international struggle is war? Well, then, let there be war! And nationalism will arouse the will for a victorious war . . . the only way to national redemption."[1]

Interpreting politics with the logic of emotions, extreme nationalists insisted that they had a sacred mission to regain lands once held in the Middle Ages, to unite with their kinfolk in other lands, or to rule over peoples considered inferior. Loyalty to the nation-state was elevated above all other allegiances. The ethnic state became an object of religious reverence; the spiritual energies that formerly had been dedicated to Christianity were now channeled into the worship of the nation-state.

By the beginning of the twentieth century, conservatives had become the

Celebration of the Unveiling of the Statue of Hermann (Arminius) at the Site of Teutoberger Wald.   The Franco-Prussian War (1870–1871) brought German unity and intensified nationalist feelings. German nationalists glorified the traditions and deeds of their ancient ancestors who overran the Roman Empire. Depicted here is the unveiling of the statue erected in 1875 for Arminius, a tribal chieftain, who had defeated a Roman force in 9 A.D. German nationalism, which grew more extreme in succeeding decades, helped give rise to the world wars of the twentieth century. (*Bildarchiv Preussischer Kulturbesitz*)

staunchest advocates of nationalism, and the nationalism preached by conservative extremists was stripped of Mazzinian ideals of liberty, equality, and the fellowship of nations. Landholding aristocrats, generals, and clergy, often joined by big industrialists, saw nationalism as a convenient instrument for gaining a mass following in their struggle against democracy and socialism. Championing popular nationalist myths and dreams, a newly radicalized right hoped to harness the instinctual energies of the masses, particularly the peasants and the lower middle class—shopkeepers, civil servants, and white-collar workers—to conservative causes. Peasants viewed liberalism and Marxism as threats to traditional values, while the lower bourgeoisie feared the proletariat. These people were receptive to the rhetoric of ultranationalists, who denounced democracy and Marxism as threats to national unity and Jews as aliens endangering the nation. Nationalism was presented as a victory of idealism over materialism and as the subordination of class and personal interests to the general good of the nation.

Volkish Thought

Extreme nationalism was a general European phenomenon, but it proved especially dangerous in Germany. Bismarck's triumphs lured Germans into a dream world. Many started to yearn for the extension of German power throughout the globe. The past, they said, belonged to France and Britain; the future, to Germany.

The most ominous expression of German nationalism (and a clear example of mythical thinking) was *Volkish* thought. (*Volk* means "folk" or "people.") German Volkish thinkers sought to bind the German people together through a deep love of their language, traditions, and fatherland. These thinkers felt that Germans were animated by a higher spirit than that found in other peoples. To Volkish thinkers, the Enlightenment and parliamentary democracy were foreign ideas that corrupted the pure German spirit. With fanatical devotion, Volkish thinkers embraced all things German—the medieval past, the German landscape, the simple peasant, the village—and denounced the liberal humanist tradition of the West as alien to the German soul.

Volkish thought attracted Germans frightened by all the complexities of the modern age—industrialization, urbanization, materialism, class conflicts, and alienation. Seeing their beloved Germany transformed by these forces of modernity, Volkish thinkers yearned to restore the sense of community that they attributed to the preindustrial age. Only by identifying with their sacred soil and sacred traditions could modern Germans escape from the evils of industrial society. Only then could the different classes band together in an organic unity.

The Volkish movement had little support from the working class, which was concerned chiefly with improving its standard of living. The movement appealed mainly to farmers and villagers, who regarded the industrial city as a threat to native values and a vehicle for spreading foreign ideas; to artisans and small shopkeepers, threatened by big business; and to scholars, writers, teachers, and students, who saw in Volkish nationalism a cause worthy of their idealism. The schools were leading agents for the dissemination of Volkish ideas.

Volkish thinkers glorified the ancient Germanic tribes that had overrun the Roman Empire; they contrasted their courageous and vigorous German ancestors with the effete and degenerate Romans. A few tried to harmonize ancient Germanic religious traditions with Christianity. Such attitudes led Germans to see themselves as a heroic people fundamentally different from and better than the English and the French. It also led them to regard German culture as unique—innately superior and opposed to the humanist outlook of the Enlightenment. Like their romantic predecessors, Volkish thinkers held that the German people and culture had a special destiny and a unique mission. They pitted the German soul against the Western intellect—feeling and spirit against a drab rationalism. To be sure, the Western humanist tradition had many supporters in Germany, but the counterideology of Volkish thought was spreading widely.

Racist doctrines had an especially strong appeal for Volkish thinkers. According to these doctrines, race was the key to history; not only physical features, but also moral, esthetic, and intellectual qualities distinguished one race from another. For racist thinkers, a race demonstrated its vigor and achieved greatness when it preserved its purity; intermarriage between races was contamination that would result in genetic, cultural, and military decline. Like their Nazi successors, Volkish thinkers claimed that the German race was purer than and therefore superior to all other races. Its superiority was revealed in such physical characteristics as blond hair, blue eyes, and fair skin—all signs of inner qualities lacking in other races.

German racial nationalists insisted that Germans, as a superior race, had a national right to dominate other peoples, particularly the "racially inferior" Slavs of the East: "The racial biological ideology tells us that there are races that lead and races that follow. Political history is nothing but the history of struggles among the leading races. Conquests, above all, are always the work of the leading races. Such men can conquer, may conquer, and shall conquer."[2]

Anti-Semitism

German racial nationalists singled out Jews as the most wicked of races and a deadly enemy of the German people. Anti-Semitism, which was widespread in late-nineteenth-century Europe, provides a striking example of the perennial appeal, power, and danger of mythical thinking—of elevating to the level of objective truth ideas that have no basis in fact but provide all-encompassing, emotionally satisfying explanations of life and history. By manufacturing the myth of the wicked Jew, the radical right confirmed the insight reached by the political philosopher Georges Sorel (see pages 472–473): that people are moved and united by myths that offer simple, clear, and emotionally gratifying resolutions to the complexities of the modern world.

Anti-Semitic organizations and political parties sought to deprive Jews of their civil rights, and anti-Semitic publications proliferated. Edouard Drumont, a French journalist, argued that the Jews, racially inferior and believers in a primitive religion, had gained control of France. Like medieval Christian anti-Semites, Drumont accused Jews of deicide and of using Christian blood for ritual purposes. Drumont's newspaper (established with Jesuit funds) blamed all the ills of France on the Jews, called for their expulsion from the country, and predicted that they would be massacred.

Romania barred most Jews from holding office and from voting, imposed various economic restrictions on them, and limited their admission into secondary schools and universities. The Romanian government even financed an international congress of anti-Semites, which met in Bucharest in 1886. In German-speaking Austria, Karl Lueger, a leader of the Christian Socialist party, founded by conservative German nationalists, exploited anti-Semitism to win elections in overwhelmingly Catholic Vienna. Georg von Schönerer,

The Protocols of the Elders of Zion. This infamous forgery, commissioned by the Russian secret police, became an international bestseller and contributed to outrages against Jews. Anti-Semitic organizations continue to publish and circulate it today. The picture is the actual cover of a French edition of the *Protocols*, c. 1934. (*The Wiener Library, London*)

founder of the German National party in Austria, wanted to eliminate Jews from all areas of public life.

Russia placed a quota on the number of Jewish students admitted to secondary schools and higher educational institutions, confined Jews to certain regions of the country, and, "to purify the sacred historic capital," expelled about twenty thousand Jews from Moscow. Some government officials encouraged and even organized *pogroms* (mob violence) against Jews. Between 1903 and 1906, pogroms broke out in 690 towns and villages, most of them in the Ukraine, traditionally a hotbed of anti-Semitism. (Ukrainian folksongs and legends glorified centuries-old massacres of Jews.) The attackers looted, burned, raped, and murdered, generally with impunity. In Russia and several other lands, Jews were put on trial for slaughtering Christian children as part of a Passover ritual—a deranged accusation that survived from the Middle Ages.

Anti-Semitism had a long and bloodstained history in Europe, stemming both from an irrational fear and hatred of outsiders with noticeably different ways and from the commonly accepted myth that the Jews as a people were collectively and eternally cursed for rejecting Christ. Christians saw Jews as the murderers of Christ—an image that promoted terrible anger and hatred.

Periodically, mobs humiliated, tortured, and massacred Jews, and rulers expelled them from their kingdoms. Often barred from owning land and excluded from the craft guilds, medieval Jews concentrated in trade and moneylending: occupations that frequently earned them greater hostility. By the sixteenth century, Jews in a number of lands were forced by law to live in separate quarters of the town, called *ghettos*. Medieval Christian anti-Semitism, which depicted the Jew as vile and Judaism as repulsive, fertilized the soil for modern anti-Semitism.

In the nineteenth century, under the aegis of the liberal ideals of the Enlightenment and the French Revolution, Jews gained legal equality in most European lands. They could leave the ghetto and participate in many activities that had been closed to them. Traditionally an urban people, the Jews, who were concentrated in the leading cities of Europe, took advantage of this new freedom and opportunity.

Motivated by the fierce desire of outsiders to prove their worth and aided by deeply embedded traditions that valued education and family life, many Jews achieved striking success as entrepreneurs, bankers, lawyers, journalists, doctors, scientists, scholars, and performers. For example, in 1880, Jews, who constituted about 10 percent of the Viennese population, accounted for 38.6 percent of the medical students and 23.3 percent of the law students in Vienna. Viennese cultural life before World War I was to a large extent shaped by Jewish writers, artists, musicians, critics, and patrons. All but one of the major banking houses were Jewish. However, most European Jews—peasants, peddlers, and laborers—were quite poor. Perhaps five thousand to six thousand Jews of Galicia in Austria-Hungary died of starvation annually, and many Russian Jews fled to the United States to escape from desperate poverty.

Like other bourgeois, the Jews who were members of the commercial and professional classes gravitated toward liberalism. Moreover, as victims of persecution, they naturally favored societies that were committed to the liberal ideals of legal equality, toleration, the rule of law, and equality of opportunity. Because they strongly supported parliamentary government and the entire system of values associated with the Enlightenment, the Jews became targets for conservatives and Volkish thinkers, who repudiated the humanist and cosmopolitan outlook of liberalism and professed a militant nationalism.

Anti-Semites invented a mythical evil, the Jew, whom they blamed for all the social and economic ills caused by the rapid growth of industries and cities and for all the new ideas that were undermining the Old Order. Their anxieties and fears concentrated on the Jews, to whom they attributed everything they considered to be wrong in the modern age, all that threatened the German Volk. In the mythical world of Volkish thinkers, the Jews were regarded as foreign intruders who could never be loyal to the fatherland; as racial inferiors whose genes could infect and weaken the German race and debase its culture; and as international conspirators who were plotting to dominate Germany and the world. This latter accusation was a secularized and updated version of the medieval myth that Jews were plotting to destroy Christendom. In an extraordinary display of irrationality, Volkish thinkers held that Jews throughout the world were gaining control over political parties, the press, and the economy in order to dominate the planet.

The myth of a Jewish world conspiracy found its culminating expression in the notorious forgery, the *Protocols of the Elders of Zion*. The *Protocols* was written in France in the 1890s by an unknown author in the service of the Russian secret police, which sought to justify the tsarist regime's anti-Semitic policies. The forger concocted a tale of a meeting of Jewish elders in the Jewish cemetery of Prague. In these eerie surroundings, the elders plot to take over the world. First published in Russia in 1903, the *Protocols* was widely distributed after World War I and widely believed.

German anti-Semites viewed the *Protocols* as convincing evidence that the Jews were responsible for starting World War I, for Germany's defeat, and for the revolution that toppled the monarchy at the war's end. Nazi propagandists exploited the *Protocols* to justify their quest for power. Even after the *Protocols* was exposed as a blatant forgery, it continued to be translated and distributed. For anti-Semites, the myth of a Jewish world conspiracy had become an integrating principle; it provided satisfying answers to the crucial questions of existence.

In the Middle Ages, Jews had been persecuted and humiliated primarily for religious reasons. In the nineteenth century, national-racial considerations supplemented the traditional, biased Christian perception of Jews and Judaism. But whereas Christian anti-Semites believed that Jews could escape the curse of their religion through conversion, racial anti-Semites, who used the language of Social Darwinism (see pages 415–416), insisted that Jews were indelibly stained and eternally condemned by their biological makeup. Their evil and worthlessness derived from inherited racial characteristics, which could not be altered by conversion. As one anti-Semitic deputy stated in a speech before the German Reichstag in 1895,

> If one designates the whole of Jewry, one does so in the knowledge that the racial qualities of this people are such that in the long run they cannot harmonize with the racial qualities of the Germanic peoples and that every Jew who at this moment has not done anything bad may nevertheless under the proper conditions do precisely that, because his racial qualities drive him to do it. . . . [T]he Jews . . . operate like parasites . . . the Jews are cholera germs.[3]

The Jewish population of Germany was quite small: in 1900, it was only about 497,000, or 0.95 percent, of the total population of 50,626,000. Jews were proud of their many contributions to German economic and intellectual life (by the 1930s, 30 percent of the Nobel Prize winners in Germany were Jews). They considered themselves patriotic Germans and regarded Germany as an altogether desirable place to live—a place of refuge in comparison to Russia, where Jews lived in terrible poverty and suffered violent attacks.

German anti-Semitic organizations and political parties failed to get the state to pass anti-Semitic laws, and by the early 1900s, these groups had declined in political power and importance. But the mischief had been done. In the minds of many Germans, even in respectable circles, the image of the Jew as an evil and dangerous creature had been firmly planted. It was perpetuated by schools, youth groups, the Pan-German Association, and an array of racist pamphlets and books. Late-nineteenth-century racial anti-Semites had constructed an ideological foundation on which Hitler would later build his movement. In words that foreshadowed Hitler, Paul de Lagarde said of the Jews: "One does not have dealings with pests and parasites; one does not rear them and cherish them; one destroys them as speedily and thoroughly as possible."[4]

It is, of course, absurd to believe that a nation of fifty million was threatened by half a million citizens of Jewish birth, or that the eleven million Jews of the world (by 1900) had organized to rule the planet. The Jewish birthrate in Germany was low, the rate of intermarriage high, and the desire for complete assimilation into German life great. Within a few generations, the Jewish community in Germany might well have disappeared.

Contrary to the paranoid claims of the anti-Semites, the German Jews and the Jews in the rest of Europe were actually quite powerless. There were scarcely any Jews in the ruling circles of governments, armies, civil services, or heavy industries. As events were to prove, the Jews, with no army or state and dwelling in lands where many despised them, were the weakest of peoples. But the race mystics, convinced that they were waging a war of self-defense against a satanic foe, were impervious to rational argument. Anti-Semites, said Theodor Mommsen, the great nineteenth-century German historian, would not listen to "logical and ethical arguments. . . . They listen only to their own envy and hatred, to the meanest instincts. Nothing else counts for them. They are deaf to reason, right, morals. One cannot influence them. . . . [Anti-Semitism] is a horrible epidemic, like cholera—one can neither explain nor cure it."[5]

Racial nationalism, a major element in nineteenth-century intellectual life, attacked and undermined the Enlightenment tradition. Racial nationalists denied equality, scorned toleration, dismissed the idea of the oneness of humanity, and made myth and superstition vital forces in political life. They distorted reason and science to demonize and condemn an entire people and to justify humiliation and persecution. They presented a dangerous racial ideology, fraught with unreason and hate, as something virtuous and idealistic. That many people, including the educated and the elite, accepted these racial doctrines was an ominous sign for Western civilization. It made plain the tenuousness of the rational tradition of the Enlightenment and showed how receptive the mind is to dangerous myths and how easily human behavior can degenerate into inhumanity.

The Emergence of the New Imperialism

The Second Industrial Revolution coincided with an age of imperialism as European states (and the United States) extended their hegemony over much of the globe. Why did Westerners strive to claim and control most of the world?

Causes

Some historians suggest that the *new imperialism* (to differentiate it from the *colonialism* of settlement and trade that flourished from the sixteenth to the eighteenth century) was a direct result of industrialization. As economic activity and competition intensified, Europeans struggled for raw materials, markets for their manufactured goods, and places to invest their capital. In the late nineteenth century, many politicians and industrialists believed that the only way for their nations to ensure their economic necessities was the acquisition of overseas territories.

Captains of industry defended the new empires to their sometimes reluctant governments and compatriots, predicting dire consequences if their nation failed to get its share of the world markets. However, their expectations often did not materialize. Historians point to the fact that most areas claimed by Europeans and Americans did not possess profitable sources of raw materials or enough wealth to be good markets. For Europeans and Americans, the primary trading and investment areas were Europe and America rather than Asia or Africa. Some individual businesses made colonial profits, but most colonies proved unprofitable for the Western taxpayer.

The economic motivations of imperialism are inseparable from the intensely nationalistic one: the desire to win glory for the nation. Nationalists in newly unified Germany and Italy demanded colonies as recognition of their countries' Great Power status. Convinced that Britain's standing depended on colonies and naval power, they wanted their nations as well to "have a place in the sun." After its inglorious defeat by Prussia in 1870, France also turned its attention overseas, hoping to recoup some prestige and to add to its manpower and wealth for future European struggles. For a time, the nationalistic competition between the Europeans led them to extend their power struggles to Africa and Asia.

With its image of national vitality and competition between the fit and the unfit, Social Darwinism was the most extreme ideological expression of nationalism. Social Darwinists vigorously advocated the acquisition of empires, contending that the strong nations—by definition, those that were successful at expanding industry and empire—would survive and that others would not. To these elitists, all white men were more fit than nonwhites to prevail in the struggle for dominance, but among Europeans, some nations were deemed more fit than others for the competition. Social Darwinists were not embarrassed by the fact that their arguments were blatantly racist. In the popular mind, the concepts of evolution justified the exploitation of "lesser breeds without the law" by superior races. This language of race and conflict, of superior and inferior people, was widely used, particularly in Germany, Britain, and the United States.

Not all advocates of empire were Social Darwinists, however. Some believed that the extension of empire, law, order, and industrial civilization would raise "backward peoples" up the ladder of evolution and civilization. Many westerners deemed it their duty as Christians to set an example and to educate others. Missionaries were the first to meet and learn about many peoples and the first to develop writing for those without a written language. Christian missionaries were ardently opposed to slavery, and throughout the century they went to unexplored African regions to preach against slavery, which was still carried on by Arab and African traders. But many of them believed that to end slavery Europeans must provide law, order, and stability.

Some of the passion for imperialism was sparked by interest in exotic places. At the end of the eighteenth century and early in the nineteenth, the expeditions of Mungo Park, a Scottish explorer, on the Niger River in West Africa stimulated the romantic imagination. The explorations of David Livingstone in the Congo Basin and of Richard Burton and John Speke (who raced with each other and with Livingstone to find the source of the Nile River) in the later 1800s fascinated many Europeans.

Control and Resistance

Aided by superior technology and the machinery of the modern state, Europeans established varying degrees of political control over much of the rest of the world. Control could mean outright annexation and the governing of a territory as a colony. In this way, Germany controlled Tanganyika (in east-central Africa) after 1886, and Britain ruled much of India. Control could also mean status as a protectorate: an arrangement whereby the local ruler continued to rule but was directed, or "protected," by a Great Power. That is how the British controlled Egypt after 1882 and maintained authority over their dependent Indian princes, and how France guarded Tunisia. There were also spheres of influence, where, without military or political control, a European nation had special trading and legal privileges that other Europeans did not have. At the turn of the century, the Russians and the British divided Persia (Iran), each recognizing the other's sphere of influence—Russia's in the north and Britain's in the south.

In some non-Western lands, the governing authorities granted Europeans extraterritoriality, or the right of foreigners to trial by their own laws in other countries. Often, too, Europeans lived a segregated and privileged life in quarters, clubs, and whole sections of foreign lands or cities, in which no native was allowed to live.

Many non-Europeans resisted American and European economic penetration and political control in varied ways, and the very process of resistance shaped their history and their self-awareness. Such resistance became a statement of both national and individual identity. It could be violent, and the many instances of violent resistance included the Sudanese Muslims' holy war led by the Mahdi Mohammed Ahmed against both Egyptian fellow Muslims, who were regarded as agents of the European nonbelievers, and the Europeans; the Boxer Rebellion in China; and the Sepoy Mutiny in India. Some resisters, however, took a different path. Also imbued with strongly nationalistic feelings, they reacted to Western penetration by fighting to strengthen the nationalism of their people, sometimes even going to Western universities, military schools, and factories in order to master the West's advanced technology.

Mohandas Gandhi, Jawaharlal Nehru, Sun Zhongshan (Sun Yat-sen), Jiang Jieshi (Chiang Kai-shek), and Mustapha Kemal Atatürk were the most famous leaders of nationalistic resistance to the West.

European Domination of Asia

Western influence in Asia expanded during the middle decades of the nineteenth century. Increased contact with Western ideas and institutions had a profound impact on Asian societies.

India

In the last part of the eighteenth century, the British East India Company became a territorial power in India. It gained the upper hand by making alliances with warring princes, by carrying on trade and collecting taxes, and by commanding armies of *sepoys* (native soldiers). Parliament regulated the chartered monopoly enterprise but in fact did not control it much until the Sepoy Mutiny of 1857–58. (The Indians call this massive act of resistance the Great Rebellion.) This major popular uprising joined Muslim and Hindu soldiers with some native princes, who finally perceived that the British, rather than neighboring princes, were the true threat to their authority. With the aid of faithful troops from the Punjab, the British repressed the uprising. The rebellion caused Parliament to abolish the East India Company and to make India an integral part of the British Empire. The British ruled some states through dependent Indian princes, but about two-thirds of the subcontinent was ruled directly by about a thousand British officials in the civil service.

At first, the civil service was entirely British, its officials confident of the superiority of their people, law, and society. Later, an elite of Indians, educated in English and trained in administration, became part of it. Indian civil servants, along with soldiers recruited from peoples with military traditions, such as the Gurkhas and the Punjabis, carried out British laws, adding their interpretations, customs, and traditions. By 1900, a civil service of 4,000 Europeans and half a million Indians ruled some 300 million Indians, representing almost 200 language groups and several religions, races, and cultures. Under British imperialism, the subcontinent gained some political unity, an English educated elite, and a focus for discontent: the common resentment of the British.

The British built a modern railroad and communications system and developed agriculture and industry to meet the needs of the world market. As a link to areas of food surplus, the railroad reduced the incidence and impact of local famines, which had plagued India's history. British rule also ended internal war and disorder. Population increased as fewer people died of starvation and lives were saved by Western medical practices. But many students of history believe that the Indian masses did not benefit from economic progress

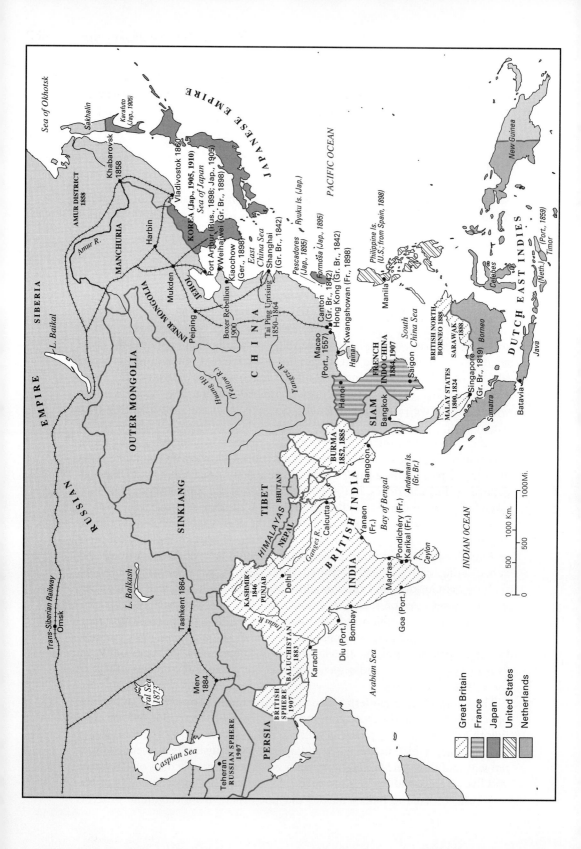

SIBERIA

Sea of Okhotsk

RUSSIAN EMPIRE

Sakhalin

Karafuto (Jap., 1905)

Khabarovsk 1858

MANCHURIA

AMUR DISTRICT 1858

Amur R.

Harbin

Vladivostok 1860

JAPANESE EMPIRE

KOREA (Jap., 1905, 1910)

Sea of Japan

Mukden

Port Arthur (Rus., 1898; Jap., 1905)

Weihaiwei (Gr. Br., 1898)

Kiaochow (Ger., 1898)

Ryuku Is. (Jap.)

East China Sea

Shanghai (Gr. Br., 1842)

Pescadores (Jap., 1895)

Formosa (Jap., 1895)

JEHOL

Peiping

INNER MONGOLIA

Boxer Rebellion 1900

Tai Ping Uprising 1850–1864

L. Baikal

OUTER MONGOLIA

C H I N A

Huang Ho (Yellow R.)

Yangtze R.

Canton (Gr. Br., 1842)

Macao (Port., 1557)

Hong Kong (Gr. Br., 1842)

Kwangshowan (Fr., 1898)

Hainan

Hanoi

FRENCH INDO CHINA 1884, 1907

South China Sea

Manila

Philippine Is. (U.S. from Spain, 1898)

DUTCH EAST INDIES

New Guinea

Celebes

Borneo

BRITISH NORTH BORNEO 1888

SARAWAK 1888

Singapore (Gr. Br., 1819)

Sumatra

Java

Batavia

Timor (Neth.) (Port., 1859)

SINKIANG

TIBET

HIMALAYAS

NEPAL

BHUTAN

BURMA 1852, 1885

SIAM

Bangkok

Saigon

MALAY STATES 1800, 1824

Rangoon

Bay of Bengal

Andaman Is. (Gr. Br.)

Calcutta

Ganges R.

Yanaon (Fr.)

BRITISH INDIA

Pondichéry (Fr.)

Karikal (Fr.)

Ceylon

KASHMIR 1846

PUNJAB

Delhi

I N D I A

Madras

Indus R.

BALUCHISTAN 1883

BRITISH SPHERE 1907

Karachi

Diu (Port.)

Bombay

Goa (Port.)

Arabian Sea

RUSSIAN EMPIRE

Aral Sea 1873

Merv 1884

L. Balkash

Tashkent 1864

Trans-Siberian Railway

Omsk

PERSIA

RUSSIAN SPHERE 1907

Teheran

Caspian Sea

PACIFIC OCEAN

INDIAN OCEAN

1000 Mi.

1000 Km.

500

500

0

0

Great Britain

France

Japan

United States

Netherlands

because they could not pay their debts in money as their landlords demanded. Furthermore, the British flooded the Indian market with cheap, machine-produced English goods, driving native artisans out of business or even deeper into debt.

The racism that excluded the Indian elite from British clubs, hotels, and social gatherings and from top government positions alienated the leaders that British rule had created. Many of the older elite of princes and landlords who may have profited from British connections resented the lack of respect for Indian traditions and culture. Educated Indians, demanding equality and self-government, created the Indian National Congress in the 1880s. The Congress party ultimately organized masses of Indians to work toward independence.

In 1919, partly in response to agitation and partly as a reward for loyal Indian service during World War I, the British granted India a legislative assembly representing almost a million of the 300 million people in the subcontinent. However, the British gave only some powers to this assembly, retaining most of the powers themselves. At the same time, agitation and unrest became very bitter. In 1919, at Amritsar in Punjab, a British officer commanded his Gurkha troops to fire into a peaceful demonstration until their ammunition was exhausted; 379 Indians died and 1,200 were wounded. Women and children were among the victims. The government punished the officer, but the British community in India gave him a fortune, honoring him for what he had done. The massacre and British behavior stung Indians to action—even those Indians who had supported the British and advocated self-government within the British Empire.

Out of this feverish period emerged a gentle but determined revolutionary leader, Mohandas K. Gandhi (1869–1948). He had led the resistance to the vicious system of racial discrimination faced by the Indian community in South Africa and, in the process, developed a doctrine of civil disobedience and nonviolent resistance. He believed that the power of love and spiritual purity would ultimately overthrow British rule in India. His was a spiritually uplifting message, and a shrewd political tactic as well. Gandhi called on the Indian elite to give up the privileges allotted by the British and to resign their positions, boycott British schools, and boycott all foreign goods. He dramatically rallied mass support with "the march to the sea": a mass refusal to pay taxes on salt. When imprisoned, Gandhi and his followers fasted for spiritual discipline. But their tactic also threatened the British, for if the confined leaders should starve to death, more civil disturbances might erupt. Gandhi also emphasized the boycott of foreign goods by spinning cotton and wearing simple native dress. To gain independence, Gandhi was even willing to sacrifice the higher standard of living that an industrial economy could bring to India.

Independence finally came after World War II had exhausted British resources and reduced British power. It was achieved without a war between

◀ **Map 16.1**   Asia in 1914

Britain and India—an accomplishment that many credit to the strength of Gandhi's moral leadership. But even his leadership could not prevent the partition of the country into Muslim Pakistan and predominantly Hindu India. Nor could it prevent conflict between Hindus and Muslims, as bloody massacres following independence clearly revealed.

China

The defeat of the Chinese by the British in the Opium War of 1839–1842, forced the Manchu dynasty to open trade with the West. Before the war, such commerce had been limited—controlled by native monopolists to whom the emperor had granted trading privileges. When the Chinese government destroyed Indian opium being traded by the East India Company, the British aggressively asserted their right to free trade and demanded compensation. In the subsequent war, Britain seized several trading cities along the coast, including Hong Kong, and the Chinese capitulated. In the Treaty of Nanking (1842), the British insisted on determining the tariffs that the Chinese might charge them. Furthermore, British subjects in China would have the right to be tried according to their own law (the right of extraterritoriality). Both provisions undermined the emperor's ability to control the foreigners in his country.

Defeat in the Opium War also forced change on the emperor. He drew on China's mandarins to revitalize the Manchu bureaucracy by cleaning out much of the official corruption, which weighed heavily on the poorest taxpayers, and by strengthening China against the westerners, sometimes by hiring westerners to train Chinese armies. Nevertheless, widespread economic discontent, hatred of the Manchu (who were regarded by many Chinese as foreign conquerors, even though the conquest had taken place some two hundred years earlier), and religious mysticism led to the Taiping Rebellion of 1850–1864. This uprising seriously threatened the dynasty, which was able to suppress the rebels with Western assistance. For this aid, Britain and France extorted additional concessions from the emperor.

For a time, the Europeans seemed content with trading rights in coastal towns and preferential treatment for their subjects. But the Sino-Japanese War of 1894–95, which Japan won easily because of China's weakness, encouraged the Europeans to mutilate China. Britain, France, Russia, and Germany all scrambled for concessions, protectorates, and spheres of influence. China might have been carved up like Africa, but each Western nation, afraid of its rivals, resisted any partition that might possibly give another state an advantage. The United States, which insisted that it be given any trading concession that any other state received, proclaimed an "Open Door" policy: that trade should be open to all and that the Great Powers should respect China's territorial integrity. The U.S. action may have restrained the Western powers from partitioning China, but it was also a way to safeguard American interests there.

Chinese traditionalists organized secret societies to expel foreigners and to punish the Chinese who accepted Christianity or any other form of westernization. In 1900, encouraged by Empress Tzu-hsi, the Society of Righteous and Harmonious Fists (called the Boxers by Europeans) attacked foreigners throughout the north of China. An international army of Europeans, Japanese, and Americans suppressed the rebellion, seized Chinese treasures, and forced China to pay an indemnity. They also made China agree to the stationing of foreign troops on its soil.

Chinese discontent with the dynasty deepened, as did unrest and nationalistic opposition to the foreigners. When the Japanese defeated the Russians in 1905, many Chinese argued that the only way to protect their country was to imitate the West, as the Japanese had done. Many signs of growing nationalism appeared. In 1911, nationalist revolutionaries, strongly present among soldiers, workers, and students, overthrew the Manchu and declared a republic. Sun Zhongshan (Sun Yat-sen, 1866–1925), who was in the United States when the revolution broke out, returned to China to become the first president of the republic and the head of the Nationalist party.

Espousing the Western ideas of democracy, nationalism, and social welfare (the three principles of the people, as Sun called them), the republic struggled to establish its authority over a China torn by civil war and ravaged by foreigners. Russia was claiming Mongolia, and Britain was claiming Tibet. The northern warlords, who were regional leaders with private armies, resisted any attempt to strengthen the republic's army because it might diminish their power. In the south, however, the republic more or less maintained control. After Sun's death, the Guomindong (Kuomintang), under the authoritarian leadership of Jiang Jieshi (Chiang Kai-shek, 1887–1975), tried to westernize by using the military power of the state and introducing segments of a modern economic system. But faced with civil war, attacked both from the right and from the communist left under Mao Zedong (Mao Tse-tung, 1893–1976), and by the Japanese after 1931, the Guomindong made slow progress. A divided China continued to be at the mercy of outside interests until after World War II.

Japan

Japan, like China, was opened to the West against its will. The Japanese had expelled Europeans in the seventeenth century, remaining isolated for the next two hundred years. By the 1850s, however, as in India and China, social dissension within Japan and foreign pressure combined to force the country to admit outside trade. Americans in particular refused to accept Japanese prohibitions on commercial and religious contacts. Like China, Japan succumbed to superior technological power. In 1853, Commodore Matthew C. Perry sailed into Tokyo Bay, making a show of American strength and forcing the Japanese to sign a number of treaties that granted westerners extraterritoriality and control over tariffs.

A flood of violence surged over Japan. Determined to preserve Japan's

Commodore Perry and the U.S. Squadron Meeting Japanese Imperial Commissioners at Yokohama, 1854.   Commodore Matthew Perry had opened Japan, against its will, to the West the preceding year. With the Meiji Restoration of 1867, a strong central government pushed Japan until it became one of the top ten industrial nations by 1900. Japan's imperialistic expansion brought it into conflict with China, Russia, and the Western imperialist powers. (*Culver Pictures*)

independence, a group of *samurai,* the warrior nobility, seized the government. This takeover—the Meiji Restoration of 1867—returned power to the emperor, or Meiji, from the feudal aristocracy, which had ruled in his name for almost seven hundred years. The new government enacted a series of reforms, turning Japan into a powerful modern unitary state. Large landowners were persuaded to give their estates to the emperor in exchange for compensation and high-level positions in the government. All classes were made equal before the law. As in France and Germany, universal military service was required, which diminished social privilege and helped to imbue Japanese of all classes with nationalism. The Japanese modeled their constitution on Bismarck's: there was a parliament, but the emperor held the most authority, which he delegated to his ministers to govern in his name without much control from the parliament.

The Meiji regime introduced modern industry and economic competition. Japanese visited factories all over the West and hired westerners to teach industrial skills. The government, like central and eastern European governments, built defense industries, backed heavy industry and mining, and developed a modern communications system of railways, roads, and telegraphs. Industry in Japan adopted traditional Japanese values and emphasized cooperation more than competition; relations between employer and employee were paternalistic rather than individualistic and deferential rather than hostile. Within little more than a generation of the Meiji Restoration, Japan moved from economic backwardness to a place among the top ten industrial nations. To underdeveloped countries, Japan became a model of a nation that borrowed from the West yet preserved its traditional values and social structure.

By 1900, Japan had ended the humiliating treaties with the West and become an imperialist power in its own right. It had won Taiwan and Korea in its war with China in 1894–95, although the Great Powers intervened, forcing the Japanese to return some of the spoils of victory while they themselves grabbed greater spheres of influence from the helpless Chinese. Their self-serving maneuvering infuriated the Japanese. Finally, in 1904, conflict over influence in Manchuria brought Japan and Russia to war, which Japan won. The victory of an Asian power over a Western power had a tremendous impact on Asian nationalists. If Japan could unite its people with nationalism and strong leadership, others should be able to do likewise. Japan's victory inspired anti-Western and nationalist movements throughout China, Indochina, India, and the Middle East.

How Japan would exercise its hard-won power was an open question in the post–World War I era. In the 1920s, the prosperous economy fortified the middle class and increased the importance of the working class, strengthening democratic institutions. But Japan's dependence on foreign trade meant that the nation was hard hit by the Great Depression of 1929, when the major states subjected its trade to tariffs. The depression weakened the elements that contributed to peace, stability, and democracy in Japan and strengthened the militarist and fascist groups, which were set on imperialism in Manchuria and China. To Asians in the 1930s, Japan seemed to champion Asian racial equality and to oppose Western imperialism. Many leaders of nationalist movements in Burma, India, Indochina, and Indonesia were attracted for a time by Japan's pose. World War II, however, brought Japanese occupation and exploitation, not freedom and equality for Asians.

The Scramble for Africa

The most rapid European expansion took place in Africa. Until the 1870s, Great Power interest in Africa seemed marginal and likely to decline even further. As late as 1880, European nations ruled just a tenth of the continent. Only three decades later, by 1914, Europeans had claimed all of Africa except Liberia (a small territory of freed slaves from the United States) and Abyssinia (Ethiopia), which had successfully held off Italian invaders at Adowa in 1896.

The activities of Leopold II, the king of Belgium, spurred expansion. In 1876, as a private entrepreneur, he formed the International Association for the Exploration and Civilization of Central Africa. Leopold sent Henry Stanley (1841–1904) to the Congo River Basin to establish trading posts, sign treaties with the chiefs, and claim the territory for the association. Stanley, an

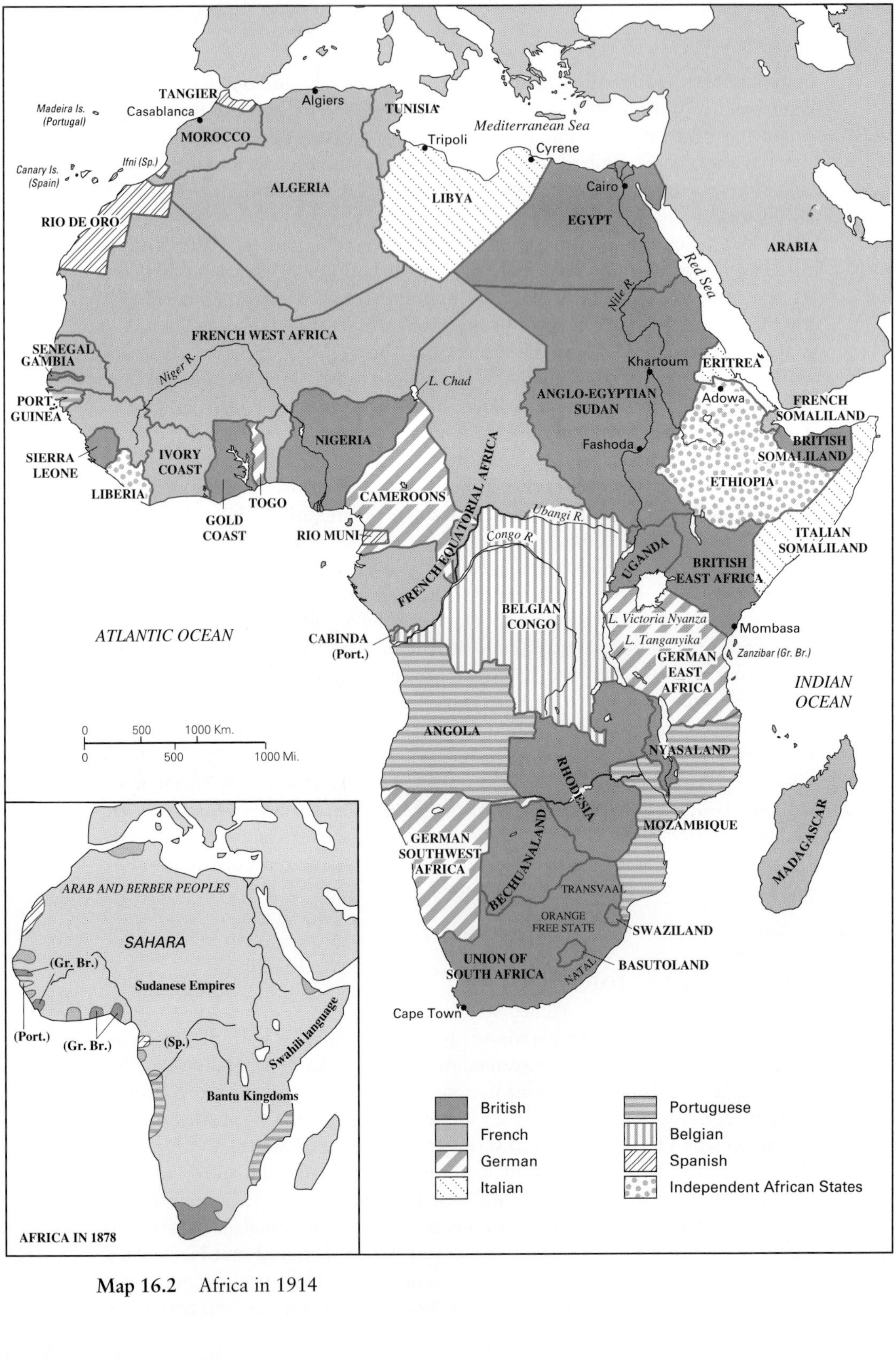
TANGIER
Madeira Is. (Portugal)
Casablanca
Algiers
TUNISIA
MOROCCO
Mediterranean Sea
Tripoli
Cyrene
Canary Is. (Spain)
Ifni (Sp.)
ALGERIA
LIBYA
Cairo
EGYPT
RIO DE ORO
ARABIA
Red Sea
Nile R.
FRENCH WEST AFRICA
SENEGAL
GAMBIA
Niger R.
Khartoum
ERITREA
L. Chad
PORT. GUINEA
ANGLO-EGYPTIAN SUDAN
Adowa
FRENCH SOMALILAND
BRITISH SOMALILAND
SIERRA LEONE
IVORY COAST
NIGERIA
Fashoda
LIBERIA
CAMEROONS
ETHIOPIA
GOLD COAST
TOGO
FRENCH EQUATORIAL AFRICA
Ubangi R.
RIO MUNI
Congo R.
ITALIAN SOMALILAND
UGANDA
BRITISH EAST AFRICA
BELGIAN CONGO
L. Victoria Nyanza
ATLANTIC OCEAN
CABINDA (Port.)
Mombasa
L. Tanganyika
Zanzibar (Gr. Br.)
GERMAN EAST AFRICA
INDIAN OCEAN
0 500 1000 Km.
0 500 1000 Mi.
ANGOLA
NYASALAND
RHODESIA
MOZAMBIQUE
MADAGASCAR
GERMAN SOUTHWEST AFRICA
BECHUANALAND
TRANSVAAL
ORANGE FREE STATE
SWAZILAND
UNION OF SOUTH AFRICA
NATAL
BASUTOLAND
Cape Town
ARAB AND BERBER PEOPLES
SAHARA
(Gr. Br.)
Sudanese Empires
(Port.)
(Gr. Br.)
(Sp.)
Swahili language
Bantu Kingdoms
AFRICA IN 1878
British
French
German
Italian
Portuguese
Belgian
Spanish
Independent African States

Map 16.2 Africa in 1914

adventurer and a newspaper reporter who had fought on both sides of the American Civil War, had earlier led an expedition to central Africa in search of David Livingstone, the popular missionary explorer, who was believed to be in danger. For men like Stanley, Leopold's private development efforts promised profit and adventure. For the Africans, they promised brutal exploitation. The French responded to Leopold's actions by immediately establishing a protectorate on the north bank of the Congo. The scramble was on.

The Berlin Conference

Bismarck and Jules Ferry, the premier of France, called an international conference of the Great Powers in Berlin in 1884 to lay some ground rules for the development of Africa south of the Sahara. The Berlin Conference established the rule that a European country had to occupy territory in order to claim it. This led to a mad race to the interior of Africa; it was a field day for explorers and soldiers. As Europeans rushed to claim territory, they ignored both natural and cultural frontiers. Even today, the map of Africa reveals many straight (and thus artificial) boundary lines, rather than the irregular lines of natural boundaries, such as rivers and mountains.

The conference declared that Leopold (as an individual, not as the king of Belgium) was the personal ruler of the Congo Free State. Before long, Leopold's Congo Association was trying to turn a profit with practices as vicious as those of the African slave traders. At the turn of the century, Edward D. Morel, an English humanitarian, produced evidence that slavery, mutilation, brutality, and murder were commonly practiced to force blacks to work for the rubber plantations in the Congo. In response to the outcry of public opinion, in 1908 the Belgian parliament declared the territory a Belgian colony, thus putting an end to Leopold's private enterprise.

The British in Africa

For much of the nineteenth century, British interest in Africa was minimal. The opening, in 1869, of the Suez Canal, which Britain viewed as a vital highway to India, greatly increased the strategic value of Egypt. Officially a part of the Ottoman Empire, Egypt had, in effect, been independent of the Ottoman sultan since the 1830s. When a nearly bankrupt Egypt could not pay its foreign debts and was threatened with internal rebellion, Britain intervened as "protector" in 1882. Prime Minister Gladstone, a "little Englander" (one who opposed empire), promised to withdraw British troops once the situation stabilized.

Not only did the British fail to withdraw from Egypt, they moved further south into the Sudan, to quell a Muslim holy war against Egyptian authority and British influence. In 1885, the Sudanese, led by the Mahdi, who viewed himself as the successor to Muhammad, captured Khartoum and killed the popular General Charles Gordon, the recently appointed governor-general of the Sudan. In 1898, the British, armed with machine guns, mowed down

The Battle of Omdurman, 1898.   A romanticized oil painting depicts the British lancers at the battle of Omdurman in heroic terms. The Muslim fundamentalists who followed the Mahdi in his attempts to expel the Egyptians and British from the Sudan were massacred in 1898 by General Kitchener. As many as 11,000 dervishes were killed, but the British suffered only slight casualties. Paintings such as this fed the public hunger for heroism and thirst for exotic places. (*Eileen Tweedy/E.T. Archive*)

charging Muslims at Omdurman. The casualties were reported to be eleven thousand Muslims and twenty-eight Britons.

Immediately after the battle, British forces confronted the French at Fashoda in the Sudan. In the diplomatic crisis that followed, Britain and France were brought to the brink of war, and public passions were inflamed. However, since France was too divided by the Dreyfus affair at home to risk a showdown with Britain, the French cabinet ordered retreat.

The British also sought territory in South Africa. Cecil Rhodes (1853–1902), who had gone to South Africa for his health in 1870 and made a fortune in diamonds and gold, dreamed of expanding the British Empire. "The British," he declared, "are the finest race in the world and the more of the world we inhabit the better it is for the human race."[6] Rhodes was responsible for acquiring Rhodesia (Zimbabwe), a sizable and wealthy territory, for Britain. He also plotted to involve Britain in a war with the Boers, Dutch farmers and cattlemen who had settled in South Africa in the seventeenth century.

During the Napoleonic wars, the British had gained Cape Town, at the southern tip of Africa, a useful provisioning place for trading ships bound for India. Despising British rule and refusing to accept the British abolition of slavery in 1833, the Boers moved northward in a migration called the Great Trek (1835–37), warring with African tribes along the way. They established two republics, the Transvaal and the Orange Free State, whose independence the British recognized in the 1850s. The republics' democratic practices did not extend to black Africans, who were denied political rights. In 1877, the British annexed the Transvaal, but Boer resistance forced them in 1881 to recognize the Transvaal's independence again.

The discovery of rich deposits of gold and diamonds in the Boer lands reinforced Rhodes's dream of building a great British empire in Africa. In 1895, his close friend Leander Jameson led some six hundred armed men into the Transvaal, hoping to create a pretext for a British invasion. Although the raid failed and both Jameson and Rhodes were disgraced, tensions between Britain and the Boer republics worsened, and in 1899 the Anglo-Boer War broke out.

The Boers were formidable opponents—farmers by day and commandos by night, armed with the latest French and German rifles. To deal with their stubborn foe, the British herded, or "concentrated," thousands of Boers, including women and children, into compounds surrounded by barbed wire, where some twenty-five thousand perished. The nasty war ended in 1902. Hoping to live together in peace with the Boers, the British drew up a conciliatory treaty. In 1910, the former Boer republics were joined with the British territories into the Union of South Africa. Self-government within the British Empire for the British settlers and the Boers did not help the majority black population; it still had to cope with the Boers' deeply entrenched racist attitudes.

Other European Countries in Africa

The cost of imperialism in Africa seemed high not only to the British, but to other imperialists as well. The Italians' defeat at Adowa (1896) by Ethiopians belied Italian dreams of empire and national glory. (Bismarck scoffed that the Italians had enormous appetites but very poor teeth.) Germans could take little heart from their African acquisitions—Southwest Africa (Namibia), East Africa (Tanzania, but not Zanzibar, which was British), the Cameroons, and Togo (part of Ghana today). The German colonies were the most efficiently governed (critics said, the most ruthlessly controlled), but they yielded few benefits, other than pride of ownership, because they were costly to govern. And the Belgians had obviously gained no prestige from the horrors perpetrated in the Congo. Serious thinkers, contemplating the depths to which Europeans would sink in search of fortune and fame, began to suggest that barbarity characterized the Europeans more than the Africans. The Europeans seemed to be the moral barbarians, as novelist Joseph Conrad and others pointed out. For the most part, honor was fleeting and profits illusory in these new African empires.

The Legacy of Imperialism

World War I was a turning point in the history of imperialism, although neither mother countries nor colonies seemed aware of it at the time. The principle of self-determination, championed for European nationalities at the peace conference, was seized on by Asian and African intellectuals, who intensified their anti-imperialist efforts. After World War II, the exhausted colonial powers were reluctant to fight rebellious colonies. Moreover, after waging war to destroy Nazi imperialism and racism, European colonial powers had little moral justification to deny other peoples self-determination.

Almost a century after the rapid division of the world among the European powers and the United States and decades after the decolonization of most of the world, the consequences of imperialism persist. Imperialism has left a legacy of deep animosity in the countries of Asia, Africa, and Latin America. Although most nations have political independence, nationalists resent Western economic and cultural influences. Much of the world is still poor and suffers from insufficient capital, unskilled leaders, and unstable governments. Many people in these poor areas believe that their countries' condition has resulted from years of Western exploitation.

To former colonial peoples, imperialism has been a source of great bitterness, not only because of its economic exploitation, but also because of its encouragement of racism and callous disregard of other cultures. Thus, non-Western nationalism has often included anti-Western elements. Today, European nations and the United States must deal in the areas of economics and politics with nations acutely conscious of their nationhood and quick to condemn any policy that they perceive as imperialistic.

Imperialism accelerated the growth of a global market economy, completing the trend that started with the commercial revolution of the sixteenth and seventeenth centuries. At the beginning of the twentieth century, in many parts of Europe, even the working classes and the peasantry were able to buy goods from faraway places—goods that had previously been available only to the very wealthy. The underdeveloped areas of the world, in turn, found markets for their crops and were able to buy European goods; at least the wealthy could.

Imperialism has also fostered the spread of Western civilization around the globe. The influence of Western ideas, institutions, techniques, language, and culture is apparent everywhere. English and, to some extent, French are international languages. African and Asian lands have adopted, often with limited success, democracy and parliamentary government from the West. Socialism, a Western ideology, has been transplanted in Third World countries. Industrialism and modern science, both achievements of the West, have become globalized. So, too, have Western agricultural techniques, business practices, medicine, legal procedures, school curricula, architecture, music, and dress. That Turkish women are no longer required to wear the veil, that Chinese women no longer have their feet bound, that Indians have outlawed untouchability, that Arabs, Africans, and Indians no longer practice slavery—all these changes have occurred under the influence of Western ideas. (To be sure, cultural forms have not moved only in one direction: African and Asian ways have also influenced Western lands.) The impact of Western ways on the Third World is one of the most crucial developments of our time.

Notes

1. Cited in Edward R. Tannenbaum, *1900: The Generation Before the Great War* (Garden City, N.Y.: Doubleday, 1976), p. 337.
2. Cited in Horst von Maltitz, *The Evolution of Hitler's Germany* (New York: McGraw-Hill, 1973), p. 33.
3. Quoted in Raul Hilberg, *The Destruction of the European Jews* (Chicago: Quadrangle, 1967), pp. 10–11.
4. Quoted in Helmut Krausnick, Hans Buchheim, Martin Broszat, and Hans-Adolf Jacobsen, *Anatomy of the SS State*, trans. Richard Barry et al. (London: William Collins Sons, 1968), p. 9.
5. Quoted in Peter G. J. Pulzer, *The Rise of Political Anti-Semitism in Germany and Austria* (New York: Wiley, 1964), p. 299.
6. Joseph E. Flint, *Cecil Rhodes* (Boston: Little Brown, 1974), p. 248.

Suggested Reading

Brunschwig, Henri, *French Colonialism: 1871–1914. Myths and Realities* (trans. 1964). The best book on French imperialism.

Craig, Gordon, *Politics of the Prussian Army* (1955). A very valuable study, with important implications for German and European history.

Ford, Colin, and Brian Harrison, *A Hundred Years Ago* (1983). An excellent social history of Britain, with fine photographs.

Hobsbawm, Eric, *The Age of Capital* (1988). A Marxist interpretation of mid-nineteenth century Europe.

Holborn, Hajo, *A History of Modern Germany, 1840–1945*, vol. 3 (1969). A definitive work.

Joll, James, *Europe Since 1870* (1973). A valuable general survey, particularly good on socialism in the individual nations.

Katz, Jacob, *From Prejudice to Destruction* (1980). A survey of modern anti-Semitism; views modern anti-Semitism as an outgrowth of traditional Christian anti-Semitism.

Kemp, Tom, *Industrialization in Nineteenth-Century Europe* (1985). Readable general survey incorporating recent scholarship.

Mack Smith, Denis, *Italy: A Modern History*, rev. ed. (1969). An excellent survey, emphasizing the theme of the failure of Italy to develop viable liberal institutions or economic solutions.

Mosse, George L., *Toward the Final Solution* (1978). An analysis of European racism.

———, *The Crisis of German Ideology* (1964). Explores the dark side of German nationalism; an excellent study of Volkish thought.

Robinson, R. E., John Gallagher, and Alice Denny, *Africa and the Victorians: The Official Mind of Imperialism* (1961). An essential book for this fascinating subject; well written and controversial.

Thornton, A. P., *The Imperial Idea and Its Enemies: A Study in British Power*, 2nd ed. (1985). An interesting study of the ideas and policies of British imperialism.

Webb, R. K., *Modern England from the Eighteenth Century to the Present* (1968). A well-informed, readable book that is balanced on controversial issues.

Review Questions

1. Why is the last part of the nineteenth century called the Second Industrial Revolution?
2. What was the difference between orthodox and revisionist Marxists?
3. Characterize the domestic histories of each of the following countries in the last part of the nineteenth century: Britain, France, Germany, and Italy.
4. To whom did Volkish thought appeal? Explain.
5. Why is racial nationalism a repudiation of the Enlightenment tradition and a regression to mythical thinking?
6. Anti-Semites attributed to Jews everything that they found repellent in the modern world. Discuss this statement.
7. Anti-Semitism demonstrates the immense power and danger of mythical thinking. Discuss this statement.
8. Account for the rise of the new imperialism in the last part of the nineteenth century.
9. Why and how were Europeans able to dominate African and Asian lands?
10. What role did each of the following play in the history of imperialism: Cecil Rhodes, Sun Zhongshan, Matthew C. Perry, Henry Stanley, King Leopold II?
11. What is the legacy of imperialism for the contemporary world?

CHAPTER 17

Modern Consciousness: New Views of Nature, Human Nature, and the Arts

$\mathcal{T}$he modern mentality may be said to have passed through two broad phases: early modernity and late modernity. Formulated during the era of the Scientific Revolution and the Enlightenment, early modernity stressed confidence in reason, science, human goodness, and humanity's capacity to improve society. Then, in the late nineteenth and early twentieth centuries, a new outlook took shape. Late modern thinkers and scientists achieved revolutionary insights into human nature, the social world, and the physical universe; and writers and artists opened up hitherto unimagined possibilities for artistic expression.

These developments produced a shift in European consciousness. The mechanical model of the universe, which had dominated the Western outlook since Newton, was altered. The Enlightenment view of human rationality and goodness was questioned, and the belief in natural rights and objective standards governing morality came under attack. Rules of esthetics that had governed the arts since the Renaissance were discarded. Shattering old beliefs, late modernity left Europeans without landmarks—without generally accepted cultural standards or agreed upon conceptions about human nature and the meaning of life.

The late modern period was marked by extraordinary creativity in thought and the arts. Yet imaginative and fruitful as these changes were for Western intellectual and cultural life, they also helped to create the disoriented, fragmented, and troubled era that is the twentieth century. ❖

Irrationalism

Some late-nineteenth-century thinkers challenged the basic premises of the philosophes and their nineteenth-century heirs. They repudiated the Enlightenment conception of human rationality, stressing instead the irrational side of human nature. Regarding reason as sovereign, the philosophes had defined human beings by their capacity to think critically; now thinkers saw blind strivings and animal instincts as the primary fact of human existence. To these thinkers, it seemed that reason exercised a very limited influence over human conduct. Impulses, drives, instincts—all forces below the surface—determined behavior much more than did logical consciousness. Like the romantics, proponents of the nonrational placed more reliance on feeling, spontaneity, and intuition than on reason. They belittled the intellect's attempt to comprehend nature and society, praised outbursts of the irrational, and in some instances exalted violence.

The new insights into the irrational side of human nature and the growing assault on reason had immense implications for political life. In succeeding decades, these currents of irrationalism would become ideologized and politicized by unscrupulous demagogues, who sought to mobilize and manipulate the masses. The popularity of fascist movements, which openly denigrated reason and exalted race, blood, action, and will, demonstrated the naiveté of nineteenth-century liberals, who believed that reason had triumphed in human affairs.

Nietzsche

The principal figure in the "dethronement of reason" and the glorification of the irrational was the German philosopher Friedrich Nietzsche (1844–1900). Nietzsche's writings are not systematic treatises but collections of aphorisms, often containing internal contradictions. Consequently, his philosophy lends itself to misinterpretation and misapplication, as manifested by Nazi theorists, who distorted Nietzsche to justify their theory of the German master race.

Nietzsche attacked the accepted views and convictions of his day as a hindrance to a fuller and richer existence. He denounced social reform, parliamentary government, and universal suffrage, ridiculed the vision of progress through science, condemned Christian morality, and mocked the liberal belief in man's essential goodness and rationality. Man, he said, must understand that life, which is replete with cruelty, injustice, uncertainty, and absurdity, is not governed by rational principles. There exist no absolute standards of good and evil whose truth can be demonstrated by reflective reason. There is only naked man living in a godless and absurd world.

Modern bourgeois society, said Nietzsche, was decadent and enfeebled—a victim of the excessive development of the rational faculties at the expense of will and instinct. Against the liberal-rationalist stress on the intellect, Nietzsche urged recognition of the dark, mysterious world of instinctual desires—the true forces of life. Smother the will with excessive intellectualizing, and you snuff out the spontaneity that sparks cultural creativity and ignites a zest for living. The critical and theoretical outlook destroyed the creative instincts. To realize his multifaceted potential, man must stop relying on the intellect and nurture again the instinctual roots of human existence.

Christianity, with all its prohibitions, restrictions, and demands to con-

Friedrich Nietzsche (1844–1900) with His Wife. Possessing the intuitive genius of a great poet, Nietzsche grasped the crucial problem afflicting the modern European soul: What path should the individual take in a world where God is dead? Nietzsche's answer to this question—the superman who creates his own values—lent itself to considerable misinterpretation and distortion and had little constructive social value. (*Photo AKG London*)

form, also stifles the human impulse for life, said Nietzsche. Christian morality must be obliterated, for it is fit only for the weak, the slave. According to Nietzsche, the triumph of Christianity in the ancient world was an attempt of the resentful slave and the slavelike plebeian to prevent their aristocratic superiors from expressing their heroic natures and to strike back at those noble spirits, whom they envied. Their way of striking back was to condemn as evil the very traits that they themselves lacked—strength, power, assertiveness, and a zest for life—and by making their own base, wretched, and life-negating values the standard of all things. Then they saddled people with guilt if they deviated from these contemptible values. This transvaluation of values engineered by Christianity, said Nietzsche, led to a deterioration of life and culture.

Although the philosophes had rejected Christian doctrines, they had largely retained Christian ethics. Unlike the philosophes, however, Nietzsche did not attack Christianity because it was contrary to reason. He attacked it because, he said, it gave man a sick soul. It was life-denying. Blocking the free and spontaneous exercise of human instincts, it made humility and self-abnegation virtues and pride a vice. In short, Christianity extinguished the spark of life in man. This spark of life, this inner yearning which is man's true essence, must again burn.

"God is dead," proclaimed Nietzsche. God is man's own creation. There are no higher worlds, no transcendental or metaphysical truths, no morality derived from God or nature, and no natural rights, scientific socialism, or inevitable progress. All the old values and truths have lost their intelligibility.

But the death of God and Christian values can mean the liberation of man. Man, Nietzsche insisted, can create new values and achieve self-mastery. He can overcome the deadening uniformity and mediocrity of modern civilization. He can undo democracy and socialism, which have made masters out of cattlelike masses, and surmount the shopkeeper's spirit, which has made man soft and degenerate.

European society, as Nietzsche saw it, lacked heroic figures; everyone belonged to a vast herd, but there were no shepherds. Europe could only be saved by the emergence of a higher type of man—the *superman,* or *over-man*—who would not be held back by the egalitarian rubbish preached by Christians, democrats, and socialists. "A declaration of war on the masses by *higher* man is needed," said Nietzsche, to end "the dominion of *inferior* men." Europe required "the annihilation of *suffrage universal,* i.e., the system through which the lowest natures prescribe themselves as laws for the higher."[1] Europe needed a new breed of rulers, a true aristocracy of masterful men.

Nietzsche conceived of the superman as a new kind of man, who breaks with accepted morality and sets his own standards. He does not repress his instincts but asserts them. He destroys old values and asserts his prerogative as master. Free of Christian guilt, he proudly affirms his own being; dispensing with Christian "thou shalt not," he instinctively says, "I will." He dares to be himself. Because he is not like other people, traditional definitions of good and evil have no meaning for him. He does not allow his individuality to be stifled. He makes his own values, those that flow from his very being. He knows that life is meaningless but lives it laughingly, instinctively, fully.

The superman's joyful and heroic assertion of the will rescues life from nothingness. He grasps that "the most fearful and fundamental desire in man [is] his drive for power,"[2] that human beings crave and strive for power ceaselessly and uncompromisingly. This will to power governs everyday life and is the determining factor in international affairs. The enhancement of power brings supreme enjoyment: "The love of power is the demon of men. Let them have everything—health, food, a place to live, entertainment—they are and remain unhappy and low-spirited; for the demon waits and waits and will be satisfied. Take everything from them and satisfy this and they are almost happy—as happy as men and demons can be."[3] The masses, cowardly and envious, will condemn the superman as evil; this has always been their way.

The influence of Nietzsche's philosophy is still a matter of controversy and conjecture. Perhaps better than anyone else, Nietzsche grasped the crucial problem of modern society and culture: that with the "death of God" traditional moral values had lost their authority and binding power. In a world where nothing is true, all is permitted. Nietzsche foresaw that the future, an age without values, would be violent and sordid, and he urged individuals to face themselves and life free of illusions, pretense, and hypocrisy. Nietzsche is also part of the general nineteenth-century trend that sought to affirm the human being and earthly aspirations rather than God or salvation. Furthermore, Nietzsche's rejection of God and metaphysics, as well as of all-embracing theories of history (Hegelianism and Marxism, for example) that attempt to impose rational patterns on the past and the present is crucial to the development of existentialism (see pages 578–580) and the movement in contemporary thought called postmodernism (see pages 651–652).

However, no social policy could be derived from Nietzsche's heroic individualism, which taught that "there are higher and lower men and that a single individual can . . . justify the existence of whole millennia."[4] Nietzsche thought only of great individuals, humanity's noblest specimens, who overcome mediocrity and the artificiality of all inherited values; the social community and social injustice did not concern him. "The weak and ill-constituted shall perish: first principle of our philanthropy. And one shall help them to do so."[5] Surely, these words offer no constructive guidelines for dealing with the problems of modern industrial civilization.

Likewise, Nietzsche had no constructive proposals for dealing with the disintegration of rational and Christian certainties. Instead, his vitriolic attack on European institutions and values helped erode the rational foundations of Western civilization. This assault appealed immensely to intellectuals in central Europe, who saw Nietzsche's philosophy as liberating an inner energy. In addition, many young people, attracted to Nietzsche, welcomed World War I; they viewed it as an esthetic experience and thought that it would clear a path to a new heroic age. They took Nietzsche's words literally: "A society that definitely and *instinctively* gives up war and conquest is in decline."[6]

Nazi theorists tried to make Nietzsche a forerunner of their movement. They sought from him a philosophical sanction for their own thirst for power, contempt for the weak, ruthlessness, and glorification of action. They also wanted this sanction for their cult of the heroic and their Social Darwinist revulsion for human equality. Recasting Nietzsche in their own image, the Nazis viewed themselves as Nietzsche's supermen: members of a master race, who, by force of will, would conquer all obstacles and reshape the world according to their self-created values. Some German intellectuals were drawn to Nazism because it seemed a healthy affirmation of life, the life with a new purpose, for which Nietzsche called.

Detesting German nationalism and militarism, Nietzsche himself scoffed at the notion of German racial superiority, disdained (despite some unfortunate remarks) anti-Semitism, and denounced state worship. He would have abhorred Hitler and would have been dismayed at the twisting of his idea of the will to power into a prototype fascist principle. The men that he admired were passionate but self-possessed individuals, who, by mastering their own chaotic passions, would face life and death courageously, affirmatively, and creatively. Such men make great demands on themselves. Nevertheless, as Janko Lavrin points out, "Practically all the Fascist and Nazi theories can find some support in Nietzsche's texts, provided one gives them the required twist."[7]

Nietzsche's extreme and violent denunciation of Western democratic principles, including equality, his praise of power, his call for the liberation of the instincts, his elitism, which denigrates and devalues all human life that is not strong and noble, and his spurning of humane values provided a breeding ground for violent, antirational, antiliberal, and inhumane movements. His philosophy leads to politics without moral limits. His philosophy, which included loose talk about the virtues of pitiless warriors, the breeding of a master race, and the annihilation of the weak and the ill constituted is conducive to a politics of extremes that knows no moral limits.

Bergson

Another thinker who reflected the growing irrationalism of the age was Henri Bergson (1859–1941), a French philosopher of Jewish background. Originally attracted to positivism, Bergson turned away from the positivistic claim that science could explain everything and fulfill all human needs. Such an emphasis on the intellect, said Bergson, sacrifices spiritual impulses, imagination, and intuition and reduces the soul to a mere mechanism.

The methods of science cannot reveal ultimate reality, Bergson insisted. European civilization must recognize the limitations of scientific rationalism. Our capacity for intuition, whereby the mind achieves an immanent relationship with the object, becomes one with it, tells us more about reality than the method of analysis employed by science. The intuitive experience—something like the artist's instant comprehension of a natural scene—is a direct avenue to truth that is closed to the calculations and measurements of science. Bergson's philosophy pointed away from science toward religious mysticism.

To his admirers, Bergson's philosophy liberated the person from the constraints of positivism, mechanism, and materialism. It showed the creative potential of intuition, the mystical experience, and the poetic imagination: those forces of life that resist categorization by the scientific mind. A protest against modern technology and bureaucracy and against all the features of mass society that seemed to stifle individual uniqueness and spontaneity, it sought to reaffirm the primacy of the individual in an increasingly mechanized and bureaucratic world. The popularity of Bergson's intuitionism and vitalism, with their depreciation of reason, symptomized the unsuspected strength and appeal of the nonrational: another sign that people were searching for new alternatives to the Enlightenment world–view.

Sorel

Nietzsche proclaimed that irrational forces constitute the essence of human nature, and Bergson held that a nonrational intuition brought insights unattainable by scientific thinking. Georges Sorel (1847–1922), a French social theorist, recognized the political potential of the nonrational. Like Nietzsche, Sorel was disillusioned with contemporary bourgeois society, which he considered decadent, soft, and unheroic. Whereas Nietzsche called for the superman to rescue society from decadence and mediocrity, Sorel placed his hopes in the proletariat, whose position made them courageous, virile, and determined. Sorel wanted the proletariat to destroy the existing order. This overthrow, said Sorel, would be accomplished through a general strike: a universal work stoppage, which would bring down the government and give power to the workers.

In Sorel's view, a general strike had the appeal of a great myth. What was important was not that the general strike actually take place, but that its image stir all the anticapitalist resentments of the workers and inspire them to carry out their revolutionary responsibilities. Sorel understood the extraordinary potency of myth for eliciting total commitment and inciting heroic action. Because it appeals to the imagination and feelings, myth is an effective way of moving the masses to revolt. By believing in the myth of the general strike, workers would soar above the moral decadence of bourgeois society and bear the immense sacrifices that their struggle called for. Sorel thought that the only recourse for workers was direct action and violence, which he regarded as ennobling, heroic, and sublime—a means of restoring grandeur to a flabby world.

Sorel's pseudoreligious exaltation of violence and mass action, his condemnation of liberal democracy and rationalism, and his recognition of the power and political utility of fabricated myths would find concrete expression in the fascist movements after World War I. Sorel heralded the age of mass political movements committed to revolutionary violence and of myths manufactured by propaganda experts determined to destroy democracy.

Freud: A New View of Human Nature

In many ways, Sigmund Freud (1856–1939), an Austrian-Jewish physician who spent most of his adult life in Vienna, was a child of the Enlightenment. Like the philosophes, Freud identified civilization with reason and regarded science as the avenue to knowledge. But in contrast to the philosophes, Freud focused on the massive power and influence of nonrational drives. Whereas Nietzsche glorified the irrational and approached it with a poet's temperament, Freud recognized its potential danger. He sought to comprehend it scientifically and wanted to regulate it in the interests of civilization. Unlike Nietzsche, Freud did not belittle the rational but always strove to salvage respect for reason.

Freud held that people are not fundamentally rational; human behavior is governed primarily by powerful inner forces, which are hidden from consciousness. These instinctual strivings, rather than rational faculties, constitute the greater part of the mind. Freud's great achievement was his exploring of the world of the unconscious with the tools and temperament of a scientist. He considered not just the external acts of a person, but also the inner psychic reality that underlies human behavior.

After graduating from medical school, Freud specialized in the treatment of nervous disorders. His investigations led him to conclude that childhood fears and experiences, often sexual in nature, accounted for neuroses: disorders in thinking, feeling, and behavior that interfere with everyday acts of personal

Freud and His Daughter, Anna, 1912.   Sigmund Freud (1856–1939), the father of psychoanalysis, penetrated the world of the unconscious in a scientific way. He concluded that powerful drives govern human behavior more than reason does. His explorations of the unconscious produced an image of the human being that broke with the Enlightenment's view of the individual's essential goodness and rationality. (*Mary Evans Picture Library*)

and social life. Neuroses can take several forms, including hysteria, anxiety, depression, obsessions, and so on. So painful and threatening were these childhood emotions and experiences that his patients banished them from conscious memory to the realm of the unconscious.

To understand and treat neurotic behavior, Freud said, it was necessary to look behind overt symptoms and bring to the surface emotionally charged experiences and fears—childhood traumas—that lie buried in the unconscious, along with primitive impulses. The key to the unconscious, in Freud's view, was the interpretation of dreams. An individual's dreams, said Freud, reveal his or her secret wishes—often socially unacceptable desires and frightening memories. Too painful to bear, they get locked up in the deepest dungeons of our unconscious. But even in their cages, the demons remain active, continuing to haunt us and to generate conflicts. Our distress is real and even excruciating, but we do not know its source.

The *id,* the subconscious seat of the instincts, said Freud, is a "cauldron full of seething excitations," which constantly demand gratification. The id is primitive and irrational. It knows no values and has no awareness of good and evil. Unable to endure tension, it demands sexual release, the termination of pain, the cessation of hunger. When the id is denied an outlet for its instinctual energy, we become frustrated, angry, and unhappy. Gratifying the id is our highest pleasure. But the full gratification of instinctual demands is detrimental to civilized life.

Freud postulated a harrowing conflict between the relentless strivings of our instinctual nature and the requirements of civilization. Civilization, for Freud, required the renunciation of instinctual gratification and the mastery of animal instincts, a thesis he developed in *Civilization and Its Discontents* (1930). Although Freud's thoughts in this work were, no doubt, influenced by the great tragedy of World War I, the main theme could be traced back to his earlier writings. Human beings derive their highest pleasure from sexual fulfillment, said Freud, but unrestrained sexuality drains off psychic energy needed for creative artistic and intellectual life; it also directs energies away from work needed to preserve communal life. Hence society, through the family, the priest, the teacher, and the police, imposes rules and restrictions on our animal nature.

But this is immensely painful. People are caught in a tragic bind. Society's demand for the denial of full instinctual gratification causes terrible frustration. Equally distressing, the violation of society's rules under the pressure of instinctual needs evokes terrible feelings of guilt. Either way people suffer; civilized life simply entails too much pain for people. It seems that the price we pay for civilization is neurosis. Most people cannot endure the amount of instinctual renunciation that civilization requires. There are times when our elemental human nature rebels against all the restrictions and "thou shalt nots" demanded by society, against all the misery and torment imposed by civilization.

"Civilization imposes great sacrifices not only on man's sexuality but also on his aggressivity,"[8] said Freud. People are not good by nature, as the philosophes had taught; on the contrary, they are "creatures among whose instinctual endowments is to be reckoned a powerful share of aggressiveness." Their first inclination is not to love their neighbor, but to "satisfy their aggressiveness on him, to exploit his capacity for work without compensation, to use him sexually without his consent, to seize his possessions, to humiliate him, to cause him pain, to torture and to kill him."[9]

Man is wolf to man, Freud concluded. "Who has the courage to dispute it in the face of all the evidence in his own life and in history?"[10] Civilization "has to use its utmost efforts in order to set limits to man's aggressive instincts," but "in spite of every effort these endeavors of civilization have not so far achieved very much."[11] People find it difficult to do without "the satisfaction of this inclination to aggression."[12] When circumstances are favorable, this primitive aggressiveness breaks loose and "reveals man as a savage beast to whom consideration towards his own kind is something alien."[13] For Freud, "the inclination to aggression is an original self-subsisting disposition in man" and it "constitutes the greatest impediment to civilization."[14] Aggressive impulses drive people apart, threatening society with disintegration. Freud believed that an unalterable core of human nature is ineluctably in opposition to civilized life. To this extent, everyone is potentially an enemy of civilization.

Freud's awareness of the irrational and his general pessimism regarding people's ability to regulate it in the interests of civilization did not lead him to break faith with the Enlightenment tradition, for Freud did not celebrate the irrational. He was too cognizant of its self-destructive nature for that. Civilization is indeed a burden, but people must bear it because the alternative is far worse. In the tradition of the philosophes, Freud sought truth based on a scientific analysis of human nature and believed that reason was the best road to social improvement. Like the philosophes, he was critical of religion, regarding it as a pious illusion—a fairy tale in conflict with reason. Freud wanted people to throw away what he believed was the crutch of religion: to break away from childlike dependency and stand alone.

A humanitarian like the philosophes, Freud sought to relieve human misery by making people aware of their true nature, particularly their sexuality. He wanted society to soften its overly restrictive sexual standards because they were injurious to mental health. One enduring consequence of the Freudian revolution is the recognition of the enormous importance played by childhood in the shaping of the adult's personality. The neurotic disorders that burden adults begin in early childhood. Freud urged that we show greater concern for the emotional needs of children.

Although Freud was undoubtedly a child of the Enlightenment, in crucial ways he differed from the philosophes. Regarding the Christian doctrine of original sin as myth, the philosophes had believed that people's nature was essentially good. If people took reason as their guide, evil could be eliminated. Freud, on the other hand, asserted, in secular and scientific terms, a pessimistic view of human nature. He saw evil as rooted in human nature rather than as a product of a faulty environment. Education and better living conditions would not eliminate evil, as the philosophes had expected, nor would abolition of private property, as Marx had declared. The philosophes venerated reason; it had enabled Newton to unravel nature's mysteries and would permit people to achieve virtue and reform society. Freud, who wanted reason to prevail, understood that its soft voice had to compete with the thunderous roars of the id. Freud broke with the optimism of the philosophes. His awareness of the immense pressures that civilization places on our fragile egos led him to be generally pessimistic about the future.

Unlike Marx, Freud had no vision of utopia. He saw the crude, destructive, tendencies of human nature as an ever present obstacle to harmonious social relations. That Freud was hounded out of Vienna by the Nazis and his four sisters were murdered by them simply for being Jewish is a telling footnote to his view of human nature, the power of the irrational, and the fragility of civilization.

Social Thought: Confronting the Irrational and the Complexities of Modern Society

The end of the nineteenth century and the beginning of the twentieth mark the great age of sociological thought. The leading sociological thinkers of the period all regarded science as the only valid model for arriving at knowledge, and all claimed that their thought rested on a scientific foundation. They struggled with some of the crucial problems of modern society. How can society achieve coherence and stability when the customary associations and attachments that had characterized village life had been ruthlessly dissolved by the rapidly developing industrial-urban-capitalist order and when religion no longer unites people? What are the implications of the nonrational for political life? How can people preserve their individuality in a society that is becoming increasingly regimented? In many ways, twentieth-century dictatorships were responses to the dilemmas of modern society analyzed by these social theorists. And twentieth-century dictators would employ these social theorists' insights into group and mass psychology for the purpose of gaining and maintaining power.

Durkheim

Émile Durkheim (1858–1917), a French scholar of Jewish background and heir to Comte's positivism, was an important founder of modern sociology. Like Comte, he brought the scientific method to the study of society. Durkheim tried to show that the essential elements of modern times—secularism, rationalism, and individualism—put society at risk of breaking apart. In traditional society, the social order was derived from God, and a person's place and function were determined by birth and custom. However, modern people, sceptical and individualistic, do not accept such restraints.

The weakening of the traditional ties that bind the individual to society constituted, for Durkheim, the crisis of modern society. Without collective values and common beliefs, society is threatened with disintegration and the individual with disorientation. Modern people, said Durkheim, suffer from *anomie*: a condition of anxiety caused by the collapse of values. They do not feel integrated into a collective community and find no purpose in life. In *Suicide* (1897), Durkheim maintained that "the exceptionally high number of voluntary deaths manifests the state of deep disturbances from which civilized societies are suffering and bears witness to its gravity."[15] The pathology of modern society is also demonstrated by a high level of boredom, anxiety, and pessimism. Modern people are driven to suicide by intense competition and the disappointment and frustration resulting from unfulfilled expectations and lack of commitment to moral principles. People must limit their aspirations and exercise discipline over their desires and passions, said Durkheim. They must stop wanting more. Religion once spurred people to view restraint and the renunciation of desires as virtues, but it can no longer do so.

Although Durkheim approved of modernity, he noted that modern ways have not brought happiness or satisfaction to the individual. Modern scientific and industrial society requires a new set of principles that would bind the various classes into a cohesive social order and help to overcome the feelings of restlessness and dissatisfaction that torment people. Durkheim called for a secular and rational system of morality to replace Christian dogma and fulfill this need.

Durkheim focused on a crucial dilemma of modern life. On the one hand, modern urban civilization has provided the individual with unparalleled opportunities for self-development and material improvement. On the other, the breakdown of traditional communal bonds stemming from the spread of rationalism and individualism has produced a sense of isolation and alienation. Twentieth-century totalitarian movements sought to integrate these uprooted and alienated souls into new collectivities: a proletarian state based on workers' solidarity or a racial state based on ethnic "purity" and nationalism.

Pareto

Like Comte, Vilfredo Pareto (1848–1923), an Italian economist and sociologist, aimed to construct a system of sociology on the model of the physical sciences. His studies led him to conclude that social behavior does not rest primarily on reason, but rather on nonrational instincts and sentiments. These deeply rooted and essentially changeless feelings are the fundamental elements in human behavior. Although society may change, human nature remains essentially the same. Whoever seeks to lead and to influence people must appeal not to logic, but to elemental feelings. Most human behavior is nonrational; nonlogical considerations also determine people's beliefs. Like Marx and Freud, Pareto was convinced that we cannot accept a person's word at face value. Instead, we find the real cause of human behavior in human instincts and sentiments. People do not act according to carefully thought-out theories; they act first from nonlogical motivations and then construct a rationalization to justify their behavior. Much of Pareto's work focused on the nonrational elements of human conduct and the various beliefs invented to give the appearance of rationality to behavior that derives from feeling and instinct.

Pareto divided society into two strata: the elite and the masses. In the tradition of Machiavelli, Pareto held that a successful ruling elite must—with cunning, and, if necessary, with violence—exploit the feelings and impulses of the masses to its own advantage. Democratic states, he said, delude themselves in thinking that the masses are really influenced by rational argument. Pareto predicted the emergence of new political leaders, who would master the people through propaganda and force, always appealing to sentiment rather than reason. To this extent, Pareto was an intellectual forerunner of fascism, which preached an authoritarian elitism. Mussolini praised Pareto and proudly claimed him as a source of inspiration.

Weber

Probably the most prominent social thinker of the age, the German academic Max Weber (1864–1920) was a leading shaper of modern sociology. Weber believed that Western civilization, unlike the other civilizations of the globe, had virtually eliminated myth, mystery, and magic from its conception of nature and society. This process of rationalization—the "disenchantment of the world," as Weber called it—was most conspicuous in Western science, but it was also evident in politics and economics. Weber considered Western science an attempt to understand and master nature through reason, and Western capitalism an attempt to organize work and production in a rational manner. The Western state has a rational written constitution, rationally formulated law, and a bureaucracy of trained government officials, which administers the affairs of state according to rational rules and regulations.

Weber understood the terrible paradox of reason. Reason accounts for brilliant achievements in science and economic life, but it also despiritualizes life by ruthlessly eliminating centuries-old traditions, denouncing deeply felt religious beliefs as superstition, and regarding human feelings and passions as impediments to clear thinking. The process of disenchantment has given people knowledge, but it has also made them soulless and their life meaningless. This is the dilemma of modern individuals, said Weber. Science cannot give people a purpose for living, and the burgeoning of bureaucracy in government, business, and education stifles individual autonomy.

The process of secularization and rationalization has fostered self-liberation, for it enabled human beings to overcome illusions and to control the environment and themselves. But it is also a means of self-enslavement, for it produces institutions, giant bureaucracies, that depersonalize life. Modern officials, said Weber, are emotionally detached. Concerned only with the efficient execution of tasks, they employ reason in a cold and calculating way; such human feelings as compassion and affection are ruled out as hindrances to effectiveness. In the name of efficiency, people are placed in "steel cages," depriving them of their autonomy. The prospect existed that people would refuse to endure this violation of their spiritual needs and would reverse the process of disenchantment by seeking redemption in the irrational. Weber himself, however, was committed to the ideals of the Enlightenment and to perpetuating the rational scientific tradition.

Like Freud, Weber was aware of the power of the irrational in social life. One expression of the irrational that he analyzed in considerable depth was the charismatic leader who attracts people by force of personality. Charismatic leaders may be religious prophets, war heroes, demagogues, or others who possess this extraordinary personality that attracts and dominates others. People yearn for charismatic leadership, particularly during times of crisis. The leader claims a mission—a sacred duty—to lead the people during the crisis; the leader's authority rests on the people's belief in the mission and their faith in the leader's extraordinary abilities. A common allegiance to the charismatic leader unites the community. Weber's analysis of this phenomenon throws light on the popularity of twentieth-century dictators and demagogues.

The Modernist Movement

At the same time as Freud and the social theorists were breaking with the Enlightenment view of human nature and society, artists and writers were rebelling against traditional forms of artistic and literary expression, which had governed European cultural life since the Renaissance. Their experimentations produced a great cultural revolution, called *modernism;* it still profoundly influences the arts. In some ways, modernism was a continuation of the Romantic Movement, which had dominated European culture in the early nineteenth century. Both movements subjected to searching criticism cultural styles that had been formulated during the Renaissance and had roots in ancient Greece.

Breaking with Conventional Modes of Esthetics

Even more than romanticism, modernism aspired to an intense introspection—a heightened awareness of self—and saw the intellect as a barrier to the free expression of elemental human emotions. Modernist artists and writers abandoned conventional literary and artistic models and experimented with new modes of expression. The consequence of their bold venture, wrote the literary critic and historian Irving Howe, was nothing less than the "breakup of the traditional unity and continuity of Western culture."[16]

Like Freud, modernist artists and writers probed beyond surface appearances for a more profound reality hidden in the human psyche. Writers such as Thomas Mann, Marcel Proust, James Joyce, August Strindberg, D. H. Lawrence, and Franz Kafka explored the inner life of the individual and the psychopathology of human relations. They dealt with the predicament of men and women who rejected the values and customs of their day, and they depicted the anguish of people burdened by guilt, torn by internal conflicts, and driven by an inner self-destructiveness. Besides showing the overwhelming might of the irrational and the seductive power of the primitive, they also broke the silence about sex that had prevailed in Victorian literature.

From the Renaissance through the Enlightenment and into the nineteenth century, Western esthetic standards had been shaped by the conviction that the universe embodied an inherent mathematical order. A corollary of this conception of the outer world as orderly and intelligible was the view that art should imitate reality, that it should mirror nature. Since the Renaissance, artists had deliberately made use of laws of perspective and proportion; musicians had used harmonic chords, which brought rhythm and melody into a unified whole; writers had produced works according to a definite pattern, which included a beginning, middle, and end.

Modernist culture, however, acknowledged no objective reality of space, motion, and time that has the same meaning to all observers. Rather, reality can be grasped in many ways; a multiplicity of frames of reference apply to nature and human experience. Consequently, reality is what the viewer perceives it to be through the prism of the imagination. "There is no outer reality," said the modernist German poet Gottfried Benn, "there is only human consciousness, constantly building, modifying, rebuilding new worlds out of its own creativity."[17] Modernism is concerned less with the object itself than with how the artist experiences it—with the sensations that an object evokes in the artist's very being and with the meaning the artist's imagination imposes on reality. Sociologist Daniel Bell makes this point in reference to painting:

> *Modernism . . . denies the primacy of an outside reality, as given. It seeks either to rearrange that reality, or to retreat to the self's interior, to private experience as the source of its concerns and aesthetic preoccupations. . . . There is an emphasis on the self as the touchstone of understanding and on the activity of the knower rather than the character of the object as the source of knowledge. . . . Thus one discerns the intentions of modern painting . . . to break up ordered space.*[18]

Dispensing with conventional forms of esthetics, which stressed structure and coherence, modernism propelled the arts onto uncharted seas. Recoiling from a middle-class, industrial civilization, which prized rationalism, organization, clarity, stability, and definite norms and values, modernist writers and artists were fascinated by the bizarre, the mysterious, the unpredictable, the primitive, the irrational, and the formless. Writers, for example, experimented with new techniques to convey the intense struggle between the conscious and the unconscious and to explore the aberrations and complexities of human personality and the irrationality of human behavior. In particular, they devised a new way, the stream of consciousness, to exhibit the mind's every level—both conscious reflection and unconscious strivings—and to capture how thought is punctuated by spontaneous outbursts, disconnected assertions, random memories, hidden desires, and persistent fantasies. Arnold Schoenberg experimented with atonality in his music and Igor Stravinsky with primitive rhythms. When Stravinsky's ballet *The Rite of Spring* was performed in Paris in 1913, the theater audience rioted to protest the composition's break with tonality, its use of primitive, jazzlike rhythms, and its theme of ritual sacrifice.

Modern Art

The modernist movement, which began near the end of the nineteenth century, was in full bloom before World War I and would continue to flower in the postwar world. Probably the clearest expression of the modernist viewpoint is found in art. In the late nineteenth century, artists began to turn away from the standards that had characterized art since the Renaissance. No longer committed to depicting how an object appears to the eye, they searched for new forms of representation.

Modern painting begins with impressionism, a movement centered in Paris and spanning the years 1860 through 1886. Such impressionists as Edouard Manet, Claude Monet, Camille Pissaro, Edgar Degas, and Pierre Auguste Renoir tried to give their own immediate and personal impression of an

The Starry Night by Vincent van Gogh (1853–1890).   Son of a Dutch pastor, Van Gogh served for a time as a lay preacher before devoting himself entirely to art. He was given to wide mood swings—from extreme agitation to melancholy. His tumultuous temperament found expression in his paintings. *The Starry Night* conveys Van Gogh's personal impression of a night sky. (*Collection, The Museum of Modern Art, New York. Acquired through the Lillie P. Bliss Bequest*)

object or an event as it appeared to the eye at a fleeting instant. In the late 1880s and 1890s, postimpressionists further revolutionized the artist's sense of space and color in order to make art a vivid emotional and personal experience. French artist Paul Cézanne (1839–1906), seeking to portray his own visual perception of an object rather than a photographic copy of it, deliberately distorted perspective. He subordinated the appearance of the individual object to the requirements of the total design. The postimpressionists produced a revolution not only of space, but also of color: thus, Vincent van Gogh (1853–1890), a Dutchman who settled in France, used color as a language in and of itself to express the artist's feelings.

After the postimpressionists, art moved still further away from reproducing an exact likeness of a physical object or human being. Increasingly, artists sought to penetrate the deepest recesses of the unconscious, which they saw as the wellspring of creativity and the dwelling place of a higher truth. Paul Klee

Harmony in Red by Henri Matisse (1908).   In this early example of French Fauvism, Matisse (1869–1954) broke away from the representational painting of his predecessors and set the tone for much of twentieth-century expressive painting. His sparing use of line, color, and rhythmic motifs transforms the visual surface into brilliant designs and established a new pictorial language. (*The State Hermitage Museum, St. Petersburg*)

(1879–1940), a prominent Swiss painter, described modern art in these words: "Each [artist] should follow where the pulse of his own heart leads. . . . Our pounding heart drives us down, deep down to the source of all. What springs from this source, whether it may be called dream, idea or phantasy— must be taken seriously."[19]

In France, a group of avant-garde artists, the *fauves* (wild beasts), used color with great freedom to express intense feelings and heightened energy. Between 1909 and 1914, a new style, *cubism,* was developed by Pablo Picasso (1881–1973) and Georges Braque (1882–1963). Exploring the interplay between the flat world of the canvas and the three-dimensional world of visual perception, they sought to paint a reality deeper than what the eye sees at first glance. One art historian describes cubism as follows: "The cubist is not interested in usual representational standards. It is as if he were walking around the object he is analyzing, as one is free to walk around a piece of sculpture for successive views. But he must represent all these views at once."[20]

Throughout the period 1890 to 1914, artists were de-emphasizing subject matter and stressing the expressive power of such formal qualities as line, color, and space. It is not surprising that some artists, such as Piet Mondrian (1872–1944), a Dutch painter, and Wassily Kandinsky (1866–1944), a Russian residing in Germany, finally created abstract art, a nonobjective art totally devoid of reference to the visible world. In breaking with the Renaissance view of the world as inherently orderly and rational, modern artists opened up new possibilities for artistic expression. They also exemplified the growing appeal and force of the nonrational in European life.

Modern Physics

Until the closing years of the nineteenth century, the view of the universe held by the Western mind rested largely on the classical physics of Newton. It included the following principles: (1) time, space, and matter were objective realities that existed independently of the observer; (2) the universe was a giant machine, whose parts obeyed strict laws of cause and effect; (3) the atom, indivisible and solid, was the basic unit of matter; (4) heated bodies emitted radiation in continuous waves; and (5) through further investigation, it would be possible to gain complete knowledge of the physical universe.

Between the 1890s and the 1920s, this view of the universe was shattered by a second Scientific Revolution. The discovery of x-rays by William Konrad Roentgen in 1895, of radioactivity by Henri Bequerel in 1896, and of the electron by J. J. Thomson in 1897 led scientists to abandon the conception of the atom as a solid and indivisible particle. Rather than resembling a billiard ball, the atom consisted of a nucleus of tightly packed protons, separated from orbiting electrons by empty space.

In 1900, Max Planck (1858–1947), a German physicist, proposed the quantum theory, which holds that a heated body radiates energy not in a continuous unbroken stream, as had been believed, but in intermittent spurts, or jumps, called quanta. Planck's theory of discontinuity in energy radiation challenged a cardinal principle of classical physics: that action in nature was strictly continuous. In 1913, Niels Bohr, a Danish scientist, applied Planck's theory of energy quanta to the interior of the atom and discovered that the Newtonian laws of motion could not fully explain what happened to electrons orbiting an atomic nucleus. As physicists explored the behavior of the atom further, it became apparent that its nature was fundamentally elusive and unpredictable.

Newtonian physics says that, given certain conditions, we can predict what will follow. For example, if an airplane is flying north at four hundred miles per hour, we can predict its exact position two hours from now, assuming

Albert Einstein (1879–1955). Einstein was a principal architect of modern physics. Forced to flee Nazi Germany because of his Jewish ancestry, he became a United States citizen. He was appointed to the Institute for Advanced Study at Princeton, New Jersey. (*Wide World Photos*)

that the plane does not alter its course or speed. Quantum mechanics teaches that in the subatomic realm we cannot predict with certainty what will take place; we can only say that, given certain conditions, it is *probable* that a certain event will follow. This principle of uncertainty was developed in 1927 by the German scientist Werner Heisenberg, who showed that it is impossible to determine at one and the same time both an electron's precise speed and its position. In the small-scale world of the electron, we enter a universe of uncertainty, probability, and statistical relationships. No improvement in measurement techniques will dispel this element of chance and provide us with complete knowledge of the universe.

The theory of relativity, developed by Albert Einstein (1879–1955), a German-Swiss physicist of Jewish lineage, was instrumental in shaping modern physics; it altered classical conceptions of space and time. Newtonian physics had viewed space as a distinct physical reality, a stationary medium through which light traveled and matter moved. Time was deemed a fixed and rigid framework that was the same for all observers and existed independently of human experience. For Einstein, however, neither space nor time had an independent existence; neither could be divorced from human experience. Once asked to explain briefly the essentials of relativity, Einstein replied: "It was formerly believed that if all material things disappeared out of the universe, time and space would be left. According to the relativity theory, however, time and space disappear together with the things."[21]

Contrary to all previous thinking, the relativity theory holds that time differs for two observers traveling at different speeds. Imagine twin brothers involved in space exploration, one as an astronaut and the other as a rocket designer who never leaves earth. The astronaut takes off in the most advanced spaceship yet constructed, one that achieves a speed close to the maximum attainable in our universe—the speed of light. After traveling several trillion miles, the spaceship turns around and returns to earth. According to the experience of the ship's occupant, the whole trip took about two years. But when the astronaut lands on earth, he finds totally changed conditions. His brother has long since died, for according to earth's calendars some two hundred years have elapsed since the rocket ship set out on its journey. Such an occurrence seemed to defy all commonsense experience, yet experiments supported Einstein's claims.

Einstein's work encompassed motion, matter, and energy as well. Motion, too, is relative: the only way we can describe the motion of one body is to compare it with another moving body. This means that there is no motionless, absolute, fixed frame of reference anywhere in the universe. In his famous equation, $E = mc^2$, Einstein showed that matter and energy are not separate categories, but rather two different expressions of the same physical entity. The source of energy is matter, and the source of matter is energy. Tiny quantities of matter could be converted into staggering amounts of energy. The atomic age was dawning.

The discoveries of modern physics transformed the world of classical physics. Whereas nature had been regarded as something outside the individual—an objective reality existing independently of ourselves—modern physics teaches that our position in space and time determines what we mean by reality and that our very presence affects reality itself. When we observe a particle with our measuring instruments, we are interfering with it, knocking it off its course; we are participating in reality. Nor is nature fully knowable, as the classical physics of Newton had presumed; uncertainty, probability, and even mystery are inherent in the universe.

We have not yet felt the full impact of modern physics, but there is no doubt that it has been part of a revolution in human perceptions. Jacob Bronowski, a student of science and culture, concludes:

> *One aim of the physical sciences has been to give an exact picture of the material world. One achievement of physics in the twentieth century has been to prove that that aim is unattainable. . . . There is no absolute knowledge. . . . All information is imperfect. We have to treat it with humility. That is the human condition; and that is what quantum physics says. . . . The Principle of Uncertainty . . . fixed once and for all the realization that all knowledge is limited.*[22]

Like Darwin's theory of human origins, Freud's theory of human nature, and the transformation of classical space by modern artists, the modifications of the Newtonian picture by modern physicists have enlarged our understanding. At the same time, they have contributed to the sense of uncertainty and disorientation that characterizes the twentieth century.

The Enlightenment Tradition in Disarray

Most nineteenth-century thinkers carried forward the spirit of the Enlightenment, particularly in its emphasis on science and its concern for individual liberty and social reform. In the tradition of the philosophes, nineteenth-century thinkers regarded science as humanity's greatest achievement and believed that through reason society could be reformed. The spread of parliamentary government and the extension of education, along with the many advances in science and technology, seemed to confirm the hopes of the philosophes for humanity's future progress.

But at the same time, the Enlightenment tradition was being undermined. In the early nineteenth century, the romantics revolted against the Enlightenment's rational-scientific spirit in favor of human will and feeling. Romantic nationalists valued the collective soul of the nation—ancient traditions rooted in a hoary and dateless past—over reason and individual freedom. Conservatives emphasized the limitations of reason and attacked the political agenda of the Enlightenment and the French Revolution. In the closing decades of the century, the Enlightenment tradition was challenged by Social Darwinists, who glorified violence and saw conflict between individuals and between nations as a law of nature. They considered the right of the powerful to predominate to be a right of nature. Echoing Sorel, several thinkers trumpeted the use of force in social and political controversies.

Furthermore, a number of thinkers, rejecting the Enlightenment view of people as fundamentally rational, held that subconscious drives and impulses govern human behavior more than reason does. Several of these thinkers urged celebrating and extolling the irrational, which they regarded as the true essence of human beings and life. They glorified an irrational vitality, which transcended considerations of good and evil. "I have always considered myself a voice of what I believe to be a greater renaissance—the revolt of the soul against the intellect—now beginning in the world," wrote the Irish poet William Butler Yeats.[23] German advocates of "life philosophy" explicitly called the mind "the enemy of the soul."

Even the theorists who studied the individual and society in a scientific way pointed out that below a surface of rationality lies a substratum of irrationality, which constitutes a deeper reality. The conviction was growing that reason was a puny instrument when compared with the volcanic strength of nonrational impulses, that these impulses pushed people toward destructive behavior and made political life precarious, and that the nonrational did not bend very much to education. The Enlightenment's image of the autonomous individual who makes rational decisions after weighing the choices (a fundamental premise of liberalism and democracy) no longer seemed tenable. Often the individual is not the master of his or her own person; human freedom is limited by human nature.

Other theorists argued that the ideas of right, truth, and justice do not have an independent value; rather, they are merely tools used by elites in their struggle to gain and maintain power. Opponents of liberalism and democracy utilized the theory of elites advanced by Pareto, as well as the new stress on human irrationality, as proof that the masses were incapable of self-government and that they had to be led by their betters. Many intellectuals of the right employed the new social theories to devalue the individualist and rational bases of liberal democracy bequeathed by the Enlightenment.

At the beginning of the twentieth century, the dominant mood remained that of confidence in Europe's future progress and in the values of European civilization. However, certain disquieting trends were already evident; they would grow to crisis proportions in succeeding decades. Although few people may have realized it, the Enlightenment tradition was in disarray.

The thinkers of the Enlightenment believed in an orderly, machinelike universe; natural law and natural rights operating in the social world; objective rules that gave form and structure to artistic productions; the essential rationality and goodness of the individual; and science and technology as instruments of progress. This coherent world-view, which had produced an attitude of certainty, security, and optimism, was in the process of dissolution by the early twentieth century. The commonsense Newtonian picture of the physical universe, with its inexorable laws of cause and effect, was altered; the belief in natural rights and objective standards governing morality was undermined; rules and modes of expression that were at the very heart of Western esthetics were abandoned. Confidence in human rationality and goodness weakened. Furthermore, science and technology were accused of forging a mechanical, bureaucratic, and materialistic world, which stifled intuition and feelings, thereby diminishing the self. To redeem the self, some thinkers urged a heroic struggle, which could easily be channeled into a primitive nationalism and martial crusades.

This radical attack on the moral and intellectual values of the Enlightenment—the denunciation of reason, exaltation of force, quest for the heroic, and yearning for a new authority—constitutes the intellectual background of the fascist movements that emerged after World War I. Holding the Enlightenment tradition in contempt and fascinated by power and violence, many people, including intellectuals, would exalt fascist ideas and lionize fascist leaders.

Thus, in the early twentieth century, the universe no longer seemed an orderly system, an intelligible whole, but something fundamentally inexplicable. Human nature, too, seemed intrinsically unfathomable and problematic. To the question "Who is man?" Greek philosophers, medieval scholastics, Renaissance humanists, and eighteenth-century philosophes had provided a coherent and unambiguous answer. By the early twentieth century, Western intellectuals no longer possessed a clear idea of who the human being was, and life seemed devoid of an overriding purpose, as Nietzsche sensed:

> *Disintegration characterizes this time, and thus uncertainty: nothing stands firmly on its feet or on a hard faith in itself; one lives for to-*

morrow as the day after tomorrow is dubious. Everything on our way is slippery and dangerous, and the ice that still supports us has become thin: all of us feel the warm, uncanny breath of the thawing wind; where we still walk, soon no one will be able to walk.[24]

This radical disorientation led some intellectuals to feel alienated from and even hostile toward Western civilization.

When the new century began, most Europeans were optimistic about the future, some even holding that European civilization was on the threshold of a golden age. Few suspected that European civilization would soon be gripped by a crisis that threatened its very survival. The powerful forces of irrationalism that had been hailed by Nietzsche, analyzed by Freud, and creatively expressed in modernist culture would erupt with devastating fury in twentieth-century political life, particularly in the form of extreme nationalism and racism that extolled violence. Confused and disillusioned people searching for new certainties and values would turn to political ideologies that openly rejected reason, lauded war, and scorned the inviolability of the human person. Dictators, utilizing the insights into the unconscious and the nonrational advanced by Freud and the social theorists, succeeded in manipulating the minds of the masses to an unprecedented degree.

These currents began to form at the end of the nineteenth century, but World War I brought them together in a tidal wave. World War I accentuated the questioning of established norms and the dissolution of Enlightenment certainties. It caused many people to see Western civilization as dying and beyond redemption. Exacerbating the spiritual crisis of the preceding generation, the war shattered Europe's political and social order. It also gave birth to totalitarian ideologies that nearly obliterated the legacy of the Enlightenment.

Notes

1. Friedrich Nietzsche, *The Will to Power*, trans. Walter Kaufmann and R. J. Hollingdale, ed. Walter Kaufmann (New York: Vintage Books, 1968), pp. 458–459.
2. Ibid., pp. 383–384.
3. Quoted in R. J. Hollingdale, *Nietzsche* (London: Routledge & Kegan Paul, 1973), p. 82.
4. Nietzsche, *Will to Power*, p. 518.
5. Friedrich Nietzsche, *Twilight of the Idols and The Anti-Christ*, trans. R. J. Hollingdale (New York: Penguin, 1972), p. 116.
6. Nietzsche, *Will to Power*, p. 386.
7. Janko Lavrin, *Nietzsche* (New York: Charles Scribner's Sons, 1971), p. 113.
8. Sigmund Freud, *Civilization and Its Discontents* (New York: Norton, 1961), p. 62.
9. Ibid., p. 58.
10. Ibid.
11. Ibid., p. 59.
12. Ibid., p. 61.
13. Ibid., p. 59.
14. Ibid., p. 69.
15. Émile Durkheim, *Suicide: A Study in Sociology*, trans. John Spaulding and George Simpson (New York: The Free Press, 1951), p. 391.
16. Irving Howe, ed., *The Idea of the*

Modern in Literature and the Arts (New York: Horizon Press, 1967), p. 16.
17. Ibid., p. 15.
18. Daniel Bell, *The Cultural Contradictions of Capitalism* (New York: Basic Books, 1976), pp. 110, 112.
19. Paul Klee, *On Modern Art,* trans. Paul Findlay (London: Faber & Faber, 1948), p. 51.
20. John Canaday, *Mainstreams of Modern Art* (New York: Holt, 1961), p. 458.

21. Quoted in A. E. E. McKenzie, *The Major Achievements of Science* (New York: Cambridge University Press, 1960), 1:310.
22. Jacob Bronowski, *The Ascent of Man* (Boston: Little, Brown, 1973), p. 353.
23. Quoted in Roland N. Stromberg, *Redemption by War* (Lawrence: Regents Press of Kansas, 1982), p. 65.
24. Nietzsche, *Will to Power,* p. 40.

Suggested Reading

Baumer, Franklin, *Modern European Thought* (1977). A well-informed study of modern thought.
Bradbury, Malcolm, and James McFarlane, eds., *Modernism, 1890–1930* (1974). Essays on various phases of modernism; valuable bibliography.
Gay, Peter, *Freud: A Life for Our Times* (1988). A highly recommended study.
Hamilton, G. H., *Painting and Sculpture in Europe, 1880–1940* (1967). An authoritative work.
Hollingdale, R. J., *Nietzsche* (1973). Lucid and insightful.
Hughes, H. Stuart, *Consciousness and Society* (1958). Good on social thinkers.

Masur, Gerhard, *Prophets of Yesterday* (1961). Studies in European culture, 1890–1914.
Nelson, Benjamin, ed., *Freud and the Twentieth Century* (1957). A valuable collection of essays.
Roazen, Paul, *Freud's Political and Social Thought* (1968). The wider implications of Freudian psychology.
Stromberg, Roland N., *European Intellectual History Since 1789* (1986). A helpful text.
Zeitlin, I. M., *Ideology and the Development of Sociological Theory* (1968). Examines in detail the thought of major shapers of sociological theory.

Review Questions

1. What is meant by the term *irrationalism?*
2. Discuss Nietzsche's attitude toward reason, Christianity, and democracy.
3. Why were Nazis attracted to Nietzsche?
4. Do you find anything positive in Nietzsche's thought?
5. In what ways did Bergson reflect the growing irrationalism of the age?
6. How did Sorel show the political potential of the nonrational?

7. To what extent was Freud a child of the Enlightenment? How did he differ from the philosophes?
8. What were the standards of esthetics that had governed Western literature and art since the Renaissance? How did the modernist movement break with these standards?
9. What constituted the crisis of modern society for Durkheim? How did he try to cope with this crisis?
10. What do you think of Pareto's

judgment that the masses in a democratic state are not really influenced by rational argument?

11. For Weber, what was the terrible paradox of reason?

12. Describe the view of the universe held by westerners around 1880. How was this view altered by modern physics? What is the significance of this revolution to our perception of the universe?

13. In what ways was the Enlightenment tradition in disarray by the early years of the twentieth century?

❖ PART FIVE

Western Civilization in Crisis: World Wars and Totalitarianism

1914–1945

German Bombers over London, 1940. (*Courtesy of the Trustees of the Imperial War Museum*)

POLITICS AND SOCIETY	THOUGHT AND CULTURE

1910
World War I (1914–1918)
United States declares war on Germany (1917)
Bolshevik Revolution in Russia (1917)
Wilson announces his Fourteen Points (1918)
Treaty of Versailles (1919)

Bohr: Quantum theory of atomic structure (1912)
Stravinsky, *The Rite of Spring* (1913)
Pareto, *Treatise on General Sociology* (1916)
Spengler, *The Decline of the West* (1918, 1922)
Dadaism in art (1915–1924)
Barth, *The Epistle to the Romans* (1919)

1920
Mussolini seizes power in Italy (1922)
First Five-Year Plan starts rapid industrialization in the Soviet Union (1928)
Forced collectivization of agriculture in the Soviet Union (1929)
Start of the Great Depression (1929)

Wittgenstein, *Tractatus Logico-Philosophicus* (1921–1922)
Eliot, *The Waste Land* (1922)
Mann, *Magic Mountain* (1924)
Cassirer, *The Philosophy of Symbolic Forms* (1923–1929)
Surrealism in art (c. 1925)
Hitler, *Mein Kampf* (1925–1926)
Kafka, *The Trial* (1925)
Heidegger, *Being and Time* (1927)
Lawrence, *Lady Chatterley's Lover* (1928)
Remarque, *All Quiet on the Western Front* (1929)

1930
Stalin orders mass purges in the Soviet Union (1936–1938)
Hitler becomes chancellor of Germany (1933)
Hitler sends troops into the Rhineland (1936)
Rome-Berlin Axis (1936)
Spanish Civil War (1936–1939)
Franco establishes a dictatorship in Spain (1939)
Nazi-Soviet Non Aggression Pact (1939)
German troops invade Poland: World War II begins (1939)

Freud, *Civilization and Its Discontents* (1930)
Ortega y Gasset, *The Revolt of the Masses* (1930)
Jaspers, *Man in the Modern Age* (1930)
Jung, *Modern Man in Search of a Soul* (1933)
Toynbee, *A Study of History* (1934–1961)
Keynes, *The General Theory of Employment, Interest, and Money* (1936)
Picasso, *Guernica* (1937)
Steinbeck, *The Grapes of Wrath* (1939)

1940
Germany invades Belgium, Holland, Luxembourg, and France (1940)
Japan attacks Pearl Harbor: United States enters war against Japan and Germany (1941)
War in Europe ends (1945)
United States drops atomic bombs on Japan; Japan surrenders (1945)

Hemingway, *For Whom the Bell Tolls* (1940)
Koestler, *Darkness at Noon* (1941)
Fromm, *Escape from Freedom* (1941)
Camus, *The Stranger* (1942)
Sartre, *Being and Nothingness* (1943)
Orwell, *1984* (1949)

CHAPTER 18

World War I:
The West in Despair

$\mathcal{P}$rior to 1914, the dominant mood in Europe was one of pride in the accomplishments of Western civilization and confidence in its future progress. Advances in science and technology, the rising standard of living, the spread of democratic institutions, and Europe's position of power in the world all contributed to a sense of optimism, as did the expansion of social reform and the increase in literacy for the masses. Furthermore, since the defeat of Napoleon, Europe had avoided a general war, and since the Franco-Prussian War (1870–71), the Great Powers had not fought each other. Few people recognized that the West's outward achievements masked an inner turbulence, which was propelling Western civilization toward a cataclysm. The European state system was failing.

By 1914, national states, answering to no higher power, were fueled by an explosive nationalism and were grouped into alliances that faced each other with ever mounting hostility. Nationalist passions, overheated by the popular press and expansionist societies, poisoned international relations. Nationalist thinkers propagated pseudoscientific racial and Social Darwinist doctrines, which glorified conflict and justified the subjugation of other peoples. Committed to enhancing national power, statesmen lost sight of Europe as a community of nations sharing a common civilization. Caution and restraint gave way to belligerency in foreign relations.

The failure of the European state system was paralleled by a cultural crisis. Some European intellectuals attacked the rational tradition of the Enlightenment and celebrated the primitive, the instinctual, and the irrational. Increasingly, young people were drawn to philosophies of action that ridiculed liberal bourgeois values and viewed war as a purifying and ennobling experience. Colonial wars, colorfully portrayed in the popular press, ignited the imagination of bored factory workers and daydreaming students and reinforced a sense of duty and an urge for gallantry among soldiers and aristocrats. These "splendid" little colonial wars helped fashion an attitude that made war acceptable, if not laudable. Yearning to break loose from their ordinary lives and to embrace heroic values, many Europeans regarded violent conflict as the highest expression of individual and national life. "If only there were a war, even an un-just one," wrote George Heym, a young German writer, in 1912. "This peace is so rotten."[1] Although technology was making warfare more brutal and dangerous, Europe retained a romantic illusion about combat.

   While Europe was seemingly progressing in the art of civilization, the mythic power of nationalism and the primitive appeal of conflict were driving European civilization to the abyss. Few people recognized the potential crisis—certainly not the statesmen whose reckless blundering allowed the continent to stumble into war.   ❖

Aggravated Nationalist Tensions in Austria-Hungary

On June 28, 1914, a young terrorist, with the support of a secret Serbian nationalist society, called Union or Death (more popularly known as the Black Hand), murdered Archduke Francis Ferdinand, heir to the throne of Austria-Hungary. Six weeks later, the armies of Europe were on the march; an incident in the Balkans had sparked a world war. An analysis of why Austria-Hungary felt compelled to attack Serbia and why the other powers became enmeshed in the conflict shows how explosive Europe was in 1914. And nowhere were conditions more volatile than in Austria-Hungary, the scene of the assassination.

   With its several nationalities, each with its own history and traditions and often conflicting aspirations, Austria-Hungary stood in opposition to nationalism, the most powerful spiritual force of the age. Perhaps the supranational Austro-Hungarian Empire was obsolete in a world of states based on the principle of nationality. Dominated by Germans and Hungarians, the empire remained unable either to satisfy the grievances or to contain the nationalist aims of its minorities, particularly the Czechs and South Slavs (Croats, Slovenes, and Serbs).

   Heightened agitation among the several nationalities, which worsened in the decade before 1914, created terrible anxieties among Austrian leaders. The fear that the empire would be torn apart by rebellion caused Austria to pursue a forceful policy against any nation that fanned the nationalist feelings of its Slavic minorities. In particular, this policy meant worsening tensions between Austria and small Serbia, which had been independent of the Ottoman Empire since 1878.

   Captivated by Western ideas of nationalism, the Serbs sought to create a Greater Serbia by uniting with their racial kin, the South Slavs who dwelt in Austria-Hungary. Since some seven million South Slavs lived in the Hapsburg Empire, the dream of a Greater Serbia, shrilly expressed by Serbian nationalists, caused nightmares in Austria. Fearing that continued Serbian agitation would encourage the South Slavs to press for secession, some Austrian leaders urged the destruction of the Serbian menace.

Chronology 18.1 ❖ World War I

1882	Formation of the Triple Alliance of Germany, Austria-Hungary, and Italy
1894	Alliance between Russia and France
1904	Anglo-French Entente
1907	Anglo-Russian Entente
1908	Bosnian crisis
June 28, 1914	Archduke Francis Ferdinand of Austria is assassinated at Sarajevo
August 4, 1914	Germans invade Belgium
September 1914	First battle of the Marne saves Paris
May 1915	Italy enters the war on the Allies' side
Spring 1915	Germany launches offensive that forces Russia to abandon Galicia and most of Poland
February 1916	General Pétain leads French forces at Verdun; Germans fail to capture the fortress town
July–November 1916	Battle of the Somme: the Allies suffer 600,000 casualties
January 1917	Germany launches unrestricted submarine warfare
April 6, 1917	United States declares war on Germany
November 1917	Bolsheviks take power in Russia
March 1918	Russia signs the Treaty of Brest-Litovsk, losing territory to Germany and withdrawing from the war
March 21, 1918	Germans launch a great offensive to end the war
June 3, 1918	Germans advance to within fifty-six miles of Paris
August 8, 1918	British victory at Amiens
October 1918	Turkey is forced to withdraw from the war after several British successes
November 3, 1918	Austria-Hungary signs armistice with the Allies
November 11, 1918	Germany signs armistice with the Allies, ending World War I
January 1919	Paris Peace Conference
June 28, 1919	Germany signs the Treaty of Versailles

Map 18.1   Ethnic Groups in Germany, Austria, and the Balkans Before World War I   ▶

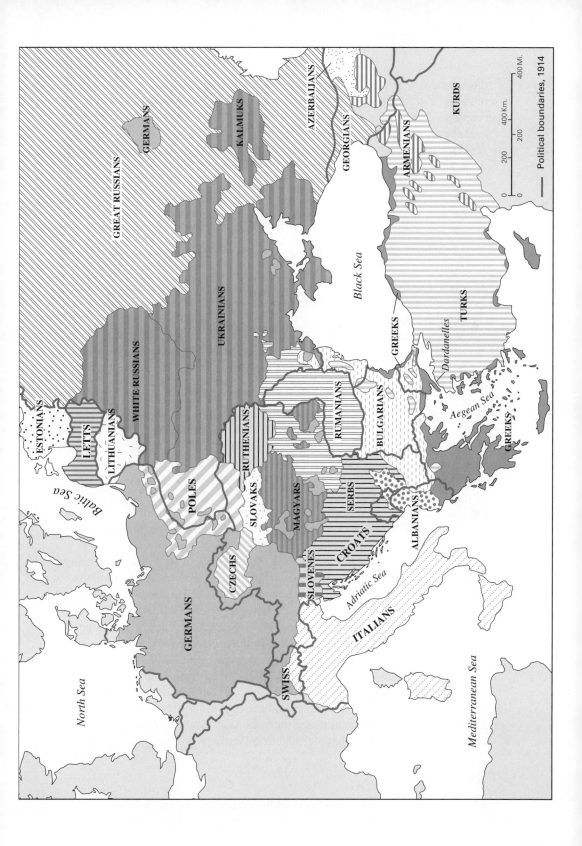

North Sea

Baltic Sea

ESTONIANS

LETTS

LITHUANIANS

GERMANS

GREAT RUSSIANS

GERMANS

KALMUKS

WHITE RUSSIANS

UKRAINIANS

POLES

CZECHS

SLOVAKS

RUTHENIANS

MAGYARS

SLOVENES

CROATS

SERBS

RUMANIANS

BULGARIANS

ALBANIANS

ITALIANS

SWISS

Adriatic Sea

Mediterranean Sea

Aegean Sea

Black Sea

GREEKS

GREEKS

Dardanelles

TURKS

BULGARIANS

GEORGIANS

ARMENIANS

AZERBAIJANS

KURDS

Political boundaries, 1914

0   200   400 Mi.

0   200   400 Km.

The tensions arising from the multinational character of the Austro-Hungarian Empire in an age of heightened nationalist feeling set off the explosion in 1914. Unable to solve its minority problems and fearful of Pan-Serbism, Austria-Hungary felt itself in a life-or-death situation. This sense of desperation led it to lash out at Serbia after the assassination of Archduke Francis Ferdinand.

The German System of Alliances

The war might have been avoided, or might have remained limited to Austria and Serbia, had Europe in 1914 not been divided into two hostile alliance systems. Such a situation contains inherent dangers. For example, knowing that it has the support of allies, a country might pursue a more provocative and reckless course and be less conciliatory during a crisis. Furthermore, a conflict between two states might spark a chain reaction, drawing in the other powers and transforming a limited war into a general war. That is what happened after the assassination. This dangerous alliance system originated with Bismarck and the Franco-Prussian War.

The New German Empire

The unification of Germany in 1870–71 turned the new state into an international power of the first rank, upsetting the balance of power in Europe. For the first time since the wars of the French Revolution, a nation was in a position to dominate the European continent. To German nationalists, the unification of Germany was both the fulfillment of a national dream and the starting point for an even more ambitious goal: extending German power in Europe and the world.

As the nineteenth century drew to a close, German nationalism became more extreme. Believing that Germany must either grow or die, nationalists pressed the government to build a powerful navy, acquire colonies, gain a much greater share of the world's markets, and expand German interests and influence in Europe. Sometimes these goals were expressed in the language of Social Darwinism: that nations are engaged in an eternal struggle for survival and domination. Decisive victories against Austria (1866) and France (1871), the formation of the German Reich, rapid industrialization, and the impressive achievements of German science and scholarship had molded a powerful and dynamic nation. Imbued with great expectations for the future, Germans became increasingly impatient to see the fatherland gain its "rightful" place in world affairs—an attitude that alarmed non-Germans.

Bismarck's Goals

Under Bismarck, who did not seek additional territory but wanted only to preserve the recently achieved unification, Germany pursued a moderate and

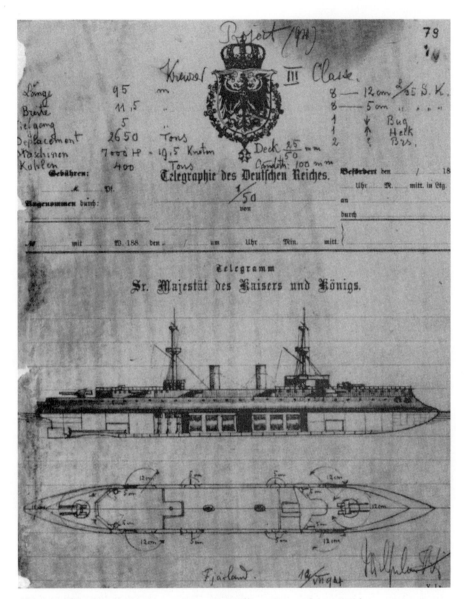

Blueprint for a Battle Cruiser.   Emperor William II was determined to construct a great navy that would challenge Britain's naval supremacy. Above is his sketch for a battle cruiser. (*Bildarchiv Militärarchiv, Freiburg*)

cautious foreign policy. One of Bismarck's principal goals was to keep France isolated and friendless. Deeply humiliated by its defeat in the Franco-Prussian War and the loss of Alsace and Lorraine, France found its nationalists yearning for a war of revenge against Germany. Even though the French government, aware of Germany's strength, was unlikely to initiate such a conflict, the issue of Alsace-Lorraine increased tensions between the two countries.

Bismarck also hoped to prevent a war between Russia and Austria-Hungary, for such a conflict could lead to German involvement, the breakup of Austria-Hungary, and Russian expansion in eastern Europe. To maintain peace and Germany's existing borders, Bismarck forged complex alliances. In the decade of the 1880s, he created the Triple Alliance, consisting of Germany, Austria-Hungary, and Italy, as well as an alliance with Russia.

Bismarck conducted foreign policy with restraint, forming alliances not to conquer new lands, but to protect Germany from aggression by either France or Russia. His aim was to preserve order and stability in Europe, not to launch war. But in 1888, a new emperor ascended the German throne. When the young Kaiser William II (1888–1918) clashed with his aging prime minister, Bismarck was forced to resign (1890). Lacking Bismarck's diplomatic skills, his cool restraint, and his determination to keep peace in Europe, the new German leaders pursued a belligerent and imperialistic foreign policy in the ensuing decades—a policy that frightened other states, particularly Britain. Whereas Bismarck considered Germany a satiated power, these men insisted that Germany must have its place in the sun.

The first act of the new leadership was to permit the treaty with Russia to lapse, allowing Germany to give full support to Austria, which was considered a more reliable ally. Whereas Bismarck had warned Austria to act with moderation and caution in the Balkans, his successors not only failed to hold Austria in check, but actually encouraged Austrian aggression. This proved fatal to the peace of Europe.

The Triple Entente

Fear of Germany

When Germany broke with Russia in 1890, France was quick to take advantage of the situation. Worried by Germany's increasing military strength, expanding industries, growing population, and alliance with Austria and Italy, France coveted Russia as an ally. In 1894, France and Russia entered into an alliance; the isolation forced on France by Bismarck had ended.

Germany's growing military might also alarmed Great Britain. Besides, its spectacular industrial growth had made Germany a potent trade rival of England. Britain was distressed, too, by Germany's increased efforts to become a great colonial power—a goal demanded by German nationalists. But most troubling was Germany's decision to build a great navy, for it could interfere with British overseas trade or even blockade the British Isles. Germany's naval program was the single most important reason that Britain moved closer first to France and then to Russia. Germany's naval construction, designed to increase its stature as a Great Power but not really necessary for its security, was one indication that German leaders had abandoned Bismarck's policy of good sense. Eager to add the British as an ally and demonstrating superb diplomatic skill, France moved to end long-standing colonial disputes with Britain. The Entente Cordiale of 1904 accomplished this conciliation. England had emerged from its self-imposed isolation.

Wishing to counter Germany's Triple Alliance with a strong alliance of their own, French diplomats now sought to ease tensions between their Russian ally and their new British friend. Two events convinced Russia to adopt a more conciliatory attitude toward Britain: a disastrous and unexpected defeat in the Russo-Japanese War of 1904–1905 and a working-class revolution in 1905. Shocked by defeat, its army bordering on disintegration, and its workers restive, Russia was now receptive to settling its imperial disputes with Britain over Persia, Tibet, and Afghanistan—a decision encouraged by France. In the Anglo-Russian Entente of 1907, as in the Anglo-French Entente Cordiale of 1904, the former rivals conducted themselves in a conciliatory, if not friendly, manner. In both instances, what engendered this spirit of cooperation was fear of Germany.

Europe was now broken into two hostile camps: the Triple Entente of France, Russia, and Britain and the Triple Alliance of Germany, Austria-Hungary, and Italy. The costly arms race and the maintenance of large standing armies by all the states except Britain increased fear and suspicion between the alliances.

German Reactions

Germany denounced the Triple Entente as a hostile anti-German coalition, designed to encircle and crush Germany; to survive, Germany must break this ring. Considering Austria-Hungary as its only reliable ally, Germany resolved to preserve the power and dignity of the Hapsburg Empire. If Austria-Hungary fell from the ranks of Great Powers, Germany would have to stand alone against its enemies. At all costs, Austria-Hungary must not be weakened.

But this assessment suffered from dangerous miscalculations. First, Germany overstressed the hostile nature of the Triple Entente. In reality, France, Russia, and Britain drew closer together not to wage aggressive war against Germany, but to protect themselves against burgeoning German military, industrial, and diplomatic power. Second, by linking German security to Austria, Germany greatly increased the chances of war. Growing more and more apprehensive of Pan-Serbism, Austria might well decide that only a war could prevent its empire from disintegrating. Confident of German support, Austria would be more likely to resort to force; fearing any diminution of Austrian power, Germany would be more likely to give Austria that support.

The Drift Toward War

Starting in 1908, several crises tested the competing alliances, pushing Europe closer to war. Particularly significant was the Bosnian affair, which involved Russia, Austria-Hungary, and Serbia. This incident contained many of the ingredients that eventually ignited the war in 1914.

The Bosnian Crisis

Russia's humiliating defeat by Japan in 1905 had diminished its stature as a Great Power. The new Russian foreign minister, Alexander Izvolsky, hoped to gain a diplomatic triumph by compelling Turkey to allow Russian warships to pass through the Dardanelles, fulfilling a centuries-old dream of extending Russian power into the Mediterranean.

Russia made a deal with Austria: if Austria would support Russia's move to open the Dardanelles, Russia would permit Austrian annexation of the provinces of Bosnia and Herzegovina. Officially a part of the Ottoman Empire, these provinces had been administered by Austria-Hungary since 1878. The population consisted mainly of ethnic cousins of the Serbs. A formal annexation would certainly infuriate the Serbs, who hoped one day to make the region part of a Greater Serbia.

In 1908, Austria proceeded to annex the provinces, but Russia met stiff resistance from England and France when it presented its case for opening the straits to Russian warships. Austria had gained a diplomatic victory, while Russia suffered another humiliation. Even more enraged than Russia was Serbia, which threatened to invade Bosnia to liberate its cousins from Austrian oppression. The Serbian press openly declared that Austria-Hungary must perish if the South Slavs were to achieve liberty and unity. A fiery attitude also prevailed in Vienna: Austria-Hungary could not survive unless Serbia was destroyed.

During this period of intense hostility between Austria-Hungary and Serbia, Germany supported its Austrian ally. To keep Austria strong, Germany would even agree to the dismemberment of Serbia and to its incorporation into the Hapsburg Empire. Unlike Bismarck, who tried to hold Austria in check, German leadership now coolly envisioned an Austrian attack on Serbia, and just as coolly offered German support if Russia intervened.

Balkan Wars

The Bosnian crisis pushed Germany and Austria closer together, brought relations between Austria and Serbia to the breaking point, and inflicted another humiliation on Russia. The first Balkan War (1912) continued these trends. The Balkan states of Montenegro, Serbia, Bulgaria, and Greece attacked the dying Ottoman Empire. In a brief campaign, the Balkan armies captured the Turkish empire's European territory, with the exception of Constantinople.

Because it was on the victorious side, landlocked Serbia gained the Albanian coast and thus a long-desired outlet to the sea. Austria was determined to keep its enemy from reaping this reward, and Germany, as in the Bosnian crisis, supported its ally. Unable to secure Russian support, Serbia was forced to surrender the territory, which became the state of Albania.

Incensed Serbian nationalists accelerated their campaign of propaganda and terrorism against Austria. Believing that another humiliation would irreparably damage its prestige, Russia vowed to back Serbia in its next confrontation with Austria. And Austria had reached the end of its patience with Serbia. Emboldened by German encouragement, Austria wanted to end the Serbian threat once and for all. Thus, the ingredients for war between Austria and Serbia, a war that might easily draw in Russia and Germany, were present. Another incident might well start a war. It came in 1914.

Assassination of Francis Ferdinand

On June 28, 1914, Francis Ferdinand was assassinated while making a state visit to Sarajevo, the capital of Bosnia. Gavrilo Princip, who was part of a team of Bosnian terrorists linked to the Black Hand, fired two shots at close range into the archduke's car. Francis Ferdinand and his wife died within fifteen minutes. By killing the archduke, the terrorists hoped to bring tensions in the Hapsburg Empire to a boiling point and to prepare the way for revolution.

For many years, leaders of Austria had yearned for war with Serbia in order to end the agitation for the union of the South Slavs. Now, they reasoned, the hour had struck. But war with Serbia would require the approval of Germany. Believing that Austria was Germany's only reliable ally and that a diminution of Austrian power and prestige threatened German security, German statesmen encouraged their ally to take up arms against Serbia. Germany and Austria wanted a quick strike to overwhelm Serbia before other countries were drawn into the conflict.

Germany Encourages Austria

Confident of German backing, on July 23 Austria presented Serbia with an ultimatum and demanded a response within forty-eight hours. The terms of the ultimatum were so harsh that it was next to impossible for Serbia to accept them. This reaction was the one that Austria intended, as it sought a military solution to the crisis rather than a diplomatic one. But Russia would not remain indifferent to an Austro-German effort to liquidate Serbia. Russia feared that an Austrian conquest of Serbia was just the first step in an Austro-German plan to dominate the Balkans. Such an extension of German and Austrian power in a region bordering Russia was unthinkable to the tsar's government. Moreover, after suffering repeated reverses in foreign affairs, Russia would not tolerate another humiliation. As Germany had decided to back its Austrian ally, Russia resolved not to abandon Serbia.

HEIR TO AUSTRIA'S THRONE IS SLAIN WITH HIS WIFE BY A BOSNIAN YOUTH TO AVENGE SEIZURE OF HIS COUNTRY

Francis Ferdinand Shot During State Visit to Sarajevo.

TWO ATTACKS IN A DAY

Archduke Saves His Life First Time by Knocking Aside a Bomb Hurled at Auto.

SLAIN IN SECOND ATTEMPT

Lad Dashes at Car as the Royal Couple Return from Town Hall and Kills Both of Them.

LAID TO A SERVIAN PLOT

Heir Warned Not to Go to Bosnia, Where Populace Met Him with Servian Flags.

AGED EMPEROR IS STRICKEN

Shock of Tragedy Prostrates Francis Joseph—Young Assassin Proud of His Crime.

Archduke Francis Ferdinand and his Consort the Duchess of Hohenberg
Slain by Assassin's Bullets.

Assassination of Archduke Francis Ferdinand. Headline from *The New York Times* reporting the assassination. (*Stock Montage*)

Serbia responded to Austria's ultimatum in a conciliatory manner, agreeing to virtually all Austrian demands. But it refused to let Austrian officials enter Serbia to investigate the assassination. Having already discarded the idea of a peaceful settlement, Austria insisted that Serbia's failure to accept one provision meant that the entire ultimatum had been rejected. It ordered the mobilization of the Austrian army.

This was a crucial moment for Germany. Would it continue to support Austria, knowing that an Austrian attack on Serbia would probably bring Russia into the conflict? Determined not to desert Austria and believing that a showdown with Russia was inevitable anyway, the German war party continued to urge Austrian action against Serbia. They argued that it was better to fight Russia in 1914 than a few years later, when the tsar's empire would be stronger. Confident of the superiority of the German army, the war party claimed that Germany could defeat both Russia and France and that Britain's army was too weak to make a difference.

On July 28, 1914, Austria declared war on Serbia. Russia, with the assurance of French support, proclaimed partial mobilization aimed at Austria alone. But the military warned that partial mobilization would throw the slow-moving Russian war machine into total confusion if the order had to be changed suddenly to full mobilization. Moreover, the only plans the Russian general staff had drawn up called for full mobilization, that is, for war against both Austria and Germany. Pressured by his generals, the tsar gave the order for full mobilization on July 30. Russian forces would be arrayed against Germany as well as Austria.

Because the country that struck first gained the advantage of fighting according to its own plans rather than having to improvise in response to the enemy's attack, generals tended to regard mobilization by the enemy as an act of war. Therefore, when Russia refused a German warning to halt mobilization, Germany, on August 1, ordered a general mobilization and declared war on Russia. Two days later, Germany also declared war on France, believing that France would support its Russian ally. Besides, German battle plans were based on a war with both Russia and France. Thus, a war between Germany and Russia automatically meant a German attack on France.

When Belgium refused to allow German troops to march through Belgian territory into France, Germany invaded the small nation, which brought Britain, pledged to guarantee Belgian neutrality, into the war. Britain could never tolerate German troops directly across the English Channel in any case, nor could it brook German mastery of western Europe.

War as Celebration

When war was certain, an extraordinary phenomenon occurred. Crowds gathered in capital cities and expressed their loyalty to the fatherland and their readiness to fight. It seemed as if people wanted violence for its own sake. War seemed to offer an escape from the dull routine of classroom, job, and home and from the emptiness, drabness, and mediocrity of bourgeois society—from "a world grown old and cold and weary," as Rupert Brooke, a young British poet put it.[2] To some, war was a "beautiful . . . sacred moment" that satisfied an "ethical yearning."[3] But more significantly, the outpouring of patriotic sentiments demonstrated the immense power that nationalism exercised over the European mind. With extraordinary success, nationalism welded millions of people into a collectivity ready to devote body and soul to the nation, especially during its hour of need.

In Paris, men marched down the boulevards singing the stirring words of the French national anthem, the "Marseillaise," while women showered young soldiers with flowers. A participant in these days recalls: "Young and old, civilians and military men burned with the same excitement. . . . thousands of men eager to fight would jostle one another outside recruiting offices, waiting to join up. . . . The word 'duty' had a meaning for them, and the word 'country' had regained its splendor."[4] Similar scenes occurred in Berlin. "It is a joy to be alive," editorialized one newspaper. "We wished so much for this hour. . . . The sword which has been forced into our hand will not be sheathed until our aims are won and our territory extended as far as necessity demands."[5] Writing about those momentous days, the British mathematician-philosopher Bertrand Russell recalled his horror and "amazement that average men and women were delighted at the prospect of war. . . . [T]he anticipation of carnage was delightful to something like ninety percent of the population. I had to revise my views on human nature."[6]

Soldiers bound for battle acted as though they were going off on a great adventure. "My dear ones, be proud that you live in such a time and in such a nation and that you . . . have the privilege of sending those you love into so glorious a battle," wrote a young German law student to his family.[7] The young warriors yearned to do something noble and altruistic, to win glory, and to experience life at its most intense.

The martial mood also captivated many of Europe's most distinguished intellectuals. They shared Rupert Brooke's sentiments: "Now God be thanked Who has matched us with His hour, / And caught our youth, and wakened us from sleeping."[8] To the prominent German historian Friedrich Meinecke, August 1914 was "one of the great moments of my life which suddenly filled my soul with the deepest confidence in our people and the profoundest joy."[9] In November 1914, Thomas Mann (see pages 571–572), the distinguished German writer, saw the war as "purification, liberation . . . an enormous hope; [it] set the hearts of poets aflame. . . . How could the artist, the soldier in the artist," he asked, "not praise God for the collapse of a peaceful world with which he was fed up, so exceedingly fed up?"[10] Besides being gripped by a thirst for excitement and a quest for the heroic, some intellectuals welcomed the war because it unified the nation in a spirit of fraternity and self-sacrifice. It was a return, some felt, to the organic roots of human existence, a way of overcoming a sense of individual isolation.

Thus, a generation of European youth marched off to war joyously, urged on by their teachers and cheered by their delirious nations. It must be emphasized, however, that the soldiers who went off to war singing and the statesmen and generals who welcomed war or did not try hard enough to prevent it expected a short, decisive, gallant conflict. Few envisioned what World War I turned out to be: four years of barbaric, senseless slaughter. The cheers of chauvinists, deluded idealists, and fools drowned out the words of those who realized that Europe was stumbling into darkness. "The lamps are going out all over Europe," said British Foreign Secretary Edward Grey. "We shall never see them lit again in our lifetime."

Stalemate in the West

On August 4, 1914, the German army invaded Belgium. German war plans, drawn up years earlier, chiefly by General Alfred von Schlieffen, called for the army to swing through Belgium to outflank French border defenses, envelop the French forces, and destroy the enemy by attacking its rear. With the French army smashed and Paris isolated, German railroads would rush the victorious troops to the eastern front to reinforce the small force that had been assigned to hold off the Russians. Everything depended on speed. France must be taken before the Russians could mobilize sufficient numbers to invade Germany. The Germans were confident that they would defeat France in two months or less.

But things did not turn out the way the German military had anticipated. Moving faster than the Germans expected, the Russians invaded East Prussia, which forced General Helmuth von Moltke to transfer troops from the French front, hampering the German advance. By early September, the Germans had reached the Marne River, forty miles from Paris. With their capital at their backs, the regrouped French forces, aided by the British, fought with astounding courage. Moreover, in their rush toward Paris, the Germans had unknowingly exposed their flank, which the French attacked. The British then penetrated a gap that opened up between the German armies, forcing the Germans to retreat. The first battle of the Marne had saved Paris. Now the war entered a new and unexpected phase: the deadlock of trench warfare.

For four hundred miles across northern France, from the Alps to the North Sea, the opposing sides both constructed a vast network of trenches. These trenches had underground dugouts, and barbed wire stretched for yards before the front trenches as a barrier to attack. Behind the front trenches were other lines to which soldiers could retreat and from which support could be sent. Between the opposing armies lay "no man's land," a wasteland of mud, shattered trees, torn earth, and broken bodies. Trench warfare was a battle of nerves, endurance, and courage, waged to the constant thunder of heavy artillery. It was also butchery. As attacking troops climbed over their trenches and advanced bravely across no man's land, they were decimated by heavy artillery and chewed up by machine-gun fire. If they did penetrate the front-line trenches of the enemy, they would soon be thrown back by a counterattack.

Despite a frightful loss of life, little land changed hands. So much heroism, sacrifice, and death achieved nothing. The generals ordered still greater attacks to end the stalemate; this only increased the death toll, for the advantage was always with the defense, which possessed machine guns, magazine rifles, and barbed wire. Tanks could redress the balance, but the generals, committed to old concepts, did not make effective use of them. And whereas the technology of the machine gun had been perfected, the motorized tanks often broke down. Gains and losses of land were measured in yards, but the lives of Europe's youth were squandered by the hundreds of thousands. Against artillery, barbed wire, and machine guns, human courage had no chance, but the generals—uncomprehending, unfeeling, and incompetent—persisted in their mass attacks. This futile effort at a breakthrough wasted untold lives to absolutely no purpose.

In 1915, neither side could break the deadlock. Hoping to bleed the French army dry and force its surrender, the Germans, in February 1916, attacked the town of Verdun. Knowing that the French could never permit a retreat from this ancient fortress, they hoped that France would suffer such a loss of men that it would be unable to continue the war. France and Germany suffered more than a million casualties at Verdun, which one military historian calls "the greatest battle in world history."[11] When the British opened a

Trench Warfare, British Troops Going "Over the Top" During the Battle of the Somme.   The soldiers still had to cross "No Man's Land" and get through the barbed wire in front of the enemy's trenches. (*Popperfoto*)

major offensive on July 1, however, the Germans had to channel their reserves to the new front, relieving the pressure on Verdun.

At the end of June 1916, the British, assisted by the French, attempted a breakthrough at the Somme River. On July 1, after seven days of intense bombardment intended to destroy German defenses, the British climbed out of their trenches and ventured into no man's land. But German positions had not been destroyed. Emerging from their deep dugouts, German machine gunners fired repeatedly at the British, who had been ordered to advance in rows. Marching into concentrated machine-gun fire, few British troops ever made it across no man's land. Out of the 110,000 who attacked, 60,000 fell dead or wounded, "the heaviest loss ever suffered in a single day by a British army or by any army in the First World War."[12] When the battle of the Somme ended in mid-November, Britain and France had lost more than 600,000 men, and the military situation remained essentially unchanged. The only victor was the war itself, which was devouring Europe's youth at an incredible rate.

In December 1916, General Robert Nivelle was appointed commander in chief of the French forces. Having learned little from past French failures to achieve a breakthrough, Nivelle ordered another mass attack for April 1917. The Germans discovered the battle plans on the body of a French officer and

Map 18.2   World War I, 1914–1918 ▶

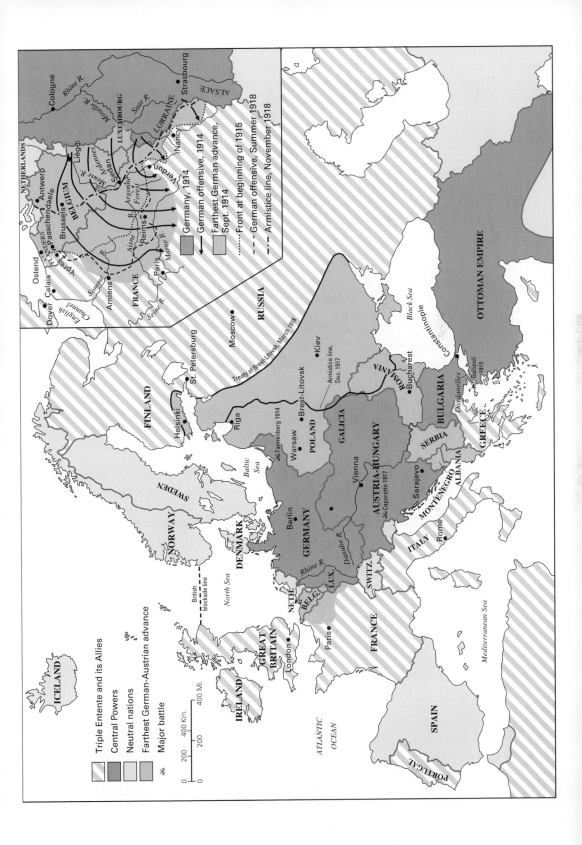

ICELAND

Triple Entente and its Allies

Central Powers

Neutral nations

Farthest German-Austrian advance

Major battle

0   200   400 Km.

0   200   400 Mi.

IRELAND

GREAT
BRITAIN

London •

British
blockade line

North Sea

NORWAY

SWEDEN

DENMARK

NETH.

BELG.
LUX.

Paris •

FRANCE

SWITZ.

SPAIN

PORTUGAL

ATLANTIC
OCEAN

Mediterranean Sea

FINLAND

Helsinki •

St. Petersburg •

Moscow •

RUSSIA

Treaty of Brest-Litovsk, March 1918

Armistice line,
Dec. 1917

Kiev •

Riga •

Tannenberg 1914

Warsaw •

Brest-Litovsk •

POLAND

GALICIA

Baltic
Sea

Berlin •

GERMANY

Danube R.

Rhine R.

Vienna •

AUSTRIA-HUNGARY

Caporetto 1917

ITALY

Rome •

ROMANIA

Bucharest •

SERBIA

Sarajevo •

MONTENEGRO

ALBANIA

BULGARIA

GREECE

Black Sea

Constantinople •

Dardanelles

Gallipoli
1915

OTTOMAN EMPIRE

Rhine R.

Cologne •

NETHERLANDS

Ostend
Dover

English
Channel

Calais

Ypres
FLANDERS

Passchendaele

Brussels •

BELGIUM

Antwerp •

Liège •

Ardennes

Sedan •

Meuse R.

LUXEMBOURG

Moselle R.

Saar R.

LORRAINE

Strasbourg •

ALSACE

Nancy •

Verdun •

Argonne
Forest

Aisne R.

Reims •

Marne R.

Paris •

FRANCE

Seine R.

Amiens •

Somme R.

German offensive, 1914

**Farthest German advance,
Sept. 1914**

Front at beginning of 1915

German offensive, Summer 1918

Armistice line, November 1918

RED CROSS OR IRON CROSS?

WOUNDED AND A PRISONER
OUR SOLDIER CRIES FOR WATER.
THE GERMAN "SISTER"
POURS IT ON THE GROUND BEFORE HIS EYES.
THERE IS NO WOMAN IN BRITAIN
WHO WOULD DO IT.
THERE IS NO WOMAN IN BRITAIN
WHO WILL FORGET IT.

British Propaganda Poster.   The warring countries employed propaganda to strengthen the resolve of the soldiers and civilians on the "home front." (*Stock Montage*)

withdrew to a shorter line on high ground, constructing the strongest defense network of the war. Knowing that the French had lost the element of surprise and pushing aside the warnings of leading statesmen and military men, Nivelle went ahead with the attack. "The offensive alone gives victory; the defensive gives only defeat and shame," he told the president and the minister of war.[13]

The Nivelle offensive, which began on April 16, was another bloodbath. Sometimes the fire was so intense that the French could not make it out of their own trenches. Although French soldiers fought with courage, the situation was hopeless. Still, Nivelle persisted with the attack; after ten days, French casualties numbered 187,000. The disgraced Nivelle was soon relieved of his command.

Other Fronts

While the western front hardened into a stalemate, events moved more decisively on the eastern front. In August 1914, the Russians, with insufficient preparation, invaded East Prussia. After some initial successes, which sent a scare into the German general staff, the Russians were soundly defeated at the battle of Tannenberg (August 26–30, 1914) and forced to withdraw from German territory, which remained inviolate for the rest of the war.

Meanwhile, Germany's ally Austria was having no success against Serbia and Russia. An invasion of Serbia was thrown back, and an ill-conceived offensive against Russia cost Austria its Galician provinces. Germany had to come to Austria's rescue. In the spring of 1915, the Germans made a breakthrough that forced the Russians to abandon Galicia and most of Poland. In June 1916, the Russians launched an offensive that opened a wide breach in the Austrian lines, but they could not maintain it. A German counteroffensive forced a retreat and cost the Russians more than a million casualties.

In March 1917, food shortages and disgust with the great loss of life exploded into a spontaneous revolution in Russia, and the tsar was forced to abdicate. The new government, dominated by liberals, opted to continue the war despite the weariness of the Russian masses. In November 1917, a second revolution brought to power the Bolsheviks, or communists, who promised "Peace, Land, Bread." In March 1918, the Bolsheviks signed the punitive Treaty of Brest-Litovsk, in which Russia surrendered Poland, the Ukraine, Finland, and the Baltic provinces.

Several countries that were not belligerents in August 1914—among them, the Ottoman Empire and Italy—joined the war later. That autumn, the Ottoman Turks entered the conflict as allies of Germany. Before the war, Germany had cultivated the Ottoman Empire's friendship by training the Turkish army; for their part, the Turks wanted German help in case Russia attempted to seize the Dardanelles. Hoping to supply Russia and, in turn, obtain badly needed Russian grain, the Allies did decide to capture the Dardanelles. In April 1915, a combined force of British, French, Australian, and New Zealander troops stormed the Gallipoli Peninsula on the European side of the Dardanelles. Ignorance of amphibious warfare, poor intelligence, and the fierce resistance of the Turks prevented the Allies from getting off the beaches and taking the heights. The Gallipoli campaign cost the Allies 252,000 casualties, and they had gained nothing.

Although a member of the Triple Alliance, Italy remained neutral when war broke out. In May 1915, on the promise of receiving Austrian territory, Italy entered the war on the side of the Allies. The Austrians repulsed a number of Italian offensives along the frontier and in 1916 took the offensive against Italy. A combined German and Austrian force finally broke through the Italian lines in the fall of 1917 at Caporetto, and the Italians retreated in disorder, leaving behind huge quantities of weapons. Germany and Austria took some 275,000 prisoners.

The Collapse of the Central Powers

The year 1917 seemed disastrous for the Allies. The Nivelle offensive had failed, the French army had mutinied, a British attack at Passchendaele did not bring the expected breakthrough and added some three hundred thousand casualties to the list of butchery, and the Russians, torn by revolution and gripped by war weariness, were close to making a separate peace. But there was one encouraging development for the Allies. In April 1917, the United States declared war on Germany.

American Entry

From the outset, America's sympathies lay with the Allies. To most Americans, Britain and France were democracies, threatened by an autocratic and militaristic Germany. These sentiments were reinforced by British propaganda, which depicted the Germans as cruel "Huns." Since most war news came to the United States from Britain, anti-German feeling gained momentum. What precipitated American entry was the German decision of January 1917 to launch a campaign of unrestricted submarine warfare. The Germans were determined to deprive Britain of war supplies and to starve it into submission. Their resolve meant that German U-boats would torpedo both enemy and neutral ships in the war zone around the British Isles. Since the United States was Britain's principal supplier, American ships became a target of German submarines.

Angered by American loss of life and materiel and by the violation of the doctrine of freedom of the seas, and fearing a diminution of prestige if the United States took no action, President Woodrow Wilson (1856–1924) pressed for American entry. Also at stake was American security, which would be jeopardized by German domination of western Europe. Leading American statesmen and diplomats worried that such a radical change in the balance of power would threaten American national interests. As German submarines continued to attack neutral shipping, President Wilson, on April 2, 1917, urged Congress to declare war on Germany. It did so on April 6.

Germany's Last Offensive

With Russia out of the war, General Erich Ludendorff prepared for a decisive offensive before the Americans could land sufficient troops in France to help the Allies. A war of attrition now favored the Allies, who could count on American supplies and manpower. Without an immediate and decisive victory, Germany could not win the war. On March 21, 1918, the Germans launched an offensive that was intended to bring victory in the west.

Suddenly, the deadlock was broken; it was now a war of movement. Within two weeks, the Germans had taken some 1,250 square miles. But British resistance was astonishing, and the Germans, exhausted and short of ammunition and food, called off the drive. A second offensive against the British, in April, also had to be called off, as the British contested every foot of ground. Both campaigns depleted German manpower, while the Americans were arriving in great numbers to strengthen Allied lines and uplift morale. At the end of May, Ludendorff resumed his offensive against the French. Attacking unexpectedly, the Germans broke through and advanced to within 56 miles of Paris by June 3. However, reserves braced the French lines, and in the battle of Belleau Wood (June 6–25, 1918), the Americans checked the Germans.

In mid-July, the Germans tried again, crossing the Marne River in small boats. Although in one area they advanced nine miles, the offensive failed against determined American and French opposition. By August 3, the second battle of the Marne had ended. The Germans had thrown everything they had into their spring and summer offensives, but it was not enough. The Allies had bent, but reinforced and encouraged by American arms, they did not break. Now they began to counterattack, with great success.

Meanwhile, German allies, deprived of support from a hard-pressed Germany, were unable to cope. An Allied army of Frenchmen, Britons, Serbs, and Italians compelled Bulgaria to sign an armistice on September 29. Shortly afterward, British successes in the Middle East forced the Turks to withdraw from the war. In the streets of Vienna, people were shouting "Long live peace! Down with the monarchy!" The Austro-Hungarian Empire was rapidly disintegrating into separate states based on nationality.

By early October, the last defensive position of the Germans had crumbled. Fearing that the Allies would invade the fatherland and shatter the reputation of the German army, Ludendorff wanted an immediate armistice. However, he needed to find a way to obtain favorable armistice terms from President Wilson and to shift the blame for the lost war from the military and the kaiser to the civilian leadership. Cynically, he urged the creation of a popular parliamentary government in Germany. But events in Germany went further than the general had anticipated. Whereas Ludendorff sought a limited monarchy, the shock of defeat and widespread hunger sparked a revolution that forced the kaiser to abdicate. On November 11, the new German Republic signed an armistice ending the hostilities.

The Peace Conference

In January 1919, representatives of the Allied Powers assembled in Paris to draw up peace terms; President Wilson was also there. The war-weary masses turned to Wilson as the prophet who would have the nations beat their swords into plowshares.

Wilson's Hope for a New World

For Wilson, the war had been fought against autocracy. He hoped that a peace settlement based on liberal-democratic ideals would sweep away the foundations of war, and he expressed these hopes in several speeches, including the famous Fourteen Points of January 1918. None of Wilson's principles seemed more just than the idea of self-determination: the right of a people to have its own state, free of foreign domination. In particular, this goal meant (or was interpreted to mean) the return of Alsace and Lorraine to France, the

Wilson and Clemenceau Arrive at Versailles, June 28, 1919.   The idealism of President Wilson (center) clashed with Premier Clemenceau's (left) determination to enhance France's security. (*Hulton Deutsch Collection*)

creation of an independent Poland, a readjustment of the frontiers of Italy to incorporate Austrian lands inhabited by Italians, and an opportunity for Slavs of the Austro-Hungarian Empire to form their own states.

Aware that a harshly treated Germany might well seek revenge, engulfing the world in another cataclysm, Wilson insisted that there should be a "peace without victory." A just settlement would encourage a defeated Germany to work with the victorious Allies in building a new Europe. To preserve peace and help remake the world, Wilson urged the formation of the League of Nations, an international parliament to settle disputes and discourage aggression. Wilson wanted a peace of justice to preserve Western civilization in its democratic and Christian form.

Problems of Peacemaking

Wilson's negotiating position was undermined by the Republican party's victory in the congressional elections of November 1918. Before the election, Wilson had appealed to the American people to cast their ballots for Democrats as a vote of confidence in his diplomacy. But instead Americans sent twenty-five Republicans and only fifteen Democrats to the Senate. Whatever the motives of the American people in voting Republican—apparently their decision rested on local and national, not international, issues—the outcome diminished Wilson's prestige at the conference table. To his fellow negotiators, Wilson was trying to preach to Europe when he could not command the support of his own country. Since the Senate must ratify any American treaty, European diplomats worried that what Wilson agreed to the Senate might reject, which is precisely what happened.

Another obstacle to Wilson's peace program was France's demand for security and revenge. Nearly the entire war on the western front had been fought on French territory. Many French industries and farms had been ruined; the country mourned the loss of half its young men. Representing France at the conference table was Georges Clemenceau (1841–1929), nicknamed "the Tiger." Nobody loved France or hated Germany more. Cynical, suspicious of idealism, and not sharing Wilson's hope for a new world or his confidence in the future League of Nations, Clemenceau demanded that Germany be severely punished and its capacity to wage war destroyed.

Seeing Germany's greater population and superior industrial strength as a threat and doubting that its military tradition would let it resign itself to defeat, Clemenceau wanted guarantees that the wars of 1870–71 and 1914–1918 would not be repeated. The latter war had shown that without the help of Britain and the United States France would have been at the mercy of Germany. Since there was no certainty that these states would again aid France, Clemenceau wanted to use his country's present advantage to cripple Germany.

The intermingling of European nationalities was another barrier to Wilson's program. Because in so many regions of central Europe there was a mixture of nationalities, no one could create a Europe completely free of minority problems; some nationalities would always feel that they had been treated shabbily. And the various nationalities were not willing to moderate their demands or lower their aspirations. For example, Wilson's Fourteen Points called for the creation of an independent Poland with secure access to the sea. But between Poland and the sea lay territory populated by Germans. Giving this land to Poland would violate German self-determination; denying it to Poland would mean that the new country had little chance of developing a sound economy. No matter what the decision, one people would regard it as unjust. Similarly, to provide the new Czechoslovakia with defensible borders, it would be necessary to give it territory inhabited mostly by Germans. This, too, could be viewed as a denial of German self-determination, but not granting the territory to Czechoslovakia would mean that the new state would not be able to defend itself against Germany.

Secret treaties drawn up by the Allies during the war also interfered with Wilson's program. Dividing up German, Austrian, and Ottoman territory, these agreements did not square with the principle of self-determination. For example, to entice Italy into entering the war, the Allies had promised it Austrian lands that were inhabited predominantly by Germans and Slavs. Italy was not about to repudiate its prize because of Wilson's principles.

Finally, the war had generated great bitterness, which persisted after the guns had been silenced. Both the masses and their leaders demanded retribution and held exaggerated hopes for territory and reparations. In such an atmosphere of postwar enmity, the spirit of compromise and moderation could not overcome the desire for spoils and punishment.

The Settlement

After months of negotiations, often punctuated by acrimony, the peacemakers hammered out a settlement. Five treaties made up the Peace of Paris: one each with Germany, Austria, Hungary, Bulgaria, and Turkey. Of the five, the Treaty of Versailles, which Germany signed on June 28, 1919, was the most significant.

France regained Alsace and Lorraine, lost to Germany in the Franco-Prussian War of 1870–71. The treaty also barred Germany from placing fortifications in the Rhineland. The French military had wanted to take the Rhineland from Germany and break it up into one or more republics under French suzerainty. The Rhine River was a natural defensive border; one had only to destroy the bridges to prevent a German invasion of France. With Germany deprived of this springboard for invasion, French security would be immensely improved. Recognizing that the German people would never permanently submit to the amputation of the Rhineland, which was inhabited by more than five million Germans and contained key industries, Wilson and British Prime Minister David Lloyd George (1863–1945) resisted these French demands.

Faced with the opposition of Wilson and Lloyd George, Clemenceau backed down and agreed instead to Allied occupation of the Rhineland for fifteen years, the demilitarization of the region, and an Anglo-American promise of assistance if Germany attacked France in the future. This last point, considered vital by France, proved useless. The alliance only went into effect if both the United States and Britain ratified it. Since the Security Treaty did not get past the U.S. Senate, Britain also refused to sign it. The French people felt that they had been duped and wronged.

A related issue concerned French demands for annexation of the coal-rich Saar Basin, which adjoined Lorraine. By obtaining this region, France would

Map 18.3   Post–World War I: Broken Empires and Changed Boundaries   ▶

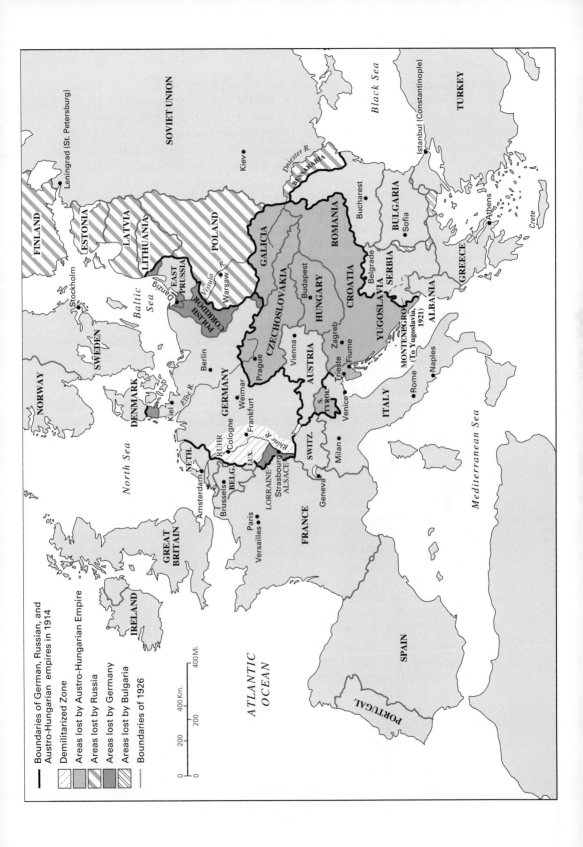

Boundaries of German, Russian, and Austro-Hungarian empires in 1914

Demilitarized Zone

Areas lost by Austro-Hungarian Empire

Areas lost by Russia

Areas lost by Germany

Areas lost by Bulgaria

Boundaries of 1926

FINLAND

SOVIET UNION

Leningrad (St. Petersburg)

Kiev

Black Sea

TURKEY

Istanbul (Constantinople)

ESTONIA

LATVIA

LITHUANIA

POLAND

GALICIA

BESSARABIA

Dniester R.

ROMANIA

Bucharest

BULGARIA

Sofia

GREECE

Athens

Crete

Stockholm

Baltic Sea

SWEDEN

Danzig

EAST PRUSSIA

Vistula R.

Warsaw

POLISH CORRIDOR

CZECHOSLOVAKIA

Budapest

HUNGARY

CROATIA

Belgrade

SERBIA

YUGOSLAVIA

MONTENEGRO (To Yugoslavia, 1921)

ALBANIA

NORWAY

Berlin

Prague

Vienna

AUSTRIA

Zagreb

Fiume

Trieste

S. TYROL

Venice

Naples

Rome

Mediterranean Sea

DENMARK

Kiel

Elbe R.

GERMANY

Weimar

Frankfurt

RUHR

Cologne

Rhine R.

SWITZ.

Milan

ITALY

North Sea

NETH.

Amsterdam

BELG.

Brussels

LUX.

LORRAINE

Strasbourg

ALSACE

Geneva

Paris

Versailles

FRANCE

GREAT BRITAIN

IRELAND

ATLANTIC OCEAN

SPAIN

PORTUGAL

0   200   400 Mi.

0   200   400 Km.

weaken Germany's military potential and strengthen its own. France argued that this would be just compensation for the deliberate destruction of the French coal mines by the retreating German army at the end of the war. But here, too, France was disappointed. The final compromise called for a League of Nations commission to govern the Saar Basin for fifteen years, after which the inhabitants would decide whether their territory would be ceded to France or returned to Germany.

In eastern Germany, in certain districts of Silesia that had a large Polish population, a plebiscite determined the future of the region. Part of Upper Silesia was ceded to Poland. The settlement also gave Poland a corridor cut through West Prussia and terminating in the Baltic port of Danzig; Danzig itself was declared an international city, to be administered by a League of Nations commission. The Germans would never resign themselves to this loss of territory, which separated East Prussia from the rest of Germany.

The victorious nations were awarded control of German and Ottoman colonies. However, these nations held colonies not outright but as mandates under the supervision of the League, which would protect the interests of the native peoples. The mandate system implied the ultimate end of colonialism, for it clearly opposed the exploitation of colonial peoples and asserted independence as the rightful goal for subject nations.

Other issues revolved around the German military forces and reparations. To prevent a resurgence of militarism, the German army was limited to one hundred thousand volunteers and deprived of heavy artillery, tanks, and warplanes. The German navy was limited to a token force, which did not include submarines. The issue of war reparations (compensation) caused great bitterness between Wilson and his French and British adversaries. The American delegation wanted the treaty to fix a reasonable sum that Germany would have to pay and specify the period of years allotted for payment. But no such items were included; they were left for future consideration. The Treaty of Versailles presented Germany with an open-ended bill, which would probably take generations to pay. Moreover, Article 231, which preceded the reparation clauses, placed sole responsibility for the war on Germany and its allies. The Germans responded to this accusation with contempt.

In separate treaties, the conference dealt with the dissolution of the Hapsburg Empire. During the final weeks of the war, the Austro-Hungarian Empire had crumbled as the various nationalities proclaimed their independence from Hapsburg rule. In most cases, the peacemakers ratified with treaties what the nationalities had already accomplished in fact. Serbia joined with Austrian lands inhabited by Croats and Slovenes to become Yugoslavia. Czechoslovakia arose from the predominantly Czech and Slovak regions of Austria. Hungary, which broke away from Austria to become a separate country, had to cede considerable land to Romania and Yugoslavia. Austria turned over to Italy the South Tyrol, inhabited by two hundred thousand Austrian Germans. This clear violation of the principle of self-determination greatly offended liberal opinion. Deprived of its vast territories and prohibited from union with Germany, the new Austria was a third-rate power.

Assessment and Problems

The Germans unanimously denounced the Treaty of Versailles, for in their minds the war had ended not in German defeat but in a stalemate. They regarded the armistice as the prelude to a negotiated settlement among equals, based on Wilson's call for a peace of justice. Instead, the Germans were barred from participating in the negotiations. And they viewed the terms of the treaty as humiliating and vindictive—designed to keep Germany militarily and economically weak.

When the United States had entered the war, the Germans protested, Wilson had stated that the enemy was not the German people but their government. Surely, the Germans now argued, the new German democracy should not be punished for the sins of the monarchy and the military. To the Germans, the Treaty of Versailles was not the dawning of the new world that Wilson had promised, but an abomination—a vile crime.

Critics in other lands also condemned the treaty as a punitive settlement in flagrant violation of Wilsonian idealism. The peacemakers, they argued, should have set aside past hatreds and, in cooperation with the new democratic German Republic, forged a just settlement to serve as the foundation of a new world. Instead, they burdened the fledgling German democracy with reparations that were impossible to pay, insulted it with the accusation of war guilt, and deprived it of territory in violation of the principle of self-determination. All these provisions, said the critics, would only exacerbate old hatreds and fan the flames of German nationalism. This was a poor beginning for democracy in Germany and for Wilson's new world.

The treaty's defenders, however, insisted that if Germany had won the war it would have imposed a far harsher settlement on the Allies. They pointed to German war aims, which called for the annexation of parts of France and Poland, the reduction of Belgium and Romania to satellites, and German expansion in central Africa. They pointed also to the treaty of Brest-Litovsk, which Germany had compelled Russia to sign in 1918, as an example of Germany's ruthless appetite. An insatiable Germany gained 34 percent of Russia's population, 32 percent of its farmland, 54 percent of its industrial enterprises, and 89 percent of its coal mines. Moreover, they maintained that the peace settlement did not repudiate Wilson's principles. The new map of Europe was the closest approximation of the ethnic distribution of its peoples that Europe had ever known.

What is most significant about the Treaty of Versailles is that it did not solve the German problem. Germany was left weak but unbroken—its industrial and military power only temporarily contained, its nationalist fervor undiminished. The real danger in Europe was German unwillingness to accept defeat or surrender the dream of expansion.

Would France, Britain, and the United States enforce the treaty against a resurgent Germany? The war had demonstrated that an Allied victory depended on American intervention. But in 1920, the U.S. Senate, angry that Wilson had not taken Republicans with him to Paris and fearing that membership in the League of Nations would involve America in future wars, refused to ratify the Treaty of Versailles. Britain, feeling guilty over the treatment of Germany, lacked the will for enforcement and even came to favor revising the treaty. Therefore, the responsibility for preserving the settlement rested primarily with France, which was not encouraging. The Paris peace settlement left Germany resentful but potentially powerful, and to the east lay small and weak states—some of them with sizable German minorities—that could not check a rearmed Germany.

The War and European Consciousness

"There will be wars as never before on earth," Nietzsche had predicted. World War I bore him out. Modern technology enabled the combatants to kill with unprecedented efficiency; modern nationalism infused both civilians and soldiers with the determination to fight until the enemy was totally beaten. Exercising wide control over its citizens, the modern state mobilized its human, material, and spiritual resources to wage total war. As the war hardened into a savage and grueling fight, the statesmen did not press for a compromise peace; instead, they demanded ever more mobilization, ever more escalation, and ever more sacrifices.

The Great War profoundly altered the course of Western civilization, deepening the spiritual crisis that had produced it. How could one speak of the inviolability of the individual when Europe had become a slaughterhouse, or of the primacy of reason when nations permitted slaughter to go unabated for four years? How could the mind cope with this spectacle of a civilization turning against itself, destroying itself in an orgy of organized violence? A young French soldier, shortly before he was killed at Verdun, expressed the disillusionment that gripped the soldiers in the trenches: "Humanity is mad! It must be mad to do what it is doing. What a massacre! What scenes of horror and carnage, I cannot find words to translate my impressions. Hell cannot be so terrible. Men are mad!"[14] The war, said British poet Robert Graves, provoked an "inward scream" that still reverberates. Now only the naive could believe in continuous progress. Western civilization had entered an age of violence, anxiety, and doubt.

The war left many with the gnawing feeling that Western civilization had lost its vitality and was caught in a rhythm of breakdown and disintegration. It seemed that Western civilization was fragile and perishable, that Western people, despite their extraordinary accomplishments, were never more than a step or two away from barbarism. Surely, any civilization that could allow such senseless slaughter to last had entered its decline and could look forward to only the darkest of futures.

European intellectuals were demoralized and disillusioned. The orderly, peaceful, rational world of their youth had been wrecked. The Enlightenment

The Survivors (1922) by Käthe Kollwitz.   With an estimated ten million dead and twenty-one million wounded, World War I shattered the hope that western Europe had been making continuous progress toward a rational and enlightened civilization. (*National Gallery of Art, Washington, D.C., Rosenwald Collection © Estates of Käthe Kollwitz, VAGA, New York, 1991*)

world-view, weakened in the nineteenth century by the assault of romantics, Social Darwinists, extreme nationalists, race mystics, and glorifiers of the irrational, was now disintegrating. The enormity of the war had destroyed faith in the capacity of reason to deal with crucial social and political questions. Civilization seemed to be fighting an unending and hopeless battle against the irrational elements in human nature. It appeared that war would be a recurring phenomenon in the twentieth century.

Scientific research had produced more efficient weapons to kill and maim Europe's youth. The achievements of Western science and technology, which had been viewed as a boon for humanity and the clearest testament to the superiority of European civilization, were called into question. Confidence in the future gave way to doubt. The old beliefs in the perfectibility of humanity, the blessings of science, and ongoing progress now seemed an expression of naive optimism. As A. J. P. Taylor concludes,

> *The First World War was difficult to fit into the picture of a rational civilization advancing by ordered stages. The civilized men of the twentieth century had outdone in savagery the barbarians of all preceding ages, and their civilized virtues—organization, mechanical skill, self-sacrifice—had made war's savagery all the more terrible. Modern man had developed powers which he was not fit to use. European civilization had been weighed in the balance and found wanting.*[15]

This disillusionment heralded a loss of faith in liberal-democratic values—a loss of faith that contributed to the widespread popularity of fascist ideologies in the postwar world. Having lost confidence in the power of reason to solve the problems of the human community, in liberal doctrines of individual freedom, and in the institutions of parliamentary democracy, many people turned to fascism as a simple saving faith. Far from making the world safe for democracy, as Wilson and other liberals had hoped, World War I gave rise to totalitarian movements, which would nearly destroy democracy.

The war produced a generation of young people who had reached their maturity in combat. Violence had become a way of life for millions of soldiers hardened by battle and for millions of civilians aroused by four years of propaganda. The astronomical casualty figures—some ten million dead and twenty-one million wounded—had a brutalizing effect. Violence, cruelty, suffering, and even wholesale death seemed to be natural and acceptable components of human existence. The sanctity of the individual seemed to be liberal and Christian claptrap.

The fascination with violence and contempt for life persisted in the postwar world. Many returned veterans yearned for the excitement of battle and the fellowship of the trenches—what one French soldier called "the most tender human experience." After the war, a young English officer recalled: "There was an exaltation, in those days of comradeship and dedication, that would have come in few other ways."[16] A fraternal bond united the men of the trenches. But many veterans also shared a primitive attraction to war's fury. A Belgian veteran expressed it this way:

> *The plain truth is that if I were to obey my native animal instincts— and there was little hope for anything else while I was in the trenches—I should enlist again in any future war, or take part in any sort of fighting, merely to experience again that voluptuous thrill of the human brute who realizes his power to take away life from other human beings who try to do the same to him. What was first accepted as a moral duty became a habit . . . had become a need.*[17]

Both Hitler and Mussolini, themselves ex-soldiers imbued with the ferocity of the front, knew how to appeal to veterans. The lovers of violence and the harbingers of hate who became the leaders of fascist parties would come within a hairsbreadth of destroying Western civilization. The intensified nationalist hatreds following World War I also helped fuel the fires of World War II. The Germans swore to regain lands lost to the Poles; some Germans dreamed of a war of revenge. Italy, too, felt aggrieved because it had not received more territory from the dismembered Austro-Hungarian Empire.

However, while the experience of the trenches led some veterans to embrace an aggressive militarism, others were determined that the horror should never be repeated. Tortured by the memory of the Great War, European intellectuals wrote pacifist plays and novels and signed pacifist declarations. In the 1930s, an attitude of "peace at any price" discouraged resistance to Nazi Germany in its bid to dominate Europe.

World War I was total war; it encompassed the entire nation and was without limits. States demanded total victory and total commitment from their citizens. They regulated industrial production, developed sophisticated propaganda techniques to strengthen morale, and exercised ever greater control over the lives of their people, organizing and disciplining them like soldiers. This total mobilization of nations' human and material resources provided a model for future dictators. With ever greater effectiveness and ruthlessness, dictators would centralize power and manipulate thinking. The first indication that the world would never be the same again, and perhaps the most important consequence of the war, was the Russian Revolution in 1917 and the Bolshevik seizure of power.

Notes

1. Quoted in Roland N. Stromberg, *Redemption by War* (Lawrence: The Regents Press of Kansas, 1982), p. 24.
2. Rupert Brooke, "Peace," in *Collected Poems of Rupert Brooke* (New York: Dodd, Mead, 1941), p. 111.
3. Quoted in Joachim C. Fest, *Hitler* (New York: Harcourt Brace Jovanovich, 1973), p. 66.
4. Roland Dorgelès, "After Fifty Years," excerpted in *Promise of Greatness*, ed. George A. Panichas (New York: John Day, 1968), pp. 14–15.
5. Quoted in Barbara Tuchman, *The Guns of August* (New York: Macmillan, 1962), p. 145.
6. Bertrand Russell, *The Autobiography of Bertrand Russell, 1914–1944* (Boston: Little, Brown, 1951, 1956), 2:4–6.
7. Quoted in Robert G. L. Waite, *Vanguard of Nazism* (New York: Norton, 1969), p. 22.
8. Brooke, "Peace," p. 111.
9. Quoted in James Joll, "The Unspoken Assumptions," in *The Origins of the First World War*, ed. H. W. Koch (New York: Taplinger, 1972), p. 318.
10. Quoted in Peter Gay, *Freud: A Life for Our Time* (New York: Norton), p. 348.
11. S. L. A. Marshall, *The American Heritage History of World War I* (New York: Dell, 1966), p. 215.
12. A. J. P. Taylor, *A History of the First World War* (New York: Berkeley, 1966), p. 84.
13. Quoted in Richard M. Watt, *Dare Call It Treason* (New York: Simon & Schuster, 1963), p. 169.
14. Quoted in Alistair Horne, *The*

Price of Glory (New York: Harper, 1967), p. 240.

15. A. J. P. Taylor, *From Sarajevo to Potsdam* (New York: Harcourt, Brace & World, 1966), pp. 55–56.

16. Quoted in Modris Eksteins, *Rites of Spring: The Great War and the Birth of the Modern Age* (New York: Doubleday Anchor Books, 1989), p. 232.

17. Quoted in Eric J. Leed, *No Man's Land: Combat and Identity in World War I* (New York: Cambridge University Press, 1979), p. 201.

Suggested Reading

Berghahn, V. R., *Germany and the Approach of War in 1914* (1975). Relates German foreign policy to domestic problems.

Fay, Sidney, *The Origins of the World War*, 2 vols. (1966). A comprehensive study of the underlying and immediate causes of the war; first published in 1928.

Fischer, Fritz, *Germany's Aims in the First World War* (1967). A controversial work, stressing Germany's responsibility for the war.

Gilbert, Martin, *The First World War* (1994). A recent survey; contains illuminating anecdotal material.

Lafore, Laurence, *The Long Fuse* (1971). A beautifully written study of the causes of the conflict.

Leed, Eric J., *No Man's Land: Combat and Identity in World War I* (1979). The impact of the war on the men who participated in it.

Marshall, S. L. A., *The American Heritage History of World War I* (1966). Probably the best account available.

Panichas, George A., ed., *Promise of Greatness* (1968). Recollections of the war by people of prominence.

Stromberg, Roland N., *Redemption by War: The Intellectuals and 1914* (1982). A superb analysis of the reasons that so many intellectuals welcomed the war.

Williams, John, *The Other Battleground* (1972). A comparison of the home fronts in Britain, France, and Germany.

Review Questions

1. How did the nationality problems in Austria-Hungary contribute to the outbreak of World War I?
2. What conditions led to the formation of the Triple Entente? How did Germany respond to it?
3. After the assassination of Archduke Francis Ferdinand, what policies were pursued by Austria-Hungary, Germany, and Russia?
4. What battle plans did Germany and France implement in 1914? What prevented Germany from reaching Paris in 1914?
5. Identify and explain the historical significance of the battles of Verdun, the Somme, and Gallipoli.
6. Why did the United States enter the war?
7. Describe Wilson's peace program. What obstacles did it face?
8. What were the provisions of the Treaty of Versailles regarding Germany?
9. Why was World War I a great turning point in the history of the West?

CHAPTER 19

The Soviet Union: Modernization and Totalitarianism

A fateful consequence of World War I, even before its final battles were fought, was the Russian Revolution of 1917. The Revolution occurred in two stages. In March, the tsarist regime was overthrown. The March revolution ushered in a period of liberal government and freedom, which soon led to a complete breakdown of law and order. Taking advantage of the chaos, the Bolsheviks, in a second stage of the Revolution, seized power in November and established a communist dictatorship.* The roots of the Russian Revolution lie in the failure of tsarist autocracy. ❖

Tsarist Autocracy

In the middle of the nineteenth century, Russia differed fundamentally from western Europe. The great movements that had shaped the outlook of the modern West—Renaissance, Reformation, Scientific Revolution, Enlightenment, and Industrial Revolution—had barely penetrated Russia. Autocracy, buttressed by the Orthodox church, reigned supreme; the small and insignificant middle class did not possess the dynamic, critical, and individualistic spirit that characterized the Western bourgeoisie, and the vast majority of the people were illiterate serfs.

After Napoleon's defeat in 1814, many returning Russian officers, asking why Russia could not share the civilized life they had seen in western Europe, turned revolutionary. The unsuccessful Decembrist uprising in 1825, during the brief interlude between the death of Alexander I (1801–1825) and the accession of Nicholas I (1825–1855), was the effort of a small group of conspirators demanding a constitution. Fear of revolution determined the character of the reign of Nicholas I and of tsarist governments thereafter.

Aware of the subversive influence of foreign ideas, Nicholas decreed an ideology of Russian superiority, called *official nationality*. The Russian people were taught to believe that the Orthodox creed of the Russian church, the

*Until March 1918, events in Russia were dated by the Julian calendar, thirteen days behind the Gregorian calendar used in the West. By the Julian calendar the first revolution occurred in February, and the second in October.

Chronology 19.1 ❖ Rise of the Soviet Union

March 1917	Tsarist regime is overthrown
November 1917	Bolsheviks, led by Lenin, seize power
1918–1920	Civil war and foreign intervention
January 1918	Bolsheviks disband the Constituent Assembly
November 1920	Remnants of the White Army are evacuated from the Crimean Peninsula
1921–1928	New Economic Policy (NEP)
1922	Stalin becomes general secretary of the Communist party
January 1924	Lenin dies
1928	First Five-Year Plan starts rapid industrialization
1929	Stalin in sole command; collectivization of agriculture starts
1936–1938	Stalin's terror purges

autocratic rule of the tsar, and Russia's Slavic culture made the Russian Empire superior to the West. To enforce this contrived invincibility, Nicholas I created the Third Section, a secret agency of police spies, and controlled access to his country from Europe. Indeed, toward the end of his reign, he drew a virtual iron curtain to keep out dangerous influences. His ideal was a monolithic country, run, like an army, by a vigorous administration centered on the monarch; all Russians were to obey his wise and fatherly commands. Nicholas's successor, Alexander II (1855–1881), was determined to preserve autocratic rule. However, he wanted Russia to achieve what had made western Europe strong: the energetic support and free enterprise of its citizens. Whether stimulating popular initiative was possible without undermining autocracy was the key puzzle for him and for his successors to the end of the tsarist regime.

Alexander's boldest reforms included the emancipation of the serfs in 1861. They were liberated from bondage to the nobility and given land of their own, but not individual freedom. They remained tied to their village and to their households, which owned the land collectively. Emancipation did not transform the peasants into enterprising and loyal citizens. For the nonpeasant minority, a package of other reforms brought new opportunities: limited self-government for selected rural areas and urban settlements, an independent judiciary, trial by jury, and the introduction of a profession novel to Russians: the practice of law.

Meanwhile, Alexander reopened the borders, allowing closer ties with Europe and westernizing Russian society. The rising class of businesspeople and professional experts looked west and conformed to Western middle-class standards. There was some relaxation in the repression of non-Russian minorities. Railroads were constructed, which facilitated agricultural exports and permitted the import of Western goods and capital. For some years, the economy boomed.

More significant in the long run was the flowering of Russian thought and literature among the intelligentsia. These were educated Russians whose minds were shaped by Western schooling and travel, yet who still were prompted by the "Russian soul." They quarreled with fierce sincerity over whether Russia should pursue superiority by imitating the West or by cultivating its own Slavic genius, possibly through a Pan-Slavic movement. Pan-Slavism, which glorified the solidarity of Russians with other Slavic peoples of eastern Europe, was a popular cause. Even more than the tsars, the intelligentsia hoped for a glorious Russia that would outshine the West.

Yet tsarist autocracy undercut their hopes. The tsar would not permit open discussion likely to provoke rebellion. Liberals advocating gradual change were thwarted by censorship and the police. The 1860s saw the rise of self-righteous fanatics ready to match the chicanery of the police and foment social revolution. By the late 1870s, they organized themselves into a secret terrorist organization. In 1881, they assassinated the tsar. The era of reforms ended.

The next tsar, Alexander III (1881–1894), a firm if unimaginative ruler, returned to the principles of Nicholas I. In defense against the revolutionaries, he perfected the police state, even enlisting anti-Semitism in its cause. He updated autocracy and stifled dissent but also promoted economic development. Russia had relied too heavily on foreign loans and goods; it had to build up its own resources. It also needed more railroads to bind its huge empire together. So in 1891 the tsar ordered the construction of the Trans-Siberian Railroad. Soon afterward, Minister of Finance Sergei Witte used railroad expansion to boost heavy industry and industrialization generally.

In 1900, Witte addressed a farsighted memorandum to Nicholas II (1894–1917), who, hopelessly unprepared and out of tune with the times, had succeeded his father:

> *Russia more than any other country needs a proper economic foundation for its national policy and culture. . . . If we do not take energetic and decisive measures so that in the course of the next decade our industry will be able to satisfy the needs of Russia . . . then the rapidly growing foreign industries will . . . establish themselves in our fatherland. . . . Our economic backwardness may lead to political and cultural backwardness as well.*[1]

Yet forced industrialization also brought perils. It propelled the country into alien and often hated ways of life, created a discontented new class of workers, and impoverished agriculture. In addition, it promoted literacy and contact with western Europe and thus helped to increase political agitation among the professional classes, intelligentsia, workers, peasants, and subject nationalities. Indispensable for national self-assertion and survival, industrialization strained the country's fragile unity.

The first jolt, the revolution of 1905, followed Russia's defeat by Japan in the Russo-Japanese War. Fortunately for the tsar, his soldiers stayed loyal. The autocracy survived, although, as a concession to the revolution, it was now saddled with a parliament, called the Imperial Duma. The new regime, inwardly rejected by Nicholas II, started auspiciously. Under its freedoms, Russian art and literature flourished and the economy progressed. Agrarian reforms introduced the incentives of private property and individual enterprise in the villages. The supporters of the new constitutional experiment hoped for a liberal Russia at last, but in vain.

The Russian Revolution of 1917

Among all classes, increased contact with "the West," as Russians called Europe, raised expectations and deepened dissatisfaction with the country's poverty and backwardness. Fears of revolution troubled foresighted Russians. During World War I, the volcano came to life. The ill-equipped and poorly led Russian armies suffered huge losses, and by 1916 the home front began to fall apart. Shops were empty, money was valueless, and hunger and cold stalked the working quarters of cities and towns. But Tsar Nicholas II, determined to preserve autocracy, resisted any suggestion that he liberalize the regime for the sake of the war effort.

The Collapse of Autocracy

The people of Russia had initially responded to the war with a show of patriotic fervor. By January 1917, however, virtually all Russians—and, most of all, the soldiers—had lost trust in their autocratic government. It had failed to protect the country from the enemy, and economic conditions had deteriorated. Autocracy was ready to collapse at the slightest blow. In early March (February 23 by the calendar then in use), a strike, riots in the food lines, and street demonstrations in Petrograd (formerly Saint Petersburg) flared into sudden, unpremeditated revolution. The soldiers, who in 1905 had stood by the tsar, now rushed to support the striking workers. The Romanov dynasty, after three hundred years of rule (1613–1917), came to an end. The Provisional Government was set up—provisional until a representative Constituent Assembly, to be elected as soon as possible, could establish a permanent regime.

The Problems of the Provisional Government

The collapse of autocracy was followed by what supporters in Russia and the West hoped would be a liberal democratic regime pledged to give Russia a

The Tsar in Exile.   Nicholas II and his children, now living in reduced circumstances, take the sun on a roof in Tobolsk, Siberia. The imperial family was later transferred to Ekaterinburg and then murdered in 1918. (*Hulton Deutsch Collection*)

constitution. In reality, however, the course of events from March to November 1917 resembled a free-for-all—a no-holds-barred fight for the succession to autocracy, with only the fittest surviving. Events also demonstrated, under conditions of exceptional popular agitation, the desperate state of the Russian Empire, its internal disunity, and the fury of the accumulated resentments. Both Germany and national minorities in Russia took advantage of the anarchy to dismember the country.

Among the potential successors to the tsars, the liberals of various shades seemed at first to enjoy the best chances. They represented the educated and forward-looking elements in Russian society that had arisen after the reforms of the 1860s: lawyers, doctors, professional people of all kinds, intellectuals, businesspeople and industrialists, many landowners, and even some bureaucrats. Liberals had opposed autocracy and earned a reputation for leadership.

The liberals had joined the March revolution only reluctantly, for they were afraid of the masses and the violence of the streets. They dreaded social revolution that could result in the seizure of factories, dispossession of landowners, and tampering with property rights. Although most leaders of the Provisional Government had only modest means, they were "capitalists," believing in private enterprise as the means of promoting economic progress.

Women Demonstrate in Petrograd, 1917.   The collapse of the tsarist regime was followed by a period of political fermentation, meetings, and concern about food shortages. Women demonstrated for increased bread supplies. The poster reads, "Comrades, workers, and soldiers, support our demands!" (*VA/Sovfoto*)

Their ideal was a constitutional monarchy, its leadership entrusted to the educated and propertied elite familiar with the essentials of statecraft.

Unfortunately, the liberals misunderstood the mood of the people. Looking to the Western democracies—including, after April 1917, the United States—for political and financial support, the liberals decided to continue the war on the side of the Allies. The decision antagonized the war-weary masses, along with the Russian soldiers, almost two million of whom had deserted. The liberals also antagonized the Russian peasants by not confiscating and redistributing the landlords' lands free of charge. As Russian nationalists who wanted their country to remain undivided, the liberals opposed national minorities who sought self-determination; hence, they lost the minorities' support.

The peasants began to divide the landlords' land among themselves, which encouraged more soldiers to desert in order to claim a share of the land. The breakdown of the railways stopped factory production; enraged workers ousted factory managers and owners. Consumer goods grew scarce and prices soared, and the peasants could see no reason to sell their crops if they could buy nothing in return. Thus, the specter of famine in the cities arose. Hardships and anger mounted. Adding to the disorder were the demands of the non-Russian nationalities—Finns, Ukrainians, Georgians, and others—for self-determination and even secession.

Freedom in Russia was leading to dissolution and chaos. The largely illiterate peasant masses had no experience with or understanding of a free society. Without their cooperation, Russian liberalism collapsed. This outcome demonstrated the difficulty of establishing Western liberal democratic forms of government in countries lacking a sense of unity, a strong middle class, and a tradition of responsible participation in public affairs.

By July 1917, when Aleksandr Kerensky (1881–1970), a radical lawyer of great eloquence, took over the leadership of the Provisional Government, it had become clear that law and order could be upheld only by brute force. In late August and early September, a conspiracy led by an energetic young general, Lavr Kornilov, sought to establish a military dictatorship. Kornilov had the support not only of the officer corps and the tsarist officials, but also of many liberals fed up with anarchy. What stopped the general was not Kerensky's government (which had no troops), but the workers of Petrograd. Their agitators demoralized Kornilov's soldiers, proving that a dictatorship of the right had no mass support. The workers also repudiated Kerensky and the Provisional Government, as well as their own moderate leaders; henceforth, they supported the Bolsheviks.

The Bolshevik Revolution

Revolutionary movements had a long history in Russia, going back to the early nineteenth century, when educated Russians began to compare their country unfavorably with western Europe. They, too, wanted constitutional liberty and free speech in order to make their country modern. Prohibited from speaking out in public, they went underground, giving up their liberalism as ineffective. They saw revolutionary socialism, with its idealistic vision and compassion for the multitude, as a better ideology in the harsh struggle with the tsar's police. By the 1870s, many socialists had evolved into austere and self-denying professional revolutionaries who, in the service of the cause, had no moral scruples, just as the police had no scruples in the defense of the tsars. Bank robbery, murder, assassination, treachery, and terror were not immoral if they served the revolutionary cause.

Lenin and the Rise of Bolshevism

In the 1880s and 1890s, revolutionaries had learned industrial economics and sociology from Marx; from Marxism they had also acquired a vision of a universal and inevitable progression toward socialism and communism, which satisfied their semireligious craving for salvation in this world, not the next. Marxism also allied them with socialist movements in other lands, giving

V. I. Lenin. Red Army soldiers leaving for battle are addressed by Lenin in Moscow in May, 1920. (*Sovfoto*)

them an internationalist outlook. History, they believed, was on their side, as it was for all the proletarians and oppressed peoples in the world.

By 1900, a number of able young Russians had rallied to revolutionary Marxism; almost all of them were educated or came from privileged families. The most promising was Vladimir Ilyich Ulyanov, known as Lenin (1870–1924), the son of a teacher and school administrator who had attained the rank of a nobleman. Lenin had studied law but practiced revolution instead. His first contribution lay in adapting Marxism to Russian conditions; to do so, he took considerable liberties with Marx's teaching. His second contribution followed from the first: outlining the organization of an underground party capable of surviving against the tsarist police. It was to be a tightly knit conspiratorial elite of professional revolutionaries. Its headquarters would be safely located abroad, and it would have close ties to the masses, that is, to the workers and other potentially revolutionary elements.

Two prominent Marxists close to Lenin were Leon Trotsky (1879–1940) and Joseph Stalin (1879–1953). Trotsky, whose original name was Lev Bronstein, was the son of a prosperous Jewish farmer from southern Russia and was soon known for his brilliant pen. Less prominent until after the Revolution, Stalin (the man of steel) was originally named Iosif Dzhugashvili; he was from Georgia, beyond the Caucasus Mountains. Bright enough to be sent to the best school in the area, he dropped out for a revolutionary career. While they were still young, Lenin, Trotsky, and Stalin were all hardened by arrest, lengthy imprisonments, and exile to Siberia. Lenin and Trotsky later lived abroad, while Stalin, following a harsher course, stayed in Russia; for four years before 1917, he was banished to bleakest northern Siberia and conditioned to ruthlessness for life.

In 1903, the Russian Marxists split into two factions, the moderate Mensheviks, so named after finding themselves in a minority (*menshinstvo*) at a rather unrepresentative vote at the Second Party Congress, and the extremist Bolsheviks, who at that moment were in the majority (*bolshinstvo*). They might more accurately have been called the "softs" and the "hards." The "softs" (Mensheviks) preserved basic moral scruples; they would not stoop to crime or undemocratic methods for the sake of political success. For that the "hards" (Bolsheviks) ridiculed them, noting that a dead, imprisoned, or unsuccessful revolutionary was of little use.

Meanwhile, Lenin perfected Bolshevik revolutionary theory. He violated Marxist tradition by paying close attention to the revolutionary potential of peasants (thereby anticipating Mao Zedong). Lenin also looked closely at the numerous peoples in Asia who had recently fallen under Western imperialist domination. These people, he sensed, constituted a potential revolutionary force. In alliance with the Western—and Russian—proletariat, they might overthrow the worldwide capitalist order. The Bolsheviks, the most militant of all revolutionary socialists, were ready to assist in that gigantic struggle.

Lenin was a Russian nationalist, as well as a socialist internationalist; he had a vision of a modern and powerful Russian state destined to be a model in world affairs. Russian communism was thus nationalist communism. The Bolsheviks saw the abolition of income-producing property by the dictatorship of the proletariat as the most effective way of mobilizing the country's resources. Yet the Bolshevik mission was also internationalist. The Russian Revolution was intended to set off a world revolution, liberating all oppressed classes and peoples around the world and achieving a higher stage of civilization.

Lenin's Opportunity

On April 16, 1917, Lenin, with German help, arrived in Petrograd from exile in Switzerland. The Provisional Government, he said, could not possibly preserve Russia from disintegration. Most of the soldiers, workers, and peasants would repudiate the Provisional Government's cautious liberalism in favor of a regime expressing their demand for peace and land. Nothing would stop them from avenging themselves for centuries of oppression. Lenin also felt that only complete state control of the economy could rescue the country from disaster. The sole way out, he insisted, was the dictatorship of the proletariat backed by *soviets* (councils) of soldiers, workers, and peasants, particularly the poorer peasants.

Lenin prepared his party for the second stage of the Revolution of 1917: the seizure of power by the Bolsheviks. Conditions favored him, as he had predicted. The Bolsheviks obtained majorities in the soviets. The peasants were in active revolt, seizing the land themselves. The Provisional Government lost all control over the course of events. On November 6 (October 24 by the old calendar), Lenin urged immediate action: "The government is tottering. It must be *given the death blow* at all costs." On the following day, the Bolsheviks, meeting little resistance, seized power. Lenin permitted elections for the Constituent Assembly that had been scheduled by the Provisional Government. In a free election, the Bolsheviks received 24 percent of the vote. After meeting once in January 1918, however, the Constituent Assembly was disbanded by the Bolsheviks.

The Bolsheviks Survive

Lenin contended that he was guiding the Russian proletariat and all humanity toward a higher social order, symbolizing—in Russia and much of the world—the rebellion of the disadvantaged against Western (or "capitalist") dominance. That is why, in 1918, he changed the name of his party from Bolshevik to Communist, which implied a concern for the human community. For Lenin, as for Marx, a world without exploitation was humanity's noblest ideal.

But staggering adversity confronted Lenin after his seizure of power. In the prevailing anarchy, Russia lay open to the German armies. Under the Treaty of Brest-Litovsk, signed in March 1918—the lowest point in Russian history for over two hundred years—Russia lost Finland, Poland, and the Baltic provinces, all regions inhabited largely by non-Russians. It also lost the rebellious Ukraine, its chief industrial base and breadbasket. Yet Lenin had no choice but to accept the humiliating terms.

Civil War

After the Treaty of Brest-Litovsk was signed, the civil war that had been brewing since the summer of 1917 broke out in full. In the winter of 1917–18, tsarist officers had been gathering troops in the south, counting on the loyalty of the Cossacks;* other anticommunist centers rose in Siberia, and still others in the extreme north and along the Baltic coast. The political orientation of these anticommunist groups, generally called Whites in contrast to the communist Reds, combined all shades of opinion, from moderate socialist to reactionary, the latter usually predominating. The Whites received support from foreign governments, which freely intervened. Until their own revolution in November 1918, the Germans occupied much of southern Russia. England, France, and the United States sent troops to points in northern and southern European Russia; England, Japan, and the United States also sent troops to

---

*Originating in southern and eastern Russia, the Cossacks became an elite corps in the tsars' armies and were used to quell uprisings.

Siberia. At first, they wanted to offset German expansion, but later they hoped to overthrow the Communist regime. In May and June 1918, Czech prisoners of war, about to be evacuated, precipitated anticommunist uprisings along the Trans-Siberian Railroad, bringing the civil war to fever pitch.

In July 1918, Nicholas II and his entire family were murdered by communists. In August, a noncommunist socialist nearly assassinated Lenin, while the White forces in the south moved to cut off central Russia from its food supply. In response, the communists speeded the buildup of their own Red Army. Recruited from the remnants of the tsarist army and its officer corps, the Red Army was reinforced by compulsory military service and strict discipline; Trotsky reintroduced the death penalty, which had been outlawed by the Provisional Government. Threatened with death if they refused, many tsarist officers served in the Red Army. They were closely watched by Trotsky's ruthless political commissars, who were also responsible for the political reliability and morale of the troops. The civil war was brutal; both sides butchered civilians and their own comrades.

In 1919, thanks to the Allied victory and the American contribution to it, the German menace ended. Yet foreign intervention stepped up in response to the formation of the Communist International (Comintern), an organization founded by Lenin to guide the international revolutionary movement that he expected to issue from the world war. Lenin sought revolutionary support from abroad for strengthening his hand at home; his enemies reached into Russia to defeat at its source the revolution that they feared in their own countries. At the same time, the civil war rose to its climax.

Hard-pressed as Lenin's party was, by the autumn of 1920 it had prevailed over its enemies. The Whites were divided among themselves and discredited by their association with the tsarist regime; the Bolsheviks had greater popular support, the advantage of interior communications, and superior political skills. The war-weary foreign interventionists called off their efforts to overthrow the Bolshevik regime by force.

The communist victory in the civil war had exacted a staggering price. Reds and Whites alike had carried the tsarist tradition of political violence to a new pitch of horror (some of it described in the famous novels by Boris Pasternak and Mikhail Sholokhov). The entire population, including the Communist party and its leaders, suffered in the war, which was followed in 1921–22 by a famine that took still more millions of lives.

War Communism and the New Economic Policy

Besides the extreme misery brought on by the world war and civil war, the Russian people had to endure the rigors of the policy known as war communism. It was introduced in 1918 to deal with plummeting agricultural and economic production, rampant inflation, and desperate hunger in the cities. Under war communism, the state took over the means of production and greatly limited the sphere of private ownership; it conscripted labor and, in effect, confiscated grain from the peasants. War communism devastated the economy even further and alienated workers and peasants. Factories were mismanaged, workers stayed away from their jobs or performed poorly, and peasants resisted the food requisition detachments that seized their grain.

There was even open rebellion. In March 1921, sailors at the Kronstadt naval base and workers in nearby Petrograd—people who in 1917 had been ready to give their lives for the Revolution—rose against the repression that had been introduced during the civil war; they called for the establishment of socialist democracy. Trotsky ruthlessly suppressed that uprising, but the lesson was clear: the Communist regime had to retreat from war communism and to restore a measure of stability to the country.

In 1921, the Communist party adopted the New Economic Policy, generally called NEP, which lasted until 1928. Under a system that Lenin characterized as "state socialism," the government retained control of finance, industry, and transportation—"the commanding heights" of the economy—but allowed the rest of the economy to return to private enterprise. The peasants, after giving part of their crops to the government, were free to sell the rest in the open market; traders could buy and sell as they pleased. With the resumption of small-scale capitalism, an air of normal life returned.

One-Party Dictatorship

While the communists were waging a fierce struggle against the Whites, they instituted a militant dictatorship run by their party. Numbering about five hundred thousand members in 1921, the Communist party was controlled by a small, tight core of professional political leaders, the best of them unusually disciplined in personal dedication. This new elite's organizational skills permitted them to preserve their revolutionary drive in the face of both failure and success. From the start, those who did not pull their weight were purged.

Under its constitution, the "Russian Communist Party (Bolshevik)," as its formal title read, was a democratic body. Its members elected delegates to periodic party congresses; these in turn elected the membership of the central committee, which originally held the reins of leadership. However, power soon shifted to a smaller and more intimate group, the *politburo* (political bureau), which assumed a dictatorial role. The key leaders—Lenin, Trotsky, Stalin, and a few others—determined policy, assigned tasks, and appointed important officials. The party dominated all public agencies; its leaders held the chief positions in government. No other political parties were tolerated, and trade unions became agents of the regime. Never before had the people of Russia been forced into such abject dependence on their government.

Impatient with the endless disputes among righteous and strong-willed old revolutionaries, Lenin, in agreement with other top leaders, demanded unconditional submission to his decisions. He even ordered that dissidents be disciplined and political enemies be terrorized. No price was too high to achieve monolithic party unity. As former victims of tsarist repression, the Communists felt no moral objection to the use of force or even of stark terror. As

Lenin admonished his followers: "cleanse the land of Russia of all sorts of harmful insects, of crook-fleas, and bedbugs," by which he meant "the rich, the rogues, and the idlers." He even suggested that "one out of every ten idlers be shot on the spot."[2] Those not shot found themselves, with Lenin's blessings, in forced-labor camps, directed by a ruthless security force, the dreaded Cheka. Staffed by hardened revolutionaries, it engaged in extreme terror not only against enemies of the regime, but also against the population at large. The Cheka established the forced-labor camps, which became notorious under Stalin's regime. The means Lenin employed for ruling his backward country denied the human values that Marx had taken from the Enlightenment and put into his vision of socialist society.

The Communists abolished the power of the Orthodox church, which was the traditional ally of tsarism and the enemy of innovation. They were militant atheists, believing with Marx that religion was the "opium of the people"; God had no place in their vision of a better society. Yet the Orthodox church and other religions survived, though much reduced in influence and closely watched—an enduring target for atheist propaganda.

The Communists also simplified the alphabet, changed the calendar to the Gregorian system prevailing in the capitalist West, and brought theater and all arts, until then reserved for the elite, to the masses. Above all, they wiped out—by expropriation, discrimination, expulsion, and execution—the educated upper class of bureaucrats, landowners, professional people, and industrialists.

The Communist party promised "to liberate woman from all the burdens of antiquated methods of housekeeping, by replacing them by house-communes, public kitchens, central laundries, nurseries, etc."[3] But traditional values, particularly in the Asian parts of the Soviet Union, hardly favored equality between the sexes, especially in political work. The practical necessity of combining work with family responsibility, moreover, tended to keep women out of managerial positions in the party and the organizations of the state, but the ideal remained alive.

The Bolsheviks never ceased to stress that they worked strenuously for the welfare of the vast majority of the population. They received much acclaim for their emphasis on providing housing, food, and clothing and making education available to the masses. They were not opposed to some private property, allowing items for personal use, provided these items were in keeping with the standards of the common people. But they outlawed income-producing private property that enabled capitalists to employ (or exploit, as the Communists said) others for their own profit. With the disappearance of private enterprise—Stalin would soon eliminate the limited free enterprise permitted under NEP—the state gradually became the sole employer, forcibly integrating the individual into the reconstruction of the country.

For Lenin, socialism meant reeducating the masses to a higher standard of individual conduct and economic productivity, which would be superior even to capitalism. In the spring of 1918, he argued that the Russian workers had

Forging Socialism.   Men and women work equally in this socialist realist propaganda poster from 1921. (*From* Art of the October Revolution, *Mikail Guerman [Aurora Publishers, Leningrad]. Reproduced by permission of V/O Vneshtorgizdat.*)

not yet matched capitalist performance: "The Russian worker is a bad worker compared with the workers of the advanced, i.e., western countries." To overcome this fatal handicap, Lenin urged competition—socialist competition—and relentlessly hammered home the need for "iron discipline at work" and "unquestioning obedience" to a single will, that of the Communist party. There was no alternative: "Large-scale machinery calls for absolute and strict unity of will, which directs the joint labors of hundreds and thousands and tens of thousands of people. A thousand wills are subordinated to one will."[4]

In these words lay the essence of subsequent Soviet industrialization. The entire economy was to be monolithic, rationally planned in its complex interdependence, and pursuing a single goal: overcoming the weaknesses of Russia, so disastrously demonstrated in the war. Leaving the workers to their own spontaneity, Lenin held, would merely perpetuate Russian backwardness. Instead, he called for a new "consciousness," a hard-driving work ethic expressed in the Russian Marxist revolutionary vocabulary.

In attempting to transform their Soviet Russia into a modern industrialized state that would serve as a model for the world, the Bolsheviks imposed a new autocracy even more authoritarian than the old. Russia must be rebuilt against the people's will, if necessary. In the view of the party leaders, the masses always needed firm guidance. The minds of the people, therefore, came under unprecedented government control. In education, from kindergarten through university, in press and radio, and in literature and the arts, the Communist party tried to fashion people's thoughts to create the proper "consciousness."

The party made Marxism-Leninism the sole source of truth, eliminating as best it could all rival creeds, whether religious, political, or philosophical. Minds were to be as reliably uniform as machine processes and totally committed to the party. Moreover, they were to be protected against all subversive capitalist influences. Soviet Russia, so the party boasted, had risen to a superior plane of social existence; it would attract other revolutionary states to its federal union, until eventually it covered the entire world. Lest Soviet citizens doubt their new superiority, the party prohibited all uncontrolled comparison with other countries.

Lenin molded the Soviet Union into an international revolutionary force, the champion of anticapitalism and of the liberation of colonial peoples. The Russian Revolution inspired nationalistic ambitions for political self-determination and cultural self-assertion among a growing number of peoples around the world, especially in Asia. It appealed particularly to intellectuals educated in the West (or in westernized schools), yet identifying themselves with their downtrodden compatriots.

To have a political tool for world revolution Lenin created the Communist—or Third—International (Comintern). The most radical successor to earlier socialist international associations, it helped organize small Communist parties in western Europe, which in time became dependable, although rather powerless, agents of Soviet Russia. In Asia, where no proletariat existed, Lenin tried to work closely with incipient nationalist movements. Lenin and the Bolshevik Revolution gained the admiration and instinctive loyalty of colonial and semicolonial peoples in what would come to be called the Third World.

World revolution, however, was never a realistic prospect. The tide of Western ascendancy was running strong. Moreover, the Comintern was never a truly international force, for it remained a tool of the Russian Communist party. But the fear it aroused served Lenin well: it made Soviet Russia appear strong when in fact the country was exhausted. At very little cost, the Comintern put prestige-conscious Russia back on the map of world politics. Having captured the attention of the world, Soviet Russia now stood out as the communist alternative to the capitalist West.

The Stalin Revolution

Lenin died in 1924, and the task of achieving the goal that he had set was taken up by Stalin. The "man of steel" was crude and vulgar, toughened by the revolutionary underground and tsarist prisons and by the roughest aspects of Russian life. Relentlessly energetic but relatively inconspicuous among key Bolsheviks, Stalin had been given, in 1922, the unwanted and seemingly routine task of general secretary of the party. He used this position to his own advantage, building up a reliable party cadre—apparatus men, or *apparatchiki,* as they came to be called—and dominating the party as not even Lenin had done. When he was challenged, particularly by Trotsky and his associates, in the protracted struggles for the succession to Lenin, it was too late to unseat him. None of Stalin's rivals could rally the necessary majorities at the party congresses; none could match Stalin's skill in party infighting or in making rough and anarchic people into docile members of the Communist party apparatus.

Modernizing Russia: Industrialization and Collectivization

To Stalin, Russia's most pressing need was not world revolution, but the fastest possible buildup of Soviet power through industrialization. The country could not afford to risk near-annihilation again, as it had done in the world war and then in the civil war. Bolshevik pride dictated that the country be made as strong as possible. Stalin set forth the stark reckoning of Russian history in a speech delivered in 1931, three years after launching a program of massive industrialization.

> *Those who fall behind get beaten. But we do not want to be beaten. No, we refuse to be beaten. One feature of the history of old Russia was the continual beatings she suffered for falling behind, for her backwardness. All beat her—for her backwardness, for military backwardness, cultural backwardness, political backwardness, for industrial backwardness, for agricultural backwardness. She was beaten because to do so was profitable and could be done with impunity. . . . You are backward, you are weak—therefore you are wrong, hence you can be beaten and enslaved. You are mighty, therefore you are right, hence we must be wary of you. Such is the law of the exploiters. . . . That is why we must no longer lag behind.*[5]

Stalin decided on all-out industrialization at the expense of the toiling masses. Peasants and workers, already poor, would be required to make tremendous sacrifices of body and spirit to overcome the nation's weaknesses. The Bolshevik Revolution had cleared the way for decisive action. Dependent as never before on their government, the Russian people could offer little resistance.

Abandoning the NEP, Stalin decreed a series of Five-Year Plans, the first and most experimental one commencing in 1928. The industrialization drive was heralded as a vast economic and social revolution, undertaken by the state on a rational plan. The emphasis lay on heavy industry: the construction of railroads, power plants, steel mills, and military hardware, such as tanks and warplanes. Production of consumer goods was cut to the minimum, and all small-scale private trading, revived under the NEP, came to an end—with

Building Industry in Russia.   Foundations were dug by hand for the huge industrial complex at Magnitogorsk in 1934. This was part of Stalin's plan to transform Russia into an advanced, industrialized country. The *kulaks*, well-to-do peasant men and women who had been condemned to hard labor, bore the brunt of the work. (*TASS/Sovfoto*)

disastrous results for the Russian economy. Having just come within sight of their pre-1914 standard of living, Russians now found their expectations dashed for decades.

Thus, a new grim age began, with drastic material hardships and profound anguish. But many people, particularly the young, were fired to heroic exertions. They were proud to sacrifice themselves for the building of a superior society. When the Great Depression in the capitalist countries put millions out of work, no Soviet citizen suffered from unemployment; gloom pervaded the West, but confidence and hope, artificially fostered by the party, buoyed up Soviet Russia. The first Five-Year Plan had to be scrapped before running its course. Subsequent Five-Year Plans, however, gradually improved the quality of planning, as well as of production. At no time, though, did the planning produce Western-style industrial efficiency. Nevertheless, Soviet Russia did industrialize at an incredibly rapid pace.

Meanwhile, a second and far more brutal revolution overtook Soviet agriculture, for the peasants had to be forcibly integrated into the planned economy through collectivization. Agriculture—the peasants, their animals, and their fields—had to submit to the same rational control as industry. Collectivization meant the pooling of farmlands, animals, and equipment for the sake of more efficient, large-scale production. The Bolshevik solution for the backwardness of Russian argiculture had long been that the peasants should become like workers. But knowing the peasants' distaste for the factory, their attachment to their own land, and their stubbornness, the party had hesitated to carry out its ambitious scheme. In 1929, however, Stalin believed that, for the sake of industrialization, he had no choice. If the Five-Year Plan was to succeed, the government had to receive planned crops of planned size and quality at planned times. With collectivization, the ascendancy of the party over the people of Russia became almost complete.

The peasants paid a ghastly price. Stalin declared war on the Russian countryside. He ordered that the *kulaks,* the most enterprising and well-to-do peasants, be "liquidated as a class." Many were killed outright, and millions were deported to forced-labor camps in the far north. Their poorer and less efficient neighbors were herded onto collective farms at the point of a bayonet.

The peasants struck back, sometimes in pitched battles. The horror of forced collectivization broke the spirit even of hardened officials. "I am an old Bolshevik," sobbed a secret police colonel to a fellow passenger on a train; "I worked in the underground against the Tsar and then I fought in the civil war. Did I do all that in order that I should now surround villages with machine guns and order my men to fire indiscriminately into crowds of peasants? Oh, no, no!"[6] Typically, however, the local officials and activists who stripped the peasants of their possessions and searched for hidden grain viewed themselves as idealists building a new society; they infused their own ruthlessness into the official orders. Their dedication to the triumph of communism overcame all doubts caused by the sight of starving people and the sounds of wailing women and children.

Defeated but unwilling to surrender their livestock, the peasants slaughtered their animals, gorging themselves in drunken orgies against the days of inevitable famine. The country's cattle herds declined by one-half, inflicting irreparable secondary losses as well. The number of horses, crucial for rural transport and farm work, fell by one-third. Crops were not planted or not harvested, the Five-Year Plan was disrupted, and from 1931 to 1933 millions starved to death.

The suffering was most cruel in the Ukraine, where famine killed approximately seven million people, many after extreme abuse and persecution. In order to buy industrial equipment abroad so that industrialization could proceed on target, the Soviet Union had to export food, as much of it as possible and for prices disastrously lowered by the Great Depression. Let the peasants in the Ukrainian breadbasket perish so that the country could grow strong! Moreover, Stalin relished the opportunity to punish the Ukrainians for their disloyalty during the civil war and their resistance to collectivization.

By 1935, practically all farming in Russia was collectivized. The kulaks had been wiped out as a class, and the peasants, ever rebellious under the tsars, had been cowed into permanent submission. In theory, the collective farms were run democratically, under an elected chairman; in practice, they followed as best they could the directives handed down from the nearest party office. People grumbled about the rise of a new serfdom. Agricultural development had been stifled.

Total Control

To quash resistance and mold a new type of suitably motivated and disciplined citizen, Stalin unleashed a third revolution, the revolution of totalitarianism. Only communist regimentation, he believed, could liberate Russia from its historic inferiority. Moreover, the totalitarian state accorded with his desire to exercise total control over the party and the nation. Stalin's totalitarianism aimed at a complete reconstruction of state and society, down to the innermost recesses of human consciousness. It called for "a new man," suited to the needs of Soviet industrialism.

The revolution of totalitarianism encompassed all cultural activity. All media of communication—literature, the arts, music, the stage—were forced into subservience to the Five-Year Plan and Soviet ideology. In literature, as in all art, an official style was promulgated. Called *socialist realism,* it was expected to describe the world as the party saw it or hoped to shape it. Novels in the social realist manner told how the romances of tractor drivers and milkmaids or of lathe operators and office secretaries led to new victories of production under the Five-Year Plan. Composers found their music examined for remnants of bourgeois spirit; they were to write simple tunes suitable for heroic times. Everywhere huge, high-color posters showed men and women hard at work with radiant faces, calling others to join them; often Stalin, the wise father and leader, was shown among them. In this way, artistic creativity was locked into a dull, utilitarian straitjacket of official cheerfulness; creativity was allowed only to boost industrial productivity. Behind the scenes, all artists were disciplined to conform to the will of the party or be crushed.

Education, from nursery school to university, was likewise harnessed to train dutiful and loyal citizens, and Soviet propaganda made a cult of Stalin that bordered on deification. Thus, a writer declared in 1935:

> *Centuries will pass and the generations still to come will regard us as the happiest of mortals, as the most fortunate of men, because we . . . were privileged to see Stalin, our inspired leader. Yes, and we regard ourselves as the happiest of mortals because we are the contemporaries of a man who never had an equal in world history. The men of all ages will call on thy name, which is strong, beautiful, wise, and marvellous. Thy name is engraven on every factory, every machine, every place on the earth, and in the hearts of all men.*[7]

But still the Russian masses resisted the enforced change to the large-scale, rigid regimentation of modern industrialism. Against that dogged resistance,

Stalin unleashed raw terror to break stubborn wills and compel conformity. Terror had been used as a tool of government ever since the Revolution (and the tsars had also used it, moderately and intermittently). After the start of the first Five-Year Plan, show trials were staged that denounced as saboteurs the engineers who disagreed with Stalin's production timetable. The terror used to herd the peasants onto collective farms was even greater. Stalin also used terror to crush opposition and to instill an abject fear both in the ranks of the party and in Russian society at large.

Purges had long been used to rid the party of weaklings. After 1934, however, they became an instrument of Stalin's drive for unchallenged personal power. In 1936, his vindictive terror broke into the open. The first batch of victims, including many founders of the Communist party, were accused of conspiring with the exiled Trotsky to set up a "terrorist center" and of scheming to terrorize the party. After being sentenced to death, they were immediately executed. In 1937, the next group, including prominent Communists of Lenin's day, were charged with cooperating with foreign intelligence agencies and wrecking "socialist reconstruction," the term for Stalin's revolution; they too were executed. Shortly afterward, a secret purge wiped out the military high command, for which the country paid a heavy price when Germany attacked in 1941.

In 1938, the last and biggest show trial advanced the most bizarre accusation of all: sabotage, espionage, and attempting to dismember the Soviet Union and kill all its leaders (including Lenin in 1918). In the public hearings, some defendants refuted the public prosecutor, but in the end all confessed before being executed. Western observers were aghast at the cynical charges and at the physical and mental tortures used to obtain the confessions.

The great trials, however, involved only a small minority of Stalin's victims; many more perished in silence. The terror first hit members of the party, especially the Old Bolsheviks, who had joined before the Revolution; they were the most independent-minded members and therefore the most dangerous to Stalin. But Stalin also diminished the cultural elite that had survived the Lenin revolution. Thousands of engineers, scientists, industrial managers, scholars, and artists disappeared; they were shot or sent to forced-labor camps, where most of them perished. No one was safe. To frighten the common people in all walks of life, men, women, and even children were dragged into the net of Stalin's secret police, leaving the survivors with a soul-killing reminder: submit or else. The toll of the purges is reckoned in many millions; it included Trotsky, who in 1940 was murdered in Mexico. The bloodletting was ghastly, as Stalin's purge officials themselves followed each other into death and ignominy.

Stalin, who had passed through the hands of the tsarist police and had participated in the carnage of the civil war, was untroubled by the waste of life. He believed that without the total obedience of the Russian people the Soviet economy could not be effectively and quickly mobilized and that terror was necessary to compel compliance. By showing party officials and the Russian masses how vulnerable they were, how dependent they were on his will, Stalin frightened them into servility. No doubt, the terror was also an expression of his craving for personal power and his sick, suspicious, and vengeful nature. He saw enemies everywhere, took pleasure in selecting victims, and reveled in his omnipotence. For good reason, Stalin has been called a twentieth-century Ivan the Terrible. Like the sixteenth-century tsar, for whom he expressed admiration, Stalin stopped at no brutality in order to establish personal autocracy.

Notes

1. Theodore H. Von Laue, *Sergei Witte and the Industrialization of Russia* (New York: Columbia University Press, 1963), p. 3.
2. V. I. Lenin, "On Revolutionary Violence and Terror," in *The Lenin Anthology,* ed. Robert C. Tucker (New York: Norton, 1975), p. 432.
3. "All-Russian Communist Party (Bolsheviks), 1919," in *Soviet Communism: Programs and Rules. Official Texts of 1919, 1952, 1956, 1961,* ed. Jan F. Triska (San Francisco: Chandler, 1962), p. 23.
4. V. I. Lenin, "The Immediate Tasks of the Soviet Government," in *Lenin Anthology,* pp. 448 ff.
5. J. V. Stalin, "Speech to Business Executives" (1931), in *A Documentary History of Communism from Lenin to Mao,* ed. Robert V. Daniels (New York: Random House, 1960), 2:22.
6. Quoted in Isaac Deutscher, *Stalin: A Political Biography* (New York: Oxford University Press, 1966), p. 325.
7. Excerpted in T. H. Rigby, ed., *Stalin* (Englewood Cliffs, N.J.: Prentice-Hall, 1966), p. 111.

Suggested Reading

Antonov Ovseenko, Anton, *The Time of Stalin: Portrait of a Tyranny* (1981). An anti-Stalinist treatment by a Soviet author.

Carr, E. H., *The Russian Revolution from Lenin to Stalin* (1970). A brief summary based on the author's multivolume study of the years 1917–1929.

Conquest, Robert, *The Harvest of Sorrow: Soviet Collectivization and the Terror Famine* (1986). The human consequences of collectivization.

Ginzburg, Eugenia, *Journey into the Whirlwind* (1967). A woman's experiences under the terror.

Koestler, Arthur, *Darkness at Noon* (1941). A revealing novel about the fate of an Old Bolshevik in the terror purge.

Lewin, Moshe, *The Making of the Soviet System: Essays in the Social History of Interwar Russia* (1985). A thoughtful analysis by a noted scholar.

Mandelstam, Nadezhda, *Hope Against Hope: A Memoir* (1976). A searing account of life during the purges by the widow of one of the victims.

Scott, John, *Behind the Urals: An American Worker in Russia's City of Steel* (1942, repr. 1973). A firsthand account of life under the first Five-Year Plan.

Sholokhov, Mikhail, *And Quiet Flows the Don; The Don Flows Home to the Sea,* 2 vols. (1934, 1940). A Nobel Prize–winning novel about the brutalizing effects of war, revolution, and civil war.

Solzhenitsyn, Aleksandr I., *One Day in the Life of Ivan Denisovich* (1963). The first account of life in one of Stalin's forced-labor camps to reach the public.

Tucker, Robert C., ed., *Stalinism: Essays in Historical Interpretation* (1977). Essays on Stalin by prominent scholars.

Ulam, Adam B., *The Bolsheviks: The Intellectual and Political History of the Triumph of Communism in* *Russia* (1965). A full account built around Lenin.

Von Laue, Theodore H., *Why Lenin? Why Stalin? Why Gorbachev?* 3rd ed. (1993). A readable survey emphasizing the global contexts.

Review Questions

1. Why did the tsarist regime collapse in March 1917?
2. Why did the Provisional Government and liberal democracy fail in 1917?
3. Why, by contrast, were the Bolsheviks successful in seizing and holding power from 1917 to 1921?
4. What were the purpose and the effects of the Five-Year Plans?
5. How did the Soviet leaders view the position of Russia in the world? What were their aims and ambitions? How did their goals compare with those of other states?
6. What were Stalin's motives and justifications for the terror purges?

❖ CHAPTER 20

The Era of Fascism: The Attack on Reason and Freedom

*I*n the immediate aftermath of World War I, it seemed that liberalism would continue to advance as it had in the nineteenth century. The collapse of the autocratic German and Austrian Empires had led to the formation of parliamentary governments throughout eastern and central Europe. Yet within two decades, in an extraordinary turn of events, democracy seemed in its death throes. In Spain, Portugal, Italy, and Germany and in all the newly created states of central and eastern Europe except Czechoslovakia, democracy collapsed and various forms of authoritarian government arose. The defeat of democracy and the surge of authoritarianism were best exemplified by the triumph of totalitarian fascist movements in Italy and Germany.

The emergence of fascist movements in more than twenty European lands after World War I was a sign that liberal society was in a state of disorientation and dissolution. The cultural pessimism, disdain for reason, and contempt for liberal values voiced by many intellectuals and nationalists before the war found expression after the war in the antidemocratic and irrational fascist ideologies, which altered European political life. Fascism marked the culmination of the dangerous trends inherent in the extreme nationalism and radical conservatism of the late nineteenth century. As a Europe-wide phenomenon, fascism was a response to a postwar society afflicted with a deep spiritual malaise, economic dislocation, political instability, and thwarted nationalist hopes. It was an expression of fear that the Bolshevik Revolution would spread westward. It was also an expression of hostility to democratic values and a reaction to the failure of liberal institutions to solve the problems of modern industrial society. To fascists and their sympathizers, democracy seemed an enfeebled old order ready to be overthrown.

In their struggle to bring down the liberal state, fascist leaders aroused primitive impulses and tribal loyalties, using myths and rituals to mobilize and manipulate the masses. Organizing propaganda campaigns with the rigor of a military operation, fascists stirred up and dominated the masses and confused and undermined their democratic opposition, breaking its will to resist. Fascists were most successful in those countries with weak democratic traditions. When parliamentary government faltered, it had few staunch defenders, and many people were drawn to charismatic demagogues who promised direct action.

The proliferation of fascist movements demonstrated that the habits of democracy are not quickly learned or easily retained. Particularly during times of crisis, people lose patience with parliamentary discussion and constitutional procedures, sink into nonrational modes of thought and behavior, and are easily manipulated by unscrupulous politicians. For the sake of economic or emotional security and national grandeur, people will often willingly sacrifice political freedom. Fascism starkly manifested the immense power of the irrational; it humbled liberals, making them permanently aware of the limitations of reason and the fragility of freedom.

The fascist goal of maximum centralization of power was furthered by developments during World War I: the expansion of bureaucracy, the concentration of industry into giant monopolies, and the close cooperation between industry and the state. The instruments of modern technology—radio, motion pictures, public address systems, telephone, and teletype—made it possible for the state to indoctrinate, manipulate, and dominate its subjects on a hitherto unimaginable scale.

The Nature of Fascism

Fascist movements were marked by an extreme nationalism and a determination to eradicate liberalism and Marxism—to undo the legacy of the French Revolution of 1789 and the Bolshevik Revolution of 1917. Fascists believed that theirs was a spiritual revolution, that they were initiating a new era in history and building a new civilization on the ruins of liberal democracy. "We stand for a new principle in the world," said Mussolini. "We stand for the sheer, categorical, definitive antithesis to the world of democracy . . . to the world which still abides by the fundamental principles laid down in 1789."[1]

Fascists regarded Marxism as another enemy, for class conflict divided and weakened the state. To fascists, the Marxist call for workers of the world to unite meant the death of the national community. Fascism, in contrast, would reintegrate the proletariat into the nation and end class hostilities that divide and weaken the state and its people. By making people of all classes feel that they were a needed part of the nation, fascism offered a solution to the problem of insecurity and isolation in modern industrial society.

In contrast to liberalism and Marxism, fascism attacked the rational tradition of the Enlightenment and exalted will, blood, feeling, and instinct. Intellectual discussion and critical analysis, said fascists, cause national divisiveness; reason promotes doubt, enfeebles the will, and hinders instinctive, aggressive action. Glorifying action for its own sake, fascists aroused and manipulated brutal and primitive impulses and carried into politics the combative spirit of the trenches. They formed private armies, which attracted veterans—many of them rootless, brutal, and maladjusted men who sought to preserve the loyalty, camaraderie, and violence of the front.

Fascism exalted the leader—who, according to the fascist view, would intuitively grasp what was best for the nation—and called for rule by an elite of dedicated party members. The leader and the party would relieve the individual of the need to make decisions. Holding that the liberal stress on individual freedom promoted competition and conflict, which shattered national unity, fascists pressed for monolithic unity: one leader, one party, and one national will.

Fascism drew its mass support from the lower middle class—small merchants, artisans, white-collar workers, civil servants, and peasants of moderate means—all of whom were frightened both by big capitalism and by Marxism. They hoped that fascism would protect them from the competition of big business and prevent the hated working class from establishing a Marxist state, which would threaten their property. The lower middle class saw in fascism a noncommunist way of overcoming economic crises and restoring traditional respect for family, native soil, and nation. Having no patience for parliamentary procedures or sympathy for democratic principles, they were attracted to demagogues who exuded confidence and promised immediate results.

Although a radicalized middle class gave fascist movements their mass support, the fascists could not have captured the state without the aid of existing ruling elites: landed aristocrats, industrialists, and army leaders. In Russia, the Bolsheviks had to fight their way to power; in Italy and Germany, the old ruling order virtually handed power to the fascists. In both countries, fascist leaders succeeded in reassuring the conservative elite that they would not institute widespread social reforms or interfere with private property and would protect the nation from communism. Even though the old elite often abhorred fascist violence and demagoguery, it entered into an alliance with the fascists to protect its interests.

The Rise of Fascism in Italy

Postwar Unrest

Although Italy had been on the winning side in World War I, the country resembled a defeated nation. Food shortages, rising prices, massive unemployment, violent strikes, workers occupying factories, and peasants squatting on the uncultivated periphery of large estates created a climate of crisis. Italy required effective leadership and a reform program, but party disputes paralyzed the liberal government. With several competing parties, the liberals could not organize a solid majority that could cope with the domestic crisis.

The middle class was severely stressed. To meet its accelerating expenses, the government had increased taxes, but the burden fell unevenly on small landowners, owners of small businesses, civil service workers, and professionals. Large landowners and industrialists feared that their nation was on the verge of a Bolshevik-style revolution. In truth, Italian socialists had no master plan to seize power. Peasant squatters and urban strikers were responding to the distress in their own regions and did not significantly coordinate their efforts with those in other localities. Besides, when workers realized that they could not keep the factories operating, their revolutionary zeal waned and they started to abandon the plants. The workers' and peasants' poorly led and futile struggles did not portend a Red revolution. Nevertheless, the industrialists and landlords, with the Bolshevik Revolution still vivid in their minds, were taking no chances.

Adding to the unrest was national outrage at the terms of the World War I peace settlement. Italians felt that despite their sacrifices—five hundred thousand dead and one million wounded—they had been robbed of the fruits of victory. Italy had been denied the Dalmatian coast, the Adriatic port of Fiume, and territory in Africa and the Middle East. Nationalists blamed the liberal government for what they called a "mutilated victory." In 1919, a force of war veterans, led by the poet and adventurer Gabriele D'Annunzio (1863–1938) seized Fiume, to the delirious joy of Italian nationalists and the embarrassment of the government. D'Annunzio's occupation of the port lasted more than a year, adding fuel to the flames of Italian nationalism and demonstrating the weakness of the liberal regime in imposing its authority on rightist opponents.

Mussolini's Seizure of Power

Benito Mussolini (1883–1945), a former socialist and World War I veteran, exploited the unrest in postwar Italy in order to capture control of the state. In 1919, he organized the Fascist party, which attracted converts from among the discontented, the disillusioned, and the uprooted. Many Italians viewed Mussolini as the leader who would gain Fiume, Dalmatia, and colonies and win for Italy its rightful place of honor in international affairs. Hardened battle veterans joined the Fascist movement to escape the boredom and idleness of civilian life. They welcomed the opportunity to wear the uniforms of the Fascist militia (Black Shirts), parade in the streets, and fight socialist and labor union opponents. Squads of the Black Shirts (*squadristi*) raided socialist and trade union offices, destroying property and beating the occupants. As socialist Red Shirts responded in kind, Italy soon appeared to be drifting toward civil war.

Hoping that Mussolini would rescue Italy from Bolshevism, industrialists and landowners contributed large sums to the Fascist party. The lower middle class, fearful that the growing power of labor unions and the Socialist party threatened their property and social prestige, viewed Mussolini as a protector. Middle-class university students, searching for adventure and an ideal, and

Mussolini with His Troops. The Italian dictator deliberately tried to sustain an image of a virile warrior. Although Mussolini established a one-party state, he was less success-ful than Hitler or Stalin in creating a totalitarian regime. (*Wide World Photos*)

army officers, dreaming of an Italian empire and hostile to parliamentary gov-ernment, were also attracted to Mussolini's party. Mussolini's philosophy of action intrigued intellectuals disenchanted with liberal politics and parliamen-tary democracy. His nationalism, activism, and anticommunism gradually se-duced elements of the power structure: capitalists, aristocrats, army officers, the royal family, and the church. Regarding liberalism as bankrupt and par-liamentary government as futile, many of these people yearned for a military dictatorship.

In 1922, Mussolini made his bid for power. Speaking at a giant rally of his followers in late October, he declared: "Either they will give us the govern-ment or we shall take it by descending on Rome. It is now a matter of days, perhaps hours." A few days later, the Fascists began their March on Rome. It would have been a relatively simple matter to crush the twenty thousand Fas-cist marchers armed with little more than pistols and rifles, but King Victor Emmanuel III (1869–1947) refused to act. The king's advisers, some of them sympathetic to Mussolini, exaggerated the strength of the Fascists. Believing that he was rescuing Italy from terrible violence, the king appointed Mus-solini prime minister.

Mussolini had bluffed his way to power. Fascism had triumphed not because of its own strength—the Fascist party had only 35 of 535 seats in parliament—but because the liberal government, indecisive and fearful of violence, did not counter force with force. In the past, the liberal state had not challenged Fascist acts of terror; now it feebly surrendered to Fascist blustering and threats. No doubt, liberals hoped that once in power, the Fascists would forsake terror, pursue moderate aims, and act within the constitution. But the liberals were wrong; they had completely misjudged the antidemocratic character of fascism.

The Fascist State in Italy

Gradually, Mussolini moved toward establishing a dictatorship. In 1925–26, he eliminated non-Fascists from his cabinet, dissolved opposition parties, smashed the independent trade unions, suppressed opposition newspapers, replaced local mayors with Fascist officials, and organized a secret police to round up troublemakers. Many antifascists fled the country or were deported.

Mussolini was less successful than Hitler and Stalin in fashioning a totalitarian state. The industrialists, the large landowners, the church, and to some extent even the army never fell under the complete domination of the party. Nor did the regime possess the mind of its subjects with the same thoroughness as the Nazis did in Germany. Life in Italy was less regimented and the individual less fearful than in Nazi Germany or Communist Russia.

Like Communist Russia and Nazi Germany, however, Fascist Italy used mass organizations and mass media to control minds and regulate behavior. As in the Soviet Union and the Third Reich, the regime created a cult of the leader. "Mussolini goes forward with confidence, in a halo of myth, almost chosen by God, indefatigable and infallible, the instrument employed by Providence for the creation of a new civilization," wrote the philosopher Giovanni Gentile.[2] To convey the image of a virile leader, Mussolini had himself photographed bare-chested or in a uniform and a steel helmet. Elementary school textbooks depicted him as the savior of the nation, a modern-day Julius Caesar.

Fascist propaganda inculcated habits of discipline and obedience: "Mussolini is always right." "Believe! Obey! Fight!" Propaganda also glorified war: "A minute on the battlefield is worth a lifetime of peace." The press, radio, and cinema idealized life under fascism, implying that fascism had eradicated crime, poverty, and social tensions. Schoolteachers and university professors were compelled to swear allegiance to the Fascist government and to propagate Fascist ideals, while students were urged to criticize instructors who harbored liberal attitudes. Millions of youths belonged to Fascist organizations, in which they participated in patriotic ceremonies and social functions, sang Fascist hymns, and wore Fascist uniforms. They submerged their own identities in the group.

Denouncing economic liberalism for promoting individual self-interest, Fascists also attacked socialism for instigating conflicts between workers and capitalists, which divided and weakened the nation. The Fascist way of resolving tensions between workers and employers was to abolish independent labor unions, prohibit strikes, and establish associations or corporations that included both workers and employers within a given industry. In theory, representatives of labor and capital would cooperatively solve their particular industry's labor problems; in practice, however, the representatives of labor turned out to be Fascists, who protected the interests of the industrialists. Although the Fascists lauded the cooperative system as a creative approach to modern economic problems, in reality it played a minor role in Italian economic life. Big business continued to make its own decisions, paying scant attention to the corporations.

Nor did the Fascist government solve Italy's long-standing economic problems. To curtail the export of capital and to reduce the nation's dependence on imports in case of war, Mussolini sought to make Italy self-sufficient. To win the "battle of grain," the Fascist regime brought marginal lands under cultivation and urged farmers to concentrate on wheat rather than other crops. While wheat production increased substantially, total agricultural output fell because wheat had been planted on land more suited to animal husbandry and fruit cultivation. To make Italy industrially self-sufficient, the regime limited imports of foreign goods, with the result that Italian consumers paid higher prices for goods manufactured in Italy. Mussolini posed as the protector of the little people, but under his regime the power and profits of big business grew and the standard of living of small farmers and urban workers slipped.

Although anticlerical since his youth, Mussolini was also expedient. He recognized that coming to terms with the church would improve his image with Catholic public opinion. The Vatican regarded Mussolini's regime as a barrier against communism and as less hostile to church interests and more amenable to church direction than a liberal government. Pope Pius XI (1922–1939) was an ultraconservative whose hatred of liberalism and secularism led him to believe that the Fascists would increase the influence of the church in the nation.

In 1929, the Lateran Accords recognized the independence of Vatican City, repealed many of the anticlerical laws passed under the liberal government, and made religious instruction compulsory in all secondary schools. Relations between the Vatican and the Fascist government remained fairly good throughout the decade of the 1930s. When Mussolini invaded Ethiopia and intervened in the Spanish Civil War, the church supported him. Although the papacy criticized Mussolini for drawing closer to Hitler and introducing anti-Jewish legislation, it never broke with the Fascist regime.

The New German Republic

In the last days of World War I, a revolution brought down the German imperial government and led to the creation of a democratic republic. The new government, headed by Chancellor Friedrich Ebert (1871–1925), a Social Democrat, signed the armistice agreement ending the war. Many Germans blamed the new democratic leadership for the defeat—a baseless accusation, for the German generals, knowing that the war was lost, had sought an armistice. In February 1919, the recently elected National Assembly met at Weimar and proceeded to draw up a constitution for the new state. The Weimar Republic—born in revolution, which most Germans detested, and military defeat, which many attributed to the new government—faced an uncertain future.

Threats from Left and Right

Dominated by moderate socialists, the infant republic faced internal threats from both the radical left and the radical right. In January 1919, the newly established German Communist party, or Spartacists, disregarding the advice of their leaders Rosa Luxemburg and Karl Liebknecht, took to the streets of Berlin and declared Ebert's government deposed. To crush the revolution, Ebert turned to the Free Corps: volunteer brigades of ex-soldiers and adventurers, led by officers loyal to the emperor, who had been fighting to protect the eastern borders from encroachments by the new states of Poland, Estonia, and Latvia. The men of the Free Corps relished action and despised Bolshevism. They suppressed the revolution and murdered Luxemburg and Liebknecht on January 15.

The Spartacist revolt and the short-lived "soviet" republic in Munich (and others in Baden and Brunswick) had a profound effect on the German psyche. The communists had been easily subdued, but fear of a communist insurrection remained deeply embedded in the middle and upper classes—a fear that drove many of their members into the ranks of the Weimar Republic's right-wing opponents.

Refusing to disband as the government ordered, detachments of the right-wing Free Corps marched into Berlin and declared a new government, headed by Wolfgang Kapp, a staunch German nationalist. Insisting that it could not fire on fellow soldiers, the German army, the *Reichswehr,* made no move to defend the republic. A general strike called by the labor unions prevented Kapp from governing, and the coup collapsed. However, the Kapp Putsch demonstrated that the loyalty of the army to the republic was doubtful.

Economic Crisis

In addition to uprisings by the left and right, the republic was burdened by economic crisis. Unable to meet the deficit in the national budget, the government simply printed more money, causing the value of the German mark to decline precipitously. In 1919, the mark stood at 8.9 to the dollar; in November 1923, a dollar could be exchanged for 4 billion marks. Bank savings, war bonds, and pensions, representing years of toil and thrift, became worthless.

Blaming the government for this disaster, the ruined middle class became more receptive to rightist movements that aimed to bring down the republic.

A critical factor in the collapse of the German economy was the French occupation of the Ruhr in January 1923. With the economy in a shambles, the republic had defaulted on reparation payments. The French premier, Raymond Poincaré (1860–1934), ordered French troops into the Ruhr—the nerve center of German industry. Responding to the republic's call for passive resistance, factory workers, miners, and railway workers in the Ruhr refused to work for the French. Paying salaries to striking workers and officials contributed to the mark's free fall.

Gustav Stresemann, who became chancellor in August 1923, skillfully placed the republic on the path to recovery. He declared Germany's willingness to make reparation payments and issued a new currency, backed by a mortgage on German real estate. To protect the value of the new currency, the government did not print another issue. Inflation receded, and confidence was restored.

A new arrangement regarding reparations also contributed to the economic recovery. In 1924, the parties accepted the Dawes Plan, which reduced reparations and based them on Germany's economic capacity. During the negotiations, France agreed to withdraw its troops from the Ruhr—another step toward easing tensions for the republic.

From 1924 to 1929, economic conditions improved. Foreign capitalists, particularly Americans, were attracted by high interest rates and the low cost of labor. Their investments in German businesses stimulated the economy. By 1929, iron, steel, coal, and chemical production exceeded prewar levels. The value of German exports also surpassed that of 1913. Real wages were higher than before the war, and improved unemployment benefits also made life better for the workers. It appeared that Germany had achieved political stability, as threats from the extremist parties of the left and the right subsided. Given time and economic stability, democracy might have taken firmer root in Germany. But then came the Great Depression. The global economic crisis that began in October 1929 starkly revealed how weak was the Weimar Republic.

Fundamental Weaknesses of the Weimar Republic

German political experience provided poor soil for transplanting an Anglo-Saxon democratic parliamentary system. Before World War I, Germany had been a semiautocratic state, ruled by an emperor who commanded the armed forces, controlled foreign policy, appointed the chancellor, and called and dismissed parliament. This authoritarian system blocked the German people from acquiring democratic habits and attitudes; still accustomed to rule from above, still adoring the power-state, many Germans sought to destroy the democratic Weimar Republic.

Traditional conservatives—the upper echelons of the civil service, judges, industrialists, large landowners, and army leaders—scorned democracy and hated the republic. Nor did the middle class feel a commitment to the liberal-democratic principles on which the republic rested. The traditionally national-istic middle class identified the republic with the defeat in war and the humili-ation of the Versailles treaty. Rabidly antisocialist, this class saw the leaders of the republic as Marxists, who would impose on Germany a working-class state. Right-wing intellectuals often attacked democracy as a barrier to the true unity of the German nation. In the tradition of nineteenth-century Volk-ish thinkers, they disdained reason and political freedom, glorifying instead race, instincts, and action. By doing so, they turned many Germans against the republic, eroding the popular support on which democracy depends.

The Weimar Republic also showed the weaknesses of the multiparty sys-tem. With the vote spread over a number of parties, no one party held a ma-jority of seats in the parliament (Reichstag), so the republic was governed by a coalition of several parties. But because of ideological differences, the coali-tion was always unstable and in danger of failing to function. This is precisely what happened during the Great Depression. When effective leadership was imperative, the government could not act. Political deadlock caused Germans to lose what little confidence they had in the democratic system. Support for the parties that wanted to preserve democracy dwindled, and extremist par-ties that aimed to topple the republic gained strength. Seeking to bring down the republic were the Communists, on the left, and two rightist parties—the Nationalists and the National Socialist German Workers' party, led by Adolf Hitler.

The Rise of Hitler

Adolf Hitler (1889–1945) was born in Austria on April 20, 1889, the fourth child of a minor civil servant. A poor student in secondary school, although by no means unintelligent, Hitler left high school and lived idly for more than two years. In 1907 and again in 1908, the Vienna Academy of Fine Arts re-jected his application for admission. Hitler did not try to learn a trade or to work steadily but earned some money by painting picture postcards. He read a lot, especially in art, history, and military affairs. He also read the racial, nationalist, anti-Semitic, and Pan-German literature, which abounded in multinational Vienna. The racist treatises preached the danger posed by mix-ing races, called for the liquidation of racial inferiors, and marked the Jew as the embodiment of evil and the source of all misfortune.

In Vienna, Hitler came into contact with Georg von Schönerer's Pan-German movement. For Schönerer, the Jews were evil not because of their re-ligion or because they rejected Christ, but because they possessed evil racial qualities. Schönerer's followers wore watch chains with pictures of hanged Jews attached. Hitler was particularly impressed with Karl Lueger, the mayor of Vienna, a clever demagogue who skillfully manipulated the anti-Semitic feelings of the Viennese for his own political advantage. In Vienna, Hitler also acquired a hatred for Marxism and democracy and grew convinced that the struggle for existence and the survival of the fittest were the essential facts of the social world.

When World War I began, Hitler was in Munich. He welcomed the war as a relief from his daily life, which lacked purpose and excitement. Volunteering for the German army, Hitler found battle exhilarating, and he fought bravely, twice receiving the Iron Cross. The experience of battle taught Hitler to prize discipline, regimentation, leadership, authority, struggle, and ruthlessness—values that he carried with him into the politics of the postwar world.

The shock of Germany's defeat and revolution intensified Hitler's commitment to racial nationalism. To lead Germany to total victory over its racial enemies became his obsession. Germany's defeat and shame, he said, was due to the creators of the republic, the "November criminals," and behind them was a Jewish-Bolshevik world conspiracy.

The Nazi Party

In 1919, Hitler joined a small, right-wing extremist group. Displaying fantastic energy and extraordinary ability as a demagogic orator, propagandist, and organizer, Hitler quickly became the leader of the party, whose name was changed to National Socialist German Workers' party (commonly called Nazi). As leader, Hitler insisted on absolute authority and total allegiance—a demand that coincided with the postwar longing for a strong leader who would set right a shattered nation.

Like Mussolini, Hitler incorporated military attitudes and techniques into politics. Uniforms, salutes, emblems, flags, and other symbols imbued party members with a sense of solidarity and camaraderie. At mass meetings, Hitler was a spellbinder who gave stunning performances. His pounding fists, throbbing body, wild gesticulations, hypnotic eyes, rage-swollen face, and repeated, frenzied denunciations of the Versailles treaty, Marxism, the republic, and Jews inflamed and mesmerized the audience. Hitler instinctively grasped the innermost feelings of his audience—their resentments and longings. "The intense will of the man, the passion of his sincerity seemed to flow from him into me. I experienced an exaltation that could be likened only to religious conversion," said one early admirer.[3]

In November 1923, Hitler tried to seize power in Munich, in the state of Bavaria, as a prelude to toppling the republic. The attempt, which came to be known as the Beer Hall Putsch, failed. Ironically, however, Hitler's prestige increased, for when he was put on trial, he used it as an opportunity to denounce the republic and the Versailles treaty and to proclaim his philosophy of racial nationalism. His impassioned speeches, publicized by the press, earned Hitler a nationwide reputation and a light sentence: five years' imprisonment, with the promise of quick parole. While in prison, Hitler dictated *Mein Kampf*, a rambling and turgid work, which contained the essence of his world-view. The unsuccessful Munich putsch taught Hitler a valuable lesson: armed insurrection against superior might fails. He would gain power not by

The Spellbinder.   Hitler was a superb orator who knew how to reach the hearts of his listeners. The masses, he said, are aroused by the spoken, not the written, word. (*Roger-Viollet*)

force, but by exploiting the instruments of democracy—elections and party politics. He would use apparently legal means to destroy the Weimar Republic and impose a dictatorship.

Hitler's World-View

Racial Nationalism   Hitler's thought comprised a patchwork of nineteenth-century anti-Semitic, Volkish, Social Darwinist, antidemocratic, and anti-Marxist ideas. From these ideas, many of which enjoyed wide popularity, Hitler constructed a world-view rooted in myth and ritual. Nazism rejected both the Judeo-Christian and the Enlightenment traditions and sought to found a new world order based on racial nationalism. For Hitler, race was the key to understanding world history. He believed that a reawakened, racially united Germany, led by men of iron will, would carve out a vast European empire and would deal a decadent liberal civilization its deathblow. It would conquer Russia, eradicate communism, and reduce to serfdom the subhuman Slavs, "a mass of born slaves who feel the need of a master."[4]

In the tradition of crude Volkish nationalists and Social Darwinists, Hitler divided the world into superior and inferior races and pitted them against each other in a struggle for survival. For him, this fight for life was a law of nature and of history. As a higher race, the Germans were entitled to conquer and subjugate other races. Germany must acquire *Lebensraum* (living space) by expanding eastward at the expense of the racially inferior Slavs.

The Jew as Devil   An obsessive and virulent anti-Semitism dominated Hitler's mental outlook. In waging war against the Jews, Hitler believed that he was defending Germany from its worst enemy. In his mythical interpretation of the world, the Aryan was the originator and carrier of civilization. As descendants of the Aryans, the Germans embodied creativity, bravery, and loyalty. As the opposite of the Aryan, the Jew personified the vilest qualities. "Two worlds face one another," said Hitler, "the men of God and the men of Satan! The Jew is the anti-man, the creature of another god. He must have come from another root of the human race. I set the Aryan and the Jew over and against each other."[5] Everything Hitler despised—liberalism, intellectualism, pacifism, parliamentarianism, internationalism, Marxism, modern art, and individualism—he attributed to Jews.

Hitler's anti-Semitism served a functional purpose as well. By concentrating all evil in one enemy, "the conspirator and demonic" Jew, Hitler provided true believers with a simple, all-embracing, and emotionally satisfying explanation for their misery. By defining themselves as the racial and spiritual opposites of Jews, Germans of all classes felt joined together in a Volkish union.

The surrender to myth served to disorient the German intellect and to unify the nation. When the mind accepts an image such as Hitler's image of Jews as vermin, germs, and satanic conspirators, it has lost all sense of balance and objectivity. Such a disoriented mind is ready to believe and to obey, to be manipulated and led, to brutalize and to tolerate brutality. It is ready to be absorbed into the will of the collective community. That many people, including intellectuals and members of the elite, accepted these racial ideas shows the enduring power of mythical thinking and the vulnerability of reason. In 1933, the year Hitler took power, Felix Goldmann, a German-Jewish writer, commented astutely on the irrational character of Nazi anti-Semitism: "The present-day politicized racial anti-Semitism is the embodiment of myth, . . . nothing is discussed . . . only felt, . . . nothing is pondered critically, logically or reasonably, . . . only inwardly perceived, surmised. . . . We are apparently the last [heirs] of the Enlightenment."[6]

The Importance of Propaganda   Hitler understood that in an age of political parties, universal suffrage, and a popular press—the legacies of the French and Industrial Revolutions—the successful leader must win the support of the masses. This could be achieved best with propaganda. To be effective, said Hitler, propaganda must be aimed principally at the emotions. The masses are not moved by scientific ideas or by objective and abstract knowledge, but by primitive feelings, terror, force, and discipline. Propaganda must reduce everything to simple slogans incessantly repeated and must concentrate on one enemy. The masses are aroused by the spoken, not the written, word—by a storm of hot passion erupting from the speaker "which like hammer blows can open the gates to the heart of the people."[7]

Hitler Gains Power

After serving only nine months of his sentence, Hitler left prison in December 1924. He continued to build his party and waited for a crisis that would rock the republic and make his movement a force in national politics. The Great Depression, which began in the United States at the end of 1929, provided that crisis. As Germany's economic plight worsened, the German people became more amenable to Hitler's radicalism. His propaganda techniques worked. The Nazi party went from 810,000 votes in 1928 to 6,400,000 in 1930, and its representation in the Reichstag soared from 12 to 107.

To the lower middle class, the Nazis promised effective leadership and a solution to the economic crisis. But Nazism was more than a class movement. It appealed to the discontented and disillusioned from all segments of the population: embittered veterans, romantic nationalists, idealistic intellectuals, industrialists and large landowners frightened by communism and social democracy, rootless and resentful people who felt they had no place in the existing society, the unemployed, lovers of violence, and newly enfranchised youth yearning for a cause. And always there was the immense attraction of Hitler. Many Germans were won over by his fanatical sincerity, his iron will, and his conviction that he was chosen by fate to rescue Germany.

In the election of July 31, 1932, the Nazis received 37.3 percent of the vote and won 230 seats, far more than any other party but still not a majority. Franz von Papen, who had resigned from the chancellorship, persuaded the aging president, Paul von Hindenburg (1847–1934), to appoint Hitler as chancellor. In this decision, Papen had the support of German industrialists and aristocratic landowners, who regarded Hitler as a useful instrument to fight communism, block social reform, break the backs of organized labor, and rebuild the armament industry.

Never intending to rule within the spirit of the constitution, Hitler, who took office on January 30, 1933, quickly moved to assume dictatorial powers. In February 1933, a Dutch drifter with communist leanings set a fire in the Reichstag. Hitler persuaded Hindenburg to sign an emergency decree suspending civil rights on the pretext that the state was threatened by internal subversion. The chancellor then used these emergency powers to arrest, without due process, Communist and Social Democratic deputies.

In the elections of March 1933, the German people elected 288 Nazi deputies in a Reichstag of 647 seats. With the support of 52 deputies of the Nationalist party and in the absence of Communist deputies, who were under arrest, the Nazis now had a secure majority. Later that month, Hitler then bullied the Reichstag into passing the Enabling Act, which permitted the chancellor to enact legislation independently of the Reichstag. With astonishing passivity, the political parties had allowed the Nazis to dismantle the government and make Hitler a dictator with unlimited power. Hitler had used

Art as History:
The Renaissance to the Present

The visual arts are a particularly rich source of information for historians of the modern West. Revolutionary changes in art styles reflect the stages and complexities of the modern age. What insights into modern history can be derived from examining these works of art?

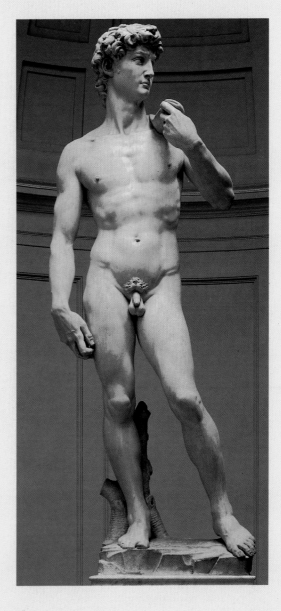

Michelangelo Buonarotti: *David*, 1504. A towering marble sculpture, Michelangelo's *David* is one of the crowning masterpieces of the High Renaissance. During the Middle Ages, artists depicted the nude figure for specific, often moral, reasons: tormented sinners at the Last Judgment, for example. Michelangelo's use of nudity breaks with this tradition. What does his heroic, idealized portrayal of the biblical David reveal about the secular spirit of the Renaissance? *(Scala/Art Resource, NY)*

Raphael (1483–1520): *Pope Leo X with His Nephews Giulio de' Medici and Luigi de' Rossi,* c. 1518.   A High Renaissance artist, Raphael combined realism and the human ideal in his portraits. In this panel, the pope's heavy features and his weak-looking nephews, who are cardinals, do not present a flattering portrayal. But Raphael's rendering of the dominant figure conveys power and dignity. How does this treatment of human character differ from Veneziano's Early Renaissance painting, reproduced in the first Art Insert? *(Scala/Art Resource, NY)*

Jan Vermeer (1632–1675): *View of Delft,* **1660.** By the seventeenth century, tiny Holland, which had enterprising merchants, sailors, and fast ships, was wealthy. Its sea ports flourished. Well-to-do bourgeois built substantial homes and furnished them with oriental rugs and handsome pictures. What does this painting convey about the Dutch town, its people, and its culture? *(Mauritshuis, The Hague)*

Jacques-Louis David: *Oath of the Horatii,* **1784.**   During the Enlightenment period, Jacques-Louis David (1748–1825) developed the neoclassic style and eventually made it the official artistic style of the French Revolution. His *Oath of the Horatii* depicts the three Horatius brothers preparing for battle, ready to die in the defense of their motherland against the enemy. The story that David chose to render in sculptural, stony terms dates back to Roman antiquity. Why did he turn to republican Rome as a source of inspiration for his art? *(The Louvre, Paris; La Reunion des Musées Nationaux)*

J. M. W. Turner (1775–1851): *Burning of the Houses of Parliament,* **c. 1835.** (top)
Turner was preoccupied with shimmering light. Although he often used literary
themes for his paintings, in accordance with romantic taste, the people, buildings, and
ships were often obscured. What does this painting reveal about his temperament and
perception of the world? *(Oil on canvas. H. 36¼" W. 48½". Philadelphia Museum of
Art: The John H. McFadden Collection)*

Paul Cézanne (1839–1906): *Still Life with Apples and Peaches,* **c. 1905.** Cézanne
did not share the French impressionists' interest in showing a "slice of life"; he
searched instead for harmony of form and color. His forms are simplified and outlined, and the different objects are seen from varying viewpoints and eye levels. They
do not conform to the laws of perspective. How does this picture reveal a movement
away from reality in art at the turn of the century? *(Oil on canvas. Copyright © 1996
Board of Trustees, National Gallery of Art, Washington; Gift of Eugene and Agnes
Meyer)*

Pierre Auguste Renoir (1841–1919): *Le Bal à Bougival,* **1883.** Joy and beauty shine in the impressionist paintings of Renoir. The impressionists in France broke with the Academy's classic themes and depicted scenes from daily life. They adopted a palette of luminous colors, as in this painting of a dancing couple. What does the emphasis on ordinary human beings as fit subjects for art disclose about French—and Western—thinking of the late 1800s? *(Oil on canvas. Courtesy Museum of Fine Arts, Boston Picture Fund.)*

Pablo Picasso (1881–1973): *Les Demoiselles d'Avignon,* **1907.** The cubists further distorted perspective, to give viewers the feeling of seeing objects and people "in the round" and over time. In this picture, Picasso painted the female nude in the strong cubist style to express the forces of nature; he goes beyond the conscious level. Can a correlation be made between some twentieth-century art and the scientific examination of the unconscious? *(Oil on canvas. 8' x 7' 8". Collection, The Museum of Modern Art, New York. Acquired through the Lillie P. Bliss Bequest)*

Frank Stella (b. 1936): *Hiraqla,* **1968.**   An abstract painting communicates with the viewer through its colors, textures, and shapes. Geometric abstract painting appeared in the years following the development of cubism and continues to be developed by artists such as Frank Stella. His canvases are often quite large, with great impact; *Hiraqla* is 120" high by 240" wide. What ideas and sensations does this painting impart? *(© 1996 Frank Stella/Artists Rights Society (ARS), New York. Polymer and fluorescent polymer on canvas, The Gund Art Foundation)*

the instruments of democracy to destroy the republic and create a totalitarian state.

Nazi Germany

Totalitarian leaders want more than power for its own sake. In the last analysis, they seek to transform the world according to an ideology, an all-embracing vision, which constitutes a higher and exclusive truth. Like religion, the totalitarian ideology provides its adherents with beliefs that make society and history intelligible and explain existence in an emotionally gratifying way. The ideology satisfies a human yearning for absolutes and creates true believers, who feel that they are participating in a great cause. Also like a religion, the totalitarian party gives isolated and alienated individuals a sense of belonging, a feeling of community; it enables a person to lose himself or herself in the comforting and exhilarating embrace of a mass movement. The nineteenth-century Russian anarchist Mikhail Bakunin had sensed the seductive power of the community when he stated: "I do not want to be *I,* I want to be *We.*"[8]

The Nazis moved to subjugate all political and economic institutions and all culture to the will of the party. There could be no separation between private life and politics. Ideology must pervade every phase of daily life, and all organizations must come under party control. There could be no rights of the individual that the state must respect. The party became the state, and its teachings the soul of the German nation.

Unlike earlier autocratic regimes, the totalitarian dictatorship is not satisfied with its subjects' outward obedience. Demanding unconditional loyalty and enthusiastic support from the masses, it strives to control the inner person: to shape thoughts, feelings, and attitudes according to the party ideology, which becomes the official creed. The aim is to create a "new man," one who dedicates himself body and soul to the party and its doctrines, a true believer stirred by a mission. Joseph Goebbels (see page 563) summed up this totalitarian goal as follows: "It is not enough to reconcile people more or less to our regime, to move them towards a position of neutrality towards us, we want rather to work on people until they are addicted to us."[9] An anonymous Nazi poet expressed the totalitarian credo in these words:

> We have captured all the positions
> And on the heights we have planted
> The banners of our revolution.
> You had imagined that that was all that we wanted
> We want more
> We want all
> Your hearts are our goal
> It is your souls we want.[10]

The Leader-State

The Third Reich was organized as a leader-state, in which Hitler, the *fuehrer* (leader), embodied and expressed the real will of the German people, commanded the supreme loyalty of the nation, and held omnipotent power. As a Nazi political theorist stated, "The authority of the Fuehrer is total and all embracing . . . it is subject to no checks or controls; it is circumscribed by no . . . individual rights; it is . . . overriding and unfettered."[11]

In June 1933, the Social Democratic party was outlawed, and within a few weeks, the other political parties simply disbanded on their own. In May 1933, the Nazis had seized the property of the trade unions, arrested the leaders, and ended collective bargaining and strikes. The newly established German Labor Front, an instrument of the party, became the official organization of the working class.

Unlike the Bolsheviks, the Nazis did not destroy the upper classes of the Old Regime. Hitler made no war against the industrialists. He wanted from them loyalty, obedience, and a war machine. German businessmen prospered but exercised no influence on political decisions. The profits of industry rose, but the real wages of German workers did not improve. Nevertheless, workers lauded the regime for ending the unemployment crisis.

Nazism conflicted with the core values of Christianity. "The heaviest blow that ever struck humanity was the coming of Christianity," said Hitler to intimates during World War II.[12] Because Nazism could tolerate no other faith alongside itself, the Nazis, recognizing that Christianity was a rival claimant for the German soul, moved to repress the Protestant and Catholic churches. In the public schools, religious instruction was cut back and the syllabus changed to omit the Jewish origins of Christianity. Christ was depicted not as a Jew, heir to the prophetic tradition of Hebrew monotheism, but as an Aryan hero. The Gestapo (secret state police) censored church newspapers, scrutinized sermons and church activities, forbade some clergymen to preach, dismissed the opponents of Nazism from theological schools, and arrested some clerical critics of the regime.

The clergy were well represented among the Germans who resisted Nazism; some were sent to concentration camps or were executed. But these courageous clergy were not representative of the German churches, which, as organized institutions, capitulated to and cooperated with the Nazi regime. Both the German Evangelical and German Catholic churches demanded that their faithful render loyalty to Hitler; both turned a blind eye to Nazi persecution of Jews; both condemned resistance and found much in the Third Reich to admire; and both supported Hitler's war. The prominent Lutheran theologian who "welcomed that change that came to Germany in 1933 as a divine gift and miracle" voiced the sentiments of many members of the clergy.[13]

The Nazis instituted many anti-Jewish measures, designed to make outcasts of the Jews. Thousands of Jewish doctors, lawyers, musicians, artists, and professors were barred from practicing their professions, and Jewish members of the civil service were dismissed. A series of laws tightened the screws of humiliation and persecution. Marriage or sexual encounters between Germans and Jews were forbidden. Universities, schools, restaurants, pharmacies, hospitals, theaters, museums, and athletic fields were gradually closed to Jews.

In November 1938, using as a pretext the assassination of a German official in Paris by a seventeen-year-old Jewish youth, whose family the Nazis had mistreated, the Nazis organized an extensive pogrom. Nazi gangs murdered scores of Jews and burned and looted thousands of Jewish businesses, homes, and synagogues all over Germany—an event that became known as Night of the Broken Glass (Kristallnacht). Twenty thousand Jews were thrown into concentration camps. The Reich then imposed on the Jewish community a fine of one billion marks. These measures were a mere prelude, however. During World War II, genocidal murder of European Jewry became a cardinal Nazi objective.

Shaping the "New Man"

The Ministry of Popular Enlightenment, headed by Joseph Goebbels (1897–1945), controlled the press, book publishing, the radio, the theater, and the cinema. Nazi propaganda sought to condition the mind to revere the fuehrer and to obey the new regime. Its intent was to deprive individuals of their capacity for independent thought. By concentrating on the myth of race and the infallibility of the fuehrer, Nazi propaganda tried to disorient the rational mind and to give the individual new standards to believe in and obey. Propaganda aimed to mold the entire nation to think and respond as the leader-state directed.

The regime made a special effort to reach young people. All youths between the ages of ten and eighteen were urged and then required to join the Hitler Youth, and all other youth organizations were dissolved. At camps and rallies, young people paraded, sang, saluted, and chanted: "We were slaves; we were outsiders in our own country. So were we before Hitler united us. Now we would fight against Hell itself for our leader."[14] The schools, long breeding grounds of nationalism, militarism, antiliberalism, and anti-Semitism, now indoctrinated the young in Nazi ideology. The Nazis instructed teachers how certain subjects were to be taught, and to ensure obedience, members of the Hitler Youth were asked to report teachers who did not conform.

In May 1933, professors and students proudly burned books considered a threat to Nazi ideology. Many academics praised Hitler and the new regime. Some 10 percent of the university faculty, principally Jews, Social Democrats, and liberals, were dismissed, and their colleagues often approved. "From now on it will not be your job to determine whether something is true but whether it is in the spirit of the National Socialist revolution," the new minister of culture told university professors.[15] Numerous courses on "racial science" and Nazi ideology were introduced into the curriculum.

Symbolic of the Nazi regime were the monster rallies staged at Nuremberg. Scores of thousands roared, marched, and worshiped at their leader's feet. These true believers, the end product of Nazi indoctrination, celebrated

Young Nazis Burning Books in Salzburg, Austria, 1938.   Heinrich Heine, the great nineteenth-century German-Jewish poet, once said that people who burn books end up burning people. (© *Topham/The Image Works*)

Hitler's achievements and demonstrated their loyalty to their savior. Everything was brilliantly orchestrated to impress Germans and the world with the irresistible power, determination, and unity of the Nazi movement and the greatness of the fuehrer. Armies of youths waving flags, storm troopers bearing weapons, and workers shouldering long-handled spades paraded past Hitler, who stood at attention, his arm extended in the Nazi salute. The endless columns of marchers, the stirring martial music played by huge bands, the forest of flags, the chanting and cheering of spectators, and the burning torches and beaming spotlights united the participants into a racial community. "Wherever Hitler leads we follow," thundered thousands of Germans in a giant chorus.

Terror was another means of ensuring compliance and obedience. The instrument of terror was the SS, which was organized in 1925 to protect Hitler and other party leaders and to stand guard at party meetings. Under the leadership of Heinrich Himmler (1900–1945), a fanatical believer in Hitler's racial theories, the SS was molded into an elite force of disciplined, dedicated, and utterly ruthless men.

Mass Support

The Nazi regime became a police state, characterized by mass arrests, the persecution of Jews, and concentration camps that institutionalized terror. Yet fewer heads had rolled than people expected, and in many ways life seemed normal. The Nazis skillfully established the totalitarian state without upsetting the daily life of the great majority of the population. Moreover, Hitler, like Mussolini, was careful to maintain the appearance of legality. By not abolishing parliament or repealing the constitution, he could claim that his was a legitimate government.

To people concerned with little except family, job, and friends—and this includes most people in any country—life in the first few years of the Third Reich seemed quite satisfying. People believed that the new government was trying to solve Germany's problems in a vigorous and sensible manner, in contrast to the ineffective Weimar leadership. By 1936, the invigoration of the economy, stimulated in part by rearmament, had virtually eliminated unemployment, which had stood at six million jobless when Hitler took power. An equally astounding achievement in the eyes of the German people was the rebuilding of the German war machine and the restoration of German power in international affairs. It seemed to most Germans that Hitler had awakened a sense of self-sacrifice and national dedication among a people dispirited by defeat and depression.

There was some opposition to the Hitler regime. Social Democrats and Communists in particular organized small cells. Some conservatives, who considered Hitler a threat to traditional German values, and some clergy, who saw Nazism as a pagan religion in conflict with Christian morality, also formed small opposition groups. But only the army could have toppled Hitler. Some generals, even before World War II, urged resistance, but the overwhelming majority of German officers preferred the new regime or were too concerned about their careers to do anything or considered it dishonorable to break their oath of loyalty to Hitler. These officers would remain loyal until the bitter end. Very few Germans realized that their country was passing through a long night of barbarism, and still fewer considered resistance.

Liberalism and Authoritarianism in Other Lands

After World War I, in country after country, parliamentary democracy collapsed and authoritarian leaders came to power. In most of these countries, liberal ideals had not penetrated deeply. Proponents of liberalism met resistance from conservative elites.

The Spread of Authoritarianism

Spain and Portugal   In both Spain and Portugal, parliamentary regimes faced strong opposition from the church, the army, and large landowners. In 1926, army officers overthrew the Portuguese republic that had been created in 1910, and gradually Antonio de Oliveira Salazar (1889–1970), a professor of economics, emerged as dictator. In Spain, after antimonarchist forces won the election of 1931, King Alfonso XIII (1902–1931) left the country, and Spain was proclaimed a republic. But the new government, led by socialists and liberals, faced the determined opposition of the ruling elite. The reforms introduced by the republic—expropriation of large estates, reduction of the number of army officers, dissolution of the Jesuit order, and the closing of church schools—only intensified the Old Order's hatred.

The difficulties of the Spanish republic mounted: workers, near starvation, rioted and engaged in violent strikes; the military attempted a coup; and Catalonia, with its long tradition of separatism, tried to establish its autonomy. Imitating France (see below), the parties of the left, including the Communists, united in the Popular Front, which came to power in February 1936. In July 1936, General Francisco Franco (1892–1975), stationed in Spanish Morocco, led a revolt against the republic. He was supported by army leaders, the church, monarchists, landlords, industrialists, and the Falange, a newly formed fascist party. Spain was torn by a bloody civil war. Aided by Fascist Italy and Nazi Germany, Franco won in 1939 and established a dictatorship.

Eastern and Central Europe   Parliamentary government in eastern Europe rested on weak foundations. Predominantly rural, these countries lacked the sizable professional and commercial classes that had promoted liberalism in western Europe. Only Czechoslovakia had a substantial native middle class with a strong liberal tradition. The rural masses of eastern Europe, traditionally subjected to monarchical and aristocratic authority, were not used to political thinking or civic responsibility. Students and intellectuals, often gripped by a romantic nationalism, were drawn to antidemocratic movements. Right-wing leaders also played on the fear of communism. When parliamentary government failed to solve internal problems, the opponents of the liberal state seized the helm. Fascist movements, however, had little success in eastern Europe. Rather, authoritarian regimes headed by traditional ruling elites—army leaders or kings—extinguished democracy there.

The Western Democracies

While liberal governments were everywhere failing, the great Western democracies—the United States, Britain, and France—continued to preserve democratic institutions. In Britain and the United States, fascist movements were merely a nuisance. In France, however, fascism was more of a threat because it exploited a deeply ingrained hostility in some quarters to the liberal ideals of the French Revolution.

The United States   The central problem faced by the Western democracies was the Great Depression, which started in the United States. In the 1920s, hundreds of thousands of Americans had bought stock on credit; this buying spree sent stock prices soaring well beyond what the stocks were actually worth. In late October 1929, the stock market was hit by a wave of panic selling, causing prices to plummet. Within a few weeks, the value of stocks listed on the New York Stock Exchange fell by some $26 billion. A ruinous chain reaction followed over the next few years. Businesses cut production and unemployment soared; farmers unable to meet mortgage payments lost their land; banks that had made poor investments closed down. American investors withdrew the capital they had invested in Europe, causing European banks and businesses to fail. Throughout the world, trade declined and unemployment rose.

When President Franklin Delano Roosevelt (1882–1945) took office in 1933, more than thirteen million Americans—one-quarter of the labor force—were out of work. Hunger and despair showed on the faces of the American people. Moving away from laissez faire, Roosevelt instituted a comprehensive program of national planning, economic experimentation, and reform, known as the New Deal. Although the American political and economic system faced a severe test, few Americans turned to fascism or communism; the government engaged in national planning but did not break with democratic values and procedures.

Britain   Even before the Great Depression, Britain faced severe economic problems. Loss of markets to foreign competitors hurt British manufacturing, mining, and shipbuilding; rapid development of water and oil power reduced the demand for British coal, and outdated mining equipment put Britain in a poor competitive position. To decrease costs, mine owners in 1926 called for salary cuts; the coal miners countered with a strike and were joined by workers in other industries. To many Britons, the workers were leftist radicals trying to overthrow the government. Many wanted the state to break the strike. After nine days, industrial workers called it off, but the miners held out for another six months; they returned to work with longer hours and lower pay. The general strike had failed. Because the workers had not called for revolution and they had refrained from violence, the fear that British workers would follow the Bolshevik path abated.

The Great Depression cast a pall over Britain. The Conservative party leadership tried to stimulate exports by devaluing the pound and to encourage industry by providing loans at lower interest rates, but in the main, it left the task of recovery to industry itself. Not until Britain began to rearm did unemployment decline significantly. Despite the economic slump of the 1920s and the Great Depression, Britain remained politically stable, a testament to the strength of its parliamentary tradition. Neither the communists nor the newly formed British Fascist party gained mass support.

France   In the early 1920s, France was concerned with restoring villages, railroads, mines, and forests that had been ruined by the war. From 1926 to 1929, France was relatively prosperous; industrial and agricultural production expanded, tourism increased, and the currency was stable. Although France did not feel the Great Depression as painfully as the United States and Germany, the nation was hurt by the decline in trade and production and the rise in unemployment. The political instability that had beset the Third Republic virtually since its inception continued, and hostility to the republic mounted. As the leading parties failed to solve the nation's problems, a number of fascist groups gained strength.

Fear of growing fascist strength at home and in Italy and Germany led the parties of the left to form the Popular Front. In 1936, Léon Blum (1872–1950), a socialist and a Jew, became premier. Blum's Popular Front government instituted more reforms than any other ministry in the history of the Third Republic. To end a wave of strikes, which tied up production, Blum gave workers a forty-hour week and holidays with pay and guaranteed them the right to collective bargaining. He took steps to nationalize the armaments and aircraft industries. To reduce the influence of the wealthiest families, he put the Bank of France under government control. By raising prices and buying wheat, he aided farmers. Conservatives and fascists denounced Blum as a Jewish socialist who was converting the fatherland into a communist state. "Better Hitler than Blum," grumbled French rightists.

Despite significant reforms, the Popular Front could not revitalize the economy. His political support eroding, Blum resigned in 1937 and the Popular Front, always a tenuous alliance, soon fell apart. Through democratic means, the Blum government had tried to give France its own New Deal, but the social reforms passed by the Popular Front only intensified hatred between the working classes and the rest of the nation. France had preserved democracy against the onslaught of domestic fascists, but it was a demoralized and divided nation that confronted a united and dynamic Nazi Germany.

Intellectuals and Artists in Troubled Times

The presuppositions of the Enlightenment, already eroding in the decades before World War I, seemed near collapse after 1918—another casualty of trench warfare. Economic distress, particularly during the depression, also profoundly disoriented the European mind. Westerners no longer possessed a frame of reference, a common outlook for understanding themselves, their times, or the past. The core values of Western civilization—the self-sufficiency of reason, the inviolability of the individual, and the existence of objective norms—no longer seemed inspiring or binding.

The crisis of consciousness evoked a variety of responses. Some intellectuals, having lost faith in the essential meaning of Western civilization, turned their backs on it or found escape in their art. Others sought a new hope in the Soviet experiment or in fascism. Still others reaffirmed the rational humanist tradition of the Enlightenment. Repelled by the secularism, materialism, and rootlessness of the modern age, Christian thinkers urged westerners to find renewed meaning and purpose in their ancestral religion. A philosophical movement, called existentialism, which rose to prominence after World War II, aspired to make life authentic in a world stripped of universal values.

Postwar Pessimism

After World War I, Europeans looked at themselves and their civilization differently. It seemed that in science and technology they had unleashed powers that they could not control, and belief in the stability and security of European civilization appeared to be an illusion. Also illusory was the expectation that reason would banish surviving signs of darkness, ignorance, and injustice and usher in an age of continual progress. European intellectuals felt that they were living in a "broken world." In an age of heightened brutality and mobilized irrationality, the values of old Europe seemed beyond recovery. "All the great words," wrote D. H. Lawrence "were cancelled out for that generation."[16] The fissures discernible in European civilization before 1914 had grown wider and deeper. To be sure, Europe also had its optimists—those who found reason for hope in the League of Nations and in the easing of international tensions and improved economic conditions in the mid 1920s. However, the Great Depression and the triumph of totalitarianism intensified feelings of doubt and disillusionment.

Expressions of pessimism abounded after World War I. In 1919, Paul Valéry stated: "We modern civilizations have learned to recognize that we are mortal like the others. We feel that a civilization is as fragile as life."[17] "We are living today under the sign of the collapse of civilization,"[18] declared humanitarian Albert Schweitzer in 1923. German philosopher Karl Jaspers noted in 1932 that "there is a growing awareness of imminent ruin tantamount to a dread of the approaching end of all that makes life worthwhile."[19]

T. S. Eliot's "The Wasteland" (1922) also conveys a sense of foreboding. In his image of a collapsing European civilization, Eliot creates a macabre scenario. Hooded hordes, modern-day barbarians, swarm over plains and lay waste cities. Jerusalem, Athens, Alexandria, Vienna, and London—each once a great spiritual or cultural center—are now "falling towers." Amid this destruction, one hears "high in the air / Murmur of maternal lamentation."[20]

Carl Gustav Jung, a Swiss psychologist, stated in *Modern Man in Search of a Soul* (1933):

> *I believe I am not exaggerating when I say that modern man has suffered an almost fatal shock, psychologically speaking, and as a result*

> *has fallen into profound uncertainty. . . . The revolution in our con-*
> *scious outlook, brought about by the catastrophic results of the*
> *World War, shows itself in our inner life by the shattering of our*
> *faith in ourselves and our own worth. . . . I realize only too well that*
> *I am losing my faith in the possibility of a rational organization of*
> *the world, the old dream of the millennium, in which peace and har-*
> *mony should rule, has grown pale.* [21]

In 1936, Dutch historian Johan Huizinga wrote in a chapter entitled "Apprehension of Doom":

> *We are living in a demented world. And we know it. . . . Everywhere*
> *there are doubts as to the solidity of our social structure, vague fears*
> *of the imminent future, a feeling that our civilization is on the way to*
> *ruin. . . . almost all things which once seemed sacred and immutable*
> *have now become unsettled, truth and humanity, justice and reason. . . .*
> *The sense of living in the midst of a violent crisis of civilization,*
> *threatening complete collapse, has spread far and wide.* [22]

The most influential expression of pessimism was Oswald Spengler's *The Decline of the West.* The first volume was published in July 1918, as the Great War was drawing to a close, and the second volume in 1922. The work achieved instant notoriety, particularly in Spengler's native Germany, shattered by defeat. Spengler viewed history as an assemblage of many different cultures, which, like living organisms, experience birth, youth, maturity, and death. What contemporaries pondered most was Spengler's insistence that Western civilization had entered its final stage and that its death could not be averted.

To an already troubled Western world, Spengler offered no solace. The West, like other cultures and like any living organism, is destined to die; its decline is irreversible, its death inevitable, and the symptoms of degeneration are already evident. Spengler's gloomy prognostication buttressed the fascists, who claimed that they were creating a new civilization on the ruins of the dying European civilization.

Literature and Art: Innovation, Disillusionment, and Social Commentary

Postwar pessimism did not prevent writers and artists from continuing the cultural innovations begun before the war. In the works of D. H. Lawrence, Marcel Proust, André Gide, James Joyce, Franz Kafka, T. S. Eliot, and Thomas Mann, the modernist movement achieved a brilliant flowering. Often these writers gave expression to the troubles and uncertainties of the postwar period.

Franz Kafka (1883–1924), a Czech Jew, grasped the dilemma of the modern age perhaps better than any other novelist of his generation. In Kafka's world, human beings are caught in a bureaucratic web that they cannot con-

Franz Kafka (1883–1924). The troubled Czech-Jewish writer expressed the feelings of alienation and aloneness that burden people in the modern age. (*The Bettmann Archive*)

trol. They live in a nightmare society dominated by oppressive, cruel, and corrupt officials and amoral torturers: a world where cruelty and injustice are accepted facts of existence, power is exercised without limits, and victims cooperate in their own destruction. Traditional values and ordinary logic do not operate in such a world. In *The Trial* (1925), for example, the hero is arrested without knowing why, and he is eventually executed, a victim of institutional evil that breaks and destroys him "like a dog." In these observations, Kafka proved to be a prophet of the emerging totalitarian state. (Kafka's three sisters perished in the Holocaust.)

Kafka expressed the feelings of alienation and isolation that characterize the modern individual; he explored life's dreads and absurdities, offering no solutions or consolation. In Kafka's works, people are defeated and unable to comprehend the irrational forces that contribute to their destruction. The mind yearns for coherence, but, Kafka tells us, uncertainty, if not chaos, governs human relationships. We can be sure neither of our own identities nor of the world we encounter, for human beings are the playthings of unfathomable forces, too irrational to master.

Before World War I, German writer Thomas Mann (1875–1955) had earned a reputation for his short stories and novels, particularly *Buddenbrooks* (1901), which portrays the decline of a prosperous bourgeois family. In *The Magic Mountain* (1924), Mann reflected on the decomposition of bourgeois European civilization. The setting for the story is a Swiss sanitarium, whose patients, drawn from several European lands, suffer from tuberculosis. The sanitarium symbolizes Europe, and it is the European psyche that is diseased. *The Magic Mountain* raised, but did not resolve, crucial questions. Was the epoch of rational humanist culture drawing to a close? Did Europeans welcome their spiritual illness in the same way that some of the patients in the sanitarium had a will to illness? How could Europe rescue itself from decadence?

In 1931, two years before Hitler took power, Mann, in an article entitled "An Appeal to Reason," described National Socialism and the extreme nationalism it espoused as a rejection of the Western rational tradition and a regression to primitive and barbaric modes of behavior. Nazism, he wrote, "is distinguished by . . . its absolute unrestraint, its orgiastic, radically anti-humane, frenziedly dynamic character. . . . Everything is possible, everything is permitted as a weapon against human decency. . . . Fanaticism turns into a means of salvation . . . politics becomes an opiate for the masses . . . and reason veils her face."[23]

Shattered by World War I, disgusted by fascism's growing strength, and moved by the suffering caused by the depression, many writers became committed to social and political causes. Erich Maria Remarque's *All Quiet on the Western Front* (1929) was one of many antiwar novels. George Orwell's *The Road to Wigan Pier* (1937) recorded the bleak lives of English coal miners. In *The Grapes of Wrath* (1939), John Steinbeck captured the anguish of American farmers driven from their land by the Dust Bowl and foreclosure during the depression. Few issues stirred the conscience of intellectuals as did the Spanish Civil War, and many of them volunteered to fight with the Spanish republicans against the fascists. Ernest Hemingway's *For Whom the Bell Tolls* (1940) expressed the sentiments of these thinkers.

The new directions taken in art before World War I—abstractionism and expressionism—continued in the postwar decades. Picasso, Mondrian, Kandinsky, Matisse, Rouault, Braque, Modigliani, and other masters continued to refine their styles. In addition, new art trends emerged, mirroring the trauma of a generation that had experienced the war and lost its faith in Europe's moral and intellectual values.

In 1915 in Zurich, artists and writers founded a movement, called Dada, to express their revulsion against the war and the civilization that spawned it. From neutral Switzerland, the movement spread to Germany and Paris. Dada shared in the postwar mood of disorientation and despair. Dadaists viewed life as essentially absurd (*Dada* is a nonsense term) and cultivated indifference. "The acts of life have no beginning or end. Everything happens in a completely idiotic way,"[24] declared the poet Tristan Tzara, one of Dada's founders and its chief spokesman. Dadaists expressed contempt for artistic and literary standards and rejected both God and reason. "Through reason man becomes a tragic and ugly figure," said one Dadaist; "beauty is dead," said another. Tzara declared:

> *What good did the theories of the philosophers do us? Did they help us to take a single step forward or backward? . . . We have had enough of the intelligent movements that have stretched beyond mea-*

*sure our credulity in the benefits of science. What we want now is
spontaneity. . . . because everything that issues freely from ourselves,
without the intervention of speculative ideas, represents us.*[25]

For Dadaists, the world was nonsensical and reality disordered; hence, they
offered no solutions to anything. "Like everything in life, Dada is useless,"[26]
said Tzara. Despite their nihilistic aims and "calculated irrationality," however, Dadaist artists, such as Marcel Duchamp, were innovative and creative.

Dada ended as a formal movement in 1924 and was succeeded by surrealism. Surrealists inherited from Dada a contempt for reason; they stressed fantasy and made use of Freudian insights and symbols in their art to reproduce
the raw state of the unconscious and to arrive at truths beyond reason's grasp.
In their attempt to break through the constraints of rationality in order to
reach a higher reality—that is, a "surreality"—leading surrealists, such as
Max Ernst (1891–1976), Salvador Dali (1904–1989), and Joan Miró
(1893–1983), produced works of undeniable artistic merit.

Like writers, artists expressed a social conscience. George Grosz combined
a Dadaist sense of life's meaninglessness with a new realism to depict the
moral degeneration of middle-class German society. In *After the Questioning*
(1935), Grosz, then living in the United States, dramatized Nazi brutality; in
The End of the World (1936), he expressed his fear of another impending
world war. Käthe Kollwitz, also a German artist, showed a deep compassion
for the sufferer: the unemployed, the hungry, the ill, and the politically oppressed. William Gropper's *Migration* (1932) dramatized the suffering of the
same dispossessed farmers described in Steinbeck's novel *The Grapes of
Wrath*. Philip Evergood, in *Don't Cry Mother* (1938–1944), portrayed the
apathy of starving children and their mother's terrible helplessness.

In his etchings of maimed, dying, and dead soldiers, German artist Otto
Dix produced a powerful visual indictment of the Great War's cruelty and
suffering. Max Beckmann's service in the German army during World War I
made him acutely aware of violence and brutality, which he expressed in *The
Night* (1918–19) and other paintings. Designated a "degenerate artist" by the
Nazis, Beckmann went into exile. In *Guernica* (1937), Picasso memorialized
the Spanish village decimated by saturation bombing during the Spanish Civil
War. In the *White Crucifixion* (1938), Marc Chagall, a Russian-born Jew
who had settled in Paris, depicted the terror and flight of Jews in Nazi
Germany.

Communism: "The God That Failed"

The economic misery of the depression and the rise of fascist barbarism led
many intellectuals to find a new hope, even a secular faith, in communism.
They praised the Soviet Union for supplanting capitalist greed with socialist
cooperation, for replacing a haphazard economic system marred by repeated
depressions with one based on planned production, and for providing employment for everyone when joblessness was endemic in capitalist lands.

Angel of Hearth and Home by Max Ernst (1891–1976).   Ernst formed part of the transition from Dada to surrealism. His paintings expressed a profound anxiety. André Breton called him "the most magnificently haunted mind in Europe." (© 1995 *Artists Rights Society (ARS), New York/SPADEM/ADAGP, Paris)*

American literary critic Edmund Wilson said that in the Soviet Union one felt at the "moral top of the world where the light never really goes out."[27] To these intellectuals, it seemed that in the Soviet Union a vigorous and healthy civilization was emerging and that only communism could stem the tide of fascism. For many, however, the attraction was short-lived. Sickened by Stalin's purges and terror, the denial of individual freedom, and the suppression of truth, they came to view the Soviet Union as another totalitarian state and communism as another "god that failed."

One such intellectual was Arthur Koestler (1905–1983). Born in Budapest of Jewish ancestry and educated in Vienna, Koestler worked as a correspondent for a leading Berlin newspaper chain. He joined the Communist party at the very end of 1931 because he "lived in a disintegrating society thirsting for faith," was moved by the misery caused by the depression, and saw communism as the "only force capable of resisting the onrush of the primitive [Nazi] horde."[28] Koestler visited the Soviet Union in 1933, experiencing firsthand both the starvation brought on by forced collectivization and the propaganda that grotesquely misrepresented life in Western lands. While his faith was shaken, he did not break with the party until 1938, in response to Stalin's liquidations.

In *Darkness at Noon* (1941), Koestler explored the attitudes of the Old Bolsheviks who were imprisoned, tortured, and executed by Stalin. These dedicated Communists had served the party faithfully, but Stalin, fearing opposition, hating intellectuals, and driven by megalomania, denounced them as enemies of the people. In *Darkness at Noon*, the leading character, the imprisoned Rubashov, is a composite of the Old Bolsheviks. Although innocent, Rubashov, without being physically tortured, publicly confesses to political crimes that he never committed.

Rubashov is aware of the suffering that the party has brought to the Russian people:

> [I]n the interests of a just distribution of land we deliberately let die of starvation about five million farmers and their families in one year. . . . [To liberate] human beings from the shackles of industrial exploitation . . . we sent about ten million people to do forced labour in the Arctic regions . . . under conditions similar to those of antique galley slaves. [29]

Pained by his own complicity in the party's crimes, including the betrayal of friends, Rubashov questions the party's philosophy that the individual should be subordinated, and, if necessary, sacrificed to the regime. Nevertheless, Rubashov remains the party's faithful servant; true believers do not easily break with their faith. By confessing, Rubashov performs his last service for the revolution. For the true believer, everything—truth, justice, and the sanctity of the individual—is properly sacrificed to the party.

Reaffirming the Christian World-View

By calling into question core liberal beliefs—the essential goodness of human nature, the primacy of reason, the efficacy of science, and the inevitability of progress—World War I led thinkers to find in Christianity an alternative view of the human experience and the crisis of the twentieth century. Christian thinkers, including Karl Barth, Paul Tillich, Reinhold Niebuhr, Christopher Dawson, Jacques Maritain, and T. S. Eliot, affirmed the reality of evil in human nature. They assailed liberals and Marxists for holding too optimistic a view of human nature and human reason and for postulating a purely rational and secular philosophy of history. For these thinkers, the Christian conception of history as a clash between human will and God's commands, provided an intelligible explanation of the tragedies of the twentieth century.

Karl Barth (1886–1968), the Swiss-German Protestant theologian, called for a reaffirmation of the Christ of faith, the uniqueness of Christianity, and the spiritual power of divine revelation. The true meaning of history, he said, is not to be found in the liberals' view of the progress of reason and freedom or the Marxist conception of economic determinism. Rather, it derives from the fact that history is the arena in which the individual's faith is tested.

A leading Catholic thinker, Jacques Maritain (1882–1973), a Frenchman, denounced core elements of the modern outlook: the self-sufficiency of the individual, the autonomy of the mind, and a nonreligious humanism. He urged that the Christian philosophy of Thomas Aquinas be revived, for he believed that it successfully harmonized faith and reason. As a strong advocate of political freedom, Maritain stressed the link between modern democracy and the Christian Gospels, which proclaimed "the natural equality of all men, children of the same God and redeemed by the same Christ . . . [and] the inalienable dignity of every soul fashioned in the image of God."[30] To survive, secular democracy needs to be infused with Christian love and compassion.

The English Catholic thinker Christopher Dawson (1889–1970) emphasized the historic ties between Christianity and Western civilization. In 1933, he wrote:

> If our civilization is to recover its vitality, or even to survive, it must cease to neglect its spiritual roots and must realize that religion is not a matter of personal sentiment which has nothing to do with the objective realities of society, but is, on the contrary, the very heart of social life and the root of every living culture.[31]

Reaffirming the Ideals of Reason and Freedom

Several thinkers tried to reaffirm the ideals of rationality and freedom that had been trampled by totalitarian movements. In *The Treason of the Intellectuals* (1927), Julien Benda (1867–1956), a French cultural critic of Jewish background, castigated intellectuals for intensifying hatred between nations, classes, and political factions. "Our age is indeed the age of the *intellectual organization of political hatreds*," he wrote.[32] These intellectuals, said Benda, do not pursue justice or truth but proclaim that "even if our country is wrong, we must think of it in the right." They scorn outsiders, extol harshness and action, and proclaim the superiority of instinct and will to intelligence; or they "assert that the intelligence to be venerated is that which limits its activities within the bounds of national interest." The logical end of this xenophobia, said Benda, "is the organized slaughter of nations and classes."

José Ortega y Gasset (1883–1955), descendant of a noble Spanish family and a professor of philosophy, gained international recognition with the publication of *The Revolt of the Masses* (1930). According to Ortega, European civilization, the product of a creative elite, was degenerating into barbarism because of the growing power of the masses, for the masses lacked the mental discipline and commitment to reason needed to preserve Europe's intellectual and cultural traditions. Ortega did not equate the masses with the working class and the elite with the nobility; it was an attitude of mind, not a class affiliation, that distinguished the "mass-man" from the elite.

The mass-man, said Ortega, has a commonplace mind and does not set high standards for himself. Faced with a problem, he "is satisfied with thinking the first thing he finds in his head," and "crushes . . . everything that is different, everything that is excellent, individual, qualified, and select. Anybody who is not like everybody, who does not think like everybody, runs the risk of being eliminated."[33] Such intellectually vulgar people, declared Ortega, cannot understand or preserve the processes of civilization. The fascists, for him, exemplified this revolt of the masses:

> *Under fascism there appears for the first time in Europe a type of man who does not want to give reasons or to be right, but simply shows himself resolved to impose his opinions. This is the new thing: the right not to be reasonable, the "reason of unreason." Hence I see the most palpable manifestation of the new mentality of the masses, due to their having decided to rule society without the capacity for doing so.*[34]

Since the mass-man does not respect the tradition of reason, he does not enter into rational dialogue with others or defend his opinions logically, said Ortega. Rejecting reason, the mass-man glorifies violence—the ultimate expression of barbarism. As Ortega saw it, if European civilization was to be rescued from fascism and communism, the elite must sustain civilized values and provide leadership for the masses.

A staunch defender of the Enlightenment tradition, Ernst Cassirer (1874–1945), a German philosopher of Jewish lineage, emigrated after Hitler came to power, eventually settling in the United States. Just prior to Hitler's triumph, in 1932, Cassirer wrote about the need to uphold and reenergize that tradition: "More than ever before, it seems to me, the time is again ripe for applying . . . self-criticism to the present age, for holding up to it that bright clear mirror fashioned by the Enlightenment. . . . The age which venerated reason and science as man's highest faculty cannot and must not be lost even for us."[35]

In his last work, *The Myth of the State* (1946), Cassirer described Nazism as the triumph of mythical thinking over reason. The Nazis, he wrote, cleverly manufactured myths—of the race, the leader, the party, the state—that disoriented the intellect. The Germans who embraced these myths surrendered their capacity for independent judgment, leaving themselves vulnerable to manipulation by the Nazi leadership. To contain the destructive powers of political myths, Cassirer urged strengthening the rational humanist tradition and called for the critical study of political myths, for "in order to fight an enemy you must know him. . . . We should carefully study the origin, the structure, the methods, and the technique of the political myths. We should see the adversary face to face in order to know how to combat him."[36]

George Orwell (1903–1950), a British novelist and political journalist, wrote two powerful indictments of totalitarianism: *Animal Farm* (1945) and *1984* (1949). In *Animal Farm,* based in part on his experiences with communists during the Spanish Civil War, Orwell satirized the totalitarian regime built by Lenin and Stalin in Russia. In *1984,* Orwell, who was deeply committed to human dignity and freedom, warned that these great principles were now permanently menaced by the concentration and abuse of political power.

"If you want a picture of the future, imagine a boot stamping on a human face forever," says a member of the ruling elite as he tortures a victim in the dungeons of the Thought Police.[37]

The society of *1984* is ruled by the Inner Party, which constitutes some 2 percent of the population. Heading the Party is Big Brother—most likely a mythical figure created by the ruling elite to satisfy people's yearning for a leader. The Party indoctrinates people to love Big Brother, whose picture is everywhere. The Ministry of Truth resorts to thought control to dominate and manipulate the masses and to keep Party members loyal and subservient. Independent thinking is destroyed. Objective truth no longer exists. Truth is whatever the Party decrees at the moment. If the Party were to proclaim that two plus two equals five, it would have to be believed.

Anyone thinking prohibited thoughts is designated a Thoughtcriminal, a crime punishable by death. The Thought Police's agents are everywhere, using hidden microphones and telescreens to check on Party members for any signs of deviance from Party rules and ideology. Posters displaying Big Brother's picture carry the words "BIG BROTHER IS WATCHING YOU." Convinced that "who controls the past controls the future," the Ministry of Truth alters old newspapers to make the past accord with the Party's current doctrine. In this totalitarian society of the future, all human rights are abolished, people are arrested merely for their thoughts, and children spy on their parents.

Existentialism

The philosophical movement that best exemplified the anxiety and uncertainty of Europe in an era of world wars was existentialism. Like writers and artists, existentialist philosophers were responding to a European civilization that seemed to be in the throes of dissolution. Although existentialism was most popular after World War II, expressing the anxiety and despair of many intellectuals who had lost confidence in reason and progress, several of its key works were written prior to or during the war.

What route should people take in a world where old values and certainties had dissolved, where universal truth was rejected and God's existence denied? How could people cope in a society where they were menaced by technology, manipulated by impersonal bureaucracies, and overwhelmed by feelings of anxiety? If the universe lacks any overarching meaning, what meaning could one give to one's own life? These questions were at the crux of existentialist philosophy.

Existentialism does not lend itself to a single definition since its principal theorists did not adhere to a common body of doctrines. For example, some existentialists were atheists, like Jean Paul Sartre, or omitted God from their thought, like Martin Heidegger; others, like Karl Jaspers, believed in God but not in Christian doctrines; still others, like Gabriel Marcel and Nikolai Berdyaev, were Christians; and Martin Buber was a believing Jew. Perhaps

Jean Paul Sartre and Simone de Beauvoir.   Existentialism is a major philosophical movement of the twentieth century. Sartre and de Beauvoir were two of its principal exponents. (*B/W Sygma-G. Pierre*)

the following principles contain the essence of existentialism, although not all existentialists would subscribe to each point or agree with the way it is expressed.

1.   Reality defies ultimate comprehension; there are no timeless truths that exist independently of and prior to the individual human being. Our existence precedes and takes precedence over any presumed absolute values. The moral and spiritual values that society tries to impose cannot define the individual person's existence.

2.   Reason alone is an inadequate guide to living, for people are more than thinking subjects who approach the world through critical analysis. They are also feeling and willing beings, who must participate fully in life and experience existence directly, actively, and passionately. Only in this way does one live wholly and authentically.

3.   Thought must not merely be abstract speculation but must have a bearing on life; it must be translated into deeds.

4.   Human nature is problematic and paradoxical, not fixed or constant; each person is like no other. Self-realization comes when one affirms one's own uniqueness. One becomes less than human when one permits one's life to be determined by a mental outlook—a set of rules and values—imposed by others.

5.   We are alone. The universe is indifferent to our expectations and needs, and death is ever stalking us. Awareness of this elementary fact of existence evokes a sense of overwhelming anxiety and depression.

6.   Existence is essentially absurd. There is no purpose to our presence in the universe. We simply find ourselves here; we do not know and will never find out why. Compared with the eternity of time that preceded our birth and will follow our death, the short duration of our existence seems trivial and inexplicable. And death, which irrevocably terminates our existence, testifies to the ultimate absurdity of life.

7.   We are free. We must face squarely the fact that existence is purposeless and absurd. In doing so, we can give our life meaning. It is in the act of choosing freely from among different possibilities that the individual shapes an authentic existence. There is a dynamic quality to human existence; the individual has the potential to become more than he or she is.

The Modern Predicament

The process of fragmentation, which had begun in European thought and arts at the end of the nineteenth century, accelerated after World War I. Increasingly, philosophers, writers, and artists expressed disillusionment with the rational-humanist tradition of the Enlightenment. They no longer shared the Enlightenment's confidence in either reason's capabilities or human goodness, and they viewed perpetual progress as an illusion.

For some thinkers, the crucial problem was the great change in the European understanding of truth. Since the rise of philosophy in ancient Greece, Western thinkers had believed in the existence of objective, universal truths: truths that were inherent in nature and applied to all peoples at all times. (Christianity, of course, also taught the reality of truth as revealed by God.) It was held that such truths—the natural rights of the individual, for example— could be apprehended by the intellect and could serve as a standard for individual aspirations and social life. The recognition of these universal principles, it was believed, compelled people to measure the world of the here-and-now in the light of rational and universal norms and to institute appropriate reforms. It was the task of philosophy to reconcile human existence with the objective order.

During the nineteenth century, the existence of universal truth came into doubt. A growing historical consciousness led some thinkers to maintain that what people considered truth was merely a reflection of their culture at a given stage in history—their perception of things at a specific point in the evolution of human consciousness. These thinkers held that universal truths were not woven into the fabric of nature. There were no natural rights of life, liberty, and property that constituted the individual's birthright; there were no standards of justice or equality inherent in nature and ascertainable by reason. Rather, people themselves elevated the beliefs and values of an age to the status of objective truth.

This radical break with the traditional attitude toward truth contributed substantially to the crisis of European consciousness that marked the first half of the twentieth century. Traditional values and beliefs, whether those inherited from the Enlightenment or those taught by Christianity, no longer gave Europeans a sense of certainty and security. People were left without a normative order to serve as a guide to living.

Such an outlook fosters nihilism. For if nothing is fundamentally true—if there are no principles of morality and justice that emanate from God or can be deduced by reason—then it can be concluded, as Nietzsche understood, that everything is permitted. Some interpreters view Nazism as the culminating manifestation of a nihilistic attitude grown ever more brutal.

By the early twentieth century, the attitude of westerners toward reason had undergone a radical transformation. Some thinkers, who had placed their hopes in the rational tradition of the Enlightenment, were distressed by reason's inability to resolve the tensions and conflicts of modern industrial society. Moreover, the growing recognition of the nonrational—of human actions determined by hidden impulses—led people to doubt that reason played the dominant role in human behavior. Other thinkers viewed the problem of reason differently. They assailed the attitude of mind that found no room for Christianity because its teachings did not pass the test of reason and science. Or they attacked reason for fashioning a technological and bureaucratic society that devalued and crushed human passions and stifled individuality. These thinkers insisted that human beings cannot fulfill their potential, cannot live wholly, if their feelings are denied. They agreed with D. H. Lawrence's critique of rationalism: "The attribution of rationality to human nature, instead of enriching it, now seems to me to have impoverished it. It ignored certain powerful and valuable springs of feeling. Some of the spontaneous, irrational outbursts of human nature can have a sort of value from which our schematism was cut off."[38]

While many thinkers focused on reason's limitations, others, particularly existentialists, pointed out that reason was a double-edged sword; it could demean, as well as ennoble, the individual. These thinkers attacked all theories that subordinated the individual to a rigid system. They denounced positivism for reducing human personality to psychological laws and Marxism for making social class a higher reality than the individual. They rebelled against political collectivization, which regulated individual lives according to the needs of the corporate state. They also assailed modern technology and bureaucracy, creations of the rational mind, for fashioning a social order that devalued and depersonalized the individual, denying people an opportunity for independent growth and a richer existence. According to these thinkers, modern industrial society, in its drive for efficiency and uniformity, deprived people of their uniqueness and reduced flesh-and-blood human beings to mere cogs in a mechanical system.

Responding to the critics of reason, its defenders insisted that it was necessary to reaffirm the rational tradition first proclaimed by the Greeks and given its modern expression by the Enlightenment. Reason, they maintained, was indispensable to civilization. What these thinkers advocated was broadening the scope of reason in order to accommodate the insights into human nature advanced by the romantics, Nietzsche, Freud, modernist writers and artists, and others who explored the world of feelings, will, and the subconscious. They also stressed the need to humanize reason so that it could never threaten to reduce a human being to a thing—a mere instrument used to realize some socioeconomic blueprint.

In the decades shaped by world wars and totalitarianism, intellectuals raised questions that went to the heart of the dilemma of modern life. How can civilized life be safeguarded against human irrationality, particularly when it is channeled into political ideologies that idolize the state, the leader, the party, or the race? How can individual human personality be rescued from a relentless rationalism that organizes the individual as it would any material object? Do the values associated with the Enlightenment provide a sound basis on which to integrate society? Can the individual find meaning in what many now regarded as a meaningless universe? World War II gave these questions a special poignancy.

Notes

1. Quoted in Zeev Sternhill, "Fascist Ideology," in *Fascism: A Reader's Guide,* ed. Walter Laqueur (Berkeley: University of California Press, 1976), p. 338.
2. Quoted in Max Gallo, *Mussolini's Italy* (New York: Macmillan, 1973), p. 218.
3. Quoted in Joachim C. Fest, *Hitler,* trans. Richard and Clara Winston (New York: Harcourt Brace Jovanovich, 1974), p. 162.
4. *Hitler's Secret Conversations, 1941–1944,* with an introductory essay by H. R. Trevor Roper (New York: Farrar, Straus & Young, 1953), p. 28.
5. Quoted in Lucy S. Dawidowicz, *The War Against the Jews 1933–1945* (New York: Holt, Rinehart & Winston, 1975), p. 21.
6. Quoted in Uri Tal, "Consecration of Politics in the Nazi Era," in *Judaism and Christianity Under the Impact of National Socialism,* ed. Otto Dov Kulka and Paul R. Mendes Flohr (Jerusalem: Historical Society of Israel, 1987), p. 70.
7. Adolf Hitler, *Mein Kampf* (Boston: Houghton Mifflin, 1962), p. 107.
8. Quoted in Hannah Arendt, *The Origins of Totalitarianism* (New York: Meridian Books, World Publishing, 1958), p. 330.
9. Quoted in David Welch, ed., *Nazi Propaganda* (Totowa, N.J.: Barnes & Noble, 1983), p. 5.
10. Quoted in J. S. Conway, *The Nazi Persecution of the Churches* (New York: Basic Books, 1968), p. 202.
11. Quoted in Helmut Krausnick, Hans Buchheim, Martin Broszart, and Hans-Adolf Jacobsen, *Anatomy of the SS State* (London: Collins, 1968), p. 128.
12. *Hitler's Secret Conversations,* p. 6.
13. Quoted in Hermann Graml et al., *The German Resistance to Hitler* (Berkeley: University of California Press, 1970), p. 206.
14. Quoted in T. L. Jarman, *The Rise and Fall of Nazi Germany* (New York: New York University Press, 1956), p. 182.
15. Quoted in Karl Dietrich Bracher, *The German Dictatorship,* trans.

Jean Steinberg (New York: Praeger, 1970), p. 268.

16. Quoted in Barbara Tuchman, *The Guns of August* (New York: Macmillan, 1962), p. 489.

17. Quoted in Hans Kohn, "The Crisis in European Thought and Culture," in *World War I: A Turning Point in Modern History,* ed. Jack J. Roth (New York: Alfred A. Knopf, 1967), p. 28.

18. Quoted in Franklin L. Baumer, "Twentieth-Century Version of the Apocalypse," *Cahiers d'Histoire Mondiale (Journal of World History),* 1 (January 1954):624.

19. Ibid.

20. T. S. Eliot, "The Wasteland," in *Collected Poems, 1909–1962* (New York: Harcourt, Brace, 1970), p. 67.

21. Carl Gustav Jung, *Modern Man in Search of a Soul,* trans. W. S. Dell and Cary F. Baynes (New York: Harcourt, Brace, 1933), pp. 231, 234–235.

22. Johan Huizinga, *In the Shadow of Tomorrow* (London: Heinemann, 1936), pp. 1–3.

23. Thomas Mann, "An Appeal to Reason," excerpted in *Sources of the Western Tradition,* ed. Marvin Perry et al., 2nd ed. (Boston: Houghton Mifflin, 1991), 2:351–352.

24. Tristan Tzara, "Lecture on Dada (1922)," trans. Ralph Mannheim, in *The Dada Painters and Poets,* ed. Robert Motherwell (New York: Witterborn, Schultz, 1951), p. 250.

25. Ibid., p. 248.

26. Ibid., p. 251.

27. Quoted in David Caute, *The Fellow Travelers* (New York: Macmillan, 1973), p. 64.

28. Richard Crossman, ed., *The God That Failed* (New York: Bantam Books, 1951), pp. 15, 21.

29. Arthur Koestler, *Darkness at Noon* (New York: Macmillan, 1941), pp. 158–159.

30. Jacques Maritain, *Christianity and Democracy* (New York: Charles Scribner's Sons, 1944), p. 44.

31. Quoted in C. T. McIntire, ed., *God, History, and Historians* (New York: Oxford University Press, 1977), p. 9.

32. Julien Benda, *The Betrayal of the Intellectuals,* trans. Richard Aldington (Boston: Beacon, 1955), p. 21. Quotations in the rest of this paragraph come from pp. 38, 122, and 162, respectively.

33. José Ortega y Gasset, *The Revolt of the Masses* (New York: Norton, 1957), pp. 63, 18.

34. Ibid., p. 73.

35. Ernst Cassirer, *The Philosophy of the Enlightenment,* trans. Fritz C. A. Koelln and James P. Pettegrove (Boston: Beacon, 1955), pp. xi–xii.

36. Ernst Cassirer, *The Myth of the State* (New Haven, Conn.: Yale University Press, 1946), p. 296.

37. George Orwell, *1984* (New York: Harcourt, Brace, 1949; paperback, The New American Library, 1961), p. 220.

38. Quoted in Anthony Arblaster, *The Rise and Decline of Western Liberalism* (Oxford: Basil Blackwell, 1984), p. 81.

Suggested Reading

Allen, William Sheridan, *The Nazi Seizure of Power* (1965). An illuminating study of how the people of a small German town reacted to Nazism during the years 1930–1935.

Bissel, Richard, ed., *Life in the Third Reich* (1987). Essays dealing with various aspects of life in Hitler's Germany; good overviews.

Blackham, H. J., *Six Existentialist Thinkers* (1952). Useful analyses of Kierkegaard, Nietzsche, Jaspers, Marcel, Heidegger, and Jean Paul Sartre.

————, ed., *Reality, Man and Existence* (1965). Essential works of existentialism.

Bracher, Karl Dietrich, *The German Dictatorship* (1970). A highly regarded analysis of all phases of the Nazi state.

Bullock, Alan, *Hitler: A Study in Tyranny* (1964). An excellent biography.

Burleigh, Michael, and Wolfgang Wippermann, *The Racial State: Germany 1933–1945* (1991). Persecution of Jews, Gypsies, mentally handicapped, and homosexuals; analysis of racially motivated social policies of the Nazi regime.

Cassels, Alan, *Fascist Italy* (1968). A clearly written introduction.

Fest, Joachim C., *Hitler* (1974). An excellent biography.

Jackel, Eberhard, *Hitler's Weltan-schauung* (1972). An analysis of Hitler's world-view.

Laqueur, Walter, ed., *Fascism: A Reader's Guide* (1976). A superb collection of essays.

Mack Smith, Denis, *Mussolini* (1982). By a leading historian of modern Italy.

Macquarrie, John, *Existentialism* (1972). A lucid discussion of existentialism.

Paxton, Robert O., *Europe in the Twentieth Century* (1975). A first-rate text, with an excellent bibliography.

Peukert, Detlev J. K., *Inside Nazi Germany* (1982). How ordinary citizens responded to Nazi rule.

Spielvogel, Jackson J., *Hitler and Nazi Germany* (1988). Clearly written, up-to-date survey.

Wagar, W. Warren, ed., *European Thought Since 1914* (1968). A valuable collection of sources.

Review Questions

1. How did fascist principles "stand for the sheer, categorical, definitive antithesis to the world of democracy . . . to the world which still abides by the fundamental principles laid down in 1789"?

2. Why did some Italians support Mussolini? In what ways was Mussolini less effective than Hitler in establishing a totalitarian state?

3. How was Hitler's outlook shaped by his experiences in Vienna? What were his attitudes toward democracy, the masses, war, the Jews, and propaganda?

4. How did the Nazis extend their control over Germany?

5. How did Nazism conflict with the core values of Christianity? What was the general policy of the Nazis toward the churches? Why did the German churches by and large fail to take a stand against the Nazi regime?

6. By 1939, most Germans were enthusiastic about the Nazi regime. Discuss this statement.

7. After World War I, in country after country, parliamentary democracy collapsed and authoritarian leaders came to power. Explain.

8. How did the United States, Britain, and France try to cope with the Great Depression?

9. What factors contributed to the mood of pessimism in the period after World War I?

10. Better than any other novelist of his time, Franz Kafka grasped the dilemma of the modern age. Discuss this statement. Do his insights still apply?

11. In *The Magic Mountain*, Thomas Mann reflected on the decom-position of bourgeois European civilization. Discuss this statement.

12. In what ways were both Dada and

surrealism an expression of the times?

13. Why were many intellectuals attracted to communism in the 1930s?

14. What did Ortega y Gasset mean by the "mass-man"? What dangers did the mass-man present?

15. Why did Julien Benda entitle his book *The Treason of the Intellectuals*?

16. What was Ernst Cassirer's attitude toward the Enlightenment? How did he interpret Nazism?

17. What were some of the conditions that gave rise to existentialism? What are the basic principles of existentialism?

❖ CHAPTER 21

World War II: Western Civilization in the Balance

$\mathcal{F}$rom the early days of his political career, Hitler dreamed of forging a vast German empire in central and eastern Europe. He believed that only by waging a war of conquest against Russia could the German nation gain the living space and security it required and, as a superior race, deserved. War was an essential component of National Socialist ideology, and it accorded with Hitler's temperament. For the former corporal from the trenches, the Great War had never ended. Hitler aspired to political power because he wanted to mobilize the material and human resources of the German nation for war and conquest.

Although historians may debate the question of responsibility for World War I, few would deny that World War II was Hitler's war: "It appears to be an almost incontrovertible fact that the Second World War was brought on by the actions of the Hitler government, that these actions were the expression of a policy laid down well in advance in *Mein Kampf,* and that this war could have been averted up until the last moment if the German government had so wished."[1] Western statesmen had sufficient warning that Hitler was a threat to peace and to the essential values of Western civilization, but they failed to rally their people and take a stand until Germany had greatly increased its capacity to wage aggressive war. ❖

The Road to War

After consolidating his power and mobilizing the nation, Hitler moved to implement his foreign policy objectives: the destruction of the Versailles treaty, the conquest and colonization of eastern Europe, and the domination and exploitation of racial inferiors. In foreign affairs, Hitler demonstrated the same blend of opportunism and singleness of purpose that had brought him to power. Here, too, he made use of propaganda to undermine his opponents' will to resist. The Nazi propaganda machine, which had effectively won the minds of the German people, became an instrument of foreign policy. To promote social and political disorientation in other lands, the Nazis propagated anti-Semitism worldwide. Nazi propagandists also tried to draw international support for Hitler as Europe's best defense against the Soviet Union and Bolshevism.

British and French Foreign Policies

As Hitler had anticipated, the British and the French backed down when faced with his violations of the Versailles treaty and threats of war. Haunted by the memory of World War I, Britain and France went to great lengths to avoid another catastrophe—a policy that had the overwhelming support of public opinion. Because Britain believed that Germany had been treated too severely by the Versailles treaty and knew that its own military forces were woefully unprepared for war, from 1933 to 1938 the British were amenable to making concessions to Hitler. Although France had the strongest army on the Continent, it was prepared to fight only a defensive war—the reverse of its World War I strategy. France built immense fortifications, called the Maginot Line, to protect its borders from a German invasion, but it lacked a mobile striking force that could punish an aggressive Germany. The United States, concerned with the problems of the Great Depression and standing aloof from Europe's troubles, did nothing to strengthen the resolve of France and Britain. Since both France and Britain feared and mistrusted the Soviet Union, the grand alliance of World War I was not renewed. There was an added factor: suffering from a failure of leadership and a political and economic unrest that eroded national unity, France was experiencing a decline in morale and a loss of nerve. It consistently turned to Britain for direction.

British statesmen championed a policy of appeasement: giving in to Germany in the hope that a satisfied Hitler would not drag Europe through another world war. British policy rested on the disastrous illusion that Hitler, like his Weimar predecessors, sought peaceful revision of the Versailles treaty and that he could be contained through concessions. Accepting the view that Nazi propaganda cleverly propagated and exploited, some British appeasers also regarded Hitler as a defender of European civilization and the capitalist economic order against Soviet communism. Appeasement, which in the end was capitulation to blackmail, failed. Germany grew stronger and the German people more devoted to the fuehrer. Hitler did not moderate his ambitions, and the appeasers did not avert war.

Breakdown of Peace

To realize his foreign policy aims, Hitler required a formidable military machine. Germany must rearm. The Treaty of Versailles had limited the size of the German army to a hundred thousand volunteers; restricted the navy's size; forbidden the production of military aircraft, heavy artillery, and tanks; and disbanded the general staff. In March 1935, Hitler declared that Germany was no longer bound by the Versailles treaty. Germany would restore

Chronology 21.1 ❖ World War II

1931	Japan invades Manchuria
March 1935	Hitler announces German rearmament
October 1935	Italy invades Ethiopia
1936–1939	Spanish Civil War
March 7, 1936	Germany remilitarizes the Rhineland
July 1937	Japan invades China
March 13, 1938	Anschluss with Austria, which becomes a German province
September 1938	Munich Agreement: Germany's annexation of Sudetenland is approved by Britain and France
March 1939	Germany invades Czechoslovakia
April 1939	Italy invades Albania
August 23, 1939	Nonagression pact between Germany and Russia
September 1 and 3, 1939	Germany invades Poland; Britain and France declare war
September 27, 1939	Poland surrenders
April 1940	Germany attacks Denmark and Norway
May 10, 1940	Germany invades Belgium, Holland, and Luxembourg
June 22, 1940	France surrenders
August–September 1940	Battle of Britain
June 22, 1941	Germany launches offensive against Russia
December 7, 1941	Japan attacks Pearl Habor: United States enters the war against Japan and Germany
1942	The tide of battle turns in the Allies' favor: Midway (Pacific Ocean), Stalingrad (Soviet Union), and El Alamein (northern Africa)
September 1943	Italy surrenders to Allies, following invasion
June 6, 1944	D-Day: Allies land in Normandy, France
May 7, 1945	Germany surrenders unconditionally
August 1945	United States drops atomic bombs on Hiroshima and Nagasaki; Soviet Union invades Manchuria; Japan surrenders

conscription, build an air force (which it had been doing secretly), and strengthen its navy. France and Britain offered no resistance.

A decisive event in the breakdown of peace was Italy's invasion of Ethiopia in October 1935. The League of Nations called for economic sanctions against Italy, and most League members restricted trade with the aggressor. But Italy continued to receive oil, particularly from American suppliers, and neither Britain nor France sought to restrain Italy. Mussolini's subjugation of Ethiopia discredited the League of Nations, which had already been weakened by its failure to deal effectively with Japan's invasion of the mineral-rich Chinese province of Manchuria in 1931. The fall of Ethiopia, like that of Manchuria, evidenced the League's reluctance to check aggression with force.

Remilitarization of the Rhineland   On March 7, 1936, Hitler marched troops into the Rhineland, violating the Versailles treaty, which called for the demilitarization of these German border lands. German generals had cautioned Hitler that such a move would provoke a French invasion of Germany, which the German army could not repulse. But Hitler gambled that France and Britain, lacking the will to fight, would take no action.

Hitler had assessed the Anglo-French mood correctly. The remilitarization of the Rhineland did not greatly alarm Britain. After all, Hitler was not expanding Germany's borders but only sending soldiers to its frontier. Such a move, reasoned British officials, did not warrant risking a war, and France would not act alone. Moreover, the French general staff overestimated German military strength and thought only of defending French soil from a German attack, not of initiating a strike against Germany.

Spanish Civil War   The Spanish Civil War of 1936–1939 was another victory for fascism. Nazi Germany and Fascist Italy aided Franco (see page 566); the Soviet Union supplied the Spanish republic. By October 1937, some sixty thousand Italian "volunteers" were fighting in Spain. Hitler sent between five thousand and six thousand men, as well as hundreds of planes, which proved decisive in winning the war. By comparison, the Soviet Union's aid was meager.

Without considerable help from France, the Spanish republic was doomed, but Prime Minister Léon Blum feared that French intervention might lead to war with Germany. Moreover, supplying the republic would have dangerous consequences at home because French rightists were sympathetic to Franco's conservative-clerical authoritarianism. In 1939, the republic fell, and Franco established a dictatorship. The Spanish Civil War provided Germany with an opportunity to test weapons and pilots and demonstrated again that France and Britain lacked the determination to fight fascism.

Anschluss with Austria   One of Hitler's aims was incorporation of Austria into the Third Reich, but the Treaty of Versailles had expressly prohibited the union (Anschluss) of the two German-speaking countries. In March 1938, under the pretext of preventing violence, Hitler ordered his troops into

Austria, which—with the enthusiastic support of the Austrians—was made a province of the German Reich.

Sudetenland, Munich, Prague   Hitler obtained Austria merely by threatening to use force. Another threat would give him the Sudetenland of Czechoslovakia. Of the 3.5 million people living in the Sudetenland, some 2.8 million were ethnic Germans. Encouraged and instructed by Germany, the Sudeten Germans, led by Konrad Henlein, shrilly denounced the Czech government for "persecuting" its German minority and depriving it of its right to self-determination. The Sudeten Germans agitated for local autonomy and the right to profess the National Socialist ideology. Behind this demand was the goal of German annexation of the Sudetenland.

While negotiations between the Sudeten Germans and the Czech government proceeded, Hitler's propaganda machine accused the Czechs of hideous crimes against the German minority and warned of retribution. Hitler also ordered his generals to prepare for an invasion of Czechoslovakia. Fighting between Czechs and Sudeten Germans heightened the tensions. Seeking to preserve peace, Prime Minister Neville Chamberlain (1869–1940) of Britain offered to confer with Hitler, who then extended an invitation.

Britain was in a somewhat different position than France regarding Czechoslovakia—the only democracy in eastern Europe. In 1924, France and Czechoslovakia had concluded an agreement of mutual assistance in the event that either was attacked by Germany. Czechoslovakia had a similar agreement with Russia, but with the provision that Russian assistance depended on France first fulfilling the terms of its agreement. Britain had no commitment to Czechoslovakia. Swallowing Hitler's propaganda, some British officials believed that the Sudeten Germans were indeed a suppressed minority, entitled to self-determination, and that the Sudetenland, like Austria, was not worth a war that could destroy Western civilization. Hitler, they said, only wanted to incorporate Germans living outside Germany; he was only carrying the principle of self-determination to its logical conclusion. Once these Germans lived under the German flag, argued these British officials, Hitler would be satisfied. In any case, Britain's failure to rearm between 1933 and 1938 weakened its position. The British chiefs of staff believed that the nation was not prepared to fight and that it was necessary to sacrifice Czechoslovakia to buy time.

Czechoslovakia's fate was decided at the Munich Conference (September 1938), attended by Chamberlain, Hitler, Mussolini, and Prime Minister Édouard Daladier (1884–1970) of France. The Munich Pact gave the Sudetenland to Germany. Both Chamberlain and Daladier were showered with praise by the people of Britain and France for keeping the peace.

Chamberlain's critics have insisted that the Munich agreement was an enormous blunder and tragedy. Chamberlain, they say, was a fool to believe that Hitler, who sought domination over Europe, could be bought off with the Sudetenland. Hitler regarded concessions by Britain and France as signs of

The Munich Conference.   Hitler and England's Prime Minister Neville Chamberlain at a fateful moment in history. Chamberlain was lauded as a keeper of the peace immediately after the Munich conference. However, Hitler used the following months to undermine the territorial integrity of Czechoslovakia. With the end of Czech independence, Hitler's intent to dominate Europe became apparent. (*Hulton Deutsch Collection*)

weakness; they only increased his appetite for more territory. Furthermore, argue the critics, it would have been better to fight Hitler in 1938 than a year later, when war actually did break out. To be sure, in the year following the Munich agreement, Britain increased its military arsenal, but so did Germany, which built submarines and heavy tanks, strengthened western border defenses, and trained more pilots. The Czechs had a sizable number of good tanks, and the Czech people were willing to fight to preserve their nation's territorial integrity. While the main elements of the German army were battling the Czechs, the French, who could mobilize a hundred divisions, could have broken through the German West Wall, which was defended by only five regular and four reserve divisions; then they could have invaded the Rhineland and devastated German industrial centers in the Ruhr.

After the annexation of the Sudetenland, Hitler plotted to crush Czechoslovakia out of existence. He encouraged the Slovak minority in Czechoslovakia, led by a fascist priest, Josef Tiso, to demand complete separation. On the pretext of protecting the Slovak people's right of self-determination, Hitler ordered his troops to enter Prague. In March 1939, Czech independence ended.

The destruction of Czechoslovakia was a different matter than the remilitarization of the Rhineland, the Anschluss with Austria, and the annexation of the Sudetenland. In all these previous cases, Hitler could claim the right of self-determination, Woodrow Wilson's grand principle. However, the occupation of Prague and the end of Czech independence showed that Hitler really sought European hegemony. Outraged statesmen now demanded that the fuehrer be deterred from further aggression.

Poland   On May 22, 1939, Hitler and Mussolini entered into the Pact of Steel, promising mutual aid in the event of war. The following day, Hitler told his officers that Germany's real goal was the destruction of Poland. "Danzig is not the objective. It is a matter of expanding our living space in the east, of making our food supplies secure. . . . There is therefore no question of sparing Poland, and the decision remains to attack Poland at the first suitable opportunity."[2]

Britain, France, and the Soviet Union had been engaged in negotiations since April. The Soviet Union wanted a mutual assistance pact, including joint military planning, and demanded bases in Poland and Romania in preparation for a German attack. Britain was reluctant to endorse these demands, fearing that a mutual assistance pact with Russia might cause Hitler to embark on a mad adventure that would drag Britain into war. Moreover, Poland would not allow Russian troops on its soil, fearing Russian expansion.

At the same time, Russia was conducting secret talks with Nazi Germany. Unlike the Allies, Germany could tempt Stalin with territory that would serve as a buffer between Germany and Russia. Besides, a treaty with Germany would give Russia time to strengthen its armed forces. On August 23, 1939, the two totalitarian states signed a nonaggression pact, stunning the world. A secret section of the pact called for the partition of Poland between Russia and Germany and Russian control over Lithuania, Latvia, and Estonia. By signing such an agreement with his enemy, Hitler had pulled off an extraordinary diplomatic coup: he blocked the Soviet Union, Britain, and France from duplicating their World War I alliance against Germany. The Nazi-Soviet Pact was the green light for an invasion of Poland, and at dawn on September 1, 1939, German troops crossed the frontier. When Germany did not respond to their demand for a halt to the invasion, Britain and France declared war.

The Nazi Blitzkrieg

Germany struck at Poland with speed and power. The German air force, the *Luftwaffe,* destroyed Polish planes on the ground, attacked tanks, pounded defense networks, and bombed Warsaw, terrorizing the population. Tanks opened up breaches in the Polish defenses, and mechanized columns overran the foot-marching Polish army, trapping large numbers of soldiers. The Polish high command could not cope with the incredible speed and coordination of German air and ground attacks. By September 8, the Germans had advanced to the outskirts of Warsaw. On September 17, Soviet troops invaded Poland from the east. On September 27, Poland surrendered. In less than a month, the Nazi *blitzkrieg* (lightning war) had vanquished Poland.

The Fall of France

For Hitler, the conquest of Poland was only the prelude to a German empire stretching from the Atlantic to the Urals. When weather conditions were right, he would unleash a great offensive in the west. In early April 1940, the Germans struck at Denmark and Norway. Denmark surrendered within hours. A British-French force tried to assist the Norwegians, but the landings, badly coordinated and lacking in air support, failed.

On May 10, 1940, Hitler launched his offensive in the west with an invasion of neutral Belgium, Holland, and Luxembourg. On May 14, after the Luftwaffe had bombed Rotterdam, destroying the center of the city and killing many people, the Dutch surrendered. Meeting almost no resistance, German panzer divisions had moved through the narrow mountain passes of Luxembourg and the dense Forest of Ardennes in southern Belgium. Thinking that the Forest of Ardennes could not be penetrated by a major German force, the French had only lightly fortified the western extension of the Maginot Line. But on May 12, German units were on French soil near Sedan. Then the Germans raced across northern France to the sea, which they reached on May 20, cutting the Anglo-French forces in two.

The Germans now sought to surround and annihilate the Allied forces converging on the French seaport of Dunkirk, the last port of escape. But probably fearing that German tanks would lose mobility in the rivers and canals around Dunkirk, Hitler called them off just as they prepared to take the port. Instead, he ordered the Luftwaffe to wipe out the Allied troops, but fog and rain prevented German planes from operating at full strength. While the Luftwaffe bombed the beaches, some 338,000 British and French troops were ferried across the English Channel by destroyers, merchant ships, motorboats, fishing boats, tugboats, and private yachts. Hitler's personal decision to hold back his tanks made the miracle of Dunkirk possible.

Meanwhile, the battle for France was turning into a rout. With authority

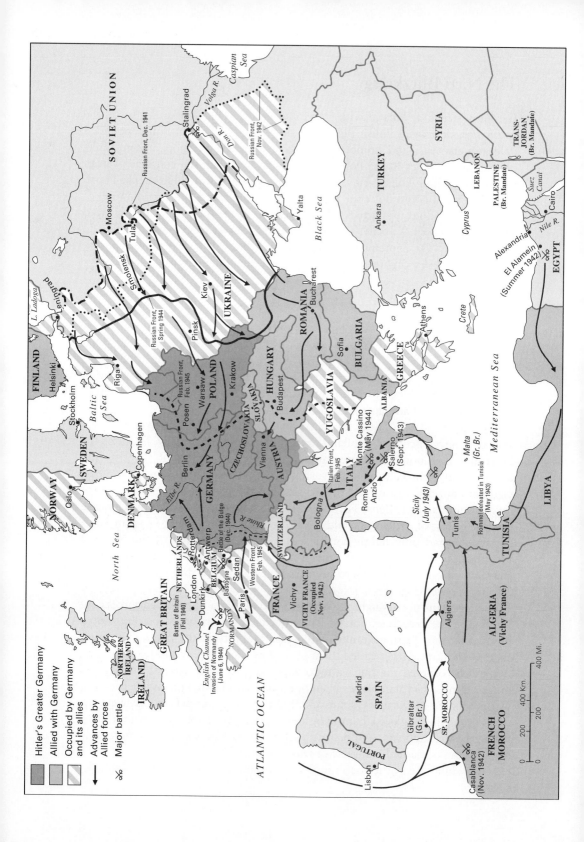

Hitler's Greater Germany

Allied with Germany

Occupied by Germany and its allies

Advances by Allied forces

Major battle

SOVIET UNION

Caspian Sea

Volga R.

Stalingrad

Russian Front, Dec. 1941

Russian Front, Nov. 1942

Don R.

Moscow

Tula

Smolensk

Russian Front, Spring 1944

Yalta

Black Sea

TURKEY

Ankara

SYRIA

TRANS-JORDAN (Br. Mandate)

LEBANON

PALESTINE (Br. Mandate)

Cyprus

Suez Canal

Cairo

Nile R.

EGYPT

Alexandria

El Alamein (Summer 1942)

FINLAND

Helsinki

Leningrad

L. Ladoga

Kiev

Pinsk

UKRAINE

ROMANIA

Bucharest

BULGARIA

Sofia

Crete

Mediterranean Sea

NORWAY

Oslo

SWEDEN

Stockholm

Baltic Sea

Riga

Copenhagen

DENMARK

POLAND

Krakow

Warsaw

Posen

Russian Front, Feb. 1945

HUNGARY

Budapest

SLOVAKIA

CZECHOSLOVAKIA

Vienna

AUSTRIA

YUGOSLAVIA

GREECE

Athens

ALBANIA

Malta (Gr. Br.)

NORTHERN IRELAND

IRELAND

GREAT BRITAIN

London

Battle of Britain (Fall 1940)

North Sea

NETHERLANDS

Rotterdam

Antwerp

Dunkirk

BELGIUM

Bastogne

Battle of the Bulge (Dec. 1944)

Sedan

Western Front, Feb. 1945

Paris

NORMANDY

Invasion of Normandy (June 6, 1944)

English Channel

FRANCE

VICHY FRANCE (Occupied Nov. 1942)

Vichy

SWITZERLAND

Berlin

GERMANY

Elbe R.

Rhine R.

Bologna

Rome

Anzio

Monte Cassino (May 1944)

Italian Front, Feb. 1945

ITALY

Salerno (Sept. 1943)

Sicily (July 1943)

Tunis

Rommel defeated in Tunisia (May 1943)

TUNISIA

LIBYA

ATLANTIC OCEAN

SPAIN

Madrid

PORTUGAL

Lisbon

Gibraltar (Gr. Br.)

SP. MOROCCO

Algiers

ALGERIA (Vichy France)

FRENCH MOROCCO

Casablanca (Nov. 1942)

0   200   400 Km.

0   200   400 Mi.

breaking down, demoralization spreading, and resistance dying, the French cabinet appealed for an armistice. It was signed on June 22, in the same railway car in which Germany had agreed to the armistice ending World War I.

How can the collapse of France be explained? The French had as many planes and tanks as the Germans, but their military leaders, unlike the German command, had not mastered the psychology and technology of motorized warfare. One senses also that there was a loss of will among the French people—the result of internal political disputes, poor leadership, the years of appeasement and lost opportunities, and German propaganda, which depicted Nazism as irresistible and the fuehrer as a man of destiny. It was France's darkest hour.

According to the terms of the armistice, Germany occupied northern France and the coast. The French military was demobilized, and the French government, now located at Vichy, in the south, would collaborate with the German authorities in occupied France. Refusing to recognize defeat, General Charles de Gaulle (1890–1970) escaped to London and organized the Free French forces. The Germans gloried in their revenge; the French wept in their humiliation; and the British gathered their courage, for they now stood alone.

The Battle of Britain

Hitler expected that, after his stunning victories in the west, Britain would make peace. The British, however, continued to reject Hitler's peace overtures, for they envisioned only a bleak future if Hitler dominated the Continent. After the German victory in Norway, Chamberlain's support in the House of Commons had eroded, and he had been replaced by Winston Churchill, who had opposed appeasement. Dynamic, courageous, and eloquent, Churchill had the capacity to stir and lead his people in the struggle against Nazism. "The Battle of Britain is about to begin," Churchill told them. "Upon this battle depends the survival of Christian civilization. . . . if we fail, then . . . all we have known and cared for will sink into the abyss of a new Dark Age."[3]

Finding Britain unwilling to come to terms, Hitler proceeded in earnest with invasion plans. But a successful crossing of the English Channel and the establishment of beachheads on the English coast depended on control of the skies. Marshal Hermann Goering assured Hitler that his Luftwaffe could destroy the British Royal Air Force (RAF), and in early August 1940, the Luftwaffe began massive attacks on British air and naval installations. Virtually every day during the battle of Britain, weather permitting, hundreds of planes fought in the sky above Britain. Convinced that Goering could not fulfill his promise to destroy British air defenses, Hitler called off the invasion. The

◄ **Map 21.1**   World War II: The European Theater

development of radar by British scientists, the skill and courage of British fighter pilots, and the inability of Germany to make up its losses in planes saved Britain in its struggle for survival. With the invasion of Britain called off, the Luftwaffe concentrated on bombing English cities, industrial centers, and ports. Every night for months, the inhabitants of London sought shelter in subways and cellars to escape German bombs, while British planes rose time after time to make the Luftwaffe pay the price. British morale never broke during the "Blitz."

The Invasion of Russia

The obliteration of Bolshevism and the conquest, exploitation, and colonization of Russia by the German master race were cardinal elements of Hitler's ideology. To prevent any interference with the forthcoming invasion of Russia, the Balkan flank had to be secured. On April 6, 1941, the Germans struck at both Greece, where an Italian attack had failed, and Yugoslavia. Yugoslavia was quickly overrun, and Greece, although aided by fifty thousand British, New Zealander, and Australian troops, fell at the end of April.

For the war against Russia, Hitler had assembled a massive force: some 4 million men, 3,300 tanks, and 5,000 planes. In the early hours of June 22, 1941, the Germans launched their offensive over a wide front. Raiding Russian airfields, the Luftwaffe destroyed 1,200 aircraft on the first day. The Germans drove deeply into Russia, cutting up and surrounding the disorganized and unprepared Russian forces. The Russians suffered horrendous losses. In a little more than three months, 2.5 million Russian soldiers had been killed, wounded, or captured and 14,000 tanks destroyed. Describing the war as a crusade to save Europe from "Jewish Bolshevism," German propaganda claimed that victory had been assured.

But there were also disquieting signs for the Nazi invaders. The Russians, who had a proven capacity to endure hardships, fought doggedly and courageously, and the government would not consider capitulation. Russian reserve strength was far greater than the Germans had estimated. Far from its supply lines, the Wehrmacht (German army) was running short of fuel, and trucks and cars had to contend with primitive roads, which turned into seas of mud when the autumn rains came. Early and bitter cold weather hampered the German attempt to capture Moscow. The Germans advanced to within twenty miles of Moscow, but on December 6, a Red Army counterattack forced them to postpone the assault on the Russian capital.

By the end of 1941, Germany had conquered vast regions of Russia but had failed to bring the country to its knees. There would be no repetition of the collapse of France. The Russian campaign demonstrated that the Russian people would make incredible sacrifices for their land and that the Nazis were not invincible.

The Russian Front. Some twenty-five million Russians perished in World War II, many of them the victims of German atrocities. (Soviet Life *from Sovfoto*)

The New Order

By 1942, Germany ruled virtually all of Europe, from the Atlantic to deep into Russia. Some conquered territory was annexed outright; other lands were administered by German officials; in still other countries, the Germans ruled through local officials sympathetic to Nazism or willing to collaborate with the Germans. On this vast empire, Hitler and his henchmen imposed a New Order.

Exploitation and Terror

The Germans systematically looted the countries they conquered, taking gold, art treasures, machinery, and food supplies back to Germany and exploiting the industrial and agricultural potential of non-German lands to aid the German war economy. The Nazis also made slave laborers of conquered peoples. Some seven million people from all over Europe were wrested from their homes and transported to Germany. These forced laborers, particularly the

Russians and Poles, whom Nazi ideology classified as a lower form of humanity, lived in wretched, unheated barracks and were poorly fed and overworked; many died of disease, hunger, and exhaustion.

The Nazis ruled by force and terror. The prison cell, the torture chamber, the firing squad, and the concentration camp symbolized the New Order. In the Polish province annexed to Germany, the Nazis jailed and executed intellectuals and priests, closed all schools and most churches, and forbade Poles to hold professional positions. In the region of Poland administered by German officials, most schools above the fourth grade were shut down. The Germans were especially ruthless toward the Russians. Soviet political officials were immediately executed; many prisoners of war were herded into camps and deliberately starved to death. In all, the Germans took prisoner some 5.5 million Russians, of whom more than 3.5 million perished.

Extermination

Against the Jews of Europe, the Germans waged a war of extermination. The task of imposing the "Final Solution of the Jewish Problem" was given to Himmler's SS. Himmler fulfilled his grisly duties with fanaticism and bureaucratic efficiency. He and the SS believed that they had a holy mission to rid the world of worthless life—a satanic foe that was plotting to destroy Germany. Regarding themselves as idealists who were writing a glorious chapter in the history of Germany, the SS tortured and murdered with immense dedication.

Special squads of the SS—the *Einsatzgruppen,* trained for mass murder—followed on the heels of the German army into Russia. Entering captured villages and cities, they rounded up Jewish men, women, and children, herded them to execution grounds, and slaughtered them with machine-gun and rifle fire. Aided by Ukrainian, Lithuanian, and Latvian auxiliaries, the Einsatzgruppen massacred some two million Russian Jews. To speed up the Final Solution, concentration camps, originally established for political prisoners, were transformed into killing centers, and new ones were built for that purpose. Jews from all over Europe were rounded up, jammed into sealed cattle cars, and shipped to Treblinka, Auschwitz, and other death camps, where they entered another world:

> Corpses were strewn all over the road; bodies were hanging from the barbed wire fence; the sound of shots rang in the air continuously. Blazing flames shot into the sky; a giant smoke cloud ascended about them. Starving, emaciated human skeletons stumbled forward toward us, uttering incoherent sounds. They fell down right in front of our eyes gasping out their last breath.
>
> Here and there a hand tried to reach up, but when this happened an SS man came right away and stepped on it. Those who were merely exhausted were simply thrown on the dead pile. . . . Every

night a truck came by, and all of them, dead or not, were thrown on it and taken to the crematory.[4]

SS doctors quickly inspected the new arrivals—"the freight," as they referred to them. Those unfit for work, including children, were immediately exterminated in gas chambers. Those not gassed faced a living death in the camp, which also included non-Jewish inmates. The SS took sadistic pleasure in humiliating and brutalizing their Jewish victims. When exhausted, starved, diseased, and beaten prisoners became unfit for work, generally within a few months, they were sent to the gas chambers.

Many of the SS were true believers, committed to racist and Social Darwinist fantasies. To realize their vision of ultimate good, they had to destroy the Jews, whom Nazi ideology designated as the source of all evil. Other SS, and their army of collaborators, were simply ordinary people doing their duty as they had been trained to do, following orders the best way they knew how. They were morally indifferent bureaucrats, concerned with techniques and effectiveness, and careerists and functionaries seeking to impress superiors with their ability to get the job done. These people quickly adjusted to the routine of mass murder.

Thus, as Konnilyn G. Feig notes, thousands of German railway workers "treated the Jewish cattle-car transports as a special business problem that they took pride in solving so well."[5] German physicians who selected Jews for the gas chambers were concerned only with the technical problems, and those doctors who performed unspeakable medical experiments on Jews viewed their subjects as laboratory animals. German industrialists who worked Jewish slave laborers to death considered only cost-effectiveness in their operations. So, too, did the firms that built the gas chambers and the furnaces, whose durability and performance they guaranteed.

An eyewitness reports that engineers from Topf and Sons experimented with different combinations of corpses, deciding that "the most economical and fuel-saving procedure would be to burn the bodies of a well-nourished man and an emaciated woman or vice versa together with that of a child, because, as the experiments had established, in this combination, once they had caught fire, the dead would continue to burn without any further coke being required."[6] Rudolf Hoess, the commandant of Auschwitz, who exemplified the bureaucratic mentality, noted that his gas chambers were more efficient than those used at Treblinka because they could accommodate far more people. The Germans were so concerned with efficiency and cost that—to conserve ammunition or gas and not slow down the pace from the time victims were ordered to undress until they were hurried into the gas chambers—toddlers were taken from their mothers and thrown live into burning pits or mass graves.

When the war ended, the SS murderers and those who had assisted them returned to families and jobs, resuming a normal life, free of remorse and untroubled by guilt. "The human ability to normalize the abnormal is

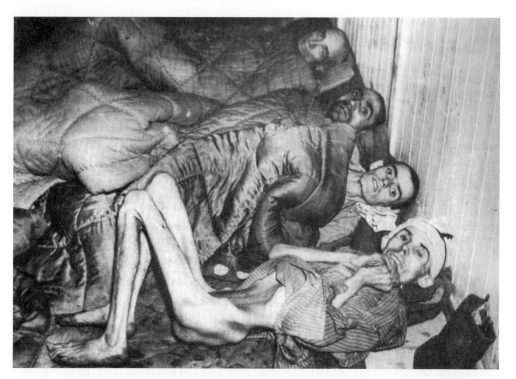

Concentration Camp Survivors.   Thousands of emaciated and diseased inmates of German concentration camps died in the weeks after liberation by the Allies. These camps will forever remain a monument to the capacity of human beings for inhumanity. (© *Topham/The Image Works*)

frightening indeed," observes sociologist Rainer C. Baum.[7] Mass murderers need not be psychopaths. It is a "disturbing psychological truth," states Robert Jay Lifton, that "ordinary people can commit demonic acts."[8]

There have been many massacres during the course of world history. And the Nazis murdered many non-Jews in concentration camps and in reprisal for acts of resistance. What is unique about the Holocaust—the systematic extermination of European Jewry—was the Nazis' determination to murder without exception every single Jew who came within their grasp, and the fanaticism, ingenuity, and cruelty with which they pursued this goal. Despite the protests of the army, the SS murdered Jews whose labor was needed for the war effort, and when Germany's military position was desperate, the SS still diverted military personnel and railway cars to deport Jews to the death camps.

The Holocaust was the grisly fulfillment of Nazi racial theories. Believing that they were cleansing Europe of a lower and dangerous race that threatened the German people, Nazi executioners performed their evil work with dedication and resourcefulness, with precision and moral indifference—a gruesome testament to human irrationality and wickedness. Using the technology and bureaucracy of a modern state, the Germans killed approximately 6 million Jews—*two-thirds* of the Jewish population of Europe. Some 1.5 million of the murdered were children; almost 90 percent of Jewish children in German-occupied lands perished. Tens of thousands of entire families were wiped out without a trace. Centuries-old Jewish community life vanished, never to be restored. Burned into the soul of the Jewish people was a wound that could never entirely heal. Written into the history of Western civilization was an episode that would forever cast doubt on the Enlightenment conception of human goodness, rationality, and the progress of civilization.

Resistance

Each occupied country had its collaborators, who welcomed the demise of democracy, saw Hitler as Europe's best defense against communism, and profited from the sale of war materiel. Each country also produced a resistance movement, which grew stronger as Nazi barbarism became more visible and the prospects of a German defeat more likely. The Nazis retaliated by torturing and executing captured resistance fighters and killing hostages—generally fifty for every German killed.

In western Europe, the resistance rescued downed Allied airmen, radioed military intelligence to Britain, and sabotaged German installations. Norwegians blew up the German stock of heavy water needed for atomic research. The Danish underground sabotaged railways and smuggled into neutral Sweden almost all of Denmark's eight thousand Jews just before they were to be deported to the death camps. After the Allies landed on the coast of France in June 1944, the French resistance delayed the movement of German reinforcements and liberated sections of the country.

In eastern Europe, resistance took the form of guerrilla warfare, as well as sabotage. In August 1944, with Soviet forces approaching Warsaw, the Poles staged a full-scale revolt against the German occupiers. The Poles appealed to the Soviets, camped ten miles away, for help. Thinking about a future Russian-dominated Poland, the Soviets did not move. After sixty-three days of street fighting, remnants of the Polish underground surrendered, and the Germans destroyed what was left of Warsaw. In the Soviet Union, Russian partisans numbered several hundred thousand men and women. Operating behind the German lines, they sabotaged railways, destroyed trucks, and killed scores of thousands of German soldiers in hit-and-run attacks. In Yugoslavia, the mountains and forests provided excellent terrain for guerrilla warfare. The leading Yugoslav resistance army was headed by Josip Broz (1892–1980), better known as Tito. Moscow-trained, intelligent, and courageous, Tito organized his partisans into a disciplined fighting force, which tied down a huge German army and ultimately liberated the country from German rule.

Italy and Germany also had resistance movements. After the Allies landed in Italy in 1943, bands of Italian partisans helped to liberate Italy from fascism and the German occupation. In Germany, army officers plotted to assassinate the fuehrer. On July 20, 1944, Colonel Claus von Stauffenberg planted a bomb at a staff conference attended by Hitler, but the fuehrer escaped serious injury. In retaliation, some five thousand suspected anti-Nazis were tortured and executed in an exceptionally barbarous fashion.

The Turn of the Tide

While Germany was subduing Europe, its ally, Japan, was extending its dominion over parts of Asia. Seeking raw materials and secure markets for Japanese goods and driven by a xenophobic nationalism, Japan in 1931 had attacked Manchuria in northern China. Quickly overrunning the province, the Japanese established the puppet state of Manchukuo in 1932. After a period of truce, the war against China was renewed in July 1937. Japan captured leading cities, including China's principal seaports, and inflicted heavy casualties on the poorly organized Chinese forces, obliging the government of Jiang Jieshi (Chiang Kai-shek) to withdraw to Chungking in the interior.

War in the Pacific

In 1940, after the defeat of France and with Britain standing alone against Nazi Germany, Japan eyed Southeast Asia—French Indochina, British Burma and Malaya, and the Dutch East Indies. From these lands, Japan planned to obtain the oil, rubber, and tin vitally needed by Japanese industry and enough rice to feed the nation. Japan hoped that a quick strike against the American fleet in the Pacific would give it time to enlarge and consolidate its empire. On December 7, 1941, the Japanese struck with carrier-based planes at Pearl Harbor in Hawaii. Taken by surprise, the Americans suffered a total defeat: the attackers sank 17 ships, including 7 of the 8 battleships; destroyed 188 airplanes and damaged 159 others; and killed 2,403 men. The Japanese lost only 29 planes. After the attack on Pearl Harbor, Germany declared war on the United States. Now the immense American industrial capacity could be put to work against the Axis powers—Germany, Italy, and Japan.

By the spring of 1942, the Axis powers held the upper hand. The Japanese empire included the coast of China, Indochina, Thailand, Burma, Malaya, the Dutch East Indies, the Philippines, and other islands in the Pacific. Germany controlled Europe almost to Moscow. When the year ended, however, the Allies seemed assured of victory. Three decisive battles—Midway, Stalingrad, and El Alamein—reversed the tide of war.

In June 1942, the main body of the Japanese fleet headed for Midway,

Map 21.2 World War II: The Pacific Theater

eleven hundred miles northwest of Pearl Harbor; another section sailed toward the Aleutian Islands, in an attempt to divide the American fleet. But the Americans had broken the Japanese naval code and were aware of the Japanese plan. On June 4, 1942, the two navies fought a strange naval battle; it was waged entirely by carrier-based planes, for the fleets were too far from each other to use their big guns. American pilots destroyed four Japanese aircraft carriers stacked with planes. The battle of Midway cost Japan the initiative. With American industrial production accelerating, the opportunity for a Japanese victory had passed.

Defeat of the Axis Powers

After being stymied at the outskirts of Moscow in December 1941, the Germans renewed their offensive in the spring and summer of 1942. Hitler's goal was Stalingrad, the great industrial center located on the Volga River; control of Stalingrad would give Germany command of vital rail transportation. The battle of Stalingrad was an epic struggle, in which Russian soldiers and civilians fought for every building and street of their city. The remnants of the German Sixth Army surrendered in February 1943. Some 260,000 German soldiers had perished in the battle of Stalingrad, and another 110,000 were taken prisoner.

In January 1941, the British were routing the Italians in northern Africa. Hitler assigned General Erwin Rommel (1891–1944) to halt the British advance. Rommel drove the British out of Libya and, with strong reinforcements, might have taken Egypt and the Suez Canal. But Hitler's concern was with seizing Yugoslavia and Greece and preparing for the invasion of Russia. Early in 1942, Rommel resumed his advance, intending to conquer Egypt. The British Eighth Army, commanded by General Bernard L. Montgomery, stopped him at the battle of El Alamein in October 1942. The victory of El Alamein was followed by an Anglo-American invasion of northwest Africa in November 1942. By May 1943, the Germans and Italians were defeated in northern Africa.

After securing northern Africa, the Allies, seeking complete control of the Mediterranean, invaded Sicily in July 1943 and quickly conquered the island. Mussolini's fellow Fascist leaders turned against him, and the king dismissed him as prime minister. In September, the new government surrendered to the Allies, and in the following month, Italy declared war on Germany. Italian partisans—their number would grow to three hundred thousand—resisted the occupying German troops, who were determined to hold on to central and northern Italy. At the same time, the Allies fought their way up the peninsula. Captured by partisans, Mussolini was executed (April 28, 1945), and his dead body, hanging upside down, was publicly displayed.

On June 6, 1944, D-Day, the Allies landed on the beaches of Normandy in France. They had assembled a massive force for the invasion: two million men

Hiroshima After the Atomic Bomb.   The mass destruction of Hiroshima ushered in a new age. Nuclear weapons gave humanity the capacity to destroy civilization. (*The Bettmann Archive*)

and five thousand vessels. The success of D-Day depended on securing the beaches and marching inland, which the Allies did despite stubborn German resistance on some beaches. By the end of July, the Allies had built up their strength in France to a million and a half. In the middle of August, Paris rose up against the German occupiers and was soon liberated.

As winter approached, the situation looked hopeless for Germany. Brussels and Antwerp fell to the Allies; Allied bombers were striking German factories and mass-bombing German cities in terror raids that took a horrendous toll of life. Desperate, Hitler made one last gamble. In mid-December 1944, he launched an offensive to split the Allied forces and regain the vital port of Antwerp. The Allies were taken by surprise in the battle of the Bulge, but a heroic defense by the Americans at Bastogne helped stop the German offensive. While their allies were advancing in the west, the Russians were continuing their drive in the east, advancing into the Baltic states, Poland, and Hungary. By February 1945, they stood within one hundred miles of Berlin.

By April 1945, British, American, and Russian troops were penetrating into Germany from east and west. From his underground bunker near the chancellery in Berlin, Hitler, physically exhausted and emotionally unhinged, engaged in wild fantasies about new German victories. On April 30, 1945, with the Russians only blocks away, the fuehrer took his own life. On May 7, 1945, a demoralized and devastated Germany surrendered unconditionally.

In the Pacific war, after the victory at Midway in June 1942, American forces attacked strategic islands held by Japan. American troops had to battle their way up beaches and through jungles tenaciously defended by Japanese soldiers, who believed that death was preferable to the disgrace of surrender. In March 1945, twenty-one thousand Japanese perished on Iwo Jima; another hundred thousand died on Okinawa in April 1945 as they contested for every inch of the island.

On August 6, 1945, the United States dropped an atomic bomb on Hiroshima, killing more than seventy-eight thousand people and demolishing 60 percent of the city. President Harry S Truman said that he ordered the atomic attack to avoid an American invasion of the Japanese homeland, which would have cost hundreds of thousands of lives. Truman's decision has aroused considerable debate. Some analysts maintain that dropping the bomb was unnecessary. They say that Japan, deprived of oil, rice, and other essentials by an American naval blockade and defenseless against unrelenting aerial bombardments, was close to surrender and had indicated as much. Because the Soviet Union was about to enter the conflict against Japan, it has been suggested that Truman wanted to end the war immediately, thus depriving the U.S.S.R. of an opportunity to extend its influence in East Asia. On August 8, Russia did enter the war against Japan, invading Manchuria. After a second atomic bomb was dropped on Nagasaki on August 9, the Japanese asked for peace.

The Legacy of World War II

World War II was the most destructive war in history. Estimates of the number of dead range as high as fifty million, including some twenty-five million Russians, who sacrificed more than the other participants in both population and material resources. The war produced a vast migration of peoples unparalleled in modern European history. The Soviet Union annexed the Baltic lands of Latvia, Lithuania, and Estonia, forcibly deporting many of the native inhabitants into central Russia. The bulk of East Prussia was taken over by Poland, and Russia annexed the northeastern portion. Millions of Germans fled or were forced out of Prussia and regions of Czechoslovakia, Romania, Yugoslavia, and Hungary, places where their ancestors had lived for centuries. Material costs were staggering. Everywhere cities were in rubble; bridges, railway systems, waterways, and harbors destroyed; farmlands laid waste; livestock killed; coal mines wrecked. Homeless and hungry people wandered the streets and roads. Europe faced the gigantic task of rebuilding. Yet Europe did recover from this material blight, and with astonishing speed.

The war produced a shift in power arrangements. The United States and the Soviet Union emerged as the two most powerful states in the world. The traditional Great Powers—Britain, France, and Germany—were now dwarfed by these *superpowers*. The United States had the atomic bomb and immense industrial might; the Soviet Union had the largest army in the world and was extending its dominion over eastern Europe. With Germany defeated, the principal incentive for Soviet-American cooperation had evaporated.

After World War I, nationalist passions had intensified. After World War II, western Europeans progressed toward unity. The Hitler years had convinced many Europeans of the dangers inherent in extreme nationalism, and fear of the Soviet Union prodded them toward greater cooperation.

World War II accelerated the disintegration of Europe's overseas empires. The European states could hardly justify ruling over Africans and Asians after they had fought to liberate European lands from German imperialism. Nor could they ask their people, exhausted by the Hitler years and concentrating all their energies on reconstruction, to fight new wars against Africans and Asians pressing for independence. In the years just after the war, Great Britain surrendered India, France lost Lebanon and Syria, and the Dutch departed from Indonesia. In the 1950s and 1960s, virtually every colonial territory gained independence. Where a colonial power resisted granting the colony independence, the price was bloodshed.

The consciousness of Europe, already profoundly damaged by World War I, was again grievously wounded. Nazi racial theories showed that even in an age of advanced science the mind remains attracted to irrational beliefs and mythical imagery; Nazi atrocities proved that people will torture and kill with religious zeal and machinelike indifference. The Nazi assault on reason and freedom demonstrated anew the fragility of Western civilization.

This assault would forever cast doubt on the Enlightenment conception of human goodness, secular rationality, and the progress of civilization through advances in science and technology. It bears out Walter Lippmann's contention that "men have been barbarians much longer than they have been civilized. They are only precariously civilized, and within us there is the propensity, persistent as the force of gravity, to revert under stress and strain, or under temptation, to our first natures."[9] Both the Christian and the Enlightenment traditions had failed the West.

Some intellectuals, shocked by the irrationality and horrors of the Hitler era, drifted into despair. To these thinkers, life was absurd, without meaning; human beings could neither comprehend nor control it. In 1945, only the naive could have faith in continuous progress or believe in the essential goodness of the individual. The future envisioned by the philosophes seemed more distant than ever. Nevertheless, this profound disillusionment was tempered by hope. Democracy had, in fact, prevailed over Nazi totalitarianism and terror. Perhaps, then, democratic institutions and values would spread throughout the globe, and the newly established United Nations would promote world peace.

Notes

1. Pierre Renouvin, *World War II and Its Origins* (New York: Harper & Row, 1969), p. 167.
2. *Documents on German Foreign Policy, 1918–1945,* vol. 6 (London: Her Majesty's Stationery Office, 1956), series D, no. 433.
3. Winston S. Churchill, *The Second World War: Their Finest Hour* (Boston: Houghton Mifflin, 1949), 2:225–226.
4. Judith Sternberg Newman, *In the Hell of Auschwitz* (New York: Exposition, 1964), p. 18.
5. Konnilyn G. Feig, *Hitler's Death Camps* (New York: Holmes & Meier, 1979), p. 37.
6. Quoted in Steven T. Katz, "Technology and Genocide: Technology as a 'Form of Life,'" in *Echoes from the Holocaust,* eds. Alan Rosenberg and Gerald E. Meyers (Philadelphia: Temple University Press, 1988), p. 281.
7. Rainer C. Baum, "Holocaust: Moral Indifference as the Form of Modern Evil," in *Echoes from the Holocaust,* eds. Rosenberg and Meyers, p. 83.
8. Robert Jay Lifton, *The Nazi Doctors* (New York: Basic Books, 1968), p. 5.
9. Walter Lippmann, *The Public Philosophy* (Boston: Little Brown, 1955), p. 86.

Suggested Reading

Adams, R. J. Q., *British Politics and Foreign Policy in the Age of Appeasement, 1935–1939* (1993). The nature, purpose, and meaning of appeasement.

Ambrose, Stephen E., *D-Day* (1994). Based on oral histories from people who were there.

Bartow, Omer, *Hitler's Army* (1992). Excellent material on the indoctrination of the German soldier.

Bauer, Yehuda, *A History of the Holocaust* (1982). An authoritative study.

Baumont, Maurice, *The Origins of the Second World War* (1978). A brief work by a distinguished French scholar.

Bell, P. M. H., *The Origins of the Second World War in Europe* (1986). An intelligent survey.

Calvocoressi, Peter, and Guy Wint, *Total War* (1972). A good account of World War II.

Hildebrand, Klaus, *The Foreign Policy of the Third Reich* (1973). A brief assessment of Nazi foreign policy.

Keegan, John, *The Second World War* (1989). A recent survey by a leading military historian.

Marrus, Michael R., *The Holocaust in History* (1987). An excellent summary of key issues and problems.

Michel, Henri, *The Second World War,* 2 vols. (1975). Translation of an important study by a prominent French historian.

Remak, Joachim, *The Origins of the Second World War* (1976). A useful essay, followed by documents.

Wiesel, Elie, *Night* (1960). A moving personal record of the Holocaust.

Review Questions

1. What were Hitler's foreign policy aims?
2. Why did Britain and France practice a policy of appeasement?
3. Discuss the significance of each of the following: Italy's invasion of Ethiopia (1935); Germany's remilitarization of the Rhineland (1936); the Spanish Civil War (1936–1939); Germany's union with

Austria (1938); the occupation of Prague (1939); and the Nazi-Soviet Pact (1939).

4. What factors made possible the quick fall of France?

5. Describe the New Order that the Nazis established in Europe.

6. In your opinion, what is the meaning of the Holocaust for Western civilization? For Jews? For Christians? For Germans?

7. Discuss the significance of each of the following battles: Midway (1942), Stalingrad (1942–43), El Alamein (1942), and D-Day (1944).

8. What is the legacy of World War II?

PART SIX

The Contemporary World

Statue of Liberty in Tiananmen Square, 1989 (*AP/Wide World Photos*)

	POLITICS AND SOCIETY	THOUGHT AND CULTURE
1940	Yalta agreement (1945) United Nations established (1945) Marshall Plan for recovery of Europe (1947) Cold war starts (1947) State of Israel established (1948) North Atlantic Treaty Organization (NATO) established (1949) Division of Germany (1949) Triumph of communism in China (1949)	Wiener, *Cybernetics* (1948) Orwell, *1984* (1949) de Beauvoir, *The Second Sex* (1949)
1950	Korean War (1950–1953) French defeated in Indochina (1954) European Economic Community (EEC) established (1957) Sputnik launched: space age begins (1957)	Camus, *The Rebel* (1951) Discovery of DNA by Crick and Watson (1951–1953) Ellul, *The Technological Society* (1954) Chomsky, *Syntactic Structures* (1957) Snow, *The Two Cultures and the Scientific Revolution* (1959) Foucault, *Madness and Civilization* (1961)
1960	Berlin Wall built (1961) Cuban missile crisis (1962) Vietnam War (1963–1973) Great Proletarian Cultural Revolution in China (1966–76)	Fanon, *The Wretched of the Earth* (1961) Pope John XXIII, *Pacem in Terris* (Peace on Earth) (1963) McLuhan, *Understanding Media* (1964) Levi-Strauss, *The Savage Mind* (1966)
1970	Détente in East-West relations (1970s) Helsinki Agreements (1975) Soviet Union invades Afghanistan (1979)	Rawls, *A Theory of Justice* (1971) Solzhenitsyn, *The Gulag Archipelago* (1974–1978)
1980	Iran-Iraq War (1980–1988) Gorbachev becomes leader of Soviet Union (1985) Explosion at Chernobyl nuclear power plant (1986) Soviet Union withdraws from Afghanistan (1988) Peaceful overthrow of communist governments in Eastern Europe (1989) Berlin Wall demolished (1989)	Gorbachev, *Perestroika* (1987)
1990	Reunification of Germany (1990) Charter of Paris for a New Europe (1990) Persian Gulf War (1991) Failed coup against Gorbachev ends rule of Soviet Communist party (1991)	

❖ CHAPTER 22

The West in a Global Age

$\mathcal{A}$ t the end of World War II, Winston Churchill described Europe as "a rubble heap, a charnel house, a breeding ground for pestilence and hate."[1] Millions had perished. Industry, transportation, and communication had come to a virtual standstill; bridges, canals, dikes, and farmlands were ruined. Ragged, worn people picked among the rubble and bartered their valuables for food.

Europe was politically cut in half, for in pursuing Hitler's armies, the Soviet troops had overrun eastern Europe and penetrated into the heart of Germany. Europe's future now depended on two countries, the United States and the Soviet Union, which soon became embroiled in a bitter cold war. The Soviet Union, exhausted by World War II and anxious about security, imposed its grim tradition of dictatorship on eastern Europe, while the United States, virtually unharmed by the war, brought the boon of its wealth and power to help rebuild western Europe. Henceforth, the United States stood out as the heir to and guardian of the Western tradition, a political giant come into its own. ❖

The Cold War

The cold war (the American financier Bernard Baruch coined the phrase in 1947) stemmed from the divergent historical experiences and the incompatible political ambitions of the United States and the Soviet Union, which clashed head-on as the new global order began to take shape. During the war, the basic disparities between the West and the U.S.S.R. had been glossed over, but once the common danger receded, the differences between political institutions and ideologies pushed again to the fore.

As the Red Army moved through eastern Europe, the fate of the peoples of that region hung in the balance. The Yalta agreement of February 1945, signed by Roosevelt, Churchill, and Stalin on Stalin's home ground in the Crimean peninsula, turned the prevailing military balance of power into a political settlement. The American bargaining position at Yalta was weakened by the expectation that Soviet help would be needed for victory over Japan. Soviet promises of free elections in Soviet-dominated eastern Europe were not kept.

Map 22.1   Western Europe After 1945

Ever worried about the security of Russia's western boundaries, Stalin sought to incorporate the countries of eastern Europe into a buffer zone for protection against Western attack. The Western allies, advancing from the Atlantic against Hitler's armies, were in no position to stop Stalin from doing as he wished. As the Red Army fought its way west in 1944–45, eastern European communists, trained in the Soviet Union, followed. The Baltic states

Chronology 22.1 ❖ Europe After 1945

1945	United Nations founded; Eastern Europe occupied by Red Army
1947	Cold War starts; Marshall Plan inaugurated
1948	Stalinization of Eastern Europe; Tito's Yugoslavia breaks with the Soviet Union
1949	NATO formed
1953	Stalin dies
1956	Khrushchev's secret speech on Stalin's crimes; the Polish October; the Hungarian uprising crushed
1957	Sputnik launched: the space age begins; the EEC established
1961	Berlin Wall built, dividing the city of Berlin
1962	Cuban missile crisis
1963–1973	Vietnam War
1964	Khrushchev ousted; Brezhnev and Kosygin installed as leaders in U.S.S.R.
1968	Czhechoslovakia's "Prague Spring": Dubček's "socialism with a human face"
1971	Détente in East-West relations
1979	Soviet Union invades Afghanistan
1980	Solidarity trade union formed in Poland
1982	Brezhnev dies, succeeded by Andropov (d. 1984) and Chernenko (d. 1985)
1985	Gorbachev becomes U.S.S.R. leader
1988	Soviet Union withdraws from Afghanistan
1989	Year of liberation in Eastern Europe
1990	Reunification of Germany; Charter of Paris for a New Europe: official end of the cold war
1991	Breakup of the U.S.S.R.

(Lithuania, Latvia, Estonia), seized after the Nazi-Soviet Pact of 1939 and then lost to Hitler, were reincorporated into the Soviet Union as "soviet socialist republics." Elsewhere, Stalin respected, at least outwardly, the national sovereignty of the occupied countries by ruling through returning native communists and whatever sympathizers he could find. In the Soviet-occupied zone of Germany, Stalin arranged for the establishment of Communist rule. This area became the German Democratic Republic, while the three other zones combined as the democratic Federal Republic of Germany. The local populations and their sympathizers in western European nations and the United States viewed the Soviet occupation of eastern Europe as a calamity. But short of starting another war, Western countries were powerless to intervene. For the next forty-five years or so, the two parts of the Continent, Eastern Europe and Western Europe, would constitute two camps of opposing ideologies, communist and anticommunist.

By the end of 1948, the lands of Eastern Europe had become Soviet satellites. The puppet regimes leveled the formerly privileged classes, socialized the economy, and implemented hasty plans for industrialization and for the collectivization of agriculture. Religion and the churches were repressed, and political liberty and free speech stamped out. Even the "proletarian masses" derived few benefits from the artificial revolution engineered from Moscow because Stalin drained Eastern Europe of its resources in order to rebuild the Soviet Union. Contact with Western Europe or the United States was banned. Each satellite country existed in isolation, its borders fortified with barbed wire and watchtowers set along mined corridors cut through the landscape. Fear reached deep into every house and into individual souls as little Stalins copied their mentor's style in East Berlin, Warsaw, Prague, Budapest, Sofia, and Bucharest. All communist parties (whatever their name) were guided by Moscow; Soviet troops remained strategically stationed in the area.

An exception to this trend was Yugoslavia under the leadership of the pugnacious Marshal Tito, who became a symbol of defiance to Stalin. During World War II, he had led the Yugoslav resistance movement against Nazi occupation. A hardened Communist, Tito was also a Yugoslav patriot committed to rebuilding and unifying his country. Thus, Yugoslavia escaped Soviet occupation. Backed by his party and his people, Tito guided his country on an independent course.

Deepening Tensions

Farther afield, in the eastern Mediterranean, Stalin was suspected of aiding communist guerrillas in the Greek civil war of 1946–47. The guerrillas were supported by the neighboring Soviet-dominated countries of Albania, Bulgaria, and Yugoslavia; Stalin's influence on the course of the war was in fact minimal. He did, however, lay claim to the Straits of Constantinople, and he unduly prolonged the wartime Soviet occupation of northern Iran.

In March 1947, fearing Soviet penetration into the eastern Mediterranean

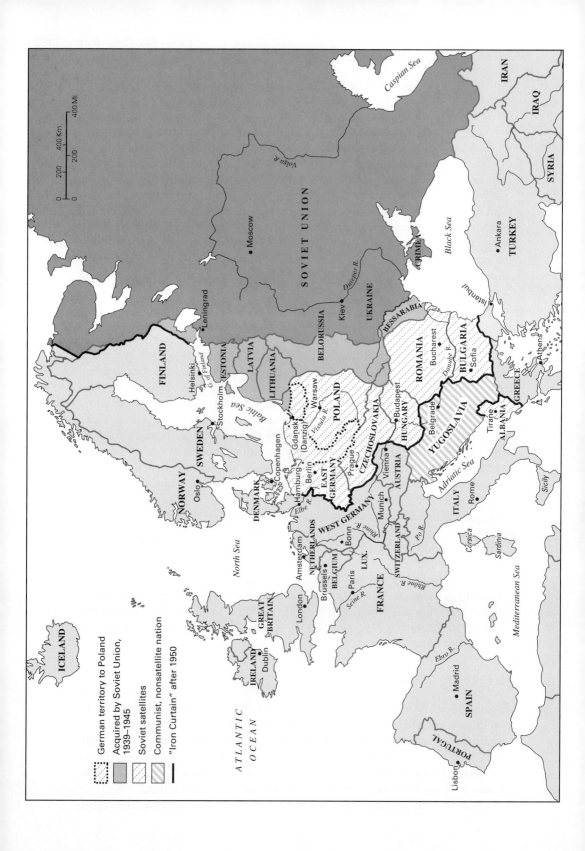

ICELAND

ATLANTIC OCEAN

NORWAY
Oslo

SWEDEN
Stockholm

FINLAND
Helsinki

Leningrad

Gulf of Finland

ESTONIA
LATVIA
LITHUANIA

Baltic Sea

DENMARK
Copenhagen

Gdansk (Danzig)

Vistula R.

POLAND
Warsaw

BELORUSSIA

SOVIET UNION

Moscow

Volga R.

Dnieper R.

Kiev

UKRAINE

Caspian Sea

CRIMEA

Black Sea

GREAT BRITAIN
London

IRELAND
Dublin

North Sea

NETHERLANDS
Amsterdam

BELGIUM
Brussels

LUX.

WEST GERMANY
Hamburg
Bonn

Elbe R.

Berlin

EAST GERMANY

Prague

CZECHOSLOVAKIA

Munich

Rhine R.

Vienna

AUSTRIA

Budapest

HUNGARY

ROMANIA
Bucharest

BESSARABIA

Danube R.

BULGARIA
Sofia

Belgrade

YUGOSLAVIA

Adriatic Sea

Tirana
ALBANIA

GREECE

Athens

Istanbul

TURKEY
Ankara

SYRIA

IRAQ

IRAN

FRANCE
Paris

Seine R.

SWITZERLAND

Rhône R.

Po R.

ITALY
Rome

Corsica

Sardinia

Sicily

Mediterranean Sea

SPAIN
Madrid

PORTUGAL
Lisbon

Ebro R.

400 Mi.

400 Km.
200

200

0
0

German territory to Poland

Acquired by Soviet Union, 1939–1945

Soviet satellites

Communist, nonsatellite nation

"Iron Curtain" after 1950

and aware of British weakness in that area, President Harry S. Truman proclaimed the Truman Doctrine: "It must be the policy of the United States to support free peoples who are resisting attempted subjugation by armed minorities or by outside pressures."[2] The Truman Doctrine was the centerpiece of the new policy of *containment*—of holding Soviet power within its then current boundaries. The United States soon furnished military and economic support to Greece and Turkey. Thus, American foreign policy underwent a sharp reversal: prewar isolation gave way to worldwide vigilance against any Soviet effort at expansion. In June 1947, the United States took another step toward strengthening the West. Secretary of State George C. Marshall announced an impressive program of economic assistance to Europe. Formally called the European Recovery Program, it became widely known as the Marshall Plan. Between 1947 and 1951, it had supplied Europe with more than $12 billion in aid—a modest pump-priming for the subsequent record upswing in U.S., Western European, and even global prosperity. Western Europe recovered, and the United States gained economically strong allies and trading partners.

These measures were accompanied by a massive ideological mobilization of American opinion against communism and a new apprehension about national security. As a result, the armed forces and the defense industries supporting them—the "military-industrial complex," in President Dwight D. Eisenhower's words—attained unprecedented political power in U.S. politics.

A spectacular test between the two superpowers took place from June 1948 to May 1949, after the Soviet authorities severed all overland access to the western sectors of Berlin. The Soviets aimed to starve into submission a half-city of about two million inhabitants who, because of their freedom, were "a bone in the communist throat" (as Nikita Khrushchev later put it). West Berlin was saved by an impressive airlift: under U.S. direction, the French, British, and Americans flew in supplies around the clock in all kinds of weather. In response to these conditions, the North Atlantic Treaty Organization (NATO) was formed (see below).

The year 1949 was a turning point in the cold war, which spread from Europe into the world at large, intensifying as it did so. The victory of the Chinese Communists under Mao Zedong seemed more threatening to the United States than the Berlin blockade. Now another communist giant had joined the Soviet Union. Even more alarming was the fact that sooner than expected the Soviet Union had exploded its first atomic bomb, breaking the U.S. monopoly of that all-powerful weapon, which had inspired American self-confidence in the immediate postwar years. Now Americans felt that they had to keep ahead of the Soviet Union in nuclear weapons as well.

◀ **Map 22.2**   Eastern Europe After 1945

The Growth of Military Alliances

The United States and the countries of Western Europe established the North Atlantic Treaty Organization in 1949 to prevent the widely dreaded westward expansion of Soviet communism. NATO combined the armed forces of the United States, Canada, Portugal, Norway, Iceland, Denmark, Italy, Britain, France, and the Benelux countries (an acronym for Belgium, the Netherlands, and Luxembourg). Greece and Turkey soon joined; West Germany was included in 1955, and Spain in 1982. The postwar rebuilding of Western Europe proceeded under the protection of U.S. military power.

The Soviet Union had its own alliance system: the Warsaw Pact, or Warsaw Treaty Organization (WTO), created in 1955. It coordinated the armies of the satellite countries with the Red Army so that they might serve as a military instrument for preserving the ideological and political unity of the bloc and for counterbalancing NATO.

Confrontations

Korean War   In June 1950, war broke out in Korea, a country divided in 1945 between a pro-Soviet Communist regime in the north and a pro-American regime in the south. Eager to restore Korean national unity and mistakenly assuming U.S. nonintervention, the North Korean army invaded South Korea, possibly with Stalin's approval. Immediately, the United States took countermeasures, gaining U.N. backing for a war against North Korea. Under the command of General Douglas MacArthur, South Korean and U.S. troops, assisted by a token force from other U.N. members, fought their way north toward the Chinese border. Fearing for his own security, Mao Zedong dispatched Chinese "volunteers" to drive back the approaching enemy in a surprise attack. Forced to retreat, General MacArthur's troops eventually withdrew from North Korea. Peace was restored in 1953, with the division of Korea reaffirmed. South Korea became an outpost of U.S. power.

The fear of Soviet global ambition redoubled Washington's resolve to contain Soviet power. Under President Eisenhower (1952–1960), the United States extended its military alliances into central and eastern Asia for reasons stated when he assumed office: "The freedom we cherish and defend in Europe and in the Americas is no different from the freedom that is imperiled in Asia." Still closer to home, in the Western Hemisphere, the United States made sure—by economic pressure, subversion, or military intervention, if necessary—that no pro-Soviet or even Marxist regime established itself.

Cuban Missile Crisis   Confrontation between the superpowers rose to a terrifying climax in 1962 during the Cuban missile crisis. In 1959, the infamous dictatorship of Fulgencio Batista had been toppled by Fidel Castro (b. 1927), a left-wing revolutionary who turned Cuba into a Communist style dictatorship. After an American attempt to overthrow him—the bungled Bay of Pigs operation—Castro was ready to turn his country into an outpost of Soviet power. Khrushchev planned to exploit this foothold within the Western Hemisphere by installing Soviet nuclear missiles in Cuba. Although the United States had for some time stationed nuclear weapons in Turkey, within easy reach of Soviet targets, the reverse situation—allowing a major Soviet threat close to home—alarmed the country. President John F. Kennedy demanded that Khrushchev withdraw the Soviet missiles from Cuba. The cold war confrontation threatened to turn into a very hot nuclear war. However, Khrushchev backed down—a move that contributed to his fall from power two years later. No Soviet missiles were stationed in Cuba.

Vietnam War   The new countries emerging from colonial rule in Asia and Africa offered seductive opportunities for Soviet global ambitions. From the U.S. perspective, the biggest challenge arose in Vietnam, where the Communist regime in the north threatened to take over South Vietnam as well. The threat had started with the partition of the country in 1954. From the north, the authoritarian regime of Ho Chi Minh (1890–1969), backed by indigenous nationalism and Soviet aid, cast its shadow over a disorganized south. Providing South Vietnam with the stability and strength needed to resist communist infiltration required increasing U.S. aid—including troops to fight off the communist guerrillas, the Vietcong. If the communists prevailed, the argument ran, all the other countries in East and Southeast Asia emerging from colonial rule would fall like dominoes to communist rule. Under President Lyndon B. Johnson, who assumed office in 1963, U.S. intervention in South Vietnam became the undeclared Vietnam War.

The U.S. government shipped to Vietnam nearly half a million soldiers, equipped with the most advanced chemical weapons and electronic equipment available. Yet victory eluded the American forces. The North Vietnamese government and its people withstood the cruelest punishment of bombs and chemical weapons ever inflicted on human beings. Nor was South Vietnam spared; virtually every South Vietnamese family saw relatives killed or maimed, and their farms and livelihoods ruined.

As domestic opposition to the war increased and Vietcong resistance could not be broken, President Richard M. Nixon, elected in 1968, realized that the war had to be ended by "peace with honor." While he initiated negotiations with North Vietnam, U.S. forces put pressure on the enemy by attacking communist bases and supply routes in neighboring Cambodia and Laos. Civilians were bombed more fiercely than in World War II. In 1973, by agreement with North Vietnam, the United States withdrew its forces from the area. In 1975, the North Vietnamese swept aside the inept South Vietnamese army and unified the country under a Communist dictatorship. Ho Chi Minh had triumphed against the mightiest nation in the world.

In the wake of the American withdrawal, Cambodian communists—the Khmer Rouge—seized power under their leader, Pol Pot. He drove more than two million people from the capital city of Phnom Penh and tried to establish a new order based on ideologically regimented rural communes. Hundreds of thousands of people died in the evacuation, and more died later in the

Bogged Down in Vietnam.   Americans defended South Vietnam against a threatened takeover by communist North Vietnam. Between 1964 and 1973, U.S. involvement in the unsuccessful Vietnam War cost tens of thousands of Vietnamese and American lives, ruined South Vietnam, and polarized U.S. public opinion over the morality of the war. (*Wide World Photo*)

countryside. In 1979, the bloodstained and starving country, together with Laos, was occupied by Vietnamese troops, visiting further catastrophe on its people.

Decolonization

Meanwhile, the cold war between the two superpowers had spread into Asia and Africa—into the Third World, as it came to be known. Western imperialism had everywhere introduced Western institutions, goods, and ideals. World War II had stirred up the non-Western peoples living under Western colonial rule to liberate themselves. When World War II ended, the militancy of anticolonial movements increased. The political agitation of the war, in which many colonial soldiers had loyally fought for their masters, sparked the desire for political independence. After all, freedom and self-determination had been prominent Allied war slogans. Exhausted by the war, European colonial powers had little strength left for colonial rule.

In this setting, a mighty groundswell of decolonization, supported by the superpowers and the ideals of the United Nations, eventually abolished all overseas empires and propelled their former subjects into independent statehood. Decolonization quickly became a major issue in the cold war as the two superpowers competed with each other for influence in the emerging states of Africa and Asia. The Soviet Union, proclaiming an ideology that called for the liberation of all oppressed peoples, tried to steer the colonial independence movements into its orbit, supporting them with advisers and weapons. The Western powers, with their superior resources, tried to guide their former colonial subjects toward a pro-Western allegiance, likewise offering military, political, and financial assistance. In their ignorance of local cultures, both sides found themselves entangled in the intricacies of local power struggles, especially in tropical Africa, which was frequently involved in protracted civil wars bordering on anarchy.

Decolonization began in 1946 in Asia, when the United States granted independence to the Philippines. In 1947, India and Pakistan attained sovereign statehood; in 1948, independent Burma and Ceylon (later renamed Sri Lanka) emerged. In 1949, Holland was forced to grant independence to Indonesia. More ominously, that year China turned Communist, encouraging anticolonialism in Asia and Africa. After granting independence to Laos in 1954, the French were driven from Cambodia and Vietnam the same year, leaving the Americans to defend South Vietnam against the communist revolutionaries of North Vietnam until 1975.

After the middle fifties, the European rulers started the process of decolonization in Africa, turning over power to indigenous leaders. In 1956, France freed its northern African colonies, Morocco and Tunisia, and four years later, Senegal, in West Africa. Algeria, however, did not gain independence until 1962, after a cruel war.

Pushed by the trend of the times, the Belgians in 1960 pulled out of the Congo, precipitating a civil war in the unprepared country. The Congo's first leader, Patrice Lumumba, appealed for Soviet help, until he was ousted by Mobutu Sese Seko, who in 1971 renamed the country Zaire. He stayed in power indefinitely, supported by Western nations eager to exploit his country's valuable raw materials.

Decolonization swept through African lands ruled by Britain. In 1957, the British Gold Coast, renamed Ghana, achieved independence—the first sub-Saharan country to do so. Its leader, Kwame Nkrumah, had already indicated his guiding policy, which also inspired other African leaders: "Capitalism is too complicated a system for a newly independent nation. Hence the need for a socialistic society" and possibly for "Emergency measures of a totalitarian kind."[3] In 1961, Nkrumah toured the Soviet bloc. Also in 1961, Tanganyika became independent, joining with Zanzibar to form Tanzania in 1964 under the leadership of Julius Nyerere. He presided until the 1980s over a socialist development program, assisted by Communist China. In 1962, Uganda was decolonized; it was led by Milton Obote as a socialist one-party state, until he was overthrown in 1971 by Idi Amin, a barbarous dictator, who lasted in power until 1980. Nigeria, an ethnically divided state, attained independence in 1960 but was soon caught in a civil war costing a million lives. In that war, Britain, Italy, and the Soviet Union, in an unusual alignment, competitively assisted the Nigerian government, while France aided the separatists. In 1964, having gained independence the previous year, Kenya turned into a republic under Jomo Kenyatta, who ruled as an authoritarian president in a one-party state leaning toward the West. The following year, a white supremacist party defied Britain by declaring unilateral independence in the British colony of Rhodesia. It finally yielded to African rule in 1980, and Rhodesia became the new state of Zimbabwe.

The Portuguese held on to their African colonies as long as possible, quitting Angola in 1975 and leaving it embroiled in a civil war between the American-supported government and a liberation movement supported by the Soviet Union, with Cuban assistance. Only the Republic of South Africa, independent since 1910, remained under repressive white minority rule during this period.

Decolonization everywhere sparked protracted and often brutal struggles of building modern states among peoples who were utterly unprepared for this effort by their colonial rulers and who were also divided by their past animosities, as well as by the competition between the superpowers. Given their lack of preparation, Western practices like capitalism and democracy proved too complex for achieving effective statehood. The Soviet model seemed more suitable; besides, it offered the new leaders the attraction of absolute power. Yet how long could that model hold its own against the capitalist rival, whose riches exerted an even stronger attraction? Decolonization inevitably expanded the influence of Western ways of life in the newly independent nations, even though one-party governments and dictatorships remain in power in many countries.

Building a New Europe

Although Europeans share a common cultural heritage, the diversity of their history and national temperaments has burdened them in the past with incessant warfare. After two ruinous world wars, many people at last began to feel that the price of violent conflict had become excessive; war no longer served any national interest. The extension of Soviet power made some form of Western European unity attractive, if not imperative.

European Unity

In 1951, the chief Continental consumers and producers of coal and steel, the two items most essential for the rebuilding of Western Europe, created the

European Coal and Steel Community (ECSC). Its six members, France, West Germany, the Netherlands, Belgium, Luxembourg, and Italy, intended to put the Ruhr industrial complex, the heart of German industrial power, under international control, thereby promoting cooperation and reconciliation, as well as economic strength.

Emboldened by the success of the ECSC, in 1957 the six countries established the European Economic Community (EEC), also known as the Common Market: a customs union that created a free market among the member states and sought to improve living conditions in them. In 1973, Great Britain, Ireland, and Denmark joined the original members in what was now called the European Community (EC); in 1986, Spain, Portugal, and Greece became members. The EC constitutes the largest single trading bloc, conducting more than one-fifth of the world's commerce. Forecasters predict that the European Community will create the largest single pool of freely flowing goods, services, and people in the world.

Recovery and New Problems and Tensions

A most striking fact of recent history in the West has been the unprecedented economic advance. Between the early 1950s and the late 1970s, production in Western Europe and the United States surpassed all previous records. However, the rapid postwar economic boom was not destined to last. It had been fed by abundant and exceptionally cheap supplies of oil, but after 1973, the Organization of Petroleum Exporting Countries (OPEC) drastically raised the price of that essential source of energy. OPEC's action aggravated adverse worldwide economic trends, which had been evident since the late 1960s (and were caused in part by the U.S. war in Vietnam). Inflation, unemployment, falling productivity, competition (especially from Japan) in automobiles and electronics, and a worldwide economic recession plagued the United States and all the governments of Western Europe. After another oil crisis in 1979, the economy recovered, and prosperity continued through the 1980s. However, unemployment in Western Europe remained high, even in West Germany, the strongest country economically.

Stimulated by the expansion of U.S. multinational corporations into Western Europe and by the opportunities offered by the European Community, many European companies have turned multinational and grown bigger than any nationalized industry. The Western European economy came to be dominated by gigantic private and public enterprises tied to other parts of the world.

Boosted by rising standards of living and by U.S. power, the overall trend of political life in the West since World War II has been toward constitutional democracy. Although Spain and Portugal retained their prewar dictatorships until the mid-1970s and Greece for a time wavered between democracy and dictatorship, by the late 1970s even these countries had conformed to the common pattern.

Western Europe did not escape serious problems and tensions after World

War II. With the rise of the public sector and the increase in social services, government and bureaucracy grew huge and more impersonal. Individuals felt dwarfed by the state and lost in a complex, interdependent society. The massive spurt of affluence had unsettling effects on European culture. Although prosperity provided more people with more material goods, it also encouraged a hedonistic self-indulgence, which ran counter to the puritan strain in Western tradition.

Young people especially were in ferment, tending to focus on the problems of modern society, particularly stark inequality and the breakdown of human intimacy and community. In their protest, some of the young sided with a romantic counterculture, disdaining traditional middle-class restraints, above all in sex, and proclaiming their solidarity with all oppressed peoples around the world.

In 1968, youthful frustration broke into politics—angrily and sometimes destructively—most significantly in France and slightly less drastically throughout Western Europe. (It also manifested itself, more mildly, in the anti–Vietnam War agitation in the United States). In May 1968, students and workers staged demonstrations and street fights in Paris, demanding educational reform and social justice. Yet no revolution followed, no sudden social change—only a conservative backlash at the next national election.

Some impatient young protesters, however, turned to terrorism, especially in West Germany and Italy. In their eyes, the entire system of state and society was inhumane and deserved destruction by any means available. The targets of their attacks were leading representatives of "the system": politicians, industrialists, judges, and the police. Terrorists of all kinds established links with their counterparts in other troubled areas of the world, creating a sort of international terrorist movement. Raw violence offered young idealists the opportunity for politically aware and self-denying heroism but it provided no answer to the intricate problems of modern society. After a few spectacular assassinations, public opinion began to favor more effective countermeasures, thus curtailing terrorist violence.

Youthful protest had also turned to environmental issues and nuclear disarmament. Both young and old gathered in mass demonstrations. They agitated against the pollution of water and air, dramatized the plight of dying forests, opposed nuclear power plants, and called attention to the threat of nuclear war.

The Leading Western European States

Impoverished by the war and vulnerable in its dependence on imported food and raw material, Great Britain lost its leading role in world politics after World War II. It peacefully dismantled its colonial empire, while British seapower was replaced by the American navy and air force. The postwar Labour government, allied with powerful trade unions, provided Britons with a measure of economic security through social programs and extensive government control over important branches of the economy. Such controls, however, placed Britain at a disadvantage vis-à-vis its European competitors.

The Iron Lady. The first British woman prime minister, Margaret Thatcher, aroused dormant patriotism in 1982 when British forces drove Argentinian invaders out of the Falkland Islands. Her government was committed to strong military and nuclear capability. (*Peter Jordan/Liaison*)

In 1979, at a low point in the economy, the voters elected a Conservative government, led by Margaret Thatcher, the "Iron Lady" and the first woman prime minister. She dominated English politics for the next decade, fighting inflation and rigorously encouraging individual initiative and free enterprise. During the Thatcher years, the British economy improved, and London regained its former luster as a financial center. Still, industries were declining, causing a rise in unemployment. Civic tensions—terrorism by the Irish Republican Army seeking to drive Britain from Northern Ireland, and resentment at the influx of Indians, Pakistanis, West Indians, and other people from former colonies—also took their toll. In addition, despite their EC membership, the English clung to their traditional insular detachment from their neighbors on the Continent.

Across the English Channel, France, liberated from German occupation, was reorganized democratically under the Fourth Republic and soon achieved respectable economic growth, despite frequent changes of government (twenty-six in twelve years). Defeat in Indochina and a civil war in Algeria between French settlers, backed by the French army, and Algerian nationalists produced a severe political crisis in 1958. It resulted in the presidency of General Charles de Gaulle, the leader of the Free French forces in World War II and president for a brief period after the war ended. De Gaulle established the Fifth Republic, with a strong executive authority, and sought to raise the country again to prominence by building its nuclear strength, making France independent of NATO, and renewing French influence in Africa. In 1962, he arranged a cease-fire in Algeria, allowing it to achieve independence. Demonstrations by students and workers in 1968, supported by the Communist party, greatly alarmed de Gaulle. He quickly called a general election, in which a frightened electorate gave him a landslide victory. However, unable to revise the constitution in his favor, he resigned in 1969.

The Fifth Republic continued with a government firmly based on a stable centrist majority, flanked by two radical parties. On the left, the Communist party gradually lost credibility because of its loyalty to Moscow. On the extreme right, the more dangerous *Front National* took hold, stirring up hatred against the increasing number of immigrants from North Africa. Under the pressure of the newcomers, the French, even more than the English, feared for their national identity.

Amid the economic and political uncertainties of the times, François Mitterand, a moderate socialist and president since 1981, maintained the Gaullist tradition. His country was the third largest nuclear power and the fourth largest economy in the world, deriving 70 percent of its energy from nuclear power plants. All along, France was a leading architect of European unity without surrendering its French character.

Italy, half the size of France, yet larger in population by a few million, became a democratic republic in 1946. Its government, however, has been weak and unstable. The average life span of an Italian cabinet to the present has been less than a year. A lengthy peninsula stretching out into the Mediterranean, the country offered a sharp contrast between north and south. The north was efficient and prosperous, whereas the south was backward and infiltrated by the Mafia. Centered in Sicily, the Mafia was a source of political corruption and even occasional terror against the government.

Division also characterized the political parties, from Communists to Christian Democrats. The Italian Communists, relatively free from corruption, well organized, and oriented toward Europe rather than Moscow, usually gained a quarter of the vote. On the other hand, the Christian Democrats—allied with the Vatican and constituting the majority party—were poorly disciplined, like the other noncommunist parties, and riven by corruption.

Yet the Italian economy proved to be a surprising success, despite the fact that the government was perennially in debt and unemployment ran high, especially in the south. Even more than France, Italy has been overrun by legal and illegal immigrants from Asia and Africa, straining the country's resources. It has been the most unruly of the major European countries, but no troublemaker for its neighbors.

In 1945, its cities in ruins, Germany had been defeated, occupied, and branded as a moral outcast. Divided among the four occupying powers—the United States, Britain, France, and the Soviet Union—the German nation was politically extinct. Extensive eastern lands were lost to Poland and the Soviet Union; some territory was returned to France. By 1949, two new and chastened Germanys had emerged. West Germany (the Federal Republic of Germany), formed from the three western zones of occupation, faced the hostile, Soviet-dominated East Germany (the German Democratic Republic). The former capital city of Berlin, inside East Germany, was similarly divided into western and eastern zones of occupation. The partition of Germany signified the destruction of Germany's traditional indentity and ambition. The national trauma reached a climax in August 1961, when the East German government suddenly threw up a wall between East and West Berlin and tightly sealed off East from West Germany. West Germany thus became the crucial frontier of the cold war, radiating Western superiority into the Soviet bloc.

The cold war proved a boon to the West Germans; it contributed to their integration into the emerging new Europe and to the reduction of old hatreds. Located next door to the Red Army, the West Germans, along with the Western armed forces stationed on their soil, were in a strategic position for defending Western Europe. Moreover, German industrial expertise was indispensable for rebuilding the Western European economy. On this basis, West Germany (far larger than its Communist counterpart to the east and the most populous of all Western European countries) began to build a new political identity.

The architect of the new West Germany was Konrad Adenauer, its chancellor from 1949 to 1963. He sought to restore respect for Germany in cooperation with the leading states of Western Europe and the United States. As a patriot, he reestablished a cautious continuity with the German past. He also had Germany shoulder responsibility for the crimes of the Nazi regime and assume the payment of indemnifications and pensions to the Jewish victims and survivors of the Nazi era, as well as the payment of reparations to the state of Israel, which had been established in 1948. Under Adenauer's guidance, the West Germans also threw themselves into rebuilding their economy; the whole world soon admired the German "economic miracle." As a result, democracy put down roots among the West German people, strengthening their solidarity with their former European enemies. West Germany was admitted to NATO in 1957, and, together with East Germany, to the United Nations in 1972. It joined France in promoting the European Community.

After the Adenauer era, German voters shifted from center-right to center-left. Chancellor Willy Brandt (1969–1974) took the initiative for an "opening toward the East," contributing to a temporary relaxation of tensions between the superpowers. During these years, West German prosperity and a generous admission policy attracted ambitious immigrants, many from Turkey; the booming economy needed additional workers. Policial extremists did not endanger political stability, except for one party, the Greens, who called attention to the destruction of the environment, industrial pollution, and the dangers of nuclear power. Loosely organized, the Greens expressed a romantic alienation from contemporary society and politics but achieved no lasting success. In 1982, the voters turned conservative, electing the leader of the Christian Democratic Union, Helmut Kohl, chancellor. Kohl continued Adenauer's policy of integrating West Germany, now the most prominent country in Western Europe, into the cold war alliance against Soviet communism.

The Soviet Union

In Soviet experience, World War II was another cruel landmark in the long succession of wars, revolutions, and crises afflicting the country since 1914. Nothing basically changed after the war. The liberation from terror and dictatorship, which many soldiers had hoped for as a reward for their heroism, never occurred.

Stalin's Last Years

Corrupted by unlimited power and unrestrained adulation, Stalin displayed in his last years an unrelenting ruthlessness and a suspiciousness that turned into paranoia. He found no reason to relax control. The country still had immense problems: the large anti-Soviet populations in Eastern Europe; the destruction wreaked by the war; the political unreliability of returning soldiers and prisoners of war; and the overwhelming strength of the United States. Stalin's indomitable ambition, undiminished by age (he was sixty-six years old in 1945), was to build up Soviet power in his lifetime, whatever the human cost. More Five-Year Plans and more terror were needed.

On this familiar note, the Soviet Union slid from war into peace, staggering through the hardships and hunger of the war's aftermath, mourning its dead, and desperately short of men. Planning, much selfless hard work, manpower released from the army, and resources requisitioned from all occupied territories brought industrial production back to prewar levels within three years—no mean achievement.

With the return to Five-Year Plans came a deliberate tightening of ideological control. The party boss of Leningrad, Andrei Zhdanov (1896–1948), lashed out against any form of Western influence. Thousands of returning soldiers and prisoners of war, who had seen too much in the West, were sent to forced-labor camps. The Soviet intelligentsia was again terrorized into compliance with the party line. And in 1948, the chief leaders of Leningrad's heroic struggle against the Nazi siege were arrested and shot. That same year Stalin tightened the reins on Eastern Europe.

Stalin continued to build Soviet power. By 1949, sooner than expected, the Soviet Union possessed the atomic bomb. By 1953, at the same time as the United States, it had the hydrogen bomb as well. Stalin also helped lay the foundation for Sputnik I (meaning "fellow traveler" of the Earth), the first artificial satellite to orbit the globe.

In his last years, Stalin withdrew into virtual isolation, surrounded by a few fawning and fearful subordinates, and his paranoia worsened. Before he died, he "recognized" a plot among the doctors who treated him and personally issued orders for their torture (which killed one of them). When on March 5, 1953, the failing dictator died of a stroke, his advisers sighed with relief, but many people wept. To them, Stalin was the godlike leader and savior of the nation.

Stalin's Successors

The most hated among Stalin's potential heirs was Lavrenti Beria, the head of the secret police and the vast empire of forced-labor camps. In December 1953, he was suddenly executed, together with his chief henchmen, for having been a "foreign spy." These cynical accusations and violent deaths were the last gasp of Stalinism; ever since, the rivals for supreme leadership have died of natural causes. Gradually, leadership was assumed by a team headed by Nikita Khrushchev (1954–1964), who breathed fresh air into Soviet life. Khrushchev was the driving force behind the "thaw" that emptied the forced-labor camps and allowed most of the nationalities forcibly resettled during the war to return to their native regions. In a speech at the Twentieth Party Congress in February 1956, Khrushchev even dared to attack Stalin himself. His audience gasped with horror as he recited the facts: "Of the 139 members and candidates of the Party Central Committee who were elected at the 17th Congress (1934), 98 persons, i.e., 70%, were arrested and shot."[4] In this vein, Khrushchev cited example after example of Stalin's terror. Without criticizing the Soviet system, Khrushchev acknowledged and rejected the excesses of Stalinism.

Khrushchev's revelations created a profound stir around the world and prompted defection from Communist ranks everywhere. Among the Soviet satellite countries, Poland was on the brink of rebellion by 1956; a workers' uprising forced a change of leadership. In Hungary in 1956, the entire Communist regime was overthrown, but the Soviet army reoccupied the country and crushed the uprising.

In foreign policy, Khrushchev professed to promote peace. But while trying to reduce the role of the army, he also made some provocative moves by threatening Western access to West Berlin and placing missiles in Cuba; U.S. pressure forced him to withdraw in both cases. In 1960, not wishing to help Communist China build atomic weapons, he withdrew, after mutual recrimination, all Soviet advisers, causing a break between the two Communist nations. Mao then charged him with "revisionism," as well as imperialism.

Eager to prod his country toward a higher level of Marxist-Leninist ideology, Khrushchev presented a new party program and impatiently pressed for reforms in industry, agriculture, and party organization. His ceaseless reorganizations and impatient manner antagonized wide sections of state and party administration. In October 1964, while he was on vacation, his comrades in the Politburo unceremoniously ousted him for "ill health" or, as they later added, his "hare-brained schemes." He was retired and allowed to live out his years in peace.

Like Stalin, Khrushchev was succeeded by a group of leaders acting in common. Among these men, Leonid Brezhnev (1906–1982) gradually rose to the fore. Under his leadership, the government of the U.S.S.R. turned from a personal dictatorship into an oligarchy: the collective rule of a privileged minority. Brezhnev's style stressed reasoned agreement rather than command. Soviet officials breathed more easily, and Soviet society in turn grew less authoritarian.

Never before in Soviet history had the country enjoyed such external security. As a result, the rigors of authoritarian rule could be relaxed, and the country could be opened, cautiously, to the outside world. For instance, young people were allowed access to Western styles of music and dress. More issues of state policy were opened to public debate and more latitude granted to artistic expression. Interest in religion revived.

The fate of Russian dissidents, however, remained uncertain. For example, Andrei Sakharov, who had helped to develop the Soviet hydrogen bomb but subsequently defended human rights, was exiled from Moscow and placed under house arrest.* The most adamant critics, like the novelist Aleksandr Solzhenitsyn or historian Andrei Amalrik, were expelled (or allowed to emigrate). Other critics who stayed were declared insane and confined in mental hospitals, following a practice begun under Nicholas I. The secret police (KGB) remained as powerful as ever.

Eastern Europe

Realizing that continued repression of the satellite countries would provoke trouble, Stalin's successors began to relax their controls. A new era dawned for Eastern Europe. The Soviet satellites began to move toward greater national self-determination, searching for their own forms of industrialization, collectivization of agriculture, and Communist dictatorship. The history of the region since 1953 was thus a series of experiments to determine what deviations from Soviet practice in domestic politics and what measure of self-assertion in foreign policy the Kremlin would tolerate.

No event proved more crucial than Khrushchev's attack on Stalin in 1956. It set off a political earthquake throughout the bloc, discrediting Stalinists and encouraging moderates in the parties, reviving cautious discussions among intellectuals, and even arousing visions of national self-determination.

The first rumbles of protest were heard in June 1956 in Poland—the largest and most troublesome of the satellite countries. The crisis came to a head in October: would Poland revolt, inviting invasion by the Red Army, or would

---

*Sakharov's six-year internal exile ended in 1986, and in 1989 he took a seat in the new Soviet legislature. He died later that year.

Khrushchev ease Soviet control? The Soviet boss yielded in return for a Polish pledge of continued loyalty to the Soviet Union. Thereafter, Poland breathed more freely, clinging to its Catholicism as a cornerstone of its national identity.

Although the "Polish October" ended peacefully, events moved to a brutal showdown in Hungary. The Stalinists had suppressed national pride in Hungary for too long. On October 20, 1956, anti-Soviet feeling boiled over in an uprising in Budapest, forcing Soviet troops to withdraw from the country. A moderate Communist government took over the reins. Eager to capture popular sentiment, it called for Western-style political democracy and Hungary's withdrawal from the Warsaw Pact. Thoroughly alarmed and supported by Mao and even Tito, the Soviet leaders struck back. On November 4, 1956, Soviet troops reentered Hungary and crushed all opposition.

But the bold uprising left its mark. The new Communist leader of Hungary, János Kádar, was a moderate. With Khrushchev's approval, he built a pragmatic regime of consumer-oriented "goulash communism," which granted considerable opportunity to private enterprise. Kádar's regime also allowed noncommunists to participate extensively in public affairs. Relaxation and decentralization of planning made possible in the 1970s a remarkable increase in popular prosperity and individual freedom. The Hungarian experiment became the envy of all other Soviet-bloc countries.

After 1956, Soviet leaders grew more circumspect in their approach to the satellite countries' internal affairs, allowing increasing diversity of political development. The post-Stalin permissiveness was never without risks, however, even under the milder regime of Brezhnev, as was shown in Czechoslovakia in 1968. A new group of Czech Communists, led by Alexander Dubček, sought to liberalize their regime to include noncommunists, permit greater freedom of speech, and rid the economy of the rigidities that for so long had prevented prosperity. Their goal was a "humanist democratic socialism," or "socialism with a human face": a Communist party supported by public goodwill rather than by the secret police.

This program panicked the governments of East Germany, Poland, and the Soviet Union. On August 21, East German, Polish, Hungarian, and Soviet troops, under the provisions of the Warsaw Pact, carried out a swift and well-prepared occupation of Czechoslovakia but failed to break the rebellious will of its reformers. While Soviet tanks rumbled through Prague, an extraordinary Czechoslovak party congress met secretly in choked fury. Never had the Soviet leaders encountered such united resistance by a Communist party. Nonetheless, the revolt ended in failure. The party was purged; all reforms were canceled; and the country was reduced to abject hopelessness. But the Soviet Union paid a high price. A cry of moral outrage resounded around the world; protests were heard even in Moscow.

Extraordinary events occurred in Poland. Industrial workers, theoretically the real masters in Communist regimes, embarrassed their government by taking the lead in pressing for freedom and a better standard of living. When a Polish cardinal became Pope John Paul II in 1978, patriotism surged. In 1980, workers, under the leadership of an electrician named Lech Walesa, succeeded, with the blessing of the church, in forming an independent labor union. Called Solidarity, the union engaged in numerous strikes. In 1981, matters came to a head: some of Solidarity's more radical members spoke of bringing free elections to Poland. In December, a military dictatorship, formed suddenly under General Wojciech Jaruzelski, imposed martial law. Walesa and other leaders of Solidarity were arrested, and protesting workers were dispersed by force.

The German Democratic Republic (East Germany) at first shared the fate of all Soviet satellites. Under the leadership of German Communists who had spent the Nazi years in the Soviet Union, industry was nationalized, agriculture collectivized, and the people regimented under the Communist party (here called the Socialist Unity party). But protests against Stalinism appeared earlier here than elsewhere. In June 1953, the workers of Berlin staged an uprising, gaining some concessions. Then followed a steady exodus of skilled manpower to West Germany, mostly through West Berlin. More than three million people escaped before the East German government, in August 1961, suddenly constructed the infamous "Berlin Wall" and built equally deadly barriers along the entire border with West Germany. For a time, all contact between East and West Germany ceased.

With renewed control over their people, the Communist leaders—first Walter Ulbricht and then, starting in the early 1970s, Erich Honecker—successfully advanced the economy. The East Germans enjoyed the highest standard of living in the Soviet bloc. In 1972, détente opened diplomatic relations with West Germany and promoted closer economic ties. After 1985, East Germans cheered the progress of reform in the Soviet Union—their leader, Honecker, denounced it as "a march to anarchy"—and hoped for similar benefits at home.

Détente—and More Cold War

In 1972, the Soviet Union and the United States agreed to limit antiballistic missiles (ABMs) designed to destroy incoming missiles. The ABM treaty reflected a new phase in U.S.-Soviet relations, soon known by the term *détente*. There were good reasons for a relaxation of tensions. The Vietnam War had made Americans more realistic. Feeling more secure, the Soviet leaders in turn softened the aggressive tone of their foreign policy.

Of broader significance were the Helsinki Agreements of 1975, signed in neutral Finland, amid considerable pomp, by all European governments, as well as Canada and the United States. The first of these agreements legitimized all borders drawn in central Europe at the end of the war; the agreements took the place of the peace that had never been officially concluded. Another agreement, especially important to the Soviet Union, stipulated the free exchange of technical and scientific data. The final agreement, and subsequently the most troublesome, called for the free movement of peoples and ideas across what Churchill had called the "iron curtain." But the Soviet government could hardly allow all those who wished to escape from oppression to leave the Soviet Union or its satellite countries.

Along with the ABM treaty, negotiations known as Strategic Arms Limitation Talks brought about an agreement, SALT I, limiting nuclear delivery systems and warheads. Hopes ran high that even more stringent reductions might be negotiated. Yet SALT II, which spelled out these hopes in specific detail, fell victim to the collapse of détente in 1979. SALT II was not ratified by the United States, but its terms were voluntarily adhered to by both sides even after détente had faded.

Several factors had undermined détente: the continuous violation of civil and human rights by the Soviet government; the establishment of a pro-Soviet regime in Ethiopia; the dispatch of Cuban soldiers and experts to Angola; and the Soviet Union's invasion of Afghanistan in 1979. In 1978, Communists had seized power in Afghanistan. The new leadership jailed and executed opponents and moved to establish a Marxist society. Worried about the Communists' ability to suppress a subsequent rebellion by Islamic traditionalists and tribal groups, the U.S.S.R., under Leonid Brezhnev, sent troops to Afghanistan in 1979 and installed a new, more strongly pro-Soviet leadership. Afghans resisted the Soviet invasion, setting off a bitter civil war. For Americans, the Soviet invasion of Afghanistan constituted dramatic proof of Soviet expansionism. Stepping up its hostility against what President Ronald Reagan called "the evil empire," the U.S. government sent military aid to the Afghan insurgents, making it difficult for the Soviet government to extricate itself with honor from this Vietnam-like venture. Now the U.S.-Soviet confrontation was extended to a highly sensitive area on the Soviet southern border.

The resumption of the cold war also revived the arms race. In 1981, the United States introduced the neutron bomb, a weapon capable of killing people by massive doses of fatal radiation without destroying their cities. In 1983, President Reagan announced the Strategic Defense Initiative (SDI), nicknamed "Star Wars," designed to build a space shield of electronic equipment over the United States capable of destroying incoming weapons. Critics pointed to its exorbitant cost, as well as its ineffectiveness. In any case, SDI propelled the arms race farther into space.

The Transformation of the Soviet Union and Eastern Europe

Brezhnev died in 1982; his immediate successors, chosen by agreement among top party officials, were old men who survived in office only for a short time. Former KGB chief Yuri Andropov (aged sixty-eight), in poor health from the start, died in early 1984. He was replaced by Konstantin Chernenko, a man of Brezhnev's generation, likewise in poor health, who lasted until early 1985.

In that year, Mikhail Gorbachev (b. 1931) took over, representing a younger and more sophisticated age group, whose members had started their careers in the calmer times after Stalin's death.

The Gorbachev Years

Self-confident, energetic, and articulate, Gorbachev was keenly aware of his country's problems and eager to confront them. He knew that the Soviet Union had to update its industrial and agricultural productivity to compete with Japan, South Korea, Taiwan, the countries of Western Europe, and the United States; in particular, the Soviet Union lagged in the design and production of computers. A sobering demonstration of inefficiency and mismanagement occurred in late April 1986 when, because of staff misjudgment, a reactor at the nuclear power plant at Chernobyl exploded, spewing dangerous radiation high into the atmosphere; poisonous fallout covered much of Europe. Wherever Gorbachev looked, the mismanagement caused by rigid, centralized planning stifled innovation.

Gorbachev demanded no less than a fundamental reorganization—*perestroika*—of the Soviet system, with the party in charge but responding more readily to the plans and hopes of Soviet citizens. Even more than his predecessors, he advocated "the democratization of society," hoping to stimulate participation by ordinary citizens, especially at their place of work and in local administration. He called for multiple candidates for elected posts, a novel experience for Soviet voters. To loosen up administrative rigidity, he also granted greater freedom to local entrepreneurs in agriculture, industry, and consumer services, demanding that supply and demand be closely coordinated, as in a free market.

Gorbachev promoted a new policy, *glasnost* (openness), in the discussion of public affairs. Let all the problems of Soviet society, hitherto kept under cover, be openly discussed: corruption, abuse of power, disregard for legality, and stifling of criticism. Domestic news began to depict Soviet reality more accurately. There was also a new candor about the Soviet past. During the seventieth anniversary of the Bolshevik Revolution, Gorbachev asserted that "the guilt of Stalin . . . for the wholesale repressive measures and acts of lawlessness is enormous and unforgivable."[5] Gorbachev then assured Soviet citizens that they should not hesitate to speak out freely. Academics, writers, and artists responded enthusiastically. As contacts with the outside world increased, Western ideals, culture, and respect for human rights entered Soviet minds as never before. Far-reaching economic changes designed to loosen the restraints of central planning and to promote a market economy accompanied the political reforms.

The End of the Cold War

Gorbachev also sought to ease international tensions. National security in the nuclear age, he stressed, called for superpower cooperation for the sake of

Mikhail Gorbachev. Soviet leader Gorbachev and his wife visit Vilnius, the capital of Lithuania, following the declaration of independence by the Lithuanian Communist Party. Gorbachev warned demonstrators, "If we should separate, it is the end of perestroika." (*Alain Nogues/ Sygma*)

common survival. Moreover, the high cost of the cold war impeded the reforms that he so urgently promoted. In the spirit of glasnost, Gorbachev frankly admitted that the adverse prospects of his country's economy forced him to advocate not only "normal international relations," but also an end to the arms race. Setting an example, with a touch of Western sartorial elegance, he traveled abroad and cautiously lifted the restrictions barring access to the outside world. Jewish emigration was eased; foreign firms were invited to help stimulate the Soviet economy; and high-level discussions between Russians and Americans became commonplace.

By the end of 1988, Gorbachev withdrew the Soviet army from Afghanistan, admitting that the 1979 invasion had been a mistake. He liberated Eastern Europe from Soviet domination, permitting the dissolution of the Warsaw Pact, the Soviet military alliance in the area, and gave approval to German reunification. He surrendered the Leninist claim to the superiority of Soviet communism and stopped support for Marxist regimes in the Third World. Unilaterally demobilizing sizable units of the Red Army in 1988, he also stopped nuclear testing. At summit meetings—with President Reagan and later with President George Bush—Gorbachev successfully pressed for strategic arms reduction. In late 1991, both the United States and the Soviet Union agreed to scrap a significant part of their nuclear arsenals.

The Collapse of Communism

1989: The Year of Liberation   *Perestroika* and *glasnost* spread among the peoples of Eastern Europe, resentful of Soviet domination and worried by growing economic hardships. During 1989 and 1990, Eastern Europeans showed their distaste for Communist leadership and demanded democratic reforms. Faced with a rising tide of popular discontent, Communist leaders resigned or agreed to reforms. People around the world cheered the opening of a new era in Eastern Europe.

In Poland, public pressure had forced General Jaruzelski to end his dictatorship and appoint a civilian government. Struggling with a deteriorating economy, Jaruzelski legalized the highly popular Solidarity union in 1989. Permitted to run against Communist party candidates in a free election, Solidarity won an overwhelming victory. The once jailed Solidarity members now sat in the Polish parliament next to their former jailers. In December 1990, Lech Walesa was elected president.

Encouraged by events in Poland, Hungary abolished its Communist bureaucracy in May 1989. By the end of the year, a multiparty system was in place, with two noncommunist parties, the Democratic Forum and the Alliance of Free Democrats, competing for leadership. Hungary had shaken off Soviet domination and embraced the ideals of democracy and free enterprise.

An even more momentous upheaval in 1989 occurred in East Germany. More than 340,000 people voted for freedom and prosperity with their feet, escaping to West Germany across the recently opened borders of Hungary and Czechoslovakia. Far larger numbers took to the streets in protest against the regime. Hoping to restore calm, Honecker's colleagues deposed their sickly, old, hard-line boss, but antigovernment demonstrations continued. On November 6, when almost a million demonstrators crammed the streets of East Berlin, the Communist government resigned. On November 9, in an explosion of patriotic fervor, the Berlin Wall was breached; tens of thousands of East Germans flocked into West Berlin, where they were welcomed with flowers and champagne. Liberated East Germany was soon reunited with West Germany, with Gorbachev's ultimate approval.

In Bulgaria, the dramatic events in Berlin led to the resignation of Tedor Zhivkov, the longest-serving Communist dictator in the Soviet bloc and an opponent of reform. Bulgaria had joined the quest for democratic government and private enterprise.

While democratic reforms triumphed elsewhere, Romania's Nicholae Ceausescu, long bent on pursuing his own dictatorial course and hostile to Gorbachev's reforms, ruthlessly enforced his own rule, ordering his soldiers to shoot into a crowd of antigovernment demonstrators. But popular resentment

The Wall Came Tumbling Down. The Berlin Wall, symbol of the division of Germany, was breached in November 1989. Young people excitedly clambered onto the partially demolished wall, while East and West Berliners thronged the streets. (*Regis Bossu/Sygma*)

was too powerful to contain and even the army turned against the dictator. On December 25, 1989, Ceausescu and his wife were tried and executed. The most hardened symbol of communist rule, defying to the last the common trend toward democratic freedom, had ignominiously fallen.

Faced with massive demonstrations in Prague and urged on by Gorbachev himself to institute democratic reform, Czechoslovakia's Communist leaders resigned on November 24, 1989. Václav Havel, a leading dissident writer and outspoken advocate of democracy who had been jailed for his views, was chosen president on December 25.

Shocked by the news of Ceausescu's execution and Havel's election, the

Yugoslav Communist party caved in. Its central committee suggested the formation of a multiparty system, which was fully adopted in January 1990.

Except for Albania, where the Communist party held on until free elections in February 1991, all of Eastern Europe had liberated itself from Soviet domination—a breathtaking change accomplished unexpectedly within a single year. Viewed as a whole, events in Eastern Europe had taken a surprisingly peaceful course, prompted by a number of favorable factors. First, Gorbachev had been willing to let the satellite peoples go their own way. Second, led by intellectuals and clergy, the people united against foreign domination and economic misery, which so vividly contrasted with the prosperity of Western Europe. Third, like Gorbachev, the Communist rulers had lost confidence in their Marxist-Leninist ideology; they knew that they had forfeited their legitimacy. Finally, the evidence of progress under freedom and democracy in the West had penetrated deep into eastern lands and had heightened popular expectations. The revolutionary changes of 1989 constituted an overwhelming victory for Western forms of government and ways of life.

Already in 1990, however, the euphoria of the previous year began to fade. New problems loomed ahead: how could democratic governments be adapted to the tension-ridden traditions of that troubled area, which, with the exception of Czechoslovakia, has had very little experience with democracy? Immediately, old ethnic divisiveness and hatreds reasserted themselves, particularly in Yugoslavia. Neofascist groups emerged in several lands, and anti-Semitism, deeply ingrained in eastern Europe, resurfaced. Everywhere, politicians found it difficult to establish effective consensus in the face of economic deterioration: rising inflation, plummeting production, unemployment, and shortages of staple foods. The chaos in the Soviet Union, to whose shattered economy the eastern Europeans were still closely tied, compounded the problem of economic reconstruction. Under these circumstances, the prospects for parliamentary democracy and an effective market economy remain uncertain.

Conditions were worst in Yugoslavia. Cobbled together after World War I as an artificial state, composed of sharply different ethnic groups dominated by Serbia, Yugoslavia was torn apart by the nationalist ambitions set off by the collapse of the Soviet Union. In July 1991, Slovenia and Croatia voted for independence; in April 1992, Bosnia seceded, ending Serbian control. Now ethnic hatred exploded, centered on Bosnia, a splintered mountainous region. Its population—44 percent Muslim, 32 percent Catholic Croat, and 11 percent Orthodox Serb—was scattered in multiethnic communities, with few ethnically consolidated areas.

The three ethnic groups ruthlessly fought each other, the Bosnian Serbs attempting to join with Serbia in a "greater Serbia." They conquered 70 percent of Bosnia, conducting a brutal "ethnic cleansing" of Muslims, while submitting Sarajevo, Bosnia's capital, to bloody bombardment. All sides, but most of all the Serbs, committed heinous atrocities, provoking moral outrage but limited foreign intervention. While the United Nations dispatched minor peacekeeping forces and imposed sanctions on Serbia, the European Community and the United States were unable to negotiate a peaceful settlement.

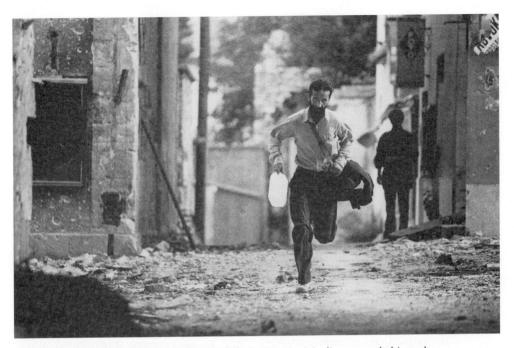

The Siege of Mostar.   Fleeing Serbian attacks in Bosnia, Muslims crowded into the city of Mostar in Croatia. The Croatians, alarmed by their numbers, tried to drive them away by shelling their area of the city. The Muslims huddled in cellars without water, light, or sanitation. Here, an inhabitant, running to escape shellfire, brings water and provisions. The siege lasted nine months and destroyed the Muslim area of Mostar. (*Laurent van der Stock/Liaison*)

Then in November 1995, the bitter enemies, pressured by the United States, which was sickened by the violence and the tarnishing of NATO's reputation, worked out an agreement at a conference held in Dayton, Ohio. It is still uncertain whether the settlement, which requires the stationing of sixty thousand NATO troops, including twenty thousand Americans, will survive ethnic and religious animosities exacerbated by brutal civil war.

The Disintegration of the Soviet Union   The transformation and spiritual rebirth that Gorbachev hoped for the Soviet Union did not occur. In October 1990, Gorbachev conceded that "unfortunately, our society is not ready for the procedures of a law-based state. We don't have that level of political culture, those traditions. All that will come in the future."[6] Meanwhile, the Soviet Union was experiencing a breakdown of effective government, economic collapse, corruption, and spiraling crime. In response to the mounting crisis, the liberals, most strongly represented in Moscow and Leningrad among the young generation open to Western ways, pressed, under Boris Yeltsin's guidance, for speedy westernization, including a multiparty system and a market economy. On the opposite side, the Communist hard-liners prepared to revive the old system, relying on the army and the security forces for restoring order and holding the country together. In August 1991, they staged a coup, imprisoning Gorbachev and deposing him as president of the Soviet Union. Their aim was to establish a new Communist dictatorship.

However, the conspirators, all of them high officials appointed by Gorbachev, grossly misjudged the people's revulsion against the Communist party. The KGB's vanguard forces defected to Yeltsin, who led a fervent popular protest at a risk to his life. The emotional outburst in favor of democracy quickly spread from Moscow to other cities, and the coup collapsed within three days. The chief victim of the coup, apart from its leaders, was the Communist party, now repudiated by Gorbachev himself and swept aside by public fury. Racked by the deteriorating economy and the growing nationalist sentiments among the various ethnic groups, the Soviet Union fell to pieces. The Baltic nations—Lithuania, Latvia, and Estonia—established their independence shortly after the coup, and a new Commonwealth of Independent States, consisting of eleven former republics of the collapsed Soviet Union, was proclaimed in December 1991. At the end of the month, Gorbachev, the last leader of the Soviet Union, resigned as president of a now defunct country. Boris Yeltsin, president of Russia, the most powerful of the new independent states, became the informal leader of the commonwealth. Its ideology discredited, its economy shattered, and its government transformed into a confederation of sovereign states, the Soviet Union had collapsed as a major force in world affairs. Only one superpower remained.

The Death of an Ideal?

The sudden and unexpected collapse of communism in eastern Europe in 1989 seemed to discredit Marxism irrevocably. Reformers in eastern European lands liberated from communist oppression expressed revulsion for the socialist past and a desire to regenerate their countries with an infusion of Western liberal ideals and institutions. Havel, the newly elected president of a free Czechoslovakia, expressed this disillusionment with the past and hope for a new democratic future:

> *The worst of it is that we live in a spoiled moral environment. We have become morally ill because we are used to saying one thing and thinking another. We have learned not to believe in anything, not to care about each other, to worry only about ourselves. . . . The previous regime, armed with a proud and intolerant ideology, reduced people into the means of production. . . . Many of our citizens died in prison in the 1950's. Many were executed. Thousands of human lives were destroyed.*
>
> *Perhaps you are asking what kind of republic I am dreaming about. I will answer you: a republic that is independent, free, democratic, a republic with economic prosperity and also social justice.*[7]

Map 22.3   Post–Cold War Europe and the Former Soviet Union   ▶

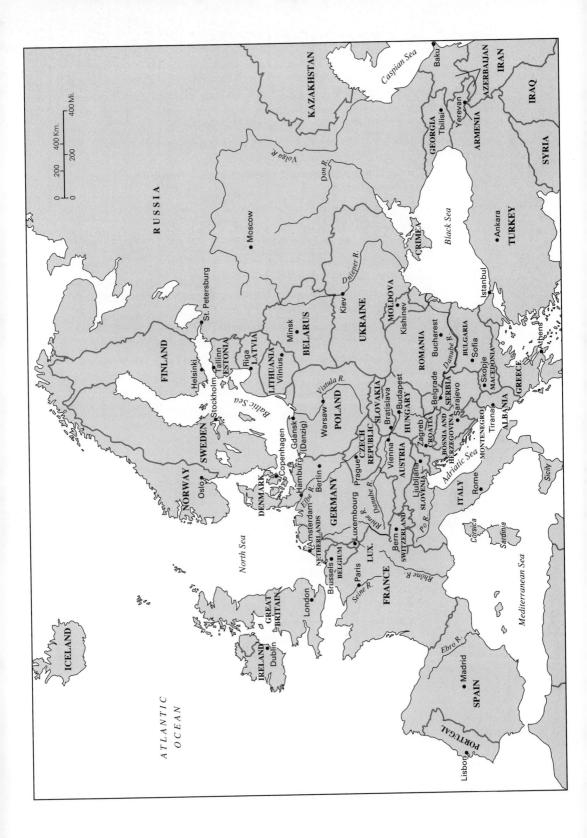

Is Marxism a failed ideology propped up only by force in the few surviving communist regimes? Is "scientific socialism," which claimed to have deciphered the essential meaning and direction of history, neither scientific nor relevant to current needs? Is it merely another idea that had been given too much credence and is now ready to be swept into the dustbin of history? Political theorist Francis Fukuyama suggests that the decline of communism and the end of the cold war reveal a larger process at work, "the ultimate triumph of Western liberal democracy":

> *The twentieth century saw the developed world descend into a paroxysm of ideological violence, as liberalism contended first with the remnants of absolutism, then bolshevism and fascism, and finally an updated Marxism that threatened to lead to the ultimate apocalypse of nuclear war. But the century that began full of self-confidence in the ultimate triumph of Western liberal democracy seems at its close to be returning full circle to where it started . . . to an unabashed victory of economic and political liberalism. The triumph of the West, of the Western idea, is evident first of all in the total exhaustion of viable systematic alternatives to Western liberalism. . . . What we may be witnessing . . . is the end point of mankind's ideological evolution and the universalization of Western liberal democracy as the final form of government.*[8]

The Post–Cold War World

The end of the cold war marked a sharp break with the past. The competition between the two superpowers and their rival ideologies, which had polarized world politics, now gave way to a new affirmation of the world's political diversity, encouraged by the victorious ideals of democratic freedom and self-determination. Ethnic and religious minorities began to struggle for recognition and independence; poiltical tensions within and between states, hitherto subdued by superpower rivalry, flared up. The collapse of the Communist dictatorships was followed by the agonies of liberation among the peoples of eastern and central Europe and the former Soviet Union. Suddenly, the world had become more unmanageable and complex. A new political constellation, however, offered an element of stability.

Global power is now concentrated in three geographical areas endowed with comparable economic and political strength, all in keen competition with each other but compelled to maintain peaceful relations by their tight interdependence. They share the common vision of a westernized modernity, as well as the uncertainties of the new global openness.

The leading role belongs to the United States, the strongest and richest country. With its 260.8 million inhabitants, it ranks third in population, after China and India, and it is still a superpower, thanks to its nuclear weapons and military bases in Europe and Asia. It proved its might during the Gulf

War in 1991, when it easily defeated Saddam Hussein, with token help from allied countries. The aggressive Iraqi dictator had invaded Kuwait in order to dominate the oil-rich Middle East. The United States expanded its commercial relations with neighboring Canada and Mexico through the North American Free Trade Agreement (NAFTA). It expects to extend this agreement throughout the Western Hemisphere. "The free trade area of the Americas will stretch from Alaska to Argentina . . . this hemisphere will be the world's largest market,"[9] said President Bill Clinton in December 1994. The United States also benefits from its innumerable economic ties around the world, which intensify its cultural outreach. Its ideals are the guide for the global future; its style of life, the envy of people around the world.

In East Asia, a more loosely related group of states with economic power and political influence has risen to prominence, headed by Japan. Although it has only limited political clout, lacks nuclear weapons or a seat on the U.N. Security Council, and is still resented by its wartime victims, Japan has gained impressive economic influence in Asia, the Americas, and Europe, more than holding its own against its Chinese neighbor. China, a nuclear power with a Security Council seat, is burdened by its huge population, 1.2 billion people. Its society, characterized in 1923 by its widely traveled statesman Sun Zongshan as "a sheet of loose sand," lacks the civic unity needed for effective democracy. Its government holds the country together by dictatorial force based on outdated communist ideology but grants sufficient freedom to private enterprise for booming economic development. Yet China's economic potential is limited by the persistent underdevelopment of its infrastructure.

Next to these two giants, the "little dragons" of the Pacific Rim—Taiwan, Hong Kong, Singapore, and South Korea—are economic powerhouses on their own, inspiring neighbors like Malaysia and Indonesia to follow their example. Inhabited by energetic and talented people energized by Western influence, East Asia is playing an increasingly prominent role in the world.

Western Europe occupies the third corner of the global triangle. The source of Western civilization and growing in economic and political unity, it constitutes a massive presence in world affairs. The largest single trading entity, in charge of one-fifth of the world's economy, it also contains two nuclear powers, France and England, both of them members of the U.N. Security Council. Linked militarily with the United States through NATO, western Europe is a center of both political and military might.

Western Europe's highly interactive historic diversity is still visible. Its member states, both large and small—all committed to democratic government in their various ways—struggle to retain their traditional identities as they cope with domestic difficulties. High unemployment, fear of refugees and immigrants, soaring government debt, social discontent, shifting parliamentary majorities, and the need to maintain economic competitiveness pose major challenges. Fearful voters, absorbed in their domestic problems, have moved to the right, slowing down the trend toward European integration. Germany's reunification, which has imposed burdensome costs on the country, has also shifted the European balance of power in Germany's favor, causing concern among its neighbors. With its population of 81 million, Germany is by far the largest state in Europe. Will it continue to integrate itself submissively into the western European community of nations, or will it try to dominate it?

Meanwhile, ambitious plans transformed the European Community into the European Union. According to the Maastricht Treaty, drafted in 1991, the European Union is scheduled to have a common currency by the end of the century and will formulate a common foreign policy. Eventually, it will approach the coherence of a unified state. Given the persistence of national ambitions among member states, however, timely realization of these plans is unlikely. Additional obstacles are raised by the European Union's projected eastward expansion. Inclusion of the prosperous and democratic Scandinavian countries will be easy. But how can Poland, the Czech republic, Slovakia, and Hungary, under consideration for admission, meet the membership requirements of a stable democratic government and a market economy? Even more worrisome, how is the new Europe to relate to the post-Soviet turmoil in the countries beyond—in the Balkans, and above all in Russia and the other lands of Eurasia? Western Europeans and their American allies look eastward with justified concern.

The New Globalism: Problems and Prospects

World War II propelled the earth's inhabitants into an inescapable, tight interdependence. The globe is becoming a single economic and financial system. Multinational corporations have offices and factories around the world. Western ideals of human rights and legal equality and Western science, medicine, technology, and business techniques have been exported to all the continents.

The new globalism is reflected in the United Nations, established in April 1945 by the victorious wartime coalition. The United Nations was designed to be a peacekeeping organization and to promote human rights. But by the last decade of this century, the global community has become an unruly association of some 160 sovereign states. The United Nations has been unable to prevent the many small wars that have flared up in Asia, the Middle East, Africa, and Central America.

Below the surface of global politics, a profound and still unfinished process of cultural transformation is at work. No other civilization in history has managed to universalize itself to the extent of imposing its achievements and its spirit on all others the way Western civilization has. For better or worse, Europeans and people of European descent have taken the initiative in creating the irreversibly interdependent world with which the present and all fu-

Map 22.4   Three Major Trading Blocs ▶

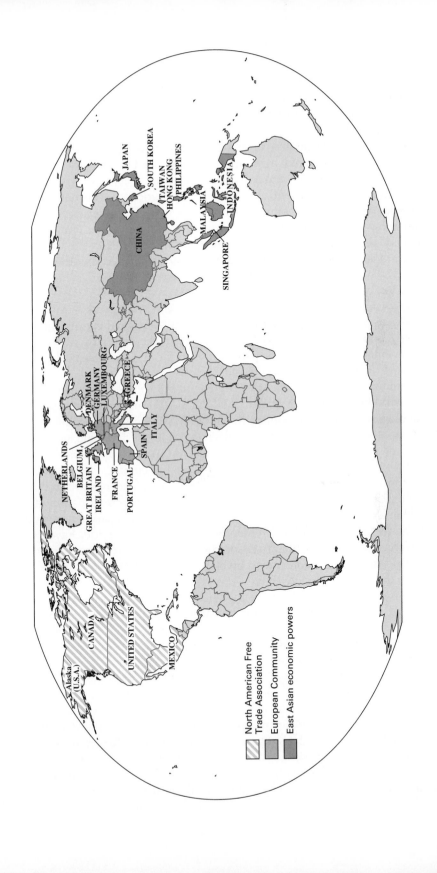

North American Free
Trade Association

European Community

East Asian economic powers

Alaska
(U.S.A.)

CANADA

UNITED STATES

MEXICO

NETHERLANDS
BELGIUM
GREAT BRITAIN
IRELAND
FRANCE
PORTUGAL

DENMARK
GERMANY
LUXEMBOURG
GREECE

SPAIN

ITALY

CHINA

JAPAN
SOUTH KOREA
TAIWAN
HONG KONG
PHILIPPINES

MALAYSIA

SINGAPORE

INDONESIA

ture generations must cope. In trying to adjust in the name of modernization to the institutions, machines, and human attitudes evolved by Western civilization, non-westerners often find themselves in permanent conflict with their indigenous traditions.

The agonizing task of fusing Western and non-Western ways in order to build a modern state and a modern economy started with the process of decolonization after the end of World War II. The newly independent states drew up enlightened democratic constitutions. The most westernized and cosmopolitan elements in the population attained the seats of power. But disillusionment arrived swiftly. Often excruciatingly poor, composed of quarreling ethnic groups that felt no attachment to the new nation, and crowded with illiterate, disease-ridden, stubborn peasants, the new countries entered the race for power and prestige with severe handicaps.

"Backwardness," in any form and by any name, represents humiliation to be escaped as fast as possible by "development"—by catching up to the "advanced" countries. Development aims to raise the standard of living and achieve industrialization, participation in scientific and technological progress, and most of all, prestige in the world. In this sense, the struggle for development among non-Western peoples represents the culmination of westernization. All humanity strives to modernize—to master institutions and technologies originally developed by the West. But how? Unfortunately, with some notable exceptions, the newcomers to modern statehood were unprepared for managing the large-scale organizations required for statehood and global competition. Each non-Western country has conducted its own experiments in modernization, limited by its own history and resources. Ranging from remarkable success to brutal failure, these efforts offer a panorama of a world in agonized transition. The experiments in westernization and modernization, in adjustment to an interdependent, competitive world, have exacted an excruciating human toll from societies culturally unprepared for drastic changes—unwilling and unable to break with their cultural heritage, yet eager to reap the benefits of modernity.

The world is inhabited by more than five billion human beings; the figure is expected to be around six billion by the year 2000 and higher thereafter. Helping to sustain them is a vast array of originally Western achievements: the nation state, industrialism, science and technology, and world-spanning organizations for business and international cooperation. Some non-Western peoples are now matching Western accomplishments. Keeping up with the latest innovations has become an ardent desire—or even an outright necessity—among all people, no matter how attached to their past they feel. Survival depends on mastery of the skills of modernity—originally Western skills—in economic productivity, in scientific and technological progress, and in the development of the most advanced weapons. These capabilities are the keys to power and prestige in the world. Thus, through westernization and economic interdependence, the new globalism has become an irresistible

Change in South Africa.   The former president of South Africa, F. W. de Klerk, talking with his successor, Nelson Mandela. The election in 1994 of a multiracial government headed by President Mandela, closed a bitter chapter of repressive white rule in South Africa. All African countries now have indigenous or multiracial governments. (*Reuters/Bettmann*)

worldwide reality. It has ominously accelerated the pace of change. Has the transformation been for better or worse?

Many people dwell on the positive aspects. Global interdependence, they argue, has vastly increased worldwide cooperation. Look at the impressive results. The volume of world trade has vastly increased, providing new material security for human life. People hitherto isolated have been exposed to new opportunities for personal development; they have become mobile in their search to improve their lot. Furthermore, global interdependence has stimulated minds over the entire world, recruiting talent from many countries. The advances in all fields of learning have been astounding. Science and technology, more closely linked than ever, have increased human control over nature beyond the wildest dreams of earlier ages. Physicists have explored the atom down to the smallest components of matter, and biologists have laid bare the genetic structures of animate matter. Human beings have set foot on the moon. Rockets with sophisticated equipment have been sent to the distant reaches of the solar system. Advances in electronics have brought the whole world to remote villages in Asia and Africa through radio and television. Computers, indispensable to scientists and engineers, have invaded everyday life in finance and business, and even in ordinary households.

In the arts and literature, the interaction of cultural influences from all parts of the world has been a creative stimulus. Even more significantly, concern for human dignity has spread. However spurned in practice, the United Nations' Universal Declaration of Human Rights sets a worldwide standard as a guide for the future. Agencies like Amnesty International keep track of human rights violations; others seek to relieve famine and offer assistance during epidemics and in the aftermath of natural catastrophes. These developments have created a mood of optimism for some people, who perceive a chance for enlightened control of human destiny over the entire world. Postwar prosperity encouraged an international effort at cooperation to bring natural resources and world population into a steady equilibrium, to provide greater equality around the world, and to avoid devastating world wars. That mood is still alive in some quarters.

In support of optimism, a Canadian observer cites encouraging statistical evidence. In the past thirty years, world per capita food production has increased by 20 percent; we live in a better-fed world, despite a 1.8 billion population increase. In developing countries, average life expectancy has increased from fifty-three to sixty-five years, while women have four rather than six children. World trade has increased by 6 percent. And in the nine years before 1993, the number of democratic countries has risen from 99 to 107. In short, "life for the majority of the world's citizens is getting steadily better in almost every category."[10]

At the same time, however, there is a contrary mood of pessimism. Despite all the progress, the bulk of humanity is still miserable. In the historically minute frame of the past one hundred years, the world has been burdened with a staggering population increase. In 1900, the world's population had reached 1.6 billion human beings. Fifty years later, those multitudes had grown to 2.5 billion; and in 1994, they had skyrocketed to 5.5 billion. Projections to the year 2025 indicate that the world's population will increase to somewhere between 7.6 billion and 9.4 billion. By the second half of the twenty-first century, according to the World Bank, total population may stabilize between 10 and 11 billion; other projections run as high as 14.5 billion.[11] This staggering population increase threatens the global environment's capacity to support human life. Individuals have to find their way among ever larger masses of people, and the masses overwhelm their governments with ever larger problems at home and in international relations. The burden is especially great for non-Western nations, whose populations grow most rapidly. In poverty-stricken sub-Saharan Africa, for example, the annual population growth rate of 3.2 percent is the highest in the world. If the rate is not checked, the current population of 600 million people in this area could more than double within thirty-five years, to 1.6 billion.[12]

As the world's population increases—by an estimated 88 million people per year in the 1990s—the world's natural resources, already strained by the population explosion of the past century, become proportionally scarcer and the natural environment is damaged. Since 1950, it has been estimated, the world lost nearly one-fifth of its cropland topsoil because of erosion; and one-fifth of its tropical rain forests, a vital reserve of animal and plant species, has been cut down. In Africa, the overly rapid population increase has led to widespread land degradation. Traditionally self-sufficient in foods, its peoples now depend on imported grain. There, as in Latin America, people eat less. In Africa, as in India, grasslands are overgrazed and cattle starve. The Saharan desert is spreading southward at an alarming rate.

Developed countries, too, suffer from environmental degradation. Chemical waste pollutes the underground water supplies, lakes, rivers, and even oceans. The beaches of the Mediterranean are notoriously dirty. Clean drinking water or water for irrigation is becoming scarcer. The radiation from nuclear waste from power plants and weapon factories poses special dangers. More visibly, exhaust from millions of cars and trucks dims the skies of most cities; air pollution is worse in the big cities of poor countries, worst perhaps in Mexico City. The fumes from coal-burning power plants produce acid rain, which destroys valuable forests in many parts of Europe and North America. Another closely watched consequence of the use of modern conveniences is the depletion of the ozone layer in the higher atmosphere, caused by chlorofluorocarbons in aerosol sprays and refrigerators. The ozone layer reduces the penetration of the sun's ultraviolet light to the earth's surface; its depletion endangers all organic life.

Inadequate supplies of food, clean water, and medical help diminish the opportunities of about half the world's population. Underfed, diseased, and untrained people perpetuate or even increase the already widespread poverty. Also, the postwar rise in living standards experienced by some peoples is receding in many countries. Since World War II, all efforts to bridge the gap between rich and poor nations have failed; in fact, the gap has widened. Modern communications have raised the expectations of poor people around the globe, but their societies suffer from staggering burdens that impede development: soaring populations, widespread illiteracy, malnutrition, disease, including acquired immune deficiency syndrome (AIDS), and huge debts. Furthermore, global military expenditures exceed the combined gross national product of China, India, and sub-Saharan Africa. The military outlays of Third World countries grow even faster, as a percentage of their GNP, than those of the developed countries. More money is spent on trading weapons on the international market than on trading grains.

Disabled by poverty, non-Western lands also have to struggle with cultural disorientation. In most non-Western parts of the world, Western influence has subverted traditional cultures. The elite, by and large, has a Western education and follows a Western lifestyle—sometimes with irresponsible extravagance—while still tied to native tradition. The bulk of the population is caught between tradition and Western ways. The old ways, with their moral obligations justified by tradition and religion, are discredited by the influx of modernity from the West. The moral vacuum, combined with the ordeals of modernizing, encourages corruption, violence, and, all too often, utter inhumanity.

Under these conditions, stable democratic governments have little chance to emerge, and without stable governments, effective self-help seems impossible. The historical record of the past thirty years shows a rising level of violence within the new states created after World War II. The brutal Communist and Fascist regimes that preceded World War II have their imitators in many parts of today's world. Terrorism born of desperation and fanaticism is a continuing threat everywhere.

All the problems just outlined—exploding population, environmental deterioration, ethnic animosity, cultural disorientation, and the failure to sustain democracy—are most serious in West Africa, as one observer notes:

> *West Africa is becoming the symbol of worldwide demographic, environmental, and societal stress, in which criminal anarchy emerges as the real "strategic" danger. Disease, overpopulation, unprovoked crime, scarcity of resources, refugee migrations, the increasing erosion of the nation-states and international borders, and the empowerment of private armies, security firms, and international drug cartels are now most tellingly demonstrated through a West African prism. West Africa provides an appropriate introduction to the issues . . . that will soon confront our civilization.*[13]

In short, "scarcity, crime, overpopulation, tribalism, and disease are rapidly destroying the fabric of our planet."[14] All promote the universal trend toward violence as the deadly tool of collective or even individual self-assertion.

The Western Tradition in a Global Age

In recent years, modern Western civilization has come under severe attack from several quarters, including religious thinkers, intellectuals loosely called postmodernists, and advocates of Third World peoples.

Some religious thinkers reject the modern age for its espousal of secular rationality, the central legacy of the Enlightenment. These thinkers argue that reason without God degenerates into an overriding concern for technical efficiency—an attitude of mind that produces Auschwitz, Stalin's labor camps, weapons of mass destruction, and the plundering and polluting of the environment. The self without God degenerates into selfish competition, domination, exploitation, and unrestrained hedonism. Human dignity conceived purely in secular terms does not permit us to recognize the *thou* of another human being, to see our neighbor as someone who has been dignified by God; and removing God from life ends in spiritual emptiness and gnawing emotional distress. These critics of the Enlightenment tradition urge the reorientation of thinking around God and transcendent moral absolutes. Without such a reorientation, they argue, liberal democracy cannot resist the totalitarian temptation or overcome human wickedness.

Postmodernists argue that modernity founded on the Enlightenment legacy, which had once been viewed as a progressive force emancipating the individual from unreasonable dogmas, traditions, and authority, has become a source of repression through its own creations: technology, bureaucracy, consumerism, materialism, the nation-state, ideologies, and a host of other institutions, procedures, and norms. An aversion to a technoscientific culture and its rational logical methodology leads postmodernists to reject the principle of objectivity in the social sciences and to give great weight to the subjective, to feelings, intuition, fantasy, to the poetry of life. Postmodernists contend that the evaluation of data and reasoned arguments, no matter how logical they seem, reveal only personal preferences and biases. In their view, science has no greater claim to truth than does religion, myth, or witchcraft. In a world marked by cultural diversity and individual idiosyncrasies, there are no correct answers, no rules that apply everywhere and to everyone. Moreover, like those who point out the dangers of reason not directed by spiritual values, postmodernists argue that reason fosters oppressive governments, military complexes, and stifling bureaucracies. Nor has it solved our problems.

Expressing disdain for Western humanism, which ascribes an inherent dignity to human beings, urges the full development of the individual's potential, and regards the rational, self-determining human being as the center of existence, postmodernists claim that humanism has failed. The humanist vision of socialism ended in Stalinism, and liberal humanism proved no more effective a barrier to Nazism than did Christianity. In our own day, they ask, has the rational humanist tradition been able to solve the problems of overpopulation, worldwide pollution, world hunger, and poverty that ravage our planet? Closer to home, has reason coped successfully with the blight, homelessness, violence, racial tensions, or drug addiction that are destroying our cities? Moreover, postmodernists contend that the Western tradition, which has been valued as a great and creative human achievement, is fraught with gender, class, and racial bias. In their view, it is merely a male, white, Eurocentric interpretation of things, and the West's vaunted ideals are really a cloak of hypocrisy intended to conceal, rationalize, and legitimate the power, privileges, and preferences of white, European, male elites.

Postmodernists and other critics of Western civilization, particularly those who identify with people of color throughout the globe, call into question the intrinsic worth of the entire tradition of humanist learning and culture. They point to the modern West's historic abuses: slavery, imperialism, racism, ethnocentrism, sexism, class exploitation, and the ravaging of the environment. They accuse westerners of marginalizing the poor, women, and people of color by viewing them as the "other." Furthermore, they condemn the West for arrogantly exalting Western values and achievements and belittling, or even destroying, indigenous peoples and cultures of the world. Finding Western civilization intrinsically flawed, some critics seek a higher wisdom in non-Western traditions—African, Asian, or Native American.

Defenders of the Enlightenment heritage, on the other hand, argue that this heritage, despite all its flaws, still has a powerful message for us. They caution against devaluing and undermining the modern West's unique achievements: the tradition of *rationality,* which makes possible a scientific understanding of the physical universe, the utilization of nature for human betterment, and the identification and reformation of irrational and abusive institutions and beliefs; the tradition of *political freedom,* which is the foundation of democratic institutions; the tradition of *inner freedom,* which asserts the individual's capacity for ethical autonomy; the tradition of *humanism,* which regards individuals as active subjects, with both the right and the capacity to realize their full human potential; the tradition of *equality,* which demands equal treatment under the law; and the tradition of *human dignity,* which affirms the inviolable integrity and worth of the human personality and is the driving force behind what is now a global quest for social justice and human rights.

The modern struggle for human rights—initiated during the Enlightenment, advanced by the French Revolution, and embodied in liberalism—continues in the contemporary age. Two crucial developments in this struggle are the civil rights movement in the United States and the feminist movement. Spokespersons for these movements have used ideas formulated by Western thinkers in earlier struggles for liberty and equality. Thus, one reason for the success of Martin Luther King's policy of direct action was that he both inspired and shamed white America to live up to its Judeo-Christian and democratic principles. In his famous "Letter from Birmingham City Jail," King expressed the immanent link between his movement and the Western tradition:

> One day the South will know that when these disinherited children of God sat down at lunch counters they were in reality standing up for the best in the American dream and the most sacred rules in our Judeo-Christian heritage, and thusly, carrying our whole nation back to those great wells of democracy which were dug deep by the Founding Fathers in the formulation of the Constitution and the Declaration of Independence.[15]

Feminist organizations, which first arose in advanced Western lands in the nineteenth century, continue their agitation for complete equality, and in recent years they have proliferated worldwide.

French social theorist Jacques Ellul answers those intellectuals who express their disdain for the West and exalt the other civilizations of the world:

> I am not criticizing or rejecting other civilizations and societies. . . . The thing . . . that I am protesting against is the silly attitude of western intellectuals in hating their own world and then illogically exalting all other civilizations. Ask yourself this question: If the Chinese

*have done away with binding the feet of women, and if the Moroc-
cans, Turks, and Algerians have begun to liberate their women,
whence did the impulse to these moves come from? From the West,
and nowhere else! Who invented the "rights of man"?*

*. . . the essential, central, undeniable fact is that the West was the
first civilization in history to focus attention on the individual and on
freedom. . . . The West, and the West alone, is responsible for the
movement that has led to the desire for freedom. . . . Today men
point the finger of outrage at slavery and torture. Where did that
kind of indignation originate? What civilization or culture cried out
that slavery was unacceptable and torture scandalous? Not Islam, or
Buddhism, or Confucius, or Zen, or the religions and moral codes of
Africa and India! The West alone has defended the inalienable rights
of the human person, the dignity of the individual. . . . The West attempted to apply in a conscious, methodical way the implications of
freedom.*

*. . . the West discovered what no one else had discovered: freedom
and the individual. . . . I see no other satisfactory model that can replace what the West has produced.*[16]

The roots of these ideals are ultimately found in the West's Greek or Judeo-
Christian heritage, but it was the philosophes of the Enlightenment who
clearly articulated them for the modern age. To be sure, these ideals are a
goal, not a finished achievement, and nothing should make westerners more
appreciative of the preciousness of these ideals and more alert to their precari-
ousness than examining their violation and distortion over the course of centuries. It is equally true that every age has to rethink and revitalize this
tradition in order to meet the needs of its own time.

Therefore, it is crucial in this age of globalism, with its heightened sense of
ethnic and cultural diversity, that westerners become sensitized to the histories and traditions of all cultures and root out permanently all racist, sexist,
and irrational ideas that have gravely poisoned Western perceptions and history. But it is equally crucial in an era of global interdependence and tension
that westerners continuously affirm the core values of their heritage and not
permit this priceless legacy to be dismissed or negated. As the history of our
century demonstrates, when we lose confidence in this heritage, we risk losing
our humanity, and civilized life is threatened by organized barbarism.

Notes

1. Quoted in Walter Laqueur, *Europe Since Hitler* (Baltimore: Penguin Books, 1970), p. 118.
2. "The Truman Doctrine," in *Major Problems in American Foreign Policy: Documents and Essays*, ed. Thomas G. Paterson (Lexington, Mass.: Heath, 1978), 2:290.
3. Kwame Nkrumah, *The Autobiography of Kwame Nkrumah* (Edinburgh: Thomas Nelson, 1957), p. x.

4. Nikita S. Krushchev in *The Crimes of the Stalin Era: Special Report to the 20th Congress of the Communist Party of the Soviet Union,* annotated by Boris I. Nicolaevsky (New York: The New Leader, 1956), p. 20.

5. Gorbachev's speech at the seventieth anniversary of the Bolshevik Revolution, quoted in the *New York Times,* November 3, 1987, p. A3.

6. Quoted in Anthony Lewis, "Et Tu Eduard," *New York Times,* December 21, 1990, p. A39.

7. *New York Times,* January 2, 1990, p. A13.

8. Francis Fukuyama, "The End of History," *The National Interest* (Summer 1989):3–4.

9. James Brooke, "U.S. and 33 Hemisphere Nations Agree to Create Free-Trade Zone," *New York Times,* December 11, 1994, sec. 1, p. 1.

10. Marcus Gee, "Surprise! The World Gets Better," *World Press Review,* 41 (July 1994):18–20.

11. Paul Kennedy, *Preparing for the Twenty-First Century* (New York: Random House, 1993), p. 23.

12. John Darnton, "'Lost Decade' Drains Africa's Vitality," *New York Times,* June 19, 1994, sec. 1, p. 10.

13. Robert D. Kaplan, "The Coming Anarchy," *Atlantic Monthly,* 273 (February 1994):46.

14. Ibid., p. 44.

15. Excerpted in James M. Washington, ed., *The Essential Writings and Speeches of Martin Luther King, Jr.* (New York: Harper Collins, 1991), p. 302.

16. Jacques Ellul, *The Betrayal of the West,* trans. Matthew J. O'Connell (New York: Seabury, 1978), pp. 16–19, 29, 49.

Suggested Reading

Beschloss, Michael, and Strobe, Talbott, *At the Highest Levels* (1993). An insider's account of the tumultuous events of 1989–1993 and the end of the cold war.

Buchan, David, *Europe: The Strange Superpower* (1993). A critical survey of diplomacy and defense in the European Community.

Colchester, Nicholas, and David Buchan, *Europower: The Essential Guide to Europe's Economic Transformation in 1992* (1990). How the concept of the European Community came about and to what degree it is likely to be achieved.

Craig, Gordon, *The Germans* (1982). Key aspects of post–World War II Germany in historical perspective.

Dahrendorf, Ralf, *Reflections on the Revolution in Europe* (1990). The prospects of economic reform and democracy in eastern Europe. Repays careful reading.

Doder, Dusko, and Louise Branson, *Gorbachev: The Heretic in the Kremlin* (1990). An excellent account of the Gorbachev revolution.

Ellul, Jacques, *The Betrayal of the West* (1978). A defense of the Western tradition.

Garton-Ash, Timothy, *The Magic Lantern: The Revolution of '89 Witnessed in Warsaw, Budapest, Berlin and Prague* (1990). A lively account of the death of communism in Eastern Europe, conveying the exhilaration of the time.

Gorbachev, Mikhail S., *Perestroika: New Thinking for Our Country and the World* (1987). The authoritative account by the Soviet leader, covering both domestic and foreign affairs.

Gwertzman, Bernard, and Michael T. Kaufman, eds., *The Collapse of Communism* (1990). Accounts from the *New York Times.*

Kaiser, Robert J., *Why Gorbachev Happened: His Triumphs and His Failures* (1991). Prominent journalist offers his insights into the difficulties of reforming the Soviet system.

Marsh, David, *The Germans: Rich, Bothered and Divided* (1990). A fine source of relevant information and perceptive analysis.

Pond, Elizabeth, *Beyond the Wall: Germany's Road to Unification* (1993). An account of the new Germany by a veteran journalist with an optimistic view of the future of Europe.

Remnick, David, *Lenin's Tomb* (1993).

A superb, Pulitzer-prize-winning account of the last years of the Soviet Union.

Rosenau, Pauline, M., *Post-Modernism and the Social Sciences* (1992). An excellent discussion of recent trends in thought.

Smith, Hedrick, *The New Russians* (1990). An American journalist looks at the effect of glasnost on everyday life in the U.S.S.R.

Review Questions

1. What do you consider the biggest changes to have taken place in Western Europe after World War II?
2. Discuss the major problems of government in France and Britain since 1945.
3. What problems in the Soviet Union did Stalin face after the end of World War II? How did he try to cope with them?
4. What happened to Stalinism after Stalin's death? Under Khrushchev? Under Gorbachev?
5. List the major events in Eastern Europe in 1989. Why was the "revolution of 1989" a relatively peaceful one?
6. What is your attitude regarding the conflict between modernization and the preservation of traditional cultures?
7. What are the major global problems confronting your generation? Do you consider yourself a pessimist or an optimist?
8. Why are some thinkers critical of Western civilization? How do defenders of the Western tradition respond to these attacks?

Index

Abbasid caliphs, 146
Abelard, Peter, 186–187
ABMs, *see* Antiballistic missiles
Absolutism, 246; in France, 253–254; destruction of in French Revolution, 323–324
Abstract art, 484, 572
Abu Bakr, 145
Abyssinia, 459
Achilles, 43
Actium, 99
Address to the Christian Nobility of the German Nation (Luther), 230
Adenauer, Konrad, 627
Adrianople, battle of, 116
Aegean civilizations, ancient, 40–42
Aeneid (Virgil), 105
Aeschylus, 67, 69
Afghanistan, 501; Soviet invasion of, 633; Soviet withdrawal from, 635
Africa: Portuguese in, 264, 265; slave trade and, 267; Italian imperialism in, 441; imperialism in, 451; in 1914, 460 (map); independent states in, 460 (map); Berlin Conference and, 461; British imperialism in, 461–463; Belgian imperialism in, 463; German imperialism in, 463; Italian imperialism in, 463; Ethiopia and, 553; battle of El Alamein in, 604; decolonization and, 621. *See also* East Africa; Near East; North Africa; Third World
African Americans, black slavery and, 267, 274
Agamemnon, 43
Age of Enlightenment, *see* Enlightenment
Age of Reason, The (Paine), 291
Agnosticism, 186
Agriculture: in Neolithic Age, 6; irrigation and, 8; in High Middle Ages, 160–162; town growth and, 162; in Late Middle Ages, 195; commons and, 268, 269 (illus.); expansion of, 268–270; open-field system and, 269; convertible husbandry and, 270; transfer between Europe and New World, 274; population growth and changes in, 345; revolution in, 346 (illus.); globalization of, 464; in Soviet Union, 535–536, 541–543, 615
Ahmed, Mohammed (Mahdi), 452
Ahriman, 22

Ahura Mazda, 22
Airlift, in Berlin, 617
Akhataten, 18
Akhenaton (Egypt), 18
Akkad, 9
Alans (tribe), 116
Albania: Serbia and, 503; Soviet Union and, 615; collapse of communism in, 638
Alberti, Leon Battista, 215 (illus.), 221
Albert the Great (Albertus Magnus), 189
Alcuin of York, 153
Alexander I (Russia), 385, 389, 525
Alexander II (Russia), 526, 527
Alexander III (Russia), 527
Alexander the Great, 45, 71, 72; division of empire, 72–73 and *map*
Alexandria, Egypt, 74; sciences in, 76
Alexius (Byzantine emperor), 172
Alfonso XIII (Spain), 566
Algeria: independence of, 621; France and, 625–626
Allah, *see* Islam; Muslims
All Quiet on the Western Front (Remarque), 572
Almagest (Ptolemy), 107
Alphabet: Phoenician, 20; Cyrillic, 144. *See also* Language(s)
Alsace-Lorraine: loss to Germany, 500; return to France, 516
Amalrik, Andrei, 630
Ambrose (Saint), 134–135
Amenhotep IV (Egypt), *see* Akhenaton
American Indians, *see* Native Americans
American Revolution: Locke and, 293; Enlightenment thought and, 303–305; French Revolution and, 316–317; liberalism and, 377. *See also* United States
Amin, Idi, 622
Amnesty International, 648
Amos (Hebrew prophet), 35
Anabaptists, 237
Anagni, pope at, 198
Anaximander (Ionia), 56
Andropov, Yuri, 633
Anglican church, *see* Church of England
Anglo-Boer War (1899–1902), 463
Anglo-Russian Entente (1907), 501
Anglo-Saxons, *see* England; Northmen